COMPLETE KICKBOXING

*The Fighter's Ultimate Guide to Techniques, Concepts
and Strategy for Sparring and Competition*

COMPLETE KICKBOXING

*The Fighter's Ultimate Guide to Techniques, Concepts
and Strategy for Sparring and Competition*

BY
Martina Sprague
&
Keith Livingston

Turtle Press   Hartford

To contact the author or to order additional copies of this book:
Turtle Press
P.O. Box 290206
Wethersfield, CT 06129-0206
1-800-778-8785
www.turtlepress.com

ISBN 1-880336-84-7
LCCN

Printed in the United States of America

10 9 8 7 6 5 4 3 2 1

Library of Congress Cataloging-in-Publication Data

Sprague, Martina.
  Complete kickboxing : the fighter's ultimate guide to techniques, concepts and strategy for sparring and competition / by Martina Sprague & Keith Livingston.-- 1st ed.
      p. cm.
  Includes index.
  ISBN 1-880336-84-7
  1. Kickboxing. I. Livingston, Keith. II. Title.
  GV1114.65.S67 2004
  796.815--dc22
                      2004003472

ACKNOWLEDGMENTS

To Tom with love -- my husband, friend, and faithful partner of 20 years.

Many thanks to Cindy Varnell Winlaw and Jennifer Lawler, my two female martial arts friends in my male dominated world. You have given me much inspiration.

And, as always, thanks to Cynthia Kim and Turtle Press for another job well done.

~ Martina Sprague

Hundreds of people have touched and shaped my life, but I am especially grateful to those who have influenced my journey through the martial arts: Mark Livingston, Tyler Mannos, Mike Stidham, Tony Martinez Sr., Tony Bullock, Karyn Turner, Kenny Yarborough, Bob Lopez, Marv Jensen, The Fullmer Brothers, Lamar Clark, Dale "Apollo" Cook, Kelly "Babe" Gallegos, Barry Benedict, Johnny Rodriguez, my countless opponents, sparring partners, teachers, family and friends.

And, finally, to my co-author, dedicated student and close friend Martina Sprague, "the student who became the master," for opening up a whole world of possibilities.

~ Keith Livingston

Martina Sprague and Keith Livingston would like to thank Mike Stidham and the Ultimate Combat Training Center in Salt Lake City for the use of the facilities. We acknowledge the following fighters for their hard work during the photo shoot:

Rachelle Bennett
Amber George
Mark Livingston
Adam Parkinson
Tracy Smith
Mike Stidham
Dave Teachout
Alex Wilsher
Cindy Varnell Winlaw

CONTENTS

What the pros are saying about Complete Kickboxing:

"Informative and well written. A must read for boxers and kickboxers alike."

~ Gene Fullmer, former middleweight champion of the world

"Packed full of valuable information on strategy, technique, and the science of fighting."

~ Jay Fullmer, former world light welterweight contender

"A great companion coach. I highly recommended it to those in or around the fight game."

~ Don Fullmer, U.S. middleweight boxing champion and world contender

PREFACE

I concede that learning a physical art form from the confines of a manual is a difficult task. Many books guide us through the steps without giving any real depth or insight. This is called learning by rote. Simply put, it is memorization without understanding. Anybody can take a person from the street and teach him the round house kick in ten minutes, but does this mean mastery of the technique? We are often misled to believe that we can learn martial arts this way. Memorizing the steps does not help you win in competition, unless you also understand the hows and whys, common errors, the many ways a technique can fail, how your opponent can take advantage of you, and how it actually feels to step into the ring to compete.

Experience is the greatest teacher. How can you know what kickboxing is really like without traveling the dusty roads? As you embark on your journey, remember that few things are properly understood without experience. Time is another factor. It is not uncommon to see a martial artist with as little as a year and a half in his chosen art attain a black belt. Although your strikes and kicks may be dazzling when performed in the air or on a stationary target, it is the years of practice, adaptation, and thinking about the art that gives you insight.

I recommend that you involve yourself with a competent instructor whose skill and experience exceeds your own, and let him guide you, give advice, and supervise your training. However, no instructor possesses all of the answers. This book is meant to be a companion teacher to enhance development, spark curiosity, and speed up the learning process. My main goal is not to impart the mechanics of technique, but rather to show you how to think properly. Resist the temptation to simply read from cover to cover. Rather, review a portion of the text, do the exercises, and take time to mentally digest the information.

A final word before you begin your journey: Hard work and the ability to push beyond pain, boredom, and fatigue are necessities for anyone desiring to attain "Olympic Quality" in his or her chosen field. There is no easy victory; keep this in mind!

And when you feel complacent, remember your competition.

INTRODUCTION

I have taught many people to fight, and some have been a real challenge. What I'm looking for is, do you understand the techniques? Can you apply the techniques in sparring? I want you to be the kind of fighter who can think and explore for yourself, until you own the techniques and the art of fighting becomes yours. I teach my students good stances and how to strike and kick with power from the start. I also teach targets and balance points. We emphasize sparring, and sometimes when they leave I wonder how they feel about it.

I enjoy teaching those who already know a little. This is when the concepts and finer details of the fight game come in. I guess I would really like to teach instructors, but I have never even approached anybody with that. As soon as you step into another school and they find out what style you're in, they start talking you down. Why is that? Insecurity, I suppose. We all tend to think that we have the only correct answer.

Some students get discouraged, because they feel they don't have a goal to work toward. But I just don't believe in giving you a sheet of paper with all the techniques, and then test you on it. Every time you come to training, you should be evaluated and tested. I guess we need something to motivate us, though. So, I have a goal for you. But it's more of a general goal that is not as specific as doing a thousand front kicks a week. Your goal is to become impossible to hit. What do you think? If your opponent can't hit you, he can't score. And if he can't score, he can't win.

You see, I can take you past my own level of skill, and I'm going to push you beyond your limit, until you are wondering how many more kicks to the gut you can take. It's going to be a bit rough, but I think you'll appreciate that in the end. When we step up a level and go harder, it will force you to rise to the occasion. That's why I feel this is the way of self-exploration. You will learn things you didn't know about yourself.

You know, you are fortunate to still have a student-teacher relationship. Sometimes, I think about how I would give anything to be in your shoes. There are many martial artists who are better than I am, who can do things that I cannot even dream of doing. But most of them don't know how to convey that knowledge to others. I often hear that I am too old for this. But doesn't that extra age make me a wiser fighter? I often wonder . . . you know, if I got back into really good shape, how far could I take it?

--Keith Livingston
kickboxing trainer and former I.K.A. light heavyweight Rocky Mountain champion.

HOW TO USE THIS BOOK

Now that you have made the decision to explore and become part of the world of kickboxing, you have also chosen to accept everything that this decision entails. As you begin your training, you will find that few people outside of our sport truly understand the strength, determination, and courage it takes to compete. The purpose of this book is to present the principles and tactics of kickboxing in an organized manner, and to give you as much in-depth insight into the sport as can fit between the confines of two covers. What makes this manual unique is that it is broken down into five interwoven parts, which will help you overcome many of the difficulties associated with learning from a book:

1. The **text** allows you to read and think about the kickboxing techniques and concepts.

2. The **fighting template** guides you through proper position and angle. As you utilize this template, remember that the lines provided are to be used as points of reference. You should be more concerned with using proper angle than positioning exactly on the line.

This is what the **fighting template** looks like:

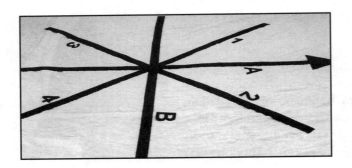

3. The **In the gym** (printed in italics) or **Glove-up with Keith** part is your instructor talking to you. This part is intended to review what you have learned and bring insight into the challenge of being an instructor.

4. The **true short stories** bring the text alive and help you relate to those who have the courage to step into the ring and compete.

5. The **summary and review** include a series of exercises and questions intended to make you think. Some of the exercises rely on what you have already learned, and others require you to challenge yourself and explore on your own.

A NOTE ABOUT THE TEXT AND ILLUSTRATIONS

Martina Sprague and Keith Livingston have more than forty years combined experience, study, and analysis of the art of kickboxing. Martina Sprague has written the majority of the text. Keith Livingston has written most of the chapter introductions and most of the true short stories, and other parts where noted. The stories are based on personal experiences and, although we have been trying to find a balance of stories that are relevant to the material discussed at the moment, we admit to that both of us have had our shares of wins and losses.

The illustrations are a combination of staged photos that demonstrate correct mechanics of technique, and actual fight photos that may be less clear or more "flawed" than the staged photos. Although kickboxers use gloves and often other protective gear on their shins and head, many of the techniques are demonstrated bare fisted for clarity. Words printed in italics refer to the name of a technique. Words or short phrases printed in bold emphasize specific information. Words that are both bold and italicized refer to the concepts that underlie the techniques, and are further explained in the quick reference section at the end of each chapter.

Much of the material you study in the beginning of this book will recur in a different light later. Because it is difficult for the new student to learn everything about a specific technique from the start, we have opted to discuss the basics in the first few sections, and expand on it in subsequent chapters. The book consists of ten major sections and two appendices. With the exception of the appendices, which you can refer to at any time throughout your training, the text is meant to be read in the order it is written, and to be used as a progressive learning tool where each section builds on the previous one. For example, you may read something about the round house kick in the second section, and read more about it in the ninth or tenth section. If you are really dedicated, you can study this book over a period of years and perfect each technique and concept as you go.

Martina Sprague   **Keith Livingston**

We have poured our hearts and souls into this book, and it is our sincere belief that no other book on the subject will be even moderately competitive. If you understand every technique and concept you are about to learn, you are miles ahead of your kickboxing counter-parts. If you master every technique and concept, you are truly Complete Kickboxing.

THREE TRUTHS ABOUT FIGHTING

Before you commence your study, let me leave you with something to think about:

1. Many of the techniques you will learn may seem basic, but it is how the practitioner uses them that determine how advanced he is. Most kickboxing matches are won with good basic techniques, coupled with superior knowledge of how to apply them. It should be understood that the word basic is not synonymous with the word beginning. Basic refers to the techniques that make up your foundation. An example is the lead jab. The jab itself may seem like a very simple technique; however, it has dozens of applications. And, if used to its fullest, it is one of the most crucial techniques in kickboxing. Just look at the sport of boxing to see that the greatest hand art in the world is comprised of only four techniques: the jab, the rear cross, the hook, and the uppercut. This is the first truth about fighting.

2. The second truth is that good mechanics in the basics will do little for you, unless you also apply the mental aspects of the fight, adapt instantly, and use hairline precision in the execution of your moves.

3. The third truth about fighting is that a tired fighter is a beaten fighter. Stop right now and take a moment to commit yourself to a disciplined training regimen.

I hope to see you in the ring someday. Don't worry, I'll know who you are. You'll be in great shape, full of confidence and skill. You'll be that fighter with his hands raised high in victory.

SECTION ONE
BASIC PUNCHING AND FOOTWORK

WHAT DOES IT TAKE?
by Keith Livingston

Kelly and I had a lot in common. We were both fourteen years old, best friends, and shared a love for boxing. So when we heard about this gym on 72nd street, we couldn't wait to go and visit, maybe even join. Although neither of us had any formal training, we had saved our money, purchased a heavy bag, boxing gloves, and jump ropes. We had been using my father's garage as our boxing ring for the past year. But we both knew that if we were to get any better, we needed a real place in which to train and a legitimate coach.

The walk from our neighborhood to the gym was long, and as we got nearer, our nervousness began to show. We discussed our plans and touched on all of the "what ifs." What if they're not open? What if they charge too much? What if we're not good enough? As I said this last "what if" to Kelly, we were standing in front of the gym and staring up at an old neon 7-Up sign: Bullock's Boxing Gym, Amateurs and Pros Welcome. Through the wall, we could hear the sound of leather on leather, mingled with the rhythmic thump of the speed bag. I took one last reassuring look at my friend and began turning the doorknob. Just as I was ready to push the door open, this voice from behind bellowed in my ear: "Hey kid, either shit or get off the pot!" I turned and stared into the belly button of the biggest and ugliest man I had ever seen. He put his massive hand on my chest and swept me to the side. As he went inside, we peeked through the opening, then followed.

The gym was small but had everything we had dreamed of. To our right was a fifteen by fifteen foot ring. Heavy bags and speed bags were lined up along the wall, and to our left hung hand wraps and jump ropes from pegs on the wall. Underneath the massage table were boxes stuffed with a variety of boxing gloves, headgear, and towels. A dozen fighters were going through their routines, and the gym smelled of sweat and years of hard work. The posters on the walls spoke of fighters long gone, fifty or more years of memories hanging silently but not forgotten.

When one of the fighters walked over to grab a jump rope, I asked, "Who is Mr. Bullock?" The fighter pointed at a small gray-haired man, who was busy massaging a fighter on the canvas table. As I watched the man's hands move in small, rhythmic karate chops up and down the fighter's back, I thought of how he looked just like Burgess Meredith of Rocky fame. I mustered the courage and yelled, "What does it take?"

The gym fell dead silent, and as the gray-haired man turned and looked me over from head to toe, the next thirty seconds became etched in my memory forever. The old man had an unlit cigar hanging from the corner of his mouth. And then came the word that I will never forget: "Guts!" Several of the fighters shook their heads in acknowledgment, and without skipping a beat returned to their workouts.

Kelly and I trained at Bullock's gym for many years, until the old man passed away, forcing the closing of the gym. Today, when prospective fighters ask, "What does it take?" I remember that day and the voice of my trainer and friend, Tony Bullock.

Two fighters landing simultaneous punches on each other.

18

THE LEFT FIGHTING STANCE

Now that you are ready to embark on the kickboxer's long and arduous journey, it should come as no surprise that the first thing you must learn is how to survive by combining offense and defense with the right mental attitude. Balance, both physical and mental, is your most important attribute. If you go into the fight without physical balance, you can't throw any of your techniques effectively. Likewise, if you enter the ring without mental balance, your emotions will quickly overshadow any logic, and you will become easy prey to even the most inexperienced opponent. The first few sections of this book focus primarily on proper mechanics of technique. This is your physical balance. Your mental balance is discussed in bits and pieces throughout the book.

Physical balance starts with stance. Standing seems like a simple concept that has been part of your subconscious since you were a year old. But what if I told you that before you can fight, you must learn all over how to stand and how to walk? Stance, in fighting, entails more than just maintaining balance. For example, standing in a way that exposes targets is incorrect. A good stance, on the other hand, provides a barrier that your opponent's strikes and kicks must penetrate. Your stance also determines your ability to move expeditiously and with ease, and to strike and kick with power.

This section covers:

• Why does a right-handed kickboxer fight from a left stance?
• Body mechanics for the left fighting stance
• What's in a good stance?
• The benefits of the boxer's stance
• Summary and review

WHY DOES A RIGHT-HANDED KICKBOXER FIGHT FROM A LEFT STANCE?

Many fighters with a traditional martial arts background have been taught to fight from a stance that places their stronger side forward (usually their right side, since most of us are right-handed). In kickboxing you will place your weaker side forward (your left side if you are right-handed, and your right side if you are left-handed). There are several arguments for and against this. For example, placing your stronger side forward allows you better speed in the strikes and kicks that are closest to your opponent. But since kickboxing relies on the "power concept," where your ultimate aim is to knock your opponent out (as opposed to the point sparring concept, where speed is your number one priority), you will stand in a way that allows your stronger punches and kicks enough time and distance to build momentum for power.

If you are right-handed, you should fight from a left fighting stance with your left foot forward and your right foot back. This gives your stronger right hand a longer distance to travel and more time to build momentum. Your left hand, which is closer to your opponent, should be used as a set-up for your more powerful rear techniques. Think of your lead hand as a "feeler," a gauge to find the distance to the target.

If you are left-handed, you should fight from a right stance, again keeping your stronger side farther from your opponent. A person who fights with his right side forward is called a southpaw. When fighting in a left stance against a southpaw, be aware of the dangers associated with this, and that you may need to make adjustments that would ordinarily not be required. We will talk about this in more detail later. Because fighting is dynamic and you are constantly moving, a stance should not be thought of as stationary. Although you stay in one stance for the majority of your fighting, there are times when it is necessary to switch from one stance to another.

Because most people are right-handed, most techniques in this book are explained from a left fighting stance, that is, with your left side forward and your right side back. If you happen to be a southpaw, you must reverse the descriptions.

BODY MECHANICS FOR THE LEFT FIGHTING STANCE

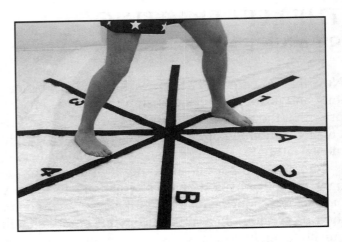

When in your fighting stance, keep your feet about shoulder width and a half apart and slightly offset (also called a toe-to-heel line). This gives you good balance, ease of movement, and the ability to throw all techniques with power and speed. Keep your knees slightly bent, your hands high to protect your head against blows, and your elbows tucked close to your body to protect your ribs. An opponent facing you should now have difficulty finding an open target.

Assume a left fighting stance by positioning your feet about shoulder width and a half apart with your knees slightly bent.

Keep your feet on a forty-five degree angle toward the front right corner and offset, with a straight line drawn from the toes of your lead foot touching the heel of your rear foot. This stance gives you good balance and full pivot when throwing your rear hand.

Keep your lead foot (left foot) to the left of centerline A, and on a forty-five degree angle in the direction of line 2. Your toes should be touching the left side of centerline A.

Keep your rear foot (right foot) to the right of centerline A, and on a forty-five degree angle in the direction of line 2. Your heel should be touching the right side of centerline A.

Angle your lower and upper body forty-five degrees in the direction of line 2. Keep your eyes forward in the direction of centerline A.

Hold your elbows forward of your body and tucked in toward your ribs. Hold your hands high (approximate height of the hands is the corner of your eyes) to protect your chin and head against blows.

Hold your lead hand forward of your body and above your lead thigh, and your rear hand a few inches farther back and in line with your rear shoulder.

Keep your shoulders and arms relaxed, and your wrists straight.

WHAT'S IN A GOOD STANCE?

A good fighting stance allows your feet, torso, arms, and head to be synchronized, so that you can throw your techniques with minimum effort and without fear of losing balance. Your feet should support the full weight of your body equally. Your knees should be bent for flexibility and balance, and be springy enough to execute quick footwork to close or widen a gap. The slightly offset position of your feet allows you to move forward, back, left, or right, or at any angle in between. Remember that movement is always used to avoid an attack or to position for a counter-attack. Maintain your guard throughout all movement, and be ready to defend against any strike or kick thrown at you.

Which fighter is in the more stable stance?

Keith's Knockout Advice

As you can see, a good stance has many facets: proper distance between the front and rear foot, proper bend in the knees and waist, proper upper and lower body angle, etc. Next time you watch a kickboxing contest, it may look as though the fighters are moving simultaneous to throwing their strikes. But if you watch closely, you will see that they actually pause for a fraction of a second to throw the strike. Yes, you will see fighters completely stationary as well, throwing or receiving barrages of punches. What should be learned from this is that your ability to position properly in your stance dictates the power, speed, and accuracy of your techniques. Because all fighters differ slightly in height, experience, style, etc., you must find your own optimum power and speed through the fine tuning of your stance. Once you find the stance that is most appropriate for you in particular, incorporate these same measurements (foot distance, bend in the knees, body angle) whenever you are moving around in the ring.

THE BENEFITS OF THE BOXER'S STANCE

In order to really appreciate a good stance, it is important to understand the inherently weak areas of the human body. Since most attacks in kickboxing are frontal (or angled slightly from one side), stability, reach, power, and protection must all be in the frontal direction. When in a neutral stance (sometimes referred to as a horse stance) both your feet are even and you stand square to your opponent. In most martial arts, the neutral stance is used as a training stance for blocking and striking, allowing you full focus on your hands. But, because of excessive exposure of the vital targets on the centerline (nose, mouth, throat, sternum, solar plexus, groin), this stance is impractical for fighting. In addition, it makes you unable to place the full weight of your body behind the strikes.

This fighter is in a neutral stance (horse stance).

The centerline refers to an imaginary line approximately five inches wide, running vertically on the front and back of your body. Striking targets on the centerline may cause serious injury or death.

This fighter is in a left fighting stance.

When in your stance, your hands should protect your forehead, eyes, and nose, in addition to protecting your temples and sides of jaw against angled attacks. Common injuries because of strikes to these areas are cuts above or under the eyes and nosebleeds. If struck to the temples or jaw, you risk getting dazed or knocked out. Since the chin is so vulnerable, guard it by tucking it down toward your chest, or by hiding it behind your lead shoulder.

Your sternum and ribs form a natural protection for your heart. Your forearms should cover any gaps at your chest, solar plexus, and ribs. Common injuries to the body are bruised or broken ribs.

Below the ribs there is little natural protection for the vital organs, namely the kidneys, stomach, liver, and spleen. These areas are protected with your elbows, which are also vicious striking weapons used to inflict as much pain as possible on your opponent, while simultaneously meeting your goal defensively.

There are additional benefits to the boxer's stance that are more difficult to attain from a neutral stance. For example:

1. The boxer's stance **provides a barrier**. Your opponent's strikes must first penetrate your lead hand, and then your rear hand in order to land on a valid target.

2. You can **use your rear leg to brace yourself** against a strong frontal attack.

3. You can **push off with your rear foot in a quick forward shuffle** to increase the momentum and power of your strikes, or push off with your lead foot in a quick shuffle back to increase the gap between yourself and your opponent.

4. You can **protect an injury** by placing the injured body part farther away from your opponent's attack.

5. You can **shift your weight forward or back to avoid a strike**, fake a strike, or draw your opponent closer.

6. The boxer's stance **gives you better overall ability to move** to a superior position out of danger of your opponent's strikes.

A boxer's stance (left fighting stance) gives you the benefit of multiple barriers that your opponent's strikes must penetrate. The punch must first pass your lead hand, then your rear hand on its way to the target.

What's wrong with these fighting stances?

too narrow

crossed and unstable

too wide

ribs exposed

The neutral stance (horse stance) does have some benefits, however. It takes great leg endurance to maintain a neutral stance for a duration of time. It has been said that in fighting the legs are the first to go. If you lack leg endurance, you can't move. Without movement, you can't fight effectively. You might also find yourself in a neutral stance by necessity, as when backed up against the ropes by a stronger opponent. The neutral stance should therefore not be discounted completely.

Your stance should present a threat. Look confident and ready. No matter how good your technique is, if you appear insecure, you are not likely to score a victory. Practice your stance until you can get into it easily and are relaxed. Your stance serves both an offensive and defensive purpose and your body must be relaxed, as tensing or tightening of the muscles causes premature fatigue, constriction of movement, and inability to strike with speed.

Eventually, you want to develop both your left and right fighting stances, so that you can choose which one to fight from, and switch from one to the other at any time during the fight. Your ability to switch stance will confuse your opponent and force him to change his plans or readjust his position.

Some fighters have a tendency to square (open their centerline) when throwing their rear hand or when stepping forward. Take time to evaluate how well you maintain your stance. The moment you square, you leave an opening which your opponent can take advantage of. We will look at proper stepping and movement shortly.

SUMMARY AND REVIEW

Stance implies more than "standing." Your stance is your foundation and determines how balanced you are. If your stance is wide you will generally have greater balance than if your stance is narrow, but there is a trade-off in mobility. On a deeper level, your stance also determines your effective power. This is something that many fighters don't think about. If your stance is off just a little, you can't throw a powerful strike.

A fighter in a left stance has his left foot forward and his right foot back. The opposite is true for a fighter in a right stance. The art you study and your objective determine which stance to fight from. If you study a full contact art, like kickboxing, you will fight from a stance that places your stronger side farther away from your opponent (your right side, if you are right-handed). The purpose of this is to give your strong hand enough distance to build power for a knockout punch. If you study point sparring, where the purpose is to score a point without hurting your opponent, you will fight from a stance that places your faster hand and foot closest to your opponent. If you are right-handed, you will fight from a right stance. If you study street fighting or fighting for self-defense, because of the unpredictability of a street encounter, you should develop both sides of your body. When in your fighting stance, your feet should be about shoulder width and a half apart and offset (also called a toe-to-heel line) for balance and ease of movement.

Getting into your stance

- Practice getting into your fighting stance quickly, each time checking that the width between your feet is correct, and that your feet are offset on the toe-to-heel line.

- The purpose of a stance is to give you stability, power, and ease of movement. Name five situations when you may get caught off guard in an unstable stance.

- If you are caught in a bad stance, how can you move to regain a good, solid stance?

- Some stances are "in-betweens" needed to reposition yourself. An example is a crossed stance in preparation for a crossover side thrust kick. When and how should in-between stances be used without jeopardizing your safety?

The crossover step is a potentially unstable maneuver that can be used as a propellant for the side thrust kick.

- Walk around randomly and when your partner (or instructor) calls for you to freeze, immediately assume a fighting stance until you can do so with ease and without fidgeting.

- Practice getting into your stance with your eyes closed. This helps you develop a feel for the stance and how to get into it comfortably and efficiently. The fighting stance should be relaxed and second nature.

- Train to anticipate danger. When a threat is imminent, be ready to respond and assume your stance quickly.

- Be aware of your surroundings, so that you don't end up cornered or with your back to the ropes, as this limits your mobility, making it difficult to assume a good fighting stance.

The horse stance is unstable in the frontal direction. You are in a very disadvantaged position when back on your heels.

Maintaining balance

- Experiment with how bending your knees affects your balance. Start from a stance where your legs are straight, and have your partner try to push you over. Gradually bend your knees, until you get in a lower and lower stance.

- The lower the stance, the more stable you are. A stance that is too low, however, inhibits ease of movement.

- When might you find yourself in a stance that is either too low or too high? Is there ever a time when a very low stance might benefit you?

- Why is the toe-to-heel line important? Experiment with balance by moving your feet off the toe-to-heel line, and have your partner try to push you over.

- If you are in a left stance, and you move your lead foot too much to the right, your stance will be crossed and maintaining balance is difficult. However, if you move your lead foot too much to the left, you will expose targets on your centerline.

When your legs are straight, your partner can easily push you off balance (left). Bending slightly at the knees and lowering your stance gives you stability (right).

Protecting the centerline

- The purpose of the fighting stance is to allow you to keep your balance, while simultaneously providing a barrier for your opponent's strikes.

The crossed stance is unstable (left). The square stance exposes your centerline (right).

- When in a good fighting stance with minimal target exposure, which targets must you still be prepared to defend?

- If your stance is too much sideways, you will limit the reach and mobility of certain strikes. Which are they?

- Stand in front of a mirror and widen your stance a little at a time. Identify targets that become exposed when you no longer maintain the toe-to-heel line.

- How can you protect the targets on your centerline if, for some reason, you are unable to maintain a toe-to-heel line?

- Name some situations where you might find yourself in a neutral stance. How can you move to re-establish the boxer's stance?

Benefiting from the neutral stance

- If your opponent is the aggressor, it is possible that you will find yourself in a neutral stance with your back to the ropes. However, there is one benefit to the neutral stance: It gives your lead techniques the same distance as your rear techniques, and therefore more power.

- When your opponent has backed you up against the ropes and is pushing against you, try throwing alternating round house kicks to his outside thigh areas. When his focus shifts to his legs, follow with alternating hooks to his mid-section or head. Varying your targets makes it difficult for your opponent to stay aggressive and defend all targets.

When in a neutral stance against the ropes (left), round house kicks to your opponent's legs (middle) or short hooks to his ribs (right), may split his focus and allow you to move to a better position.

- When in a good fighting stance, you are stable in the frontal direction; when in a neutral stance, you are stable in a direction perpendicular to your opponent. How can you disrupt your opponent's balance when he is in a neutral stance?

- How can you take advantage of your perpendicular stability when you are in a neutral stance?

Maintaining stance when moving

- Face your partner as if to engage in sparring. Start moving around, focusing on maintaining a boxer's stance. When moving with your partner, move so that you always expose your side (not your centerline) to him.

- If your opponent were trying to exploit the weaknesses of your centerline, which direction would he move: to your right or to your left?

- What kind of footwork can you use to reposition for a strike to your opponent's centerline, without jeopardizing your own centerline?

Drawbacks of the boxer's stance

- The drawback of fighting from a boxer's stance is that your lead leg is more exposed than your rear leg, which makes this an easy and quick target for your opponent. This is especially important in arts that allow kicks or sweeps to the legs, like kickboxing and Muay Thai.

Your lead leg is exposed to a kick when fighting from a left fighting stance.

- Experiment with penetrating your opponent's guard when both you and your opponent are in good fighting stances.

- If your lead leg or arm gets hurt and it is necessary to switch stance in order to protect that side, when would it be wisest to switch: when moving forward or when moving back? Why?

- Which techniques are especially easy to throw with power from a boxer's stance? Is there a possibility that you might telegraph your intents if your stance is too much sideways?

- Assume a boxer's stance and practice circular movement around the heavy bag while maintaining your stance.

- The foot that is farthest from the center of the circle must take a bigger step than the foot that is closest, or you will eventually end up in a crossed stance. If your step is too big, however, you will end up in a square stance with your centerline exposed.

- Stay on the balls of your feet for a springier step with easier mobility.

THE JAB

So, there! Kickboxing is a stand-up art (as opposed to grappling, which is a ground art), and hopefully you have now broadened your views on standing and stance. You should also have practiced getting into your stance, and gained some insight into why a stance is both offensive and defensive. We will now start working on offense (punching, in particular). Is offense more important than defense? Hardly. But the fact is that defense alone does not win a kickboxing match. Just keeping your opponent from scoring ain't gonna cut it! That is, unless you can simultaneously score on him. Remember, this isn't self-defense. This is sports competition. So you must now learn how to throw a punch properly. You can throw all punches with either your lead or rear hand, but your rear punches are generally used as finishing, or knockout, techniques.

The jab is a straight punch thrown with your lead hand. It is also the most basic and often used punch in kickboxing.

The jab has two primary missions:

1. **Seek out** your opponent and establish distance. Once this is achieved, you know that you can reach him with your rear hand as well.

2. **Create openings** for your slower and more powerful rear techniques, like the rear cross and rear leg round house kick.

Because your lead hand is closer to your target than your rear hand, it is naturally faster than most other techniques, and should therefore be used often and effectively.

This section covers:

• Body mechanics for the jab
• What's in a good jab?
• Guarding your hands against injury
• Glove-up with Keith
• What is proper breathing, and how is it attained?
• Tips on relaxation, reach, and speed
• Summary and review

BODY MECHANICS FOR THE JAB

Throw the jab by extending your lead hand straight out from the guard position along centerline A. Find your aim by sighting down your second big knuckle.

Pivot your lead foot with your heel toward line 1. This increases the power by placing the weight of your body behind the strike. The toes of your lead foot should now point toward line 2.

Keep your elbows tucked close to your body until it is time to deliver the strike. This keeps your ribs protected against your opponent's counter-strikes. As you extend your arm, point your elbow toward the ground, and hold your fist in the vertical position until just prior to landing the strike.

Rotate your fist to a horizontal position palm down, just as it is about to impact the target. This gives you more extension for power. Simultaneously, rotate your shoulders into alignment with the jabbing arm. After impacting the target, bring your hand straight back to the point of origin.

Fist in vertical position.

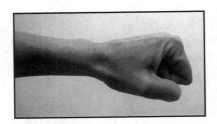

Fist in horizontal position.

WHAT'S IN A GOOD JAB?

Untrained fighters often tend to throw their strikes using arm power only. A well executed jab, on the other hand, relies on the synchronization between your lower and upper body. The punch originates in your lower body, where you can rely on the strength of your legs. Your foot pushes off against the floor and pivots to add momentum to your hips, which, in turn, strengthen your shoulders and add power to the punch. The quick jab is used as a "feeler," and the power jab is used to hurt your opponent. Rotation of your foot and body should be more pronounced when throwing the power jab.

Pivot your body in the direction of the punch for power and reach. Think of it as "setting down" on your punches.

It is extremely important that you do not raise your elbow prior to punching. By raising your elbow, two things occur:

1. You **leave your ribs exposed** for your opponent's counter-attack.

2. The **punch will lack power** because the mass of your body is no longer directly behind it.

Although the jab is not primarily a knockout punch, you should have a precise target in mind. A punch thrown without proper intent is likely to land on your opponent's glove or arm. A common mistake when using the quick jab as a feeler is to get lazy with the technique and throw it half-heartedly. By twisting your wrist to the horizontal position just prior to impact, your hand becomes like a drill pushing through your opponent's guard. Not only does this increase the power of the strike but also the accuracy, enabling you to take small and well-guarded targets. Accurate jabbing also causes a lot of anxiety in your opponent.

Keith's Corner

One day when I was sitting in my office filing new student applications, I got the sense that I was being watched. I looked up from the pile of papers on the desk, and yes, there were not just one pair of eyes watching me, but twenty! Crowded in my doorway and down the hall was a line of the most sinister looking Vietnamese kids I had ever seen. Being a law enforcement officer, it wasn't difficult to surmise that I was about to be confronted by one of the local gangs. Two of the gang members breached the doorway and approached cautiously. I stood and extended my hand for introductions. My hand was disrespectfully ignored. The two who had entered spoke in Vietnamese, yet it was evident that I was being evaluated and sized up. Finally, the one to my right spoke: "We fight you!"

"What? Why?" I asked, a bit taken aback. Pointing to the man at his right, the Vietnamese kid said, "He Vietnamese champion. He fight you." Being just a little annoyed that my afternoon was interrupted, I decided to be a smart-ass. "Where does he want to fight, here on my desk, or out by the flag pole after school?"

After a brief exchange in their native tongue, the supposed champion cracked a smile and laughed. The interpreter also smiled and pointed to my gym. "No, we fight you in ring." I gave my future opponent the once over. "I don't think so, he's not big enough," I said. "But I can line him up with one of my students, who is more his weight class."

Just then, my partner Tyler showed up for the afternoon training. With a puzzled look, he waded through the crowd. "What's up, Keith?" I explained that the kid had thrown down a challenge, and I was trying to convince him that it wasn't prudent to spar so far out of your weight class. Tyler looked him up and down, and in his normal engaging style said, "You can't weigh but a buck thirty, you'll get hurt." The interpreter was becoming incensed. "He champion, and he fight you!" By now a dozen of my fighters had surrounded the gang, and everyone was taking defensive postures. Feeling the testosterone levels rising, it was time to do what law enforcement has been trained to do: de-escalate.

"Okay . . . okay, you can fight me," I said. The man to my right quickly translated, and a hush went through the Vietnamese and American crowd. As I changed, the crowd encircled the ring, Vietnamese on one side, and my students on the other. Tyler walked into the dressing room and reminded me that we were currently threatened by a lawsuit over a similar situation. I had recently been confronted by a student with something to prove. Unfortunately, he had been knocked out and suffered a concussion. But that's another story. Tyler and I made an agreement. I wouldn't hurt the kid. "Tell you what," I said to Tyler. "I'll just use the jab, and you pay me a dollar every time it lands." We shook hands, and I headed for the ring.

I'm not trying to sound cocky, it's just that I was confident that he couldn't hurt me. I had a weight advantage of nearly 50 pounds and a substantial reach advantage. Okay, and I have a pretty good jab. As I walked to the ring, I quickly evaluated my opponent, who was warming up and showing his stuff. His stance was traditional Thai, and he appeared to be mainly a kicker. I would now teach the young Vietnamese champion the value of good basics, specifically the jab.

The first round netted me forty-two dollars and several confused looks from the spectators. Every time he set for a kick, I would knock him off balance with a stiff jab or two, and sometimes three. The left side of his face was particularly vulnerable, and after the second round his eye was beginning to shut. Net for round two was forty-six dollars. By round three, the young champion was both frustrated and embarrassed. Net fifty-one dollars. Round four never happened. The Vietnamese champion, eye shut and bleeding from the nose, decided that the fight was over. I turned to my students and told them, "Sometimes simple is better, and the jab is the foundation of all other techniques."

Disappointed, the gang began to file out of the gym, but the champion stayed behind. He walked up to me and extended his hand. We shook. "You train me?" he asked. "I'll be glad to," I said. The Vietnamese champion bowed and left. As I walked back into the gym, I was not surprised to see everyone working the jab so diligently. Another day had ended well.

GUARDING YOUR HANDS AGAINST INJURY

Powerful punching relies on your ability to properly clench your fists. To make a proper fist, curl the fingers into the palm of your hand with your thumb overlapping the first two fingers. Keep your wrist straight to prevent injury to your hand and joints. Impact the target with your first two knuckles. Keep your hand and body relaxed until just prior to impact.

To further protect against injury, you may wrap your hands with reusable hand wraps or gauze. In competition, gauze must be used. The wrap is intended to support your joints and the areas of your hand that are most pone to injury: wrist, thumb, and knuckles. If you already have an injury: a sprained finger or a bruised knuckle, for example, you can use pieces of a sponge to provide additional protection for the injured part.

Wrap around your wrist and back over the knuckles. The wrap should cover your punching knuckles, but not those on your fingers.

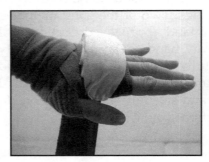

Since the knuckles absorb most of the force in the execution of a punch, you may use gauze to build some extra padding over the knuckles.

First wrap around the wrist three or four times.

When wrapping the knuckles, spread your fingers to give your hand better mobility. Then bring the wrap back around your wrist and secure.

Then over the back of your hand and around the thumb.

Straighten your fingers and wrap over the back of your hand again in an X-pattern.

The finished wrap should extend about three inches up the wrist and be a little tight when making a fist, but not so that it restricts blood circulation. If the wrap is too tight, your fist will go numb. Aside from being a mental distraction, this also decreases the power in your punches.

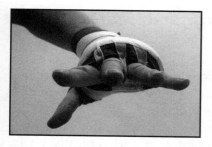

When wrapping for competition, you may also place tape between your fingers and around your hand and wrist. This gives your hand added stability and a more secure wrap.

Clench your fist a few times before the wrap is finished, or do some light shadow boxing to determine whether your hand is agile enough to function well in combat.

There are many variations to wrapping hands. Some fighters like to wrap between their fingers for more support. Personally, I like to wrap in competition the same way I wrap in training, with not too much wrap around the thumb and no wrap at all between the fingers. I do like to build up my knuckles with a few folded layers of wrap. My belief is that if you train the way you compete, you can compete the way you train. The idea is that the competition wrap with gauze should feel the same as when you wrap with the reusable wraps. There is enough pressure in competition not to have to worry about the comfort of your hands. In training, I use reusable hand wraps and do the wrapping myself. In competition, I use gauze and have my trainer do the wrapping. There have been a couple of times when I have gone to competition without my trainer. I have then wrapped my own hands with gauze. It is not difficult, but takes a little more effort than with the reusable wraps.

Glove Up with Keith

Grab your hand wraps and a roll of tape. I want to show you how to properly wrap your hands.

Start with your right hand and wrap around your wrist three or four times, then over the back of your hand and around the thumb. Wrap the back of your hand again so that the wrap makes an X- pattern, then around your wrist and back over your knuckles. Spread your fingers when wrapping the knuckles. Come back around your wrist again. Take the tape and pull off a strip about five inches long. Tear half of it into three equal parts lengthwise. These will go in between your fingers. Take the roll of tape and wrap around your hand and wrist. I sure use a lot of tape, man! Almost six rolls a week! The wrap should feel just a little tight when making a fist.

Get in a left fighting stance. Check your stance. Make sure the mechanics are correct and your balance is good. Jab only. When punching air, don't go too fast, or you'll get sloppy. Work on correct technique and form. Jab only, now. This is used to establish distance. Your strike should come straight out and then straight back to the guard position. Don't loop it, or you'll lose time and power. Looping the strike also exposes your jaw. Your hand should stay vertical until the very last moment. Your foot should end its pivot at the same time your hand snaps to the horizontal position.

Some fighters throw the jab without really aiming for anything, hoping that the punch will land on a good target. Many fighters are also headhunters, obsessed with the idea of knocking out their opponent. The jab can be thrown effectively to the body and still be used as a set-up for your rear cross or a second jab high. When jabbing to the body, lower your shoulders to the level of the punch. Failing to do so will expose your jaw. It is equally important to keep your jaw tucked behind your shoulder when coming back up for your follow-up strike.

A common mistake when jabbing is to raise the elbow prior to extending the arm. If I were to reach forward to grab something, I wouldn't raise my elbow first, would I? Well, this works the same way. And, most importantly, don't forget to breathe!

Which is a good jab, and why?

Wrong: Lacks pivot

Wrong: Chin exposed

Correct: Good stance & guard

Wrong: Ribs exposed

Wrong: Too upright

WHAT IS PROPER BREATHING, AND HOW IS IT ATTAINED?

Everybody is looking for the secret, the one thing that makes the martial artist superior to others and able to do astonishing feats with seemingly no effort. But those who have studied the arts for many years have overcome their disappointment and typically go by the saying that "the secret is that there is no secret; there is only hard work." But, you know, after all my years of training, I have discovered that there is, in fact, one secret to fighting, and I am now going to let you in on it. Are you ready? The one secret to successful and seemingly effortless fighting is proper breathing. A properly timed breath adds power and speed to your strikes. Breathing at the right moment also takes power from your opponent's strikes. Finally, proper breathing keeps you from getting winded.

Breathing, in itself, is an automatic function. But how one breathes is important as well. Some fighters new to the sport breathe without purpose. The onlookers hear a forceful grunt every time the fighter moves, yet the fighter is "sucking air" after the first round. When oxygen starvation sets in, it happens fast, which I became painfully aware of in my first kickboxing match. I was in awesome shape. I could spar an intense ten rounds in the gym and think nothing of it. But when I got back to my corner after the first two-minute round of competition, I was so winded that I didn't think I could get out for the second round, let alone fight!

You can learn proper breathing by exhaling with each punch or kick. A short grunt, as you let the air from your lungs, will help remind you to breathe properly.

Let's put **BREATHING** to the test. Try these exercises:

Exercise 1

Hold your breath for fifteen seconds while punching the heavy bag. Let me guess, you are quite winded now, with your punches drained of energy and your muscles restricted. Now, do the same drill again for fifteen seconds, but exhale at the exertion of each punch, and inhale as you retract the technique. This shouldn't have been quite as unpleasant as holding your breath.

So what? you say. Who is stupid enough to hold their breath while fighting? Yet, improper breathing is essentially the same as holding your breath. In order to increase endurance and power, all parts of your body must be synchronized. This includes breathing. Holding your breath, even for short instances, is destructive and few things are as incapacitating as oxygen starvation in the midst of battle. Still, it is not uncommon for students to repeatedly and unknowingly hold their breaths, particularly during sparring when the threat is high and you are a little tenser than normal. The way to correct this is to be very conscious of your breathing during every aspect of training, whether it is bag work, focus mitts, shadow boxing, jump rope, running, weight lifting, or stretching. At times, it is also necessary to take deep, full breaths. Deep breathing, filling your lungs completely with oxygen, should be done when you are outside of striking range of your opponent.

Exercise 2

Whenever you are up against the unknown, as is the case in competition, the adrenaline rush coupled with fear makes you tenser than normal. Without consciously working on proper breathing, you will breathe using the upper portion of your chest only, with the air going in and out in short, snappy breaths, depriving the rest of the body of oxygen. Next time you spar or work the heavy bag, make a conscious effort to breathe from the abdominal cavity. Whenever there is a lull in the fight, take a few long, deep breaths. Between rounds, pay attention to how fast you can recover and get your heart rate back down.

The rest period between rounds is one minute. During this minute, you must have time to recover, fix any cuts, drink water or rinse out your mouth, and listen to advice from the corner. As a guideline, if you can drop your heart rate to 110 beats per minute within 30 seconds of getting to your corner, you are in pretty good cardiovascular shape.

Now that we have established the importance of breathing, let's summarize what proper breathing will do for you. Proper breathing will:

1. Help you with **power and speed**, allowing you to use less effort with greater results.

2. Help you **absorb the impact** of a strike. Exhaling at just the right moment can decrease the effects of your opponent's strikes. Exhaling the moment your opponent strikes your mid-section, for example, helps take the power out of the strike. On the other hand, if you are caught with the strike as you breathe in, the strike will be more damaging and can literally knock the wind out of you.

3. Help you **maximize endurance**. Proper breathing will sustain you throughout the competition.

The diaphragm is the muscle that is responsible for movement of air in and out of the lungs. When your diaphragm moves down, expanding the abdominal and chest cavity, you inhale; when it moves up, you exhale. When the diaphragm spasms, it feels as though the wind has been knocked out of you. Your lungs are unable to function until the diaphragm recovers.

Keith's Knockout Advice

The positive action of any technique is the extending motion, and the negative action is the contracting motion. It is during the positive phase that it is crucial to exhale. The exhalation should be timed with the technique. You should begin to exhale at the initiation of a punch, and end your breath the moment the punch reaches full extension. The principle of proper breathing holds true for anything you do, whether it is running, lifting, walking, or shadow boxing. Yet, each field of athletics has its own unique breathing techniques. Weight lifters, for example, exhale during the positive motion of the routine and inhale during the negative motion. Runners, on the other hand, utilize deep controlled breathing throughout their run. Kickboxers are unique in that we supplement our skills training with many other athletic routines. We are not only martial artists, but also weight lifters and runners who utilize many other aerobic and anaerobic methods of training.

As I have already stated, a tired fighter is a beaten fighter. Conditioning is therefore one of the most critical elements to success in the ring. The scary part is that one can be in superior condition and still starve the body of oxygen. Many novice fighters who are in great shape find themselves tired within seconds after the opening bell. And many experienced fighters can last round after round while seemingly not in very good shape. I'm not saying that, as you gain experience and learn proper breathing, you should ignore conditioning. Rather, it is the well-conditioned and experienced fighter, who also utilizes proper breathing, that we generally call a champion.

And here is the second part of the secret: The experienced fighter watches his opponent's breathing pattern and tries to land his techniques during his opponent's inhalation phase. Why? Because it causes the diaphragm (the muscle that separates the lungs and heart from the stomach and intestines) to spasm. Your opponent is then unable to breathe until the diaphragm returns to normal.

A properly timed strike to the mid-section can knock the wind out of your opponent.

Some other aspects of breathing that are worthy of mention are the relaxing effects. During stretching routines, taking in a full breath and exhaling fully as you stretch the muscle improves the overall stretch and is a great stress reducer. Another simple drill for immediate stress reduction is to take in a full breath, hold the breath for a second or two, and then blow it forcibly from your lungs. Do this four times before any stressful situation, and you will immediately feel better.

Since retiring from competition, I no longer maintain the level of fitness required for competitive kickboxing, and the majority of the martial artists I work with are younger and better conditioned than I am. However, my experience as a fighter makes me appear well-conditioned and allows me to spar round after round. Recently, I was asked why, for an "old man," could I still spar so many rounds with the younger and better conditioned kickboxers. Initially, I answered, "experience." But when I had thought about it a while longer, I replaced experience with "proper breathing."

Once you have mastered correct breathing, you can fight longer and perform at a greater intensity. Experience is nothing more than accomplishing an objective with less effort, which means working smarter, not harder. It shouldn't take years to become proficient at what we do. We often try to reinvent the wheel, even though many successful athletes have already done the work for us. Study those who have gone before you. Cast aside their mistakes and tap into their successes.

TIPS ON RELAXATION, REACH, AND SPEED

Relaxation: Kickboxing students often tend to tense or raise the shoulders prior to punching. Somehow, we believe this helps elevate the strike to the height of our opponent's head. But tensing or raising the shoulders gives the strike away and inhibits speed. This is because your body is required to do two moves (raise the shoulders and extend the arm) for a technique that could have been done in one move. When you are tense, it is difficult to set your strikes in motion. When your shoulders and arms are rigid, your opponent will see the move easier. If you are too relaxed, on the other hand, your guard will be drooping and your techniques will lack stiffness and power. So, just how relaxed should you be? There is a fine line here. You don't want to tense to the point that you stifle movement, yet you don't want to relax to the point that your techniques are sloppy. Picture a kind of controlled tenseness that allows you to be in the ready state both to throw and defend against a blow. When shadow boxing, work on relaxing your shoulders and letting them bounce lightly with each step or move. We will talk more about shadow boxing in Section 3.

Reach: You can increase your reach significantly by pivoting on the foot that is on the same side as the punching arm. You can also increase reach through a crouched stance. Try this: Stand upright and extend one arm toward the wall until your fist is barely touching. This is your maximum reach. Now, crouch and extend your arm until it is straight and your fist is touching the wall. Adjust your distance back as necessary. You should have gained a minimum of six inches of reach. When you crouch, your upper body must move forward in order to maintain balance, thus the increase in reach.

The concept of crouching can be applied to straight punches to the body. Lower your upper body to the level of the punch to protect your head against blows, placing the weight of your body behind the blow for power and extending your reach. It is now possible to be at one range when striking to the head, and at a longer range when striking to the body. On a more advanced level, this can be used deceptively. Your opponent gets a feel for where your maximum range is for head shots, and stays slightly out of reach. But you still have reach to strike his mid-section.

PIVOT

When you pivot on the foot on the same side as the punching hand, your reach extends an additional few inches.

When you crouch, your reach increases by several inches.

CROUCH

35

Jab to the head . . .

followed by a jab to the mid-section. Note how the reach increases through the crouch.

Push-pull principle with a rope:

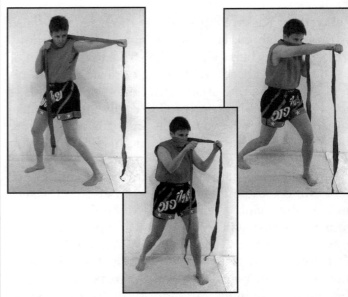

How does this apply to a kick? (I know, we haven't learned about kicks yet, but keep this paragraph in mind for when we do). Let's look at the side thrust kick. When your lead leg extends to kick, your rear leg simultaneously pushes off against the floor, with your upper body inclining slightly to the rear.

Allowing your lead and rear leg to work in unison can increase the power of a kick.

Speed: The speed of your strikes is increased through the push-pull principle. Let me explain. We have a tendency to focus only on the arm or leg that is doing the punching or kicking. Thus, when we throw a jab, our full effort is in the extension of the jabbing arm. Likewise, when we throw a kick, our full effort is in the extension of the kicking leg. You can increase speed and explosiveness by allowing the "non-striking" side of your body to aid the "striking" side. Think of it this way: When your left hand extends to jab, your right hand and shoulder simultaneously pull to the rear. If you were holding the ends of a rope around a pulley, you could more easily see the effect of your hands working in unison. The most effortless move comes when both hands do equal amount of work. Consider pushing with your lead hand only. Sure, because of the rope, your rear hand is forced back, but all your effort is in your lead hand. The push-pull principle states that whenever your lead hand pushes, your rear hand pulls, dividing the workload. You can increase speed and explosiveness by using both sides of your body equally.

The push with your foot and the incline in your body should not be the result of your lead leg extending, but rather a combined effort between your lead and rear leg. Because of the weight of your leg and gravity counter-acting any upward movement, much of the work in kicking is done when lifting the knee prior to extending the leg. Rather than focusing on raising the knee, with all work coming from the muscles in your leg, focus on pushing off with the supporting foot to help launch the kick off the floor. This is a variation of the push-pull concept, where you use opposing forces to divide the work over more than one body part, resulting in less effort and a more explosive kick.

SUMMARY AND REVIEW

The jab is thrown with your lead hand and is used as a feeler to gauge distance for your more powerful rear techniques. Because your lead hand is closer to the target than your rear hand, it has the added benefit of speed, making scoring relatively easy. Even though the jab is not the ultimate knockout strike, it should never be thrown half-heartedly. You can increase power and reach in the jab by pivoting the heel of your lead foot toward the target. This places your body weight behind the strike. A very quick jab can be thrown effectively without a pivot, and will then serve as a distraction.

Retrieving the jab to the point of origin

• Observe yourself in the mirror and practice throwing the jab straight and with good form. Keep your elbow down until just prior to impact, when your hand rotates into the horizontal position. Minimize target exposure by bringing your hand back to the point of origin between each strike.

• Note targets that are exposed when you do not bring your hand back to the point of origin. Many fighters tend to loop the punch slightly downward, opening targets on their head.

• When bringing your hand back, keep your elbow down to protect your ribs and mid-section. Observe yourself in a mirror to ensure that you do not point your elbow to the outside and expose your ribs.

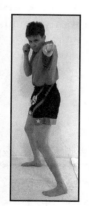  

Jab   **Incorrect retrieval**   **Correct retrieval**

• When you get tired, it is more difficult to bring your hand back to the point of origin, especially when wearing gloves that weigh down your hands. Look for your opponent's tendency to bring his hand back slightly low.

Using the jab as a set-up

• You can throw the jab as a set-up or distraction for another strike. Practice hand speed by whipping your hand as if it were a wet towel. The speed should originate in your shoulder. Keep your fist relaxed, closing it gradually, until it snaps fully closed at the moment of impact.

• How does whipping your strike at your opponent's gloves, instead of at his face, serve as a distraction?

• Can you get your opponent to raise or lower his guard by whipping the strike at a high or low target? What strategic benefit does it give you?

Whipping a strike high may make your opponent raise his guard, allowing you to throw a strike low to his mid-section.

• Multiple jabs can serve as a distraction, forcing your opponent to focus on defending his head. Practice multiple jabs to the head with a partner. After two or three jabs, follow with a strike or kick to a different target area: a front kick to the mid-section, for example.

• Broken rhythm, or a slight pause or twitching of your shoulder prior to throwing the jab, can make your opponent tense. Can you draw a reaction through a sudden, unexpected move?

Jabbing to different targets

- It is difficult, if not impossible, to defend all targets simultaneously. You are more likely to land a strike by throwing high-low and low-high combinations, than if you consistently focus on the same target.

- Practice jabbing to different targets with a partner. Jab low to the mid-section, and follow with a jab high to the head. Vary the targets enough to confuse your opponent.

Closing distance with the jab

- The jab can also be used as a quick distance closer, often called a "stick and move" or an "elongated jab." Execute the stick and move from long range by taking a step forward with your lead foot only, simultaneously sticking a jab in your opponent's face. Quickly step back to long range and continue moving. This is especially beneficial when fighting somebody who has a significant reach advantage.

- Practice closing distance by stepping forward with your lead foot only. This widens your stance momentarily. Simultaneously throw a jab and spring back to long range.

The elongated jab

- When is it appropriate to jab and follow with a strong rear technique, rather than a stick and move?

- Against which type of fighter would you use the stick and move strategically?

- Close distance with the elongated jab when circling your opponent from long range, and quickly get back to long range before your opponent has a chance to counter-strike.

- Is it more beneficial to circle to one side than the other? Why? If your opponent cuts you off, how can you start circling the other way without stepping into his power strike?

- Work on switching from circular to linear movement. Use circular movement while working on your set-up; use linear movement when you feel that you have the upper hand and can safely press forward.

Throwing multiple jabs

- You can also close distance with multiple quick jabs. Use explosive moves when your opponent is at a distinct disadvantage; use short and patient moves when working on strategy.

- Each time you jab, take a tiny step forward to close distance gradually, until you are within reach to follow with a strong combination.

- Have patience while working your way to the inside. Multiple jabs in conjunction with many small steps seem more threatening than one sudden explosive move.

Circling with the jab

- Practice circling the heavy bag both left and right, throwing a jab each time you step. Stay in a boxer's stance to keep your centerline protected. In contrast to closing distance with the jab, when circling, your distance to the target should remain constant.

- Which is easier: circling left from a left fighting stance, or circling right from a left fighting stance? Why?

- When circling toward your opponent's power side (usually the side from which he throws his rear techniques), be careful not to circle into his counter-strike. What strategic benefits do you get from circling toward your opponent's lead side?

Jabbing with broken rhythm

- Some jabs should be faster than others, with a varied beat between strikes. Broken rhythm confuses your opponent and makes it difficult for him to block your strikes.

- Practice multiple jabs with broken rhythm. Count the beats in your head, speeding up and slowing down with the count. This makes you more aware of your rhythm.

- The jab should be like a gun ready to fire. Keep the strike in contact with the target a minimal amount of time, and snap it back to the guard position in preparation for a second strike.

Gauging distance for the power jab

- The jab can be used either as a feeler to gauge distance, or to confuse your opponent. A hard, stiff jab has the ability to knock your opponent back.

- Have your partner hold focus mitts while you practice the jab for power. The pivot in your lead leg with your heel toward your opponent should now be more pronounced. Focus on throwing the jab absolutely straight with the weight of your body behind it.

- The power jab is a little slower than the quick jab. Speed is sacrificed for power, because of the greater movement in your body.

- If you don't throw the jab absolutely straight, power is sacrificed. Why?

Power jabs can knock an opponent back or out.

- Each time your partner steps, distance increases or decreases and the angle changes. For a maximum power jab, step with your partner until the distance for you is optimal.

- Practice power jabs on focus mitts with your partner moving back, forward, and to the side.

- Can you decide the direction of the fight? When you speed up the jab and take tiny steps forward, it is more difficult for your opponent to sidestep the attack.

- If your opponent steps forward to stifle your jab, try taking a step back and time the jab to his forward motion.

Jabbing the double-end bag

- The double-end bag is a small bag attached with a bungee cord to both the floor and the ceiling. When you strike the bag, it swings back at you. If you don't strike it straight, it will swing wildly.

- Work on circling the double-end bag, throwing a jab each time you step. Practice timing your strikes to the movement of the bag.

- If the bag starts to swing wildly, instead of stopping it with your hands, use footwork to step into position to again strike it straight.

- Is it easier to step to your right or left around the double-end bag? Why?

Jabbing the double-end bag.

Retreating with the jab

- The jab is useful as a distraction when creating distance between yourself and your opponent.

- With your opponent backed up against the ropes, work your way out with multiple jabs to keep him occupied.

- Your opponent is most likely to counter-strike when there is a short pause between combinations. Because the jab is so quick, it helps keep him on his toes while you move back to long range.

- You are more vulnerable when stepping back than when stepping forward. One reason is because you can't use your momentum against your opponent. What is another reason?

Using the jab strategically

- Use the jab strategically. If both you and your opponent are equally aggressive, you will simply trade blows. There is a time for offense and a time for defense.

- Engage in light sparring with your partner, limiting your strikes to the jab only. Try to take different targets to confuse your opponent. Experiment with the elongated jab (stick and move) from a distance.

- Work on circling your opponent with the jab, then moving back to the center of the ring after you have backed him up against the ropes.

THE REAR CROSS

We have now talked about how to get started with offense, and the significance of the jab as the most basic, yet perhaps most versatile, kickboxing technique. We have looked at a variety of ways to use the jab, including speed, set-up, and power. Still, it doesn't surprise me if your next question is: "When do I get to knock 'em out?" It is not necessarily the power of a strike that determines its knockout capability. Other factors, such as accuracy, choosing the best target, and timing are equally important. But power, even if it doesn't result in a knockout, will certainly help get your opponent's attention. Because of its power potential, the next punch you will learn is the rear cross. A second reason to learn the rear cross at this time is because it follows naturally and smoothly off of the jab.

3 views of the Rear Cross

The rear cross is a straight strike thrown with your rear hand. The primary purpose of the rear cross is to knock your opponent out. When a jab and a rear cross are put together into a combination, they are commonly referred to as a one-two punch combination. From now on, whenever your trainer calls "one-two," he wants you to throw the jab, immediately followed by the rear cross.

Jab   Rear Cross

The power of the rear cross is derived by a series of events that occur simultaneously. Your foot, hips, and shoulders must rotate together at precisely the same time. This places the weight of your body behind the punch. Initiate the rear cross with the elbow pointed toward the ground. Do not raise the elbow prior to punching.

This section covers:

- Body mechanics for the rear cross
- The non-working hand
- In the gym
- What's in a good rear cross?
- Summary and review

BODY MECHANICS FOR THE REAR CROSS

Throw the rear cross by pivoting your rear foot in the direction of line 1 (your heel should be off the floor). Simultaneously rotate your hips and shoulders into alignment with centerline A.

Keep your upper body, from the knuckles on your right hand to your left shoulder, in a straight line toward your opponent. This brings the centerline of your upper body above your lead leg.

Synchronize your moves with the rotation of your fist to the horizontal position just prior to impact. Keep your elbow pointed toward the ground until the punch is fully extended. This protects your ribs and ensures that your body weight is behind the punch for power.

THE NON-WORKING HAND

The hand that is not striking or blocking at the moment is referred to as the **non-working hand**. In order to minimize target exposure, it is important to keep the non-working hand near the chin, or to bring it forward to a checking position in front of the face. After you have thrown the punch, the "punching hand" should also return to its point of origin, as should the body. Do not return your punch to a higher or lower position than it originated from, providing that it was properly positioned to begin with.

IN THE GYM

Rear cross, now! Remember, the strike starts at the floor with your foot and hip pivoting for power. Pivot all the way forward, bending your rear knee slightly to drop your weight into the punch. Dig in with the ball of your rear foot. If you allow your foot to slide on the canvas, your punch will not be as effective. Keep your elbows in front of your body to avoid punching with arm power alone. Throw alternating jabs and rear crosses that complement one another. When the jab comes back, it should pull the rear cross out. Rotate your shoulders a little more.

I'm coming around with the focus mitts now, and will call out a number. That's how many strikes I want you to throw. Make sure that you have a target for your strikes. For example, if I call out three, and you throw a jab, a rear cross, and another rear cross, but your first rear cross moves your opponent back, you need to do something to close that distance. If I step back when you jab, you need to step forward with your next strike. Faster now! Snap the punch more! Stay relaxed in your shoulders. Tensing deprives the punch of full penetrating force. Throw a lot of double and triple jabs to keep your opponent occupied. Be a bit quicker with your follow-up strike, or it won't land.

Let's reiterate the point of origin concept: wherever a technique leaves from, it must return to. There are two main reasons for this:

1. In order to reset your body for a follow-up technique, your hand or foot must return to the original position.

2. Any time you throw a strike or kick, you automatically create an opening on yourself. To minimize target exposure, it is imperative that you bring your "tools" back to the guard position.

Try these exercises on **POINT OF ORIGIN**:

Exercise 1

Observe yourself in the mirror while throwing jabs and rear crosses, each time making note of targets that are exposed when you fail to bring your hand back to the point of origin. For example, throw a jab, but instead of bringing your hand back to your jaw along the same path it left on, bring it back slightly low to your ribs or hip instead.

Exercise 2

Experiment on the heavy bag by throwing multiple strikes with the same hand. Try double and triple jabs, or double rear crosses. First, retrieve your hand to other positions than point of origin. Repeat the exercise, but retrieve your hand to the point of origin along the same path it left on. How does retrieving your hand to point of origin affect your ability to fire successive strikes rapidly? How does it affect your power?

Measure distance with the jab, and follow with the rear cross.

Which fighter has the non-working hand in a good position?

Wrong: Low and too far back

Correct: Guarding the chin

Wrong: Too low

Wrong: Head exposed

Wrong: Ribs exposed

WHAT'S IN A GOOD REAR CROSS?

An accurately placed rear cross can score a knockout. The effectiveness of the strike also depends on your timing. Since the rear cross usually follows the jab, it is essential to note your opponent's reaction to the jab. Some fighters defend the jab by slipping it (moving your head to the side) and firing a fast counter-strike. Others like to parry or block. Ideally, you should throw the rear cross the moment you feel the jab land. If your opponent slips or parries the jab, his head is not likely to be in position for your rear cross. But if your jab lands, it may stun your opponent for a fraction of a second and allow you to land the rear cross.

A rear cross that lands with power is likely to stagger your opponent. His head will now be exposed with his chin up, his hands low, and his mind split between defense and offense. This is a good time to think of the finish. Because of the power of the rear cross, your opponent may have taken a step back. In order to land your next strike, you must now take a step forward to close distance. You can further increase power by timing your rear cross to your opponent's movement. If your first strike lands and knocks your opponent back, follow with a second rear cross as he regroups and comes toward you.

A rear cross can stagger your opponent.

SUMMARY AND REVIEW

The rear cross has a longer distance to travel than the jab, and therefore more time to build momentum for power. While the jab is often used for speed and set-up, the rear cross is used to knock your opponent back or out. The rear cross works great in combination with the jab. When throwing the strike, pivot your rear foot with your toes toward the target. Throw the punch as straight as possible from point of origin, with movements synchronized so that your hand lands on target at precisely the same time as the pivot in your rear foot and upper body ends.

Powering up the rear cross

- Practice the rear cross for power on focus mitts or a heavy bag by pivoting your rear foot to the front, simultaneously bending your rear knee (setting down on the strike). Retrieve your hand to point of origin as soon as the strike has landed.

- Think of the strike as a gun ready to fire. The move should be quick and straight with full follow-through.

- Be careful not to raise or slide your rear foot forward. For maximum power, dig the ball of your foot into the floor.

Throwing the double rear cross

- The rear cross is a power strike designed to knock your opponent out. Practice the double rear cross on the heavy bag, throwing the strike as straight as possible with the full weight of your body behind it.

- Bring your hand back to point of origin between strikes, making the beat between them as short as possible. If your opponent gets dazed or off balance from the first strike, the second strike should finish him.

- It is easy to cheat and reset your hand halfway between strikes. Don't get ahead of yourself by thinking of the second strike before the first is complete.

- Because the first strike is likely to move your opponent back, you may need to step forward with the follow-up strike.

Jab/rear cross practice on the double-end bag

- When the jab and rear cross are thrown in combination, they are often referred to as a "one-two combination." Practice the one-two combination on the double-end bag, taking tiny steps around the bag with each strike.

- Stay in a good boxer's stance. Work on timing the strike to the movement of the bag. Ideally, you want to strike the bag as it comes toward you, but before it is all the way up by your face.

JAB

REAR CROSS

- Step in one direction first, then reverse and go the other way. Take two or three steps between strikes. This simulates adjusting to your opponent's timing and openings.

- Mix it up, sometimes throwing multiple jabs, sometimes a one-two combination, and sometimes double rear crosses.

Speeding up the jab/rear cross combination

- The jab is a set-up for the stronger rear cross, but if you allow your opponent too much time to regroup after you land the jab, you defeat the purpose of the jab, and your rear cross may not have the intended effect.

- Work the heavy bag and practice shortening the beat between the jab and the rear cross. Make sure that your body mechanics are correct with good pivots and the weight of your body behind each strike.

- When speeding up your combinations, don't fall back on using arm power only by neglecting the movement in your lower body.

- Your intent and commitment to a technique should be total. Don't throw your strikes half-heartedly.

Setting up the rear cross with the jab

- The jab is often thrown as a distance closer, allowing you to get within reach with your stronger rear technique.

- Have your partner hold focus mitts. Practice the double jab followed by a rear cross. When your partner steps back, take tiny steps forward to stay within punching range.

- The jabs should be quick with the intent of annoying your opponent and getting a feel for distance. When following with the rear cross, set down on the strike by bending your rear knee and using the weight of your body for power.

- Fake a strike by twitching your shoulder and watching for your partner's reaction. Does he tense or move the mitt in anticipation of the strike? This is a good indication of how he will react in sparring.

Target practice for the jab and rear cross

- Practice taking different targets with your jab/rear cross combination on the heavy bag. Jab low to the mid-section and follow with a rear cross to the head, or jab high and follow with a rear cross low, and then throw your second rear cross high.

- The more you mix it up, the more confusing and difficult it is for your opponent to defend against the strikes.

- When striking low, cover high with your non-punching hand against your opponent's counter-strikes.

- When up against an aggressive hand combination, what types of kicks can you use to stop your opponent's advance or disturb his rhythm? More about kicks in Section 2.

Broken rhythm in the jab/cross combination

- A steady rhythm enables your opponent to block everything you throw. Broken rhythm makes it more difficult for him to defend against the strikes.

- Work on broken rhythm, sometimes using a shorter and sometimes a longer beat between the jab and the rear cross.

- Add a fake or shoulder twitch. This will confuse your opponent and help you break his rhythm.

Heavy bag practice with flurries

- When your opponent is tired or hurt, a fast flurry of punches could create **sensory overload**, leaving him unable to defend himself.

- Work for twenty seconds at a steady pace on the heavy bag, then explode with a ten-punch jab/cross combination, then go back to a steady pace for twenty seconds.

- Work two-minute rounds and develop a feel for when there is 10-15 seconds left in the round. Explode with a flurry until the bell rings.

- When your opponent throws a flurry, work on defense and let him tire himself. When he is tired and his punches lose their sting, retaliate with a double rear cross.

Be aware of the position of your guard. Fighting with your guard down, especially in the early stages of training, develops bad habits that you may pay for later.

- For muscular endurance, throw alternating jabs and rear crosses as fast as you can on the heavy bag for twenty-second intervals, with a ten-second rest in between. Start with a set of four twenty-second intervals, and build up to a set of ten.

- When you get tired, don't give in to your desire to slow down. How can you synchronize your breathing to assist your endurance?

Sparring practice with the jab and rear cross

- Engage in light contact sparring, using the jab and the rear cross only. Be unpredictable, throwing multiple jabs high and low, followed by single or double rear crosses.

- Explode with flurries for five seconds, then go back to a slower pace.

- Incorporate good footwork (we will talk more about footwork in the next sub-section) and strike when stepping forward or back. Avoid getting cornered by your opponent.

BASIC FOOTWORK

Let's talk about footwork next. Because fighting is so dynamic, now that you know how to throw the first two basic strikes, you must also learn how to maneuver yourself around the ring. Basic movement consists of four major directions: forward, backward, left, and right. Later, you will learn to incorporate many different directions and angles, but for now, let's start with these four basic ones.

This section covers:

- When moving, does it matter which foot you step with first?
- What's in good footwork?
- Adding momentums
- Summary and review

WHEN MOVING, DOES IT MATTER WHICH FOOT YOU STEP WITH FIRST?

In general, you should step with the foot closest to the direction of travel first, and readjust the width of your stance with your rear foot. When stepping forward, step with your lead foot first, and when stepping back, step with your rear foot first. The same concept applies to stepping left and right. When stepping left, step with your lead foot first, and when stepping right, step with your rear foot first (remember, this assumes that you are in a left fighting stance). This concept is called the basic movement theory. The primary reason for the development of the **basic movement theory** is to keep you from crossing your feet. It also allows you to move smoothly and with good balance, without telegraphing your intents to your opponent. When, then, do you step forward and when do you step back?

Stepping forward is usually utilized by the aggressive fighter; if you have dazed or knocked your opponent back, and you need to close distance in order to land your next strike. As you initiate your step with your lead foot, your stance will be slightly wide for a moment. Your rear foot should now follow and close the gap, so that the distance between your feet remains constant.

When stepping forward with a strike, your stance will be slightly wide for a moment.

Stepping back, on the other hand, is utilized when you are either overpowered, or when you need to use a strategic move to outsmart your opponent. Stepping back is therefore not a weakness.

A step back can make your opponent's strike miss.

Stepping left or right is used to sidestep an attack, or to create a more superior angle for your own strikes and kicks. This lateral movement allows you to move off the line of attack. It may also decrease the distance to your opponent, giving you reach on a taller fighter without jeopardizing your own safety.

A lateral step off the attack line helps you establish a superior position toward your opponent's back.

Try these exercises on **THE BASIC MOVEMENT THEORY**:

Exercise 1

From a left fighting stance, move forward several times, each time stepping with your lead foot first and adjusting the width of your stance with your rear foot. Your rear foot should move forward the exact same distance as your lead foot, so that the distance between your feet remains constant. Repeat the exercise moving back and stepping with your rear foot first.

Exercise 2

Have a partner mirror your moves, so that each time you step forward, he steps back, keeping the distance between you constant. This helps you develop a feel for distance.

Exercise 3

Experiment with moving left and right, again stepping with the foot closest to the direction of travel first. If you violate the concept of basic movement, your stance will be either too narrow, or your feet will be crossed. This may result in a loss of balance. To demonstrate this, cross your feet and have your partner try to push you over. Now, get in a good fighting stance where the distance between your feet is correct, and again have your partner try to push you over. Which stance were you more comfortable with? When were you most stable?

Exercise 4

Repeat the exercises above, but add a strike to your movement. For example, step forward with your lead foot, adjust the width of your stance with your rear foot, and throw a jab. This helps you develop the ability to strike while moving.

Exercise 5

Face your partner and have him mirror your moves and step back each time you step forward. In order to land your strikes now, you must speed up and be a step quicker than your partner. Most people find it more difficult to fight moving backward than for-ward, and the distance between you and your partner will gradually decrease until you are within striking range.

WHAT'S IN GOOD FOOTWORK?

Footwork is sometimes referred to as "ring generalship." You have many options on how to move, depending on the characteristics of your opponent. However, don't allow your feet to move without purpose. Observe your opponent's footwork to determine what kind of fighter he is. Then use footwork to close distance when you are the aggressor, to increase distance when you need to defend, or to change the angle to position for a maximum power strike.

A fighter without footwork is like a woodworker with his tools nailed to the workbench.

Footwork can also take place at many different speeds, making a quick attack or retreat possible. There is **stalking footwork**, consisting of many small steps forward to gradually move your opponent back in preparation for your attack. And there is **quick footwork**, also called "on your bicycle." Use this type of footwork to stay off the attack line of an aggressive opponent, to circle him, and to quickly move in and out, flicking jabs from many different angles. Try to stay on the balls of your feet when moving. You may dip the heel momentarily, but you should avoid becoming flat footed. Staying light on your feet allows you to switch direction faster, to launch a kick faster, or to bring a knee up in defense against a leg attack.

It should be understood that fighting is a "gain/ lose" situation, where sometimes you need to give something up in order to gain a greater advantage. The concept of basic movement may be violated if it benefits you, and if you are aware of the consequences of doing so.

Footwork should ultimately be used to maneuver into a more desirable position. For example, when both you and your opponent are in left fighting stances and facing each other, your positions are equally superior. If you are of equal size and ability, it makes little sense to fight from this position, as you will simply be trading blows. The weaker fighter, in particular, must therefore find a way to fight from a superior position, where he isn't disadvantaged by his opponent's greater strength. By using proper footwork, you can quickly move into such a position and execute your techniques from an angle where you are not at risk of getting struck. Remember that power and speed are of little use if you can't land your strikes.

Fighters in equally superior positions.

Try these exercises on **FOOTWORK** and **position of superiority**:

Exercise 6

Stay away from your opponent's power side, usually the side from which he throws his rear techniques.

1. If both you and your opponent are in left fighting stances, how would you move to stay away from his power side?

2. How would you eliminate the use of one or both of your opponent's hands just by positioning differently?

3. If your opponent switches to a right fighting stance while you stay in a left, how does this affect your ability to move into a superior position?

Exercise 7

In order to create more power and open up targets for your strikes, you may need to change the angle at which you are facing your opponent. This can be accomplished in several ways:

1. You can change the angle by taking a step with your rear foot only, with your lead foot only, or with both feet.

2. You can change the angle by waiting until your opponent takes a step, creating a new angle.

Because fighting is so dynamic, there are many opportunities when the angle for a maximum power strike is right. Have your partner stand stationary while you experiment with changing the angle. For example, keep your lead foot stationary and move your rear foot forward one inch at a time, until you have switched from a left to a right fighting stance. Pause after each one-inch step and note the openings. Also note how changing the angle changes your reach.

Repeat the exercise, but keep your rear foot stationary while moving your lead foot back one inch at a time. Are you ever in a position where your opponent has the advantage? Is your back ever turned toward your opponent?

Exercise 8

Stand stationary and have your partner move around you by using proper footwork. Observe how targets open and close. When is the best time to strike? Move with your partner and try to position for a maximum power strike without jeopardizing your own safety.

Keith's Corner

One day early in my career, everybody was standing around the ring watching the fight. One of the observers kept telling the rest of us about the awesome footwork of his buddy. "What's so good about it?" I asked. "He can move, man!" the other observer responded. I smiled. "Anybody can move, man!" I took a step to my right and a step to my left. "See?" Disgusted with my sarcasm, the man walked away. So, my question remained, what is good footwork?

The fighter who dictates the fight can force his opponent to step in a given direction at a given time. Good footwork can force your opponent against the ropes or into a corner. Good footwork can tire and frustrate your opponent. Many good athletes have great footwork. Michael Jordan, for example, has a great shot, but it is his footwork that creates the slam dunk. A receiver may make great catches, but it is his ability to run and evade tacklers after the catch that makes him truly great. One of the greatest boxers of all times (or perhaps the *greatest*), Muhammad Ali, also had the greatest footwork.

Good footwork is not the same as "fancy footwork." It is not absolutely necessary to have full control of the Ali shuffle. In fact, personal style has very little to do with it. Rather, good footwork is one's ability to take the appropriate foot action at the appropriate moment. Good footwork is about controlling and manipulating distance, limiting your opponent's offensive and defensive capabilities while maximizing your own. Good footwork enables you to destroy your opponent's power, or to completely suffocate his offensive tools. Good footwork helps you create distance at the precise moment, causing your opponent to miss. In essence, good footwork allows you to hit without being hit (this is your goal, remember?). This includes the ability to give your opponent the impression that you are within striking range, giving him the confidence to initiate a strike, only to find it miss and get countered or smothered by your footwork.

ADDING MOMENTUMS

The fighter who controls footwork controls the fight. But controlling footwork extends beyond just your own footwork. You must also learn to control your opponent's footwork. Once you achieve this, your strikes become more effective. The concept of **adding momentums** works on the principle of your opponent "walking into" your strike. One way to add momentums is to wait until your opponent steps toward you, and to time your strike to his forward motion. Because most people tend to mirror their opponent's moves, you can also try taking a half-step back to lure your opponent forward. This gives you a feel for his rhythm as he attempts to close distance. Now, quickly reverse direction by taking a half-step forward, simultaneously throwing a strike.

A half-step back (a step with your rear foot only) increases distance and may lure your opponent to come forward into your counter-strike.

The opposite of adding momentums is called **canceling momentums**. *Going with the motion* of your opponent's strike decreases the power of that strike. For example, when your opponent throws a jab, instead of blocking (or worse, taking) the jab, execute a *rearward slip* to make the jab miss (more about slipping in Section 3).

When defending against an angled attack to your head, you can cancel momentums by moving your head to the side and "rolling under" the strike. This upper body movement is called *bobbing and weaving*, and will be explained in more detail in Section 3. Going with the motion of a strike requires being very relaxed and aware of what your opponent is doing.

Summary and review

The basic movement theory states that whenever moving, you should step with the foot closest to the direction of travel first. When moving forward, step with your lead foot first; when moving back, step with your rear foot first. The purpose of the basic movement theory is to keep you from crossing your feet. Position of superiority means placing yourself in a position that enables you to use your techniques effectively, while eliminating the use of some or all of your opponent's techniques. This is especially important when you are up against a stronger or faster fighter.

Basic movement stepping forward

- From a left fighting stance, start at one end of the room and step forward with your lead foot first, readjusting the width of your stance with your rear foot so that the distance between your feet remains constant. Keep stepping forward in this manner until you reach the other end of the room.

- Take a series of steps at different speeds, then stop and look at your stance to determine if you have balance and a proper toe-to-heel line.

- The offense-minded fighter often has the upper hand in a fight. Whenever possible, step forward rather than back. This allows you to pressure your opponent to the rear.

- What are the benefits of lateral movement? Is it possible to close distance and move laterally simultaneously?

- Throwing a strike simultaneously to closing distance gives your opponent more to worry about, making you less vulnerable to a counter-attack.

- Varied rhythm confuses your opponent and allows you to take advantage of a weakness in his defense.

Basic movement stepping back

- Repeat the above exercise stepping back. Step with your rear foot first, readjusting the width of your stance with your lead foot.

- There are basically three times when you want to step back: to defend against your opponent's attack, to create distance for a long range technique, or as a strategic move to lure your opponent forward into close range.

- When stepping back, it is equally important to keep your opponent occupied. Try throwing a kick every time you step back.

Mirroring your opponent's moves

- As far as distance is concerned, we have a natural tendency to mirror our opponent's moves. For example, if your opponent steps forward, you have a natural tendency to step back, so that he doesn't crowd you. If he steps back, you have a natural tendency to step forward to close distance.

- Experiment with mirroring your partner's moves, so that each time he steps forward you step back, and vice versa. This gives you a feel for distance.

- If somebody pushes you, you have a natural tendency to resist; you will push in the opposite direction. Can defeating this natural tendency work to your advantage? When going with the motion of a push or a pull, how can you increase the momentum of your counter-strike?

Using range strategically

- When moving forward, add a strike to your movement. Since your opponent will mirror your moves, and since it is easier to move forward than back, the distance between you and your opponent will gradually decrease, until you are within reach to land your strikes.

- If you have longer arms than your opponent, stay at a distance that allows you optimum reach for your hands. This makes your opponent's strikes short of reach.

- If your opponent has longer arms than you, stay at a distance that allows you optimum reach for your kicks, but out of range for his strikes.

Fighting from kicking range keeps you out of reach of your opponent's punches.

Circling strategy

- Most fights employ circular movement. We have a natural tendency to circle with our opponent in order to protect our back. But this allows your opponent to command the direction of the fight, and may move you into a disadvantaged position where you are either cornered or with your back to the ropes.

A pivot-step away from the ropes can help you get back to center of the ring.

- Whenever you get within two feet of the ropes, try to move back to the center of the ring.

- When your opponent starts to circle, cut him off by stepping the opposite direction.

- A fight is to a great degree mental. If you can take charge mentally from the start, you have already won much of the battle.

Cutting off the ring with lateral movement

- Lateral movement (side to side) may give you an advantage over circular movement, because you eliminate the tendency to circle yourself into a trapped position with your back to the ropes.

- When your opponent starts to circle, practice "cutting off the ring." You do this by stepping to the side and toward the direction he is circling.

- As distance between you decreases, time a strike to your opponent's forward motion, so that he walks into the strike.

Superior positioning when striking

- When you are in the superior position, you eliminate the use of one or both of your opponent's hands. Your opponent also has a tougher time defending strikes that come from different angles.

- Position away from your opponent's power side (the side from which he throws his rear techniques).

- Try to move into a position that gives you free strikes to your opponent's centerline.

- Instead of approaching your opponent from the front, approach slightly from the side, preferably toward the side from which he throws his lead techniques.

- You can also gain superiority by breaking your opponent's focus. If you overwhelm him with strikes to many different targets, he is unable to defend them all. This allows you to take advantage of a weakness in his defense.

- Some positions are equally superior. You must now rely on the element of surprise to disrupt your opponent's physical and mental focus.

Approach your opponent at an angle toward his weak side.

Adjusting to your opponent's movement

- Experiment with adjusting to your opponent's movement, so that you maintain superiority slightly away from his power side. Whenever your opponent moves, adjust to his position to protect your centerline.

- How can you keep your opponent from gaining the superior position? It takes longer to react than to act. If you initiate the technique, it gives you the benefit of time. Try to be the one in charge.

- The available targets have a lot to do with your position in relation to your opponent. Experiment with different angles, making note of how targets open and close depending on whether you attack straight or from the side.

- Pausing shortly before attacking may give you a better perception of available targets. Work on striking with broken rhythm, sometimes slowing down or pausing, and sometimes exploding with a combination.

THE HOOK

If kickboxing relied on striking and kicking only, it wouldn't be called "the sweet science" (actually, we borrowed this term from boxing). One reason it is classified as a science is because it takes place at many different ranges and angles, making sound strategy a crucial part of the fight game. A variety of techniques have been developed to accommodate the many situations a fighter may encounter. The jab and rear cross, for example, are essentially long range techniques, meaning that they are thrown at a range from where you can barely reach your opponent. But no fighter is complete if he is limited to long range only. Imagine the frustration if your opponent moved forward to nullify the power in your perfect rear cross, and you had nothing to follow up with. So, now that you have learned the two basic strikes for long range fighting, it is time to learn the two basic strikes for *short range fighting*. Because competition kickboxing takes place in a confined area (the ring), there are many times when you will get in a clinch or within a foot's distance of your opponent. Fighting at close range is also referred to as *inside fighting*.

Lead hook

Rear hook

The two basic and most often used strikes for fighting on the inside are the hook and the uppercut. Both can be thrown with either your lead or rear hand. Let's start with the hook, which is an extremely powerful kickboxing weapon.

This section covers:

- Body mechanics for the hook
- Where does the power come from?
- Glove-up with Keith
- Punching 101
- What's in a good hook?
- Some pointers on hooking strategies
- Broken rhythm
- Summary and review

BODY MECHANICS FOR THE HOOK

Throw the lead hook by moving your upper body slightly to the left of centerline A, simultaneously dropping in the knees. This positions your upper body above your lead leg.

Keep your guard up and your elbows tucked close to your body. A common mistake is to throw the arm wide, often called the "haymaker" or "John Wayne" punch. In order to derive maximum power and protection, keep the hook short and tight.

Start to turn back toward line 2. Begin the pivot in your foot by pushing off with the ball of your lead foot. Simultaneously raise the heel of your lead foot and begin to turn the knee and hip of your lead leg, bringing the strike back along centerline B.

Raise your elbow gradually, until your arm is at a ninety-degree angle in front of your face. The blow should impact your opponent's right side.

Throw the rear hook by doing the opposite of what you just learned. Move your upper body slightly to the right of centerline A, simultaneously dropping in the knees. This positions your upper body above your rear leg.

Begin the pivot back toward line 1 by pushing off with the ball of your rear foot. Simultaneously raise the heel of your rear foot and begin to turn the knee and hip of your rear leg, bringing the strike back along centerline B. The blow should impact your opponent's left side.

WHERE DOES THE POWER COME FROM?

You attain power by keeping the elbow of the hooking arm in front of the body. A properly thrown hook is not a wild swing, but a tight strike that relies on *body rotation*. The elbow leaves the body only long enough to bring mobility to the technique. Hooks can be thrown to the body or head and cause significant injury. Many fights are won by knockout with a hook to the jaw. The hook is also used to "wear down your opponent's body"; in other words, to bring his guard down to protect his ribs and open targets on his head.

Vertical hook

Horizontal hook

There are *vertical* and *horizontal* hooks. Normally, the vertical hook is thrown to the body, and the horizontal hook is thrown to the head (vertical and horizontal refer to your hand position on impact).

Targets for the hook are the mid-section and the head (including the jaw, nose, and temples). When hooking to the body, impact your opponent's ribs, solar plexus, liver on his right, or spleen on his left. Your hand position on impact can be either vertical or horizontal, or halfway between an uppercut and a hook. In other words, the path of the strike should be at a forty-five degree angle upward. This is probably the most effective hand position when hooking to the body, because it allows you to spring from your knees, placing the mass of your body behind the blow.

When hooking to the body, impact the ribs, solar plexus, liver, or spleen.

When hooking to the head, raise the elbow of the hooking arm by *gradually* rotating your shoulder until your arm is horizontal and parallel with the floor. Upon impact, the "V" of the elbow joint should be in front of your face.

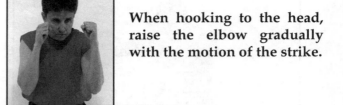

When hooking to the head, raise the elbow gradually with the motion of the strike.

The hook can be thrown stationary or stepping. Stepping in the direction of the strike adds body momentum and power, providing that the step is done quickly and all components of the technique happen simultaneously. This can be thought of as "throwing within movement." When throwing a stepping lead hook, step forward with your *rear foot* at a forty-five degree angle toward the right front corner, simultaneously pushing off with the ball of your lead foot, raising the heel and turning the knee, hip, and shoulder into the technique. Avoid stepping, pausing, and then punching. This is a "one-step" process. When throwing a stepping rear hook, step forward with your *lead foot* at a forty-five degree angle toward the front left corner, simultaneously pushing off with the ball of your rear foot, raising the heel and turning the knee, hip, and shoulder into the technique. Your stance in these stepping hooks will be slightly wide for a moment. Upon impact, bring the non-stepping foot forward to close your stance. This places you "inside" of your opponent, or at close quarter range.

In addition to creating power, a step enables you to reach openings that are normally not available for the hook. For example, because of the way your opponent carries his elbows, it may be difficult to reach his mid-section or solar plexus. By stepping to the side, the line of attack changes slightly, and a target that initially seemed unavailable may now be exposed.

When your opponent blocks your strikes with his elbows (left), stepping slightly to the side may enable you to strike his centerline (below).

Glove Up with Keith

We're going to work on inside fighting today. Inside fighting, or fighting at close range, is an important part of the fight game that most martial artists don't know how to use properly. When watching a karate tournament, if you ever see a fight go to the inside, I'd sure like to know about it.

The first technique we're going to work is the hook to the head. Start by pivoting your foot and body and gradually raising your elbow. Keep your arm tight until impact. Let your fist go through the target by angling the strike slightly down, keeping your arm and shoulder relaxed and snappy. You should feel the snap coming from your shoulder and, like ripples on water, transferring through your arm. When throwing two hooks to the same side, reset your body to the point of origin between strikes.

Jab, rear cross, lead hook now! Make sure that there is no separation between strikes. Think of it as a tram going up a mountain. When the gondola at the top starts on its way down, the one at the bottom starts on its way up. Staying relaxed helps with speed. The faster the body, the faster the strike. Some fighters throw the jab and rear cross, and then pause briefly before throwing the hook. But you can increase speed and power by eliminating that pause.

PUNCHING 101

Power is defined as the force with which you strike your opponent, and is derived from several sources working in harmony toward a common goal. If your goal is to impact a target with maximum force, you must train your body mechanics to work harmoniously toward this goal. You must strike by utilizing your body's mass in conjunction with the speed of the technique. This, in turn, is combined with proper position and leverage. Balance is therefore an element of power. Center your upper body over the foundation of your lower body and project all energy in the same direction. When throwing a punch, if your upper body is moving to the rear while your arm is moving forward, a loss of power results due to the conflict with the direction of energy. You can increase power in your punch combinations by relying on the following two principles:

1. **"Set down" on the foot opposite of the striking hand.** If you strike with your left hand, the majority of your weight should be on your right foot. By allowing that foot to stay planted, you also allow for better balance (a more solid stance), and therefore greater ability to create a powerful punch.

2. **Bring your hand all the way back to the guard position** before throwing a second strike with the same hand. This gives you more time to build momentum.

One of the best ways to learn balance and proper body mechanics for punching is through the concept of **weight transfer**. When throwing a punch combination, your weight should shift from one foot to the other depending on which strike you throw. For example, in a one-two-three punch combination (jab, rear cross, lead hook), your weight should shift as follows:

1. When throwing the jab, your weight will be on your *rear foot*, with the heel of your lead foot off the floor.

2. When throwing the rear cross, your weight should shift to your lead foot, with the heel of your rear foot off the floor, and the heel of your lead foot planted.

Caution: Do not raise all the way up on your toes, as this may result in a loss of balance. Your foot should stay planted, allowing you to "dig" with the ball of your foot. The weight shift should not be so dramatic that you compromise balance.

Being flat footed (left), or up on the toes of both feet simultaneously (right), destroys your body mechanics and decreases the power of your strikes.

3. When throwing the lead hook, your weight should again shift to your rear foot, with the heel of your lead foot off the floor, and the heel of your rear foot planted.

What's wrong with these fighters' punching mechanics?

Contradictory body mechanics

When throwing the lead hook, if the heel of your rear foot is still off the floor from throwing the rear cross a moment ago, your punch will lack power. Your balance will also suffer. When punching, never be up on the balls of both feet simultaneously.

Legs too straight

If your weight is equal on both feet, you will be punching with arm power only. If your weight is on the foot on the same side as the punching arm, you will have a conflict with the direction of energy, and maximum power cannot be attained. For example, throwing a rear cross while simultaneously placing weight on your rear foot has the effect of moving your upper body slightly to the rear, with some power going forward and some backward. There may also be a loss of balance, because your weight is no longer directly above your foundation.

Off balance

Keith's Knockout Advice

Each technique starts with position. In other words, if you are not close enough to strike your opponent, everything else is of little value. To begin, find a wall and a roll of tape. Measure from the floor up the wall approximately six feet and run the tape vertically back down to the floor. The tape represents your opponent's centerline. Now position yourself in a fighting stance in front of the tape. The tape should be in line with your centerline as well.

Let's start with the jab. Power begins at the ground, generates through the body, comes out the hand, and releases into your opponent. Any break or pause in the following movements result in power loss:

Start by raising the heel of your lead foot. This causes the ball of your lead foot to dig into the floor.

Rotate your lead knee, hip, and shoulder to the inside (toward your centerline). Simultaneously start the jabbing arm forward, keeping your elbow pointed toward the ground.

As your arm moves forward, use the momentum to continue rotating your knee, hip, and shoulder to the inside.

Approximately 3 inches prior to impact, rotate your hand from a vertical to a horizontal position. Your hand, shoulder, hip, and knee should end their rotation upon impact with the target.

Your weight has now transferred from your lead foot to your rear foot, and your rear arm has rotated with your body. Now, with the majority of your weight on your rear foot, you are ready to throw the rear cross:

As the jab starts to return to its point of origin, simultaneously drop the heel of your lead foot and raise the heel of your rear foot off the floor, starting the rear cross forward.

Use the momentum of the returning jab to aid in the rotation of your body for the rear cross.

With the heel of your rear foot raised off the floor and your rear cross coming forward, rotate your rear knee, hip, and shoulder to the inside.

Rotate your hand from a vertical to a horizontal position just prior to impact. Your entire body should finish its rotation at the moment of impact.

With the heel of your lead foot raised off the floor, rotate your lead knee, hip, and shoulder to the inside, simultaneously throwing your lead hook to your opponent's head or body.

You have now transferred the majority of your body weight from your rear foot back to your lead foot. You are now ready to throw the lead hook:

The hook can be thrown with the hand vertical, horizontal, or inverted (palm forward).

As the rear cross begins to return to its point of origin the lead hook begins its route to the target.

Once again, as your rear cross begins to return, the heel of your rear foot drops and the heel of your lead foot raises off the floor.

Use the returning momentum of your rear cross to increase the momentum of your lead hook.

Throw all of your punch techniques using the weight transfer described above. If you want to throw two or more punches with the same hand, snap your body and punch back to the point of origin after impact. Practice two or more punches with the same hand, and different combinations of punches. The purpose of this drill is to learn weight transfer from one foot to the other, body rotation, body position, how to use momentum from one punch to complement the next, how to place the mass of your body behind your strikes, and how to throw fluent combinations. As you become comfortable, take it to the heavy bag, focus mitts, and finally the ring. Not until you can apply it in sparring should you consider yourself the owner of the technique.

WHAT'S IN A GOOD HOOK?

You can attain power in the hook by relying on the following principles:

1. Keep your arms tight to your body.

2. Use body rotation to place the weight and momentum of your body behind the blow. The faster the body, the faster the strike.

3. Apply the concept of weight transfer.

Because the hook is an angled attack that relies on the rotation of your body, keeping your arms tight lessens the rotational inertia and makes the technique faster. It also keeps the sides of your body protected while initiating the technique. Since the arms are naturally faster than the body, it is easy to cheat and throw with arm power only. But since the body is so much more massive than the arms, relying on body rotation throughout the technique vastly increases power. Synchronization between your body and arm is of utmost importance. The arm should not be allowed to lead or "finish the technique on its own"; nor should the body be allowed to move with the arm lagging behind.

What's wrong with these hooks?

Too straight

Too wide

Head exposed

Applying weight transfer, especially between alternating hooks, will further help you utilize the full weight of your body coupled with superior balance. When throwing the lead hook, the heel of your lead foot should come off the floor and not set back down until the strike is complete and your arm returns to its point of origin, and the rear hook starts on its way out. The heel of your rear foot should now come off the floor, allowing you to dig with the ball of that foot, repeating the procedure.

Note: When punching, never be up on the balls of both feet at the same time. The transition from one foot to the other should be smooth and in tune with your strikes.

SOME POINTERS ON HOOKING STRATEGIES

Most kickboxers are familiar with the one-two-three punch combination (jab, rear cross, lead hook), but less often do we see fighters throw a lead hook after a jab and be successful with it. This is one of the more difficult combinations, because:

1. **Both strikes are thrown with the same hand.** In order to gain power in this combination, you must reset your body before starting the second strike.

2. **The strikes employ different directions of motion.** The jab is thrown straight, and the hook is thrown at an angle perpendicular to the jab.

The jab followed by a lead hook is a combination that employs two different directions with the same hand, and is therefore more difficult to find a natural flow in.

When practicing this combination, first throw the jab, then step forward with your lead foot to close distance. Now throw the hook, simultaneously digging with the ball of your lead foot, turning the knee, hip, and shoulder in the direction of the strike. A common mistake when throwing the lead hook is to drop your guard below the level of your chin. This must not happen, as you will open a knockout target for your opponent's counter-strike. Keep your chin tucked down behind your shoulder.

You can also think of the hook as a hooking upper-cut thrown at a forty-five degree angle upward with your elbows tight to your body, using body weight for power. Because the change in angle (direction) between the jab and the hooking uppercut is very slight, the beat between strikes will decrease, making this a fast combination.

Hooks are very effective when thrown in pairs. When the first hook lands, snap your body back to the point

of origin as rapidly as possible. Think of it as a door opening and closing. Once you have achieved point of origin, the second hook should snap back out (opening the door again).

When hooking multiple times with the same hand, the heel of the foot on the same side as the punching hand should stay off the floor between strikes. You can decrease the beat between multiple punches by snapping only your body and arm (not your leg) back to the point of origin.

Keith's Knockout Advice

Once you get proficient at multiple hooks, vary your targets by going body-head, head-body, body-body, or if throwing triples, body-body-head, or head-head-body. The possible choices of combinations are many and should be dictated by the openings that occur. If you throw the first hook to your opponent's body and his hand comes down, then, of course, you want to throw the second hook to his head where the opening is. If the first hook does not create the desired effect, you may want to throw two or three hooks to the body, until your opponent's hands begin to drop. This is what we mean by "wearing down the body." Once your speed builds, you may be able to land two hooks to the same target before the opening closes again.

Try this **JAB/LEAD HOOK** exercise on the heavy bag:

Exercise 1

1. Jab to the head, followed by a lead hook (same hand) to the head.

2. Jab to the head, followed by a lead hook to the body.

3. Jab to the head, followed by a double lead hook (one to the body, one to the head).

4. Jab to the body, followed by a lead hook to the head.

5. Jab to the body, followed by a lead hook to the body.

6. Jab to the body, followed by a double lead hook (one to the body, one to the head).

If you throw all strikes with the same rhythm, your opponent will soon adapt and easily block your attack. The most difficult strikes to defend are those thrown with broken rhythm.

BROKEN RHYTHM

Keith's Corner

Rhythm, also referred to as cadence, is the specific beat by which you throw your strikes; it is a consistent, predictable pattern of timing. If your heart beats one time every second, that would be the rhythm of your heart. If your heart suddenly stopped beating for two seconds and then started again, it would be considered a break in the rhythm. In a fight, both your and your opponent's striking rhythm play a crucial role. If you can establish your opponent's pattern and rhythm, he becomes predictable. A predictable opponent is a beatable opponent. The opposite also holds true. If you can disguise your rhythm and not become

trapped in predictable patterns, you are more difficult to defeat. To take it one step further, if you can make your opponent believe that he has established your rhythm and timing, you can set him up by "changing up." For example, you throw a triple jab:

jab . . . jab . . . jab

and your opponent defends with:

block . . . block . . . block

timed to your jabs at the exact same rhythm.

You have now created several opportunities for yourself. For example, you could try:

jab . . . jab . . . . . (pause) . . . . . jab

or

jab . . . jab . . . (feint with shoulder, forcing opponent to move his hand to block) . . . jab

These are just a few examples of many possibilities. You can also vary your speed continually to achieve broken rhythm. Start with a medium speed:

jab . . . . . jab . . . . . jab

then, suddenly, and without warning:

jab . jab . jab

In order to succeed with this, you must have a good understanding of your opponent's defensive and offensive rhythm. Most fighters vary the speed of their strikes, but within those variations emerge a predictable pattern. It is the fighter who can vary speeds within the same combinations who has mastered and understands rhythm. To illustrate this, let's examine a punch combination which consists of a jab . . . jab . . . left hook to body . . . left hook to head . . . right cross to head. If you were to watch a fighter throw this combination a hundred times, you would probably observe varied speeds, but within those variations would be the same pattern, with each speed having its own pattern and rhythm. There would be a slow-speed rhythm, and a fast-speed rhythm, but no varied speeds within each of the separate combinations.

So, you see, speeding up suddenly allows you to beat your opponent to the punch. Changing your rhythm can disrupt your opponent's timing and create sensory overload. Usually, a couple of unexpected strikes with broken rhythm will make your opponent unable to keep up.

Sensory overload is a state of confusion and chaos often experienced when a fighter is attacked with explosive combinations, where the attacker attempts to take as many targets as possible in the shortest amount of time.

A steady rhythm can benefit you, however, if used as a set-up. Having your opponent lulled into a steady rhythm may give him a false sense of security and lead him to believe that he can block everything you throw. Once your opponent is in tune with your rhythm, throw an explosive combination. One of the best ways to learn broken rhythm is to count the beats in your head, speed up and slow down the count, and make your physical body do the same.

Try these exercises on **BROKEN RHYTHM**:

Exercise 2

When working the heavy bag, listen to the "thuds" of your strikes to determine the rhythm. Is there a steady beat, or is the rhythm broken? Usually, the strikes that get in are off a beat. Practice broken rhythm by adding a slight pause in the middle of a punch combination, or by speeding up some strikes and slowing down others. Counting the beats in your head helps you be more aware of your rhythm.

Exercise 3

It is essential to know when to implement a pause to achieve broken rhythm. In general, when on the outside working your way in, throw continuous combinations to overwhelm your opponent (more about moving from the outside to the inside in Section 5). Once you have found a gap in your opponent's defense, you may need to pause briefly in preparation for taking the opening. Work on changing your ca-

dence without sacrificing power or technique. Under no circumstances should you leave your fist on the target, as this leaves you open for counter-strikes. Remember that the purpose of changing your cadence is to unnerve your opponent.

Summary and review

The hook is essentially an inside fighting technique (close range). Unlike the jab or rear cross, which are thrown straight, the hook is thrown with a twist of the body and should land on the side of your opponent's head or body. You can throw hooks with either your lead or rear hand.

Stepping laterally with the hook

- Utilizing the basic movement theory, circle the heavy bag to the right from a left fighting stance, throwing a lead hook each time you step. Stay in a good boxer's stance to avoid exposing your centerline. When you have worked a complete circle around the bag, circle to the left and throw the rear hook each time you step.

- Stepping hooks can be thrown as a two-count where you step first and let your body set for the hook, or as a one-count where you throw the strike within the movement of the step.

- Snap the hook back to point of origin after impact. This keeps your head protected and allows you to reset into your fighting stance for a second strike.

- Watch your balance. When in close, it is easy to get in the habit of leaning against your opponent and becoming top heavy forward.

If you lean on your opponent, she may step back and throw a counter-strike timed to your loss of balance forward.

Throwing the double hook

- Throw double hooks with the same hand: one low and one high. The purpose of the low hook is to bring your opponent's guard down and open up targets on his head.

- When throwing the low hook, guard high with your other hand.

- The beat between hooks should be short, but don't sacrifice body rotation for speed.

The importance of hand position when throwing the hook

- Your hand position and choice of target for the hook can affect your power, and may determine the strike's destructive capabilities.

- Throw low hooks with your hand turned at a slight upward angle. Then throw high hooks with your hand turned to the vertical position or all the way to the horizontal position.

- Keeping your palm at a slight upward angle for the body hook allows you to drive the hook into the soft internal organs, relying on the weight of your body for power. Turning your hand horizontally allows you to drop your weight with the strike.

Throwing alternating hooks

- Repeat the stepping exercise but, when stepping right, throw a left hook followed by a right hook. When stepping left, throw a right hook followed by a left hook.

- The first hook is now thrown within the movement of the step. This adds the momentum of your body to the strike, and places you in a superior position to your opponent's side.

- When throwing alternating hooks, snap your body back to point of origin to reset for the next strike. Use body momentum from the first hook to gain power in the second hook (pulley effect, remember?)

Throwing the body hook with power

- Have your partner strap on a body shield. Practice throwing body hooks with power. Throw both single and double hooks, and hooks to alternating sides of your partner's body.

- Find specific targets for the body hook. Which will hurt more: getting hit to the ribs or getting hit to the softer organs? Why?

- For maximum penetration, you must throw the hook absolutely straight on impact. A common mistake is to loop the hand back toward you. Even though the strike is thrown with a twist of the body, there should be no circular motion on impact.

- Also practice this exercise with your partner stepping forward and back. Be aware of distance, so that you can close or gap as appropriate.

- Without using a body shield, take turns with your partner to throw hooks to the body. This not only gives you a realistic feel for the target, it also allows you to work on body conditioning.

- Keep the contact controlled and appropriate for the size, strength, and experience of the person you are striking. Even though the contact is controlled, don't sacrifice correct mechanics.

Start slow, working on full body rotation and target accuracy.

Closing distance with the hook

- The hook is essentially an in-fighting technique. Work the heavy bag and practice closing distance with a jab followed by a step forward, throwing the hook when you are within range to do so.

- Which is easiest: a lead jab followed by a lead hook, or a lead jab followed by a rear hook? Why?

- When jabbing high, the hook to the body may be a good follow-up after gap closure. This is because your opponent will be looking at defending high and may leave his body open.

- Repeat the exercise, but with a partner who moves forward, back, and side-to-side. You may now need to throw more than one jab before being within striking range for the hook.

- If your partner steps to the side, how can you utilize his movement to increase the power of your hook? Try to make your partner step into your strike's

path of power. For example, if your partner steps to your right, throw a right hook; if he steps to your left, throw a left hook.

- Have your partner push against you with his shoulder in an attempt to move you to the rear. How can you use a lateral step to gain superiority while simultaneously throwing a hook?

Following up off the hook

- Once you have landed a hook, think of an appropriate follow-up. Experiment with distance to find techniques that work from the inside. Some examples are round house kicks, especially to the legs, uppercuts, and elbow strikes.

- Take as many diverse targets as possible. For example, throw a hook followed by an elbow strike, an uppercut, a round house kick to the legs, and a second round house kick to the head.

Hook followed by elbow strike. Note how the hooking arm simply folds into the elbow strike. We will discuss the elbow in Section 7.

- Your follow-up strike should be a beat faster than your initial strike, to allow you to land the strike while your opponent is still stunned from the hook.

Hooking an opponent on the ropes

- The hook is great against an opponent who is cornered or backed up against the ropes. With your partner on the ropes, experiment with changing the angle at which you are facing him and note how targets that initially seemed inaccessible now become available. Vary your targets for the hook, throwing to the solar plexus, stomach, and ribs.

- Which is faster: multiple hooks with the same hand, or multiple hooks with alternating hands? Why? Make sure to bring your hands back to point of origin between hooks.

- How can you best transition to long range techniques (jab, rear cross) when moving back to the outside?

Strategy for stepping back with the hook

- If your opponent is backed into the ropes, he will first try to defend against your strikes and then throw a counter-strike. When you are within striking range, you must stay as busy as possible.

- Back your partner up against the ropes, throw a hook combination, and move back to long range by throwing a jab or front kick simultaneous with your step back.

Throw a hook (left) or front kick (right) to keep your opponent occupied when gapping and moving from close to long range.

- It is easier to act than react. Force your opponent to react to your strikes, never giving him the opportunity to initiate offense.

Increasing explosiveness in the hook from short range

- Fighters often get tired toward the later rounds, and may lean on each other to get a few seconds rest. Practice throwing short hooks with minimal or no "wind-up" while pushing against your partner. Such a strike must be explosive in order to be effective. Avoid using arm power alone.

- How can you increase the explosiveness of a strike that is thrown from very short range?

- Keep your strikes as tight as possible, relying on the movement in your body for power.

Throwing the double hook as a knockout attempt

- The double hook, especially when thrown to the body, is often used to bring your opponent's guard down and open up targets on his head. If the first hook staggers your opponent, you can throw the double hook to the head as a knockout attempt.

- Practice double hooks with the same hand, increasing the power of the second hook by resetting your body between strikes. Think of it as a door opening and closing.

- Is there ever a time when it might be beneficial to sacrifice body rotation for speed in the double hook?

Hooking the double-end bag

- Practice timing of your hooks to the movement of the double-end bag. Start with some straight jabs and rear crosses. As the bag swings, follow with a hook. The bag will now start swinging perpendicular. Take a short step to the side to again line the bag up with your centerline, and repeat the exercise.

- Try the jab followed by a lead hook off the same hand. Why is it more difficult to gain speed in this combination than when using alternating strikes?

- Can you increase the speed by resetting your body halfway only? What are the drawbacks of this?

Jab/cross/hook combination practice

- You can increase the speed in your combinations by using the pulley effect, where one strike helps the other. The jab-cross-hook is often referred to as a "one-two-three" combination.

- Practice the one-two-three combination on focus mitts, decreasing the beat between strikes so that, as the jab starts on its way back, the rear cross starts on its way out. When the rear cross starts on its way back, the lead hook starts on its way out.

- Practice the one-two-three combination, taking short steps forward with each strike to close distance and back your opponent up.

- When your opponent is against the ropes, explode with a longer combination in an attempt to create sensory overload.

THE UPPERCUT

The next close range technique you will learn is the *uppercut*. This is a vicious power technique thrown deceptively from below, making it difficult to detect in close quarters. The uppercut can tear your opponent down without prior warning. Unfortunately, it is vastly underused, and many fighters don't know how to throw it properly once they do get to the inside.

This section covers:

- Body mechanics for the uppercut
- In the gym
- What's in a good uppercut?
- Following up off the uppercut
- Punching in combinations
- Counter-striking
- Summary and review

BODY MECHANICS FOR THE UPPERCUT

Lead uppercut   **Rear uppercut**

When initiating the uppercut, keep the punching arm close to the body, using body power. Keep your legs slightly bent, so that you can push off with the ball of your foot and drive the strike into the target with an upward, explosive surge. Many fighters tend to throw with the arm only. Since the uppercut is a short traveling technique, it does not need any extra wind-up to be effective.

The uppercut can be broken down into the *straight uppercut* and the *hooking uppercut*. The straight uppercut is thrown vertically straight along the centerline of your opponent's body. The hooking uppercut is thrown at an angle between a straight uppercut and a hook, and is used mostly for striking the body.

Targets for the straight uppercut are the solar plexus and the point of the chin. Targets for the hooking uppercut are the sides of the body, both sides of the jaw, and the point of the chin.

Throw the lead uppercut by moving your upper body to the left of centerline A, simultaneously dropping in the knees and bending slightly at the waist.

Raise your lead knee, hip, and punch together by pushing off with the ball of your lead foot and raising your heel off the floor. The punch should come straight up along centerline A, with your lead knee and hip pointed in the direction of line 2.

Throw the rear uppercut by moving your upper body to the right of centerline A, simultaneously dropping in the knees and bending slightly at the waist.

Bring your rear knee and hip toward line 1, simultaneously throwing the punch straight up along centerline A.

When throwing the *hooking uppercut*, the moves are identical as described with the exception that the punch itself is thrown at a forty-five degree angle upward in the direction of line 2 (for the lead), or line 1 (for the rear); in other words, at an upward diagonal angle toward the target. The strike is initiated with your hand in the vertical position, as if you were going to throw a hook. Gradually rotate your hand palm up on impact with the target.

The hooking uppercut is effective for striking to the soft internal organs of the body, especially if your opponent carries his elbows slightly high. Try it with alternating hands. First, throw to the ribs. As your opponent moves his elbow to protect his ribs and kidneys, throw to his solar plexus or liver with your other hand.

IN THE GYM

When you watch kickboxing in its purest form, you will see very few flashy kicks and movements. Most fighters stay strictly with the basic techniques. That is, the jab, the rear cross, the hook, the uppercut, the front kick, and the round house kick.

The uppercut is an in-fighting technique that comes straight up along the centerline of your body, landing on your opponent's chin. Try not to straighten your back. Even though the strike comes straight up and through the target, your body should stay compact. Pretend that your elbow is initially connected to your body. Then the elbow frees itself, allowing your hand to continue through the target, while your body stays down low.

There is also a variation called a hooking uppercut. When striking with your lead hand, first set the weight of your body to the left. The strike should land on your opponent's liver on the right side of his body. The opposite is true for your rear hand. If your opponent's elbow is in the way, you might have to go for the solar plexus instead, or strike with your other hand until he moves his elbow for protection.

Straight uppercut　　**Hooking uppercut**

The hooking uppercut is thrown at an upward angle, as if you were trying to punch through your opponent's body and out his opposite shoulder, allowing you to drive the organs up and cause intense pain. This strike will drop more fighters than a strike to the jaw.

WHAT'S IN A GOOD UPPERCUT?

What makes the uppercut such a potentially devastating strike is not only that it is thrown with your entire body weight behind it and to a target that is likely to cause a knockout but, more importantly, that it has the ability to land unseen. The normal kickboxing guard will not defend against it. All other strikes are designed to go either through the guard or around it. But the uppercut sneaks in behind the guard. When properly thrown from close range, your opponent's guard may actually be blocking his view. When throwing the uppercut, keep in mind that you are leaving the side of your head exposed. You should therefore rely on a short move in your body to launch the technique. Your hand should leave the guard position for a very short time only. When uppercutting to the body, keep your head close to your opponent's head to protect against his counter-strikes. If you can sneak the strike into the middle of another combination, you can land it almost every time.

To throw an effective uppercut, you must:

1. **Position** for the punch.
2. Know when to **strategically** throw it.

The uppercut can be thought of as a "lifting" or "opening" technique, bringing your opponent's head up to create an opening for your left and right straight punches. You can also throw the uppercut to the body and create enough internal damage to drop your opponent to the ground. Some fighters tend to extend their elbows slightly in front of their body. When this happens, you can throw the uppercut underneath your opponent's arms and into his solar plexus. Observe the position of your opponent's arms and elbows to determine when and where to throw the strike.

In order to throw a powerful and explosive uppercut, it is important to place the entire weight of your body behind the strike. You do this by springing from your knees and hips.

Caution: Do not straighten your knees on the strike's upward path, as this exposes your chin and decreases your balance. Bring power to the punch by doing the following:

The uppercut is a "lifting technique." When your opponent's head comes up, follow with a strike to the jaw in an attempt to knock him out.

1. **Pivot to the side to set for the strike**. Your body and punch should follow an X-pattern. If you want to throw a right uppercut, pivot at a forty-five degree angle to the right prior to throwing the punch, **but the punch is thrown as your body moves on a forty-five degree angle to the left**, thus the X-pattern. The reverse is true for the left uppercut.

2. **Bend at the knees.** This allows you to push off with the ball of your foot and create a lifting effect. Springing from the knees increases the power and explosiveness of the strike.

3. **Make the movement of the uppercut short.** All movements in your body should be compact and snappy.

Dropping your hand slightly below the level of the chin before letting the punch go may enhance relaxation and speed. As long as you keep your body compact and avoid swinging your arm wide or dropping the punch all the way down to your hip, this usually does not create a problem in your defense.

What's wrong with these uppercuts?

Too extended

Too upright

Too low and wide

Ribs exposed

FOLLOWING UP OFF THE UPPERCUT

Because the uppercut is likely to bring your opponent's head up, you must be ready to take advantage of this opportunity to knock him out. When the uppercut lands, follow with hooks to the body or head, or with a second uppercut thrown with your other hand. One of the more effective combinations is *straight left and right punches* to your opponent's head.

Follow the uppercut with straight punches to the head.

You must throw these straight punches with *acceleration* in order to be effective; in other words, the last strike should be faster than the first and second strike. This acceleration is difficult to defend against, particularly after the stunning effect of the uppercut. Now, when your opponent is dazed, you can finish with a powerful hook to his jaw.

PUNCHING IN COMBINATIONS

Keith's Knockout Advice

Perhaps no other aspect of kickboxing is as important as mastery of combinations. Rarely does a fighter knock his opponent down or out with one single blow. Yes, sometimes it is one strike that eventually takes the fighter out, but it is essential that you examine the events that led up to the knockdown or knockout. In the majority of cases, you will see several other strikes that established the foundation for this one strike. In addition, if a fighter goes down as the result of one blow, he is still likely to get back to his feet and continue the bout. But if you examine bouts where a fighter goes down as the result of a combination, he is not as likely to recover. Even if he does get back up, he will usually suffer from jelly-like legs and disorientation, and the spectators will sense that the end is near. There are always exceptions, but your goal is to increase the odds of winning, and to do it with the least amount of resistance.

To illustrate the importance of striking in combinations, I draw from my experiences both in and out of the ring. The first example is a bit graphic, but necessary to bring the point home. I have been a police officer for many years, and have seen several assaults, beatings, and vicious murders. Experience has taught me that combinations in any form usually produce deadly results. Recently, I was called to investigate the brutal beating of a club owner. The assault was captured on video and graphically illustrated the end result of a series of punches and kicks. The victim was attempting to remove several drunk and disorderly patrons from the club. One of the patrons was not happy about being eighty-sixed. As they came into view of the video, the patron struck the owner to the back of the head. The owner fell to the floor, but was still conscious and trying to defend himself. During the next thirty seconds he received twenty-three kicks to the body and head, with an additional seventeen punches. Watching the video, it is obvious that he was unconscious by the fourth blow. As a result, he suffered broken ribs, a ruptured spleen, a collapsed lung, and bleeding inside the cranial cavity. Had the attacker stopped after the first blow, the owner would most likely have recovered without requiring medical attention.

As a police officer, I look at all of my defensive measures (including the handgun) in combination. Police officers are not taught to fire their weapon one time and hope for the best. Rather, a combination of rounds is employed to eliminate the threat. I have seen many people survive a single gunshot wound, but few survive multiple rounds. The reason that combinations are so effective is because more strikes equal greater trauma. If you watch truly accomplished fighters, you will see that the first strike does the initial damage, with the follow-up strikes creating the final outcome. I have followed boxer Felix Trinidad's career for many years. His success has come largely from his ability to throw combinations. You can literally watch the punches build on one another until the climax, which is usually a knockout. Recently, I watched him land a beautiful right uppercut. His opponent buckled, but before he could recover he was hit with a left hook. Still upright, but obviously hurt, he struggled to clear his head. Trinidad would have none of that. He finished his opponent with a right cross. The entire sequence lasted less than four seconds, with each punch building on the last punch's effect.

As you can see, there is a difference between throwing many single strikes and punching in combinations. Combinations are always more effective because the momentum is allowed to build throughout. Combinations also present a greater threat, where your opponent feels overwhelmed. Even if your opponent is a master at blocking and evading, if you throw enough strikes, some will land. Try the following combination on weight transfer and double strikes:

Jab, rear cross, lead hook high, rear uppercut, lead uppercut, rear cross, rear cross, lead hook low, lead hook high.

The above combination employs all of the four major strikes to both high and low targets. By varying the targets and the direction of the strikes, it is almost impossible for your opponent to defend against all of them.

Try this exercise on **WEIGHT TRANSFER AND THE FOUR MAJOR STRIKES** (lengthy and more complex combinations should be practiced for rhythm, power, and balance):

Exercise 1

1. **Double jab, rear cross.** Step to a forty-five degree angle forward with the second jab, and set your weight above your rear foot prior to throwing the rear cross.

2. **Jab, rear cross, lead hook.** Transfer your weight with each strike to set for the next.

3. **Double jab, double lead hook.** As the second jab comes back, pivot your body to set for the lead hook. Leave the heel of your lead foot off the floor between the two hooks to increase the speed.

4. **Double rear cross, double lead hook.** This is for fighting a southpaw, a left-handed opponent, where it benefits you to take up a stance at an angle to the outside of his centerline (more about southpaws in Section 5). Step with your lead foot to a forty-five degree angle forward with the first rear cross. Leave your heel off the floor between double strikes, and push off with the inside knife edge of your foot.

5. **Jab, lead hook, rear hook, jab.** Let the motion of your lead hook pivot your body into position for the rear hook. Let your rear hook set up the jab.

6. **Jab, rear uppercut, lead hook, rear cross, jab.** All alternating strikes. Let one strike set up the next by using the principle of weight transfer.

7. **Rear cross, lead uppercut, lead hook, rear cross.** Step with your lead foot to a forty-five degree angle forward with the first rear cross, letting the strike pivot your body into position for the lead uppercut. Leave the heel of your lead foot off the floor between the lead uppercut and the lead hook.

8. **Rear cross, double rear hook, rear uppercut.** All strikes thrown with the rear hand. Use pivot and snap to set for the next strike. Leave the heel of your rear foot off the floor between strikes for better speed.

Uppercut followed by . . .

a rear cross and a hook to finish.

Think about this: Always train and fight in combinations. If you hurt your opponent with a good blow, don't stop and marvel. Rather, continue the barrage until you are victorious. It is not your job to decide when your opponent has had enough. That is up to the referee or corner team. You have made the choice to participate in a dangerous and, in some people's mind, barbaric sport. You know the consequences, as does your opponent. It is usually the first solid strike that I refer to as the stunning blow, the blow that allows the other strikes to land with greater ease and effect. You will recognize the stunning blow when it comes. You can literally sense your opponent's injury. Each additional strike will further decrease his energy and will to continue. You will sense, with certainty, the knockout seconds before it comes. If you find yourself on the receiving end, you must learn to channel your energy, recover, and turn the fight around. When this happens, you will be faced with a choice: succumb to defeat or rise to the occasion.

COUNTER-STRIKING

Keith's Corner

True counter-punchers are a breed unto themselves. I am not talking about the occasional counter-puncher; I am talking about the purest, the one who builds his career on the counter-punch, the fighter who can frustrate you by countering your lead with the speed and accuracy of the mongoose fighting the King Cobra. The snake possesses the deadlier weapon and, in theory, should easily kill the mongoose. But, in order to survive, the mongoose has learned the value of the counter-strike. And, more often than not, it is victorious over the cobra. It happens like this: The mongoose waits for the snake to commit to a strike, and then, in a flash, makes the snake miss. This is when the snake is the most vulnerable, and the mongoose counters and kills the snake.

In order to join this elite group, you must develop three things: footwork, timing, and speed. Through mastery of these skills, you become a formidable fighter. Picture yourself in the ring. Every time your opponent throws a punch or kick, your footwork allows you to be at just the right distance, your timing sets the counter-punch into motion at just the right time, and your speed ensures that the blow lands before your opponent can react.

Great counter-punchers also possess one other skill: They are brilliant strategists and masters of illusion. Just when your opponent is positive that his strike will land, he finds nothing but air, and then . . . *Whack!* he has been countered. Knowing that it will lure out offense, great counter-punchers purposefully place themselves within striking range. As soon as their opponent commits, they withdraw and counter. The opponent thinks that he is on the offensive, when he really should be more concerned with defense.

I am not suggesting that everyone is engineered to be a great counter-puncher, or even that you will be defeated by one. But every fighter should understand the mechanics of great counter-punching, and ultimately not fall victim to the game.

Try these exercises on **COUNTER-PUNCHING**:

Exercise 2

Whenever your opponent throws a strike, he automatically creates an opening on himself. For example, if he throws a left hook, there will be an opening on his left side. In order to take that opening, you must come off your block with a fast counter-strike, preferably while his strike is still in motion. If you counter too late, you may get hit, or your opponent may block your counter-strike.

Where is the opening?

Solar plexus exposed

Head exposed

Ribs exposed

Centerline exposed

Certain punches tend to go together. For example, the rear cross generally complements the jab, and the uppercut generally complements the hook. As a result, we have a tendency to fight within these parameters. For example: jab-cross-hook or jab-jab-cross, or hook-uppercut. How often do you see a leading rear cross, followed by a jab or double lead uppercut? How often do you see a rear uppercut followed by a rear cross? Unorthodox? Maybe. Unsound? Hardly!

Exercise 3

Have your partner throw jabs and rear crosses, while you practice counter-striking to the opening created. In order to beat him to the punch, your counter-strike must be slightly faster than your opponent's strike. You can decrease the risk of getting struck by moving your upper body slightly off the attack line. Be aware of your openings, particularly when moving toward your opponent's power side.

If your opponent is a "puncher," try counter-striking with kicks. This gives you reach while staying out of range for his strikes. If your opponent is a "kicker," try jamming his kicks to get to the inside and counter-striking with punches. The best time to counter-strike is when your opponent is still on one leg and unable to move away (more about kicks in Section 2).

Summary and review

The uppercut is an inside fighting technique employing awesome power. The uppercut is thrown straight up along your centerline with the palm of your hand turned toward you. The primary target for the uppercut is the chin, but you can also throw it diagonally to your opponent's mid-section. The uppercut should be taken "through" the target. Don't stop short on impact. Because the elbow comes up to chest level when throwing the strike, you also leave your lower ribs and abdomen exposed. It is therefore imperative that you bring your hand back to the point of origin immediately after landing the strike.

Uppercut practice in the air

- Practice the uppercut in the air, utilizing correct technique by springing from your knees, placing the full weight of your body behind the blow.

- Observe yourself in a mirror and throw the strike along your centerline with a short explosive surge.

- If your legs are straight prior to throwing the strike, you will be using arm-power only, and maximum power cannot be attained.

- What type of strike would best lend itself as a set-up for the uppercut?

Throwing the twisting uppercut

- The twisting uppercut is thrown to your opponent's mid-section and follows a diagonal path upward. This strike is kind of in-between the hook and the uppercut, and should land on your opponent's liver on his right side, or spleen or stomach on his left side.

- Get within one foot of your partner and, utilizing light contact, take turns practicing the twisting uppercut to the mid-section. Alternate left and right strikes, or throw two strikes to one side and one or two strikes to the other side.

- After impact, re-twist your hand back to the original position in preparation for a maximum power follow-up strike.

- Some of the power of the uppercut comes from the turn of your hand. Be careful not to telegraph the strike by twisting your hand prior to throwing it.

Throwing uppercuts to the body

- When throwing many uppercuts to the body, it is easy to neglect bringing your hands back high between strikes, giving your opponent the opportunity to counter to your head. Be aware of the position of your guard at all times.

- Alternate twisting uppercuts to the mid-section on the heavy bag. Bring your hands back to the point of origin after each strike.

- When striking the body, rather than dropping the hands, drop your weight by bending at the knees.

Setting up the straight uppercut with the twisting uppercut

- When your opponent feels a need to protect his mid-section, he will create a barrier with his elbows. But this also creates an opening for the straight uppercut along his centerline. The twisting uppercut can therefore be used as a set-up for the straight uppercut.

- Have your partner hold a focus mitt face down, as if it were your opponent's chin. From close range, alternate twisting uppercuts to your partner's mid-section, followed by a straight uppercut to the focus mitt.

- How can you decrease the beat between these uppercuts?

- Depending on your position, you may throw uppercuts to the mid-section and chin with the same hand, or with alternating hands.

Twisting uppercut to the mid-section, followed by a straight uppercut to the chin.

Focus mitt practice for the uppercut

- Have your partner hold focus mitts. Practice uppercuts for power by springing from your knees, but without straightening your upper body or exposing your chin. If you alternate between rights and lefts, a short bob and weave will help you set for each strike.

- When your body finds the rhythm, you can speed up your strikes without losing power.

- Each strike should have full follow-through. Don't stop short on impact.

- When your opponent's head comes up, distance is automatically created for your rear cross. If you have already hurt your opponent with the upper-cut, the rear cross is likely to end the fight.

- Have your partner hold one focus mitt in position for the left uppercut, and the other in position for the rear cross. Throw the uppercut first and, as your opponent's "head" comes up, follow with the right cross to his "chin."

The uppercut brings the head up, exposing the chin to a rear cross.

- Watch for your opponent's reaction. If his head does not come up, the right cross will not be an appropriate follow-up, and a second uppercut may work better.

Closing distance with the uppercut

- You can also throw the uppercut following a long range technique, but would then need to take a step forward to close distance.

- Have your partner hold focus mitts for a lead jab and a rear uppercut. Throw a couple of jabs first, each time taking a tiny step forward to bring you within range. After the second or third jab, explode forward with a rear uppercut.

The jab helps you set up and establish distance for the uppercut.

- The uppercut must follow explosively off of the jab. Positioning your hand low prior to throwing the uppercut may telegraph your intent.

- Practice many quick, short jabs to close distance for the rear uppercut.

Setting up the uppercut with a hook

- Because both the uppercut and hook are in-fighting techniques, the uppercut is a natural follow-up off the hook. This combination employs two different directions: horizontal for the hook, and vertical for the uppercut.

- Practice a lead hook followed by a rear uppercut.

- The lead hook followed by the lead uppercut is also a good combination, but a little slower because both strikes are thrown with the same hand.

Your elbow should come down to protect your ribs after landing the hook.

Double-end bag practice for the uppercut

• Practice the jab followed by the rear uppercut on the double-end bag, each time taking a tiny step to the left or right to move off your opponent's attack line. When you get comfortable with this combination, reverse it and throw a rear cross followed by a lead uppercut.

• Because of the construction of the double-end bag, it is better than the regular heavy bag for working the uppercut. When you strike the bag with the jab, the bag will swing straight back and toward you. When you follow with the uppercut from underneath, the bag will move straight up toward the ceiling.

• After landing the uppercut, look for your opponent's reaction, then throw a third strike to an appropriate target.

Uppercutting the double-end bag.

• A rear cross followed by a lead uppercut is normally not a logical combination, because the rear cross will snap your opponent's head back. However, if the timing is altered slightly, or if you take a step forward with the uppercut, you may still land it unexpectedly.

Weight shifts for power and set-up

• Your weight should shift to your rear foot with the jab, to your lead foot with the rear cross, to your rear foot with the lead hook, and back to your lead foot with the rear uppercut.

• Practice a one-two-three-four combination in the air (jab, rear cross, lead hook, rear uppercut). Make sure that your weight shifts with each strike. Think of it as one strike helping the other. As your jab comes back, your rear cross should already be on its way out.

• Start slow, feeling the weight shift between strikes. How does the weight shift affect your reach?

• Pay attention to balance. It is easy to inadvertently become top heavy to the front.

QUICK REFERENCE TO CONCEPTS

ADDING MOMENTUMS: Striking when your opponent steps toward you allows you to add his momentum to yours. Technically, this doubles your power without increasing your efforts. But you must be aware of your opponent's offense and avoid stepping into his strikes.

ATTACK LINE: The attack line is created by linear movement between you and your opponent. When you move back in a straight line, it allows your opponent to attack more effectively. This linear attack can be thwarted by side-stepping or pivoting off the attack line, thereby forcing your opponent to adjust to the new position. On the contrary, if you are the aggressor and your opponent is moving back in a straight line, you have the upper hand and should keep him on the attack line.

BALANCE: This may be the most important concept of the fighting arts, because without balance you can't throw a powerful strike or move to a superior position. In order to maintain physical balance, your center of gravity (the point in your body around which all of your weight is equally distributed) must fall above the area of your foundation. The wider your foundation in the direction of the applied force, the more stable you are. You must also have mental balance, or your emotions will quickly overshadow logic, making you easy prey even to the most inexperienced opponent.

BASIC MOVEMENT THEORY: When moving, step with the foot closest to the direction of travel first. This helps you maintain balance by keeping you from narrowing your stance or crossing your feet.

BEAT: You can increase the speed of a combination by decreasing the beat between strikes. However, a short or steady beat is not always to your advantage. An irregular beat may benefit you the most through the confusion it causes your opponent.

BODY ROTATION (SYNCHRONIZATION): The rotation of your body places your weight behind the strikes, and is beneficial through the power it provides. For maximum power and speed, the rotation of all your body parts must be synchronized and happen simultaneously.

BROKEN RHYTHM: A steady rhythm can be used as a set-up; however, it also has its drawbacks. Once your opponent gets in tune with your rhythm, he can cover his openings and block your strikes. To stay unpredictable, change your rhythm by speeding up or slowing down. A good way to learn broken rhythm is to count the beats in your head, speed up and slow down the count, and make your physical body do the same.

CADENCE: This is the specific rhythm by which you throw your strikes; it is a consistent, predictable pattern of timing. If you can establish your opponent's pattern and rhythm, he will become predictable. A predictable opponent is a beatable opponent. The opposite is also true: If you can disguise your rhythm and avoid getting trapped in predictable patterns, you will be more difficult to defeat.

CANCELING MOMENTUMS: This is the opposite of adding momentums. When you go with the motion of your opponent's strike, you decrease the force. This is also why it is not as beneficial power-wise to strike an opponent who is in the process of stepping away from you, as it is to strike an opponent who is in the process of stepping toward you. Canceling momentums for the benefit of defense requires good timing.

CENTERLINE: The centerline refers to an imaginary line approximately five inches wide, running vertically on the front and back of your body. Striking targets on the centerline can cause serious injury or death.

COUNTER-STRIKING: Whenever your opponent throws a strike, he automatically creates an opening on himself. In order to take full advantage of that opening, you must come off your block with a fast counter-strike.

DIRECTION OF ENERGY: This is the ability to direct all of your energy into a target to create a specific effect. To produce optimum results, all your body's energy and mass must flow in one direction. Power loss most often results from opposing movements in body mechanics.

FIGHTING STANCE: Your stance determines your effective power. If you are right-handed, fight with your left foot forward and your right foot back. This allows your right hand, which is stronger, a longer distance to travel and more time to build momentum. Your left hand, which is closer to your opponent, is used as a set-up for your more powerful rear techniques. If you are left-handed, the opposite is true.

HORSE STANCE (NEUTRAL STANCE): When in a neutral stance, both your feet are even and you stand square to your opponent. In most martial arts, the neutral stance is used for blocking and striking when training, allowing you full focus on your hands. However, in kickboxing, the neutral stance may be detrimental because you are leaving your centerline exposed, and because of your weakened stability in the direction of power.

NON-WORKING HAND: The hand that is not striking or blocking is referred to as the non-working hand. To minimize target exposure, it is important to keep the non-working hand near the chin or bring it forward to a checking position in front of the face.

POINT OF ORIGIN: Wherever a technique leaves from, it must return to. There are mainly two reasons for this: First, in order to reset your body for a follow-up technique, your hand or foot must return to its original position. Second, any time you throw a strike or kick, you automatically create an opening on yourself. To minimize target exposure, it is imperative that you bring your "tools" back to the guard position.

POSITION OF SUPERIORITY: This is the ability to move to a position that minimizes your opponent's strength and places him in a position of vulnerability. By moving to your opponent's side, you can eliminate half of his tools while keeping all of yours. By moving behind your opponent, you can eliminate most of his tools.

POWER: In kickboxing, power is the force with which you strike your opponent. If your goal is to impact a target with maximum force, you must train your body mechanics to work harmoniously toward this goal, and strike by utilizing your body's mass in conjunction with the speed of the technique. This, in turn, should be combined with proper position and leverage.

PUSH-PULL PRINCIPLE: We have a tendency to think only of the arm or leg that is doing the punching or kicking. For example, when we throw a jab, our full effort is in the extension of the jabbing arm. Likewise,

when we throw a kick, our full effort is in the extension of the kicking leg. But you can increase speed and explosiveness by allowing the non-striking side of your body to aid the striking side. The idea is to divide the workload equally between your body parts.

QUICK FOOTWORK: This type of footwork is generally used by the lighter or faster fighter, and may also be used by the underdog to gain an edge on his opponent. Quick footwork involves frequent switches in direction, usually in combination with the jab.

ROTATIONAL INERTIA: Inertia means resistance to change in motion. It is the force that makes you exert an effort when setting yourself into motion, or when stopping your momentum. Rotational inertia is resistance to change in anything that is rotating. The farther away your mass is from the center of rotation, the more inertia it produces. This is why it is difficult to gain speed in a spinning technique if your arms or legs are thrown wide.

SENSORY OVERLOAD: This is a state of confusion and chaos often experienced when attacked with explosive combinations, where the attacker attempts to take as many targets as possible in the shortest amount of time.

SOUTHPAW: A southpaw is a fighter who fights from a non-conventional stance with his right foot forward. Generally, those who are left-handed fight from the southpaw stance, placing their left hand to the rear for power. It may benefit a right-handed fighter to develop the ability to switch to southpaw.

STALKING FOOTWORK: Use this type of footwork if you are the stronger or heavier fighter, or if you are mentally in charge of the fight. The stalking fighter moves his opponent back with many short steps and fights from his own optimal range, with the goal of smothering his opponent's techniques.

TOE-TO-HEEL LINE: When in your fighting stance, your feet should be about shoulder width and a half apart and slightly offset on the toe-to-heel line. This means that a line drawn from the toes of your lead foot straight back should touch the heel of your rear foot. This gives you good balance, ease of movement, and the ability to throw all techniques with power and speed.

WEIGHT TRANSFER: When throwing a punch combination, your weight should shift from one foot to the other, depending on which strike you throw. For example, in a one-two-three punch combination (jab, rear cross, lead hook), your weight should shift to your rear foot with the jab, to your lead foot with the rear cross, and back to your rear foot with the lead hook. The purpose of the weight shift is to avoid opposing body mechanics that may disrupt balance and power.

PUNCHING FUNDAMENTALS REVIEW

THE JAB

THE REAR CROSS

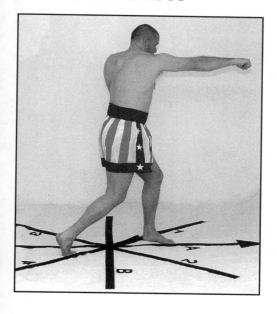 

THE HOOK

THE UPPERCUT

SECTION TWO
BASIC KICKING

KNOW YOUR OPPONENT
by Keith Livingston

The hype surrounding the Robinson vs. Smith fight had been building for months. In fact, it was the kickboxing equivalent to the Sugar Ray Leonard and Thomas Hearns championship bouts. Robinson, a kickboxing purist, and Smith, a lightening fast full contact karate practitioner were about to square off for a world championship unification bout. Both fighters had amassed perfect records and destroyed everyone in their paths.

Just a month earlier, I had watched Robinson and Smith compete on the same card but against different opponents. Robinson had showed awesome power and incredible conditioning, but it took him seven rounds to dispatch his opponent. I found it interesting that Robinson had kept his techniques to a minimum, just enough to do the job. What struck me the most was that he hadn't thrown a single leg kick during the entire seven rounds. And this came from a fighter whose reputation was built on his terrifying leg destruction kicks. By the seventh round he seemed bored with his opponent's impotence, and finished him with a thundering right hook to the body.

Smith, on the other hand, had been all business. Charging from his corner with a fierce determination, he had overwhelmed his opponent with a barrage of punches and kicks and finished the match in just minutes. As he stood over his fallen victim, he turned and grinned at Robinson in the front row, knowing that he was next.

To the casual observer, Smith was the favorite. But as a kickboxing trainer, I sensed something different. I had studied both fighters extensively, and believed that Robinson had shown exactly what he wanted the Smith camp to see. I was also convinced that Robinson could have finished his opponent in the first round. But Robinson's people were crafty. They knew that the Smith camp would be studying Robinson, looking for weakness. Smith was from the East Coast, and Robinson from Las Vegas. Chances were they knew very little about one another. Unlike boxing, it is difficult to obtain video footage and accurate intelligence on other kickboxers.

So, here I was, sitting front row of possibly the biggest fight in kickboxing history; two finely tuned competitors about to play to a sold out auditorium. The anticipation was evident as the crowd buzzed and argued the merits of each fighter. The lights dimmed. Smith was the first to emerge from his dressing room. As he made his way to the ring, the crowd went wild with a mixture of cheers and boos. Then Robinson began his advance to AC/DC's song "Thunder." Clearly the crowd favorite, he entered the ring to the delight of the cheering fans.

After the ring introductions and the usual stare down, the fight was underway. Robinson exited his corner with a wry grin, stopped in the middle of the ring, assumed a traditional Muay Thai stance, and waited. In his typical fashion, Smith charged forward. Just as Smith was about to find his range, Robinson stepped to a forty-five degree angle, simultaneously pivoting his upper body and digging a kick deeply into Smith's outer thigh. Smith stumbled backward with watery eyes, and the color drained from his face. Knowing the pain from a well-placed kick, I could feel my own leg tensing in sympathy.

Before Smith could recover, Robinson was airborne. Time slowed as I once more watched Robinson's kick find the perfect spot on Smith's leg. Smith dropped from the pain and the force of the blow. As the referee began the count, Smith gallantly tried to rise, but his leg refused the command and he collapsed. In less than thirty seconds, Robinson had brought an end to the most eagerly anticipated fight of the nineties.

Smith, with his great arsenal of techniques, may have been the more skilled fighter, but on this particular night none of it mattered. Smith was a full contact karate fighter, and since full contact karate does not allow for kicks to the legs, Robinson knew his opponent's greatest weakness. What I had seen strengthened my belief that sometimes less is better. One technique comprised of only two strikes had felled one of the best fighters in the world. The lesson? Always make an effort to know your opponent!

THE ROUND HOUSE KICK

We have now talked about and practiced the four basic strikes (jab, rear cross, hook, uppercut). But knowing how to box is not enough if you want to call yourself a kickboxer. Because kickboxing combines kicks and strikes, we will now look at the three basic kicks: the round house kick, the front kick, and the side thrust kick. Which kick you use depends on your position, on your distance to the target, and on what you are trying to accomplish.

The benefit of a kick compared to a punch is that you can reach any target on your opponent's body. This is true not only distance-wise, because the legs are longer than the arms, but also target-wise. While the hands can be used for punching to the head and body only, the legs can be used for kicking both to the head, body, and legs. In this sense, kicks are more versatile than punches. But our legs are also heavier than our arms and generally not as precise. Kicks are therefore a little slower than punches, and require more energy to launch.

In general, your lead leg is used much like the jab: to gauge distance. Because your lead leg is closer to the target than your rear leg, it is faster and needs less movement. But your rear leg has the potential to create a more powerful kick. Which part of the foot you connect with (instep, shin, heel, ball of foot) depends on the path of the kicking leg and on the distance to the target. You can throw all kicks with either the lead or rear leg. However, because of excessive movement with the side thrust kick, you will, with few exceptions, throw this kick with the lead leg only.

Throughout your training, we will explore those kicks that are the most practical for competition kickboxing, and learn their application from beginning to advanced stages. Remember that all techniques are explained from a left fighting stance, and that you must reverse the descriptions if you are a southpaw.

This section covers:

- The universal kick
- Body mechanics for the round house kick
- In the gym
- High and low targets
- The sciatic nerve and the benefits of low kicking
- Power principles for the round house kick
- Side-shuffle with leg kick
- Summary and review

Round house kick

Front kick

Side thrust kick

THE UNIVERSAL KICK

The round house kick is probably the most frequently used kick in competition kickboxing. Its popularity stems from the fact that it can be thrown with ease and speed from almost any stance, distance, or angle. It also has multi-faceted application and awesome power. This kick is therefore referred to as the "universal kick."

Use the instep, shin, or ball of foot when impacting with the round house kick. If impacting with the instep or shin, stretch your toes and align your foot with your knee. Whether you use the instep or shin depends on the distance to the target. If fighting at long range, use your instep; if fighting at close range, use your shin. You can also impact with the ball of your foot. This enables you to penetrate a tight defense and take well-guarded targets. When impacting with the ball of the foot, curl your toes back to avoid injury.

Targets for the round house kick are the inside and outside thighs, hamstrings, quadriceps, calves, stomach, ribs, upper arms, and head. Practice this kick both stationary and stepping.

If you are too close for impacting with the instep or ball of foot, you can impact with the shin instead. This is also good for taking two targets simultaneously: your opponent's solar plexus with your shin, and his ribs with your instep.

Because the ball of the foot is smaller than the instep, the kick will have more penetrating force. Use this kick to take well- guarded targets.

TARGETS FOR THE ROUND HOUSE KICK

Depending on your distance to the target, you can impact with your instep or shin when round house kicking.

You can also wrap the round house kick to the back of your opponent's head. This requires a slightly deeper aim than if kicking to the side of the head. In general, kicking completely to the back of the head is not allowed, so make sure you know the rules before attempting this.

BODY MECHANICS FOR THE ROUND HOUSE

Initiate the *lead leg round house kick* by bringing your lead knee up along centerline A, with your lower leg chambered.

Extend your leg along centerline A. This should force a slight pivot in your rear foot in the direction of line 4, or to a reverse forty-five degree angle, which will bring your hips through toward line 2.

Impact the target with the instep, shin, or ball of your foot. If impacting with the instep, your toes must be stretched until the upper portion of your foot is tight (think of it as a springboard). This can be likened to a punch: *If your fist isn't tight on impact, your strike will be weak and you will risk injury to your hand and wrist.* Likewise, if your foot is "floppy" on impact, the kick will be weak and you will risk injury to your ankle.

Initiate the *rear leg round house kick* by bringing your rear knee up and thrusting it forward along centerline A. As your knee comes up, pivot your hips toward line 1.

Your rear leg, from the knee down, should be angled forty-five degrees upward toward the front left corner. Extend your lower leg along centerline A. This will force your lead foot to pivot in the direction of line 3, or to a reverse forty-five degree angle. Impact the target with the instep, shin, or ball of your foot.

A common mistake is to neglect to chamber the leg. We often think that we bring the kick up chambered, when it is really already half extended. Extending the leg too soon results in target exposure to your groin and inside thigh. It also fails to conceal the kick.

Which kick is properly chambered?

Correct

Good chamber, but centerline exposed

Incorrect

IN THE GYM

Let's work on kicks next. Start with the round house kick. What I'm looking for is penetration, the final snap at the end of the kick. Try to increase the height of the kick. Chest level first, then shoulder height, and finally to the head. When initiating the kick, your knee should be angled upward. As the kick impacts the target, bring your knee horizontally across, so that you're kicking with the instep or shin rather than with the side of the foot. It's kind of like punching . . . like turning your fist to the horizontal position right before impact.

Lead leg round house kick now! Remember, this works like a jab. The kick should be quick and used as a feeler to gauge distance to the target, or as a set-up for your more powerful rear techniques. Throw doubles. Stay loose.

What do you need to work on? Make sure that you bring your leg up chambered, or you'll lose power. Keep the leg chambered until it is time to extend the kick. You are also taking a cheat step with your rear foot, but that's okay, as long as your opponent doesn't pick up on it.

The lead round house kick is a bit trickier than the rear, because you can't build as much momentum. If you take a cheat step now, make sure to use some kind of set-up first to conceal the step: a jab, for example. How high should you kick? Because your opponent's body is a lot of mass to move, kicking to the body may not do you much good, unless you impact with the shin. Eventually, I would like to see you kick to the head.

Rear leg round house kick now! Turn your supporting foot forty-five degrees to the outside. This helps bring your hips through. You are throwing the kick a little wide. Try to accelerate it more at the end. See how much more power that gives you, and how much easier it is to kick when you're relaxed?

Now try multiple rear leg round house kicks. Bounce your foot off the floor between kicks. Multiple kicks help break your opponent's timing. Five now! Can you do six? How about seven? Throwing multiples requires relaxation for quick reversal of direction.

HIGH AND LOW TARGETS

Kickboxers distinguish their round house kicks from traditional karate fighters by the way they make contact with the shin rather than the instep. Because of the circular path of the round house kick, and the fact that the instep is a relatively weak impact weapon in comparison to the shin, heel, or ball of foot, impacting your opponent's body or legs with the instep usually doesn't do enough damage to end a fight. If you can make it a habit to impact with the shin, the kick will be many times stronger and have a deeper effect than the stinging impact of the instep. When kicking with the shin, your foot will actually be kicking air behind the target. You should still keep your foot tight and pointed. This binds the muscles and reduces the risk of injury. Another advantage of impacting with the shin is that the kick can be thrown from close range, making it quick and difficult to detect. If your opponent steps back to create distance, you still have the option of reaching him with the instep.

When impacting with the shin, your foot will be kicking behind the target.

Kickboxers are often seen dropping one hand low behind their back when throwing mid-level and high kicks. The benefit of this is that the lower position of the hand counter-acts your tendency to lose balance and aids the development of power. It can't be disputed, however, that dropping your guard exposes targets that your opponent can take advantage of. My recommendation is therefore to keep your guard high whenever possible.

Dropping your guard aids with balance but exposes your head. Keep your guard high whenever possible.

Kicking to the head is more difficult and tiring. The head kick should be explosive and powerful, and can be thrown more easily if you incline your body slightly to the rear. When thrown at the right moment and to a precise target, a round house kick to the head can quickly stop your opponent's advance or produce an instant knockout. Throw the head kick primarily when your opponent is tired, bent over, or is fighting with his guard down. Targets on the head are the jaw, chin, nose, and temples.

The round house kick to the head can cause an instant knockout. Look for a time when your opponent is keeping his guard low.

Note: You can increase the height of the round house kick by bending the supporting leg slightly. This works well if you have limited flexibility. The same concept is true for your other kicks. Although bending the supporting leg may seem like a contradiction because it lowers your body slightly, it also makes your muscles more flexible and allows you to kick higher.

Round house kicks to the body are usually not rib breakers, but they can have the effect of draining energy from your opponent. Generally, most fighters can take a round house kick to the body without too much of a problem, and some fighters use their opponent's round house kick as an opportunity to move to close range for a counter-attack. When kicking above the waist, be aware that you are exposing targets on your legs, and that your balance and mobility may be weak.

The lowest two sets of ribs are called floating ribs. The floating ribs are attached to the spine but not to the sternum, and are therefore weaker and easier to break than the other ribs.

Keith's Knockout Advice

When kicking to the body, accuracy and timing are vital elements of success. Your objective is to land blows to the solar plexus, liver, spleen, and ribs. Because it is easier to defend the body than the legs, you must look for and create openings to the targets mentioned above. You must time the kick to land before your opponent is able to defend the opening. Secondary targets for the round house kick are the upper arms. When kicking to the upper arms, aim for the upper part of your opponent's triceps. The nerves in this part of the arm are very sensitive, and a kick to this area will assist in making your opponent arm weary.

Caution: When kicking to the arms, be careful not to kick your opponent's elbow. Kicking an elbow with power can break the bones in your foot or shin instantly.

The round house kick is often used as a low kick to the legs. When used as a leg destruction kick (often called a cut kick, because of the way it cuts across the leg), it is easy to land and extremely painful. A few well-placed kicks to the back of the leg and slightly above the knee joint are likely to wear your opponent down within seconds. Choosing your targets precisely allows you to do enough damage to send your opponent to the canvas. You can also throw low kicks effectively after a punch combination in close quarters, where the kicks are often unexpected and difficult to detect and defend against.

You can increase power in the leg destruction kick by turning your knee to a forty-five degree angle downward on impact. You can increase the speed by initiating the kick with a step. Throw the lead leg round house kick by stepping with your rear foot to a forty-five degree angle toward the front right corner. Simultaneously raise your lead leg in a chambered position and impact the target by extending the leg along your centerline. Impact should come simultaneous with the step. The lead leg round house kick is particularly useful if thrown to the inner thigh.

Throw the rear leg round house kick by stepping with your lead foot to a forty-five degree angle toward the front left corner. Simultaneously raise your rear leg and impact the target by extending the leg along your centerline. Let's look at, in greater detail, what it is that makes the legs such great targets.

Round house kicks to the upper arms can make your opponent arm weary.

THE SCIATIC NERVE AND LOW KICKING

A well-placed leg kick to either the outside or inside thigh area can cause extreme pain and end a fight instantly. Leg destruction kicks should therefore be an important part of your training routine. In addition, since the legs are a fighter's support, a good kick to the legs can destroy your opponent's balance and mobility. In many cases, a single, solid blow to the thigh area that impact the sciatic nerve can produce a "dead leg" and inhibit your opponent's ability to move, or cause collapse of the leg and drop him to the ground. Note that not all bouts allow kicks to the legs.

The sciatic nerve is the longest and thickest nerve of the human body. It emerges from the spinal cord and runs down through the buttocks and to the back of the thighs, to their lower third where it divides into the tibial and the peroneal nerves, both which serve the lower leg and foot.

TARGETS FOR THE LEG DESTRUCTION KICK

Try these exercises on **LOW KICKING**:

Exercise 1

Hang a heavy bag with its bottom about twelve inches off the floor. Start from kicking range (long range) and launch a series of round house kicks to a point on the bag that is the same height as your thigh. Throw a number of kicks with your rear leg (start with twenty), and then switch to your lead leg. Make sure to extend your leg fully on impact, without slowing the kick down or stopping its momentum.

Exercise 2

Move to close range (about a foot and a half from the bag), and throw a series of round house kicks impacting with your shin instead of your instep. Build speed and power by accelerating the kick on its way to the target, so that the greatest speed occurs at the moment of impact. You can increase power by angling the kick slightly downward, dropping your body weight into the kick.

Drop your weight to increase the power of the leg destruction kick.

Exercise 3

When you start to get comfortable kicking from a stationary position, begin moving around the bag as if you were engaged in a fight. Alternate kicks with your lead and rear legs, throwing to both the outside and inside of your "opponent's" thighs. When kicking to the inside thigh, allow your kick to wrap around to the back of the leg where the nerve is more sensitive. As the bag swings, you may need to step from close range to long range and vice versa, or from side to side to create a better angle for the kick. This helps you develop a feel for timing and distance. You can also throw leg destruction kicks to your opponent's calf.

Be aware of the target when kicking to the inside thigh. The kick above is too shallow and the kick below is too deep.

Exercise 4

The leg kick is also effective for taking two targets simultaneously. Face a partner and kick to the back of his lead leg with your shin, simultaneously kicking the back of his rear leg with your instep.

Take 2 targets on the leg with your shin and instep.

POWER PRINCIPLES FOR THE ROUND HOUSE KICK

In order to land the round house kick successfully, you must:

1. **Avoid telegraphing your intents.** Don't take an unnecessary step or pivot your hips prior to throwing the kick.

2. **Throw the kick with determination and full extension.** Your opponent will lose respect for a kick that is thrown half-heartedly.

Full extension, in turn, is also comprised of two elements:

1. The actual **physical extension** of your leg.

2. The **extension of power**, as your kick goes through the target.

By *kicking through the target*, we mean *releasing all energy at the appropriate moment*. Sometimes too much effort is placed on the early stages of the kick. Yes, you will need to expend some energy to lift your foot off the ground, but powerful kicking relies on acceleration, with the final "snap" coming at the appropriate moment. There is a difference between just lifting your leg to throw the kick, and actually releasing the power at the appropriate time. Work on the following principles:

1. **Raise your leg in the chambered position**. A common error is to raise the leg straight. Because the motion of the round house kick is half-circular, raising the leg chambered helps you accelerate the kick by decreasing the *rotational inertia*. It also makes it easier to rotate your hips.

2. When extending your leg to kick, **impact should come slightly before** the leg is fully extended, allowing you to extend through the target.

3. After the kick is complete, **pull your leg back to the chambered position** before setting your foot down. Dropping the knee too soon may cause the kick to slide off the target before the power has been released in the proper direction (*splitting the power*). Your leg is also vulnerable right after impact, as this is when a skillful opponent is most likely to counter your kick.

4. Practice the round house kick with a **step with your supporting foot** to a forty-five degree angle forward. This creates a better angle and more power. Again, the step and kick should be synchronized.

5. For greater mobility, **your upper body and legs should be relaxed**, allowing you to spring from your knees. For proper energy transfer, keep your foot in connection with the target only as long as is necessary.

> Bringing your foot off the ground, chambering the leg, and throwing the kick may seem like three separate moves, but they need to be synchronized into one fluid motion.

What's wrong with the fighters' kicking mechanics?

Not enough pivot

Contradictory body mechanics

Guard too low

Poor balance

Think about this: The best time to strike or kick is when your opponent is throwing a kick and is on one leg. This is called *completion of motion*. Once your opponent has committed to a kick, he is unable to change his position until the motion of the kick is complete and he has replanted his foot. Also, when your opponent is throwing a kick and is on one leg, this leg is his only point of support. If you can take out his supporting leg, he will be unable to fight until he has regained balance. Take advantage of this by counter-striking while your opponent is in the process of kicking and is unable to move away.

Try this exercise on **COMPLETION OF MOTION**:

Exercise 5

Attack your opponent's supporting leg with a round house kick. Vary your targets from calf to thigh. If your opponent throws a strike, practice side-stepping the strike and take both of his legs simultaneously: the near leg with your shin and the far leg with your instep.

SIDE-SHUFFLE WITH LEG KICK

The *side-shuffle* is a quick step either left or right used to obtain a better angle of attack. Again, in accordance with the **basic movement theory**, you should move the foot closest to the direction of travel first. The side-shuffle is particularly effective for leg kicking. For example:

1. Shuffle right and throw a right round house kick to the outside of your opponent's lead thigh.

2. Quickly step right, then shuffle left and, within the movement of the left shuffle, throw a right round house kick to the inside of your opponent's rear thigh.

Side-shuffle with leg kick.

Summary and review

The round house kick follows a slightly circular path and impacts the target from the side. When kicking from long range, impact with the instep or ball of your foot; when kicking from close range, impact with the shin. The round house kick works well from a variety of angles. It is therefore popularly referred to as the "universal kick."

Round house kick practice in the air

- Start from a left fighting stance and throw a series of round house kicks with your lead leg. Work on proper body mechanics and full extension of the leg on impact.

- Bring your foot back to the point of origin between each kick. Check your stance to ensure that it is not too narrow or too wide.

- Repeat the exercise with your rear leg, then switch to a right fighting stance and do the exercise again, starting with your lead leg.

- Start at one end of the room and throw a series of alternating (left/right) round house kicks until you get to the other end of the room.

- It is easy to get in the habit of dropping the hands low to aid with balance. Pay attention to where your hands are, so that you don't expose targets on your head.

Kick/punch combinations and target practice

- Start at one end of the room and put together kick combinations with the round house kick. Take a step forward with each kick until you get to the other end of the room.

- Repeat the exercise, but add punch combinations. Try to throw at least one kick for every five punches.

- Get with a partner and take turns round house kicking to low, medium, and high targets. Identify all targets for the round house kick by touching each target lightly with the kick.

Defending the round house kick

- Identify the proper defense against the round house kick for each low, medium, and high target (we will talk more about defense in Section 3).

- Have your partner throw round house kicks which you defend against.

- Throw a counter-strike or kick after each defensive move.

Identifying the correct impact weapon

- The round house kick impacts the target with the instep, shin, or ball of your foot. When would you use the shin versus the instep? When would you use the ball of the foot versus the instep? Why?

- Because the shin is often used as an impact weapon when round house kicking, you should work on toughening this sensitive part of your leg. Start by kicking a heavy bag a number of times, impacting with the shin.

- When you get comfortable with the contact, have your partner hold a padded stick vertically straight. Kick the padded stick, focusing on kicking "through" the target.

Practice the cut kick on a heavy bag to toughen your shins.

Contact drill partner practice

- Engage in contact drills with a partner, using light contact. Take turns throwing the round house kick to the legs and mid-section.

- Contact drills accomplish two things: They teach you to throw the technique with precision, and they help your partner get used to taking the impact. This is why both parts of this exercise are important.

Throwing alternating strikes and kicks

- Alternating strikes flow more naturally than strikes from the same side, because they allow your body to reset between strikes.

- Have your partner hold focus mitts. Throw a lead leg round house kick followed by a rear hand strike.

- Repeat the exercise, but throw a rear round house kick followed by a lead strike (a jab, for example).

- Now, throw any combination of alternating strikes and round house kicks, starting with either a strike or kick.

A lead leg round house kick followed by a rear cross are alternating strikes that flow naturally.

Switching stance with the round house kick

- If you plant your foot forward after throwing the rear round house kick, you will close distance and possibly end up at close quarter range. Your stance will also shift from left to right (southpaw).

- Face your partner and throw a rear round house kick. Plant your foot forward and follow with a hand combination suitable for close range fighting.

- How can you switch back to a left fighting stance without sacrificing safety or opening your centerline?

Leg kicking practice

- A good target for the round house kick is your opponent's legs, especially the outside thigh area. If your opponent can't walk, he can't fight.

- Practice round house kicks at thigh level on a swinging heavy bag. When the bag swings, use footwork to adjust your position for the next kick.

- Have your partner hold a focus mitt at thigh level. Practice the round house kick for power by taking a lateral step prior to throwing the kick. Since the target has "give," you should be able to kick all the way through.

THE FRONT KICK

The front kick is a popular and highly effective kick. The primary difference between the front kick and the round house kick is that the front kick is thrown linearly straight forward. It has therefore the additional strategic benefit of adding momentums. This means that if the kick is timed to your opponent's advance, he will be walking into the kick's line of power. This allows you to use the kick for maximum destruction with minimum effort. The front kick is also used to keep an aggressive opponent at a distance.

A front kick to the body can keep your opponent at a distance.

Use the ball of your foot to impact the target. You can also impact with the heel by bringing the whole upper portion of your foot back. Utilizing the ball versus the heel depends on your intended target. As you go through these kicks, practice both and make note of the different effects. Under rare circumstances, as when your opponent leans forward, you can also impact with the instep, but you must then stretch your toes and keep your instep aligned with your lower leg.

Impact with the instep to your opponent's face when he is bent over.

The front kick can be further broken down into the front snap kick and the front push kick. We will deal with the front snap kick first. Targets for the front snap kick with the ball of the foot are the liver, spleen, stomach, solar plexus, chest area, and chin. Front kicks to the legs are not allowed.

TARGETS FOR THE FRONT SNAP KICK

Solar Plexus or Ribs

Chest

Chin

This section covers:

- Body mechanics for the front kick
- In the gym
- Stepping front kick
- The front push kick
- Body mechanics for the front push kick
- Sparring principles for the front kick
- The secret of the switch-step
- Summary and review

BODY MECHANICS FOR THE FRONT KICK

Initiate the *lead leg front kick* by thrusting your lead knee forward along centerline A, pointing it at the intended target. For example, if you intend to kick your opponent in the solar plexus, you should point your knee at his solar plexus. When extending your lower leg, it will automatically be in line with your knee, and therefore in line with your intended target. The higher you raise your knee, the higher you will kick.

As you thrust your knee forward, keep your lower leg chambered until it is time to extend the kick. Curl your toes back to avoid injury. Note how the instep of the kicking leg is aligned with the shin, forming a straight line for stability.

As you extend your leg, it should force a slight pivot in your supporting foot toward centerline B, or at a ninety-degree angle. This brings your hips through and increases the power of the kick. Impact your opponent with the ball of your foot.

When practicing the front kick, try to make all moves occur simultaneously. The pivot of your supporting foot should end precisely at the same time as the kick impacts the target.

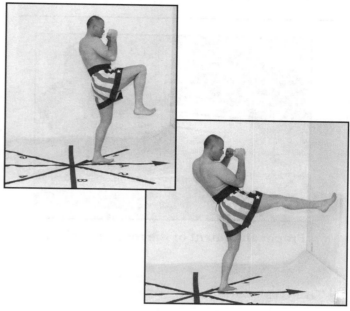

Initiate the *rear leg front kick* by thrusting your rear knee forward along centerline A. This should force a slight pivot in your supporting foot toward line 1. Extend your lower leg and impact your opponent with the ball of your foot.

A common error when throwing the front kick is turning the supporting foot to the outside *before* the knee comes up. A more proper way is to bring the knee up first, and let the motion of the kicking leg produce the pivot in the supporting foot. This eliminates any extra movements that may give the kick away. The fastest and most powerful kicks are those that flow in one continuous motion without pauses or extra steps. Another common error is failing to keep the foot and ankle aligned. Failure to do so is equivalent to keeping your wrist bent when punching. We also have a tendency to let the foot follow a vertical path instead of a *diagonal upward* path into the target. This may result in injury to your toes, even if they are curled back. Practice proper alignment of the foot by walking on the balls of your feet, as if you were wearing high heel shoes.

You must throw the front kick absolutely straight. Since your supporting leg is angled slightly outward, you may have a tendency to throw the kick at an outward angle as well. But if the kick doesn't follow a straight path through the target, the power will split into two or more directions.

Proper alignment of the foot and ankle.

IN THE GYM

Let's look at the front kick next. Start with your rear leg. Kick more diagonally into the target. The only time you really want to kick vertically straight is when kicking to your opponent's chin. Keep your leg chambered when lifting your foot off the ground, or you will lose momentum. Even though you're kicking faster now, you must still extend the kick all the way on impact.

Lead leg, now! If you throw your lead leg front kick without chambering your leg first, the kick will be worthless. Curl your toes back more. Your knee is pointed slightly toward your centerline, which keeps the kick from coming straight. As your foot comes off the floor, start pivoting your knee so that it points straight to the target when the kick connects.

Now, add a step to the lead leg front kick. The step must be very short and quick to be effective. Step forward with your rear foot first and throw your lead kick. Try it with the rear front kick now. To cut the time and movement, instead of stepping with your lead foot, then stepping with your rear foot, and then throwing the kick, make the step and the kick one fluid motion. Now, step back to lure your opponent into coming toward you, then immediately step forward with your front kick and meet his momentum with yours.

STEPPING FRONT KICK

The front kick is more dynamic if you initiate it with a step. Rather than allowing the momentum from your kicking leg to cause the pivot in your supporting foot, position your supporting foot at a forty-five degree angle within the step. Simultaneously thrust your kicking leg forward along your centerline, with your knee pointed at the intended target.

The stepping front kick requires a bit more practice than the stationary front kick. Practice the front kick stepping forward, backward, left, and right.

Stepping Forward

1. To step straight forward with your lead leg front kick, step with your rear foot first, pointing it at an outward forty-five degree angle to the right front corner. Your stance will now be slightly narrow.

2. Simultaneously raise your lead leg up along your centerline, keeping your lower leg chambered.

3. Extend your lower leg and impact the target with the ball of your foot.

4. After impact, replant your foot in a good fighting stance. The distance between your feet should allow for maximum mobility and balance. If your stance is too wide your mobility will suffer; if your stance is too narrow, your balance will suffer. You should have advanced about one shoulder length.

The basic movement theory states that whenever moving, you should step with the foot closest to the direction of travel first. As you can see, you violated this concept in the stepping exercise you just did, where you were taught to step forward with your rear foot first. But because fighting is a "give/take" situation, you must sometimes give something up in order to gain a bigger advantage. In this case, the concept of basic movement was given up in order to achieve a faster kick. Had you stepped with your lead foot first, almost twice as much movement and time would have been required. Try it! It is also important to remember that the basic movement theory was created primarily to keep you from crossing your feet.

Stepping Backward

1. To step straight backward with your lead leg front kick, step with your rear foot first, pointing it at an outward forty-five degree angle to the front right corner. Your stance will now be slightly wide.

2. Simultaneously raise your lead leg up along your centerline, keeping your lower leg chambered.

3. Extend your lower leg and impact the target with the ball of your foot.

4. Replant your foot in a fighting stance. You should now have retreated about one shoulder length.

Stepping Left And Right

In order to create a better angle for the front kick, you can practice it with a small step to the side with your supporting foot. This is especially beneficial when fighting a southpaw (a fighter who fights with his right side forward) from a left fighting stance.

1. To step left with the front kick, step with your lead foot to the left first. Bring your rear leg up along your centerline and extend your lower leg to kick.

2. To step right with the front kick, step with your rear foot to the right first. Bring your lead leg up along your centerline and extend your lower leg to kick.

Step right and kick with the lead leg.

Try this exercise on **STEPPING AND EVADING** your opponent's kicks:

Exercise 1

Have your partner throw front and round house kicks, while you experiment with different ways to evade or jam his kicks. If you choose to sidestep the kick, it is still important to stay within range to counter-strike. How can you gain a superior position without rushing in mindlessly, or placing yourself in danger?

THE FRONT PUSH KICK

The objective of the *front push kick* (the name itself is somewhat deceiving, since it is more of a thrust than a push) is to create distance between yourself and your opponent, to keep an aggressive opponent away (the kick is then used as a defensive move), or to unbalance your opponent. Unlike the front snap kick, which connects with the target and then snaps back from the knee, the front push kick sticks to the target long enough to drive the momentum through. The front push kick differs from the front snap kick in that it derives most of its power from extension in the hips and the leg, rather than just the leg.

The front push kicks drives through the target from the hips.

The front push kick is generally reserved as a body kick. Your goal is to stop your opponent's advance by thrusting the kick at his body and sending him back or knocking him off balance. If you use the kick to unbalance your opponent, it has the greatest effect if your opponent's base is narrow, as when he is on one leg in the process of stepping or kicking. When you unbalance your opponent, you buy yourself time. You must therefore take advantage of this and immediately follow with another move before your opponent has recovered. If your goal is to keep your opponent at a distance, throw the push kick to his chest. If you kick to a natural bend in the body (the mid-section), your opponent is more likely to bend forward than move back. Which part of your foot contacts the target depends on the height of the target. If you kick to the mid-section, impact with the ball or bottom of your foot; if you kick to the head, impact with the heel of your foot. You can also angle your entire foot back and impact with both the heel and bottom. Ideally, you want to drive your heel into your opponent's solar plexus, and the bottom of your foot into his sternum.

You can also use the front push kick strategically to create distance. Let's say that your opponent is superior on the inside (in close quarters). By timing your kick to his advance, you can keep him at long range where you have the upper hand. If you get backed up against the ropes of the ring, use the ropes to support yourself while delivering the front push kick to your opponent's body. This can create the distance you need to move away from the ropes and into a superior position.

Incline your body slightly to the rear and throw a front push kick underneath your opponent's jab.

Also try the front push kick against your opponent's guard (his hands), either to distract and irritate him, or to knock his hands into his face. The push kick can be an effective defense against your opponent's jab, especially if you've got his timing down. When he extends his jab, incline your body slightly to the rear and throw the push kick underneath his jab to the open target on his mid-section. Because he has momentum coming forward, the kick is likely to be very damaging. Try a parry in conjunction with the kick for additional safety.

The push kick is a great counter-move against the round house kick. Because the round house kick comes from the side, and the push kick comes straight, they don't have conflicting paths. Because the push kick follows a straight path with meeting momentums, your kick is likely to be more damaging than his, even though both you and your opponent are on one leg in the process of kicking.

Lastly, you may want to try the kick with a jump to close distance. It is then best thrown with your lead leg. Initiate the technique by jumping (or stepping) forward with your rear foot. In addition to closing distance, this adds the momentum of your body to the kick.

BODY MECHANICS FOR THE FRONT PUSH KICK

Initiate the *rear leg* front push kick just as you did the front snap kick, by bringing your rear knee up along your centerline and pointing it at the intended target.

As you extend your lower leg, curl your toes back to impact either with the ball or heel of your foot. You must also extend your hips forward by dropping your upper body slightly to the rear. This extends your knee and hips until they are in line with your upper body, creating a thrust.

<u>Note:</u> Don't incline your upper body to the rear until your kick connects. If you incline too soon, your body mechanics will contradict, splitting the power in opposite directions.

The momentum from your rear leg will now force your lead foot (your supporting foot) to pivot at forty-five degrees toward the front left corner. When you extend your leg to kick, the thrust from the kick should cause your supporting foot to slide a few inches forward.

Initiate the *lead leg* front push kick by bringing your lead knee up along your centerline and pointing it at the intended target. Extend the lower portion of your leg, simultaneously inclining your upper body slightly to the rear and extending your hips forward to create the desired thrust. To increase the dynamics of the front push kick it, too, can be thrown with a step.

SPARRING PRINCIPLES FOR THE FRONT KICK

Although the mechanics for the front kick are quite simple, in order for it to be effective in sparring, you must:

1. Throw it with full **extension**.
2. Throw it **straight**.

Fighters often make the mistake of throwing the kick vertically, allowing the foot to slide against the target. Because an effective defense against the front kick is the elbow block (more about blocking in Section 3), the fear of getting your toes smashed by your opponent's elbows may keep you from throwing the kick with full extension. This may result in slowing the kick down, or "holding back." A kick that is held back will do no damage and is a waste of time and effort. If you hesitate, your opponent can anticipate your move, so once you initiate a kick, you must have confidence in the technique and let it go to completion regardless of the consequences. Bear in mind that kickboxing requires you to make instant decisions and act decisively. If you ignore this, your opponent will lose respect for the technique.

The front kick with the *lead leg* is almost synonymous with the jab. Use it to annoy your opponent by jabbing the tip of your foot into his mid-section. A quick front kick to the solar plexus is also likely to make your opponent winded.

An object lacks stability unless its weight is centered above its foundation. It is therefore necessary to move your upper body above your supporting leg when kicking. A common error when throwing the lead leg front kick is to lean back excessively. Leaning back makes the kick a few inches short of reaching its target.

Against an experienced fighter, a series of five or six front kicks is useless, as he will pick up on the technique and either move out of reach or alter his timing to jam your toes with his elbow before counter-striking. It is better to throw one or two front kicks, and then move on to some other technique.

THE SECRET OF THE SWITCH-STEP

You can throw the front kick with either the lead or rear leg, with the lead leg usually being quicker, but the rear leg more powerful. There is another interesting concept of the front kick, which applies to both offense and defense: Because of the quickness and straight path of the lead leg, it can be used effectively to keep an aggressive opponent at a distance. Every time he tries to move in, you stick him with your lead leg front kick to stop his advance. Because you throw the kick with your lead leg, you also maintain your stance throughout the execution of the kick. This makes a follow-up easy. The rear leg, on the other hand, requires that you either switch stance by planting the kicking foot forward, or that you pull back into your conventional stance after kicking. But this requires time and also moves your upper body back. However, because of the longer distance the rear leg must travel, it is an excellent offensive weapon, especially when used as a thrust kick.

Now, here is a secret: You can give your lead kick the power of the rear kick without sacrificing the lead kick advantages of quick delivery, concealment, reach, and stance. Sounds like a dream? It's not. As long as the move is quick, you can switch the positions of your feet without actually switching stance. Think of it as a quick "hop" into a crossed stance. Yes, the crossed stance is not as stable as the regular fighting stance, but you will only be in it for a split second. By switching the positions of your feet, your lead foot becomes your rear foot with all of its power advantages. Because your lead foot is also your foundation when throwing a rear kick, and because your upper body must be above your foundation in order to remain balanced, this places your foundation approximately a foot and a half closer to your target. You have now increased your reach considerably, along with increasing the power in your kick. Since your upper body doesn't switch stance, your opponent will most likely not notice that the switch is taking place, as long as you can keep his focus away from your feet.

By switching the positions of your feet, you can increase the power and reach of the lead leg front kick.

If you want to throw a round house kick instead of a front kick using the switch-step, your rear foot needs to go in front of your lead foot; if you want to throw a side thrust kick, your rear foot needs to go behind your lead foot. You can also extend the reach of a kick by pushing off with your supporting foot simultaneous to extending the leg. This makes you slide a few inches forward, enabling you to use momentum to your advantage.

The switch-step is basically a very short and quick shuffle where you switch the positions of your feet. The switch-step allows you to place your lead foot to the rear quickly, and follow with a kick off this leg. The switch-step is beneficial whenever we wish to throw a lead kick, yet desire the power of a rear kick. The switch-step can be used with any kick, but is perhaps most beneficial with knee strikes. Because of the close proximity to your opponent when kneeing, especially in a tie-up, it may be difficult to throw the lead knee with power (we will talk about knees in Section 7).

Summary and review

The front kick is essentially a long range technique designed to strike your opponent's upper body or head. Throw the front kick by bringing your knee straight up along your centerline and pointing it at the target. Extend your lower leg from the knee and impact the target with the ball of your foot. When impact is complete, snap your leg back to the chambered position before replanting your foot.

Front kick practice in the air

- Assume a fighting stance and throw ten front kicks in the air with the lead leg, then ten with the rear leg.

- Use a slow to medium pace and work on correct body mechanics, good balance, and full extension of the kick.

- Start at one end of the room and throw a series of front kicks, alternating legs, until you get to the other end of the room.

- Keep your hands in the high guard position. It is easy to get in the habit of lowering the hands as a counter-weight to balance.

- In order to keep your head protected, keep your hands high and bend your knees, or crouch slightly to aid with balance.

A front kick to the mid-section makes your opponent bend forward.

- Throw a series of front kicks with your lead leg only, each time taking a short step forward with your rear foot to advance the kick.

- When you get to the other end of the room, throw a series of front kicks with your rear leg only, each time taking a short step forward with your lead foot to advance the kick. Reset into your stance after each kick.

Target practice for the front kick

- Face your partner and throw front kicks in slow motion to specific targets, identifying and touching each target lightly with the ball of your foot.

- Determine your opponent's expected reaction to each kick. Will it push him back? Make him bend over?

- Your opponent's reaction will determine what kind of follow-up punch or kick to use.

A front kick to the chest will make your opponent move back.

Kicking shield practice for the front kick

- Have your partner hold a kicking shield. Throw a lead leg front kick with power. As your partner moves back, take an adjustment step and immediately follow with a strike.

- If you can strike your opponent when he is on the defensive, as when he is taking a step back, you are likely to catch him off balance or with his guard down.

- Repeat the exercise. As your partner moves back, follow with a rear front kick with power. When alternating lead and rear kicks, you will automatically advance forward.

- Repeat the exercise. As your partner moves back, follow with another lead front kick. You must now take an adjustment step with your rear foot.

Front kick combination practice

- Start at one end of the room and put together punch combinations including at least one front kick, advancing forward with each strike or kick until you get to the other end of the room.

- Try to get a feel for combinations that are "natural." In a natural combination, each punch and kick flows easily off the previous one, there are no awkward movements in your body mechanics, and you are never at a danger of losing balance.

- Face your partner and take turns, using light contact only, to throw a combination including at least one front kick. As your partner moves back, move forward so that you are always within reach to follow with a punch or kick.

Heavy bag practice for the front kick

- Work the heavy bag with hand combinations. Try to throw at least one front kick for every five strikes.

- As the bag swings, make adjustments in your stance and distance, timing the bag's movement to your kick.

- Have your partner hold a kicking shield. Time twenty-second intervals and execute front kicks with the lead leg only, then with the rear leg only at the next interval, then alternating lead and rear.

- Make sure that the mechanics are correct for each kick. Even though you are kicking fast, you don't want the kicks to be sloppy.

Front kick sparring practice

- Engage in light sparring with your partner, using the front kick only, while your partner uses hand techniques only.

- The hands are short to medium range techniques, while the front kick is essentially a long range technique. How can you keep your partner at bay with the front kick?

- Engage in "three-step sparring," using the front kick and round house kick only. Face your partner and throw a three-kick combination, while your partner moves back to give you distance. Then have your partner do the same to you.

THE SIDE THRUST KICK

The *side thrust kick* is one of the more powerful kicks used in kickboxing. Since the side thrust kick requires a bit more movement than the round house and front kick, it is usually thrown with your lead leg only. The side thrust kick can be used both offensively and defensively to keep an opponent at a distance. You can impact the target with either the heel or bottom of your foot. The heel gives you a smaller area with more penetrating force, and the bottom of the foot gives you a larger area, with the damage spreading over a wider range, but with less penetrating force. A common error is to contact with the ball of the foot or with the toes. If this is done, it is an indication that the kick is not thrown straight, which may result in power loss. You can also impact with the outside knife edge of the foot, but this is generally reserved for point sparring competition or street encounters. Targets for the side thrust kick are the stomach, ribs, chest, forearms, and head. This kick is not thrown to the legs.

The side thrust kick can knock your opponent off balance, and is one of the more powerful kicks used in kickboxing.

This section covers:

- Body mechanics for the side thrust kick
- Stepping side thrust kick
- Glove-up with Keith
- The rear leg side thrust kick
- Sparring principles for the side thrust kick
- Some pointers on the power of kicks
- What's in a good kick?
- The application of "fancier" kicks
- Summary and review

BODY MECHANICS FOR THE SIDE THRUST KICK

Initiate the side thrust kick by bringing your lead leg up and chambering it so that your knee is pointed to a reverse forty-five degree angle toward line 4. Your supporting foot should pivot to a ninety-degree angle in the direction of centerline B.

Extend your leg straight along centerline A, and impact your opponent with the heel of your foot. As your foot thrusts forward, and simultaneous to impact, the force of your lead leg extension should pivot your rear foot (supporting foot) into alignment with line 4 with your toes to the rear.

STEPPING SIDE THRUST KICK

The side thrust kick is often thrown with a step to close distance and create more power. A common error is to use *too much* movement. Since the kick starts from long range, it is especially important to conceal it. The step should therefore start in your supporting foot (rear foot), which is farther from your opponent and more difficult to detect. However, this violates the basic movement theory, so your stance will be narrow for a moment.

To initiate the stepping side thrust kick, step with your rear foot first, bringing it into contact with your lead foot. You should now be standing with your feet side by side.

The moment your rear foot plants, bring your lead leg up and chamber for the kick. Do not chamber your leg prior to throwing the kick. Any additional movement can give the kick away.

The rest of the technique is identical to the stationary side thrust kick.

Maximum power in the stepping side thrust kick is achieved by carrying the momentum of the step through the target in one fluid motion. At no time should you allow your momentum to stop. Once your rear foot plants, your lead foot should already be chambering and kicking forward. Strive to make the step as "clean" as possible. You can do this by taking a

half-step only, by bringing your rear foot forward half the distance to your lead foot. Taking a large step or crossing your feet is not recommended, because:

1. Crossing your feet may **telegraph** the kick to your opponent.

2. Crossing your feet may result in a **loss of balance**.

3. Crossing your feet may **redirect the path** of the kick, so that the power is no longer projected straight through the target.

For additional power and reach, allow your supporting foot to slide a few inches forward on impact.

Glove Up with Keith

When throwing the stepping side thrust kick, it is important to carry your momentum all the way through the target. If I were going to run through the wall over there, I wouldn't start, and then come to a stop as I got to the wall, and then bump my shoulder into it. No, I would start running, and continue to run without stopping until I was all the way through the wall.

There are basically two times when you would use the stepping side thrust kick. What are they? Okay, against multiple opponents. Use it against one opponent to kick him back to create time to eliminate your second opponent. But we're not concerned with multiple opponents in kickboxing. When is the other time you would use it? When you need to close distance? Yes, but that's kind of a given. The second time is as a finisher, when your opponent is already dazed or knocked back against the ropes.

Step faster now. I want to see a faster gap closure. Make sure there is no separation between step and kick, no break in momentum.

If you throw a stepping side thrust kick and your opponent hunches over and freezes up, that's a good time to throw a second regular side thrust kick. Like this! See? That one knocked you clear over there. Then, maybe add a spinning back kick to the end of your combination.

Your side thrust kick looks pretty good. The only problem is that you're kicking a little too high, which makes the kick slide off the target at an upward angle. This results in power loss. Throw the kick parallel with the floor to direct the power straight through the target. You feel that you are having a hard time getting comfortable with this kick? That it is too slow? I think you are putting too much effort into it. You're also cocking your hips before your foot is off the ground. Lift your foot up first and cock as you throw the kick. Try to time it so that your opponent walks into the kick.

Your kick is mechanically correct, but when you pull back and chamber your leg like that, your opponent will most likely see it coming. Try a faster kick by impacting the target with the bottom or knife edge of your foot. The knife edge kick is not designed to hurt your opponent, but more to annoy him. Kind of like a jab. What would you do if you're too close and need to create distance? Sometimes you will think that you are too close when you're really not. If you bring your lead knee to the rear simultaneous to chambering the leg, it will create the distance you need. As your opponent moves back after being kicked, you can follow with a second stepping side kick.

THE REAR LEG SIDE THRUST KICK

The side thrust kick thrown with the rear leg is not very often seen in kickboxing. One reason is because this kick is quite "lengthy" and requires a good set-up. Another reason is because the fighter has not analyzed when the best time is to throw the kick. Most fighters who attempt the rear leg side thrust kick throw it from long range and without concealing its movement. Or they throw it in the center of the ring, where their opponent has distance and time to get away. You can conceal the rear leg side thrust kick from long range by initiating it with a rear leg round house kick. As your hips come through, convert the round house kick into a side thrust kick.

Another good time to throw the rear leg side thrust kick is from close range with your opponent backed up against the ropes and unable to get away. An opponent against the ropes seldom expects this kick. The kick is therefore "naturally concealed." When kicking from this tight a distance, first keep your opponent busy with a hand combination. Then step to the side, or slightly to the rear, with your lead foot. This creates distance and an angle off your opponent's centerline.

When in close, bring your lead knee to the rear to create distance.

Step to the rear with your lead foot. As distance is created, throw the rear leg side thrust kick.

After the kick has landed and before your opponent has had time to regroup, follow with additional strikes. You can now step back to your right and off your opponent's centerline, and follow with either a round house kick off your lead leg, or with a punch combination.

Step to your right with your right foot, and throw a left round house kick.

SPARRING PRINCIPLES FOR THE SIDE THRUST KICK

Because a properly thrown side thrust kick requires quite a bit of rotation in the hips and upper body, you risk telegraphing the kick or placing yourself in an inferior position with your back turned toward your opponent. This is true especially if the kick lacks speed or is thrown without a proper set-up. You can set up the side thrust kick with a hand combination to distract your opponent's focus away from your feet. An aggressive hand combination can drive your opponent back and create the distance you need to throw the kick effectively. Against an opponent who rushes you, you can use the side thrust kick as a deterrent by timing it to his forward momentum.

Time the side thrust kick to your opponent's forward momentum.

Extend the power of the side thrust kick through the target by utilizing the big muscles in your buttocks. Many fighters make the mistake of trying to use the leg muscles to extend the kick, but this takes a lot of energy. It is better to keep the kick contracted initially, and let the power and explosion come from the muscles in your butt and hip. You may also find that the side thrust kick has greater power if your body stays compact. Leaning back excessively, or getting up on your toes creates a conflict with balance and the direction of energy.

The side thrust kick is excellent for funneling your opponent into a corner. When he reaches the ropes of the ring, step off to the side and away from the closest corner. This creates an angle that allows you to kick your opponent back into the corner. Once he is cornered, you must be aware of his escape routes. Use tiny steps left and right to keep him in the corner, simultaneously throwing punch combinations to the body and head.

SOME POINTERS ON THE POWER OF KICKS

Many fighters kick with awesome power when kicking a stationary target, such as a heavy bag or kicking shield. But this is only impressive if you can transfer that power to the actual fight. Power is increased when:

1. **The kick is relaxed.** Don't try too hard. Trying implies tensing. If all your energy is released at the appropriate time, your strikes and kicks will be more explosive and, therefore, more devastating. Stay relaxed until the moment of impact, so that the energy can flow through your body and transfer into the target.

2. **The speed is increased.** You must train to throw your punches and kicks faster and faster, and to decrease the beat between each strike. To throw faster, "think" faster. When speed increases, power automatically increases.

Power loss most often results from opposing movements in body mechanics, and is commonly manifested as leaning back when kicking, particularly if you lack flexibility in your legs and hips. Leaning lessens power through an increase in distance, because your body is moving away from the target instead of toward it. The higher you kick, the harder it is to keep all of your body momentum going in the direction of the kick. However, if you eliminate leaning entirely, you may also lose power, because you limit the flexibility in your kick. I usually teach to "crouch" (stay compact) in the direction of the kick, so that you can grab the "love handles" on that side of your mid-section. This ensures proper direction of energy and sets you deeper in your stance for better balance.

Note: Your body must be relaxed to throw a fast and powerful kick. As you increase the height of the kick, some leaning is necessary. Try to find the happy medium between crouching and leaning.

Try this exercise on **DIRECTION OF ENERGY**:

Exercise 1

Any time a strike or kick is not lined up with your centerline, you lose power. A common error when kicking is to swing the leg out wide. Experiment on the heavy bag throwing round house kicks wide. Now tighten the kicks by keeping your leg lined up with your centerline. A tight kick:

1. Is more **powerful** than a wide kick.

2. Helps **protect** your centerline.

3. Helps **conceal** the kick.

4. **Cuts the time** it takes for the kick to reach the target.

The best way to improve your kicks is, of course, to practice those kicks. Since kicking relies mainly on four major muscle groups, proper strengthening of these muscle groups makes for stronger and faster kicks. The buttocks (gluteus muscles), the front of the thighs (quadriceps), the back of the thighs (hamstrings), and the calves must all work together to create well-balanced, fast, and powerful kicks. Once you have built strength and flexibility in these four muscle groups, power is generated in your lower body by using *hip rotation* and *body momentum*. You can increase power by utilizing the strength in your legs, and ending with a snappy twist of your hips (hip rotation). You can also increase power by using the momentum of your whole body (as when stepping forward with a kick).

A "tight kick" is not the same as a "tense kick." Tensing is the opposite of relaxing and is destructive to fighting. A tight kick or punch is thrown with your leg or arm close to your body, denying your opponent time or space to take the created opening.

When your body mechanics are correct, the only way to increase power is through speed. The finer details of speed branch off into the *acceleration* of the kick. Power is increased if the kick can build speed on its way to the target, so that the greatest speed happens at the moment of impact.

There are several elements to consider when practicing acceleration of kicks. Your mental attitude, for example, plays an important role. Kicking "with an attitude" means that you kick with intent and are therefore more likely to accelerate the kick. Another important factor is your target. When speeding up a kick, the area where your foot lands on your opponent will usually change. This happens because when the speed changes you get a different timing and, therefore, different visual cues. When practicing target accuracy, be aware of this error and make the necessary adjustments.

Try this exercise on **ACCELERATION OF KICKS**:

Exercise 2

The faster your foot leaves the ground, the more powerful your kick will be. Have a partner hold a kicking shield while you throw kicks at a constant speed. Now, try to accelerate the kicks so that the greatest speed occurs at the moment of impact. Ask your partner if he felt any difference in power. Speed originates in your body and not in your hand or foot. The faster you can move your body, the more speed and power you can attain.

WHAT'S IN A GOOD KICK?

Throwing a powerful kick is not as simple as lifting your foot off the floor, thrusting it at the target, and expecting the desired results. If you do not possess good technique, your chances of success are slim. To throw a powerful kick, all parts of the kick must be accomplished simultaneously. Once you initiate the kick, all moves involved in throwing it should be completed at the same time. If you neglect this important concept and break the kick into separate parts, the kick will lack power and be way too slow for competition. It is okay to break the kick down into its component parts at the beginning stages while you are learning

and analyzing it. But as you progress and become more advanced, you must make the kick flow in one continuous motion from initiation to impact. Also, remember that the fighters who kick with power do so because they get their whole body, rather than just the leg, involved in the technique.

When throwing a multiple hand combination, your speed and power should build so that your strongest punch comes at the end of the combination. When throwing a multiple kick combination the same concept is true. Still, I often see fighters throw their strongest kicks at the beginning of the combination, and many fighters don't throw multiple kicks at all. Throwing multiple kicks in fluid combinations, with an increase in speed for each kick, is an enormous asset to the serious kickboxer. A good kick combination enables you to take many different targets within a short period of time. Work on *blending* your kicks in with your punch combinations.

Try these exercises on **MULTIPLE KICKS**:

Exercise 3

Practice multiple kicks on the heavy bag. As the bag swings, do not stop and reset it, but adjust your foot position for the new angle and distance. You will discover that throwing multiple kicks effectively requires very good timing, coordination, body mechanics, and speed.

Exercise 4

When sparring, concentrate on your hand techniques only, letting your kicks "come by themselves." As your experience grows, your subconscious mind will automatically "see" the openings and allow you to kick without telegraphing your intents. Planning the kick too long in advance can allow your opponent to "read your mind."

THE APPLICATION OF "FANCIER" KICKS

In contrast to karate point sparring, the "fancy" kicks seen in traditional martial arts are usually not practical for fighting in the ring. Many of the flying and spinning kicks, though pleasing to watch, have less penetrating power and are easier to defend against than the simple and direct kicks, such as the round house kick, front kick, and side thrust kick. You should therefore practice these three basic kicks meticulously. **But bear in mind that even for simple techniques to work, speed, power, and accuracy is required. Never throw your techniques half-heartedly!**

As you gain experience, and particularly if you have previous knowledge of martial arts, some of those spectacular kicks (flying side kicks, jump spinning back kicks, crescent kicks, spinning heel kicks) do have application in competition kickboxing. A flying or jumping kick, just by the way it is executed, can "freeze" your opponent, making him unable to defend effectively against the attack. The unorthodox, even if it lacks precision or power, is usually feared more than that which we are used to seeing and defending against.

Keith's Corner

As I began my training many years ago, I was fascinated by the spinning techniques. They were pretty to watch, and seemed to be a measure of one's overall ability. Because most schools teach these techniques in the advanced stages of training, if you were doing them, you were looked upon as an advanced student. So, I spent a lot of time and energy trying to perfect spinning techniques. Later, when I became a competitive kickboxer, I discovered that sometimes less is better. I adopted the Lee philosophy of "hacking away at the non-essentials." To me, spinning kicks became non-essentials, as I found them energy consuming, dangerously ineffective from a throw to connect rate, and often resulting in nagging injuries. In fact, the only positive about them was that the crowds loved them. But I was fighting for myself first, and for the crowd second. I had seen too many fights where the crowd dictated to the fighter, resulting in fatigue and another notch in the loss column.

I went back to basics and strung together an impressive number of wins. Only occasionally would I pull a spinning kick out of the tool bag. If my opponent were out of gas or on the verge of a knockout, I would give the crowd a nice finisher. But now, some twenty-five years into the business, I've come full circle, and it is with a much different perspective. My attitude toward spinning kicks over the last few years has changed, but I'm coming from a completely different application. So, to answer the question whether spinning kicks are important to a student's learning and progression, yes, I have found the spinning kick to be one of the very best teachers of the principles of balance, position, and momentum. In fact, I teach spinning kicks very early in my program. I have found that mastery of one's body in motion gives better balance, understanding of power, and an increased enhancement of all techniques. As a result, my beginning students have more confidence, and the less technical techniques come easier. However, I have not changed my position about the ring application. Spinning techniques are occasional tools to be utilized with common sense and under the right circumstances.

Summary and review

The side thrust kick is a powerful and damaging kick often used to knock your opponent back and create distance. Preferably, you should impact the target with the heel of your foot. One drawback of the side thrust kick is that it requires flexibility in the hips. Since it is easier telegraphed than the front kick and round house kick, it is mostly thrown with your lead leg. To execute a side thrust kick, raise your lead knee up in the chambered position and pivot on your supporting foot with your heel toward the target. Simultaneously extend your leg, impacting the target with the heel of your foot. Targets for the side thrust kick are the mid-section and head.

Side thrust kicking with proper form

- Practice the side thrust kick with proper form in the air from a stationary position. Angle your foot back so that you impact the target with the heel of your foot. Extend your leg fully upon impact.

- Practice the side thrust kick on a partner for target accuracy. Face each other and lock your lead hands. This gives you support for balance.

Lock lead hands and take turns practicing the side thrust kick on each other.

- Take turns kicking in slow motion to the rib area underneath your partner's extended hand. Pay attention to impacting with the heel of your foot.

- Make sure your leg is extended fully on impact. This might require that you lean your upper body slightly to the rear.

- Pull your leg back into the fully chambered position before re-planting your foot on the floor.

Target practice for the side thrust kick

- Practice target accuracy by kicking to different medium and high targets. A good medium target is the solar plexus or chest, and a good high target is the head.

- Practice the kick in the air first, then on a focus mitt held at different levels, and finally on a partner.

- Why is it important to plant the foot between each kick? Not planting the foot requires very good balance and flexibility, and is likely to make the kick less powerful than if you plant the foot briefly (touching) before launching the next kick.

- When planting the foot between kicks, which is better: planting it in your toe-to-heel stance, or planting it so that your hips are already chambered for the next kick? Why?

- Practice the side thrust kick by kicking over the back of a chair. This exercise teaches you to chamber the leg properly before kicking.

Throwing the stepping side thrust kick

- Practice the side thrust kick in the air across the room. In order to move forward, you must take a step before throwing it.

- If you step with your lead foot first, you can increase the speed of the step by pushing off with your rear foot. Stepping with your rear foot first is slightly quicker, because you only have one step and one kick, rather than a step, a step, and a kick.

- How much distance can you gain with the stepping side thrust kick? Experiment on a heavy bag or partner.

- Practice the stepping side thrust kick in combination with other kicks. What other kicks can you use to maintain a smooth flow in your combinations?

- Think about what is logical. A side thrust kick following a round house kick with the shin may not be logical, because the distance is too tight. A round house kick with the instep following a side thrust kick may or may not be logical. It depends on how far your opponent moved back after taking the side thrust kick.

- Determine your opponent's reaction to getting kicked in the mid-section, chest, or head. His reaction may determine your follow-up kick or punch.

Heavy bag practice for the side thrust kick

- Practice the side thrust kick on a swinging heavy bag. Is it easier to land the kick when the bag is swinging toward your front or back (butt)? Why? It is important to think about this, because the least awkward movement gives you the fastest and most deceptive kick.

- If you can throw the kick without having to position your hips, you are more likely to conceal it. When is the best time to throw the side thrust kick: when your opponent moves to your left or to your right? Consider that this differs depending on whether you are in a right or left stance.

- Use footwork to move around the swinging heavy bag, and throw the side thrust kick when the bag is coming toward you, simulating an opponent moving to close range. This increases the power of the kick by adding his momentum to yours.

Side thrust kicking with power and precision

- Practice the side thrust kick on a shield held by a partner to give you a realistic feel for your power. Can you move your opponent (the shield holder) back?

- Have the shield holder move around while you shadow box in the air. Try to position for the side thrust kick on a moving target.

- Practice the side thrust kick on a smaller target (double-end bag or focus mitt) for precision. Can you impact with your heel rather than the ball or bottom of your foot?

Practicing the side thrust kick on a small target helps you work on accuracy and penetrating force with the heel of your foot.

- Have your partner throw a lightweight object (a sparring glove, for example) toward you. Try to time your side thrust kick to strike the object. This is an exercise in both precision and timing.

- If you miss the object, why did you miss it? Determine whether you have to initiate your kick sooner or later.

- If you strike the object, can you kick it all the way back to the thrower? How straight does it move through the air? This is an indication of how straight your power is focused.

Side thrust kick sparring practice

- Have your partner move to the left, then right. When is it easiest to land the side thrust kick?

- If you are in left stance, and you throw the kick with your lead leg, it is easiest to land it when your opponent moves toward your left. This is because your hips are already set for the kick in this direction.

- Engage in light contact sparring, throwing the side thrust kick every time your opponent moves to your left.

- If your opponent moves to your right, which kick would lend itself to this movement? Try a rear leg round house kick (providing that you are still in a left stance). You conserve time and energy when you throw a kick that your opponent walks into.

Gaining height with the side thrust kick

- How can you attain greater height in the side thrust kick, especially if you lack flexibility? Try bending your supporting leg slightly at the knee and crouching in the direction of the kick. First, hold on to a wall with one hand and have your partner raise your leg up in the side kick motion. Keep your supporting leg absolutely straight.

- When you can't raise your leg any higher, bend slightly at the knee of the supporting leg. How many inches did your kick increase in height? This is true for all kicks. By bending the supporting leg slightly, you increase the flexibility in the kicking leg.

When keeping your supporting leg straight, you limit the flexibility of the kicking leg, as seen above.

Increasing the speed of the side thrust kick

- How can you increase the power of the side thrust kick? One way is by increasing the speed. You can increase the speed by utilizing your body weight and momentum through a step.

- You can increase the speed by pulling your leg back into the chambered position (rather than dropping the foot straight down) after impact. Think of your leg as a piston that shoots out from the hip, and then quickly retracts again. An additional benefit is that this allows you to reset quickly for a follow-up technique.

Defending the side thrust kick

- Practice defending against the side thrust kick (we will talk more about defense in Section 3). Because the kick comes straight toward you, be careful not to walk into the kick.

- The side thrust kick is difficult to block. How would you go about blocking it, or is there a better way to defend against it?

- Experiment with jamming and gapping. If you can move in while the kick is in its initial stages, you can jam it and follow with a punch combination. If you see the kick coming, you can gap and let the kick miss.

- What are the advantages of jamming versus gapping? Can you move to the side and attack your opponent's supporting leg? Is it better to move to your left or right? Why?

When your opponent kicks, try to move to the side and attack her supporting leg.

Lead vs. rear leg side thrust kick

- The side thrust kick is most effective when thrown with the lead leg. Why? Determine when you can throw it effectively with the rear leg.

- Experiment with timing the rear leg side thrust kick to your opponent's movement, so that when he moves back, you pivot your hips through and throw the rear leg side thrust kick.

- Initiate the attack with a lead leg round house kick from close range, then plant the kicking foot to the rear in the opposite stance. Your rear leg has now become your lead leg. Throw the side thrust kick with this leg.

- How can you increase the speed of the above combination? Can you decrease the beat between kicks by planting your kicking foot in position to follow with another kick?

QUICK REFERENCE TO CONCEPTS

ACCELERATION OF KICKS: You can increase the power by accelerating the kick so that the greatest speed happens at the moment of impact.

ADDING MOMENTUMS: When your opponent steps toward you, his momentum is added to that of your kick. This results in an increase in kicking power.

BASIC MOVEMENT THEORY: When moving, step with the foot closest to the direction of travel first. This helps you maintain balance by keeping you from narrowing your stance or crossing your feet.

COMPLETION OF MOTION: The motion of your kick must come to completion before you can move to a new position or throw another kick. For example, if your opponent throws a round house kick, he is unable to move away from his present position, until the motion of the kick is complete and he has replanted his foot on the floor. To take advantage of this concept, counter-strike while your opponent is in the process of kicking and is unable to move away from you.

DIRECTION OF ENERGY: The ability to direct all of your energy into a target to create a specific effect. To produce optimum results, all your body's energy and mass must flow in the same direction. Power loss most often results from opposing movements in body mechanics.

DYNAMICS OF POWER: Power is derived from several sources working in harmony toward a common goal. If you are off balance, or if you lean back when kicking, a loss of power results due to the conflict with direction of energy. Power is also increased when speed is increased.

EXTENSION WHEN KICKING: A kick cannot reach maximum power unless the leg is fully extended through the target at impact. To increase the power in your kicks, bring your leg up chambered with the knee high, and with the final extension coming at the moment of impact.

KICKING THROUGH THE TARGET: If you are slightly out of reach, your kick will lack penetrating force; if you are slightly too close, you will be jamming your own kick. Correct distance and the ability to release the power at the appropriate moment allow you to extend the power of your kick through the target; you will not merely be kicking the surface.

MULTIPLE KICKS: When throwing multiple kicks, try to throw a fluid combination with an increase in speed for each kick. This allows you to take many different targets within a short time period.

ROTATIONAL INERTIA: Inertia means resistance to change in motion. The farther the mass is from the center of rotation, the greater the inertia. In practical terms, this means that whenever you kick, you should attempt to keep your leg chambered as long as possible through the acceleration of the kick. This enables you to accelerate the kick easier for maximum power.

SECTION THREE
BASIC DEFENSE

CAN'T LOSE, IF YOU CAN'T BE HIT
by Keith Livingston

I was fortunate. During the prime of my career, I did not only have a full time kickboxing coach, but I had a full time boxing coach; a crusty old sea dog named Tony Bullock. Tony was a throw back to an age now all but forgotten. He always said what he meant, and meant what he said. In other words, you knew where you stood, and if you didn't, you weren't listening. When Tony threw a compliment your way, you knew you were training hard. Just don't bask in the moment too long, or pretty soon you'd hear the old man bark: Jesus Christ, you hit like an old woman! What the hell's the matter with you?!

My training in those days was somewhat unconventional. I would fluctuate between the kickboxing gym and the boxing stable. While the kickboxing centers were usually more upscale and the clientele a little softer, I found the quality of sparring at the boxing gym a bit more demanding with a genuine flavor to the environment. Let's face it, whereas kickboxing gyms are filled with the middle class that are generally paying for their lessons, boxing gyms are filled with kids from the streets that come in with a certain toughness. While martial arts studios are forced to be kinder and gentler for fear of liability, I've never heard of a boxing gym getting sued for injury. Tony Bullock's idea of insurance was a simple sign on the wall: Caution, you may get your ass kicked in here!

I recall a particular fight that I was about to undertake. My opponent was known for his awesome power and his ability to knock you out with either hand. As I began my training, my kickboxing coach and I were discussing various strategies. We watched video after video of my opponent dropping fighter after fighter to the canvas. Our strategy was to stay outside and box to a decision. I was not entirely satisfied working the outside game. I was primarily an inside fighter with a powerful punch myself. But my coach insisted that we would have to out-box this one.

Week one found me arriving at Bullock's and eager to spar. I always arrived early, wanting to spend a few minutes alone with the old man. As I entered the humid gym, I noticed Tony sitting in his well-worn chair next to the fifteen by fifteen foot bloodstained ring. As usual, he was bitching to himself about world events as he flipped through the newspaper. As I walked in, he peered over the top, wearing his Navy issued reading glasses from World War II. "Goddamm world's goin' to hell in a hand basket . . . Just give me a few minutes with these gangs!"

I purposely sat down next to Tony and began wrapping my hands. It wasn't long before he neatly folded the paper and placed it in his lap. "What's eatin' ya kid?" I explained about my upcoming bout, our strategy, and my discomfort at trying to out-box the other fighter. Tony took a cigar out of his shirt pocket, broke the end off, and chewed it up. And after packing it into the corner of his mouth, he spat. "Simple," he said. "Don't get hit!"

The next three weeks in the boxing gym, I experienced some of the most valuable training of my career. It started with a rope strung from one corner of the ring to the other. The drill was simple: Bob and weave from corner to corner, first moving forward, and then moving backward. Simple, that is, until I discovered I would be there until all the other fighters had come and gone. The next day when I arrived at the gym, there was a spider web of ropes inside the ring, six of them strung east and west, and six strung north and south, forming a series of boxes throughout the ring. Tony smiled, spat, and instructed me into the ring. My new drill was comprised of lateral movement, as well as forward and backward. Again, I was the first one there and the last to leave.

At the beginning of week two when I entered the gym and found the ropes missing, I was relieved. However, my relief was short lived. Tony suited me up with the heaviest headgear he had, which included a steel brace to protect the nose. He ordered me to place my hands in the rear of my shorts and grab my jock strap. For the next five rounds various fighters took turns sparring with me. I was literally unarmed, but the drill taught me to watch body movement prior to a punch. It taught me evasiveness, distance closure, and to block and push off with my shoulders. By the end of the week, I hardly even got hit anymore.

Week three was my week. Not only was I becoming an elusive target, but now I got to hit back. I was able to make my sparring partners miss with regularity and make them pay with my counter-attack. Through weeks four and five, I worked the double-end bag with left and right slips. My mitt work incorporated slipping, ducking, and bobbing and weaving. I continued the rope drills, along with extensive sparring. My final lessons taught me to vary my defensive rhythm and speed, which played havoc with my sparring partners. The last week of my training was spent adjusting my newly found defense into the kickboxing style. My kickboxing coach was amazed at the new dimension and depth of training I had acquired.

The fight itself was a huge success. In the first few rounds, my opponent became frustrated and angry over his inability to land a solid punch. In round three I admit I got a little cocky, taunting him by placing my hands behind my back and making him miss with ease. In round four, I slipped his left jab and threw a rear uppercut, which sent him down like a used dishrag. I was almost disappointed when he failed to make the count. A few days later when I returned to the boxing gym, Tony looked up from his paper. "How did ya do, kid?" I smiled and winked. "Can't lose, if ya can't be hit!"

The referee is tending to a fallen fighter.

UPPER BODY BLOCKS

Now that you have learned some offensive skills of basic punching and kicking, it's time to learn good defense. A successful fighter must be complete in all aspects of fighting, and offense cannot survive without defense, and vice versa. Defense can be broken down into three major target areas: lower body, upper body, and head. In addition, there are two parts to basic defense:

1. Blocking and parrying
2. Head and body movement

Which part of your body you use (hand, forearm, elbow, shin) when blocking or parrying depends on the type of strike you are defending and on your target. All blocks can be done with either the lead or rear hand (or leg). In addition, blocks can be either *linear*, as when meeting the strike straight on, or *circular*, as when redirecting the path of the strike.

Head and body movement can be either linear or circular and is determined by the type of strike you are defending, and whether the movement is used defensively (bobbing and weaving, slipping, ducking), or offensively (jamming, gapping). In this section, *shadow boxing*, which is a training routine against an imaginary opponent, will also be part of your movement exercises.

This section covers:

- Making your opponent pay a price
- The vicious elbow
- Body mechanics for the reverse elbow block
- In the gym
- Body mechanics for the downward elbow block
- Glove-up with Keith
- Body mechanics for the inward elbow block
- Forearm blocks
- The shoulder block
- What's in a good block?
- Summary and review

MAKING YOUR OPPONENT PAY A PRICE

Many fighters think that defense is simply the ability to avoid getting hit. But good defense has many other purposes. Your goal defensively is to make your opponent *pay a price*. The objective of good defense is four-fold:

1. **Protect you from harm.** If the defensive move fails to defend, it is of little value. A good block requires *a minimum amount of movement with minimal target exposure*. To accomplish this, block everything that comes above the waist with your hands, forearms, or elbows, and everything that comes below the waist with your legs. If you get in the habit of dropping your hand to block a low kick, you will leave yourself open at the head. Blocks can therefore be broken down into upper and lower body blocks.

2. **Create offense.** Blocking, in itself, will not win the fight. It is impossible to protect against all strikes. You will get hit. You should therefore strive to use the momentum of good defense to launch a counter-attack.

3. **Destroy your opponent's weapons.** Although the very nature of blocking is defensive, if you execute your blocks properly, they can be highly destructive to your opponent's offensive weapons. For the purpose of this training segment, you should change your mind-set about blocking from a defensive attitude to an offensive attitude. Begin thinking of your blocks as strikes, and not simply as a means of thwarting your opponent's attack. By selecting the right block and executing it in the proper manner, we can punish our opponent's offensive weapons and eventually render those weapons harmless. Elbow blocks and shin blocks, especially, can be used to inflict enough harm on your opponent's strike that he becomes reluctant to use it again.

4. **Tire your opponent.** It takes more energy to fight offensively than defensively. Defense, with its shorter and more compact moves, should therefore be used in between offense to replenish your energies and tire your opponent. Superior defense, which encourages your opponent to throw lengthy combinations without landing anything of value, is likely to frustrate and tire him in seconds. In sports competition, particularly when the fight may be lengthy, the person who tires first will most likely lose. When your opponent is exhausted and frustrated, his defense is lacking. This is a good time to explode with offense.

It is easy to get in the habit of being offensive minded and simply trade blows with your opponent. But since one properly placed punch or kick can easily end the fight, you should be careful and look out for your safety at all times. Still, being overly cautious and trying to avoid every strike thrown at you will never win the fight. There is a fine line that needs to be drawn, where you adopt the attitude of the offensive minded fighter, yet keep defense in the back of your mind at all times, and if possible, use it to feed your offensive techniques.

THE VICIOUS ELBOW

The elbow is one of the hardest bones in the human body, and perhaps the most effective blocking weapon the kickboxer possesses. By utilizing the elbows as weapons against your opponent's feet, shins, and fists, you can inflict damage to those offensive tools.

Using your elbow allows you to keep your hands high for protection. Don't drop your hand to block.

A properly executed elbow block can take away your opponent's fighting spirit, and may even crack his shinbone.

We will explore the following three elbow blocks:

1. Reverse elbow block
2. Downward elbow block
3. Inward elbow block

Although there are other types of elbow blocks, I have found these three to be the most effective as *striking blocks*. Let's look at the *reverse elbow block* first, which is designed to protect your ribs and kidney area, and is generally used to defend the round house kick.

BODY MECHANICS FOR THE REVERSE ELBOW BLOCK

Keith's Knockout Advice

As we have already learned, round house kicks utilize the top portion of the foot and shin as impact weapons. The elbow is capable of defeating both. Timing is critical, as your intent is to maximize the impact. To execute the reverse elbow block against a round house kick, bring your elbow straight back as if you were trying to elbow somebody standing directly behind you. Impact your opponent's instep, ankle, or shin by driving your elbow into the target. For maximum effect, strike the target squarely with the point of the elbow. After a few of these blocks, your opponent will see the futility and pain associated with trying to round house kick you, and you will have eliminated one of his offensive weapons.

Execute the reverse elbow block by jamming your elbow into your opponent's instep, ankle, or shin. This is a short and snappy block that does not require much upper body movement. Return your hand to point of origin, as soon as you have completed the block.

Pivot your body either in the direction of the block, or in the opposite direction. Pivoting in the opposite direction may seem contradictory, but gives you more protection along your centerline. As your hand drops with the block, tuck your chin down behind your shoulder. As a rule of thumb, and for maximum protection, pivot in the same manner as when throwing a strike. If you block with your lead elbow, use the "jab pivot"; if you block with your rear elbow, use the "rear cross pivot."

Jab pivot with reverse elbow block.

Rear cross pivot with reverse elbow block.

When pivoting, transfer weight from one leg to the other and set your body for a follow-up strike. Blocking with your lead elbow sets you for a rear cross, rear hook, or rear uppercut. Blocking with your rear elbow sets you for a jab, lead hook, or lead uppercut. If choosing to pivot in the same direction as the block, the opposite is true, and you should throw the counter-strike with the same hand that is blocking. Since most fighters drop their guard slightly when throwing the round house kick, try countering with a rear cross to the head.

IN THE GYM

Reverse elbow block! Drop your weight slightly with the block. This technique is great when throwing a follow-up strike off that same hand. When your opponent throws a round house kick, he is likely to drop his guard on that side and leave an opening at the head. I notice that you have a tendency to block with the muscle on your arm rather than with the point of the elbow. Blocking with the point of the elbow, and directing the block toward your opponent's shin or ankle, allows you to inflict maximum damage. Which way you pivot depends mostly on what kind of follow-up strike you have in mind. Are you setting for a rear hand strike or a lead hand strike, or for a kick?

BODY MECHANICS FOR THE DOWNWARD ELBOW BLOCK

When your opponent has learned his lesson with the round house kick, you can do the same to his front kick by utilizing the *downward elbow block*. Most front kicks are thrown to the mid-section. This bit of knowledge is helpful when it comes to defending the kick. Since the groin and legs are illegal targets for the front kick, we know that the kick will go either to the body or head. The head is a difficult target to kick, because the kick must first pass the body on its way to the head. It can therefore be said that *all front kicks can be blocked as they reach our mid-section*. Never wait until the kick reaches head height to block it.

Execute the downward elbow block against a front kick by dropping your elbow straight down with the full force of your body behind it. Impact your opponent's toes, instep, ankle, or shin with the point of your elbow. Return your hand to the point of origin as soon as the block is complete.

Glove Up with Keith

Downward elbow block! Throw this block as if you were going to break a board with your elbow. Allow your opponent's kick to reach maximum speed, then, just before impact, drop your elbow straight into the target. Remember to think of the block as a strike, and to strive for maximum impact. I have personally fractured my opponent's instep and toes with this block, rendering him incapable of throwing the kick a second time, and virtually causing him so much pain that he lost his will to fight. Where do you think you are in most danger when executing this technique? At the head? Okay, make it a habit to tuck your chin down behind your shoulder for protection.

When elbow blocking with your rear hand, use the rear cross pivot; when elbow blocking with your lead hand, use the jab pivot. If I hold a focus mitt for you to block, but you fail to drop your weight, you won't have enough power to knock it out of my hand. Drop your weight now! See how much more effective that was? The downward elbow block also works well against punches to the mid-section.

You can use the downward elbow block against a low jab. If your elbow impacts your opponent's fist or wrist, he will feel it through 14-ounce boxing gloves.

When blocking with the elbow, keep your chin tucked for protection and drop your body weight with the block. If your head does not follow your body, you will leave an opening for a counter-attack.

BODY MECHANICS FOR THE INWARD ELBOW BLOCK

The inward elbow block is a variation that is used less frequently against a strike or kick to the mid-section. It differs from other blocks because your elbow does not drop straight down, but swings like a pendulum toward the centerline of your body. Use this block against a side thrust kick. I recommend that you impact your opponent's toes rather than his heel, because the toes are more sensitive and injury prone.

When using the inward elbow block, pivot your body off the attack line and impact your opponent's toes rather than his heel.

The inward elbow block also works well when defending against punches on the inside (in close quarters). Use sharp and small moves when blocking punches to your body. This allows you to block without dropping your hand at all. Use body movement instead of arm movement. Pivoting your body when blocking places more weight behind the block, making it more effective. It also allows you to cover your ribs with your non-blocking arm, simultaneously defending against strikes thrown to the outside of your body.

Use the inward elbow block to redirect the path of an uppercut.

Try these exercises on **ELBOW BLOCKS**:

Exercise 1

Get in front of a mirror and note the openings that occur when using large arm movements for blocking. Next, note how much better you stay protected when keeping your arms tight to your body and blocking by pivoting your body.

Exercise 2

Think of every block as if it were a strike. Use the elbow block to protect you from harm, and to destroy your opponent's weapons by inflicting as much pain as possible. When your opponent throws a round house kick, instead of taking the kick on the side of your arm, block it by dropping the point of your elbow into his ankle. When the pain starts to bother him to the point that he stops kicking or becomes overcautious in his attempts to protect himself, move forward with explosive offense.

Exercise 3

Aside from protecting you from harm, good defense also creates offense. Every time your opponent throws a punch or kick, he automatically leaves an opening on himself, so your block is a "cue" that an opening exists. Instead of *freezing* (tensing) when your opponent's strike hits your blocking arm or leg, you should immediately come back with offense. Practice *offensive defense* by learning to see the opening every time your opponent throws a strike, and by following that strike back and beating him to the punch.

Where is the opening?

Midsection

Supporting leg

Ribs

Thigh and midsection

FOREARM BLOCKS

Although the elbow is the most vicious blocking weapon, the forearms and shoulders can also be used to protect you from harm against an upper body attack. The movement of the forearm block is similar to that of the inward elbow block, but instead of swinging your elbow like a pendulum toward the target, your forearm should stay vertically straight. To increase the power of the forearm block, pivot your upper body in the direction of the block and impact your opponent's punch or kick with the "fleshy" part of your forearm.

Forearm blocks can be broken down into inward and outward. The inward forearm block is used to block a strike that comes toward the centerline of your body (jab, rear cross, or front kick), and the outward forearm block is used to block a strike that comes toward the outside of your body (hook or round house kick).

To execute the inward or outward forearm block, wait until your opponent's strike is almost at the target (don't reach for it). Then take a small step or pivot your body off the attack line, and deflect the strike with your forearm.

Use the inward (left) or outward (below) forearm block to defend the round house kick.

You can also use the inward forearm block against a jab to your mid-section. A good follow-up is the spinning back fist. The slight rotation of your upper body to the inside helps you set for the continued rotation of the spinning back fist (more about this strike in Section 9).

Use the inward forearm block against a low jab, and follow with a spinning back fist.

Although the reverse elbow block is one of the best blocks for defending against a round house kick thrown to the body, many fighters tend to use the inward forearm block instead (blocking with the arm that is on the opposite side of the kick). This can be dangerous, because it turns your body partly away from your opponent, exposing targets on your back and side of head. Your opponent can now throw the round house kick a few times, then fake the kick to draw a block, and follow with a rear cross to your jaw.

There are also double forearm blocks. These are used much like the inward and outward forearm blocks, but against stronger techniques that need extra reinforcement. To execute the double forearm block against a side thrust kick, evade the kick by pivoting your body off the attack line. Allow both of your forearms to impact the target simultaneously. This prevents the kick from going through your guard. Note how the fighter has pivoted off the attack line, so that the kick passes in front of his body.

Impact your opponent's shin, using the sharp edge of your forearms (about one inch from the elbow).

Try this exercise on **FOREARM BLOCKS**:

Exercise 4

When your opponent kicks, your natural tendency is to step back and make the kick miss. But this places you in a disadvantaged position too far away to counter-attack. Since regaining that distance is difficult, try stepping forward rather than back, and jam your opponent's kick with your forearms. You are now within striking range. As soon as you have completed the block, reset your body to the point of origin and throw a counter-strike. Note that, in order for jamming to be effective and safe, you must start your gap closure at the initiation of your opponent's kick, before his kick reaches maximum power.

THE SHOULDER BLOCK

A more unorthodox way to block punches is using your shoulder. The shoulder block is similar in motion to the reverse elbow block. As the punch comes toward you, rotate your body in the "jab pivot" with your weight transferring to your rear leg. Simultaneously tuck your chin down behind your lead shoulder. This increases the distance between you and your opponent. Take the punch on your lead shoulder. Your body is now chambered for a follow-up strike with your rear hand.

Block a punch with your lead shoulder and throw a rear cross.

WHAT'S IN A GOOD BLOCK?

Keith's Knockout Advice

As you perfect the elbow and forearm blocks, you will take away your opponent's offensive weapons, and in some cases render him incapable of continuing the fight. Your elbows will protect you from most of your opponent's kicks. The message you should send him is this: *You will pay a price each time you kick.* Your goal is to make the price greater than the value, until your opponent stops using his kicks.

If your block isn't committed, a strong punch or kick will get through your defense. Don't throw your elbow blocks half-heartedly.

Summary and review

The elbows are vicious striking weapons, but many fighters forget that they are equally vicious blocking weapons. The elbow is very sharp and strong and has the ability to focus the power into a small area, inflicting great pain on the target. Using your elbow instead of your hand to block a strike or kick also allows you to keep your arms close to your body for protection. There are essentially three types of elbow blocks: reverse, downward, and inward.

Reverse elbow block partner practice

- Have your partner whack your rib and kidney area with a focus mitt, while you block with the reverse elbow block.

- From a fighting stance with your guard high, drop your elbow straight back, as if you were elbowing somebody standing directly behind you. Drop your weight slightly with the block.

- Return your hand to the high guard position as soon as the block is complete.

- Move with your partner, and have him alternate left and right strikes to your rib and kidney area with the focus mitt.

- Look at your partner's upper body to determine from which side the strike is coming. Do not look at his hands.

- Relax your shoulders as much as possible, letting the reverse elbow block come naturally.

Reverse elbow blocking a kick

- Have your partner wear shin guards and throw round house kicks to your rib area. Block the kicks using the reverse elbow block.

- Focus on blocking with the elbow and not with the forearm. Although the forearm will protect you against the kick, the elbow will inflict more damage.

- Practice throwing a counter-strike the moment your block impacts the target, preferably while your partner is still on one leg. The best time to strike your opponent is when he is in the process of kicking. This is because he is in an unstable stance and unable to move.

- Try throwing a round house kick to your partner's supporting leg, preferably to his inside thigh area, simultaneously blocking his round house kick with your elbow.

Target practice for the reverse elbow block

- Because the round house kick is effective from a variety of ranges, you can block either to your opponent's instep, ankle, or shin, depending on how far away he is when executing the kick.

- Have your partner throw round house kicks from long range. Impact his instep with your elbow.

- Have your partner throw round house kicks from short range. Impact his shin with your elbow.

Reverse elbow block sparring practice

- Engage in light sparring with your partner throwing round house kicks. Have your partner mix his rhythm and combinations, throwing both multiple kick combinations, and single kicks with a slight pause in between.

- Practice using your peripheral vision to pick up on the movement of your partner's kick. This helps you see the kick coming.

- Use reverse elbow blocks to block as many kicks as possible, immediately following with a counter-strike or kick.

Counter-striking off the reverse and downward elbow block

- Have your partner mix round house kicks and front kicks. Practice the reverse and downward elbow blocks against these kicks.

- Each block should be short and quick with minimum movement. Return your hand to point of origin as soon as the block is complete. This helps you protect your openings.

- Because the front kick is a long range technique (as opposed to the round house kick, which works from both long and short range), a counter-punch may not be effective. After blocking with a downward elbow, look for ways to step to a new angle closer to your opponent but off his attack line. What kind of counter-strikes can you throw?

After blocking a front kick with your elbow, step off the angle and throw a counter-strike.

• Look at ways to counter-kick (rather than punch) after you have utilized the downward elbow block against the front kick.

Partner practice using the downward elbow block

• Have your partner wear shin guards and throw kicks to your mid-section. Block the kicks with a downward elbow.

• Execute the block by dropping your elbow straight down along your centerline. Drop your weight slightly with the block. As soon as the block is complete, return your hand to the point of origin.

• Impact your partner's toes, instep, ankle, or shin. This takes a bit of precision, since both your elbow and your partner's foot are relatively narrow.

Partner practice using the inward elbow block

• Have your partner wear gloves and throw straight strikes to your mid-section. Block each strike with an inward elbow block. This block allows you to keep your hands high for protection.

• Execute the inward elbow block by keeping your fist stationary, allowing your elbow to swing like a pendulum toward your centerline. The movement should be short and snappy.

• The inward elbow block works best against a straight strike to your mid-section, and is similar to a parry in that it redirects the path of the strike.

Counter-striking off the inward elbow block

• Whenever your opponent throws a straight strike to your mid-section, he will automatically leave an opening at the head.

• After executing the inward elbow block, practice counter-striking to the opening at your partner's head.

• Try counter-striking both with the hand on the same side as the block, and with the hand on the opposite side of the block. Which is quicker? Why?

• Try a counter-kick after you have completed the inward elbow block. For example, take a step back and throw a front kick to your partner's gut.

Block a punch with an inward elbow block, and throw a front kick to the mid-section.

Partner practice using the inward forearm block

- Have your partner wear shin guards. Block his round house kicks with inward forearm blocks. Use the forearm that is on the opposite side of his kick. If he kicks with his left leg, block with your left arm, and vice versa.

- The inward forearm block is used mostly against a round house kick, but can be used against a variety of mid-level and high attacks.

- Execute the inward forearm block by pivoting your upper body with your forearm vertically straight and toward your centerline. Your forearm should impact your opponent's shin.

- Avoid blocking directly with the bone of the arm, or with the small bones in your wrist. You can make the block stronger by turning your arm slightly, so that you absorb the impact on the fleshy part of your forearm.

- Forearm blocks do not inflict as much damage as elbow blocks. But because the forearm is bigger than the elbow, these blocks are easier to use and do not require as much precision to execute.

Inward forearm block practice against a punch

- You can also use the inward forearm block against a punch. You must now move your upper body slightly to the side to avoid getting hit.

- Practice the inward forearm block against your partner's jab. Impact his forearm with your forearm.

- Experiment with suitable follow-up strikes. How can you take advantage of the slight rotation the block has caused in your body?

Partner practice using the outward forearm block

- The outward forearm block is used mostly to block a kick or hook to the head. Use the outward forearm block to block your partner's round house kicks to your head.

- Execute the outward forearm block from a fighting stance with your guard held high. Bring your arm up to the side of your head, simultaneously tucking your chin down toward your chest for protection.

- When fighting at close range, expect hooks to your head. Practice the outward forearm block against your opponent's hooks. Keep your arm tight to your body. If you leave a gap between your arm and head, you risk getting your own arm swatted into your head. If you raise your arm too high, you risk exposing your mid-section.

Use the outward forearm block against your opponent's hooks.

Forearm and elbow block sparring practice

- Engage in some light contact sparring. Have your partner be the aggressor by throwing round house kicks both mid-level and high.

- Block the round house kicks to the mid-section with an inward forearm block, and the round house kicks to the head with an outward forearm block.

- When you get comfortable with blocking, try following up with a counter-strike or kick.

- Face your partner and start at one end of the room. Have him throw round house kicks randomly, advancing with each kick. Practice using both the reverse elbow block and the inward forearm block, and experiment with suitable follow-up strikes.

- The reverse elbow block is likely to do more damage, while the inward forearm block is easier and sets you up nicely for a follow-up technique.

Reverse elbow block (top). Inward forearm block (above). Either can be used to defend the round house kick.

Partner practice using the double forearm block

- Practice the double forearm block against your partners round house kicks. The double forearm block works like an inward forearm block, but is stronger because you are blocking with both arms at the same time.

- The disadvantage of the double forearm block is that both your arms are tied up in the block, so counter-striking is a little slower.

The double forearm block is a strong block that impacts your opponent's shin near the ankle and near the knee simultaneously.

LOWER BODY BLOCKS

Since many of the kicks used in kickboxing are leg kicks, and since the legs are a fighter's support, it is crucial to learn how to defend against lower body attacks. Lower body blocks can be broken down into:

1. Shin blocks
2. Leg checks

This section covers:

- Shin blocks (defending the legs)
- Following up off the shin block
- Generating momentum through shin blocks
- In the gym
- Leg checks
- Summary and review

SHIN BLOCKS (DEFENDING THE LEGS)

You can execute the shin block with either your lead or rear leg. In general, your lead leg is faster since it is closer to your opponent. Shin blocks can be further classified as "outside" or "inside." The *outside shin block* is used to defend against an attack to your outside thigh area, which may be the most sought after target on the legs.

To execute the outside shin block, chamber your lower leg and point it at a forty-five degree angle toward line 1. Bring your knee all the way up to your

elbow to ensure that there is no gap at your rib area. A skilled opponent will exploit any visible gap.

Meet your opponent's kick with the muscle to the outside of your shin. You do this by extending your leg slightly outward and forward. This extension eliminates most of the power in your opponent's kick and reduces the risk of injury to your shin. It also helps you push your opponent off balance. Ideally, you should block the kick before it is fully extended.

The *inside shin block* is used to defend against an attack to your inside thigh area.

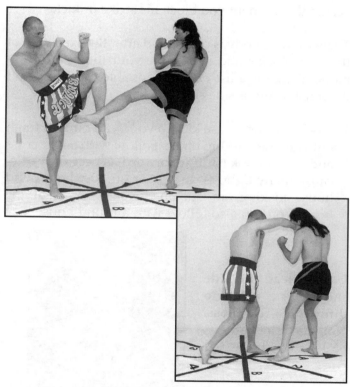

To execute the inside shin block, chamber your lower leg and point it in the direction of line 2. Bring your knee all the way up to your elbow.

Keep your lower leg vertically straight, bringing your shin forward and past your centerline, impacting your opponent's shin or ankle with the muscle slightly to the inside of your shin.

When the block is complete, set your foot down and throw a rear cross along centerline A. As you can see, shin blocks allow you to defend against lower body attacks without a need to drop your hands.

FOLLOWING UP OFF THE SHIN BLOCK

Most kickboxers find shin blocks easy to learn. But it's not enough to block the attack. In order to take full advantage of your opponent's position, you must also throw a follow-up technique. Furthermore, it is easy to be so pre-occupied with blocking that you forget to follow up. Many fighters are happy if they just keep their opponent's kick from landing. But defense should always be seen as a way to create offense. The advanced fighter stays ahead of the game and does not allow his mind or body to freeze when he executes a block. The best time to counter-strike is when your opponent's mind and body are frozen, which usually occurs the moment you block his strike or kick.

The way your body is positioned after the execution of the shin block could determine your follow-up technique. Below is a list of some possible follow-ups off the outside and inside shin blocks:

1. Block a round house kick to your lead outside thigh with an outside shin block. Follow with a rear cross and a lead hook (shuffle forward as necessary). Because many fighters drop their guard when round house kicking, an opening usually exists at the head. You can also follow with a round house kick to the legs.

Use a lead outside shin block prior to throwing a rear cross. Note how the fighter's body is set for the rear cross.

2. Block a round house kick to your lead inside thigh with an inside shin block. Follow with a lead leg side thrust kick (off the same leg) to your opponent's gut. You can plant your foot before throwing the side thrust kick, or come right off the shin block without setting your foot down first. Because the kick will most likely knock your opponent back, you must now follow with a technique that allows you to regain that distance (a stepping side thrust kick, for example).

Use a lead inside shin block prior to a side thrust kick. Note how the fighter's body is set for the kick.

The shin block should be executed at the initiation of your opponent's kick. As soon as you see the first twitching in his hip, initiate the block and, if possible, step forward to jam his kick. This eliminates much of the power and places you at close quarter range, where you can follow with a punch combination. However, since it is not always possible to say whether your opponent's kick will come high or low, you may feel a need to raise the leg in the shin block motion even when the kick is intended for your body or head. Be aware of the danger associated with this move, as your opponent can take advantage of your positional weakness and attack your supporting leg.

3. Block a round house kick to your rear outside thigh with an outside shin block. Follow with a lead front push kick. Follow with additional strikes and kicks as distance increases. You can also block the attack with a lead inside shin block.

Use a rear outside shin block prior to a front push kick. Note how the fighter's body is set for a push kick.

4. The rear leg inside shin block is a bit more time consuming and therefore not as practical. Block a round house kick to your rear inside thigh with a rear inside shin block. Follow with a side thrust kick off that same leg. You have now switched stance.

Note how the fighter's body is set for a side thrust kick.

When shin blocking, bring your knee up high enough to avoid leaving a gap between your knee and elbow. This forms a solid block along the entire side of your body, which can also be used as an effective upper body block against a side thrust kick. When your opponent kicks to your mid-section, your block will impact either the heel or bottom of his foot.

A good shin block leaves no gap at your mid-section (left). If you don't raise your knee high enough (right), your opponent can land a kick to your ribs.

There is one more shin block worth mentioning, which can also be used against a side thrust kick to your mid-section. As the kick comes toward you, bring your lead leg straight up along your centerline and high in front of your body (same motion as if you were going to throw the front kick). Crouch forward slightly for protection and stability. Block the kick with your shin vertically straight in front of your centerline. Before your opponent's kick is fully extended, push off with your supporting foot to jam the kick.

Use the straight shin block against a side thrust kick.

GENERATING MOMENTUM THROUGH SHIN BLOCKS

Once you get good at shin blocking and following up, look at how to use the momentum generated from re-planting the blocking leg to help you launch a powerful kick with your other leg:

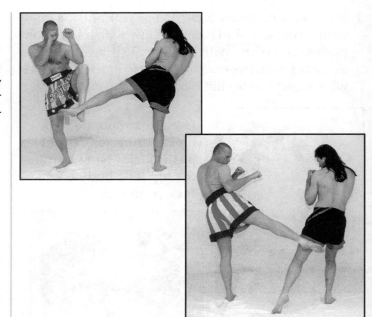

Execute a lead outside shin block. Set your foot back down and shuffle forward with a rear leg cut kick to the front of your opponent's thighs. There should be no stop in momentum between the lead shin block and the rear cut kick.

Execute a lead inside shin block. Bring the blocking leg back and replant your foot in position to throw a rear leg cut kick to the back of your opponent's thigh. The power of the kick is derived from the pivot in your body when bringing your blocking leg back.

Execute a lead outside shin block, set your foot back down and follow with a lead leg cut kick to the back of your opponent's calf. As your foot plants on the floor between kicks, use the "tap and go" concept (more about this in Section 8), reversing direction by allowing your foot to bounce off the floor.

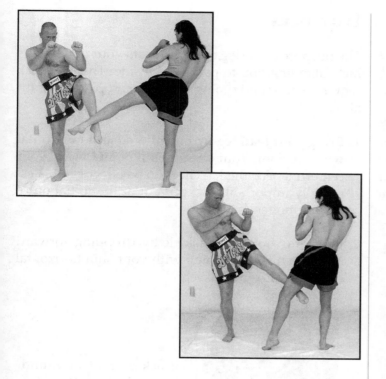

Execute a lead inside shin block, set your foot back down and follow with a lead cut kick to the inside of your opponent's thigh. Again, rely on the tap and go concept. Keep the beat between kicks as short as possible.

Use the lead inside shin block as a set-up for the spinning back kick. Since the inside shin block is slightly circular in motion, it can help you build momentum for a spinning technique.

IN THE GYM

The inside shin block is a defensive move that can be used effectively as a set-up for a side thrust or spinning back kick. Since the kick is likely to knock your opponent back, you must follow with a technique that allows you to regain that distance: a stepping side thrust kick, for example. If this were in competition, where would your opponent be right now? On the ropes, right? So, unless you want to kick your opponent through the ropes and onto the judges' table with another side thrust kick, you must now work your way to the inside.

The side thrust kick is a good follow-up off the inside shin block.

LEG CHECKS

The purpose of the leg check is to jam your opponent's kick, allowing you to get to the inside. The leg check requires speed and timing. When your opponent initiates a kick:

1. **Bring your lead leg up chambered and horizontal with the floor.** Your knee should point toward your centerline. For the leg check to be effective, it is especially important to execute it at the initiation of your opponent's kick.

2. **Jam your opponent's kick** by dropping forward and into his upper thigh with your shin horizontal or diagonal across his leg.

Block a front or round house kick with a leg check.

If your opponent is open at the ribs, you can also use the leg check as a strike against his body. When leg checking to the body, extend your leg at impact to knock your opponent off balance.

Keith's Knockout Advice

A big part of the fight game is mental and is comprised of frustrating and confusing your opponent. See it as a strategic mind game. The more you can take your opponent out of his fight plan, the better you'll be at executing your own. I like to use a variety of leg checks to literally keep my opponent's kicks in check. Leg checks can be pesky little techniques that will both anger and frustrate your opponent. Rules in kickboxing vary from state to state, and from promoter to promoter, so make sure that leg checking is legal prior to using these techniques. Regardless, they should be added to your tool bag, in the event that you find yourself in a match that allows them.

The leg check is accomplished by bringing your leg up with your lower leg horizontal to your body, using your shin to check. As your opponent prepares to kick, place your shin across his middle thigh, disabling his ability to raise his leg. You can vary this technique by simply raising your leg as you close on your opponent, creating a barrier against his kick. Timing is hard to master, but well worth the practice. Most kickboxers that I execute these checks on have never even seen them before, giving me a clear advantage.

The leg check is also commonly thrown like a lead leg front push kick, impacting with the ball of your foot to the middle of your opponent's thigh muscle. Throw the check when he is preparing to raise his leg for the kick, or whenever you feel like it. Once you develop the timing to catch his leg during its upward motion, your check will knock his kick back down, causing him frustration and pain to the middle thigh. When you use the leg check randomly, it tends to make your opponent hesitant to throw his kick, causing him to pay undue attention to the distraction, resulting in a loss of attention to his fight plan.

Summary and review

While the elbow and forearm blocks are used to block an attack to your upper body, shin blocks are used to block an attack to your lower body. The primary advantage of the shin block is that it allows you to keep your hands high for protection. The shin block is executed by bringing your knee up to your elbow with your lower leg in the vertical position. The leg check, too, can be used to protect your lower body against attack. The leg check is a quick move executed with your leg in a horizontal position, and with your knee either toward your centerline to protect the targets on the centerline, or away from your centerline to protect the legs. When the leg check is used against an attack to your legs, use your knee as the impact weapon. When the leg check is used to thwart your opponent's kick or to knock him off balance, use the entire shin horizontally across your opponent's leg or body.

Use the leg check against the body

Shin toughening exercises

- To develop effective shin blocks, start by toughening your shins on the heavy bag. Throw round house kicks to the lower end of the bag where the filling has settled. Impact the bag with your shin.

- Because the shins are bony with very little padding, most people find even light contact to the shins very uncomfortable. Try using light shin pads as a transition to harder contact.

- As you get used to the contact, increase the intensity or start kicking harder targets.

- Have your partner strike at your legs with a foam padded stick (lightly at first).

Shin blocking and countering the leg kick

- You can make the shin block more effective by bringing the block slightly forward and into your opponent's kick.

- Start at one end of the room and alternate left and right shin blocks against an imaginary opponent, advancing forward with each block until you get to the other end of the room.

- Have your partner alternate left and right round house kicks to your legs, advancing with each kick. Practice alternating shin block, stepping back each time your partner advances.

- Execute a shin block against your partner's kick. As your blocking leg lands, follow with a counter-strike to your partner's mid-section. If you can time the strike to land while your opponent is on one leg, you are likely to knock him off balance.

- Execute a shin block against your partner's kick and experiment with suitable follow-up kicks. First, counter with the leg that is not blocking. Then, counter with the leg that is blocking.

Heavy bag practice using the shin block

- Work the heavy bag, executing shin blocks against an imaginary opponent, and countering with punches on the bag.

- Experiment to get a feel for which follow-up strikes feel most natural. Identify the strikes that would most easily cause a knockout.

- When working the heavy bag, we often get into an offensive mode, where we tend to neglect defense. Make a conscious effort to incorporate blocks and movement into your bag work, even though there is no risk of getting struck back.

Throw shin blocks to an imaginary opponent when working the heavy bag.

Leg checking from close range

- From close range, check your partner's kick by timing the leg check to the initiation of his kick.

- Your shin should come horizontally across your partner's thigh. Look for a suitable follow-up combination, preferably a set of close range strikes.

- Practice the leg check with your knee impacting the outside of your opponent's thigh. This has an effect similar to the cut kick to the outside thigh.

Use your knee to check your opponent's outside thigh area.

Shin block sparring practice

- Engage in light contact sparring with your partner. Practice shin blocks against round house kicks thrown from close range with the shin rather than the instep.

- Block and follow with a short range punch combination (uppercuts and hooks).

- Step back to long range and have your partner occasionally fake a round house kick. Note your reaction. Remember, you are vulnerable when on one leg.

- If your opponent fakes a kick that makes you raise your leg to block, he can take advantage of your position of weakness.

Fake a round house kick, and throw a rear cross to knock your opponent out.

Heavy bag practice using the leg check

- Practice the leg check on the heavy bag. Your shin should impact at about mid-section height horizontally across the bag.

- Use a shuffle-step (fast gap closure) prior to the leg check.

- Set the heavy bag swinging and time the leg check to the bag's forward momentum. If you can time the leg check to your opponent's forward motion, you will add his momentum to yours and stifle his attack.

- Shadow box around the bag, then explode with a shuffle-step forward followed by a leg check to the mid-section. As soon as your foot re-plants on the ground, follow with a punch combination. Move back to long range and repeat the procedure.

Leg check the heavy bag and follow with a punch combination.

- Have your partner hold a kicking shield. Practice the leg check on the shield, using your forward momentum to knock your partner back.

PARRIES

The parry is an open handed deflection of your opponent's strike. The parry is designed not to block or stop an attack, but to redirect the path enough to make the strike miss. Since the parry is not a hard block, it requires very little energy.

This section covers:

- Body mechanics for the parry
- In the gym
- Using defense to trigger offense
- In the gym
- What's in a good counter-strike?
- The trap and redirect
- In the gym
- The catch
- Summary and review

When parrying punches, start by looking for movement in your opponent's body. Do not look at his hands. It is important that you don't initiate the parry too soon (don't reach for the strike; let it come to you), or extend your hand beyond your shoulder, as this leaves unnecessary openings on your head and body. You can decrease the risk of getting struck by your opponent's punch by pivoting your body off the attack line.

BODY MECHANICS FOR THE PARRY

Use the inside parry against a strike thrown to your facial area. To parry your opponent's jab with your lead hand, bring your hand at a forty-five degree angle forward from left to right toward line 2. Your hand should be open if possible.

Turn the palm of your hand at a forty-five degree angle forward, using the heel of your palm to deflect the strike. Stop when your hand gets in line with your rear shoulder.

When you have completed the parry, bring your hand back to the point of origin.

Because the parry is primarily a defensive move, your hand should move only enough to redirect the path of the strike. Keeping the parry short with minimal forward movement of your arm allows you to bring your hand back to the point of origin quickly. Since the parry places your opponent in an inferior position, either with his back turned partly toward you or with his centerline exposed, it is especially beneficial when used in conjunction with a follow-up strike.

To execute a parry with your rear hand, do the opposite of the above. As the punch comes toward you, and just before impact, bring your rear hand at a forty-five degree angle forward from right to left toward line 1.

Continue the parry past your face until your hand is in line with your lead shoulder. This will deflect the blow. When you have completed the parry, bring your hand back to the point of origin.

IN THE GYM

Try counter-striking off the parry. Parry with your lead hand and counter with your rear. Parry a little closer to your opponent's wrist and not by his elbow. When counter-striking, aim directly for the target and not for your opponent's gloves. What are your targets? Jaw and nose. If you want to make his eyes water, go for the nose; if you want to take him out, aim for the jaw. Stay in a good defensive stance. Your hands are too close together and a little low. A good fighting stance places you out of reach of most of your opponent's counter-punches. Have patience. If you rush in, you will get hit.

I want you to really believe in defense. When you get tired, rely on your defensive fighting more. You will not only get winded, you get arm weary, too. You'll get mentally fatigued. And when you're tired, you will get hit more. Good defense allows you to rest and replenish your energies. Good defensive skills will tire your opponent. He will get frustrated and weary, and will eventually not be able to defend himself. And it will be like fighting a child.

When you parry your opponent's punch, you disturb his rhythm. Take advantage of it and exploit the gap at his chin and mid-section.

USING DEFENSE TO TRIGGER OFFENSE

Once you have deflected your opponent's strike, you must take charge of the fight and turn defense into offense. Use the momentum of your defense to launch a counter-attack. The effectiveness of a strike is determined by your ability to "set" for the strike and use your body weight for power. Another important element is your ability to throw the strike directly off of a block. The pick and counter is one of the most useful kickboxing parries. When your opponent jabs, come over the top of his hand with your rear hand, cupping his hand in yours. This redirects the path of the strike down and slightly away from your centerline. Before your opponent has time to retrieve his punch, counter with a lead jab to the open target on his jaw. Your parrying hand should make a tiny circle down and back to the guard position.

When countering off the parry, either draw the parrying hand slightly toward you and counter with a jab or rear cross off that same hand, or throw a strike off your other hand. In either case, your parry and strike should happen at two different speeds. If the strike has the same beat as the parry, your opponent will already have withdrawn his hand to the guard position, and the opening will no longer exist. If he is quick, he may also strike with his free hand before your punch reaches him.

Try this exercise on the **PICK AND COUNTER:**

Exercise 1

Using proper footwork, move with your partner while he throws jabs at you randomly. Try to pick as many of his jabs as possible. Make sure that the distance between you and your partner is realistic, so that if your timing or accuracy is off, your partner's jabs will land. As you gain proficiency at picking, add a counter-strike with your lead hand. To make this more difficult, have your partner throw his jabs with broken rhythm, adding pauses between them, and throwing doubles and triples in rapid succession.

Learning to pick your opponent's jab is not that difficult. The danger lies in becoming so concerned with defending that you fail to follow up. If you give your opponent time to reset, you will miss the opening, and will most likely get struck by his next punch. Once your opponent learns that you will pick his jabs but fail to counter, he can easily time his strikes to your defensive moves and allow your defense to trigger his offense. New kickboxing students tend to block separately from striking. In other words, there is a slight pause prior to the follow-up strike. In order to speed up your strikes, catch your opponent off balance, and offset his rhythm, you must combine your blocks and strikes and think of your combinations as part of your defense. Use the block or parry as a cue to trigger a counter-strike. As soon as your block or parry touches your opponent's strike, you should be thinking about countering.

To counter your opponent's strike effectively, your counter-strike must be faster than your parry.

Try this exercise on **COUNTERING IN COMBINATIONS**:

Exercise 2

As you pick your opponent's jab with your rear hand, you also gain momentum to throw a counter-jab with speed and power. This is part of the push-pull principle, where the returning motion of your "picking" hand provides power for your striking hand. When your jab has landed and that hand starts on its way back to the guard position, your rear cross should be starting its motion forward. Your hands will make tiny circles on their return path. This allows your strikes to complement one another. As one hand starts on its way back, it pulls and gives momentum to the other hand on its way out.

IN THE GYM

After you parry or block, you must follow with a good counter-strike to the opening you have created. Work on breaking your rhythm. Add more movement, or you will become predictable. I want you to try something different today. Keep your hands open and slightly extended along your centerline. Use your hands to paw your opponent's punches away. Just circle your hands like this, and then transform that circling of your hands into a strike: either a jab or a rear cross. See how you're building momentum for your follow-up strike?

A common mistake is to fail to follow up off the block. You block and then wait for your opponent's reaction. But by then it's too late.

You're raising your elbow with the rear cross, and every time you throw the jab, your right hand is dropping below your chin. Keep your elbow resting against your ribs. The moment your elbow falls behind your ribs, your hand will automatically drop.

When your elbow falls behind your body, your guard will drop.

WHAT'S IN A GOOD COUNTER-STRIKE?

Keith's Knockout Advice

A great counter-puncher can make his opponent's strikes miss, can fight from a variety of angles, and can respond to the attack quickly. All of the great counter-punchers I have known made their technique part of their opponent's technique. In other words, there is little or no delay between the opponent's punch or kick and your counter-strike. The pick and counter (pick and jab) is possibly one of the quickest counter-strikes available. Because the jab is such a fast weapon, I like to consider it first when counter-striking, and then allow my stronger techniques to follow. In order to execute a proper pick and jab, you must be in range to be hit with your opponent's jab. As he jabs, allow his strike to pass your lead hand, using your rear hand to parry it downward. Simultaneously start your lead jab forward. As your lead hand starts on its way out, continue to parry your opponent's strike downward. The moment your jab impacts the target, your parrying hand should be circling back toward your body and return to the high guard position. When this technique is done correctly, your opponent's arm will be fully extended by the time your jab lands on the opening on his head.

As you start the downward parry of your opponent's punch, you should also rotate your shoulders and body into alignment with your jabbing arm. This should be done in one simultaneous motion. Practice it slowly at first for proper technique. Then practice until the move becomes habit and can be done in a blinding flash. After your jab has landed, follow with another technique that feels natural to throw from that position. Each additional technique should be thrown without hesitation. Continue to build off the jab until you are able to throw three- and four-punch combinations with increasing speed, and without pausing between strikes.

THE TRAP AND REDIRECT

Some defensive techniques are a bit more difficult than others, and are generally not worked as often as the simple pick and counter. One such technique is the trap and redirect. This technique is designed to block your opponent's strike, and also to throw him off balance and open a target for a counter-strike. The technique is similar in concept to the pick and counter, but when you have picked your opponent's strike, you continue to circle your hand down and to the outside until your arm is straight at the elbow, and your opponent's hand has been moved all the way off the attack line. This does two things:

1. **Places you in a superior position** with your opponent's back turned partly toward you.

2. **Hinders your opponent's follow-up strike.** When his body is turned, his strike will lack flexibility, reach, and power.

Trap and redirect your opponent's jab (above), and counter with a rear leg cut kick (right).

You can get proficient with the trap and redirect by using it frequently in training. This will increase your arsenal of techniques and help you defend successfully against your opponent's strikes.

IN THE GYM

Have we talked about the trap and redirect yet, where you parry and hook your opponent's arm away from his body? If I hook your lead hand with my lead hand, and parry it down and to the outside, it will open up targets on your jaw, ribs, and legs. It will also eliminate the threat of your rear hand. That's what I mean when I say that defense creates offense. By trapping and redirecting your rear hand, I will open up targets on the inside of your body. Or if you throw a left-right combination, I can trap your lead hand first and then your rear hand, and then counter with a punch or a kick.

Also try countering with the same hand that is trapping. When trapping with your rear hand, try countering with that same hand. Trap and redirect and make a tiny circle with your hand back to the point of origin. Then throw your rear cross, using the momentum from the trap and redirect.

Trap, redirect, and counter with the same hand.

THE CATCH

The catch differs from the parry in that it meets power with power. The catch can therefore be classified as a block. The catch is generally executed with the rear hand, but can be done with either hand.

To catch your opponent's strike with your rear hand, start by bringing your hand forward at a forty-five degree angle toward line 1. Keep your palm open and facing your opponent.

Extend your hand slightly forward along centerline A, and meet your opponent's strike before it is fully extended, stopping it in its track.

To catch your opponent's strike with your lead hand, start by bringing your hand forward at a forty-five degree angle toward line 2.

Extend your hand forward along centerline A, meeting the strike and stopping it in its track.

The catch must be timed to impact as your hand moves forward. If your hand is stationary at impact, the force of your opponent's punch could swat your own hand back into your face. The beauty of the catch is that it hinders your opponent from throwing a counter-strike. If he tries to counter with a jab, for example, you simply execute the catch again. Because the catch meets power with power, it also has a tendency to knock your opponent back, stalling his attempts to counter.

A variation to the straight catch is the downward catch, which is used to defend strikes that are thrown upward along the centerline of your body. The downward catch is the same in principle as the straight catch: Extend your hand to meet your opponent's strike straight on. Try it against an uppercut aimed for your chin.

Straight Catch

Downward Catch

Use fakes and deception (more about this in Section 10) to land strikes on an opponent who uses the parry or catch extensively.

Keith's Corner

To put it simply, the catch is a block that is accomplished by catching your opponent's striking hand in your open glove, much like a baseball catcher catches the ball thrown by the pitcher. You should never settle on the fact that you caught the punch, but must remember that your opponent is open for a counter. As you train, always practice what I call the "catch and throw." As soon as you catch your opponent's strike, you counter with a punch or kick to the open target. Remember, your counter-strike must be immediate: Catch and throw with no hesitation. Work this into all aspects of your training, including mitt work, bag work, and sparring.

During mitt training, have the trainer throw a punch that you catch and counter with no hesitation. The cadence should be bang-bang, with no beat in between. When training on the heavy bag, visualize your opponent's strike, simulate the catch, and counter immediately. Sparring gives you the most variations. Try catching and countering with the same hand, catching with one hand and countering with the other, and countering with kicks instead of punches. Train for proficiency with both hands. For example, if you catch your opponent's rear cross with your rear hand, this opens up your counter lead hook. On the other hand, had you defended with a lead catch against the same punch, you would have been better positioned to counter with a rear cross. Becoming proficient with either hand places you in control and opens up a myriad of possible counters.

The second part of good defense is comprised of head and body movement. When you move your head to the side to avoid a punch, you are slipping. When you move your upper body side to side and below the path of a punch, you are bobbing and weaving (or rolling). We will study this in the next sub-section.

Summary and review

A parry is an open handed deflection of your opponent's strike. When your opponent is committed to a punch, he has momentum coming forward. When you parry his punch, the punch will pass over your shoulder. This places you at close quarter range. Because you have taken your opponent by surprise and his arm is still extended, he is open at both the midsection and the head. This is a good time to launch a strong body attack. Parries are most effective against your opponent's weaker lead hand strikes (jabs), but can also be used against rear crosses. The pick and counter and the catch are both variations of the parry.

Parrying and countering the jab

- Have your partner throw jabs at you from a left fighting stance. Use your rear hand parry to deflect the jabs.

- The parry is useful for getting your opponent's timing down.

- Once you get a feel for the rhythm of your opponent's jab, parry with your rear hand and immediately throw a jab.

- After each parry, bring your hand back to the point of origin.

- Repeat the exercise, but parry your opponent's jab with your lead hand instead. When you get the timing down, follow with a rear cross.

- Countering with the opposite hand is more effective than countering with the same hand that parries. There are two reasons for this: First, your body will be chambered for a counter-strike with the opposite hand. Second, it allows you to decrease the beat between parry and counter-strike.

- Move with your partner as he throws jabs at you. Vary the rhythm so that sometimes you parry his strike, and sometimes you parry and counter.

Sparring practice using the parry

- Parry your opponent's one-two combination (jab/ rear cross), using your rear hand parry against the jab, and your lead hand parry against the rear cross. Throw a counter-strike after the second parry.

- If both you and your opponent are in left fighting stances, it is more beneficial to use your rear hand for parrying the jab. This is because the parry has a tendency to turn your opponent slightly to the side, giving you a superior position toward his back. If you parry with your lead hand, you will place yourself in an inferior position in the path of his rear cross.

Parrying your opponent's jab with your rear hand turns his body to an inferior position with his back partly toward you.

- Engage in light contact sparring and work on parrying your partner's jabs and rear crosses, and on counter-striking to different targets. Experiment with both low and high targets, and with counter-kicking rather than striking.

DEFENSIVE MOVEMENT

There are two ways to defend against an attack: You can block it, or you can use movement to evade it. Using movement gives you the benefit of keeping your hands and legs free for counter-striking. Movement is further broken down into defensive movement and offensive movement. We will look at defensive movement first.

This section covers:

- Slipping
- Bobbing and weaving
- Glove-up with Keith
- Summary and review

SLIPPING

When fighting an opponent who favors long range techniques, moving from the outside to the inside can be tricky. You can jam your opponent's kicks to eliminate most of the power, but when fighting a good puncher you may need to rely on upper body movement to avoid strikes. You must learn to slip punches, duck jabs, and bob and weave underneath hooks.

Slipping is a sideways movement of your head that allows your opponent's punch to pass over your shoulder. A slip usually precedes a bob and weave. Watch your opponent's upper body (shoulders in particular), and initiate the slip when you see the first movement of a punch.

Note how the weight shifts from one foot to the other when slipping. You should also keep one hand up as a check, with the other hand ready to counter-strike.

Be careful not to slip *toward* your opponent's punch. Some fighters jab a little more to one side than the other. At the beginning of the round, feel your opponent out so that you know which side his jab is most likely to land on. Avoid slipping to that side.

When you slip your opponent's punch successfully, there will automatically be an opening for your counter-punch to his chin.

There is also a *rearward slip*, where you move your head back instead of to the side, increasing distance and making your opponent's punch short of reach. When slipping to the rear, be careful not to shift your weight to your rear leg, or your balance may suffer. Another danger occurs when your opponent throws a double jab. Once you have slipped his first jab to the rear and your head comes forward again, as it must in order for your body to correct itself, he can time his second jab to your head movement and add your momentum to his.

Be careful not to move into your opponent's double jab.

Try this exercise on **SLIPPING**:

Exercise 1

Try parrying in conjunction with slipping. For example, parry your opponent's jab to the inside of his arm with your lead hand, simultaneously slipping to the left. Or parry to the outside of your opponent's arm with your rear hand, simultaneously slipping to the right. If he throws a rear cross, the opposite is true. Throw a counter-strike immediately following the slip. Use very little separation between slip and counter. Think of it as "following your opponent's punch back in."

Parrying and slipping simultaneously gives you double protection.

BOBBING AND WEAVING

When fighting an opponent at close range, use bobbing and weaving instead of slipping. Bobbing is the vertical movement of your body, and weaving is the horizontal movement of your body. There are four objectives of good bobbing and weaving:

1. **Avoid** getting hit.

2. **Confuse** your opponent.

3. **Set** for a counter-strike.

4. **Move from the outside to the inside** safely, from where you can follow with a hook or uppercut combination.

Bobbing and weaving is also referred to as *rolling*. Roll from your knees and not your waist, keeping your

chin down and your eyes focused on your opponent. Stay visually aware of what your opponent is doing and where your targets are. Keep your guard up to avoid getting hit with a hook to the head.

Note how the fighter shifts his weight from one foot to the other when initiating the bob and weave, and how he bends primarily at the knees when rolling under his opponent's hook.

If your opponent throws more than one strike, you risk getting hit when resetting from the bob and weave into your stance. You should therefore roll *toward* your opponent and to inside range. Once you have closed the gap, your opponent must create distance to strike effectively. This leaves you in charge of the fight. When you are ready to move back to long range, do so while simultaneously keeping your opponent occupied with strikes or kicks.

Try these exercises on **BOBBING AND WEAVING**:

Exercise 2

Stretch a rope at shoulder height from wall to wall across the room or ring. Start at one end bobbing and weaving under the rope until you arrive at the other end. Move the foot closest to the direction of travel first (concept: BASIC MOVEMENT THEORY), readjusting the width of your stance with your rear foot. Return to the other end by bobbing and weaving backwards. Bend at the knees and not the waist to keep your chin protected and your eyes on your opponent.

Exercise 3

Work the same drill with **broken rhythm**. Take a couple of short steps between each bob and weave, or do a couple of quick rolls without stepping. Also add punch combinations in the air. For example, bob and weave from right to left under the rope and throw a lead hook followed by a rear cross. Then bob and weave back to the right, and throw a rear cross followed by a lead hook. Mix offense with defense. When you get to the end of the rope and your imaginary opponent has his back to the ropes of the ring, experiment with different ways to finish him.

Instead of waiting for your opponent to throw a punch that you can roll under, stay unpredictable by using a lot of upper body movement even when he doesn't throw a punch. When the punch comes, work the roll in with the rest of your movement. Also use broken rhythm when working your way to the inside. When it is time to move out, either roll out or jab out.

Some fighters avoid a punch by ducking it. You do this by lowering your body straight down, letting the punch pass over your head. There is no sideways movement of your body or head when ducking.

Duck a punch by lowering your body straight down.

Glove Up with Keith

Get your headgear and mouthpiece. I'm going to throw some punches while you keep your guard down. There are three ways in which you can slip a punch and avoid getting hit: You can slip to the inside, you can slip to the outside, and you can slip by moving your head back. Note that when you move your head back, you put more weight on your rear leg. To avoid losing your balance, you can add a bob and weave, and then do a quick roll back out and off the line of fire. If you want to throw some body shots, then stay on the inside. Roll toward your opponent more.

Drive the body shots at an upward angle into your opponent's body to push his organs up. These kinds of strikes will keep him from fighting back. You can fight with a broken rib, you can fight with a broken nose, because you usually have so much adrenaline that you don't feel the pain until after the fight is over. The reason they sometimes stop a fight because of a broken nose is not because of the pain, but because you are swallowing too much blood. But you can't fight without air. When you get hit with a good body shot, it will knock the wind out of you. That's why they say, "take the wind out of your sails." Your lungs are your sails, and if there is no wind, you won't get anywhere.

You can't slip all of your opponent's punches. Some will connect, and some will graze by or touch the side of your head or forehead, but that's okay. They won't do much damage there. If you slip nine out of ten punches, that's pretty good.

I will vary my rhythm now. This is when it gets hard. But even when fighting with varied rhythm, there is a rhythm. Use quick moves with your head and upper body. Try quick rolls, keeping your eyes on your opponent. Don't bend all the way over. Just bend at the knees while keeping your body upright. Use a shallow, quick roll, just enough to make the punch miss.

Now, slip left, slip right. Then slip and roll and counter with body punches. Make those hooks to the body tighter, almost like an uppercut. Now, slip left, roll right, hook right, then roll left and hook left. If this move seems awkward, it's because you're not re-chambering after the first hook. What are your targets? Floating ribs? It depends on what your intentions are. Breaking the higher ribs will usually hurt more, because every time you breathe there is movement in that area.

Summary and review

Many martial arts use rigid stances. The fighter's legs are rigid, his back is straight and rigid, his guard is still and rigid, and his head is rigid. Imagine that you are going to fire a rifle at a target. Is it easier to strike a stationary or a moving target? Since the head is such an attractive target in kickboxing (even if you have a real ugly mug), you should learn different ways to move the head in order to elude your opponent and make it difficult for him to land a strike. Once you have learned to make the head an elusive target through small and quick moves, also look at how to move your whole upper body to evade a strike or kick.

In general, upper body movement is most effective against a strike but could, on occasion, be used to evade a head kick.

Slipping practice in front of a mirror

- Place a two-inch wide piece of tape vertically down a mirror. Stand about one arm's length from the mirror, so that when you look at your reflection, the tape runs down the centerline of your body. Experiment with how much you need to move your head to the side in order to move it completely off the tape. The tape represents your opponent's punch.

- Many fighters move their head excessively, using up energy needlessly. What other dangers are associated with too much head movement? Are you placing yourself in the path of another strike?

- Short movements are faster than large movements. When utilizing short movements, you might still take part of the strike. But rather than hurting you, it may only stun you. With practice, you can learn not to let it bother you at all.

Upper body movement in shadow boxing

- Practice head and upper body movement in shadow boxing. Try to make it a natural part of your footwork, strikes, and kicks.

- We often think that it is necessary to move only when threatened by a strike. But continuous slipping is beneficial when disguising your strikes as well.

Partner practice with slipping

- Have your partner throw punches at you. Keep your guard down and force yourself to use head movement to avoid the strikes. Slip either left or right.

- Is there a time when it is better to slip left? Right? In general, moving your head to the "outside" (away from opponent's centerline) is a little safer, because you won't be directly in his line of power.

- What benefits does slipping to the outside give you regarding your follow-up strike?

Upper body movement and target practice

- Have your partner throw strikes that you avoid with head and upper body movement. When the strikes miss, throw a counter-strike. Ideally, you want to counter while your opponent's arm is still extended.

- Fights are not won through defense alone. When your opponent misses, he is likely to take another swing at you. Knowing this in advance, gives you the opportunity to beat him to the punch.

- What targets are best suited for your counter-strike? Can you counter-kick? Also try a double slip and counter.

Blocking and slipping practice

- Have your partner throw punches at you. Keep your guard up and work on blocking or parrying the punches in conjunction with head movement.

- Your opponent's punch must penetrate your guard, and then find the target behind the guard. If the target (your head) is moving, accuracy in your opponent's punch is decreased.

- Practice double slips to avoid two successive punches. Never assume that your opponent will throw only one strike.

Double slip two jabs. Don't breathe a sigh of relief when the first misses, and then get hit by the next.

Double-end bag practice with slipping

- Work the double-end bag, incorporating slips. First, throw a punch to set the bag in motion. When the bag comes back, move your head enough to make it miss.

- When you get good at this, start working the counter-strike in with your head movement.

- Try slipping slightly to the rear instead of to the side. Time your head movement to the motion of the bag, so that when your head comes forward again, your "opponent" is in the process of withdrawing his strike.

- Add the counter-strike. Time your strike to the forward movement of your head. Why is it a bad idea to counter when your head moves to the rear? Why is it a bad idea to counter after your head has reset to the normal position?

Bobbing and weaving practice under a rope

- String a rope at about shoulder height from one end of the room to the other (or have two students hold each end of the rope). Start at one end and bob and weave under the rope. Weave from left to right, then reverse and weave from right to left.

- Bobbing and weaving requires both a lowering (ducking) of your upper body, and head movement (slipping) underneath the rope. There should also be a slight sideways movement of your upper body.

- Bobbing and weaving helps you avoid a strike that is thrown from the side and aimed at your head (hook, round house kick, spinning heel kick, etc.) Each time you bob and weave under the rope, take a short step forward, starting with your lead foot and adjusting your stance with your rear foot. Why is it important to stay in your stance and not step forward the way one would normally walk?

- When you get to the other end of the rope, bob and weave backwards. When is it beneficial to move forward, and when is it beneficial to move back?

Bobbing and weaving practice in shadow boxing

- Use bobbing and weaving in shadow boxing. Shadow box for one minute, using only defensive and evasive moves. Then shadow box for one minute, adding counter-punches and kicks.

- Shadow boxing, using defense only, requires better visualization skills than when offense is also used.

- Mix up your movement for variety. For example, bob and weave from left to right, and throw a punch that you are chambered for. Next, move around throwing punches and kicks. Next, visualize your opponent throwing hooks or round house kicks at your head. Bob and weave under the attack, and throw a counter-kick that you are chambered for. Next, do a couple of quick bob and weaves from left to right and back. Mixing it up teaches you to be unpredictable.

Bobbing and weaving under a hook

- Have your partner throw hooks to your head. Avoid the strikes by bobbing and weaving under them.

- Is it better to weave toward or away from the punch? Why? Weaving toward the punch places you in the superior position to your opponent's outside. When he misses with the punch, you will be positioned slightly toward his back. He must now readjust his stance before being able to strike you. If you weave in the same direction as the strike, you risk getting struck when coming back up in your stance.

Bobbing and weaving toward the hook places you in the superior position toward your opponent's back.

- Note how the bob and weave chambers your body. Which type of strike seems most natural to throw off of the bob and weave? Which type of kick lends itself to your upper body movement?

- When your opponent throws a hook or round house kick aimed for your head, and misses, where does he leave himself open? Knowing in advance where the opening is helps you train for a logical follow-up technique.

Upper body movement partner practice

- Have your partner throw a jab followed by a hook. Slip the jab by moving your head slightly to the side. Then, bob and weave under the hook.

- Use your peripheral vision to pick up on the movement of the hook. Ideally, you want to bob and weave in the opposite direction of the slip. Why? Because your head and upper body movement have already chambered for this.

- Since you are not absolutely sure of which strike your opponent will throw next, you must be ready to adapt. Should head and upper body movement be used when your opponent is not counter-striking? Why, or why not?

Focus mitt practice with upper body movement

- Have your partner hold a focus mitt in one hand and wear a glove on the other hand. When he throws a hook with his gloved hand, bob and weave under it and counter-strike to the focus mitt.

- The idea is to make the bob and weave subconscious, where you implement offense automatically without having to think about your next move.

- Try the double bob and weave. This simulates an evasive movement against two successive looping strikes: a left hook followed by a right hook, for example, or a left hook followed by a right round house kick.

- Why is it illogical to reverse the above combination and throw a right round house kick followed by a left hook? If your opponent misses with the round house kick, he will not be in position to throw a left hook, because he will have his back turned partly toward you. If he initiates with the hook and misses, he can use the miss to chamber for the round house kick, with his feet in position for this move.

Bobbing and weaving with counter-striking

- Practice bobbing and weaving with both high and low counter-strikes. Try to get away from being a headhunter.

- Start on the heavy bag. Bob and weave under an imaginary punch, and counter with a strike or kick to the mid-section. Move around and throw some punches and kicks. Then bob and weave again and counter with a strike or kick to the head.

- Get with a partner in a light contact sparring match. Avoid his hooks by using upper body movement. Vary your counter-strikes to high and low targets.

Bobbing and weaving with gapping

- Most fighters tend to favor offense. Bobbing and weaving lends itself to this, as you can first avoid your opponent's strike, and through that avoidance position for a counter-strike. But you should also practice avoiding a strike and moving back to long range. You do this by taking a step back simultaneous to the bob and weave.

- When your opponent misses with his strike, and you have moved to long range, he is likely to step forward to attempt to close distance. If your timing is good, you can stop his forward movement with a front kick.

- Can you throw a side thrust kick after moving to long range? How about a round house kick? Why are the front kick or side thrust kick more beneficial than the round house kick?

- Try bobbing and weaving and counter-striking while in close, then moving out with a couple of quick straight strikes to your opponent's head. You are vulnerable when backing up, so it is especially important to throw strikes to keep your opponent occupied.

- If you counter-strike now, you are better off using your longer reaching legs. For example, bob and weave with a step to the rear, and counter with a front kick to the mid-section.

Bob and weave with a step back, and counter with front kick.

OFFENSIVE MOVEMENT

In order to control the fight, you must be the one who dictates what, when, and how. It is through movement and superior footwork that appropriate distance is achieved. Offensive movement is comprised of distance awareness and jamming and gapping techniques.

This section covers:

- Distance awareness
- "Short" blocking with your elbows
- Jamming and gapping
- Summary and review

DISTANCE AWARENESS

The different distances at which a fight takes place can be broken down into three zones, commonly called:

1. The safety zone
2. The out-fighting zone
3. The in-fighting zone

When in the *safety zone*, the distance between you and your opponent is so great that neither fighter can strike the other.

When in the *out-fighting zone*, the distance between you and your opponent allows you to reach each other with long range techniques only (any of the three basic kicks, plus the jab and the rear cross).

When in the in-fighting zone, the distance between you and your opponent is very tight, normally within one foot of each other, and most long range techniques are no longer effective. You must now rely on short range techniques, mainly the hook and the uppercut.

It is through movement and footwork that you will learn to maneuver from the "outside" to the "inside." More about this in Section 5.

Try these exercises on **THREE ZONES OF FIGHTING**:

Exercise 1

The fighter who controls distance controls the fight. Learn to judge and control distance by mirroring your opponent's moves, so that each time he steps forward to close a gap, you step back to again widen the gap. This keeps you in the safety zone where neither fighter can strike the other.

Because most fighters find it easier to step forward, in order to stay in the safety zone when moving back, you must be a step quicker than your opponent.

Exercise 2

The out-fighting zone is where you and your opponent can reach each other with long range techniques only. Experiment to find the type of combinations that are most suitable for fighting in the out-fighting zone. Also explore proper defense against a fighter using long range techniques.

When your opponent tries to increase distance and move to the safety zone, close the gap with a shuffle-step and explode with a combination. Be aware of any set-ups your opponent may be using, so that you don't let him lure you into closer range. Closing distance without a follow-up is not recommended.

Next, experiment with moving from the out-fighting zone to the safety zone by using proper footwork. Be in charge of distance, so that you are the one deciding when to move in and out.

If you have reach on your opponent, you will be at a distinct advantage. You and your opponent will now work from two different distances, with you in the safety zone and him in the out-fighting zone. This allows you to land techniques while preventing your opponent from scoring.

Exercise 3

The in-fighting zone is where you are very close to your opponent, touching, or almost touching. Techniques suitable for the in-fighting zone are close range techniques, like uppercuts and tight hooks. Some fighters stay covered so well on the inside that it is difficult to find an opening. Experiment with moving your opponent's focus away from his upper body by kicking his legs. Leg kicks at close quarter range, utilizing the shin of your leg, usually work well for splitting your opponent's mind and body focus. When his focus shifts to his legs, look for openings on his head.

"Short" blocking with your elbows

The most obvious way to increase distance is by stepping back. But you can throw many long range techniques effectively and with power from a tight distance without stepping, simply by relying on the movement of your upper body. An example is the rear cross. You can chamber for the rear cross by pivoting your upper body to the side, while your feet remain at close fighting range. Use this concept in conjunction with *elbow blocking*:

1. As your opponent throws a hook to your right side, pivot your body to the right and block the strike with your right elbow. Keep your arm tight and in front of your body. There is very little movement in the elbow itself, with the power of the block coming from the rotation of your body. You have now chambered for a follow-up rear cross.

2. You can also chamber for a follow-up hook by pivoting your body and relying on short blocking with your elbows. As your opponent throws a hook to your left side, block with your left elbow while pivoting to the left. You have now increased distance and are set to throw a left hook. If your opponent throws the hook low to your ribs, his arm will be blocking his own rib section, and an opening will exist high to his head.

You can also counter with the arm that is not blocking. When working on these blocking principles, there should be very little pausing between your block and counter. As you strike, allow your body to pull the striking arm out by shifting your weight to your opposite foot. By keeping your arms tight and letting your body do the work, you eliminate throwing "arm punches," and power is increased considerably.

Jamming and gapping

Aside from blocking, another effective defense against a kick is to move in and jam the kick. Jamming is a *rapid closure of distance*. Jam with the intent of smothering your opponent's long range techniques and to lessen the power of an imminent strike. Effective jamming requires superior timing. If your closure happens too soon, your opponent will adapt and counter-strike or step back to create a gap, rendering the jam ineffective. If your closure is too slow, you risk getting struck on the way in and will experience *added momentums* first hand. Jamming is most effective against a round house kick, since the power of the kick comes from the side (as opposed to a front kick, where the power is focused straight ahead).

Jam a round house kick (above) or a front kick (right) to get to close quarter range and render your opponent's techniques ineffective.

To inhibit your opponent's ability to move (concept: *completion of motion*), you must time your jam to the *initiation* of his technique. Correct timing places your opponent at a distinct disadvantage:

1. His **techniques** are rendered **ineffective**.
2. His **mobility** is **reduced**.
3. His **balance** is **diminished**.

Jamming is usually more effective against kicks than strikes, because a fighter's legs are generally slower and less precise than his hands. Your opponent also has faster recovery when striking than when kicking, and can therefore retain better balance and mobility. When jamming strikes, you must utilize better timing, head and body movement, and faster counter-strikes. When your jamming technique is effective, immediately follow with a counter-strike.

Gapping means creating distance, and is the opposite of jamming. If your opponent tries to smother your techniques, you must move out of range and create the gap needed to strike effectively. This is particularly true if he is superior at close range.

Try this exercise on **JAMMING**:

Exercise 4

Experiment with jamming your opponent's kick before it is fully extended. When your opponent throws a round house kick, shuffle forward and jam the kick. Follow with a punch combination.

A common mistake is to try to block the kick first, before moving to close range. But this is time consuming. The best time to move in and counter is when your opponent is on one leg and in the process of kicking. If your timing is good, there shouldn't even be a need to block the kick. Because of the structure of the knee joint, stepping straight toward your opponent will make his round house kick unable to "curve" around your body on impact, and the power will be nullified.

Experiment with taking a half-step forward with your lead foot only. You do this by pushing off against the floor with your rear foot.

The half-step allows you to reverse direction and move in and out quickly.

If you have difficulty determining if you opponent's kick will go high or low, you can use jamming or gapping as defense instead of a shin or elbow block. Your technique must now be a beat faster than your opponent's. To gap, shuffle back as soon as you see the first initiation of a kick. Gapping places you on the outside, where you can follow with a long range technique. As discussed earlier, the best time to counter is when your opponent's kick misses and he is still in motion, off balance, and unable to follow up.

There are also times when you need to close a gap, even if your opponent doesn't throw a kick; for example, when he is moving back faster than you are moving forward. You must now speed up your footwork to close the distance between you.

Summary and review

The shuffle-step is faster and more explosive than the regular step forward or back. Use the shuffle-step when you need a quick closure or widening of distance. To execute a forward shuffle, push off with your rear foot, simultaneously taking a big step forward with your lead foot. As your lead foot lands, bring your rear foot forward to adjust your stance. The reverse is true for the rearward shuffle.

Shuffle-step practice across the room

• Start at one end of the room and take a series of shuffle-steps forward. Make sure that your balance is good and that the distance between your feet remains correct between each step. When you get to the other end of the room, take a series of shuffle-steps back to increase distance.

• A strike or kick should usually follow a shuffle-step. When shuffling forward, the shuffle increases the momentum and power of the strike; when shuffling back, the strike serves as a defensive move to keep your opponent occupied.

Gap closure with the forward shuffle

• The forward shuffle can be used effectively whenever your opponent creates a gap. Have your partner hold a kicking shield. Throw a front or side thrust kick with as much power as possible, attempting to move your partner back. As distance is created, quickly shuffle forward and follow with a punch combination.

• When your opponent gets kicked back or is off balance, his natural reaction is to come forward again. When you have landed your kick, instead of shuffling forward, wait for your opponent's reaction and time your next kick to his forward momentum.

Focus mitt practice with the shuffle-step

• Have your partner hold a focus mitt. Stand slightly out of reach of the mitt. Shuffle forward with your lead foot only and throw a jab, without moving your rear foot. Immediately shuffle back to long range.

The half-step shuffle with a jab helps you get back to long range quickly.

• The purpose of this type of shuffle is to get within range to throw a strike, and then quickly get back to safety. Your stance will be slightly wide for a moment.

• Can you increase the speed of the half-step by using weight transfer, placing more than half your weight on one foot for a moment?

• A good time to use this type of shuffle is against an opponent who is stalking you. By striking him from many different angles, you decrease the risk of being struck.

- Repeat the exercise above, but have your partner move around as if you were actually engaged in a fight. Shadow box until you find it suitable to shuffle forward and throw a jab to the focus mitt. Then shuffle back to long range and continue shadow boxing.

- Pay attention to the width of your stance. When your stance gets too wide, it is difficult to execute the shuffle. Why?

- How can you use footwork to shuffle side-to-side, and what are the advantages?

Gapping with the rearward shuffle

- Use the rearward shuffle to create a gap after a close range combination. Have your partner hold focus mitts. Get within a foot's distance of the mitt and throw a hook or uppercut combination. When you have finished your combination or when your opponent starts to counter-strike, quickly shuffle back, simultaneously throwing a front kick to keep him at bay.

- Any kick that meets your opponent's forward momentum will work when stepping back to long range. For example: front kick, side thrust kick, spinning back kick. The round house kick is not as effective, because it doesn't strike your opponent straight.

Be aware that your opponent can use a fake to draw you forward and into his powerful rear hand. When you decide to jam, move decisively. If you hesitate, an alert opponent will take advantage of you.

Shuffle-step sparring practice

- Engage in light contact sparring, with your partner being the aggressor. Each time you feel a need to move outside of his punching range, execute a rear shuffle, simultaneously throwing a jab to keep him occupied.

- It is more difficult stepping back than forward. Your rearward shuffle must therefore be quicker than your opponent's forward shuffle.

- Can you shuffle back at an angle to thwart your opponent's linear attack?

- Engage in light contact sparring where you are the aggressor, and your partner tries to stay away from you by using a lot of footwork. Experiment with forward shuffles to close distance to where you can throw a strong combination.

- Use lateral movement to cut your opponent off. Shuffle in and strike with aggressive combinations.

- Can you use the forward shuffle in conjunction with a kick? Can you use it in conjunction with a block?

SHADOW BOXING

Since everybody is built differently and moves differently, in order to derive the most benefit from your kickboxing training, you must now find what works for you in particular. This can be achieved through experimentation in sparring and shadow boxing.

Shadow boxing is a form of self-exploration that allows you to express yourself freely in movement. Now that you have learned specific stances and moves that are considered correct for competition kickboxing, you must also understand that the moves you have learned are not law, and may be altered as necessary to better suit yourself and the fighting environment. For example, if the situation warrants, you may use a neutral stance (horse stance) instead of a boxer's stance, as long as you understand the consequences of doing so.

When shadow boxing, visualize your opponent in front of you and work both offensive and defensive moves. Shadow boxing teaches you about rhythm, movement, angles, and balance. In short, shadow boxing teaches you to look and feel like a fighter.

This section covers:

- Some pointers on shadow boxing
- Learning to relax
- A list of sparring principles
- Summary and review

Don't get too set in your ways. Train with an attitude of improving overall skill instead of specific techniques.

SOME POINTERS ON SHADOW BOXING

Shadow boxing can be broken down into two parts:

1. Analysis
2. Application

The analysis is where you concentrate on proper form, making sure that everything you throw is mechanically correct. The analysis should be slower and more precise than the application.

When you have achieved good balance, correct technique, and full extension in your punches and kicks, begin to visualize your opponent in the ring with you. This is called application and consists of a combination of offense, defense, and a variety of foot maneuvers.

To practice application, incorporate the following concepts into your shadow boxing drill:

1. Throw strikes that come **naturally**. Usually, what feels good also works well.

2. Make sure that your techniques are **logical**. For example, a tight hook may not be a logical follow-up off of a rear cross, unless you also take a step forward to close distance.

3. Work both **offensive and defensive** moves, implementing all of your blocks, strikes, kicks, and movement. Since combinations are not limited to punches and kicks, but should be thought of as a whole fighting system, every move (like slipping, bobbing and weaving, and shuffle-steps) should be incorporated into your shadow boxing.

4. Stay **light on your feet**. Staying on the balls of your feet aids your mobility. A flat-footed fighter will have difficulties with both movement and balance. Do not stay only in one place. Use the whole ring.

5. **Exaggerate** all moves. Speed is not as important in shadow boxing as is proper form. Working on full extension now keeps you from stopping short in the actual fight.

6. **Visualize** your opponent. The subconscious mind stores what you learn. If possible, get so deeply into visualization that an outsider watching you will think that you are engaged in an actual fight.

7. Look at shadow boxing as a way of **expressing yourself** freely in movement. Do not worry about following any specific pattern, or what any onlookers may be thinking.

Try these exercises on **SHADOW BOXING**:

Exercise 1

Think of every move as a part of a combination. It is not necessary to throw your strikes continuously. Upper body movement increases your awareness and helps you attain a better position. Don't stay in one spot, but work all angles. Incorporate rolls, pauses, head movement, and footwork. Other defensive moves, like elbow blocks, forearm blocks, and shin blocks should also be thought of as part of your combinations.

Next, slow down to half-speed to work on good form and technique. Make sure that your upper body is relaxed. Every once in a while, speed up with a combination to simulate the different speeds and spurts that occur in a fight.

Exercise 2

Shadow box, using *defensive moves only*. Block or use movement to avoid any strikes or kicks that you visualize being thrown at you. Blend your footwork in with other defensive moves. Incorporate shuffles and lateral steps to force your imaginary opponent to adjust.

It is impossible to block every punch and kick, but being comfortable with defense will frustrate your opponent and lessen the risk of injury to you.

Exercise 3

Shadow boxing should not be done without plan or intention. Make sure that what you throw is logical. For example, a jab is normally not logical after an uppercut combination on the inside. Why? First, the uppercut combination is a short range technique, while the jab is a long range technique. Second, a jab is not a power strike, but a set-up strike and should precede a power combination, such as the uppercuts. Even if your opponent steps back to the out-fighting zone, it would be better to follow with a wide hook or a rear cross, both of which are power punches. Find the logical follow-ups off:

1. Jab
2. Rear cross
3. Hook
4. Uppercut
5. Front kick
6. Round house kick
7. Side thrust kick
8. Elbow block
9. Forearm block
10. Shin block
11. Leg check
12. Parry
13. Slipping
14. Ducking
15. Bobbing and weaving
16. Shuffle-step (jamming/gapping)

Now, put together the above techniques in logical combinations.

Learning to relax

Most people have a natural tendency to tense when threatened. In order to answer the threat successfully and within the brief period of time allotted, it is essential that you learn to relax. Freezing when your opponent comes toward you with a barrage of blows inhibits your ability to respond.

The benefits that come with relaxation are many. A relaxed strike allows for better energy transfer and is more damaging than a tense strike. A relaxed strike feels heavier and hurts more than a tense strike, which is often slowed down subconsciously before hitting its target. Relaxing also helps you cope better through a physically tiring workout or spar.

Few fighters are naturally relaxed. Most of us must learn to relax. Next time you shadow box, work on these relaxation concepts:

1. Practice speed and focus of power by **keeping your hands open**. As you extend your arm to punch, gradually close your fist as if you are "squeezing air," until your fist snaps fully closed on impact.

2. Keep your **shoulders relaxed by letting them bounce** back and forth. Think of it as a whip, where your shoulder is the handle and your fist is the tip that snaps at the moment of impact.

3. Work on **upper body movement**, as this tends to confuse your opponent. If you are rigid, your opponent will see what is coming more easily.

4. Tensing takes almost as much energy as throwing punches. To learn relaxation, get into the kind of mind-set that you are just not going to worry about what your opponent is doing. Trying implies tensing. If you try to throw a relaxed strike, you will most likely tense. **Adopt the "I don't care" attitude.**

A relaxed strike has a "soft" hardness to it. Relaxation also increases your speed. When your speed changes, your opponent's timing must also change to match the openings. Staying relaxed makes your strikes harder, faster, and more deceptive.

Try these **RELAXATION** exercises:

Exercise 4

Grab a set of light dumbbells (three pounds, for example) and alternate left and right strikes in the air as fast as you can for three one-minute rounds with a thirty-second rest between rounds. To get the most benefit from this exercise, bring your hands all the way back to your shoulders between each punch. **Do not hyperextend your elbow by snapping the strike on its way out!** Once your arms get a little tired, you will be less likely to tense when punching.

Exercise 5

Wear boxing gloves and punch the heavy bag with jabs and rear crosses for three one-minute rounds. Do not try to hit with power. Focus on relaxation by striking as fast as you can and without stopping. When your arms and shoulders begin to hurt, do not give in to your desire to slow down. This exercise is supposed to tire your muscles to aid with relaxation of those muscles.

A LIST OF SPARRING PRINCIPLES

1. **Do** throw all strikes and kicks with extension.

2. **Do** stay crouched in your stance. Bend at the knees and not at the waist. This helps you avoid taking a retaliatory hook on the back of your head or an uppercut on your chin or nose.

3. When throwing the jab, **do** keep your right hand high and, like a gun, ready to fire.

4. **Do** guard low to the body with your elbows to defend a strike or kick to your mid-section.

5. **Do** throw overwhelming combinations to high and low targets.

6. **Do** work with broken rhythm. Pause briefly to break the rhythm before firing back. Have patience.

7. When backed up against the ropes, **do** fire back and move.

8. **Don't** rush in. Be methodical when working your way to the inside.

9. **Don't** switch stance at long range. This exposes your centerline and inside thigh area.

10. **Don't** step forward with your rear foot when throwing your rear hand. Shuffle-step instead and set (lower your weight) for power and reach. Don't lean back.

11. **Don't** bring your hand back low after throwing a punch. This will leave openings on your head.

12. **Don't** move back to the outside if you land a strong technique. When staggering your opponent, follow with a second strong technique to finish the fight.

13. **Don't** throw just one strike as a follow-up. Counter all of your opponent's strikes with a combination.

Summary and review

Shadow boxing is a good warm-up exercise that helps you get into the right mind-set for the rest of the workout. When shadow boxing, work on specific techniques, or on staying relaxed and fast and on visualizing your opponent. Shadow box two to five minutes prior to your workout.

Analysis of technique in shadow boxing

- Shadowbox, working on correct execution of technique. Utilize only the strikes, kicks, blocks and movement that you are familiar with. Do each technique slow and with control and full extension. Feel every movement of your body, and be attentive to any time that your balance seems to suffer.

- Are there any particular techniques that seem to disrupt your balance?

- Be careful not to kick and punch at the same time, as this is destructive to your foundation and therefore to power.

- When a technique is hurried, it will lack extension. Work on full range of motion until the techniques are mechanically sound. You can then work on speed.

Finding the natural follow-ups

- Find the natural follow-ups to each strike or kick. If you throw a long range technique that is intended to back your opponent up, a short range follow-up is illogical. Any technique that compromises balance is not advisable.

A side thrust kick followed by an uppercut is an illogical combination.

A hook followed by an uppercut is a logical combination.

- Generally, combinations that feel right will work well; for example, alternating strikes or kicks, or a spinning technique following a round house kick. Combinations that require a constant start and stop of movement are more difficult to find a natural flow in.

- Multiple strikes with the same hand or foot, especially in different directions, are especially difficult to find a natural flow in. This is because they require a constant start, and stop, and restart of motion.

- How can you combine body movement with strikes and kicks without contradicting the direction of the strike?

Defense practice in shadow boxing

- Shadow box, working on defense only: blocks, parries, and movement. Visualize an imaginary opponent throwing strikes and kicks at you. How can you block these techniques?

- Good defense is often lacking in new kickboxing students. Most of us find it easier to be aggressive and slug at each other, than to work on proper timing of our techniques.

- Defending and countering a strike requires two different timings: a slower timing for the defense, and a faster timing for countering to the opening.

- The best time to counter-strike is when your opponent is throwing a kick and is on one leg. How can you use a block to trigger a counter-strike, and take the opening before your opponent has replanted his foot in a solid stance?

Visualization practice in shadow boxing

- Close your eyes and visualize your opponent. Work on blocking and countering his strikes.

- Training through visualization has proved almost as effective as real training. When you can't see, you are forced to work on balance and your sense of touch.

- Before going to sleep at night, take ten minutes to visualize a match with your most feared opponent. Work on increasing your confidence.

Kicking practice in shadow boxing

- Shadow box using only kicks, blending many kicks together into smooth combinations. Keep your hands high for protection.

- We often get in the habit of punching only or kicking only for long periods of time. How can you flow from punching to kicking and back to punching without disrupting your timing?

Controlling the center of the ring

- Mark off a twelve by twelve foot area and shadow box within its perimeter. Try to stay as close to the center as possible. Never get with your back within one foot of the perimeter.

- The fighter who controls the center of the ring can make his opponent move around him in large circles and use up energy.

- If you are the weaker or smaller fighter, it may not be possible to control the center. Having your back to the ropes places you in a disadvantaged position.

- Whenever you get with your back within one foot of the ropes, use a pivot-step to regain the center of the ring.

- Because your opponent has a tendency to mirror your moves, if he is not careful he will pivot with you, trading places until he has his back to the ropes.

- The pivot-step should be quick and executed with authority. Fire a strike from your superior position immediately upon completing the pivot.

Footwork practice in shadow boxing

- Shadow box, using a quick forward shuffle followed by a jab, then shuffle back quickly. Move around and repeat the procedure.

- If your opponent is moving toward you in a straight line, instead of standing toe-to-toe with him and duking it out on the inside, rely on strategy to keep him at bay.

- A stronger opponent will use his strength to move forward in a straight line. If you can strike from many different angles, you can confuse your opponent and gain superiority.

Closing distance and gapping with the jab

- Shadow box throwing multiple jabs, each time taking a tiny step forward to gradually close distance. When your imaginary opponent gets with his back to the ropes, unleash a ten-strike combination.

- Use the jab as a distance closer. If you can explode with a lengthy combination, you might create sensory overload in your opponent, where he is unable to defend all strikes.

- When it is time to move back to long range, throw a strike or kick to keep your opponent occupied.

- How can you change your strategy when trying to back an opponent up who won't give?

Quick footwork in shadow boxing

- Without worrying about stance, stay relaxed in your upper and lower body, dancing around in the ring and flicking jabs at your imaginary opponent.

- Use quick footwork to frustrate your opponent, or to rest between combinations.

- It is not uncommon for a fighter to subconsciously imitate his opponent's moves. If your opponent uses the same strikes against you that you are using against him, should you stay with your original plan? How can you change it?

- How can you exploit an opponent who is playing "cat and mouse" with you?

Partner practice in shadow boxing

- Shadow box with a partner as if you were sparring, but without using any contact at all. Look out for his offensive techniques and experiment with how to avoid and counter them.

- Also, look at what kind of defense your opponent is using. Try to throw techniques that are comfortable and naturally follow one another. Mark off a ring area and practice staying within the confines of the ring, without getting your back against the ropes.

- A relaxed fighter can throw his strikes with speed and power, and usually has the upper hand mentally. When you have learned to stay relaxed in shadow boxing, how can you carry that into the actual fight?

- Pay attention to when you are tense. Tensing inhibits your fighting ability and slows your responses.

QUICK REFERENCE TO CONCEPTS

BROKEN RHYTHM: A steady rhythm can be used as a set-up; however, it also has its drawbacks. Once your opponent gets in tune with your rhythm, he can cover his openings and block your strikes. To stay unpredictable, change your rhythm by speeding up or slowing down. A good way to learn broken rhythm is to count the beats in your head, speed up and slow down the count, and make your physical body do the same.

COMPLETION OF MOTION: The motion of your kick must come to completion before you can move to a new position or throw another kick. For example, if your opponent throws a round house kick, he is unable to move away from his present position until the motion of the kick is complete, and he has replanted his foot on the floor. To take advantage of this concept, counter-strike while your opponent is in the process of kicking and is unable to move away from you.

COUNTERING IN COMBINATIONS: While it is easy to time your defense and counter to single strikes, combinations are both deceptive and overwhelming. Throwing your strikes in combinations allows you to build speed, so that the highest speed, and therefore the greatest power, happens at the end of the combination. When defending and countering your opponent's strike or kick, try to counter with a combination. This sends the message that for every strike he throws, he will pay five- or ten-fold.

FREEZING: Freezing is the involuntary and often damaging tensing of muscles that happen when stunned or confronted with a threat. Freezing inhibits further muscle movement until you can relax. Making your opponent freeze is therefore a good strategic move that allows you to take advantage of his moment of weakness. There are many ways to freeze your opponent's weapons. For example, a sudden, unexpected move will usually solicit a reaction. If he is defensive-minded, he will most likely freeze for a second. Touching any part of your opponent's body can also cause him to tense. Touching his gloves may cause his arms to freeze long enough that you can land a strike without being countered. However, you must also strive to eliminate your own tendency to freeze. Think like this: Every time your opponent lands a strike, whether to a valid target or just to your arm,

use that as a cue to come off with a counter-strike. In other words, use your opponent's offense to trigger your own offense.

OFFENSIVE DEFENSE: Defense is taken to a new level when you start using it offensively. An offensive move executed with the right timing will interfere with your opponent's technique enough to keep it from landing. Likewise, a defensive move that simultaneously serves to harm your opponent (an elbow block to his shin, for example) will destroy his offensive weapons.

RELAXATION: Relaxed striking and kicking increases your speed and therefore your power. When your speed changes, your opponent's timing must also change to match the openings. Staying relaxed makes your strikes more deceptive. Relaxation also helps you avoid the natural tendency to freeze when getting struck.

THREE ZONES OF FIGHTING: The safety zone is where you and your opponent are at a distance where neither can strike the other. The out-fighting zone is where you and your opponent are at a distance where you can reach each other with long range techniques only (two to three feet from each other). The in-fighting zone is where you and your opponent are touching or very close to each other, and where most long range techniques are no longer effective.

SECTION FOUR
LONG RANGE FIGHTING

A ONE-LEGGED MAN IN AN ASS-KICKING CONTEST
by Keith Livingston

Truly great kickboxers don't label themselves as close or long range fighters. Instead, they seek to adapt to the situation. Early in my career I became known as an "in your face" type of fighter. Hooks and uppercuts were my forte. I lived by the old adage "chop down the body and the head will fall." I would constantly pressure forward, hunting my opponent's rib cage with a devastating barrage of close range tactics. But during the eighth week of a twelve-week training cycle, the unthinkable happened. I was working my hooks on a particularly hard heavy bag. I threw a twisting right hook, and cringed as my hand folded backwards. I could feel the immediate throbbing, even though my hand was expertly wrapped and taped. Discomforting thoughts flooded my mind. Was the hand broken? Would it heal with less than four weeks till fight time? How would it affect the remainder of my training? Should I withdraw or continue?

Tony must have noticed my watery eyes, because he immediately came to my aid. He gingerly removed the glove and tape, and then the moment we were both waiting for: the hand wrap. As he pulled the wrap, my hand swelled instantly. Tony's eyes said it all: withdraw. I responded with a resounding "no!" We had come too far and trained too hard. I would simply alter my training and allow the hand to heal. Tony examined my hand, carefully choosing his words he spoke: "You'll just have to learn to become a one-legged man in an ass-kicking contest."

Through the doctor's examination the next day, we learned that I had a hairline fracture. Thus began a regimen of ice packs, non-use, and altered training. Tony's advice was simple: "The lead jab is the most important technique in all of boxing. You will master this technique while your right hand is healing. Your left hand will become a wrecking ball, with the speed of a venomous snake and the sting of an angry wasp."

Fighters are creatures of habit, and at first it was difficult not to throw my right hand. But after a couple of inadvertent mishaps and pain, I learned. Our first session required that I shadow box round upon round, using only the left jab. By the time of the final round, I could barely throw the punch, so tired was my arm. Next, I worked the speed bag and heavy bags endlessly, which slowly helped to improve my strength, accuracy, and left arm endurance. Tony taught me to throw the jab from odd angles and to varied targets. My sparring techniques were limited to the left jab, uppercut, and hook. During the final phase of training, I learned to fight from the southpaw stance and use my left arm as I had once used my right. Things were coming together, including the rehabilitation of my right hand.

On fight night, I felt strong and confident in my new-found ability. At the opening bell, I advanced on my opponent, allowing my subconscious to take over. There was one problem, however. The subconscious chose my right hand. As it slammed against my opponent's jaw, there was a sickly vibration in my hand, and the pain was so intense I felt as though I might pass out. I finished the first round by smothering my opponent with close body contact.

When I returned to the corner, Tony asked me if I wanted to quit. I seriously considered it, but shook my head. In round two, I regained my composure and decided to put my new talents to the test. I was surprised at the ease with which I pumped the jab, and I soon established a crimson flow from my opponent's nostrils. With each successive blow, the blood spatter took flight. By the end of the round, I was covered in blood . . . his! In round three, I continued to pump the jab unmercifully, shutting my opponent's right eye. Now that he was thoroughly frustrated, I was able to use the uppercut and hook with lethal accuracy. Round four would be the deciding and final round. I came out in the unorthodox southpaw stance, measured him with my right hand, and let go with a double left cross, which sent him reeling into the ropes. I advanced landing another left cross, followed by a double left hook. One slammed his rib cage while the other careened off of his temple, sending him down for the count. I was elated, having learned the value of my one good hand, and truly become a one-legged man in an ass-kicking contest.

JABBING STRATEGY

Your opponent rushes toward you, swinging his arms like a windmill. You cover up in defense of the oncoming barrage of blows. But only seconds into the first round, his punches lose their sting. He is pawing at your chest, unable to focus his power. His mouth is wide open, and his breathing is labored. His feet seem to be lagging behind the rest of his body, as he takes a few stumbling steps forward, desperately waiting for the bell to save him . . .

On the amateur level, you will be judged on how many strikes you land. You must therefore stay as active as possible. But when a fighter of lesser experience gets overly aggressive, he will run out of steam and his techniques will get sloppy. Most aggressive fighters tend to plow forward in a straight line, at risk of walking into a more skilled opponent's punches. A fighter who is skilled at long range can use footwork to avoid the aggressive attacker, and time his counterstrikes to his opponent's forward motion.

What differentiates the champions from the rest of us is their ability to control distance. Fighters who rush in carelessly, or who are comfortable only at close range, can easily be defeated by the strategic long range fighter's fakes and distance manipulations. Your basic long range techniques are comprised of the jab, rear cross, round house kick, front kick, and side thrust kick, along with both linear and circular movement (other long range techniques, including spinning techniques, are discussed in Section 9).

This section covers:

- Thoughts on long range fighting
- Using the jab offensively (how to reach your target)
- Choosing your targets
- Lateral movement
- Using the jab defensively (stick and move)
- Distance and the elongated jab
- Glove-up with Keith
- Multiple relaxed jabs
- Summary and review

THOUGHTS ON LONG RANGE FIGHTING

Keith's Corner

Technique aside, long range fighting is about footwork; about controlling the center or outer perimeter of the ring, never allowing yourself to get pinned to the ropes. Long range fighting is about *side-stepping* and *out-stepping* your opponent; it's about timing and understanding the cadence of your steps.

When you watch great long range fighters, like Ali, you will see that their techniques are secondary to their footwork. Footwork accomplishes letting your opponent move into range for your long range techniques, but not any closer. It is footwork that makes the techniques effective. If your footwork is wrong and allows a short range opponent to penetrate that distance, your jab will no longer work. The long range fighter must be proficient at striking from a variety of angles, and must employ quick footwork to maneuver himself into a superior position.

I'm not suggesting that you should fight exclusively at long range, as it is almost impossible to keep an aggressive opponent at long range for the duration of the fight. In order to be effective, you must be proficient at both long and short range fighting. However, you should be the one who decides when to move from long range to short range, and vice versa. Now that you have learned how to execute basic offensive and defensive moves, let's look at how to put that knowledge to work by employing some fighting strategy.

USING THE JAB OFFENSIVELY (HOW TO REACH YOUR TARGET)

Although the jab is not your most powerful strike, at long range it is in a sense your most superior strike. Superiority is determined not only by how much strength or power a fighter has, but also by how he utilizes movement to better employ that power. It is difficult to land a long range technique without some sort of set-up against a skilled opponent. The jab is perhaps the most versatile kickboxing technique, and can be used to set up all long range techniques. Unless you are trapped in a habitual pattern, your opponent will not know which technique you will throw after the jab. Much of this section is devoted to the jab, and how to use it as a set-up.

The jab must be thrown with speed, with your stronger rear technique following only a half-beat behind.

A fighter skilled at using the jab may be able to keep his opponent at a distance for most of the round. But since the ultimate aim in kickboxing is to knock your opponent out, you can't rely on the jab alone. The primary mission of the jab is to create openings for your stronger rear hand. The intent of the rear cross is to knock your opponent out, or to cause enough damage to set him back. When you do damage with a long range technique, it also gives you the perfect opportunity to move into close range.

Your first jab may strike your opponent's gloves only. But your second and third jabs are likely to land on a valid target, if you take a small step forward to close distance. Once you feel the jab land, immediately follow with the rear cross. **Do not switch stance or step through with your rear foot** when throwing the rear cross. This exposes your centerline and inside thigh.

If the rear cross seems short of reaching its target, you probably need to:

1. **Shuffle forward**. Your opponent may have taken a step back after being hit with the jab.

2. **Bend at the knees**. This not only increases your reach; it also keeps your jaw better protected. A common mistake is to lean back slightly when throwing the rear cross. Be aware of this pitfall which decreases your reach, lessens your power, and exposes your jaw.

3. **Pivot your upper body**. If your shoulders are rigid, you will cancel the power and reach the rotation in your lower body has created.

Because it is easier to step forward than back, the distance between you and your opponent is likely to decrease with each of your jabs.

Why are these jabs short of reach?

Too far away

Too upright

No pivot

A good way to close distance is with a *shuffle-step*, which is a longer step than what you use when stepping forward or back. You can increase the speed of the shuffle by pushing off with your rear foot against the floor and bringing your lead foot forward as fast as possible. Also use the shuffle when moving back to long range, although the danger of getting struck when distance is increased is slightly less.

Try these exercises on **SHUFFLE-STEPS**:

Exercise 1

Shuffle forward several times, each time throwing a jab. On the last shuffle, set down in your stance and throw a rear cross. Be careful not to widen your stance, as this hinders your mobility. If you throw the rear cross from a wide stance, you may also have a tendency to straighten your rear leg with the strike, raise your upper body, and expose your jaw. This lessens the power.

Exercise 2

Stay on the balls of your feet for easy mobility. Work on a variety of strikes when moving around. If you shuffle forward without throwing anything, you risk walking into your opponent's strike. In addition, a step without a strike or kick serves little purpose. When stepping back to create distance, it is also important to keep your opponent occupied by throwing strikes in broken rhythm.

CHOOSING YOUR TARGETS

One day a newcomer was practicing strikes on the heavy bag with such force that you could feel the vibrations throughout the walls. Several fighters were watching in awe as this small kickboxer landed strike after strike, until the chain holding the one-hundred pound bag broke, dropping the bag to the floor with a loud thud. But when the newcomer entered his first full-contact match a few weeks later, his technique reminded us more of the "windmill" strategy; in other words, no strategy at all. Many fighters throw a good jab on a stationary object, such as the heavy bag. But when it comes to using the jab effectively in sparring, skill (or full understanding of the purpose of the jab) is often lacking. You should never throw the jab without intent. It is easy to get in the habit of flicking jabs at your opponent, yet failing to land, because you are misjudging either distance or target. If your jab does not create an opening for your rear cross, you may need to choose a different target; for example, a low strike to the body. If none of your jabs creates the desired results, you may need to step back out and regroup for a different technique.

Target areas can be broken down into high (head), middle (body), and low (legs). These areas can be further broken down into specific targets. The body, for example, is a large target area with many smaller targets. Since your opponent's reaction differs depending on where you strike on the target area, it is important to choose your specific targets with care. For example, striking the soft internal organs on the middle target area may knock the wind out of your opponent, causing him to buckle over. Striking higher to the chest is more likely to knock him back, creating distance. The reaction you get from your opponent determines the target for your follow-up strike. Jabbing without specific intent is therefore a waste of time. It is important to have an understanding of the many different targets, how the human body functions, and your opponent's expected reactions.

Try this exercise on **TARGET AREAS**:

Exercise 3

Every time you throw a strike, you automatically create an opening on yourself. Being aware of this is especially important when throwing punches to the body. Get with a partner and experiment with body punches. Have your partner counter to the opening at your head. Keep your jaw protected by lowering your shoulders to the level of the punch. Think of your shoulder as a shield against your opponent's blows.

Standing upright exposes your head (left). Lower your shoulders to the level of the punch when striking the body (below).

LATERAL MOVEMENT

You can also use the jab effectively against a bigger opponent. Instead of going toe-to-toe with a stronger fighter and trying to out-muscle him on the inside, use the jab often and in rapid succession to keep him at a distance. An aggressive opponent who steps toward you in a straight line can be evaded through *lateral movement* in conjunction with the jab. The smaller fighters are often faster than the heavyweights, who are usually sluggers. It is through this extra speed that you can tip the scale to your advantage.

If you take as many strikes as you throw, engaging in battle becomes futile. By initiating your moves *on an angle*, you avoid trading blows with your opponent, and force him to make an adjustment before he can counter-strike.

Try this exercise on **LATERAL MOVEMENT**:

Exercise 4

Take up an angle slightly to the *outside* of your opponent (slightly toward his back). This enables you to land your jab and still eliminate the threat of his rear hand. This lateral movement also gives you reach on a taller fighter.

Jab from a superior position from the side.

Many fighters are headhunters. But since there are so many good targets on the body, you're doing yourself a disservice by striking only to the head.

USING THE JAB DEFENSIVELY (STICK AND MOVE)

You have now learned how to use the jab offensively by stepping forward or to the side and throwing a rear cross off of the jab. But you can also use the jab to circumvent your opponent's long range techniques, annoying and irritating him through the use of circular movement. The primary purpose of the jab will now shift toward the stick and move concept, which works on the principle of striking your opponent with the jab (stick), and quickly moving out of reach (move). Your footwork must be quick and synchronized with the strike. When backing out, your movement can be either linear or circular. However, the quick reversal of motion requires that you stay light on your feet. Practice quick footwork by moving forward and back and changing direction often. You can increase the speed in your footwork by:

1. Staying **relaxed**
2. **Bending** slightly at the knees
3. Staying on the **balls of your feet**

When "on your bicycle," as this quick footwork is called, there is no left or right fighting stance, and you will be switching stance often. The stick and move is also used when your opponent is trying to crowd you with a linear attack. Your circular movement now allows you to strike from many different angles, forcing your opponent to constantly readjust his position. When you decide to follow with a strong combination, you must set down on your strikes. You will be up on the balls of your feet when on your bicycle, but more "rooted" and linear when actually throwing your combination. The skilled kickboxer can combine quick footwork with power combinations.

Footwork should be smooth and natural and practiced at every opportunity. As your opponent comes forward, use footwork to jam, gap, or move to the side. Advanced footwork is more mental than physical, and can be thought of as *deception within movement*. By utilizing footwork in conjunction with distance and timing, you will frustrate your opponent, continually making his strikes miss.

Try this exercise on **FOOTWORK**:

Exercise 5

A moving target is more difficult to strike than a stationary target. A good fighter must be light on his feet, unpredictable in his moves, and able to switch direction often. Engage in light contact sparring, using the whole floor space and incorporating all aspects of footwork: shuffle-steps, pivot-steps, and fast switches in direction.

To catch an opponent backing up, you must be a step quicker. A fighter who understands and applies good footwork is difficult to beat.

DISTANCE AND THE ELONGATED JAB

I can't stress enough the importance of being in control of distance. Controlling distance allows you to move out of reach of an aggressive opponent, smother his long range techniques, and move to a position of superiority. But the most interesting part about fighting is, perhaps, the ability to use distance coupled with superior timing to deceive your opponent into thinking that he is safe.

One of the problems we often encounter when judging distance is that we judge to the "wrong target." We see what is closest to us. For example, instead of measuring the distance from your hands to your opponent's jaw or nose (which is a foot or more behind his guard), your brain will automatically judge the distance from your hands to your opponent's hands when he carries his guard high. This is one reason why so many fighters strike their opponent's gloves even if they have enough reach to strike his face. You must therefore train your brain to see beyond the first barrier. This can be likened to reading a book, where you see the black print on the white page. What you need to do now is learn to read between the lines, to see what is not there.

Timing is part of the distance measuring process. There are two timings you must be aware of:

1. The **timing of your strike** to your opponent's movement and distance.

2. The **timing of your movement** and distance to your opponent's counter-strike.

Fighting, at this stage, becomes very complex, and it is impossible to avoid getting hit completely. But sound strategy helps you outsmart your opponent most of the time. One of the best ways to make your opponent believe that he is out of reach is with the elongated jab. When throwing this technique, you can be as much as two to three feet away and still land the strike.

To throw the elongated jab:

1. Take a **short step forward** with your lead foot *only*, thereby widening your stance.

2. **Push off** with your rear foot and **stretch your body** by pivoting your hip and shoulders in the direction of the jab.

3. **Tuck your chin down** behind your shoulder for protection.

When out of reach (left), the elongated jab helps you land your strike without stepping closer (below).

Your reach has now increased by about two feet. After the jab has landed, bring your lead foot back to reset your body into your stance and maintain good mobility and balance. Use footwork to change your position. Then throw the elongated jab again. The elongated jab is especially effective against an aggressive opponent, who will get frustrated when you keep nailing him with jabs before he even gets within range.

The danger of the elongated jab is, of course, that if you do it too often against a smart fighter, he will pick up on your rhythm and time his counter-strikes to your forward movement. You must therefore change your rhythm frequently to upset his timing. Try timing the step with your lead foot to your opponent's forward motion, so that he steps into your jab and adds his momentum to yours.

If your opponent's head snaps back when you land the jab, instead of stepping out of reach again, you should bring your rear foot forward to narrow your stance and follow with a rear cross or other power punch.

There are two types of fighters: punchers and boxers. When the bell sounds for the first round, you can usually tell what kind of fighter you are up against just by the way he comes out of his corner. A puncher will walk toward you in an aggressive manner and start to slug away with punches, while a boxer will use more movement and set-ups before charging forward.

Try this exercise on **DISTANCE**:

Exercise 6

Use the concept of *half-stepping* to give an opponent the perception that you are moving back. For example, take a step to the rear with your rear foot only. This will widen your stance, moving your upper body slightly to the rear, and creating the illusion that you have increased distance. When your opponent moves forward to close the gap, step forward with your rear foot and strike as he is moving toward you. When you change distance constantly, your opponent will have difficulty determining when he is within firing range.

Glove Up with Keith

We are going to talk about distance today. First, I want you to get used to where your circle of safety is. Know when you're within striking range, and when you're not. Now, get outside of striking range and push off with your rear foot, lunging toward your opponent with a quick jab to his face. As the strike lands, push off with your lead foot and move back to your zone of safety. Move in fast, strike, and move back out fast. If you are aware of distance and can control it, there is a lesser need to block, since you will know when your opponent's strikes can't reach you. Push off more when sticking that jab! Come back out faster! Now, pivot off the line of fire. Stay on the balls of your feet when moving. You can't move very fast when you're flatfooted.

Instead of moving straight back, pivot on the ball of your lead foot until you are off the attack line. Move forward and stick a jab in your opponent's face, then pivot off the angle and throw another jab. Your opponent must now reset his stance before he can land a technique. As soon as he has reset, move and stick another jab in his face.

Jab and pivot off the attack line.

Take a half-step back to increase distance, and strike when your opponent comes forward.

These kinds of stick and move jabs should be thrown mostly when your opponent is the aggressor, or during a lull in the fight. This technique is a great feeler to see where your opponent is mentally. I watched a boxing match once, which everybody thought was real boring because the boxers seemed unable to hit each other. But that was only because both were masters at controlling distance. Distance is really just another word for footwork. Mastering distance is mastering footwork.

MULTIPLE RELAXED JABS

Now that you have worked on the elongated jab, let's look at doubling up on the technique. Multiple quick jabs not only help you determine the distance to your target; they also keep your opponent occupied and frustrated.

A relaxed, snappy jab will not do as much damage as the stiff jab, but it can be thrown faster and serves as a gauge and set-up for your rear techniques. In conjunction with footwork, it also helps you stay out of reach of an aggressive opponent. The relaxed jab can be thrown from a longer distance than the power jab and still reach the target. In a sense, it is therefore similar to the elongated jab, but without the step. To throw the relaxed jab:

1. Be about **six inches farther from your target** than you normally would. This gives your opponent the *illusion* that you are out of reach and therefore harmless.

2. **Push off with your rear foot** while pivoting your body into alignment with the jabbing arm.

3. **Snap your arm** like a wet towel (out-in). Stay relaxed in your shoulders and elbow for speed.

4. As you complete the technique, **reset your body** into your fighting stance. This places you about six inches out of reach. Use footwork to move to a superior position and repeat the procedure.

Every time you jab, take a tiny step to the side to adjust your position. This constant movement helps you control distance, forcing your opponent to readjust his stance in order to land a good blow. As little as an inch in sideways movement is often enough to get off your opponent's centerline where his power is focused.

Many fighters have a lazy jab, which does little damage to their opponent. Even though the jab is primarily used as a set-up for your stronger rear techniques, it can (and should) be thrown with power and speed. In order to throw the jab with power, you must ensure full extension in the technique. A common mistake is to extend the arm, while keeping the shoulders and upper body rigid. To avoid this contradiction in movement, work on **dropping** your lead knee to the inside, **rotating** your shoulders for full extension, and **pushing off** with your rear foot.

Another common mistake is to lean back. This happens because your body is upright. To throw a good jab with power and still protect your openings, work on crouching. An added benefit is that crouching makes you look more threatening. Throw the strike straight with your elbow down and your hand rotating to the horizontal position right before impact.

Jabbing from a crouched stance (left) makes you appear more threatening than jabbing from an upright stance (right).

Summary and review

It is quite common to see kickboxers who are headhunters. Target accuracy, and varying your targets, is important to the successful outcome of the fight. This requires that you have knowledge of which strikes and targets are likely to cause injury.

Target identification and practice

- Identify all targets on the centerline (nose, mouth, throat, heart, solar plexus, groin, back of neck, spine, tailbone). Striking targets on the centerline can cause serious injury.

- In kickboxing, the throat, groin, back of neck, and tailbone are illegal centerline targets. Identify the most appropriate strikes and kicks for striking to legal targets.

- Contact drills help you with target accuracy and choosing the right strike for the target. Face your partner and take turns throwing a combination (using light contact) to three or four different targets. Have your partner mirror your moves, so that when you have finished your combination, he throws an identical combination on you.

- Light contact drills get you used to taking a punch or kick without it inhibiting your fighting ability.

- How can a strike to one target help you set for a strike to a different target? Your opponent's reaction helps determine your next strike.

- Giving your opponent multiple points of pain is likely to inhibit his ability to fight back. One strike to one target (one point of pain) is easier for your opponent to focus on and defend, than many strikes to different targets.

Partner practice using random combinations

- Face your partner at one end of the room and throw random combinations to different targets. Each time you strike, your partner should take a step back, allowing you to advance with your next strike. When you get to the other end of the room, switch so that your partner can practice his combinations on you.

- This exercise allows you to be the aggressive fighter, punching and kicking while moving forward. It also helps your partner get used to dealing with a threat.

- Use your peripheral vision to pick up on your opponent's strikes and movement. Don't focus directly on his striking weapon.

- How can you side-step a strong frontal attack and counter from a superior position?

Partner practice using defense and random combinations

- Repeat the exercise, punching and kicking in combinations across the room, but have your partner use an appropriate block against each strike.

- You can't block everything your opponent throws. The more experienced you get, the more composed you will be, and the more likely you are to subconsciously defend the attack.

- Is there ever a time when you need to block two strikes simultaneously? How can you do this without jeopardizing your balance?

- How do you react when you have to take a strike? How can you stay in charge of the fight, even when you get hit?

Controlling distance

- Target awareness plays a crucial role when controlling distance. Experiment with distance awareness, and identify strikes that are effective from close and long range.

- All punches and kicks don't work equally well from all distances. There are long range techniques and short range techniques, techniques intended to move your opponent back, and others intended to make your opponent crouch forward.

- When you are at close range and desire to move to long range, how can you get your opponent to increase distance between you? Which techniques are distance increasers intended to move your opponent back?

- Which techniques work well in conjunction with a step to the rear?

Following up based on distance awareness

- Identify the most appropriate follow-up strikes, based on whether your opponent creates distance or decreases distance after your first strike lands.

- When you land a strike, knowing how your opponent is likely to react helps you determine your follow-up technique.

- If you are too aggressive when closing distance, your opponent may take advantage of your advance, so that you step into his strike. Work on closing distance utilizing many small steps in conjunction with strikes.

- How can you decrease or increase distance without exposing targets unnecessarily? What is the best way to step when moving forward or back? How can you use lateral or circular movement in conjunction with a strike?

Finding your range

- Distance is not solely dependent on your actual physical distance to your target. Distance also increases or decreases depending on whether you throw the strike below or above the horizontal.

- Extend your strike horizontally toward your partner. Now raise your arm to a slightly higher target and note how your reach decreases. A strike that is thrown above or below the horizontal requires being closer to your target.

The side thrust kick is a good distance increaser. However, this kick is difficult to throw from very close range.

- Identify strikes that are commonly thrown above the horizontal (a kick to the head, for example). Find your range for throwing them accurately.

- Distance also increases when throwing strikes below the horizontal. However, when your opponent is in a fighting stance, his lead leg is naturally closer to you than his upper body. This allows you to reach his leg with a kick from long range, without closing distance.

Heavy bag practice with varied targets

- Work the heavy bag, throwing punches and kicks to both high and low targets. The more you vary your targets, the more difficult it is for your opponent to defend against your strikes.

- How can you vary targets if you are limited to hand strikes only? How can you vary targets if you are limited to kicks only?

- We often have a tendency to imitate our opponent. If your opponent throws mostly kicks, try breaking his focus by moving in and countering with punches. If he throws mostly punches, try staying at long range and countering with kicks.

- If you have an injury that renders one or more of your weapons useless, what can you do to still confuse your opponent with varied targets?

Heavy bag practice with kick and distance awareness

- Work the heavy bag, experimenting with positioning for kick and distance.

- The round house kick is seen as a universal kick, which can be thrown from any range. If you are far from your target, impact with your instep; if you are close, impact with your shin; if you are very close, impact with your knee.

- Is it possible to throw a front kick from very close range? Experiment with increasing distance by stepping to the side rather than straight back.

INCORPORATING ANGLES

The *attack line* is created through linear movement between yourself and your opponent. When you move back in a straight line, it allows your opponent to attack more effectively. To thwart this linear attack, side-step or pivot off the attack line, forcing your opponent to readjust. This gives you a positional advantage, because when your opponent has to reposition himself, he uses up time, giving you additional time.

This section covers:

- Pivoting off the attack line
- In the gym
- The dangers of switching stance at long range
- Getting past long range techniques
- Leaving a jab behind
- Summary and review

Pivoting off the attack line

The pivot-step is perhaps used best against a fighter who is crowding you. In order to move off the attack line completely, you must change your stance until it is perpendicular to your opponent's. There are two ways to do this:

1. **Pivot on the ball of your lead foot**, swinging your rear foot ninety degrees (one-quarter of a turn) to the left or right.

2. **Pivot on the ball of your rear foot**, swinging your lead foot three-quarter of a turn to the left or right.

Pivot until you are perpendicular to the attack line, and throw your strike. A pivot is often just a few inches of movement.

If you were to move your lead foot only half a turn, you would not have stepped off the attack line, but merely switched from a left stance to a right and created distance. Likewise, if you were to move your lead foot only one quarter of a turn, you would still be on the attack line, even though you would be facing a different direction. TRY IT! Once you have pivoted off the attack line, use the opportunity to strike your opponent before he has readjusted his stance.

The fighter on the right increases distance by pivoting to an angle perpendicular to his opponent, and countering with a round house kick.

The fighter on the right increases distance by pivoting 180 degrees. This may tempt your opponent to come forward and into your lead leg side thrust kick.

Strive for as much space as possible, and be careful not to end up in a position where you can't use your mobility. In regards to footwork, most fighters have a natural tendency to mirror their opponent's moves. In other words, if you step forward, your opponent will step back, and vice versa, keeping the distance between you constant. This bit of knowledge can be used to lure your opponent into a position of weakness. By taking a half-step back, you can lure your opponent to come forward and into your strike. The same concept applies to circular movement, where your opponent is likely to circle with you, as if engaged in a dance where you are the leader.

I recall a particular fight where I used the pivot-step repeatedly to reverse positions with my opponent, placing her with her back against the ropes, and scoring a win based on good strategy. Every time I was getting within a foot's distance of the ropes, I would start to circle back to the center of the ring, with my opponent mirroring my moves and circling herself into the ropes.

Try these exercises on **PIVOT-STEPS**:

Exercise 1

Instead of remaining on the attack line when your opponent charges forward, take a pivot-step to force him to readjust his position. For maximum effect, pivot your rear foot ninety degrees off the attack line. This places you at an angle perpendicular to your opponent, allowing you to throw a counter-strike from a superior position.

Exercise 2

If you are the aggressor, it is important to keep your opponent on the attack line. Any time he tries to side-step or pivot, you must beat him to the move by staying one step ahead and cutting off his escape routes. Experiment with cutting off your opponent's attempts to side-step your attack, until you have backed him up against the ropes of the ring.

IN THE GYM

We fighters have a natural tendency to mirror our opponent's moves. If I step toward you, you will step back, because you will feel as though I'm crowding you or entering your private space. I can use this to my advantage by slowly entering your zone of safety without your knowing it. When I step toward you and you step back, I will gradually take bigger steps. If you don't pick up on it, I will soon be within striking range.

Even if you're not within distance, throw the jab anyway to give your opponent something to think about. Double up on your jabs! And keep your mouth closed! If you have a hard time breathing through your nose, breathe through your mouth when outside of striking range, and bite down on your mouthpiece when within striking range.

You have to stay relaxed for this to work. Tensing is death. My advice is to stay as aggressive as possible, almost to the point that you are a little bit angry. As long as you keep your opponent moving back in a straight line, you can maintain control of the fight. Don't try to match your strength against a bigger and stronger opponent. When you're against the ropes, try to circle back to the center of the ring. Stay mobile. The person who moves last is dead• The rule is: If your opponent is moving back, stay on the line of fire; if you are moving back, angle off.

THE DANGERS OF SWITCHING STANCE AT LONG RANGE

My instructor nailed my inside thigh so hard that I couldn't walk without a limp for a week• "Last time I told you nicely not to step through with the rear cross," he said. "But since the information apparently didn't sink in, I had to show you!"

You may switch from a left to a right fighting stance to increase or decrease distance, or to create a better angle for your techniques. However, you must be careful not to rush your opponent. When fighting at long range, do not switch stance by stepping forward in the manner one would normally walk. Switching from a left to a right stance when on the outside creates the following problems:

1. It **exposes your rear inside thigh** to your opponent's cut kick.

2. It **exposes your centerline** to your opponent's front kick.

3. It **exposes your face** to your opponent's powerful rear hand.

The best time to switch stance is on the inside (in close quarters), where it is more difficult for your opponent to use his kicks against you. In addition, you can keep him busy with your hands and therefore conceal the switch better. If you still feel a need to switch stance at long range, switch stepping back, as this increases the distance and lessens the dangers mentioned above.

GETTING PAST YOUR OPPONENT'S LONG RANGE TECHNIQUES

Although the jab is generally considered a set-up strike for your stronger rear hand, you can also use it to get past your opponent's long range techniques. You do this by slipping in conjunction with jabbing when moving from the outside to the inside.

Start by throwing a jab to get a feel for distance. When your opponent counters, slip his jab, using just enough head movement to avoid the strike. Large bobs and weaves are seldom necessary and may even be dangerous. When slipping left from a left fighting stance, move your head slightly to the left and set your weight over your lead leg. You are now loaded for a hook or uppercut with your lead hand.

Be aware of the momentary weaknesses in your defense when switching stance.

Slip your opponent's jab to the left and throw a lead hook to his mid-section.

By slipping, you accomplish two things:

1. **Avoid** your opponent's long range strike, while keeping both hands free to counter.

2. **Chamber** for a short range technique, by setting your body at an angle.

Because a single blow seldom ends a match, be prepared to follow with a combination of punches and kicks. For example, let's say that you start by throwing a lead hook to the mid-section. As you pivot to the right with the hook, you can simultaneously chamber for your next strike: **an uppercut with your rear hand.**

Follow the hook with a rear uppercut.

The superior kickboxer can fight well at both long and close range. Stay on the inside only long enough to take advantage of your opponent's openings. If your opponent starts landing strikes, move back to long range. When backing out, stay off the attack line by moving out on an angle. **Try stepping back and to the right with your right foot.** This places you to the outside of your opponent (away from his centerline). He must now readjust before he can fire back. Take advantage of this by **throwing a strong finishing strike**.

Step out at an angle and throw a rear cross.

Once back on the outside, continue circling your opponent while throwing jabs to keep him at a distance. When the time is right, come in with a new combination, but do not step straight in. Use lateral movement (side to side). If you get backed up against the ropes, use a pivot-step to get off the attack line and back to the center of the ring.

LEAVING A JAB BEHIND

Once you have worked your opponent over on the inside and it is time to move out, you should *work your way out*. Many fighters simply take a step back without throwing anything, or they raise their body upright when moving out, exposing their jaw or centerline. Since moving back creates distance, this is the perfect opportunity for your opponent to counter with a strong rear technique. Your opponent's counter-strike is almost a given and will almost always land for the simple reason that there is only one move required for your opponent (throwing the strike), while there are two moves required for you (stepping back and countering your opponent's strike). This is why it is so important to keep your opponent occupied while you are in the process of moving out.

When moving back to long range, give your opponent a present: **Leave a jab behind**. Since the primary pur-

pose of this type of jab is to distract your opponent, you need not be too concerned with whether it lands on a good target or not. Because the jab is faster than the rear cross (and as long as you throw it while in motion), you should be successful at keeping your opponent at a distance.

> When moving out and leaving a jab behind, move out on an angle. As little as a one-inch step to the side is usually enough to offset your opponent's rhythm and force him to readjust his stance.

Summary and review

Use the pivot-step to attain a superior position by changing the angle at which you are fighting your opponent. You can also use the pivot-step to get back to the center of the ring when you are cornered. The pivot can be as small as a few inches, to a full 180 degrees. Pivot on the ball of one foot, swinging your other foot to a new position. This places your centerline off the attack line.

There are many benefits to switching stance in the middle of the fight. Offensively, it makes it more difficult for your opponent to anticipate your techniques. Defensively, it allows you to protect a part of your body that has been injured. When switching stance, be careful not to expose targets on your centerline.

Footwork practice

- Take some masking tape and mark the floor with a number of Xs about two and a half feet apart. Place your feet on two different Xs.

- Practice moving around, switching direction while stepping on the Xs only. Your legs should never be crossed.

- A pivot-step as small as one inch can be helpful when establishing a superior position for striking or kicking.

Partner practice with pivot-step

- Face your partner in a good fighting stance. Pivot on the ball of your lead foot, taking a one-inch step to your right with your rear foot. Note how this slightly new angle gives you a different perspective and new targets.

- Keep taking one-inch steps with your rear foot to your right, each time noting the new targets, until you have changed the angle a full ninety degrees.

- Repeat the exercise, stepping with your rear foot to the left.

Superior positioning with pivot-step

- Face your partner from a good left fighting stance. Have your partner take a series of pivot-steps both left and right, while you remain in your stance.

- At each step, observe how he is gaining the superior position. Note how you must pivot with him in order to land a good technique.

Sparring practice with pivot-step and counter-striking

- Engage in light contact sparring, with your partner pressing forward. Instead of moving back when he presses forward, pivot with your rear foot a full ninety degrees to the right. Throw a rear cross to your opponent's jaw.

- Throw your follow-up strike as soon as your foot plants from the pivot. Do not delay, or your opponent will have time to adjust and regain superiority.

- The fighter that dominates the center of the ring dominates the fight. When up against a stronger opponent, it is likely that you will end up with your back to the ropes. When you get within a foot's distance of the ropes, take a pivot-step back to the center of the ring.

Switching stance through the pivot-step

- Use the pivot to switch from a left to right stance, and vice versa. You do this by pivoting on the ball of your rear foot, swinging your lead foot a full 180 degrees.

- This is perhaps the safest way to switch stance, because it creates distance between you and your opponent.

- As distance is created and your opponent comes forward, throw a front or side thrust kick timed to his advance.

Pivot 180 degrees to switch stance, and throw a front kick.

Target awareness when switching stance

- On the command of your instructor or partner, switch from a left to a right fighting stance, either by executing a quick jump or by taking a step forward or back in the way one would normally walk.

- When stepping forward, pay attention to target exposure and decide how you can best protect these targets while in the process of switching stance.

- Switching stance stepping back is often safer than switching stance stepping forward. Why? What are the drawbacks of switching stance stepping back?

- Identify all targets that are exposed when switching stance. Pay particular attention to how to protect against an attack to these targets.

- Switch stance when you are the least vulnerable to attack. For example, switch when you are outside of your opponent's reach. Or switch when you are very close to your opponent and you can keep him occupied with a vicious punch combination.

- Is it possible to switch stance without your opponent knowing it? Pay attention to how long it takes for your opponent to notice that you have switched stance.

Switching stance through a kick

- Most kicks lend themselves to switching stance while throwing a technique. For example, throw a round house kick with your rear leg and, after impacting the target, set your foot down forward in the opposite stance. If you are uncomfortable with fighting from a right stance, throw another technique and switch back to a left stance.

- Be careful not to telegraph the move when switching stance, or your opponent can counter-strike when you are the most vulnerable: when your centerline is exposed due to the step required to switch stance.

- The switch should not be isolated, but should happen as a result of throwing a technique.

- How can you distract your opponent's focus away from your legs? Try concealing the switch by throwing a multiple punch combination to his head.

Superior positioning

- Switching stance may enable you to gain a superior position to your opponent's outside (away from his centerline and toward the side from which he throws his lead techniques).

- When both you and your opponent are in left fighting stances, and you suddenly switch to a right stance, how does this affect your ability to strike different targets on your opponent? Which targets on yourself must you be careful to protect?

- If part of your body has been hit a lot and you switch stance to protect that part, it may jeopardize the other side of your body. If possible, never show your opponent that you are hurt.

EFFECTIVE COUNTER-STRIKING

Once you understand effective counter-striking, you can take kickboxing to a new level. Let's say that your opponent throws a lot of multiple jabs. You can use head movement to slip his jabs, but you can't slip constantly throughout a two-minute round and avoid getting hit. Nor will you score any points if you don't land any blows. You must now start thinking about counter-striking.

This section covers:

- Preparing for your opponent's counter-strike
- Eight ways to defend the jab
- How does an improper guard originate?
- Countering the counter
- Summary and review

PREPARING FOR YOUR OPPONENT'S COUNTER-STRIKE

When throwing the jab, you automatically leave an opening for your opponent's counter-strike. There are several ways that your opponent can counter your jab. For example:

He can pick it with his rear hand and counter with a jab to your jaw. Or he can catch it in his lead hand and counter with a rear cross over the top of your arm.

He can slip it and counter with a hook. Most fighters, when countering with a hook, throw it to the body.

He can counter with a front kick to the ribs underneath your extended arm.

When your opponent counters with a front kick, he will place most of his weight on his rear leg (this moves his upper body to the rear, making your jab short of reach), and kick with his lead leg to the open area at the ribs underneath your extended arm. Countering with a kick requires slightly better timing than countering with a strike. This type of counter is powerful, but it does have a tendency to keep your opponent at long range, where it is a bit more difficult for him to follow up.

Be aware of your opponent's most likely counter-strikes and train to respond appropriately. For ex-

184

ample, if there is some distance between you and your opponent, he will most likely counter with a long range technique. When throwing the jab, bring your free hand in front of your face as a check, and prepare to catch or pick your opponent's counter-strike.

If the distance is tighter and your opponent slips your jab and sets for his next strike by tilting his body to the side, he will most likely counter with a hook. As you pick up on this move, there are a number of things you can do to defend yourself:

Block the hook with your elbow and "counter the counter" with a hook to your opponent's jaw with your free hand.

If you are fast, you can beat your opponent to the punch by countering with a hook or rear cross underneath his punch, and before he throws his hook to your body.

Slip to the right and counter with a rear hook or cross underneath your opponent's jab.

You can also step back to create distance the moment your opponent sets for his counter-strike. He will now throw his strike and miss, placing himself in an inferior position. Ideally, you want to initiate your counter-strike before your opponent has fully retrieved his hand, and while there is still an opening at his jaw. Imagine your opponent's jab coming out, grabbing your hand, and pulling it back towards him, as you counter-strike.

Because the jab is such a versatile punch that can be used in attack, defense, or retreat, let's talk about some more ways in which you can defend and counter this strike.

EIGHT WAYS TO DEFEND THE JAB

1. **Catch the jab** in the palm of your hand by extending your hand slightly toward your opponent. This defense is rather easy, as long as you watch for the initiation of your opponent's jab in his upper body. Avoid looking directly at his hand. You must also prepare to defend against your opponent's follow-up strike; for example, a second jab, rear cross, front kick, or round house kick. The benefit of the catch is that it tends to stop your opponent's forward momentum, disturb his balance, and offset his timing.

Catch the jab in the palm of your hand.

2. **Redirect the jab** by parrying it, preferably with your rear hand. This places you to the outside of your opponent and eliminates the use of his rear hand. If your opponent has a lot of momentum behind the jab, he is likely to be off balance forward and will end up in close quarter range. You can now counter with a lead hook to his head, or with a lead leg round house kick to his mid-section.

Redirect the jab with your rear hand. Follow with a lead hook or lead leg round house kick.

3. **Trap and redirect the jab** with your lead hand by coming over the top of your opponent's hand. This exposes targets on his side and head. The rear cross is a good follow-up.

Trap and redirect the jab, and counter with a rear cross.

4. **The vertical forearm block** can be used both against jabs, rear crosses, and hooks. Watch your opponent's shoulder for the initiation of a strike. Do not reach for the strike, as this may tempt him to fake to create an opening, and then throw a hook around your now extended guard. The forearm block should be short and snappy. When moving your forearm across your centerline and to your opposite shoulder, you will momentarily expose the side of your head. You must therefore move your arm back to the point of origin as soon as possible after blocking.

Block the punch with a vertical forearm block. This is similar in principle to the parry, with your body perpendicular to your opponent.

5. Another forearm block that is effective but not seen as often is the **double vertical forearm block**. When your opponent throws his jab, bring both of your forearms together vertically in front of your face. This creates a barrier that your opponent's strikes must penetrate. The double vertical forearm block is a very strong technique that works best if you extend your arms slightly to meet your opponent's strike. If your opponent throws multiple jabs, once you have gotten his timing down, you can step forward and jam his jab with the double forearm block.

Block with the double vertical forearm block. This is similar to the catch, where you meet power with power.

6. **Slip the jab**, preferably to the outside (away from your opponent's centerline). This places you in a superior position, allowing you to counter with a hook or rear cross. Be aware of your opponent's counter-strikes when he realizes that he missed with the jab. If you slip toward your opponent's centerline, be ready to defend against his rear cross.

7. **Duck the jab** by bending at the knees and lowering your body straight down. Simultaneously strike to the opening at your opponent's mid-section. Lowering your upper body at a slight diagonal angle forward increases the momentum and power of your strike. This assumes that your opponent throws a jab to your head. Although the head is the most sought after target, a crafty opponent will jab low to the body as well. A low jab can be defended with an elbow block.

8. **Fade with the jab** by moving your upper body slightly to the rear. This increases distance, allowing you to add body momentum to your counter-punch. Be aware of your opponent's attempts to throw a second jab or rear cross when the first one misses. Be careful not to come forward and into his follow-up punch.

Fade to the rear and counter when your body comes forward.

HOW DOES AN IMPROPER GUARD ORIGINATE?

You can't win by using defense alone, and you know beforehand that you will get countered. A skilled counter-puncher is most likely to strike a fraction of a second after you strike, because this is when you automatically leave an opening. Your opponent is also likely to strike in the slight pause between your combinations, when his mind shifts from defense to offense.

You can cover many of your openings by using a proper guard. In between punch combinations, keep both hands in the high guard position, and return them to the point of origin as soon as you have thrown a strike. Fighters often tend to get lazy with their guard and carry it low, particularly the rear hand. This is especially prevalent whenever the fighter throws the jab. He keeps the right hand high when at long range evaluating the situation. But when he throws the jab, he drops his right hand slightly low to a position in front of the face or to the side of the body.

Many fighters tend to drop the rear hand slightly low when throwing the jab.

One reason for dropping the guard is because the fighter carries his elbows behind his body. Whenever he throws the jab and pivots his upper body, the elbow of the non-punching hand automatically drops to the rear, dropping the hand and exposing the jaw. Make a conscious effort to keep your elbows in front of your body.

Note how the guard automatically drops when the elbows are carried behind the body.

You can also keep your rear hand against your cheek as a reminder that it is high. Any time you don't feel the pressure of your hand against your cheek, you know that you have accidentally dropped your hand low, and that you need to bring it back up to the high guard position.

When throwing multiple jabs, we also tend to drop the lead hand low. This is mostly because the fighter points his elbow to the outside when retrieving the jabbing arm. This exposes the ribs and results in dropping that hand low. When your elbow rotates to the

outside, your hand will automatically drop to a level below the chin. When throwing multiple jabs, ensure that your elbow comes straight back, and that you pivot your upper body with each jab.

Note how the guard automatically drops when the elbows are extended away from the body.

It is equally important to keep your guard high when striking to the body. Keep the elbow of the non-punching hand close to your body, and bring your punching hand back to the high guard position as soon as you have landed the strike.

To increase the speed with which you bring your hands back to the guard position, imagine a strong rubber band tied from your shoulder to your wrist. When your arm is fully extended, the rubber band is also fully extended with a great deal of tension on it. Allow the imaginary rubber band to help you retrieve your hand with speed to the high guard position.

Most of us are not aware of that we carry our guard low until we take one of our opponent's punches or kicks to the head. As little as an inch in vertical drop in your hands may mean the difference between safety and a knockout.

COUNTERING THE COUNTER

Once you have learned effective counter-striking and defense, it is time to take the fight to a new level. If you know beforehand what to expect, you can counter the counter. In short, this means that you always stay one step ahead of your opponent, ready to follow-up off of either your own or your opponent's strikes. When throwing combinations, think of every move as part of the combination. Don't let a slip or bob and weave offset your momentum and make you pause. Most fighters get tense when they see their opponent's punch coming toward them. But to be an effective counter-striker or defender, you must eliminate this tendency to freeze. Don't try to avoid your opponent's strikes. Acquire the mind-set that your defense "comes by itself," while you continue with offense.

It is also important to vary your rhythm. For example, bob and weave at a slightly faster speed than you throw your strikes. This keeps your opponent from timing his counter-strike to your defensive move. You should also speed up or slow down your strikes depending on the situation. Be careful not to sacrifice power or technique for speed.

Since the rear cross is a sequel to the jab, you know that you can expect it whenever your opponent throws a jab. It is therefore not enough to defend the jab and counter-strike. You must now go one step further and think about how to counter your opponent's counter-strike. This is where fighting becomes mentally challenging. We will look at how to "play chess" with your opponent in more detail in Section 10.

Summary and review

The counter-strike is an important defensive/offensive move with a high success rate. When your opponent throws a strike, it is not enough to block or slip it, as this only accomplishes half of your objective. Defense, by itself, does not win the fight, and one of the best times to land your offense is with the counter-strike. The counter-strike also gives you a mental advantage by establishing an aggressive mind-set and posing a threat.

Mitt work with defense and counter-striking

- Have your partner hold a focus mitt in his right hand, while jabbing you with his gloved left hand. Block or parry the jab, and counter-strike to the focus mitt. The beat between parry and counter-strike should be very short.

- Practice parrying and counter-striking with both your left and right hand. For example, parry with your right and counter with your left, or parry with your left and counter with your right. You can also counter with the same hand that is parrying, but this requires a slightly longer beat between parry and counter.

- Practice slipping your opponent's jabs and countering to the focus mitt. Is it easier to counter off of a block or off of a slip? Why?

Mitt work with defense and counter-kicking

- Repeat the exercise above, but counter with a kick instead of a strike. Experiment with low, medium, and high kicks. Keep your balance forward and project the power of your kick into the target.

- Counter with a strike followed by a kick. How can you transition smoothly between strike and kick?

Counter-striking partner practice

- Have your partner throw kicks that you block and counter. Try to land your counter-strike while your opponent is in an inferior position on one leg. His foundation is now narrow, and he is unable to move out of the way until the motion of his kick is complete.

- Move to close range with your counter-strike. Since your opponent is pre-occupied with blocking or with regaining his balance, you get the opportunity to close distance and throw a hook or uppercut combination.

- How can you mix strikes and kicks from close range? The round house kick with the shin lends itself to the shorter distance.

Evasion and counter-striking

- Practice an evasive move in conjunction with your counter-strike. When your opponent jabs, parry and pivot off the attack line. Throw a strike from your superior position to the side.

- When you have parried and pivoted off the attack line, throw a round house kick to your opponent's mid-section, taking two targets simultaneously: his ribs with your instep, and his solar plexus with your shin.

Take two targets by throwing a round house kick with the shin from a side angle.

- Throw a high counter-kick to your opponent's jaw from an off angle to the side. A front kick, for example, can easily go between his guard.

Countering strike and kick combinations

- Have your partner throw a combination of strikes and kicks. Practice parrying or blocking the strikes until your opponent wears himself out. Note that most fighters don't throw combinations in excess of five or six strikes.

- Have your opponent's last strike trigger your counter-strike. Counter with a combination, driving forward with each strike.

Quick footwork and counter-striking

- Have your partner throw a jab. Execute a parry or quick slap to his hand, simultaneously using quick footwork to move off the attack line.

- Note whether this frustrates your opponent. Move in and strike when his focus is split.

- Repeat the parry and quick footwork, countering with a kick from a side angle. Throw a front or side thrust kick to your opponent's ribs.

Parry and pivot off the attack line. Throw a side thrust kick to the ribs.

LONG RANGE KICKING

Since the hands are faster and more precise than the feet, we tend to rely on our hands and neglect kicking. But since we are kickboxers, we must make a conscious effort to kick. Some competitions also penalize you for failing to meet the minimum kick requirement. As you start implementing kicks with your hand combinations, you will find one or two kicks that are comfortable to throw at any given time, while all other kicks seem awkward for that particular combination. The front kick, for example, is awkward in close quarters right after a hook or an uppercut. And the side thrust kick may turn your body to an inferior position (with your back partly toward your opponent) and slow your follow-up technique. The round house kick, on the other hand, can be thrown effectively from both long and close range, and in conjunction with most hand combinations. The way your body is positioned in the stance also lends itself better to the round house kick than to any other kick. Much of this section is therefore devoted to long range kicking with the round house kick.

I have yet to meet a kickboxer who does not use the round house kick extensively. The round house kick is a fundamental building block that you should place at the top of the priority ladder. Without the round house kick, you limit your effectiveness severely.

The advantage of kicking is that the legs are longer than the arms, allowing you to keep an opponent at a distance. The disadvantage is that the legs are slower, not as precise, and require more energy. The best long range fighters are proficient with both punches and kicks, and can switch from one to the other during the course of the fight.

This section covers:

- Mixing it up
- In the gym
- The power of the lead leg round house kick
- Third arm concept
- Adding circular to linear
- Glove-up with Keith
- Summary and review

MIXING IT UP

Many kickboxers isolate their kicks (separate them from the rest of the technique), pausing slightly before and after the kick, or they use the kick to initiate a hand combination. The reasons for this are:

1. It is easier to isolate the kick than to blend it in with the rest of the technique. Because **kicking takes more effort than striking** and the feet are not as precise as the hands, you need slightly more time to prepare.

2. A kick is usually considered a long range technique and is therefore thrown from the outside either to keep an opponent at a distance, or as a set-up in an attempt to get to the inside. It is therefore **more difficult to find a useful range** for kicks in conjunction with punches.

It is okay to isolate a kick if used for a greater purpose, as when faking. For example, if your opponent drops his guard when he sees the kick, you have created an opening high for your strikes.

When you isolate the kick, you also risk telegraphing it and giving your opponent the opportunity to defend against it. Because kicks require more movement and take longer to throw than punches, you must set them up with some other technique. For a kick to be truly effective, you should blend it in with your hand combination.

The round house kick is the easiest kick to set up with a jab, for the simple reason that you can throw it comfortably from any range and within most hand combinations. The front kick is also rather easy to set up, because both the jab and the kick are linear and acting in the same direction. The side thrust kick takes a little more effort, because you must first line up your hips properly. It is therefore especially important to use a set-up before throwing the side thrust kick. Many fighters also like to take a step with their lead foot laterally toward their centerline to line up the hips with the attack line. You can conceal the step with a jab.

The sophisticated kicks, such as the spinning back kick, outside crescent kick, axe kick, and spinning heel kick are more difficult to blend with a hand combination. Such kicks usually offset your rhythm, slow you down, or allow your opponent time to move out of range. You should therefore use these kicks conservatively and always with a proper set-up. With practice, however, these kicks can become an important part of your fight game. Some of the more sophisticated kicks are incredibly powerful and can be devastating when thrown at the proper time.

IN THE GYM

Throw kicks the way you throw strikes: in combinations. Don't throw just one strike or kick at a time. It's combinations that win the fight. Also, work on alternating hands and feet, eliminating the beat between strikes and kicks. As soon as one foot plants on the floor, the other should already be on its way out. Speed it up! Don't hesitate when you see the opening. Remember that you are in charge of the fight. What if the distance isn't right? Either don't throw the kick, or adjust the distance. If you're in close with your opponent, you can throw the round house kick with your shin instead of your instep.

When throwing the rear leg round house kick, your opponent can counter to your centerline. Why? Maybe you don't pivot all the way when throwing the kick, leaving your centerline open. Or maybe the kick is too slow and your opponent sees it coming. I think you're telegraphing the kick by isolating it. Try to conceal it within a combination. Or maybe the problem is not in you at all. Maybe your kick is perfect, and the problem is that your opponent simply is in the habit of countering it. If you can use the kick as a fake, you can draw a counter-strike from your opponent and create an opening in his defense.

Why did that round house kick miss your opponent? Because you jabbed, and your opponent moved back, so you didn't have the reach. You should have thrown a side thrust kick instead.

When blending kicks in with hand combinations, choose a four- or five-punch combo and work your kicks in somewhere in the middle. This teaches you about distance, angle, fluidity, power, and balance.

THE POWER OF THE LEAD LEG ROUND HOUSE KICK

We often use the lead leg as a set-up for our stronger rear techniques. The lead leg is less powerful than the rear leg because it has less distance to travel for building momentum. Many fighters also feel that the lead leg seems less flexible because of its position. This may be because, when throwing the kick, your upper body is forward of your foundation (your rear leg). To maintain balance when throwing a lead leg kick, you must first center your upper body above your supporting leg.

When throwing a kick with your lead leg, you must move your upper body back and above your rear leg for balance.

Since centering your upper body above your supporting leg requires a slight move of your upper body to the rear, the kick often seems short of reach, which can give the feeling of power loss or flexibility loss. A more effective way is to center your supporting leg under your upper body. You do this by taking a small step forward with your rear foot. The kick now has good reach with greater ease of movement.

Taking a step forward with your rear foot prior to throwing the lead kick, gives you better reach and power.

Since the step may telegraph the kick, it is especially important to use some kind of set-up. The step should be very short and quick, and synchronized with the kick into one move. Even if your opponent sees the kick coming, there should not be enough time for him to move out of range.

When throwing the lead leg round house kick multiple times, we tend to set our foot down wide in a neutral (or nearly neutral) stance, exposing our centerline. This could be a result of low flexibility in the hips, where you feel that your kick lacks power if thrown from a sideways stance. But if you pull your leg back to a square stance, your opponent can time his counter-strike to the opening on your centerline. When practicing the lead leg round house kick, stay in a good sideways stance, even at the expense of losing power.

Changing the angle at which you are facing your opponent might help you throw the lead leg kick easier. In order to do this, you might have to take an extra

step back with your lead foot to a square stance to create a better angle, or forward with your rear foot (also to a square stance). The problem is that an experienced opponent will see the step and take advantage of a time when you are either slightly off balance or leaving your centerline open. But there are ways that you can turn the weakness of your lead leg round house kick into a strength. If you know that you can create an angle from which you can comfortably throw this kick, try to find a way to conceal your step. One of the easiest ways is with a jab. First, throw the jab. Then, initiate a step with your rear foot *as the jab starts on its way back*. Bring your free hand in front of your face as a check against any counter-blows. You should now be set to follow with your lead leg round house kick.

Throw the jab.

Step as you retrieve the jab.

Throw the lead leg round house kick.

Do not retrieve the jab and *then* step. You must step *before* you bring your hand back to the guard position. This ensures that your opponent is still thinking about your jab, while you are stepping into position to throw the kick.

THIRD ARM CONCEPT

Since your lead leg is closer to your opponent and faster than your rear leg, you should think of it as a "third arm." Although, in daily life, you may use your feet for little more than walking, when fighting, your legs become powerful weapons with the ability to create openings and shift your opponent's focus from your upper to your lower body. Stay as versatile as possible, and avoid becoming obsessed with using only your hands. Use your lead leg much in the same way as you use your lead arm:

1. **To set** your opponent up.

2. **To gauge** the distance to your target, so that you can follow with a more powerful rear technique.

Your feet are also excellent for distracting your opponent and splitting his mind and body focus. When both of your hands are busy, think of your legs as extra arms and use them to work your opponent's lower body.

Try these exercises on the **THIRD ARM CONCEPT**:

Exercise 1

Overwhelm your opponent with punches to get him to focus on your upper body. When he gets in tune with your rhythm and blocks most of what you throw, attack his lower body with your legs. This will split his focus.

Exercise 2

Remember that more is not necessarily better, unless you know how to use that "more" effectively. Work on blending your leg movements in with your arm movements, so that your legs become part of the whole, allowing them to function as additional arms.

ADDING CIRCULAR TO LINEAR

You increase the power in your kicks by staying relaxed which, in turn, allows you to place the full weight of your body behind the kicks in one synchronized motion. We tend to emphasize keeping our guard high at all times; however, as your experience grows, you may need to relax your arms a little in order to create more momentum for your kicks. Because of the circular path of the round house kick, when throwing this kick, you must allow your hip and upper body to pivot all the way through the circle until impacting with the target. When stepping or jumping with the round house kick, synchronize the step or jump with the circular motion, so that there is no separation between the different components of the kick.

You can also increase the power in your kicks by adding circular movement to linear movement. A common example is the spinning back kick, which gets its momentum (and therefore power) from the rotation of your body. **But the kick itself must be thrown straight at the moment of impact, or the power will split in different directions.** The round house kick also uses the circular-linear concept, but in a less obvious way. To apply this concept to the rear leg round house kick, think in the following terms:

Start the kick with **linear motion** by stepping to a forty-five degree angle forward with your lead foot in the direction of line 1. As you step, pivot your lead foot to a forty-five degree angle outward (**circular motion**).

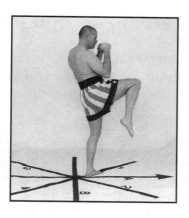

Bring your rear knee up straight along centerline A (**linear motion**).

Rotate your hips toward your centerline (**circular motion**), simultaneously pivoting your supporting foot in the direction of centerline B.

Extend your leg at the knee along centerline A (**linear motion**).

Bring your kick through the target by rotating your hips and supporting foot in the direction of line 3 (**circular motion**).

Glove Up with Keith

It's time you start analyzing your sparring sessions. What are your strengths and weaknesses? If all you can think of are the bruises and sore ribs, the sparring has become useless. Look at it objectively and see what can be done. When you're driving home after a workout, think about what you did well and what you need to work on. Maybe your opponent's kicks are getting in time and time again. So, why is that? Well, maybe you don't see the kicks coming. Or maybe you don't see them as a threat, so you get in the habit of ignoring them. But you must remember that you are not training for your buddies in the gym. You are training for this fighter who wants to win as badly as you do, and if you fail to block one of his kicks, it could mean the end of the fight.

Or maybe you notice that your arm got tired when you jabbed a lot. Ask yourself why. Maybe you are in an occupation that is physical, and you were tired from work. Or you could be tensing when throwing the jab. But if you get tired after three rounds in training, then how can you go six rounds in competition?

Either way, you need to analyze what you did well and what you did badly, and then work to correct those things. A skilled fighter doesn't make corrections after the fight. A skilled fighter can find his faults while fighting and adapt within the round. I would suggest that you write down your strengths and weaknesses after every sparring session, so that they become more concrete. Then, work actively to improve them.

Summary and review

Most of us favor one side of our body over the other. Likewise, most of us favor our hands over our feet. But since the legs are capable of being extremely destructive, we should try to implement them in our strategy as much as possible. In fact, you should use your legs as if they were extra arms. With enough training and conscious effort, this will become second nature.

Third arm concept bag work practice

- Start by going one round on the heavy bag, throwing a good mix of strikes and kicks, but without making a conscious effort to throw any particular technique. Work what comes naturally.

- Have your partner keep track of approximately how many kicks you throw in comparison to strikes. Next round, make an effort to throw twice as many kicks. For example, if you threw one-hundred punches and twenty kicks in the first round, then throw forty kicks in the next round, regardless of how many punches you throw.

- Have your partner call out "kick" approximately once for every four punches. Respond to his command with a kick that flows naturally within your punch combination.

- Pretend that you have only one arm, and that you have to use your kicks predominantly. This might be similar to how you would feel if you had hurt one arm and couldn't use it.

Long range kicking sparring practice

- Engage in light contact sparring with your partner. Have him throw only punches while you throw only kicks.

- Time your kicks to the openings in your opponent's defense. How can you position to use your longer reaching legs as defense against his strikes?

- Pretend that you have no arms, and experiment with moving out of the way and countering with a kick before your opponent has a chance to strike.

- Try to achieve a healthy mix of strikes and kicks. Pay attention to how you can flow from one to the other. How can you use your strikes to set up the correct distance for your kicks?

KICKING STRATEGY

An effective kicker does not throw his kicks half-heartedly. When you hesitate, your opponent can easily defeat your kick. When you indicate that you are going to kick, yet hesitate in the execution of the technique, your opponent can take advantage of the extra time you are giving him. He can now close distance, placing you at a range where you are less comfortable. If you prefer long range fighting, you must do whatever you can to keep your opponent from closing distance. Keeping an aggressive opponent at long range takes precision timing. As little as an inch too close can mean the difference between superiority in fighting and an ineffective technique.

A skilled kickboxer thinks of the follow-up. But if you are in a hurry to punch after your kick has landed, you may sacrifice balance and power as a result. Because the feet are in general slower and not as precise as the hands, you must ensure that you have a firm base, and that you are not on one foot or up on your toes when reverting back to the hand combination.

Although the round house kick is the most frequently used kick in kickboxing, it is also the easiest kick to defend against. In most traditional martial arts, the round house kick is frequently used as a high kick to the head, but it can be equally effective to the legs or to the body. Because it takes less effort to throw a low kick, it is easy to build speed in the technique, even when you are tired. This extra speed makes the kick more difficult to time and defend against. Your opponent's legs are therefore the easiest targets to round house kick. A kickboxer must have strong legs and a solid stance, and after taking a few of these kicks, your opponent will have difficulty moving.

When kicking to the body, be careful not to kick your opponent's elbows, which are devastating blocking/striking weapons. You can throw the round house kick to the body after stepping off the angle to the side, as your opponent is extending his arm to punch.

This section covers:

- Seven ways to defend and counter the round house kick
- First touch concept
- Throwing and defending the front kick
- Six strategic ways to use the side thrust kick
- Setting up a kick with a kick
- Thoughts on kicking
- Summary and review

SEVEN WAYS TO DEFEND AND COUNTER THE ROUND HOUSE KICK

1. **Block the kick with your elbow or arm.** Blocking with the elbow is best because of the damage you can inflict. If blocking with the arm, try blocking with the upper portion of the arm. As long as you keep your elbows tight to your body, you have little to fear, where even the most devastating round house kick is unlikely to do significant damage. If you block with the lower portion of the arm, a very powerful kick could break your arm. Moving in and countering while your opponent is on one leg is usually a good move.

Block a round house kick with the elbow or upper arm.

2. **If the round house kick is thrown to the head, you can block it with an outside forearm block**. Be aware that a good kicker allows his foot to wrap around to the back of the head or neck area. Your block must therefore cover the whole side of your head. Simultaneously, tuck your chin down behind your shoulder.

Use the outside forearm block to block a high kick.

3. The problem with blocking is that it momentarily freezes your weapons, so that you can't counter-strike until the block is complete. **An alternative to blocking the round house kick is to jam it and counter-strike**, to pivot off the attack line, or to use other movement to avoid the kick.

Jam the kick and counter-strike.

4. **Defend the round house kick by moving in.** Shuffle forward to close distance before the kick is fully extended. You will still take the kick on your arm, but most of the power will be eliminated. Because the knee joint only works one way, by moving forward, you can keep the kick from wrapping around your body. Your opponent will kick behind you.

Move in against the natural movement of the knee joint.

5. When moving in to jam the kick, **your effectiveness as a fighter increases if you can simultaneously throw a counter-strike.** This can be either a straight right to your opponent's mid-section (with the effect of knocking the wind out of him), or a straight right to your opponent's chest or head (with the effect of knocking him back or out). Countering with a punch allows you to keep your full foundation. You can also counter with a round house kick to your opponent's supporting leg. This works especially well if your opponent is in the habit of throwing a lot of round house kicks mid- or head level.

Counter with a round house kick to the supporting leg.

6. **You can also step back at the initiation of your opponent's kick.** Because your opponent is unable to move forward until the motion of the kick is complete, stepping to a safe distance helps you regroup for a counter-attack. However, this is perhaps the least desirable method of defense, because you cannot strike your opponent until you have again stepped forward to close distance. Unless your timing and footwork are very fast, this technique is more time consuming than blocking and countering, or jamming and countering.

Step to long range and allow the kick to miss.

7. If your opponent is in the habit of round house kicking to the head, or if you can pick up on the move early enough, **you can duck or bob and weave under the kick.** This requires better timing. Always think of the counter-strike. When ducking a kick, a good counter is a straight punch to your opponent's mid-section, while he is still on one leg.

Duck and counter to the mid-section.

FIRST TOUCH CONCEPT

Counter-striking is most effective when done within the motion of an evasive move. This way you not only avoid your opponent's kick, you also speed up your counter-strike by striking while the motion of your opponent's kick is not yet completed. If you choose to block the kick, you can counter with either the same hand that is blocking, or with the opposite hand. Countering with the same hand takes slightly longer, but allows you to use the concept of *first touch* to trigger your counter-strike. Think of it as your hand "bouncing" off of your opponent's kick.

Let's say that your opponent throws a round house kick that you block with your right elbow. As soon as you feel the kick hit your arm, you know that the energy has already dispersed into the block. You can now throw a rear cross to his face, preferably before he has replanted his kicking foot. Or you can counter with your opposite hand, again using first touch to trigger your counter-strike. You can also counter with a kick.

If countering with a kick, the best target is the legs, as they are almost a given. Whenever your opponent kicks, his supporting leg is his only foundation, and he can't move until the motion of his kick is complete. Always think of the follow-up. Again, be careful not to isolate the kick. If you throw a round house kick, you can easily follow with a punch combination as soon as your foot plants. If you throw a front or side thrust kick, you may need to wait for your opponent's reaction, and then follow with either another linear attack as he comes forward, or step off the angle and counter with a punch combination.

The best time to counter is when your opponent is on one leg, or when his kick is "in the process," and he is unable to move out of the way. Do not give your opponent the opportunity to regain balance or superior positioning.

Try this exercise on the **FIRST TOUCH CONCEPT**:

Exercise 1

Use first touch as a signal to counter-strike. The moment your block touches your opponent's punch or kick, immediately throw your counter-strike or kick. First, try countering with the same hand or leg you used for blocking. Then, try countering with the opposite hand or leg. For example:

1. Block a round house kick to your rear leg with a **rear outside shin block**, and use that same leg to counter with a **front kick** to your opponent's gut.

2. Block a round house kick to your lead leg with a **lead outside shin block**, shuffle forward and counter with a **rear cross** to your opponent's jaw.

THROWING AND DEFENDING THE FRONT KICK

The front kick is a little more difficult to defend than the round house kick, because it is a linear attack and impact is usually more devastating. The best time to throw the front kick is when your opponent is moving toward you and into the kick's path of power. Another good time is when he is extending an arm to punch. Because your front kick has longer reach than your opponent's arm, you can score with this technique if you incline your body slightly to the rear as the punch comes toward you. Now, extend your leg and kick to the open area at your opponent's ribs. If your opponent's punch is committed, he will tend to move forward for more penetrating force. If your timing is good, this increases the effectiveness of the kick, setting your opponent back, knocking him off balance, or knocking the wind out of him.

Throw the front kick under your opponent's extended arm.

Defend the front kick with a downward elbow block. Aim your elbow at your opponent's toes, and block the kick with the tip of your elbow. Since his toes will be curled back, the block will have devastating results, either jamming or breaking his toes. You can also block front kicks with your forearm or with your shin by raising your knee high.

Use the elbow (left) or shin (right) to block a front kick.

As stated earlier, there should be no need to block high against a front kick thrown to the head. Because the front kick must first pass the body on its way to the head, all front kicks should be blocked and countered prior to reaching head level. When front kicking to the head, the aim is usually the chin. If the kick lands, it could have devastating results.

A front kick to the chin can knock your opponent out.

SIX STRATEGIC WAYS TO USE THE SIDE THRUST KICK

1. The side thrust kick is usually thrown to the body, but can be thrown to the head. **If you kick to the body, your opponent's reaction will differ depending on your specific target.** For example, if you kick to the mid-section, he will crunch up or get the wind knocked out of him. If you kick to the chest, he is likely to lose balance to the rear. If you kick higher to the head, he may also lose balance, or, if the kick is accurate, you can score a knockout.

2. Block side thrust kicks to the body with your forearms or elbows. Blocking with the elbow takes greater precision, but is more devastating to your opponent. **Also try side-stepping the attack and countering from an angle**.

3. Because of the way your hips are positioned when throwing the side thrust kick, it takes slightly longer to reset your body after landing the kick. When your opponent kicks, you can take advantage of him by **countering with a strike or kick while he is in the process of resetting his body**.

4. The side thrust kick is most effective whenever your opponent moves toward the outside of your body (toward your back). Because of the alignment of your hips with the attack line, the kick is difficult to throw if your opponent moves toward your centerline. When throwing the side thrust kick, **observe which direction your opponent moves, and use the kick whenever he is moving toward your back**. He is now moving into the kick's path of power. If your opponent moves toward your centerline instead, it is better to throw the rear leg round house kick.

Throw the side thrust kick when your opponent moves toward your back (top). Throw the rear round house kick when your opponent moves toward your centerline (bottom).

5. If stepping prior to throwing the side thrust kick, you can **throw it as a distance closer**, especially if you have already thrown some other technique that has set your opponent back. The stepping side thrust kick is a quick and devastating move that is difficult to defend against, especially when fighting in a confined area (a ring).

6. If your opponent is with his back against the ropes of the ring, you can use the side thrust kick to keep him there. When you have worked him over with an inside combination and start stepping back to the center of the ring, he is likely to come forward and try to counter. As your opponent steps forward, **time the side thrust kick so that the power of the kick meets his forward momentum**. You have now knocked him back against the ropes again, which buys you time to move out or step in with a hand combination. A double side thrust kick is also great against an opponent who has already been hit once and who is stunned by the first kick.

Throw a close range combination and step back to finish with the side thrust kick.

SETTING UP A KICK WITH A KICK

The most common way to set up a kick is with the jab. But you can also set up a kick with a kick. A properly thrown kick is initiated by raising your knee high before starting to turn your hips. This keeps your opponent from guessing which kick that is coming. With your knee high, you can now throw any of the three basic kicks: round house, front kick, or side thrust kick. Because all these kicks start from the knee high position, the side thrust kick, for example, can be set up with the round house kick.

The knee high position looks identical for any of the three basic kicks.

Try this exercise on **SETTING UP THE FRONT AND SIDE THRUST KICK**:

Exercise 2

Start by throwing the lead leg round house kick a few times. Since the round house kick strikes from the side, once your opponent gets in the habit of defending against it, he is likely to leave an opening along his centerline. Once you have trained your opponent to block the round house kick, you can land a front or side thrust kick to his mid-section. As long as you bring your knee up high prior to kicking, the specific kick you throw will be concealed by the position of your knee.

THOUGHTS ON KICKING

There is more to kicking than what can be learned from kicking a stationary target, and you should practice kicks meticulously in sparring. Speed, timing, correct choice of target, defense . . . all need to be mastered. Limiting your practice to power kicking on the heavy bag may instill a false sense of confidence. It's an entirely different ball game when up against another fighter who wants to score as badly as you do. Successful long range kicking also requires stamina.

Long range kicks are great when used as counter-techniques against your opponent's kicks or hand techniques:

1. When you have landed a kick, **return the kicking foot to your stance as soon as possible**. Failing to withdraw the leg (setting your foot down straight in front of your opponent, or letting it stick to the target) allows your opponent to take advantage of you, either by disrupting your balance, kicking your supporting leg, or catching your kicking leg (if this is allowed).

2. If your opponent has a traditional martial arts background, or is in the habit of throwing a lot of fancy spinning kicks, he is likely to drop his guard or become careless with covering his openings. This allows you to **take advantage of the open target on his head**. This may be a good time to use a high side thrust, round house, or front kick.

3. If you can **disrupt your opponent's balance so that he falls**, you will not only score points, you will also make him winded. A tired fighter needs a great deal of energy to get back to his feet. In competition, falling in front of a large audience may also disturb the fighter mentally. You have now taken his focus. If you can get him to fall again within the same round, he is likely to become cautious with executing his techniques.

4. If your opponent throws a lot of kicks to your lead leg, **stay light on your lead foot and go with the motion of your opponent's kick**. You can now use the momentum your opponent has created to throw a side thrust kick while he is still on one leg.

Go with the motion of your opponent's kick, using his momentum to set your side kick in motion.

5. High and fancy kicks can look frightening, but they are often easier to defend against than low kicks. High kicks take more energy to throw than low kicks, so your opponent will wear himself out faster. High kicks are also easier to see than low kicks, and there is a **sure target on your opponent's supporting leg any time he kicks high**.

6. Ultimately, you want to **use your feet as if they were hands**. Instead of having two weapons that are limited to striking medium and high targets, you now have four weapons that can strike low, medium, and high targets on both sides of your opponent's body. When you get so comfortable using kicks that you can easily blend them in with a hand combination, your possible moves are almost unlimited. The jab is similar in concept and motion to a lead leg front kick, the rear cross is similar to a rear leg front kick, and hooks are similar to round house kicks. You can now use your kicks deceptively as if they were hands. For example, throw a jab followed by a rear cross. Then, throw a jab followed by a rear leg front kick.

Summary and review

The first touch concept uses your opponent's strike or kick to trigger your counter-attack. This works because many fighters have a tendency to freeze momentarily simultaneous to blocking. The quicker you throw your counter-strike, the less time you give your opponent to follow up off of his initial attack. If you can fire a strike or kick almost at the exact moment you block your opponent's strike, you will take the lead in the fight. You will also create a threatening impression, making your opponent reluctant to strike again.

First touch concept partner drills

- Engage in light contact drills with your partner. Have him throw round house kicks to your upper arms. The moment you feel his kick impact your arm, fire a strike with your non-blocking hand. For example, if he kicks to your left side, throw a right cross; if he kicks to your right side, throw a jab, or move in and throw a hook.

- Listen to the beat between block and counter-strike. The shorter the beat, the more likely you are to land your counter-strike. However, the beat should not be so short that you start anticipating your opponent's kick. You must keep a solid guard until you have defended and it is time to fire back.

- Repeat the exercise, but counter with the same hand that is blocking. This is slightly slower than countering with the opposite hand.

- Allow your opponent's kick to make contact with your block first. If you anticipate the kick, you will get in the habit of countering before you have blocked, increasing the risk of him landing the kick on a valid target.

- Experiment with turning your body slightly in the direction of the block. This helps you set for the strike, increasing power through a longer distance.

Partner practice with shin blocks and first touch concept

- Have your partner throw round house kicks to your legs instead of to your arms. Block the kicks with shin blocks. Experiment with firing a counter-punch as soon as possible after blocking.

- Do not counter-punch while your foundation is narrow. Allow your foot to plant before countering, or you will contradict your body mechanics, starving the strike of power.

- To speed up your counter-punch, try blocking the kick with a shin block and setting that foot down slightly forward, so that distance between you and your opponent closes. This allows you to launch your counter-punch slightly before your foot has planted, relying on the forward momentum of your body to increase the power of the strike. Think of it as blocking and "falling" forward with the strike.

- Repeat the exercise, but throw a counter-kick instead of a strike. When you have blocked your opponent's kick with your shin, which counter-kick is easiest to throw? If you block with your lead leg, the fastest counter will be with your rear leg.

Distance practice and counter-kicking

- Experiment with front, round house, and side trust counter-kicks with your rear leg. Are any of these difficult to throw because of distance?

- When you block with your lead leg and set that foot back down, it becomes your foundation and your upper body must move forward with your rear leg kick. This might place you uncomfortably close to your opponent.

- Experiment with setting your blocking foot down at an angle to the side. As soon as you plant your lead foot, kick with your rear leg. How can you adjust your distance for optimum reach by planting your lead foot closer or farther from your centerline?

QUICK REFERENCE TO CONCEPTS

ATTACK LINE: This is a line created by linear movement between yourself and your opponent. When you are moving back in a straight line, it allows your opponent to attack more effectively. To thwart his linear attack, side-step or pivot off the attack line, forcing your opponent to readjust to your movement.

CHOOSING YOUR TARGETS: Since your opponent's reaction differs for each target you strike, it is important to choose your targets with care. Whenever possible, choose targets to create a specific effect which, in turn, determines your follow-up technique.

CIRCULAR TO LINEAR: You can increase the power in your kicks by adding circular movement to linear movement. One of the most common examples is the spinning back kick, which gets its momentum (and therefore power) from the rotation of your body. But the kick itself must be thrown straight at impact, or the power will split in different directions.

COUNTERING THE COUNTER: This means consistently staying one step ahead of your opponent. Some strikes naturally follow others, and you will see your opponent throwing the same combinations time and time again. Once you learn which strikes your opponent is likely to throw, you can plan your counter-strike, as well as your counter-strike to your opponent's counter-strike.

FIRST TOUCH CONCEPT: When your opponent kicks, use the moment you first touch (the moment his kick impacts your block) as a cue to counter-strike to the opening.

HALF-STEPPING: By taking a step back with your rear foot only, you will create the illusion that you have increased distance, luring your opponent to come forward and into your strike.

LATERAL MOVEMENT: Taking up a position slightly to one side of your opponent's centerline, preferably toward his weak side or the side from which he throws his jab, helps you land your strikes without risk of getting struck back. Fighting from an angle is therefore considered superior positioning.

LEAVING A JAB BEHIND: Whenever you move back to long range or finish a combination, give your opponent something to think about. Leaving a jab behind gives you a strategic advantage, allowing you to move about relatively safely, without your opponent taking advantage of your retreat. It doesn't have to be a jab that you leave behind; you can also leave a kick behind. Ending with a punch or kick from whichever side of your body is forward allows you to reset your fighting stance or chamber for an additional strike with your strong rear hand.

THIRD ARM CONCEPT: A fighter must stay as versatile as possible and not become dependent on using his hands only. Think of your lead leg, which is faster and closer to your opponent than your rear leg, as a third arm, and use it according to the same principles as your lead hand: to set your opponent up, and to gauge distance for your more powerful rear techniques.

WORKING YOUR WAY OUT: When you have finished a combination on the inside and it is time to move back to long range, do so while throwing a strike or kick. Moving back without throwing anything gives your opponent the opportunity to strike you. It has been said that the best defense is offense. This is an opportunity to put that into practice.

SECTION FIVE
SHORT RANGE FIGHTING

ON THE INSIDE
by Keith Livingston

I spent most of my career in a unique but special place: on the inside. You see, I never had great hand speed or fancy footwork, but I could hit! I learned early to get in my opponent's chest, glue myself to his body, and make him taste hell. There's nothing quite like it. The pace is always fast and furious, with each fighter attempting to impose his will upon the other. Forget the finesse. Being on the inside is being in the trenches, no holds barred, head banging, body aching, bone crushing fun. The inside is where you either fall or rise to the occasion. It's pure and it's real, and I love it. Let's stand toe-to-toe and get it on.

The inside game is a battle of will, fortitude, and heart. It's only on the inside that you can smell, taste, and sense another man's fear in his sweat, breath, and eyes. One of my most memorable fights was with "Crazy" Ike Jenkins, a skilled kickboxer from St. Louis. Ike and I met for the first time in Las Vegas. You learn a lot about a man when you stand inches apart and trade blows, looking into each other's eyes, exploring each other's soul, and watching for the slightest hint of weakness. I know we both left that day with respect and admiration for each other.

I became addicted to this battle of will and attrition. It's difficult to explain; perhaps it's the whole pleasure/pain dichotomy. At times I would find myself growing stronger with each body punishing shot I absorbed. It was as though I would grow impervious to the pain and would actually look forward to the next blow, knowing that my opponent could sense the futility of his strikes. My rule was simple: If my opponent hit me, I retaliated with three of my own. If my opponent caused me pain, I caused him more pain. This simple rule sent a simple message: You cannot hurt me, and therefore you cannot beat me. Your most dangerous opponent is one who has no fear of dying. This way of thinking may seem extreme, but it is truly the warrior attitude.

WORKING YOUR WAY IN

Keith's Corner

I have often stated that an entire art form could be created around inside fighting. Many kickboxers with a traditional martial arts background completely ignore this aspect of fighting and concentrate solely on fighting at long range. I believe this leaves students ill prepared when they suddenly find themselves at close quarters.

Inside fighting takes you into a new realm comprised of hooks, uppercuts, leg kicks, knees, arm traps, and shoulder butts. You also learn defense at its very best. Additionally, inside fighting teaches you to move from long range to close range comfortably and with confidence. This is particularly beneficial if your opponent is superior at long range.

Many people would say that the bigger and stronger fighter controls the fight on the inside. I disagree. I feel that the fighter who has the ability to use distance and tactics to his advantage controls the fight both on the outside and on the inside. The simplest way to defeat your adversaries is to fight beyond their limitations. If your opponent has little knowledge of inside fighting and you exploit this limitation, the fight is over before it has even begun.

The tough inside fighter is difficult to beat.

This section covers:

- Thoughts on inside fighting
- Getting from here to there (how to close distance)
- In the gym
- Working your way in against a fighter with longer reach
- Mind and body focus
- Freezing your opponent's offensive weapons
- Distance in close quarters
- Protecting your centerline in close quarters
- Choosing your kick combinations when moving in
- Jamming your way to the inside
- Summary and review

THOUGHTS ON INSIDE FIGHTING

Keith's Knockout Advice

The inside is typically where you want to be against an opponent with longer reach, but this is only true if your opponent is superior at long range. Remember, the fighter who controls distance controls the fight. If you are controlling the inside game, then your opponent is obviously not controlling the outside game. Some fighters can be hit to the head all day without showing any sign of weakness. But if your opponent comes to the fight a little out of shape, a punishing body attack will tend to take his endurance quicker. A good strike to the liver, solar plexus, or spleen could win a fight quicker than a strike to the jaw.

We often think of safety in distance. But this is only true if you are more than an arm's or leg's reach away. There is also safety in closeness. When we get hurt, we tend to choose distance, to try to get away. This choice is not always appropriate because when you are hurt, it is only a matter of time before your opponent will attempt to knock you out. It is better to get close and try to eliminate your opponent's power strikes. You can also use closeness to tie him up, giving yourself time to recover.

The difference between the inside and outside is that the inside is a total power game, a seek and destroy kind of a game. A good inside fighter generally equates to a power fighter. On the outside, the jab is the dominant technique. It may therefore appear as though outside fighting is more strategic. But all the

principles that apply to outside fighting also apply to inside fighting. When you get to the inside with a good defensive fighter, you can't just punch away and hope to win. There has to be some method to your madness. You must vary your rhythm, timing, and strike patterns. For example, on the outside, you may jab high and throw a rear cross low. But on the inside, you may throw an uppercut to the head to open up the body. There are specific techniques which are more appropriate at close quarter range, such as hooks to the body, uppercuts, tight hooks to the head, short jabs and crosses, and overhand strikes. These inside techniques tend to favor power and allow for a better body attack. On the outside, you can land a lot of strikes to your opponent's centerline. But on the inside, you can be successful with both the center and sides of your opponent's body.

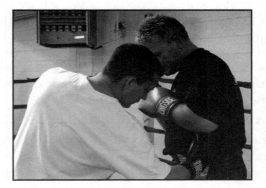

Close range fighting gives you potentially more targets than long range fighting.

GETTING FROM HERE TO THERE (HOW TO CLOSE DISTANCE)

It is now time to move from the out-fighting zone to the in-fighting zone, where you are very close to your opponent and many long range techniques are no longer effective. Once you get past your opponent's long range techniques, you have taken from him many of his weapons. Getting past this long range barrier and to the inside is perhaps the toughest part about inside fighting, and a threat that you must learn to deal with.

A common mistake when moving in is to be so concerned with getting there that you abandon your long range techniques, rush in, and take some good blows in the process. Don't let your emotions interfere. An angry fighter will harbor negative energy and lose focus. Few things will destroy a fighter faster than uncontrolled emotions.

> **The emotional fighter will forget most of his tactics. Exploding with a combination is not the same as rushing in thoughtlessly.**

Distance should be closed when your opponent is experiencing a moment of weakness; for example, right after you have successfully defended and countered his long range technique. You can also close distance methodically by taking small steps forward, slipping punches, weaving under hooks, and countering off your opponent's strikes. Start by throwing your outside techniques at a controlled pace, gradually speeding them up. Try a series of multiple jabs at a pace that is slightly faster than your opponent's. This will break his timing, making him more concerned with defense than offense.

You can further increase the speed of the jab by pivoting your lead foot only a minimum amount. You may find it even more beneficial not to pivot at all, but to push off with your rear foot by digging into the floor with the ball or inside knife edge of that foot.

> **If you throw a single jab, your opponent can pick up on your rhythm and time his counter-strikes to your openings. There is a difference between many single jabs and one multiple jab combination. Think about it!**

Try these exercises on **WORKING YOUR WAY IN:**

Exercise 1

When your opponent jabs, pick his jab with your lead hand, immediately throwing your rear cross over the top of his jab. Strike while there is still an opening at his head. Also duck his jab and counter with a rear cross to his mid-section. **Close distance while there is a weakness in your opponent's defense.**

Duck the jab and throw a rear cross to the mid-section, simultaneously taking a step forward. Note how your body should be slightly off the attack line to the side.

Exercise 2

Throw double jabs. When the second jab lands and your opponent's head snaps back, retrieve your hand while simultaneously shifting your weight to your lead foot. Your body is now slightly off the attack line and chambered to throw a lead hook to your opponent's solar plexus. **You have now closed distance by going from a long range technique to a short range technique.**

Jab and, when your opponent's head snaps back, throw a lead hook.

Exercise 3

Throw a jab and a rear cross. When you retrieve your hand from the rear cross, simultaneously shift your weight to your rear foot and off the attack line, and throw a rear hook to your opponent's ribs. **You have now closed distance by pivoting your body off the attack line and moving in with a short range technique.** Note how the distance between your lead and rear hook differs. If you are too far away for the rear hook, you may need to take an additional small step forward.

Set up a rear hook with a jab and a rear cross.

Once you have closed distance with the hook, make an effort to stay at close range until you have done some damage to your opponent. Shift your weight back to your lead leg again and throw a double lead hook, one low and one high. Taking different targets will break your opponent's focus. Remember to reset your body between these double strikes (like a door opening and closing). Be careful not to expose your centerline.

When you have landed a series of good blows and it is time to move back out, do so by using a pivot-step (pivoting ninety degrees and perpendicular to your opponent), or by using lateral movement. This creates both angle and distance, allowing you to follow with a long range combination.

Any time you feel that you are too close or too far away, or that the angle is not right, take small adjustment steps until you can throw your strikes with power and precision. Be dynamic. Pausing between steps and strikes allows your opponent to get in tune with your rhythm and block your strikes.

IN THE GYM

When fighting an opponent who has reach on you with a fast jab, your strategy should be to go to the inside. Be careful not to fight your opponent's game. When you get to the center of the ring, don't let your opponent dictate the fight. Work your way in methodically. Try catching your opponent's jab, then step forward and counter-strike. Since your opponent has reach on you, catching and countering without stepping forward will not land your strike.

We're going to start on the outside and work our way in. Keep your guard a little higher. Now, catch your opponent's jab. Make the catch forceful by meeting the strike as it comes toward you. Now that it is time for you to climb another step on the ladder, you must understand that everything you have learned is not absolute. For example, if a different stance works better, then use it. It's like we talked about the other day, about switching to a neutral or a right stance when throwing hooks on the inside. When fighting in sport kickboxing, we're going to take it as far as we can without breaking the rules.

Keep catching your opponent's jab and working your way in until you are within striking range. This also helps you destroy the range for an opponent with longer reach. Crowd him. You can also try playing with his hands. Hit his gloves and pull his hands out of the way to create an opening. Keep your glove attached to your opponent's and follow it around as he tries to strike you. This will frustrate him greatly. Then take advantage of the openings. Also be aware of the openings you may have created on yourself in the process.

WORKING YOUR WAY IN AGAINST A FIGHTER WITH LONGER REACH

Having long arms and legs is usually an advantage in kickboxing. But your long reach is only as good as you are at using it. You can exploit the strength of your opponent's longer reach by developing superior inside fighting techniques. Let's say that your opponent uses his jab extensively to keep you at a distance. In order to work your way in without getting hit, you must do at least one of the following:

1. **Slip the jab.** This allows you to close distance without disrupting your timing by blocking the strike.

2. **Use your longer reaching legs.** Once you land a kick, follow with additional strikes or kicks or you will be back to where you started, trying to defeat the jab on the outside. The kick serves as an "opener," and helps you get from the outside to the inside.

3. **Use lateral movement.** We have already talked about using lateral movement against the aggressive fighter. We will now look at how to use it to get to the inside and stay there.

Lateral movement is part of both long and close range fighting. As little as an inch in sideways movement is often enough to establish a superior position off the attack line. Use lateral movement to defend against the aggressive fighter, to gap after a successful combination, or to defeat your opponent's long range techniques. Lateral movement when closing distance has two primary benefits:

1. Moving from side to side confuses your opponent and makes it harder for him to time his strikes to the openings.

2. Moving from side to side changes your viewpoint, giving you a fuller picture and allowing you to see more openings.

When closing distance, either close on a short zigzag path, or move laterally to one side while simultaneously moving forward.

MIND AND BODY FOCUS

Many fighters are one-dimensional: They are headhunters. When working your way in, bear in mind that the easiest way to defeat a strong opponent is to separate his *mind and body focus*. Try to attack a different target than you initially intended. For example, if you intend to throw a strike to the jaw but your opponent has superior timing, you can divert his focus from his upper body to his lower body by attacking his legs. When your opponent becomes disrupted and starts to focus on your lower body attack, you can go for that knockout punch to the jaw.

Try these exercises on **MIND AND BODY FOCUS**:

Exercise 4

Spar, using light contact only. Make note of whether you and your partner are headhunters, or if you vary your targets enough to disrupt your opponent's mental and physical coordination.

Exercise 5

How do you react when your opponent tries to separate your mind and body focus? In fighting, logic must prevail. Emotions, particularly feelings of frustration or embarrassment, are destructive and keeps a fighter from using sound strategy. It is therefore important to keep your focus on the fight at hand. Make note of your mental and physical reactions to your opponent's attempts to split your mind and body focus.

Freezing works on the principle of your opponent momentarily tensing the part of his body that is struck. This makes him unable to use it against you.

FREEZING YOUR OPPONENT'S OFFENSIVE WEAPONS

Because much of a fight is mental, any strike to your opponent's arms or hands may enable you to momentarily *freeze* his weapons. This concept can benefit you when working your way in.

Try these exercises on **FREEZING**:

Exercise 6

Your opponent's mind will momentarily go to the part of his body that is struck. This buys you time and allows you to follow with an offensive move. To create an opening at the head, strike your opponent's arm or glove and note his reaction. Did he lower his guard? Did he extend his hand slightly? Now, when you know how he will react, you can set him up for a strike to his jaw. Next, strike the top of your opponent's gloves and make note of his reaction. Did he raise his guard enough to create an opening at his ribs?

Exercise 7

Work to eliminate your own tendency to freeze. If your opponent picks your jab and counters with a strike to your face, your best course of action may be to ignore this strike and continue on your original mission of multiple jabs. This will most likely break his rhythm and allow you to land your second or third jab.

DISTANCE IN CLOSE QUARTERS

The fighter who controls distance controls the fight. This is true both in long and short range fighting. When moving from the outside to the inside, use distance to smother your opponent's weapons or to create a gap at the appropriate moment. To smother your opponent's weapons, work on the following principles:

1. When your opponent kicks, rather than staying at the tip of his kick where most of the power is, **shuffle forward to smother the kick**. Try blocking the kick with an elbow or forearm block, followed by an immediate shuffle-step forward.

2. When blocking kicks to the legs, use the inside or outside shin block, followed by an **immediate shuffle-step forward**.

3. Side thrust kicks need to be side-stepped either to the inside or outside of your opponent's centerline, creating a superior position for inside fighting by **changing the angle**.

4. Also experiment with leg checks to **jam your opponent's kicks**.

Sometimes, you can place your opponent in an inferior position by creating distance before closing the gap. For example, if you knock your opponent back against the ropes with a side thrust or front push kick, shuffle forward and finish him on the inside as he struggles to recover.

At times, it may appear as though you are too close for a long range technique. However, some long range techniques can be thrown effectively on the inside simply by using a different striking surface. For example:

1. The round house kick is an effective inside technique if you **impact the target with your shin** instead of with your instep.

2. A front kick can also be thrown effectively in close quarters, if you **stay compact** and bring your knee up high before extending your leg to kick.

Chamber your leg prior to throwing the front kick in close quarters.

PROTECTING YOUR CENTERLINE IN CLOSE QUARTERS

Because some of the most vital targets are on the centerline, and the uppercut is such a powerful inside technique, you must be careful to protect your centerline when moving in. Some fighters make the mistake of squaring their body. This happens because the fighter attempts to close distance by stepping forward with his rear foot instead of using the shuffle-step (staying in your stance). Some fighters square their body only, while their feet and hands stay in a good fighting stance. To break this habit, observe yourself in a mirror and make note of any openings along your centerline. **Practice keeping a good fighting stance until you can do so by feel.**

Stepping forward with your rear foot exposes your centerline.

Squaring, when very close to your opponent, is okay if it gives you more power in your lead hand. But a gap as little as a few inches will leave your centerline exposed to uppercuts. To protect your chin, keep your head slightly to one side of the center. In a left fighting stance, keep your head to the right and against your opponent's left shoulder.

Keep your head to the right and off the centerline.

When in a left stance against an opponent who is also in a left stance, stay slightly to your opponent's left (to the outside and away from his power hand). Your angle should be so that you are never directly on the attack line. If your opponent looks straight ahead, he should be looking past your left shoulder. In order for him to strike you, he must first make an adjustment to his left.

Stay slightly to your opponent's left and off the attack line.

When fighting the southpaw, the opposite of the above is true. You should now stay slightly to your opponent's right and away from his left power hand. If in a left stance against a southpaw, position your lead foot to the outside of your opponent's lead foot. This will guide him back toward your stronger rear hand. Your right hand will now function like a jab. Throw it often as a feeler, and follow with a lead hook to your opponent's jaw.

When fighting a southpaw, position your lead foot to the outside of your opponent's lead foot.

CHOOSING YOUR KICK COMBINATIONS WHEN MOVING IN

Since we are kickboxers, we must strive to use our kicks with as much ease as we use our hands. Different kicks have different purposes, and all kicks are not equally effective when moving in. A side thrust kick, for example, is used mostly to keep your opponent away, or to nail him against the ropes. Because this kick increases the gap, it is not your best choice when trying to get from long to close range. Likewise, any kick that turns your back partly toward your opponent (cut kick, spinning back kick) is difficult to blend with a follow-up hand combination.

A good time to kick is between the time your opponent extends his hand to throw a jab and the punch lands. If your opponent throws multiple jabs in rapid succession, you must have superior timing to get past his jabs and to the inside.

The best kicks for moving from long to close range are the front kick (if used as a feeler), and the round house kick. Kicking your opponent's legs can be effective, since it will distract his focus away from your hand techniques. Let's say that your opponent is keeping you away with his jab. Split his focus and close the gap by:

1. **Establishing distance**, so that you are slightly out of reach of the jab.

2. **Throwing a kick**, preferably a round house kick to the outside or inside thigh area. If this is a rear leg kick, and you set your foot down in a slightly narrow stance, you can again widen your stance when lunging forward with a punch combination.

3. **Moving in with a hand combination** while your opponent is still stunned from the kick.

You can also place the punch combination between your kicks by:

1. Throwing a rear leg round house kick to your opponent's outside thigh.

2. **Moving in with the punch combination**.

3. Finishing with a front kick to his gut.

Or you can place the punch combination at the end of your kick combination by:

1. Throwing a lead leg round house kick to your opponent's inside thigh.

2. Following with a rear leg round house kick to his outside thigh.

3. **Moving in with a punch combination**.

Getting to the inside requires timing. Good timing, in turn, requires a relaxed body and mind. Do not anticipate your opponent's strikes. Use a lot of upper body movement and footwork. When the distance and angle are right, move in without warning.

JAMMING YOUR WAY TO THE INSIDE

But what if your opponent is a good kicker and uses his legs to keep you at bay? There are mainly three ways to defend against a kick:

1. **Block the kick** and follow with a punch or kick combination.

2. **Shuffle back** to make the kick miss. Then immediately shuffle forward, while your opponent is regaining balance, and follow with a punch combination.

3. **Jam your opponent's kick**. Because jamming automatically places you at close range, this is perhaps the best alternative for the inside fighter.

When jamming, initiate your gap closure before your opponent's kick is fully extended. When shuffling to the inside, your lead foot should be on your opponent's centerline and between his legs. This ensures you a superior inside position, where you are crowding his space and simultaneously knocking him off balance. Staying compact also makes it more difficult for your opponent to retaliate.

Summary and review

The difficult part about fighting at close range is moving in and achieving the superior position. You must also know when it is appropriate to close distance. Every fighter cannot be fought from close range. This may be especially true if you're up against somebody who is heavier than you, or who is a skilled short range fighter. It is therefore important to feel your opponent out during the first round to determine his skill level and whether he is more comfortable at close or long range. There are many ways to close distance, including lateral movement, shuffle-steps, and jamming. You must also take into account your opponent's physical and mental characteristics. Do you have to get past his longer reach? Does he fall for fakes, freezing, or other mind-games?

Determining when to close distance

- Distance should generally be closed when your opponent experiences a moment of weakness. Engage in light contact sparring with your partner and be observant of his moments of weakness.

- Does he tend to throw his strikes in groups of threes or fours, with a slight pause in-between? This might be a good time to move in.

- Does he react to a sudden, unexpected move? This might be a good time to move in.

- Is he more worried about defense than offense? Move in while keeping him occupied with quick jabs.

Awareness practice when closing distance

- Be aware of your openings when moving to close range. Engage in light contact sparring and pay attention to the following: Do you tend to throw strikes from long range, then pause, and then move in without throwing anything? This is your moment of weakness, which can be exploited by your opponent.

- When moving in, do you stay in a good boxer's stance, or do you tend to square your body? If squaring, is your opponent able to take advantage of the openings on your centerline? Be especially aware of his front kicks.

- When are you most vulnerable to a hook to the side of your head? A hook to the body? How can you protect these areas while moving in, simultaneously throwing your offense?

Sparring and behavior awareness practice

- How logical is your advance? Engage in light contact sparring, paying attention to the following in your behavior: Are you determined to get to the inside at any cost? When does the price become greater than the value?

- If your opponent counters your advance, do you try again, or do you remain at long range? Why?

- Is there a way in which you can "lure" your opponent to come to close range, saving you the trouble of initiating the advance? What kind of mind-games can you engage in without jeopardizing your own safety?

OFFENSE ON THE INSIDE

The purpose of working your way to the inside is to throw powerful inside techniques, so once there, you must make an effort to stay there until something decisive happens; until your opponent gets knocked out or you choose to move back to long range for some other reason.

This section covers:

- The effects of striking the body
- Ten ways to power up the body hook
- "Short" punching in close quarters
- The importance of the crouched stance
- The shoulder butt
- Switching to southpaw stance on the inside
- The arm trap
- Chipping ice
- Kicking in close quarters
- Different angles for the shin kick
- Summary and review

THE EFFECTS OF STRIKING THE BODY

You will use predominantly short range techniques on the inside. Hooks and uppercuts can be thrown to the body or head. Double (or alternating) hooks to the body can be effective for dropping your opponent to the ground. First, throw a hook to his left side (floating rib or spleen). Then, follow with a hook to his right side (liver or solar plexus). Lower your shoulders to the level of the punch to protect your chin and keep the weight of your body behind the strikes. You must also protect against uppercuts. You do this by placing your head slightly off center and against your opponent's shoulder. The distance and angle now make strikes to your centerline ineffective.

Body shots derive their effectiveness from striking the organs in the lower body. When a good blow lands to your mid-section, the diaphragm (the muscle that separates the chest from the abdomen), which is responsible for movement of air in and out of the lungs, goes into spasms. When this happens, your lungs are unable to function until the diaphragm recovers. Getting the wind knocked out of you is seldom dangerous and is a condition that usually corrects itself within a few seconds to a minute, but you won't be able to breathe until the spasms stop. Unless you are saved by the bell, such a blow might end the fight. Strikes to the body could also stimulate the vagus nerve, which runs from the brain to the abdominal region, producing an instant knockout.

If your opponent has a good defensive guard, scoring with body shots can be difficult. Reaching a good target may also be difficult because your angle is not appropriate for the strike. Try pivoting your upper body slightly to the side before throwing the punch. You will be amazed at the targets that are exposed when the angle changes a bit.

When it is time to take your opponent out, you must establish a good angle for a powerful strike. The twisting uppercut is a useful inside technique that is particularly beneficial when striking the body.

To throw the twisting uppercut:

1. **Start with your hand in the vertical position**, as if you were going to throw a hook.

2. **Gradually rotate your hand palm up**, with the final snap at the moment of impact.

3. **Drive the strike at an upward angle**, as if you were trying to punch through your opponent's body and out his opposite shoulder.

The twisting uppercut drives through your opponent's body at a diagonal angle.

> The twisting uppercut allows you to keep your body weight behind the strike. Because this is a "short" strike, there is no wasted time, and you can be more explosive than when throwing a regular uppercut or hook.

A good time to throw the twisting uppercut is when your opponent carries his elbows just a little high, exposing his ribs. Let your strike follow his elbow and upper arm to the target. Try alternating twisting uppercuts. First, throw to your opponent's ribs. As he moves his elbow to protect his ribs and kidneys, throw with your other hand to his solar plexus or liver.

Any time you get into a set pattern for an extended period of time, your opponent will get in tune with your rhythm and block everything you throw. You should therefore vary your techniques enough to avoid getting into a habitual pattern. For example, throw a couple of right hooks to the body, followed by a right hook to the head. Next, you may want to change one of your hooks to an uppercut aimed at the jaw. Speed up or slow down to change the rhythm. Add a slight pause between blows, or try to strike faster than your opponent.

> Whenever you strike to only one target area, your opponent can block all day long, because he has only one area to focus on.

What makes a great inside fighter great is his ability to "feel" his opponent's intentions. Touching shoulder with your opponent allows you to feel small movements in his body. Experience also tells you that when your opponent raises his elbow to throw a hook, there is an automatic opening at his ribs or solar plexus. Knowing this in advance can help you beat him to the punch. As soon as you feel the first movement in his shoulder, you can "translate" that into a particular strike. You can now counter to the created opening before his strike lands. Remember that your opponent can feel your intentions as well. Don't become predictable. When on the inside, you become very close physically and mentally to your opponent. Inside fighting is essentially about counter-punching. You let your opponent initiate a strike that you can counter. As the game goes on, you will add more strikes to your combinations. When you hurt or daze your opponent with a blow, be prepared to follow with strong offense.

> The benefit of initiating the attack is that it places you mentally in charge of the fight. The benefit of counter-striking is that you can take advantage of the opening.

TEN WAYS TO POWER UP THE BODY HOOK

Visualize this: The bell sounds for the start of the round. Eager to get the game under way, you rush to the center of the ring and tie up shoulder-to-shoulder with your opponent. With his slightly longer reach, your opponent's strikes lack full power at close range, and the moment he gaps a little, you connect with a jab and cross that jolt his head. When his hands come up to protect against further assault, you unleash a devastating left hook to his body, dropping him to the canvas and ending the fight.

On April 19, 2003, boxer Miguel Cotto won over Joel Perez with a left body hook in the fourth round of a ten rounder. You could literally see the pain on Perez' face as he took a few steps back and went down to one knee. Most fighters tend to be headhunters, but a good blow to the abdomen or solar plexus is just as effective at ending the fight. When you knock the wind out of your opponent, he will drop to his knees instantly. Try these ten ways to maximize the power of the body hook:

1. **Keep the elbow of the hooking arm down and close to your body**. This allows you to use body weight to maximize power. Keep your hand in the vertical position with your palm turned toward you or slightly upward. Don't rotate your fist palm down, as this brings your elbow up and keeps you from placing your full weight behind the blow.

2. **Choose a specific target, not the mid-section in general.** Generally, the stomach/spleen on the left and the liver on the right are great targets for dropping your opponent to the canvas.

3. **Be selective with your strikes.** Although throwing a barrage of blows serves a strategic purpose of overwhelming your opponent, we often tend

to sacrifice proper body mechanics for speed. Being selective with your strikes and targets results in throwing fewer strikes but with greater power. It also helps you keep your cool and conserve energy.

4. **Take a short step to the side and slightly forward with the foot opposite that of the striking hand.** If you throw a left hook, step with your right foot forward and to the side of your opponent's body. This places you off your opponent's attack line, and allows you to use body momentum to your advantage. It also gives you a better angle for penetrating a tight guard.

5. **Use weight shift when you can't step and need to control your opponent with strikes at close range.** If you're fighting somebody who is strong or skilled at close range, you will end up expending much energy pushing against your opponent just trying to keep your ground. A small weight shift to one foot sets your body a few inches off your opponent's attack line, and may give you a better position and more targets, without going directly against his body weight.

6. **Throw the strike absolutely straight.** This doesn't mean that your arm should be straight (since it is a hook, it won't be), but impact must be straight in order to focus the power into one point. Many fighters tend to loop the hooking arm slightly toward their own body as the punch lands, splitting the power and starving the strike. When practicing body hooks, snap your hand back in the exact same direction it came from after landing the strike. This eliminates the conflict with the direction of energy, protects you better against your opponent's retaliation, and helps you reset your body's balance for a follow-up strike.

7. **Avoid leaning into the technique.** This is especially common when trying to move your opponent back through the use of your body weight. Although it may seem as though leaning places more weight behind the blow, it actually has an adverse effect both in balance and in starving the strike of distance. Leaning is especially detrimental at close range, where you need that extra distance for power. To avoid leaning, imagine a stiff pole going vertically through your head and body. Rotation of

your body for the hook should be around this vertical axis.

8. **Press the attack.** Normally, the fighter who is back-pedaling is at a disadvantage, because he can't use his momentum optimally. Use short lateral steps rather than your body weight alone when forcing your opponent to the rear. If he attempts to escape the attack, cut him off by moving in the direction he is moving. If he moves to your left, take a step to your left to cut off his escape route and simultaneously throw a body shot with your right hand. Manipulate your opponent by using your shoulders to press him to the rear, while landing hooks to his body.

9. **Synchronize body and strike.** Since the body is so much more massive than the arms, relying on quick body rotation increases the power of the hook. Don't allow your arm to lead or "finish the technique on its own"; nor should you allow your body to move with the arm lagging behind.

10. **Feel your opponent's intentions.** Use short punching when the situation only allows you to move a few inches. Being shoulder-to-shoulder with your opponent allows you to feel his moves without seeing the target, to know where the opening is, and to beat him to the punch.

In full-contact fighting, your purpose is to control your opponent, destroy his fighting spirit, demonstrate real power, and finish as quickly as possible. When you make your advance, throw jabs and crosses in conjunction with short steps forward. This helps you control distance and fight at a range that is optimum for you, without risk of jamming your own strikes. When you land a strike that stuns your opponent, move forward and slightly to the side, using your body momentum to land a hook to your opponent's exposed mid-section. If you can control your opponent to where he has no place to go, it is easier picking your shots. When he can't move with your strikes, he will absorb all of your power. Make sure your strikes always carry a heavy impact. A bigger opponent will feel threatened by your power punches on the inside, where his longer reach is smothered and keeps him from launching an effective close range technique.

"SHORT" PUNCHING IN CLOSE QUARTERS

The body mechanics for hooks and uppercuts require that you set your weight over the leg on the same side as the punching arm prior to throwing the strike. This gives you a more powerful strike.

When you "set" for a strike, the strike is "loaded."

However, setting for the strike has some disadvantages:

1. **It is time consuming** and may telegraph the technique.

2. **You risk leaving one side of your head or body exposed** to your opponent's counter-strike.

3. **If your opponent has a weight advantage** and pushes you back, it is difficult to set for the strike.

Uppercuts and hooks can be thrown effectively on the inside by using short punching techniques. Short punching means that you don't set for the punch first, but start from the point of origin and thrust upward from your knees and hips. These short strikes are very fast and usually unexpected. As your opponent's head snaps back from the impact of your strike, you have sufficient time to set for your follow-up technique.

Spring from your knees when throwing the short uppercut.

> **Correct body mechanics may be the most important part of powerful striking. While muscular strength and endurance enable you to throw more strikes faster, it is correct body mechanics and timing that enable you to throw with power.**

Short punching is generally thought of as counter-punching. If your opponent covers well, you may have difficulty creating enough power in your short strike to penetrate his guard or knock his head back. However, if you can feel your opponent's intentions, and he moves his body or pulls his hand back to throw a punch, you can use this as a signal for your short punch technique.

A good way to practice short punching is through the first touch concept. As your opponent comes to the inside and his gloves touch yours:

1. **Take a subtle step** with your rear foot to the side.

2. **Throw a lead twisting uppercut** to your opponent's solar plexus.

3. **Follow with a rear hook** to his ribs.

For first touch to be effective in conjunction with short punching, you must throw your strikes while your opponent has momentum coming forward. The purpose of the above exercise is not necessarily the types of strikes you throw, but the movement involved in creating a good angle.

You can also practice first touch when your opponent tries to gap from an inside attack. Throw your short uppercut or hook as soon as you feel the pressure release from his glove against yours.

> **Setting for a punch requires two moves of your body: outward to shift your weight, and back inward to throw the punch. Short punching requires only one move: inward to throw the punch. The short uppercut should be thrown without any "wind-up." Your hand should start from its position at the chin, with the power of the strike derived from your compact body springing upward.**

THE IMPORTANCE OF THE CROUCHED STANCE

In order to create a powerful strike, regardless of whether it is a jab, rear cross, hook, or uppercut, your body must stay compact. Crouching, with your knees bent, chin down, and elbows tucked close to your body is perhaps especially important in close quarters. The only part of your body that is exposed now is the upper portion of your head, where most fighters can take blows without it bothering them too much. Crouching also increases your reach. You can test this on the heavy bag. Stand upright and extend your arm straight toward the bag. Establish a distance from where your knuckles are barely touching the bag. This is your maximum reach. Without moving, crouch by bending the knees, again extending your arm straight toward the bag. Did your reach increase by two to three inches?

You can increase your reach by crouching.

Take a look at the following pictures to see the difference between the upright (left) and crouched (right) stance. Which fighter seems more mobile? Better protected? More threatening?

Crouching also allows you to pivot and dig with the balls of your feet into the floor for power. Your compact body can now deliver blows with precision and speed. Check your stance to make sure that you are not straightening your rear leg when punching, caus-

ing a wide stance. A stance that is too wide hinders mobility, reach, and power.

Stay crouched when pausing or backing out to long range. Raising your body to the upright position now, when your opponent is most likely to retaliate, could have devastating effects.

Crouching does not imply bending at the waist, as this may expose your facial area to blows. Crouching means staying compact by bending at the knees and tucking your chin down toward your chest. This automatically moves your upper body forward, resulting in an extension of reach.

THE SHOULDER BUTT

If your opponent is a good inside fighter, you must be careful not to stay in a position where it becomes a matter of his strength against yours. When very close to your opponent, you can manipulate distance with the shoulder butt. The purpose of this technique is to create distance without having to step back to long range. This allows you to stay on the offensive. To execute the shoulder butt, extend your lead shoulder forward and down, without extending your arm. This momentarily drops your hand below the level of your chin. It is therefore important to tuck your chin down behind your shoulder before commencing the move.

When very close to your opponent, use your shoulder to push him back and create distance.

If it is difficult to land your strikes when shoulder-to-shoulder with your opponent, try pivoting your body slightly to the side. Your strikes are also more effective if you release from your opponent briefly before throwing the technique. Remember that, just as you can feel your opponent's intentions when touching on the inside, he can also feel your intentions.

Keith's Knockout Advice

The shoulder butt is a lesser known close quarter defensive tactic. With just a little nudge of the shoulder, properly positioned, you can create all kinds of balance and positional problems for your opponent. However, be cautious not to cross the fine line between a legal and an illegal technique. For example, it is illegal to strike an opponent with the shoulder, especially to the head, but it is legal to push off with the shoulder while fighting at close range.

There are several applications of the shoulder butt theory. In order to position correctly, step slightly right or left of your opponent's centerline. Step right if you are fighting from an orthodox stance and left if you are fighting southpaw. This places your lead shoulder into your opponent's centerline. Keep your head to the right or left of your opponent's head. Again, which way you move depends on your stance. Use your shoulder to bump your opponent. The bump causes a momentary balance disturbance and, therefore, a brief recovery time for your opponent. This is an opportunity for you to throw a strike. The strike creates a momentary shock recovery, enabling you to bump again. This eventually leads to your opponent placing more weight forward to keep your shoulder in check. When this happens, allow him to push against your shoulder. As soon as you feel his weight coming forward, take a quick step either right or left (depending on your stance) and throw your next strike while he is battling his loss of balance.

Since you can feel your opponent's movement through your shoulder, it allows you to know which side the punch is coming from prior to delivery. As soon as you feel the initiation of your opponent's strike, bump him with your shoulder. If your timing is good, this will disrupt his punch.

Finally, during the in-fight, you will discover that fighters move each other by pushing with their shoulders. Use this to your advantage. As your opponent attempts to establish dominance by pushing you back, practice side-stepping and striking. As you become proficient at this, try bumping and striking in combinations. Use your shoulder to create distance when you need to throw long range techniques, then quickly re-establish yourself on the inside. The bottom line is to mix it up, keeping your opponent frustrated and guessing.

SWITCHING TO SOUTHPAW STANCE ON THE INSIDE

Strategy at close range is just as important as at long range. Switching stance can create a better angle and distance. However, if fighting from a neutral stance, you must be very offensive minded to ensure that your opponent doesn't counter with an uppercut or front kick along your centerline. Close quarter fighting lends itself to switching stance, because the switch itself is easier to conceal. Since inside fighting involves a lot of strikes to both sides of the body, there are times when it benefits a right-handed fighter to switch to southpaw stance to create more power in his left hand.

To switch stance in close quarters, start from a left fighting stance and work your opponent over with strikes to the body and head. Your head should be off to one side of his centerline.

Step across your opponent's centerline with your right foot in the direction of centerline B. Your stance is now slightly narrow and potentially unstable. But because you are so close to your opponent and keeping him occupied with strikes, he is less likely to see the switch.

Step back with your left foot in the direction of line 3. You are now in a right fighting stance, and your left hand has become your power hand.

Step out slightly with your right foot along line 2, so that it is outside of your opponent's lead foot. You have now established outside dominance. Simultaneous with the step, throw a left cross to his jaw.

To switch back to a left fighting stance, do the opposite of the above. Start by stepping up with your left foot until your head passes your opponent's centerline. Then step back with your right foot into a left fighting stance. You can now throw a right cross.

THE ARM TRAP

If you have spent a considerable amount of time on the inside and have been unsuccessful at pushing your opponent back, another strategic move you can try is the arm trap. Since a trapped fighter will usually begin to struggle, the main purpose of this move is to tire your opponent.

The arm trap controls, tires, and frustrates your opponent.

When trapping your opponent's arm:

1. **Establish the centerline** by getting your hands between your opponent's hands.

2. **Wrap one of your arms over the top of his arm to pin it**. You can pin either above the elbow or at the wrist. Pinning above the elbow gives you better control, while pinning at the wrist allows you more room for a follow-up technique.

3. Move your head to the same side as the arm that is trapped. As your opponent struggles, **lower your weight to tire him**.

If your opponent traps you, relax the arm that is trapped and ease it out of the hold. When you relax, your opponent has a tendency to relax as well. In the meantime, use your free hand and legs for punching and kicking.

Note: Trapping is usually not allowed in competition. If the arm trap is lengthy, the referee is likely to break you apart. Don't wrap your arms around your opponent's body or lean on him for extended periods.

Keith's Corner

The arm trap, or tie-up, is another technique that is under utilized. When used, it is generally when a fighter is hurt or tired and, in my opinion, by then it is probably too late. Of course, tying up when you're hurt is better than the alternative of being knocked out. But consider for a moment using the tie-up when you're not hurt or tired.

The tie-up is accomplished in several ways. You can trap your opponent's glove by wrapping your arm around his wrist, or you can pin his arm just above the elbow. You can also do the bear hug with your arms wrapped around his body. However, I don't recommend the bear hug, as it has little practical application in kickboxing. Use the arm trap judiciously, as many referees will take points away if they see you holding for long periods of time.

During the in-fight, you will find numerous opportunities to tie up your opponent, which will provide you with some interesting possibilities. You can manipulate your opponent's balance and position by hooking his glove. Visualize for a minute that you and your opponent are both fighting from left orthodox stances. Your opponent moves to the inside, and you immediately tie up his left glove with your left arm. Several things can occur now. If he elects to try to pull free, let him struggle for a moment. This causes him to expend energy. Remember to move with your opponent, and not against his resistance. When you feel ready to attack, you have several options. For example, you can strike to the open areas with your free hand, or quickly release your opponent's trapped hand and bang the opening before he can recover his guard. One of my favorites is to step toward the trapped hand, and at the moment I release it, throw a lead uppercut to the wide opening up my opponent's centerline. Another version is to step to the rear bringing your opponent forward, release the trapped hand while he is attempting to recover balance, and again bang away with a quick combination. I recommend releasing the trapped hand prior to throwing, as some referees will penalize you for holding and hitting. Speed and decisiveness are essential. Don't give your opponent time to recover his defensive position.

You can also hook your arm over your opponent's elbow, pulling him close. If you push him toward your centerline, you will move his free hand away from you and gain the superior position. You can now lift his elbow and expose his ribs to body shots. Finally, you can continually move your opponent forward, back, left, and right, depending on your position or the punch you throw.

CHIPPING ICE

Fighting at close quarter range doesn't mean that you abandon your long range techniques. When in close, your opponent will look for and try to defend against uppercuts and hooks, and possibly leg kicks and knees (more about knees in Section 7). Your offense is therefore somewhat predictable. Having the ability to throw long range techniques on the inside gives you a strategic advantage. Not only does your opponent have more to defend against, a long range strike is also unexpected at close quarter range.

With the exception of the round house kick, most long range strikes follow a straight path (jab, rear cross, front kick, side thrust kick). A straight strike can derive the same power as a curved strike, but with more leeway for mistakes. The power of the straight strike is focused in only one direction, but a curved strike that continues to curve on impact will split the power in two or more directions.

You can throw the jab and rear cross from a very tight distance of approximately one foot and still be effective, especially when used to annoy your opponent. This is often referred to as chipping ice. First, close distance by slipping your opponent's jab. Start chipping away at his body with jabs and rear crosses from short range. When he lowers his elbows to defend against these quick straight strikes, throw a hook, with the full weight of your body behind it, to the opening at his head.

Sometimes it is advantageous to throw a rear cross after an inside combination, such as a series of uppercuts. You create distance and power for the rear cross by shifting your weight to your rear leg, bringing your upper body above your rear knee. Keep your jaw tucked down behind your shoulder.

Fade to the rear by bringing your upper body above your rear knee, and throw a rear cross.

Shifting your weight to the rear without actually taking a step is called fading, and increases the distance for the rear cross in close quarters. If you want to follow with an inside technique, such as a lead hook, you must again shift your weight to your lead leg after landing the rear cross.

KICKING IN CLOSE QUARTERS

Many fighters feel that because kicks are essentially long range weapons they are difficult to throw in close quarters. But the front kick can be an excellent inside fighting technique with deceptive capabilities. When throwing the front kick on the inside:

1. **Crouch** (stay compact).

2. **Raise your knee high** prior to throwing the kick.

The tight distance has the advantage of creating the illusion of being too close, and this kick is therefore seldom expected in close quarters. You must still throw the kick with extension in the leg. Experiment on the heavy bag to find your distance for the front kick at close quarter range.

The round house kick is also an effective inside technique. You may initially intend to throw a round house kick at long range, when your opponent moves in to jam the kick. You can now throw a round house kick impacting with the shin instead. The trick is to understand how the extension of the kick works. While your shin impacts the target, your foot is actually "kicking air" behind the target.

Throw a round house shin kick to your opponent's thigh from close quarter range.

The shin kick can be even more powerful than a regular round house kick, especially when thrown to the outside thigh. Kicking with your instep will sting your opponent's leg, but kicking with your shin has a deeper effect because of the bonier and more solid anatomy of the shin. In order to throw this kick without injuring yourself, you must condition your shins properly. A good time to throw the round house kick to your opponent's legs is when he steps out to create distance, as he will be unable to block while in the process of stepping.

Try this exercise on **SHIN CONDITIONING**:

Exercise 1

A good way to condition your shins is to gradually expose them to contact. Start by kicking the lower end of a heavy bag (the hard part where the filling in the bag has settled). Do this twenty times with each shin every other day. Once you start developing tolerance to the pain, you can begin to kick harder and harder targets. If a bone bruise develops, give yourself adequate time to heal before continuing the exercise.

DIFFERENT ANGLES FOR THE SHIN KICK

You can throw the shin kick high across your opponent's body or low across his legs. The beauty of the kick is that it can be thrown at angles that normally don't work well with the regular round house kick. The extension of the shin kick comes at a ninety-degree angle to your target. This allows you to throw the kick from a very tight distance, which makes it a good inside fighting technique. In addition, it allows you to take targets that are square to you. For example, kick across the front of both of your opponent's thighs when he is in a neutral stance. If kicking high, kick across his abdomen and ribs.

Throw the shin kick to both of your opponent's thighs simultaneously (left), or across her abdomen and ribs (right).

When throwing the shin kick at these angles, you may need to take a short lateral step with your supporting foot to allow the knee of the kicking leg space to the side of the target. If very close to your opponent, you can impact with your shin diagonally upward instead of horizontally across the target. Before replanting your foot on the floor, your leg should make a tiny circle forward (similar to the outside shin block). This lessens the force against your shin, increases the power through more snap and extension, and sets your body for a follow-up kick with the same leg.

Explosiveness and acceleration increase the power and efficiency of the kick.

Try this exercise on **SHIN KICKS IN CLOSE QUARTERS**:

Exercise 2

Work your inside techniques on the heavy bag. Let the bag swing freely, so that the distance and angle constantly change. Throw a lead or rear leg round house kick at rib height, impacting with the shin. If you have difficulty finding a good angle, use footwork to attain a different stance. As long as you keep your opponent busy with hand combinations, switching stance at close range is seldom noticed.

Once you have thrown an effective inside combination, or if your opponent is superior at defense and you cannot find an opening for your strikes, you may take the fight back to long range and re-evaluate the situation. Move back out and throw a couple of long range strikes, then quickly move back in again. If this doesn't work, start kicking your opponent's legs to break his focus. Then go back to striking the head or body. Vary your targets.

Note that when you back out, the pressure on your opponent is lessened. This is when he is most likely to retaliate. You should therefore work your way out with jabs or a front kick, or with some other strike to keep him occupied. Crouching is important when working your way out as well. Don't straighten your body or back out with your guard down.

Summary and review

You are vulnerable to your opponent's power strikes at close quarter range, particularly the hook and uppercut. If you are comfortable fighting at long range, you may feel as though your strikes are starved of power once you do get to the inside. This happens if you attempt to throw long range techniques from close range, or if you don't have a good opening for the hook or uppercut. But because you are vulnerable at close range, you must take the offensive stand. In addition to throwing techniques that are mechanically correct, vary your targets to split your opponent's mind and body focus.

Stance awareness at close range

- Engage in light contact sparring with your partner, experimenting with different stances at close quarter range. When shoulder-to-shoulder with your opponent, how does a crouched stance (knees bent and upper body slightly forward) affect your ability to hold your ground?

- Is there a point at which your stance is too crouched? What dangerous strikes must you be aware of when bent forward at the waist? Any strike or kick that comes along your centerline can have devastating effects. Watch for the uppercut and the front kick or knee strike.

Don't bend over at close quarter range. Watch for the knee strike.

- How do you stay protected when at very close range? Is it possible to cover your centerline and the sides of your body simultaneously? When shoulder-to-shoulder with your opponent, you can usually feel any small movement in his body, which will forewarn you of the strikes to come.

Target practice at close range

- Many fighters tend to be overly aggressive on the inside, or to wail away at their opponent without rhyme or reason. Experiment with landing strikes to particular targets.

- Be observant of your opponent's defense and movement. It is difficult to defend all parts of the body simultaneously. Look for openings along the centerline, to the sides of the body, to the sides of the head, and to the legs. The shin kick is quick and deceptive, and can easily be landed from close quarter range.

- When you have backed your opponent up against the ropes, how can you keep him there solely through the use of strikes? Experiment with the hook within the movement of a lateral step. For example, if your opponent attempts to move to your right, take a step to your right to cut him off, and throw the left hook to his mid-section.

Experiment with the arm trap to reverse positions on the ropes.

- Make note of how a short lateral step makes you see more openings. You may be able to land a strike that ordinarily cannot be thrown to the centerline from a position to the side. The lead hook is such a strike.

Creating openings at close range

- Pay attention to your opponent's reaction when struck at close quarter range. When you strike to the body, does he tend to move his arms in an attempt to block the strikes? How can you use this to create an opening to a different target?

- Does he tend to cover up without striking back? To move back or try to gap? To press forward? What can you do to exploit his moves?

- If your opponent is a good inside fighter, what is your reaction? When is it wise to move back to long range? What do you need to be aware of when gapping?

DEFENSE ON THE INSIDE

Another aspect of inside fighting you must consider is defense against an aggressive opponent who is superior at close range.

This section covers:

- Getting backed up
- What to do when backed up against the ropes
- Glove-up with Keith
- Eight ways to defend the hook and uppercut
- Timing your opponent's upper body movement
- Summary and review

GETTING BACKED UP

The aggressive opponent will press forward and try to back you up. He will restrict your mobility, limit the effectiveness of your techniques, and block your escape routes. When you get with your back against the ropes, it becomes difficult to create distance in defense of an oncoming barrage of blows. The ropes are also seen as the inferior position by the judges, and you may therefore not score as well, even if your opponent's strikes don't hurt you. During your career, you will fight in different size rings ranging from 16 X 16 feet to 25 X 25 feet. When fighting in a 16-foot ring against a stronger or more aggressive opponent, it is only a matter of seconds before you find yourself with your back to the ropes.

Your natural tendency when your opponent starts to push you back is to resist. But this doesn't work if your opponent has the weight and strength advantage. Instead of resisting, work on going with the motion of your opponent's push. When he pushes, step back with your lead foot (you have now switched stance) and immediately throw a rear leg front kick to his gut (the same leg that stepped will do the kicking). If you do this move explosively, it will cause your opponent to "fall" forward and into your kick (because of his forward momentum when pushing against you). If the kick hurt your opponent, you can stay on the inside and take advantage of the situation by firing a strong hand combination.

The strategic fighter dominates the center of the ring in an attempt to keep his opponent from backing him up.

If your opponent squares (gets in a horse stance) when trying to back you up, you can still go with the pressure and step back with your lead leg. When he is in a square stance, his centerline is exposed and his balance jeopardized. Your best retaliation is a straight attack, like a front kick or rear cross. Timing and speed are important. If you delay your attack, you have again given your opponent the opportunity to crowd you. Remember, it takes less time to act than to react. You should therefore be the one who decides when to attack. Relying on the *first touch* concept works well to trigger explosiveness in your step. When your opponent attempts to back you up, the moment you feel his shoulder pressing against yours, explode with a pivot-step off the attack line. Follow with a hook or a rear cross. Always think of the follow-up! Then move back to the center of the ring. Dominating the center is energy efficient and results in less movement for you, forcing your opponent to move around you.

When using first touch, understand that your opponent will most likely press against one of your shoulders more than against the other. In other words, he will not be pressing directly into your centerline. Feeling the push helps you determine which direction to move. When you go with the pressure, your opponent's momentum will carry him into your retaliatory strike. When following with a combination from your now superior position on the inside, you can use the movement of the pivot-step to set for the combination. For example, if your opponent presses against your left shoulder, go with the pressure and pivot to the right. You have now chambered your body to the left and can throw a left uppercut to your opponent's chin. When we start talking about strategy in more detail in Section 10, you will also see how the element of time plays a crucial role.

227

Pivot off the attack line and throw an uppercut to your opponent's chin.

When moving back to long range, be aware of your opponent's offense, as this is when he is most likely to retaliate. Back out with a swift increase in distance. When your opponent turns toward you, immediately follow with one or more counter-strikes.

WHAT TO DO WHEN BACKED UP AGAINST THE ROPES

When you have taken all the necessary precautions of lateral movement, first touch, and positional awareness, there are still times when you will find yourself with your back to the ropes. Your opponent will now try to take advantage of your position with a strong inside attack. Your primary concern is to keep him from knocking you out. You should therefore do the following, in this order:

1. **Keep your cool.**

2. **Defend** (block) the strikes.

3. **Fire back.**

4. **Move.**

Use elbow and forearm blocks to **defend the strikes,** until you have **collected your thoughts** enough to come back with offense. If you stay relaxed, you can block most of your opponent's strikes. Remember to keep your chin down so that it won't become an easy knockout target.

Since you cannot stay on the ropes forever, you will have to **fire back.** This keeps your opponent occupied

while you work back to the center of the ring. To be successful with offense on the inside, your strikes must be faster than your opponent's strikes. Keep your rear hand close to your chin. Since your opponent is likely to throw the hook on the inside, keeping your hand too far forward, even if it is held high, allows him to loop the hook around your arm and land it on your chin or temple.

If you keep your hand too far forward, your opponent can loop his hook around your guard.

Finally, once you have thrown a combination to your opponent's openings, you must **move away from the ropes** and back to the center of the ring. You can move out with a big pivot-step, or you can move out methodically by taking small steps and using lateral or circular movement. Remember, your opponent is likely to mirror your moves, so you can also use this strategically to circle him into the ropes.

When backed up or cornered, it is especially important to keep a good boxer's stance. If you are in a neutral stance when your back hits the ropes, the only way you can regain a fighting stance is by stepping forward with one foot. This is not practical against a stronger opponent who is pressing you back. If you have difficulties moving to a superior position, try the arm trap, as discussed earlier. Pin your opponent's arm by looping your own arm over the top of his. This ties up his offensive weapons, tires him, and allows you to reverse positions by turning him into the ropes.

It is a mistake to think that when it gets rough, if you just back down on your power a little, your opponent will back down as well. When fighting toe-to-toe, the fight will escalate until the weaker fighter starts moving back. The stronger fighter will then feed on this and move ahead with even more vicious offense.

If your opponent is the one who decides to move back to long range, try to throw a rear cross to his jaw the moment he steps back. This strike is almost a given, because there is only one move required for you (throwing the strike), while there are two moves required for your opponent (stepping back and defending, or stepping back and striking). The best time to retaliate with a powerful long range technique from close quarters is therefore when your opponent steps back.

One may ask why a fighter who has backed his opponent against the ropes would want to step back to long range. The most common reason, especially in the amateur ranks, is because he has worn himself out with a lengthy body attack, and is thinking of his own safety against a counter-attack.

When your opponent steps back, be aware of your own openings so that you don't walk into his strikes.

Glove Up with Keith

What should you do when you're against the ropes and your opponent is pounding away at you with a twenty-punch combination? Hit him back? But what if you try hitting him back, and every time you do so you leave an opening on yourself, which he takes advantage of? Then kick him to keep him off you. Use a lot of straight kicks. Or try something totally unorthodox, like running. If you can, try to crowd your opponent and push him back until you have created an escape path. You can't play the other man's game, though. If you visit a point-sparring karate school and you point spar, whose game are you playing? If a point-sparrer walks into a boxing gym, I guarantee you that the boxer won't play the point-sparrer's game.

EIGHT WAYS TO DEFEND THE HOOK AND UPPERCUT

1. Defend a hook to the head with an **outside forearm block**. When your opponent throws the hook, raise your arm up by the side of your head and take the punch on your upper arm or forearm. Keep your elbow bent with your fist pointing to the rear, and your chin tucked down behind your shoulder. The problem with blocking is that you risk getting your own hand swatted into your head, and you will therefore absorb a considerable amount of the force. But if your hand stays tight to your head, the actual force at impact is less. On the other hand, if you extend your hand or forearm to meet your opponent's hook (providing that your block is convincing), your head will absorb none of the force. Simultaneous to blocking, counter with a hook or uppercut with your free hand to your opponent's head or body, using first touch to trigger your strike.

Defend a hook to the head with an outside forearm block.

2. One of the best defenses against a hook is a **straight punch**. As long as your timing is good, a straight punch will always beat a looping punch, because the quickest route from point A to point B is a straight line.

Throw a rear cross the moment your opponent initiates the hook.

3. **Bob and weave** under the hook. Since the hook strikes from the side, it is important to bob and weave in the opposite direction of the hook (toward the hook). This places you in a superior position to the outside (slightly toward your opponent's back). If you bob and weave in the same direction as the hook, you may still get hit when coming back up.

4. If you see the hook coming, **go with the motion of the hook (same direction)**, lessening its impact. Continue to bob and weave back the other way to get to the superior position toward your opponent's outside (back).

Go with the motion of the hook and continue into a bob and weave.

5. The uppercut is perhaps the most powerful and dangerous close quarter strike. If you can **anticipate the strike and upset your opponent's timing**, you will have a clear advantage. When very close to your opponent, watch for and expect the uppercut.

Use a downward catch to stop the uppercut from reaching your chin.

6. Defend the hook by **anticipating the strike and stepping to long range**. Take advantage of your position by firing a fast counter-combination. Be aware that your opponent's compact stance and momentum will carry him forward. Stepping to long range against a hooking attack is therefore more difficult than staying at close range and relying on blocking or upper body movement.

7. You can also defend the uppercut by **fading slightly to the rear**, so that the strike passes vertically in front of your face. An experienced fighter will often follow the uppercut with a hook. You must therefore be prepared to defend against the hook as well.

Fade by placing your weight on your rear leg. Watch for your opponent's follow-up strike.

8. Defend the uppercut by **throwing a counter-punch**. When your opponent throws the uppercut, either catch it or fade and counter with a hook to the opening on his jaw. A counter-strike is generally faster if you rely on movement rather than on blocking. This is because blocking ties up your weapons momentarily, while movement allows you to keep your hands free and counter before your opponent has had time to reset into his fighting stance.

TIMING YOUR OPPONENT'S UPPER BODY MOVEMENT

As mentioned earlier, defense is not simply a way to avoid getting hit. The defensive position should therefore not be seen as a weakness. The defensive fighter who takes charge of the fight can create an offensive type of defense by taking advantage of his opponent's aggressiveness. If your opponent is closing distance methodically by slipping or bobbing and weaving, and you anticipate and time your strikes to his movement, you can get him to "roll into" your strikes. This works particularly well when your opponent is trying to get to the inside, because his momentum is coming forward and into the power of your strikes.

Say, for example, that you throw a jab, which your opponent slips. If the purpose of his slip is to get to the inside, he will most likely follow the slip with a roll (bob and weave). You can now time an uppercut to his jaw or nose the moment he rolls toward your uppercutting hand.

When your opponent slips and rolls in an attempt to get to the inside, throw an uppercut to his jaw.

If you are slow retrieving the jab, your opponent can slip it and follow with an uppercut underneath your jabbing arm to your chin. It is therefore important to move your non-working hand to a position in front of your face, and tuck your chin down behind the shoulder of your jabbing arm.

Whether you throw your left or right uppercut depends on the direction of your opponent's slip. If he slips to your right, throw a left uppercut, because his bob and weave is toward that hand. If he slips to your left, throw a right uppercut. Your opponent's reaction will determine which type of strike you throw following the uppercut.

Another way to blend offense with defense is when your opponent throws a jab that you slip. Let's say that you slip his jab to the right. As your body turns, your lead shoulder will protect you, and you will place more weight on your rear foot. Your rear hand is now chambered for a hook to your opponent's body. Preferably, you want to throw your hook before he has time to withdraw his hand from throwing the jab. This enables you to come underneath his arm to the open target at his ribs.

Slip the jab to the right and throw a rear hook.

If you slip to the left instead, you will place more weight on your lead foot and will be chambered for a lead hook or uppercut. In the next sub-section, we will look at how to incorporate upper body movement, both offensively and defensively, into the inside game.

Summary and review

Defense at close quarter range involves more than blocking. If it is your opponent's choice to go to the inside, it probably means that he is either an aggressive fighter, or that he has the weight advantage. In either case, the second element of defense involves fighting from an inferior position, often when backpedaling or when cornered. Once your opponent achieves close quarter range, you must be on your guard against hooks and uppercuts, which are both devastating finishing strikes.

Close range focus mitt practice

- Have your partner hold focus mitts while constantly stepping forward, crowding you and pushing you back with whatever means he has available.

- How realistic is it to throw an uppercut or hook when crowded by your opponent? What are your chances of side-stepping or pivoting off the attack line?

- Be aware of your position. Don't get any closer than two feet to the ropes. What technique can you successfully use while circling back to the center of the ring? How quick must you be in order to better your position?

- Try to dominate the center of the ring for one two-minute round. Dominating the center does not mean that you have to remain there, only that your back is always toward the center.

Sparring practice on the ropes

- Engage in light contact sparring with your partner, allowing him to back you up against the ropes. Block his strikes and rely on the concept of first touch to trigger your counter-strike. When your opponent strikes, where does he leave an opening?

- Try countering with the opposite hand that is blocking, and then with the same hand that is blocking. Don't throw your counter-strikes without a purpose. Be observant and choose your targets with care.

- When your opponent strikes low to your body, is it necessary to drop your guard in order to block his strikes with your elbows? Can you crouch instead of dropping your guard, and still achieve a good block?

- Be careful with getting your weight to the rear. Try to stay in a crouched stance both for protection and stability.

- Analyze how to move to get away from your disadvantaged position on the ropes.

SLIPPING TO CLOSE QUARTER RANGE

Advanced short range fighting consists of more than just punching and kicking. Your upper body movement can serve as effective defense while closing distance. When thinking defensively, we often tend to think of blocking. But, as discussed earlier, the problem with blocking is that:

1. You might "freeze" for a fraction of a second as your opponent's strike hits the blocking weapon, making you **unable to respond with a counter-attack.**

2. The blocking weapon will be "tied up" in the technique until the block is complete, **reducing your number of effective weapons**.

Advanced defense consists of slips and counter-strikes, where your opponent's strike is allowed to pass over your shoulder without touching any part of your body. Both of your hands are now free to counter-strike. This may seem like an insignificant detail, but can be tremendously helpful when working your way from long to short range. By slipping and keeping your hands free to strike, you can bypass your opponent's long range techniques, simultaneously creating a need for him to defend against your explosive short range strikes.

This section covers:

• Slipping and counter-striking
• In the gym
• Slipping and staying off the attack line
• Weight transfer in conjunction with slipping
• Thinking of slipping as offense
• Loading your kicks for battle
• Summary and review

SLIPPING AND COUNTER-STRIKING

As already discussed, the slip is executed by moving your head side-to-side, using the least amount of movement necessary to avoid getting hit. Large moves are easy for your opponent to counter, and also take longer to reset than moves that are short and snappy.

Focus your eyes on the target. A common mistake is to turn the head slightly to the side, exposing the side of your jaw to your opponent's retaliatory hook or rear cross. Effective slipping also consists of counter-strikes to help you transition from long to short range. For example:

1. **Slip left and counter with a left uppercut** underneath your opponent's jab and to his jaw. When throwing the uppercut, keep your head to the left of the centerline (off the attack line).

2. **Follow with a second strike: a rear hook, for example**. Once you have closed distance, you must take advantage of your position while there is still an opening in your opponent's defense. When initiating the hook, your head should still be off the centerline. Not until the hook is complete should you bring your head back to the point of origin. This ensures clearance from your opponent's punch.

3. If your opponent is in the habit of throwing double jabs, **try slipping to the left first, and then back to the right**. Be aware of your opponent's follow-ups to avoid slipping into his strikes.

The faster you can slip and counter, the easier it is to take the created opening. Try countering within the movement of the slip. Because your slips must be timed to your opponent's rhythm to avoid his strike, your counter-strike must be slightly faster than the slip, or your opponent will have time to withdraw his hand and cover the opening. The best way to learn slipping is to work on getting in tune with your opponent's rhythm without consciously anticipating his strikes. A tense fighter is easy to freeze with a sudden unexpected move. The more relaxed you are, the easier and quicker you will react.

The beat between slips should be varied for deception. When working your way from outside to inside, you may slip even if your opponent doesn't throw any strikes.

The slip and counter is similar in concept to the pick and counter, but rather than parrying your opponent's jab, you move your head to avoid the punch. Typically, with a right-handed opponent, you should move your head to the right. This protects you against his stronger rear hand. You can now counter with a jab within the movement of the slip.

With a left-handed opponent (a southpaw), the opposite is true. You should now move your head to the left to avoid moving into his stronger left hand, and counter with a rear cross within the movement of the slip.

Keith's Knockout Advice

Let's examine the mechanics of the slip and counter against a right-handed opponent in a left stance:

1. As your opponent jabs, **move your head to the right just far enough for the jab to miss**. A good rule of thumb is to move your head into alignment with your right shoulder. Be careful not to slip too soon, or your opponent will redirect the path of his jab and still hit you. I don't need to tell you the consequences of slipping too late!

2. **As your head begins to move right, simultaneously initiate your jab**. As your opponent's arm reaches full extension, your jab should be landing on target. This technique requires excellent timing and reflex.

Practice the technique slowly at first, then progressively faster. If fighting a southpaw, your lead foot should be to the outside of your opponent's lead foot. The technique itself is identical, with the exception that you should counter with a straight right generally followed by a lead hook.

Both the pick and counter and the slip and counter are attempting to keep your opponent in motion longer; the pick and counter by redirecting the punch, and the slip and counter by avoiding the punch entirely and letting it pass over your shoulder. Remember from your physics classes in school that an object in motion tends to stay in motion unless acted upon by some outside force. Both actions that you have learned (pick and counter and slip and counter) will keep your opponent in motion longer. Your opponent will be unable to initiate a new action (new technique) until the first action is complete.

IN THE GYM

What is the danger of slipping to the left against a right-handed fighter? You will be slipping into his power hand. When slipping to the right, however, you will be on your opponent's outside in a superior position away from his attack line.

When I throw my jab, I want you to slip to your right and follow my arm in with a right cross to my jaw. Come over the top of my arm. Any time your opponent throws a strike or kick, there is automatically an opening on that side of his body.

Try to stay relaxed. Make your slips very short and quick. Don't do the same thing too many times, or you'll become predictable. If your opponent throws a jab that you parry four times, you will get into a habit that is easy for your opponent to exploit. Also be aware of openings you might be creating on yourself.

When you spar with other students, you should consciously try to improve on specific things. Working with less experienced students is a good opportunity to practice these concepts. Try to get away from that ego thing where you have to show everybody what you know.

SLIPPING AND STAYING OFF THE ATTACK LINE

Using continuous head movement confuses your opponent and minimizes the risk of getting hit. This is also a good opportunity to move from long to close range. Be careful never to leave your head on the attack line. Keep your head off to one side until you have finished your combination and decide to move back to long range. A common mistake when slipping is to move the head off the attack line for the slip, and then move the head back to the attack line again when counter-striking. You may move your head through the attack line and to the other side to set for a strike, but you should never leave your head on the attack line!

Try this exercise on **CROSSING THE ATTACK LINE**:

Exercise 1

Observe yourself in a mirror while slipping from left to right. The only time your head should be on the attack line is when it is crossing over from one slip to the next. When counter-striking, your head should be off to one side. To keep from getting into a set pattern, practice slipping and counter-striking with broken rhythm.

Slipping left.

Slipping right.

Take a look at the following slip and counter techniques that will help you get to the inside:

Slip to the left (toward line 1) and counter with a left hook to your opponent's mid-section (in the direction of line 2). Be aware of his right hand.

Throw a second left hook high to the head, while keeping your own head off the attack line.

Slip to the right (toward line 2) and counter with a right hook to your opponent's mid-section (in the direction of line 1).

Immediately slip left (toward line 1) and counter with a left hook to the mid-section (toward line 2).

Add a roll (bob and weave) while retreating to safety. Make sure to use an angle off the attack line when stepping back.

WEIGHT TRANSFER IN CONJUNCTION WITH SLIPPING

Slipping can also be thought of as *weight transfer*. When positioning your upper body over your lead leg, as is the case when slipping left, your weight transfers to that leg and your head automatically moves off the attack line and closer to your opponent. Your weight transfer will cause your opponent's strike to miss your head. Now, when your weight has shifted to your lead leg, your body is chambered for a lead hand strike: a hook, for example.

The same can, of course, be applied to your rear hand. When your opponent throws a jab, transfer your weight to your rear leg by positioning your upper body over that leg. This moves your head to the right

of the attack line, causing your opponent's strike to miss. Depending on distance, your right hand is now chambered for a hook or a rear cross.

Keep the weight transfer short and snappy. Large bobs and weaves are seldom necessary and may even be dangerous. Taking a two-count to do a large roll allows your opponent to pick up on your timing. Do all rolls from the knees with your upper body slightly crouched. Start the rolls at the end of your slip, cross the centerline and end with your weight transferred to your other leg.

When shadow boxing, practice weight transfer and short rolls by rocking your upper body back and forth over your lead and rear leg. When you get comfortable with this, add steps and punches. It is not necessary to throw your punches with full extension for this exercise. Think of it as "throwing with your shoulder." This should also help you relax your shoulders.

THINKING OF SLIPPING AS OFFENSE

Although slipping is primarily a defensive move, you can also use it offensively to close distance for short range fighting and help you launch an effective body attack. Many fighters feel that it is easier to think "offense" than "defense." If you think of slipping as a set-up for offense, you will be more concerned with your own strategy than with what your opponent is doing. You will therefore not anticipate his punches as much, and slipping will come more naturally.

Try these exercises on weight transfer and **USING SLIPPING OFFENSIVELY**:

Note: When working on these slipping and countering exercises, try to stay relaxed and move methodically without too much fidgeting. Stay within range to counter, and try to pick up on any change in distance between yourself and your opponent.

Exercise 2

Transfer your weight to your lead leg, and within the movement of your weight transfer throw a rear cross. The weight transfer automatically creates a slip to your left, making your opponent's strike pass over your right shoulder. Your rear cross counter-strike will sneak underneath his strike and to the open target at his ribs.

Transfer your weight to your lead leg and throw a rear cross underneath your opponent's jab.

Exercise 3

Transfer your weight to your rear leg. This creates a slip to your right. You can now counter with a lead hook. The weight transfer to your rear leg automatically helps you throw the lead hook within the movement of the slip.

Transfer your weight to your rear leg and throw a lead hook underneath your opponent's jab.

Exercise 4

Transfer your weight to your lead leg, creating a slip to your left and countering with a lead hook. This move takes slightly longer, because the hook is not thrown within the movement of the slip.

The weight transfer allows you to chamber for the lead hook.

Exercise 5

Transfer your weight to your rear leg, creating a slip to your right and countering within the same movement with a jab to the opening underneath your opponent's punch.

Transfer your weight to your rear leg, and throw a jab underneath your opponent's jab.

Once you have slipped and countered, you must stay within range to fire a strong combination. Ideally, try to keep the distance constant, so that you are always within firing range. If you are too far out, there is no need to slip your opponent's punches; however, you will also be unable to reach him with short range techniques.

LOADING YOUR KICKS FOR BATTLE

We have now worked a variety of inside combinations off of a slip. As you can see, slipping can be used effectively to "load" your hands for punches. But slipping can also be used to load your legs for kicks. Slipping is therefore deceptive and can be used to set up kicks by making your opponent think of your hands. To understand this better, start thinking of your kicks as if they were hands. For example:

1. Think of your **lead leg front kick** as a **jab**.

2. Think of your **rear leg front kick** as a **rear cross**.

3. Think of your **lead leg round house kick** as a **lead hook**.

4. Think of your **rear leg round house kick** as a **rear hook**.

When slipping left from a left stance, you can either load your lead hand with a jab or a hook, or your lead leg with a front kick or a round house kick. The same is true for your rear hand and leg when slipping to your right.

In general, then, it can be said that when slipping left, you will set for your lead strikes and kicks, and when slipping right, you will set for your rear strikes and kicks. The only kick that does not follow this rule is the side thrust kick, where the opposite is true. When slipping left from a left stance, it would be too awkward to set for the lead leg side thrust kick. To load for this kick properly, you must slip right, which is the opposite of the above.

The rear leg side thrust kick needs a good set-up. One of the best ways to set for this kick is to bring your rear leg out a little wide, so that it looks as though you will throw a rear leg round house kick. As your hips pivot through your centerline, you must now change the direction from circular to linear so that the kick strikes the target straight. Practicing the kick in this way enables you to land your rear leg side thrust kick any time you can land a rear leg round house kick.

Start a rear leg round house kick, but as your hips come through . . .

. . . convert it to a rear leg side thrust kick.

When kicking, it is equally important to keep your head off the attack line. For example, if you slip left and kick, your head may cross the attack line but should not stay on it. Or if throwing multiple kicks with the same leg, your head should stay to one side of the attack line until the combination is complete.

Slipping, then, can be used deceptively to conceal a kick. Knowing this is useful when working your way to the inside. Because upper body movement is often used as a means to close distance, and because most kicks are long range techniques, they are seldom expected in conjunction with slipping. A kick that is hidden within a slip or upper body movement is more likely to land, than a kick thrown isolated with no upper body movement.

We will learn more about deception and faking in Section 10, which will take you into an entirely different ball game. But before we do that, I suggest you compete in an amateur kickboxing contest to learn what it's really like in the trenches.

Summary and review

Slipping is normally seen as a defensive move, allowing you to keep your hands free for counter-striking. Slipping is a great way to get to close quarter range. When your opponent throws a punch, his focus and concerted effort is in that punch. When it misses through your slip, you will offset his timing, possibly disturb his balance, and create an opportunity to move in for the kill.

Partner practice with slipping

- Have your partner throw jabs in slow motion. Slip either left or right, and throw a counter-strike. Why is it better to slip right against a right-handed fighter's jab? What types of follow-up strikes or kicks are you chambered for?

- If you slip left, you will be slipping toward the attack line of your opponent's strong rear hand. Is this necessarily bad? When is he most likely to throw his rear cross?

- If you counter-strike with a rear cross within the movement of the slip, you are likely to beat your opponent to the punch, because his focus is still on his jab that missed.

Shifting weight when slipping

- Shadow box, using only footwork and slipping. Try to feel the weight shift with each slip. The weight shift should not be so much that you risk losing balance, but you should feel one foot "dig" slightly into the floor.

- You can achieve the weight shift by pushing off with the foot on the opposite side of the slip. If you slip left, initiate the slip by pushing off with the ball of your right foot. This moves your upper body off the attack line and slightly forward, if you are in a left stance.

- Proper weight transfer is difficult to achieve without a slight bend in the knees. Think of it as "rocking" back and forth from your lead to your rear foot. The move is similar in feel to a slalom skier going down a hill.

Sparring practice with slipping and distance closure

- Engage in light contact sparring and work on establishing an aggressive mind-set for slipping. The slip should accomplish more than just avoiding your opponent's strike. Try to focus on the offensive move, until the slip comes almost automatically and you can use it to gain the inside position.

- Staying relaxed in your shoulders and upper body is imperative to avoid pausing between the slip and counter-strike. Relaxation comes easier once you stop focusing on it. Thinking "offense" may therefore be a good distraction.

- The shorter the slip, the quicker you can set for and throw the counter-strike or move to the inside. Listen to the rhythm, and try to decrease the beat between slip and counter.

QUICK REFERENCE TO CONCEPTS

DISTANCE IN CLOSE QUARTERS: The person who controls distance, controls the fight. Use distance manipulation to smother your opponent's weapons, or to create a gap at the appropriate moment.

FADING: Shifting your weight to the rear without actually taking a step gives you the advantage of an increase in distance for your powerful rear techniques. When you move your upper body forward again, your power will increase through the use of body momentum.

FREEZING: You can momentarily freeze your opponent's offensive weapons by hitting or touching that weapon. When your opponent tenses the body part that is struck, he is momentarily unable to use it against you.

FIRST TOUCH CONCEPT: As your opponent comes to the inside, use the moment you first touch as a cue to create distance or explode with a combination.

MIND AND BODY FOCUS: To defeat your opponent, you must split his mind and body focus. In other words, you must interrupt his concentration by continuously distracting and disrupting his mental and physical operation. One way to do this is by kicking your opponent's legs until he attempts to defend against your lower body attack and leaves an opening at his head.

POINT OF ORIGIN: Bring your strikes back to the point of origin as soon as they have landed. Be careful not to pull a strike to the rear of the point of origin prior to throwing it, as this would telegraph the move. Try to throw your strikes from the point of origin, without any prior movement.

SHORT PUNCHING: Short punching allows you to throw your strikes with minimal "wind-up" from close range. Short punching relies on the weight of your body. There should be no prior twist in your body; rather, the momentum and power comes from pushing off with your foundation, moving your whole body a short distance forward or, if throwing the uppercut, upward by springing from the knees. Be careful not to use your arms only. A powerful strike relies on the movement of your body.

SECTION SIX
YOUR FIRST COMPETITION

A TEAM EFFORT
by Keith Livingston

I remember with clarity the first really big punch I took. The reason I remember so clearly is because time stood still, allowing me to take in and engrave that moment forever.

Almost every new student asks me what it is like in the ring. Well, except for a few common denominators, it's different for everybody. Although we have all heard of fight or flight syndrome, tunnel vision, and distorted reality, those are just terms that label what a person might encounter in a threatening or highly stressful situation. Still, the feelings vary with experience, attitude, and level of training. As a young martial artist with a background in Tae-Kwon-Do, I had many hours of sparring, and had competed in the more traditional tournament settings. But nothing had prepared me for my first full-contact match.

I had become dissatisfied with the traditional competitions, and yearned for a new test of my abilities. As fate had it, I stumbled across a full-contact karate event televised on ESPN. I was intrigued and felt the adrenaline rush as I contemplated entering. I was not overly impressed with the fighters I had seen, which further encouraged my decision and filled me with a false sense of security. Little did I know that there were much better martial artists, and that I was about eight weeks away from meeting one. My martial path would soon be changed forever.

The second fateful event occurred as I was discussing my plans with another student, and heard this voice behind me: "You're not ready!"

I turned toward the stern look of my instructor. "With all due respect, this is something I've thought about and would like to try," I said.

"Forget it. It's not for you!"

"How the hell would you know?" I shot back.

The stunned class fell silent, and my instructor ordered me into his office. Before I could apologize, he lifted the pant legs on his gi, exposing the pink scars around both knees. "Because I've been there!"

Emotions flooded my mind. Why had he never told me? Was he any good? Would he consider training me? Before I could verbalize my thoughts, he reached into the desk drawer and scribbled something on a piece of paper. He slapped the paper into my palm and said the last words we spoke to one another: "Train hard and trust nobody. Good luck!"

I knew that my attempts at further conversation were futile, so I grabbed my gear and left. When I reached the parking lot, I unfolded the paper and looked at the name and the long distance phone number. When I finally committed to making the call, I felt the same nervousness as when calling a woman for a first date. You're not quite sure what to say, and you have no idea to where it will lead.

After a few rings, the promoter answered. I introduced myself and asked if she might be looking for fighters. Then the third fateful event happened: "As a matter of fact, we're doing a show at the Special Event Center in Salt Lake City, and I'm looking for area fighters."

For the next half hour I told her about myself, my training, and my eagerness to fight. And I made my first deal: three rounds against a Denver fighter named Lance Reese. The promoter described him as good, not great but good. She obtained my address and told me that I would be receiving a contract in the mail, along with specific fight information. "I will see you in Salt Lake in seven weeks, and good luck," she said.

I spent the entire first week looking for a place to train, and discovered that there were no formal kickboxing or full-contact karate training facilities in Salt Lake in those days. I had heard that there were some fighters training at a local spa, but what I found was an unorganized group of karate practitioners sparring and hitting bags. I watched one fighter as he pounded the heavy bag. I saw little rhyme or reason to his technique: a blend of karate, kickboxing, and . . .? Off by himself was another martial artist who at least seemed to have a grasp on what he was doing.

I watched as he began sparring with another fighter, whom he defeated with ease. I decided I would train with him, and introduced myself and my goal of fighting full-contact. "Let's spar, see what you've got!" he said after listening to my story. For the next ten minutes I received a severe beating. My head throbbed and my rib cage hurt, but I was still standing. The fighter introduced himself as Kenny. He told me that he worked out Monday, Wednesday, and Friday and that I was welcome to join him.

For the next seven weeks I trained with Kenny. In hindsight, I've learned several things: First, three days a week does not a fighter make. Second, there is more to fighting than sparring. And third, if you're going to buy gold, buy from a gold dealer. I'm not knocking Kenny; he taught me a lot. But he was not a trainer, and he was not a kickboxer. A very good free stylist, yes, but not a kickboxer.

During the last week, I lay awake at night pondering the fight. The mind is a funny thing. It's either your ally or your enemy. I tended to think about the worst possible outcome, including injury, death, and even worse: embarrassment! The idea of non-performance seemed overwhelming. I had been in several street fights that were much more violent than an organized fight with rules. But I was terrified of losing in an event I had not trained for properly. I was terrified of my peers and the 3500 bloodthirsty spectators. I know now that the fear of the fight is far worse than the fight itself.

The last night, my adrenal glands were working in overdrive, and sleep was impossible. The morning of the fight, I fixed myself a big breakfast, which I simply stared at. I think I finally choked down a piece of toast. These mind games would have an adverse effect on me. Not only was I worried about the fight, I hadn't eaten, and I had had very little sleep. I tried a variety of things to ease the stress. I watched television, listened to the radio, took showers, went for walks, you name it, but nothing seemed to help. A few hours from fight time, I thought about various ways that I could miss the event gracefully. My car could break down on the way, or I could suddenly get sick. I was experiencing fight or flight syndrome. In the end, my pride wouldn't allow it, and I resigned myself to the inevitable.

I met Kenny at the arena. He had agreed to work my corner. We found some unoccupied space in the dressing room, and I began to change. There were a wide variety of emotions from the other fighters. Some were obviously trying to hide their fear, while others were genuinely relaxed and at ease with the situation. A black fighter lying on a table actually seemed to be sleeping! As I began to warm up, he opened one eye and spoke: "Relax, there's over an hour left. Save some for the fight." I later learned that he was world champion Alvin Prouder.

By fight time, the adrenaline was surging out of control. My mouth was dry, my skin cold and clammy, and I wanted to puke. But as I walked into the coliseum, it was too late to turn back. Upon entering the ring I scanned the screaming crowd, but my ears locked onto a specific voice: "C'mon Keith, knock him out!"

Through the deafening roar, I could barely hear the ring announcer: "Fighting out of the red corner, from Salt Lake City, Utah, Keith Livingston . . . This is Keith's first full-contact fight."

When I stared across the ring at my opponent, my heart was beating so loud it was booming in my ears. "And fighting out of the blue corner, hailing from Denver, Colorado, with an impressive record of twelve and one, his only loss coming at the hands of world bantamweight champion Felipe Garcia, ladies and gentlemen, please welcome Lance Reese . . . Reese!"

At first I thought I must be in the wrong fight. How could I be fighting someone almost undefeated to boot? But during the referee's instructions, it became clear that not only was I in the right fight, but that I had been brought to slaughter.

The sour smell of perspiration filled my nostrils, and the single voice of the crowd blended into an indiscernible roar as the opening bell rang. The first blows were exchanged. In the first round I took a severe beating and was sent to the canvas by a thundering right cross. I now had to make a decision: lie down and quit, or get up and fight.

As I rose to my feet, so did the crowd. When I realized what had happened, a controlled anger swept through me. Every punch, every kick I threw became a blow for the journeyman fighters of the world: the overmatched, the underpaid, those who had been taken advantage of by promoters looking to further their own interests and, most of all, the under appreciated.

One minute and twenty-nine seconds into the second round, I experienced the mother of all punches. I attempted to land a rear leg front kick, but my opponent saw it coming from a mile away. In fact, he could probably have timed it with a calendar. As I was coming forward with my hands down, he was already stepping left and throwing a rear cross. On impact, the combined momentum lifted me off my feet and sent me to the canvas as though I had been dropped from the ceiling. A stick of dynamite went off inside my head, and as my body crumbled on the canvas, time stood still.

I managed to rise once more, but in the end he won the decision, and my first fight became perhaps the most valuable lesson of my kickboxing career. The mind requires conditioning, as does the body. Never again would I come to a fight under trained. But, more importantly, I had learned that there are two types of fighters: those who rise to the top, and those who help the others rise to the top. When you see an undefeated fighter, his opponents have more than likely been less than credible. It's not until two fighters on their way to the top meet that you truly see a competitive bout. Not only do you need to know your opponent and yourself. You must also know the promoter, your trainer, and your manager. Although kickboxing is considered an individual sport, it takes a team effort to win.

Singing the National Anthem prior to a bout.

PREPARING TO FIGHT

Suppose that somebody offered you a nice sum of five-hundred dollars for a one hour job, would you do it? At first, you would probably think you'd be a fool not to. But let's assume that you were told that the one-hour job you just agreed to might involve some risk, that you would most certainly get bumped and bruised, and that you might possibly get a life long injury; even meet sudden death as a result. Would you still accept the offer? Now, what if somebody waved a twenty-thousand dollar check at you and said that the money might be yours, but first you must commit yourself to years of hard work where you will risk injury daily. And even then, receiving that check will not be certain. Would you still want the job?

Few people outside of our sport understand the preparation required to become a professional kickboxer, and you will hear remarks such as, "I can't believe he made that much money for twenty minutes of work." Admittedly, the top fighters in our sport make some big bucks; however, they didn't earn it for just twenty minutes of work. And, compared to many other sports, the pay is meager, indeed. Remember the age-old saying that there is no free lunch? The fighters who do make it big did not get there by accidentally bumping into a promoter on the sidewalk, and signing a contract with him over a coffee break. The fighters who finally get rewarded with a large sum of money have spent many painstaking nights fighting for no more than a hundred dollars or, as amateurs, fighting for no more than plastic trophy.

Many people would risk their lives for a huge paycheck, but few would do it for free. Most fighters hang on to the dream of someday making it big, but more fail than succeed. As you make your decision to become a professional kickboxer, remember that the terrain is rugged, the road is long, and before earning the right to walk that final step, you must first walk the miles ahead of you.

This section covers:

- How to get started
- An insider's story
- What to look for when choosing a gym
- How to find competition
- The importance of practice

- Nutrition and eating habits
- Thoughts on eating
- Thoughts on sleeping
- Performance enhancing drugs

How to get started

Kickboxing is a rough sport, where you deliver blows intended to knock your opponent out. You will also learn how to take powerful strikes without getting stunned. Although it is a contact sport, the injuries are relatively few and usually limited to bruises, black eyes, nosebleeds, and sprained fingers and toes. Kickboxing is a sport in which none of the Eastern philosophies is emphasized. Those who truly go into kickboxing do so primarily to compete, and not to learn self-defense, confidence, meditation, etc., which many of the martial arts schools advertise. Before you decide to do this, you should therefore define exactly what it is that you want.

Keith's Knockout Advice

You are now at a point where maybe you would like to possibly compete. An appropriate question to ask is, "How do I get started? Where do I go from here?" Hopefully, you have read and practiced the techniques and concepts in this manual. Additionally, it is important to remember that this is meant to be a companion teacher and provide a sound foundation. It is not meant to be your only source of information.

If you desire to go beyond the pages of this book, you must now find a training center, a coach, and eventually a manager. This is the tricky part. In the world of martial arts, there are many pretenders. I see training centers all the time that advertise kickboxing; however, only a handful are legitimate and have competent instructors. When looking for a school, you are likely to find a ton of martial arts schools, but few that specifically teach kickboxing. Many martial artists also confuse the various styles of karate with kickboxing. They're not the same. Just because a person throws kicks and punches, he is not necessarily practicing kickboxing. Also be aware that cardio-kickboxing and kickboxing aerobics are not the same as kickboxing. Almost every fitness center and many martial arts schools advertise kickboxing, and many people have generalized the word to any workout that includes kicking and punching.

An insider's story

Keith's Corner

During the early nineties, I owned and operated a kickboxing gym called North American Kickboxing. My gym had a reputation as a no nonsense school of hard knocks. Typically, all of my students were sparring full-contact within the first ninety days, as I've always believed that the only way to learn to fight is to do it. I modeled my gym after the boxing gyms I had been in and around. You sign up, learn some basics, and before you know it, you're sparring and competing. I've always believed that students are capable of learning advanced techniques early in their development.

A student's training must be individualized as much as possible. The problem is that most schools lump everyone together, and expect all students to learn at the same pace. A good instructor must evaluate a student's overall make-up, including body structure, intellectual maturity, competitiveness, mental attitude, and heart. For example, if a student lacks coordination, more time working the basics is in order. But if, in the same class, you have a student with excellent physical attributes, would it be fair to hold him back in order that you might keep the class training together? The student with the enhanced physical attributes will soon become bored and drop out of class.

On the flip side, if you tailor your teaching toward the fast learner, the slower students will become frustrated and eventually leave. My experience is that martial arts studios generally move at the pace of the slowest student.

Good instructors evaluate each student individually, and train him accordingly. Most studios, out of necessity, continue to lump students into categories or belt levels. But I recommend that even in a group teaching environment, instructors find ways to individualize their students' training. This approach requires more instructors for the group. A class of thirty students should have a minimum of three trainers, who have met and evaluated the students prior to the class. Each student's progress and aptitude should be charted with clearly defined goals. The student should be an integral part of this process, and should be allowed to define his or her goals within the art.

It has been my experience that the average student can be expected to last ninety days before losing interest and leaving your gym. This usually happens because of the group teaching mentality. The same could be said for health spas. The reason is simple. The student gets excited, signs up, and is thrown into a group setting, becoming just another member. Good instructors make their students feel that the training is individualized, keeping them excited for years rather than months.

I would like to impart a little advice as you begin, or continue, your journey in the martial arts. Everybody has a story, some true, and some less true. If I had a nickel for every time somebody told me that they "used to be a martial artist," I would be a rich man. I've heard it all: from hearts being torn from chest cavities, to secret death blows, and even magical powers that can strike you from a distance. I've seen instructors that move objects, like phone book pages, or send pencils spinning wildly across the tabletop. I've seen every possible con to separate the student from his hard earned cash. I've met the best of the best and certainly the worst of the worst. I've had conversations with people that haven't met me, but still recall with great detail the fight where they knocked me out. It's always enjoyable to wait until after the story to introduce myself. I've actually had people so embarrassed by their account that they tried to convince me that we did fight. Fortunately, I learned early not to believe anything I hear, and only about half of what I see. When I hear these fantastic tales, my response is simple: "Show me." Yet, my heart is still beating safely inside my chest, I've yet to suffer the fabled death blow, and sure I've been hit, but never from the other side of the room. Usually the correspondence goes something like this:

"Show me."
"I can't, it would result in your death."
"I'll take my chances."
"I can't be responsible for your death."

The individual who claims to possess the power to strike me from a distance then says that he will show me, but it requires a one-year contract with his studio. When I agree to sign the contract after he shows me the magical strike, he refuses. Not once in twenty-four years have I seen proof of these incredible feats.

Oh, and the martial artist who could move objects with his mind, he was debunked on national television. He was also completely humiliated in the ring by Dale "Apollo" Cook, a man who can truly fight. My advice is simple: Look for a reputable gym that turns out a quality product. Forget about the secret or magic techniques. If it sounds unbelievable, it is!

WHAT TO LOOK FOR WHEN CHOOSING A GYM

Keith's Knockout Advice

Although the hand techniques of kickboxing are identical to those of boxing, it has been my experience that boxers are generally tougher and more skilled than kickboxers. I believe this is because they have had tougher and more knowledgeable trainers. When choosing a school, first sit in on a few sessions and observe the instructor. There are four things you must consider when selecting a training center and a coach:

1. **Are the students at the center competing**, and if so, are they winning? Does the instructor do a good job at organizing events in which they can compete?

2. **Is the facility properly equipped?** Does it have heavy bags, speed bags, boxing equipment, conditioning apparatus, and preferably a ring?

3. **Does the coach show genuine interest** when interacting with his students, or does he care only about the money he is taking in? Is the instructor really teaching, or is he just putting students through their paces? Remember, an instructor doesn't have to be the world champion in order to be a good teacher. Performing and teaching are two different things. A good instructor can take you beyond his own level of skill and toward world champion caliber.

4. **Is the instructor compassionate and safety minded?** A good instructor should be tough and drill you on your work, but he should not be cruel. He should also know how to treat minor injuries and how to give emotional support when needed. Is the overall image of the school professional?

Many areas of the country don't have kickboxing centers. The best alternative is therefore a good boxing gym. There are many benefits to training at a boxing gym, as well as some disadvantages. The benefits are that the boxing gyms are relatively inexpensive and sometimes even free of charge. Additionally, I have found the training to be superb, the coaches knowledgeable, and the facilities properly equipped. I would recommend that you go to a boxing gym on occasion in addition to your training at the kickboxing facility.

The disadvantages of the boxing gyms are that they are for boxing. When training at the boxing gym, please leave your kicks at home. Never kick the bags in a boxing only gym! I have also found that boxing gyms are generally tougher than kickboxing gyms. I don't mean to imply that this is a disadvantage, but you should be prepared for the school of hard knocks when entering the world of boxing. If you do supplement your training with straight boxing, and you are given the opportunity to compete, I highly recommend that you take advantage of it. The more ring experience you gain, the better overall fighter you will become. Good boxing skills are essential to the kickboxer.

How to find competition

Keith's Corner

Once you have found a facility and a coach and gained some ring experience with your peers, your next step is to begin competing. So, how does one line up fights? In general, once your coach feels that you are ready, he will begin to find competitions for you to enter. Most competent coaches double as corner men and will see to the majority of the competition arrangements.

A manager is not really needed until you become a professional fighter and need to negotiate prize money and travel expenses. When selecting a manager, you must be cautious and fully aware of each other's expectations. Remember, the contract you sign is legal and binding. Generally, the manager receives one-third of the fighter's prize money. In addition, you must pay your trainer and corner personnel.

The fighter should not concern himself with anything other than training and competing. A good manager who can negotiate on your behalf is therefore vital. A good manager keeps abreast of your potential opponents and matches you accordingly. The manager generally starts you out with fights he knows you will win. Once you begin to fight with confidence, the manager will scout stiffer and stiffer competition.

A good manager will never overmatch his fighter for the sake of money.

A good manager must also be a master at promoting his fighter. If the manager can keep his fighter in the public eye, the public will demand to see the fighter, placing pressure on the promoter to use the fighter, and eventually increasing the fighter's net worth. The manager usually gains exposure through media, such as television and newspapers. To date, the marketing of kickboxing has been lacking. How many kickboxers can you name? If you don't believe in the value of marketing, just look at Ali. Marketing more than fighting made him known the world over. I would challenge you to find a single person who has not heard of the great Ali.

Finally, be careful of blanket contracts that give a manager the right to compensation for all aspects of your career. Who knows, I might see you in the movies some day.

The importance of practice

The serious kickboxing competitor must establish good habits and a disciplined training routine early. But, as in any activity you pursue, there are times when you get utterly bored with the routine, when you feel that you just can't set foot in the gym one more day. However, understand that it is not possible to win in kickboxing by being an armchair fighter; in other words, by dreaming about it in the safety of your living room. To master the art, you must practice often. Twice a week does not cut it for a person with ambitions to win.

But what if you feel that you will go crazy if you go to the gym every day? Right now, as you are imagining yourself the champion of the world, such a statement may sound rather ironic. Your passion is kickboxing! However, as time goes by and you begin to feel the wear on your body and mind, it is possible that you will wake up one morning and say that you have had enough. You must now know how to push beyond boredom, frustration, and physical and mental pain.

If your objective is to win in kickboxing, the price you must pay is measured in time, sweat, muscle pain, and mental determination. Your dedication to the sport must be unflinching. However, the thrill that you felt in those early days may begin to fade. You may feel that you have hit a plateau, that you are just not making progress as fast as you should. Instead of adding new techniques, begin to refine and polish those that you already know. This is when boredom sets in for most people.

Setting goals is the first step to winning. Knowing how to get there is the next step. The third step is executing the plan with consistency every day.

Try these exercises to break up the **MONOTONY OF TRAINING**:

Exercise 1

Your training does not need to be comprised of only long hours of punching and kicking and sparring. Try channeling your energy toward specifics tasks, such as improving endurance, coordination, balance, and reflexes. Sports that involve a lot of running and jumping, for example, help build endurance, explosiveness, and leg strength. Weight lifting increases your muscular strength. Once in a while, you may even take an evening off to play chess with your best friend (or worst enemy) to help sharpen your mind.

Exercise 2

When in the gym, analyze and compare yourself to the other fighters, and compete silently. How does your endurance compare to that of the other fighters? Can you wear your opponents down without getting tired yourself? How fast are you compared to the others? Can you move around your opponents in circles and strike before they see it coming? What about power? Can you overpower most of your opponents

or, if not, what strategy can you use to gain an advantage? What about determination? When the others are ready to quit, can you take that extra step? (This is the only time when finishing last is acceptable).

NUTRITION AND EATING HABITS

Food is your source of energy and helps build muscles, bones, and other tissues. To function well, you need a balanced mixture of protein, carbohydrates, fats, vitamins, minerals, and water. The problem top athletes face is which types of foods to eat and which to avoid. Many advertisements for sports bars and food supplements promise winning results in weight loss, or increased stamina and strength. Taking a pill may seem far easier than planning and cooking a good meal. But the question is, will a simple pill really make up for nutritional deficiency and compensate for bad habits in your lifestyle? Will these supplements really improve your performance, or will they simply empty your wallet? Let's start by looking at what your body needs:

Proteins provide the framework for your muscles, bones, and blood, and are essential for growth and repair of tissue. Proteins are found in chicken, beef, pork, fish, eggs, and dairy products.

Carbohydrates provide your body and brain with fuel and are broken down into simple carbohydrates (sugars), and complex carbohydrates (starches). Simple carbohydrates may give you a quick spurt of energy, while complex carbohydrates provide your body with vitamins, minerals, and other nutrients. Carbohydrates are found in bread, potatoes, spaghetti, rice, grains, fruits, and vegetables.

There has been a lot of controversy about whether you should eat lots of proteins and cut the carbohydrates. Proteins help you build muscle, but carbohydrates give you endurance and energy. Both are important to fighting. My suggestion is, don't cut the carbohydrates.

Fats store vitamins A, D, E, and K, and help insulate you from extreme temperatures, as well as giving you stamina. Fats are found in butter, cheese, oils, milk, meat, and nuts.

Vitamins put proteins, carbohydrates, and fats to use, and are also involved in the manufacturing of blood cells and hormones. Vitamins are found in a wide variety of foods, and especially in fruits and vegetables.

Minerals help build bones and teeth, help your muscles to operate, and help your nervous system to transmit messages. Minerals are obtained through ordinary intake of food.

Water is used to digest food and transmit nutrients to, and waste products from, cells. Water also acts as a cooling agent and is important in the production of sweat, which evaporates from your skin to cool your body. To prevent dehydration, drink when you are thirsty, as well as during and after exercise to replace water lost from sweating. In addition to pure water, water is also found in milk and fruit juices.

Should you limit drinking to before or after workouts, or is it okay to drink during the workout as well? Some schools discourage this, because they don't want the distraction, or they equate drinking to lack of discipline during training. Others say that being thirsty, and having to work through this uncomfortable experience, makes us stronger. Or they say that water settles in your stomach and makes you sick during training. But research shows that it is good to drink before, during, and after exercise. Furthermore, you can become dehydrated before you feel thirsty. If you do a lot of sparring or bag work, you should drink between rounds. Drinking small amounts often keeps you hydrated and less likely to get sick than gulping down a gallon of cold water all at once.

Some schools also believe that raising the temperature in the training area by a few degrees makes students sweat more and lose more weight. I don't recommend this, either. Excessive temperatures, along with exercise and sparring gear, don't make for a good combination. In rare instances, heat exhaustion can kill you.

Calories are the measure of the amount of energy that can be derived from food. If you take in more calories than required, and you don't work them off in a physical activity, you body will convert the excess to fat. How many calories you need depends on your sex, age, body composition, percentage of body fat, and metabolic rate (the number of calories needed to sustain your body at rest). How active you are physically also affects your calorie requirement. If you are into heavy physical activity, you will need 400-600 calories more a day than if you are into low activity.

To calculate your ideal body weight, use the following formula:

Men: Height (in inches) times 4 minus 128
Women: Height (in inches) times 3.5 minus 108

For example, if you are a man of 5 foot 11 inches, convert that to 71 inches and time it by four. Your new number is now 284. Subtract 128, and your ideal body weight is 156 pounds.

It is important to understand that rather than aiming for one ideal number, there is a range of ideal body weights for every height. Also consider your muscle mass and skeletal structure. Do you have a small, medium, or large frame? The need to lose weight is determined more accurately through body composition, especially in athletes, who are more muscular than the average person, and therefore tend to weigh more.

THOUGHTS ON EATING

Many people ignore the fact that they abuse their bodies with junk food, too little exercise, and other destructive habits. But becoming a "health-nut" may be equally destructive. Your diet should be consistent whether you are training for a fight or not. Breakfast, as everybody knows (or so it has been said), is the most important meal of the day. However, breakfast is typically filled with high cholesterol foods: bacon, sausage, and other things that you should stay away from. I don't believe that it is necessary to completely eliminate these high fat foods from your diet, but instead be careful with how much you consume, as there are better ways to get proteins.

Contrary to popular belief, I don't feel that breakfast is the most important meal of the day. I eat a very light breakfast, consisting of one slice of toast and a cup of tea. Around noon, I eat a well-balanced meal. At night I eat the leftovers from lunch, or a small sandwich, or soup and crackers and an apple. I snack every few hours on candy, nuts, and salty snacks, such as pretzels and crackers. Before bedtime, I eat milk and cereal, or cheese and crackers with tea. I eat something light containing carbohydrates about one hour before I work out, and again within one hour after completing the workout. Eating before working out fuels my body and removes hunger pains. I also drink one or two carbonated soft drinks a day, even though others say it's bad for you. My diet stays the same whether I am training for an upcoming fight or not. I do not change my diet just because I am competing. I try to maintain a healthy diet that has longevity and works whether I am competing or not. That way I don't have to make a major life-style change. Competing is stressful enough, without the added burden of dietary adjustments.

I don't follow any established dieting program. Most of what I do comes from experimentation with how I feel and with what works for me in particular. In general, I eat a low to medium fat diet, about 40 – 50 grams of fat/day. I eat a variety of foods, and always one home cooked, well-balanced meal a day, usually favoring vegetables, pasta, and chicken over red meats. I don't deprive myself of anything I like to eat, but I also don't overindulge in anything. For example, I like to drink one or two Diet Cokes a day, and I always eat some chocolate or other sweets every day. Because I have a job that is physically demanding in addition to my martial arts workouts, I sweat a lot, so I always have some salt cravings. I eat pretzels, salty nuts, soy sauce in foods, and potato chips a couple of times a month. I stay away from fast foods more because I simply don't like it, than because it is supposed to be bad. I might eat a hamburger and French fries twice a year.

Nutrition is certainly important. If I don't eat properly, I don't have the energy to train hard. This is true both if I eat too little or too much, or the "wrong" kinds of foods, usually meals lacking in balance: too much meat and not enough vegetables, for example. Or the other way around: too many vegetables and not enough calories or fat. Eating almost exclusively vegetables makes me hungry quicker which, in turn, steals energy and keeps me from training all out.

I emphasize proper eating habits more than exactly what to eat. For example, I feel it is good to eat whenever you are hungry, but also to stop eating whenever you get full. I stress the importance of not depriving yourself of the foods you really like. Few people have the discipline to maintain a diet that makes them feel deprived. In addition, I have not found weight loss easier when restricting certain foods. I find it more beneficial to restrict the size of the portions and to engage in activities that don't make you think of food all the time. I have found that if you are limited to eating only certain foods at only certain times of the day, you think about eating more often and are therefore more likely to cheat on your diet. I emphasize making sure that you get the nutrition you need. When you step up the intensity in your training, your body needs more calories and a higher fluid intake in order to "rise to the occasion." I stress listening to what your body needs, and experimenting in small steps to see if it makes a difference for the better or worse, and then make the necessary adjustments.

When training for a fight, it is not necessary to cut all the good foods you normally enjoy. Everything that sounds like it's bad is not going to affect you negatively. Much of it has to do with the amounts you consume, rather than with what you consume. The key is to listen to your body more than you listen to the "experts." Coffee, for example, sounds like a poison, but in small amounts of one or two cups a day, it can give you a good energy boost. The same goes for soft drinks or candy bars. Although I don't believe in making these your primary source of food and drink, as long as you eat regular balanced meals, if your body says Coke, and if you feel good when you drink one, by all means . . . You can even experiment to see what your optimal amount is. I like to eat a candy bar or some other sweet snack, but I don't like to eat a candy bar within an hour before a hard workout. I'd rather eat it one or two hours after the workout. My decisions are not based on knowing beforehand what is supposed to be best for me; only by listening to my body and doing what makes me feel good, strong, and satisfied. If I skip out on the candy or soft drink, I feel as though my body is missing something, even if I eat a well-balanced nutritious meal. In short, I don't feel as good as I would have, had I had my chocolate and Coke. I feel that anything that is too restrictive or extreme, for example, cutting almost all fats, or cutting all sweets, or living on an almost all liquid diet, has a negative effect on you. Not eating in the evening is hard, too. If I go to bed hungry, I can't sleep, which affects my energy level the next day.

I don't smoke or drink alcohol, and never have. I lead an active lifestyle and have a high energy level. I am five foot six inches tall and weigh 120 pounds. My weight has remained constant (give or take a pound or two) for fifteen years. I am of the opinion that most nutritional supplements, such as Creatine and protein sports bars, are both harmless and worthless. Eat them instead of a candy bar if you want to, but it's going to cost you three times as much! Also, I think we tend to fear getting off the supplements and losing some of our athletic ability. Using supplements for many years may make you a "slave" to them. In general, my philosophy is that, in our society, we can get all the nutrition we need from regular food sources, as long as they are chosen with some forethought and care.

When you hear about a new exercise or dieting program, look hard at all the facts and your personal lifestyle and experiences. Is this program going to enhance the specific attributes you need for kickboxing? Does it use a time schedule that will work well with your schedule: your work hours, family obligations, etc.? If it involves eating, is it something that you can actually be excited about, or will it interfere with the cooking plans and eating habits of your family?

Keith's Corner

Typically, a fighter's diet should be high in carbohydrates, as this is the body's fuel, but there is some controversy here, too. I think the problem is that every human being is different. In other words, you have to experiment. Some people gain a lot of weight when they go high on carbs. It is therefore important to determine over a period of time what types of meals seem to give you energy, and what types of meals make you sluggish. I don't believe it is necessary to cut all the fats, or to get rid of all the foods that are nice and tasty. However, you need to eat appropriate portions and not stuff yourself with one big meal.

When I train for a fight, I eat four to five eggs in the morning (minus the yolk, which is high in cholesterol), because egg white is a good source of protein. I also eat oatmeal and toast. If you get yourself on a schedule where you are having dinner at an appropriate time, let's say no later than six, you will be hungry enough for a big breakfast when you wake up in the morning. The problem with us Americans is that we snack on potato chips and other crap constantly, all day long, without stopping. What works for me is no lunch at all, or if I have lunch, it is something light and nutritious, like a tuna fish sandwich and vegetables. For dinner, I don't worry so much about what I eat, as long as I eat sensibly.

As long as you are exercising, your weight will mostly take care of itself. I am five foot eleven inches tall, and my weight fluctuates between 185 and 200 pounds. I am consistently between 195 and 200 pounds when I'm not training. When I'm training, I am consistently between 185 and 190 pounds. I don't have much of a sweet tooth, but sometimes your body needs it. Again, it comes down to sensibility. If you eat five candy bars in a row, it might not be a good thing. But I have also found that if I feel that I need some chocolate in my system, or if I just have the munchies, as long as I don't sweat it, I'll be alright. It's when you start to obsess and say no, that your plans become difficult to follow. If you get a craving for a candy bar, then eat the damn candy bar!

There has also been a lot of talk about the drawbacks of carbonated soft drinks. I think that the fighter who is not drinking them is better off. Personally, I like to have a carbonated drink right before the fight as an energy boost. Again, I think it boils down to personal preference. As far as supplements go, I always felt that Creatine gave me more endurance, more muscular strength. The problem is that I think you can achieve the same things through your diet. I would not recommend to my students to buy supplements. I may recommend Creatine simply because it worked for me, but again, I think that everybody is different. Either way, you should be careful and use these things in moderation. We live in a society of quick fix, where we want fast results. But I think that you're better off doing it the natural way, and get lasting results over a period of time instead of right up front.

I smoked for a lot of years, and found that after I quit I was able to get into shape faster and maintain that condition much longer. Smoking is obviously a factor when training for a fight, and we all know about the health effects of smoking. Every little edge counts in this game. If you can last just seconds longer than your opponent, it could mean the difference between winning and losing. It's that close.

As far as drinking goes, it's really not conducive to the sport. If you get stone drunk three nights before a fight, it will definitely affect your performance, because your body has to correct itself. When you go out and get smashed, you are going to be high, even though alcohol is a depressant. In order for the body to balance itself, at some point afterwards, you are going to be low. You may be able to recover within the three days, but again, from personal experience, I think that you are not going to perform as well. If you get drunk one night two months before a fight, it may not affect the fight itself, but it will probably affect your training schedule for the next week, and may put you behind. The downside to beer is mostly the potential for weight gain, and the potential for it to become an addiction that will eventually destroy not only your fighting career, but your life. Yes, I think you can probably drink in moderation and get away with it, but why give your opponent the edge? The bottom line is common sense and discipline. If you are training for a fight and you are serious about reaching the top, smoking, drinking, and silly eating habits should not even be a factor. Don't punish yourself if you slip here and there, but if you want to make it to the world championships, this isn't even an issue.

THOUGHTS ON SLEEPING

Many people don't understand the importance of sleep. They think that if they can get by on fewer hours a night, they will have more time for training, a social life, work, etc. But lack of sleep does more than just make you sleepy. Lack of sleep limits your endurance. You can't go as many rounds in sparring or on the heavy bag when your body is suffering from sleep deprivation. Lack of sleep could also take more than a day to make up for. I once knew a martial artist who felt he was wasting time when he was sleeping. He would limit his sleep to just a few hours a night, then get up at five o'clock in the morning and put in a grueling workout before going to his regular job, and not be back in bed until one or two at night. But, guess what? He would sit and nod off in his car in a parking lot, or wherever else he had a few extra minutes.

Everybody doesn't need the same amount of sleep to function well. If your buddy gets by on five hours a night, it doesn't mean that you will. I feel good after about eight hours of sleep. If I cut to seven hours for two nights in a row, I actually feel the effects: I don't have as much energy, and I can't go as long during workouts. If you train a lot, you should listen to your body's signals for rest. For example, some people think that if you train for five hours a day, you are more admirable and have better work ethics than if you train for only an hour and half every other day. Without listening to the experts, listen to how you feel. Set your training schedule and pace for what makes you stronger, not for what sounds better. You may find that you can actually advance faster by doing less, plus it will do wonders for your social life.

Sometimes you may need to take a longer break of a week or two. When I go on vacation, I often worry about missing my workouts, and that I will feel sluggish when I start up again. But I have found the opposite to be true. My body welcomes the much needed rest, and I feel recharged when getting back to the gym after a week off. If this works for you, you might want to plan to take a week off every three to four months.

Also, get away from the idea that you have to be soaked in sweat and almost unable to walk to your car after every workout. Some training sessions can and should be lighter than others. Exploring and refining the techniques is important in addition to hardcore sparring. These workouts are not a waste of time. They can enhance learning, as well as giving your body a break. Just make sure that the workout is productive; that you are actually working on something and not just socializing. Find the good medium. Don't deprive yourself of things your body needs, like sleep, or coffee, or chocolate, or good hard sparring. But also don't overdo it. Drinking a twelve pack of Coke a day will most likely be too much, and so will three hours of sparring a day. More is not necessarily better; nor is less. There is a happy medium that allows you to feel at your peak at all times. But guess what? It's your job to find it. Somebody else's program or training schedule will not work for you.

PERFORMANCE ENHANCING DRUGS

Keith's Corner

When I was training for the Ultimate Fighting Championships in 1994, I used DHEA (a hormone that is naturally produced by your adrenal glands, and which increases your blood testosterone level) in conjunction with DMSO as a carrier. To get quick results, I used more than I should have. In combination with dehydration, over training, and a rigorous weight lifting program that was way too advanced for my level, these factors had a cumulative adverse effect.

During early usage, I noticed some psychological effects, including increased aggression. About two weeks after starting usage, I developed intense lower back pain, bloating, and blood in the urine. At the emergency room a few days later, I was diagnosed with complete kidney failure. I spent a week in the hospital and underwent dialysis (artificial cleaning of the blood, because of kidney malfunction). Little by little, my kidneys healed and restarted on their own. Within a month, I was back to training (but not for the UFC, which I had missed). Now, almost ten years later, my training is completely drug free, and I have no symptoms from this earlier mishap. Others may not be so lucky!

Listen to your body and mind. If something feels out of whack, it probably is. If you have an injury, lighten up a little on the training. If you lack energy, or are hungry or tired, then eat more or better, or get some rest. I can't remember who said it, but I think it was some Chinese philosopher: "When you're hungry, eat. When you're tired, sleep." I think that's probably good advice to follow.

TRAINING WITH EQUIPMENT

Training with equipment is an integral part of the fight preparation process. Through proper equipment training, you will develop power, speed, accuracy, and timing, along with proper technique and conditioning. As your experience grows, you will become more and more comfortable with beating the heavy bag. You will throw your strikes and kicks with extension and speed. You will learn to judge distance and make adjustments to the swinging bag, keeping a fast and strong pace throughout the round. A common problem, however, is how to transfer this bag work to the ring.

This section covers:

- Choosing a heavy bag
- Working the heavy bag
- Glove-up with Keith
- Working the double-end bag
- Drills for the speed bag
- Mitt work
- Kicking drills
- Thoughts on bag work
- Training for a three-round fight
- In a nut-shell

CHOOSING A HEAVY BAG

Keith's Corner

Choosing the proper bag is almost as important as the training process itself. I have found that leather bags are the best, while canvas bags are the least desirable. Leather has a better feel and is less likely to damage your gloves. Because kickboxers often train barefoot, the rough surface of the canvas bag tends to scrape and cut feet. Some would have you believe that this is a good way to condition your feet for the sport. My feelings are that all it does is set you back in your training while waiting for your feet to heal. If canvas is all you can afford, I recommend that you wrap the whole bag with duct tape. When buying a bag, you may also want to consider vinyl or synthetic leather.

The weight of your heavy bag should be relative to your size and experience. Starting out with a bag that is too heavy can have a negative impact on your joints and muscles. Many bags come unfilled. This allows you to adjust the weight accordingly. Unfilled bags can be stuffed with rags or old bed sheets. When you are starting out, make sure that the bag has a few inches of give to it. Your training will be of little benefit if you feel like you are punching and kicking a rock. The bag should be heavy enough not to swing wildly when hit.

WORKING THE HEAVY BAG

Keith's Knockout Advice

The heavy bag has a variety of uses. Perhaps the two most important benefits of heavy bag training are **power** and **conditioning**. A regular heavy bag routine teaches you to hit the bag with power, and to work in rounds.

Your heavy bag workout should be a sustained effort: Punch and kick with maximum intensity. A starting routine should be a minimum of three 2-minute rounds, with a 1-minute rest between rounds. Do this routine until it becomes fairly easy, then increase by one round, working up to a maximum of twelve rounds. By working rounds, you will simulate the actual fight. Work both long and short range fighting, throwing hard combinations to both the body and head. If you are fighting a minimum mandatory eight kick per round fight, make sure to throw at least twice that many kicks per round on the heavy bag.

Heavy bag work is essential for building power, learning to punch properly, and learning to control various distances. Don't punch the bag simply for the sake of punching. Always have a plan or a goal. In other words, work on specific techniques or concepts. Master a few punches at a time and build your repertoire.

Make sure that you throw your techniques correctly, so that you don't develop bad habits and improper technique. Work on fighting at different distances, using techniques that appropriately complement the fighting distance that you are seeking. Build technique first and power last.

When working the heavy bag:

1. **Throw strong combinations** including both punching and kicking, along with inside and outside fighting techniques.

2. Set your bag up so that it **allows at least 180 degrees of movement** around the bag. Standing in one spot and pounding away at the bag does not represent the fight realistically.

3. **Work a variety of angles** from different ranges, while incorporating footwork.

4. **Incorporate head and body movement.** Visualize your opponent trying to counter your offensive techniques.

Glove Up with Keith

Most fighters in the amateur ranks don't know how to throw a punch properly, and are often seen swinging wildly. But if you can't punch and kick with conviction in the real fight, it doesn't matter how hard you can punch and kick the bag. Maybe you can beat the heavy bag at full intensity for two minutes without getting tired. But after a well fought two-minute round in competition, you will feel as though you're ready to die. So, how do you keep from getting tired?

The answer is: experience. When all the unknown factors are resolved, you will fight more relaxed and get less tired. You must learn to fight in the moment only. When you start getting concerned with when the round is over, or with that you still want to have a life after this fight, that's the beginning of your destruction. I think that few people understand what Bruce Lee meant when he said, "forget about winning or losing; lay your life before him."

WORKING THE DOUBLE-END BAG

Keith's Knockout Advice

Good head and upper body movement is essential to kickboxing. A good way to develop upper body movement is through the use of the double-end bag. This is a small bag about the size of a person's head, and is attached from the top and bottom with a bungee cord. When struck, the bag swings back at you, and if not struck straight, it will swing back wildly in different directions. It takes good coordination to strike the double-end bag for a duration of time.

The double-end bag teaches you to punch and slip, and is most useful in developing speed, timing, and rhythm. Many new fighters find the bag extremely difficult to master and experience frustration. Again, I urge you to begin slowly, mastering a few techniques at a time. As with the heavy bag, you must have a plan and specific goals. I teach my students to begin with a jab, as this enables you to get a feel for the bag and establish your timing. Next, add the rear cross. After mastering the one-two punch combination, try a double jab, followed by a rear cross. After gaining comfort with a few punches, add head movement to your combinations. For example, throw a jab and a rear cross, and as the bag comes toward you, move your head right, then left. This simulates avoiding your opponent's counter-punches. The combinations are almost unlimited. As you advance, add the hook, uppercut, and overhand punches. Always work head movement within your combinations.

Try this exercise on the **DOUBLE-END BAG**:

Exercise 1

1. **Strike the bag with a jab**. To keep it going straight back and forth, you must throw your punches straight.

2. Once the bag is responding correctly and comes toward you, think of it as your opponent's punch and **slip left or right**,

making the punch miss. Then **counter with another jab**.

3. Next, **add a rear cross**. You are now throwing two punches. **Continue slipping** and countering, adding punches until you are throwing combinations.

4. **Slip left and right at your discretion**. The objective is to keep the bag moving constantly. The harder you strike the bag, the faster it will swing back toward you. You must now **change the timing** of your head and upper body movement to fit the movement of the bag.

5. When you become comfortable with the straight punches, **try some hooks**. This is more difficult than on the heavy bag, because you must time your hook to the bag's forward and reverse movement.

6. If your timing is off, you will get struck in the face. **Your distance to the bag should be so that the bag will impact your head if you do not use sufficient upper body movement**. This gives you a direct indication of how well you are doing.

7. You can also **practice uppercuts** on the double-end bag. To throw the uppercut, come with your fist directly underneath the bag. This requires superior timing if the bag is already swinging from your previous strikes.

8. When you get comfortable with the four basic strikes, **try some spinning back fists**. If your timing is off, you will either be out of reach, or strike with your forearm instead of with your fist. When you have learned to land the spinning back fist, put together combinations that allow you to throw additional strikes.

9. The double-end bag is also an excellent device for **practicing footwork**. Start by throwing a jab, slipping the counter-punch, and taking a tiny step to the side. Continue this exercise until you have stepped a complete circle around the bag. Every time you step, you must time your next jab to the bag's movement. Stepping and striking is more difficult than throwing the strike stationary because, as your angle to the bag changes, the bag will no longer swing straight toward you but slightly to the side. To keep the bag from swinging wildly, your timing must be very good.

Also use the double-end bag for precision kicking.

Drills for the speed bag

Keith's Corner

Punching the speed bag develops timing, rhythm, and accuracy. But perhaps the most important benefit is increased shoulder strength. Because the bag hangs rather high with its lower end level with your chin, it helps you develop the endurance and muscular strength required to keep your guard up throughout the fight. The smaller the bag, the faster it moves. When working the speed bag:

1. **Strike the bag with the edge of your hand**. Allow the bag to bounce off the board and swing back toward your hand, and bounce off the board one more time. Then hit the bag straight with the same hand. Continue alternating hands until you build up a fast pace. Set a timer and work in rounds.

2. Next, **strike the bag straight**, alternating hands. Or strike the bag twice with the same hand before alternating.

3. **Strike the bag with the back of your hand**, either alternating hands or striking it twice with the same hand in a figure eight pattern.

4. Because the speed bag is hung high and is about the same size as a human head, you can use it to **practice head kicks**.

5. Also **try uppercuts and hooks**. A common drill is to get the bag going in a pattern with alternating left and right strikes, and then stop it against the board with a sudden, explosive hook or uppercut.

MITT WORK

Keith's Knockout Advice

Mitt drills are designed to enhance a fighter's ability to throw combinations. When working the mitts, start by throwing specific combinations. This allows you and the mitt holder to get comfortable with each other, and also gives the mitt holder the opportunity to correct mistakes you may be making.

Next, throw combinations according to the positions of the mitts. The mitt holder will position the mitts, then call out various numbers representing the number of punches or kicks to be thrown. For example, if the mitt holder calls "three," you would throw a

three-strike combination according to the mitt position. If the mitt holder calls "kick-three," you would incorporate a kick into the three-strike combination. You can also respond with an appropriate punch for the position, without the mitt holder calling out numbers.

Once you and the mitt holder are comfortable with this, incorporate movement by the mitt holder. For example, the mitt holder will sweep his left mitt toward your head like a hook, and you will bob and weave and counter with a combination on the mitts. Both you and the mitt holder should utilize proper footwork throughout the drills.

If you are the mitt holder: It takes skill to be a good mitt holder. The purpose of holding mitts is not limited to giving the fighter a striking target. The mitt holder should know what he is doing to protect both himself and the fighter from injury. If he is too far away, or holds the mitts at an angle that isn't appropriate for the strike, the fighter risks overextending and injuring his joint. The mitt holder also risks injury to joints, and if the mitts aren't held tightly enough or close enough to the body, he risks injury by the power of the fighter's strike pushing the mitts into the holder.

Many untrained people think that the mitt is supposed to be a moving target, and that the kickboxer should strike the mitt only when it is shown to him. Thus, the mitt holder holds the mitts behind his back, and then quickly brings one mitt into view, giving the fighter a moving target to try to hit, and then withdraws the mitt again. But this is, in my opinion, a poor way to work the focus mitts. A good mitt holder holds the mitts stationary at the proper angle, and then uses footwork and adjustments in distance to provide a challenging workout that brings out the fighter's power and timing. A good mitt holder can move or respond with a strike of his own, and generally act as an opponent. A good mitt holder can also pressure the fighter by forcing him to move back or to the side. There should also be an element of intimidation in the drill. If the mitt holder is the one who constantly retreats, it does not give a true reflection of the fight, and is therefore not a valuable training tool for full contact kickboxing.

KICKING DRILLS

Keith's Corner

The air shield (or kicking shield) has traditionally been used for kicking only. With some experience, however, you and your partner can learn to strike the shield with punches as well. It is important to combine punching and kicking whenever possible. Remember, you will fight the way you have trained.

Prior to working with the air shield, work slowly with your partner on holding positions. Make sure the holder understands where and how you want the shield positioned. The holder will position the shield either to the left, right, or center. The holder must provide variety through many different positions. By positioning the shield to the side, the holder provides a target for round house kicks, crescent kicks, knee strikes, hooks, etc. The frontal position is natural for front kicks, side thrust kicks, spinning back kicks, knee strikes, jabs, rear crosses, etc. Bending the top portion of the shield allows you to work uppercuts, knee strikes, etc.

The drills are similar to mitt drills, with the holder calling out position and number. For example, "left-three" would be three kicks of your choice thrown to the left position. The shield holder can also call out two positions and two numbers, "right-two, center-one," for example. Your response is now two kicks to the right position, and one to the center. You can also respond with an appropriate kick for the shield position, without the holder calling out a number.

A stopwatch or timer when working mitts may seem like an insignificant piece of equipment. However, not only does it keep track of the length of the rounds, it also helps you develop a feel for the time intervals. Getting a feel for how much time that remains of the round helps you end with an impressive power combination.

Air shield work should be mobile, working various distances and angles. As with all types of bag work, you should attempt to make the drills as realistic as possible, utilizing movement, distance, combinations, power, and speed.

The air shield can also be used for endurance training. From a stationary position, have the shield holder call out a kick. Begin kicking non-stop for a pre-determined period of time. Start with twenty seconds, then increase until you are doing sixty seconds of continuous work for each kick. Work speed and power without sacrificing proper form to get a great cardiovascular workout.

In addition to providing aerobic fitness, bag work develops your fighting skills. Start slow, be familiar with your equipment, and know your capabilities. Bag work should be done at least three times per week. Always have a goal and a direction. Work with a partner whenever possible. This gives you better routines, because your partner can observe and assist with proper technique.

Thai pads are an alternative to the kicking shield. Thai pads are used for developing strong "Thai-style" round house kicks. Thai fighters typically impact with their shins when round house kicking. Thai pads are smaller than the regular kicking shield, but bigger than the focus mitts. Thai pads are used for power and endurance training. For example:

1. Assume a fighting stance and begin executing rear **leg round house kicks** with maximum power.

2. When you reach a designated number of kicks, **switch stance** and do the same on the opposite side.

3. **Increase** the number of kicks weekly.

THOUGHTS ON BAG WORK

When sparring, we tend to let down on our power or aggressiveness whenever we get a little tired or hurt. Let's say, for example, that you throw some awesome leg kicks in the beginning of the first round, but your opponent retaliates with a leg kick of his own. Once your leg starts hurting and you start fearing your opponent's retaliation, you will most likely avoid throwing subsequent leg kicks with extension and power. These are the things we don't notice when beating the heavy bag. Since the bag can't block or retaliate, the fledgling kickboxer must work to eliminate his tendency to back down when he gets hurt. If you start out strong, don't let your opponent take the fight from you.

We often hear such things as "he was born to be a fighter" or "he has killer instinct." What we mean is that the successful fighter has the ability to *take the fight to the end*, to finish, no matter how tired he is. This type of fighter also knows when it is time to bump the fight up a notch. The judges will remember those last few seconds of the round best, so it is important to finish strong. When your opponent gets hurt, this is not the time to go to your corner and take a breather. When working the heavy bag, keep in mind that bags don't hit back. Although bags and punch mitts give you superior cardiovascular conditioning, mental conditioning is developed through sparring.

You must practice punching and kicking meticulously to reach success in the ring. Simply hitting the heavy bag for a few months without getting actual fighting experience might instill a false sense of confidence. Yes, you can attain power by kicking the heavy bag, but other factors such as toughness, stamina under pressure, timing, and ability to make split second decisions must be practiced in actual sparring. It is highly recommended that before going into the advanced sections of this book, you compete in a full-contact event for a minimum of three rounds. Win or lose, learning is greatly enhanced when you face the unknown and go up against fighters that you know little or nothing about.

TRAINING FOR A THREE-ROUND FIGHT

If you want to make it as a fighter, if you want to be even moderately good, you have to pay your dues. Training for a three-round amateur fight should start about eight to ten weeks prior to fight time. The following is a suggested training schedule, which should help you acquire the endurance and strength you need. I know it is a lot to ask, but why give your opponent the edge?

Every day (evening)

1. **Shadowbox:** 3 rounds.
2. **Jump rope:** 3 rounds.
3. **Flexibility exercises:** 15 to 20 minutes until all muscles have been stretched.
4. **Abdominal exercises:** sit-ups, leg lifts, crunches (increase reps weekly).

Mon/Wed/Fri (morning)

1. **Running:** 2-3 miles. Sprint, then jog, gradually increasing sprint distance. This will train your body to speed up and slow down, and to recover while on the move.

Mon/Wed/Fri (evening)

1. **Heavy bag:** 3 rounds.
2. **Air shield:** 3 rounds.
3. **Focus mitts:** 3 rounds.
4. **Focus mitts with body gear** (a pad that the mitt holder wears around his body to shield him from blows) for punching and kicking in combinations: 3 rounds.
5. **Speed bag:** 3 rounds.

Tues/Thur/Sat (morning)

1. **Swimming:** Swim normally, gradually increasing time and distance. Sprint, gradually increasing time and speed.
2. **Strength building exercises:** weight circuit.

Tues/Thur/Sat (evening)

1. **Sparring:** 3-9 rounds. Sparring is one of the most important exercises when preparing to fight. If training for a 3-round fight, it is recommended that

you triple the number of rounds to nine to build endurance. Choose sparring partners who will simulate your opponent's style, or who will help you improve on specific skills. Start by sparring opponents that you can easily dominate. Then graduate to tougher and tougher opponents.

Caution: If your workouts become unproductive, you may need a few days of rest. Spending eight hours a day at the gym may seem impressive, but will hardly benefit your body. It is more satisfying to have a short and intense training session, where you still have time for your regular duties and obligations to home and family. Most amateur and professional kickboxers also have regular day jobs. Make sure you find a balance between training and working.

IN A NUT-SHELL

MONDAY

Morning: Run

Evening: Shadowbox
Jump Rope
Stretching
Ab Work
Bag Work

TUESDAY

Morning: Swim
Weights

Evening: Shadowbox
Jump Rope
Stretching
Ab Work
Sparring

WEDNESDAY

Morning: Run

Evening: Shadowbox
Jump Rope
Stretching
Ab Work
Bag Work

THURSDAY

Morning: Swim
Weights

Evening: Shadowbox
Jump Rope
Stretching
Ab Work
Sparring

FRIDAY

Morning: Run

Evening: Shadowbox
Jump Rope
Stretching
Ab Work
Bag Work

SATURDAY

Morning: Swim
Weights

Evening: Shadowbox
Jump Rope
Stretching
Ab Work
Sparring

RULES OF THE RING

The rules in competition kickboxing vary from sanctioning body to sanctioning body, and from country to country. The main sanctioning bodies are I.K.A. (International Kickboxing Association), I.K.F. (International Kickboxing Federation), W.K.A. (World Kickboxing Association), and I.S.K.A. (International Sport Karate Association). There are several other sanctioning organizations; however, these are the most widely recognized.

This section covers:

- The ring
- Amateur and professional fights
- Weight divisions
- Corner work
- In the gym
- Protective gear
- Treating injuries

THE RING

You will be fighting in a square ring (is this a contradiction?) that can be anywhere from 16 X 16 feet to 25 X 25 feet. This is the area inside of the ropes. If you have the weight advantage, a small ring is usually to your advantage, because it limits your opponent's mobility, and you will soon find him with his back to the ropes. The opposite is true if your opponent has the weight advantage. However, you don't get to choose the ring size, so you need to be prepared to fight in both small and large rings.

The ring will be elevated by a few feet, with a set of stairs leading up to your corner. One corner of the ring is blue, the opposing corner red, and the other two corners white. Generally, the "visiting fighter" fights from the blue corner, and the fighter with the "home corner advantage" fights from the red corner. You should go back to your corner between rounds, where your corner team will tend to your needs. The white corners are neutral. The referee will direct you to a white corner when giving your opponent an eight-count after a knockdown.

Your corner team should place a stool in the corner for you to sit on between rounds. They should also have water and spit bucket ready. Your trainer and corner personnel are allowed inside the ring between rounds, but should quickly remove the stool and spit bucket at the sound of the bell. It is also the corner team's responsibility to ensure that water is not spilled on the canvas (or if it is, to wipe it up), as water might contribute to an accidental slip.

The perimeter of the ring is marked with three or four ropes that should be fairly tight, with the top rope about shoulder height, or high enough to avoid the risk of a fighter being knocked backwards over the ropes and onto the judges table (although this happens occasionally). When entering the ring, your trainer should spread the ropes for you, so that you can enter between them. Some fighters prefer to climb over the top rope for a more flashy entrance. If a fighter gets a foot caught on the ropes when kicking, the referee should call a break in the action, until the fighter has regained his balance.

The floor of the ring is usually constructed of wooden boards with a pad on top, and then covered with tightly stretched canvas. The ring floor should have some springiness to make it comfortable to move around on, and to decrease the risk of injury to a fallen fighter.

Keith's Corner

The ring size is determined by the inside dimensions. A 20-foot ring is actually 22 feet. It's rare to find a competition ring less than 18 feet. The ring size is generally determined by the promoter, and may be whatever he or she has available. I have heard of some top fighters that negotiate the ring size as part of their contract. The edge of the ring floor should protrude a foot or more outside of the ropes. This decreases the risk of a fighter against the ropes accidentally stepping off the edge. The event personnel should ensure that the ring floor is in good shape. In my last fight, I stepped in an uneven spot in the ring and injured my knee severely, with the result of the fight being discontinued.

There should also be a bell or gong clearly signaling the start and end of each round. The bell will usually sound five seconds before the start of the round, so that the fighters have time to step from their respective corners and toward the center of the ring, with a second bell or gong at the actual start of the round.

AMATEUR AND PROFESSIONAL FIGHTS

Most rules vary from state to state and are often left up to the fighters and promoters. In general, you can expect the following:

Rounds

1. Amateurs fight three 2-minute rounds.

2. Professionals fight four to ten 2-minute rounds (sometimes 3-minute rounds).

3. Championship bouts are ten or twelve 2- or 3-minute rounds.

4. There is a 1-minute rest period between rounds.

Equipment

1. The fighters should be dressed in kickboxing shorts and a T-shirt, sleeveless shirt, or sports bra (females), or no shirt (males). Because kickboxing evolved from full-contact karate, the fighters in the old days usually wore long gi pants and a karate belt when fighting. This is not commonly seen anymore, but is not necessarily against the rules. Exactly how to dress is pretty much up to your discretion, as long as the clothing doesn't obstruct movement or presents a problem to either fighter. To my knowledge, no jewelry is allowed, especially piercing.

2. Footpads and shin guards are usually worn in amateur fights but not in professional fights, but there is no rule against wearing them if the fighters choose to do so. When fighting without footpads, ankle supports or tape around the feet or ankles may be worn.

3. Gloves should be 8-12 ounces depending on the fighter's weight division, but may be as much as 14-16 ounces depending on how liability conscious the promoter is. Tape can be used to cover the laces, but if the tape comes loose during the fight, the fight must be stopped and the fighter directed to his corner, where his corner team will fix the tape.

4. Headgear is mandatory in amateur fights, but is not worn in professional fights.

5. Groin protector (for males) and mouthpiece are required. Groin protector for females is optional.

6. Vaseline can be used in a thin layer on the face and front of the headgear, but caution must be used so that it does not get into the fighter's eyes, or into his opponent's eyes.

Rules

1. It is illegal to strike or kick to the groin, to clinch, to catch or grab a leg, and to hold the back of the opponent's head while striking. Thai-boxing matches usually allow clinching, catching a leg, and throwing.

2. In fights that allow leg kicks, a fighter is generally allowed to kick to both the outside and inside thigh

area, and to the calves. Kicking to the knees is illegal.

3. Fights that do not allow leg kicks usually have a minimum kick requirement of eight kicks per round. Fights that do allow leg kicks usually have a minimum kick requirement of six kicks above the waist per round. Some fights have no minimum kick requirement.

4. In fights that allow knee strikes, a fighter is allowed to knee to the body only (unless the opponent bends over or positions his head at body height). A fighter is not allowed to grab the opponent when kneeing, unless he is fighting under Thai-rules. Elbow strikes are illegal in most fights in the United States, except when fighting under Thai-rules. Elbow pads may be required.

5. Some fights allow the fighter to use sweeps to tire his opponent or to throw him off rhythm, but a sweep does not necessarily count as a knockdown.

6. Rules vary from state to state. Some states use the three knockdown rule or the standing eight-count. The three knockdown rule states that a fighter who is knocked down three times in a round loses that match. The standing eight-count gives a fighter who is dazed or knocked down eight seconds to recover.

Scoring

1. The fight is scored by three judges at ringside. Scoring is done according to a "10-point must system." The winner of the round gets 10 points, and the loser gets 9 points, unless additional points are deducted for a knockdown or foul.

2. The fighters are scored on the number of punches and kicks thrown. The judges will consider the force and impact of such blows.

3. The fighters are scored on the effectiveness of their defense and on their ability to counter-attack.

4. The fighters are scored on their skill and crispness. If the fighters' skill level is very closely matched, the fighter who shows more aggressiveness will have an advantage over the one who is on the defensive.

5. Points are deducted from the fighter knocked down or for fouls, or for not meeting the minimum kick requirement.

6. If a fighter is knocked down, the referee will signal the other fighter to a neutral corner, and will begin the ten-count. If the fighter rises to his feet by the count of eight, the referee will ask the fighter if he wants to continue. If the fighter rises to his feet before the count of eight, the referee will continue to count to eight, and then ask the fighter if he wants to continue. A slip is not considered a knockdown.

7. A knockout (KO) is scored if a fighter fails to resume the fight after a ten-count. A technical knockout (TKO) is scored if:

   - a fighter fails to answer the bell for the start of the next round
   - the referee deems that, for the sake of safety, the fighter should not continue
   - the fighter says that he does not want to continue
   - the corner "throws in the towel"
   - a fighter loses by default
   - a fighter is disqualified

8. A unanimous decision is announced if all three judges scored the bout in favor of the same fighter. A split decision is announced if two judges scored the bout for one fighter, and the third judge scored the bout for the other fighter. A majority decision is announced if two judges scored the bout for the same fighter, and the third judge scored the bout even. A draw is announced if one judge scored the bout for one fighter, one judge scored the bout for the other fighter, and the third judge scored the bout even.

The Referee

1. The referee shall be in the ring throughout the bout. Generally, the referee is not a judge, but may give warnings or ask the judges to deduct points for fouls. A foul consists of head butting, biting, holding the opponent's neck, attacking an opponent who has slipped or been knocked down, spitting, or other un-sportsmanlike conduct.

2. The referee shall summon the fighters to the center of the ring and give instructions prior to the first bell. At this time, the fighters should touch gloves to show proper sportsmanship.

3. The referee shall tell the fighters when to start and end the bout, and call time out when needed.

4. The referee shall separate the fighters from a clinch and ensure that the fighters otherwise follow the rules.

5. The referee may stop the contest if he feels that a fighter is getting hurt unnecessarily. The referee must use good judgment and not stop the contest unless one fighter really is unable to defend himself effectively. However, the referee must also be cautious not to allow the contest to continue, if this would endanger the fighter. The referee must therefore execute hairline precision when making decisions. During an eight-count, when deciding whether to stop or allow the fight to continue, the referee is typically looking at the fighter's eyes, balance, and ability to answer simple questions, such as, "Can you continue?" Fights that are stopped without an eight-count are generally stopped when the fighter is being overwhelmed, hurt, or is not fighting back. The referee knows the fighter is hurt when his eyes and facial expression depict injury, his balance is poor, and he is beginning to get rubber legs and arms. The referee can also stop the fight if the fighter is being so completely beaten and dominated that there is no possible way for him to win, and it is more prudent to stop the fight than risk injury to the fighter.

I refereed twelve three-round amateur matches once, and consider it harder work than fighting. The referee must be constantly sharp to ensure that nothing escapes her. She must also stay out of the way and let the fighters fight, yet be close enough to break them apart, or to stop or pause the match. The referee must also call a time out to fix tape on a fighter's gloves, or to pick up a mouthpiece that has fallen out, or to ask a corner to dry up water that has been spilled on the canvas. I felt as though I did more legwork during this night of refereeing than I do when running in preparation for a fight.

Weight divisions

In kickboxing, just as in boxing, you fight in weight divisions. It is therefore important to keep a record of your weight, and decide how many pounds you need to lose or gain in order to get to the desired weight class. Reaching your desired weight is more critical when fighting in the professional ranks. Refer to the table below to determine your weight division (females listed in parenthesis):

Heavyweight: no upper weight limit
Cruiserweight: not over 195 (168) pounds
Light Heavyweight: not over 175 (159) pounds
Middleweight: not over 160 (150) pounds
Welterweight: not over 147 (141) pounds
Lightweight: not over 135 (132) pounds
Featherweight: not over 126 (123) pounds
Bantamweight: not over 118 (114) pounds
Flyweight: not over 112 (105) pounds

The weigh-in takes place either the evening before your fight, or in the morning the day of your fight. It is not uncommon for a fighter to discover that he needs to lose two or three pounds in order to "make weight." A fighter can lose a couple of pounds of weight in a few hours through dehydration (by not eating or drinking anything, and by building up a sweat). The weight lost through dehydration is called water weight.

Sweating can be brought on by strenuous or rapid exercise. Wearing a shirt both increases sweating and acts as an absorbent. Do not wear an airtight sweat suit that traps body heat. Being unable to regulate body temperature could have an adverse effect on your health, with serious complications or even death as a result! If using sweating as a weight reduction method before a fight, don't push yourself too hard, as this may cause fatigue and illness. Work on exercises that could easily be done in your dressing room, like shadow boxing and jumping rope. Swallowing small amounts of warm (or nearly hot) water will usually help you sweat easier. All other unnecessary fluid intake should be eliminated.

Once you have made the desired weight class, you can replace the water lost before getting into the ring to fight. Although your weight at the weigh-in may fall within your division, at the start of the fight, you may actually be heavier since by then you will have replaced the water loss. This procedure may seem strange; however, it is acceptable and common. If reducing weight over a period of time, keep the weight loss slow and gradual, with no more than a pound or two per week. Don't starve yourself. As an athlete, you need to fuel your body with nutritious foods.

When fighting as an amateur, if the fighters and trainers agree, you can fight out of your weight class. In my first amateur fight, my opponent outweighed me by 40 pounds. In my fourth amateur fight, my opponent outweighed me by 24 pounds. However, giving up that much weight can be detrimental and is not recommended. If the fighters are nearly equal in skill, a weight difference of only a few pounds can make a difference. Facing an opponent who is much bigger than you can also have an adverse mental effect. I have seen fighters try to sneak pre-views of their opponents before the fight, and then comment on how "big" they were. Even when the fighters are nearly equal in weight, some fighters seem bigger than others, because of their muscular build.

CORNER WORK

I've seen corner teams act as if they were on the brink of madness. I've seen them yelling and screaming, and even slapping their fighters: "What's the matter with you?! Don't just stand there and take it! Fight back, damn it! You're gonna lose this fight, you worthless piece of sh . . . t!" Whatever works, I guess. But logically, a corner team must be calm, so that it can offer effective advice in the one minute between rounds. The corner's job is to look for weaknesses in your opponent, and to offer strategy. In one of my matches, after the first round, my corner told me to throw my rear leg cut kick a lot. They had recognized that my opponent was open for it and that she didn't have a

good defense. I did so, and it won me more openings, and eventually a knockout.

Just how much should the corner talk to the fighter? When you come back from a round, if you're not tired, you're not the norm, and I envy you. The first thing the corner must do is help you catch your breath. If you can't breathe, you are not likely to listen to advice. The corner can help you breathe by removing your mouthpiece and letting you rinse your mouth with water. Personally, I also like something cold on my head or back of neck. Pouring water on the back of the neck helps me recover quicker.

If you are part of the corner team, and it is your job to offer advice, don't give the fighter twenty things to remember: "Throw your right cross more, and the uppercut, too. And what about that bobbing and weaving we've worked so hard on? Your opponent is throwing a lot of hooks. Bob and weave, then side-step and follow with a knee strike. And don't turn your head! And I haven't seen a single high kick yet. You've got the hook kick and the spinning heel kick, and . . . damn it, that's the bell! Hurry and put your mouthpiece in!"

How much will your fighter remember? It is better to give your fighter one, or at the most, two specific things to work on. Keep the directions short and to the point. This is not the time to teach your fighter how to fight, but rather to let him know which technique or strategy that will work. Maybe you have seen that his opponent carries his left hand a little low. If you have worked the overhand strike with your fighter, this may be a good time to tell him to use it. Showing confidence in your fighter also helps. Rather than telling him how worthless he is, pat him on the shoulder and send him on his way.

Keith's Corner

All agree that the majority of fights are won by the fighters. However, the difference in many fights is a proficient and well-schooled corner team. Going into a bout with a bunch of your buddies working the corner, is like racing at the Indianapolis 500 with a bunch of your buddies working the pit. The corner team is much like a pit crew at the Indianapolis 500. While the driver is on the track, he is on his own. But without his pit crew to fuel up his car, change his tires, and repair any mechanical problems, he is not likely to finish the race.

The corner team plays a crucial role between rounds. It is the corner team's responsibility to help the fighter recover from the round just fought, to stop nosebleeds, to fix any facial lacerations, and to offer strategy to the fighter. Much like a pit crew, each member has a clearly defined function. The crew member changing the tires has no business stopping and giving advice to the driver, or the tires don't get changed. The same can be said of a corner team. If a person's job is to fix a cut, then he needs to keep his mouth shut and fix the cut. I've seen many confused fighters getting advice from three or four different people upon returning to their corner between rounds. Assignments need to be made and adhered to before the fight. Corner teams should practice prior to the fight, so that they can function as a unit, and are able to complete all tasks in sixty seconds or less. You never see an Indy pit crew send their car onto the track with a missing tire. Usually, the corner team consists of two or three people, but occasionally one person does it all:

Trainer: The trainer is in charge. He is responsible for coordinating the rest of the corner team's actions and providing the fighter with proper advice between rounds. The trainer must identify his fighter's immediate needs and tend to those needs prior to the start of the next round. It is also the trainer's responsibility to throw in the towel, or to stop the contest, if he feels that his fighter is getting hurt unnecessarily, and the referee has allowed the contest to continue.

Cut Man: The cut man's responsibility is to stop any "bleeders" that the fighter has acquired during the round. Most common are cuts above the eyes and nosebleeds. Depending on the seriousness of the cuts, the referee or ring doctor may decide to end the contest. A bout is usually not stopped because of a nosebleed. The cut man may offer advice to the trainer while the round is in progress, but should not speak to the fighter between rounds. The trainer collects all information, and is the only person allowed to speak to the fighter.

Third Person: The third person acts as a trainer's and cut man's assistant. He carries tape, Vaseline, towels, water bottle, and spit bucket. The trainer will state his needs and the third person will immediately provide for it. For example, the trainer may state "water," and the third person will immediately hand the trainer the water bottle. When the trainer is finished, the third person takes the water bottle back. The third person should also place and remove the stool and spit bucket.

As you can see, each person's role is critical to effective corner work. There are several variations to the way a corner is run, which depend on the trainer and how many people he is allowed to have in the corner. It is not uncommon for one person to do all of the above in less than one minute, and to do it well.

In the Gym

You will have just enough time to catch your breath and get some water between rounds. It is therefore important to have good people in your corner, who can get you ready for the next round and give constructive advice. When it gets tough, it is a mistake to think that if you back down a little, your opponent will back down as well. Instead, the fight will escalate until one fighter starts backing up. The other fighter will feed on this and move ahead. If you can keep the intensity up throughout the fight, you can chase your opponent all over the ring and impress the judges. Your corner will look for weaknesses in your opponent's offense and defense, and suggest technique or strategy.

If you get knocked down, come to one knee and wait for the referee to give you an eight-count. The purpose of the eight-count is to let your opponent cool off a bit, and to allow you to get yourself together. If you stand up too fast, and you're wobbly, the referee will discontinue the fight. Look the referee in the eyes to show him that you are alright. He may also ask you whether you wish to continue. Make sure that your answer is definite and clear and not open to misinterpretation. Nodding by blinking your eyes, for example, may be interpreted as an unsure response.

PROTECTIVE GEAR

Unlike the boxer, the kickboxer does not wear shoes when fighting. Depending on the sanctioning body, you may be allowed to wear footpads and shin guards, or you may fight barefoot. Tape around the feet and ankles may be worn. Taping varies between sanctioning bodies and promoters. It's typically not enforced very well, as long as the amount is not outrageous. A good rule of thumb is using three feet of tape on each ankle.

Because the shins are bony with very little muscle covering the bone, most people find blows or even light touches to the shins uncomfortable. This is something you need to get used to, so it is a good idea to condition yourself well in advance to not wearing protection on your feet and shins.

Although kicks to the groin are not allowed in kickboxing, accidents do happen, and you should therefore wear a protective cup (mandatory for males; optional for females). Mouthpiece should be worn. It is also a good idea to wear the mouthpiece during training. This helps you get used to breathing through your nose. Whenever possible, keep your mouth shut to protect your teeth and jaw. You run a greater risk of injury or knockout if you take a blow to the jaw when your mouth is open.

Headgear should be worn when training and in competition, if the sanctioning body so requires. The headgear should be of the professional boxing type, and not the type that traditional martial artists use. With the exception of cheek protectors, there should be no padding on the chin or facial area.

Kickboxer in full gear. Note the footpads, shin guards, headgear, and gloves.

Fourteen ounces is not a lot of weight, you say? Carry those gloves on your hands for ten rounds of battle, and then tell me if you've changed your mind.

When working the heavy bag, you may use bag gloves that are lighter and thinner than regular boxing gloves. When sparring, wear sixteen or fourteen ounce boxing gloves. In competition, the size of the gloves is usually decreased to twelve or ten ounces. Wearing heavier gloves in training helps you build strength in your shoulders and arms. Striking the heavy bag bare fisted is not recommended. Gloves lessen the impact on the fists, and protect against sprains and knuckle injuries. It is difficult to throw a strike with conviction when your hands are hurting. Both bag gloves and fight gloves should have the fingers covered and the thumb attached.

TREATING INJURIES

Injuries happen to any athlete in any sport. The most common injuries in kickboxing are nosebleeds, bruises and sprains, with an occasional fracture to a rib, toe, or nose, and an occasional concussion. Deep tissue bruises from elbow blocks to your shins, ankles, and top of your feet and toes also kind of go with the territory. Nosebleeds, black eyes, sprained fingers and toes, and bruises are considered minor and generally do not require professional medical attention. You should still know how to treat these minor injuries properly to help you return to competition sooner. Most of these injuries can be treated with ice, light compression, and adequate time to heal.

In general, after an injury such as a bruise or a sprain, the area should be iced and gently compressed. Cold and compression primarily help control swelling and bleeding. Application of cold also has an anesthetic effect. Leave ice packs on for 20 to 30 minutes, then remove and leave a pressure bandage in place. Do not place ice directly against the skin. This can cause frostbite. Make sure the ice is wrapped in a protective cloth. It is also a good idea to elevate the injured part to a level higher than the heart to facilitate drainage and help prevent swelling. It is not a good idea to massage bruises.

Most medical professionals recommend against the use of heat for immediate first aid. However, the application of heat can be of benefit later during rehabilitation.

If you think you have a concussion or a fracture, it is

recommended that you see a doctor who can give you advice on treating these injuries, and what precautions to take before getting back to training. Typically, you should not spar or compete within four weeks of a knockout.

In my twelve years of kickboxing, I have had the following injuries:

- Many bruises, primarily on the legs.

- One nosebleed from an uppercut in competition.

- 6-7 black eyes.

- One sprained toe.

- One hyper-extended elbow.

- Fluid in the knee from clashing knees with my opponent. I went to the doctor and had the fluid drained.

- Two broken blood vessels in the eye. These were no worse than regular bruises; they just looked nasty.

- Three busted eardrums that healed by themselves in about two weeks, with no hearing loss.

- One blood clot in the skin from a bone bruise on the shin, which disappeared without treatment in about three months.

- Two torn hamstrings (one in each leg), which I still feel the effects of several years later.

- One whiplash injury with severe headache, which required some chiropractic treatment and medication.

In Keith Livingston's twenty plus years of kickboxing, he has had the following injuries:

- Broken ribs, twice, that healed by themselves, although he couldn't laugh or breathe without pain for several weeks.

- Broken toes, a dozen times, both from sparring and competition. Usually, in competition, you don't dis-

cover that a toe is broken until after it's over.

- Cuts above both eyes, which should have had stitches, but didn't.

- Bit through his lower lip when hit with an uppercut. He couldn't eat for a week, and had to suck from a straw.

- Black eyes. The longer you're in it, the fewer of those you seem to get. Somehow, your body tends to adjust.

- Torn ACL, and torn MCL. He got a leg brace, but probably should have had surgery.

- Busted right hand from punching in competition, and a hairline fracture from training, which he just wrapped. Later, when he fought, he broke the bones in the hand and had to get a cast.

- Twisted ankles from stepping wrong inside the ring, and from running in training.

- Three concussions as a result of fighting. The first was the worst and caused blindness for a couple of hours, and a headache that lasted several days.

- One busted eardrum, which healed by itself.

- Muscle pulls, hyper-extended elbows, torn shoulder muscles, and a dislocated hip joint, which required some chiropractor treatment.

- Deep thigh bruises from leg kicks, to the point that his leg swelled so badly he had difficulty pulling his pants on.

How do you deal with training when you have an injury? Most injuries in kickboxing are minor and to specific areas. I recommend protecting the injured part against further injury, while continuing to train the rest of the body. If you break a hand, does it mean that you have to take three months off? Perhaps you can use this time to perfect your kicks? Although you may not want to practice difficult flying or spinning kicks where you risk losing balance, there are still plenty of kicks you can work on. Or work on footwork and movement, or hit the cardiovascular training hard. Continued training, providing that it doesn't aggravate the injured part, helps you maintain your conditioning and fighting mechanics. I have also found that if I baby an injury, I actually feel worse or sicker than I am. If you can go about your life normally, you are likely to recover faster from the injury.

MENTAL ISSUES

The most important training tool for the kickboxer is contact sparring. Contact sparring exposes you to the realities of fighting and brings out your strengths and weaknesses. It is through contact sparring that you will gain confidence in your ability and trust in your technique.

In order to master kickboxing, you must spar often. Getting hit is one of the greatest fears of most new kickboxers. The only way that I know of to alleviate this fear is by gradually increasing the level of contact during your sparring sessions. First, find a level that you and your sparring partner are comfortable with. Then, make increases based on improved skill level. As you increase the level of contact, your mind and body will also grow and adapt to this new environment.

This section covers:

- Getting hit
- The fighter's mentality
- Resolving fears
- Getting knocked out
- Mental training exercises

GETTING HIT

You will get hit in kickboxing. Will it hurt? Yes, it will. Do you get tougher, and is it easier to deal with pain when you get more experienced? Most likely. You don't stop feeling the pain, but it won't bother you as much. Work this drill: Every time you take a blow, instead of freezing and waiting to see what happens next, use it as a cue to strike back. Show your opponent that he will pay a price for hitting you. Some fighters, when hit, go on the defensive and start worrying about next time they get hit. This is the beginning of the end. Of course, there is a time when it is smart to be on the defensive, but you must know the difference. When your opponent strikes you, he is also vulnerable, and will leave an opening somewhere on his body. Some fighters are in the habit of pausing briefly after they have landed a hit to see if it did any damage. This is a good time for you to take advantage of that fighter. With a little bit of training, you can

condition yourself to taking most of what your opponent dishes out without giving it second thoughts. Taking a hit and thinking nothing of it has a lot to do with mental conditioning. Also, the better conditioned your body is physically, the better you can take a blow without going into shock. You must therefore train both physically and mentally.

I used to take pride in the fact that it didn't bother me to get hit to the head, and that I had never had a nosebleed, until I accidentally blocked my sparring partner's powerful round house kick with my nose. Although I had taken literally hundreds of head shots throughout my years of training, this kick was a most shocking experience that made me freeze for a few seconds, giving up valuable time to my opponent. And, yes, even the best noses do bleed on occasion.

Should you look your opponent in the eyes when sparring? Should you look at his gloves? Looking at the eyes is fine for intimidation purposes, and I would never look directly at a glove. Since the movement of a punch originates in the body, if you look at the glove you will see the punch too late. I like to look at my opponent's upper chest, as this allows me to pick up on any movement in his shoulders prior to him throwing a punch. I use my peripheral vision to observe my opponent's legs. Your distance to your opponent also matters. It is more difficult to see a kick coming if you are very close to your opponent, than if you are farther away.

As you rise to your new environment and become comfortable with the level of contact, you must make yourself uncomfortable again. Every time you step up a level and go a little harder, you are forced to rise to the occasion and push beyond what you think is your limit. Yes, you can learn good form without the roughness, but if you allow yourself to become comfortable during training, you will stagnate. How will you react the first time you get hit? Can you take a good blow if you have never been hit before?

And this is why kickboxing isn't for everybody. In fact, it takes a rare type of person to keep going when it gets rough. This is called determination and, more often than not, it is the mental part of you that will say "no."

Try this exercise on **DETERMINATION**:

Exercise 1

Your mental determination plays a crucial role in competition fighting. With increased confidence comes determination and the ability to face a situation logically. The next time you take a couple of hard hits, note how this affects your determination to continue. Does getting tired or hurt increase or decrease your will to take the fight to the end? Remember that the moment you look at the clock to see when the round is over, your determination will suffer.

THE FIGHTER'S MENTALITY

Keith's Corner

An interesting difference between American fighters and our Eastern counterparts is that we Americans train from the outside and in, giving us the appearance of a physically stronger body, while the Eastern martial artists train from the inside and out, keeping most of their strength hidden within.

When training for a full-contact fight, you will often be fatigued both physically and mentally. If you get hurt early in the fight, you may have a hard time coming back. You must therefore rely on your mental capacity and learn to draw strength from within. Be honest with yourself. Know who you are, and strive to understand your faults and weaknesses.

The death of a martial artist comes when he no longer puts his martial art at the forefront. Many times we get so preoccupied with our injuries or, if in competition, with the length of the round (waiting for the bell to sound) that our primary concern (the fight) goes out the window. A fighter may have skill, natural talent, and intelligence, but if he is worried about getting injured or knocked out, or how tired he will be at the opening of the next round, the whole battle may be lost.

During that two- or three-minute round, you must be prepared to give everything to the fight. During the rest period between rounds, you must regroup and get your mind ready for the next round. Each round should be looked upon as if it were a single fight. When starting the next round, it should be as though you are starting anew again.

What separates the average martial artist from the winner is heart: the ability to cope with the fight mentally until the end, the ability to go beyond pain, frustration, and anger. Don't step in and take an ass-whipping, but stay aggressive and fight with intent from start to finish

There will be times when you just want to throw in the towel, but on fight day your adrenaline will act as a painkiller. If you have the conditioning, skill, and heart, you can fight anybody anywhere.

When fighting in competition, you must focus on the round at hand only, for the full duration of that round.

RESOLVING FEARS

Most fighters experience some degree of fear before fighting. I have often felt that if I could eliminate the fear factor, nothing could stand in my way. There are two kinds of fears: the kind that gets you in shape for the fight and makes you give your utmost to win, and the kind that cripples you and splits your ability to focus.

It is okay to be scared as long as you can control your emotions. But when it is time to step up in the ring, you must cut all negative feelings and not let your opponent intimidate you. When you are seconds away from the sound of the first bell, the fighter part of you should say: "Go for it! I don't care who you are, or what you look like." In the hours before my first fight, somebody unknown to me walked up and asked whom I was fighting. When I told him, he said: "Oh, I've heard that she is a monster!" As it turned out, not only did the fight go the length with no knockout and no injuries, my opponent was also a decent human being, and not at all equitable to a monster. Never forget that to your opponent, you are that mysterious unknown fighter.

Keith's Knockout Advice

When afraid, your mental and physical performance is reduced to a level below your actual capability. But fear does not need to be crippling if you seek to actively confront it with the intent to eradicate the source that causes it. The most common fears about fighting are:

1. **Fear of the unknown.** In order to resolve this fear, you must first identify where the fear is coming from. Ask yourself what exactly it is that you fear. You may have heard that your opponent is this hotshot fighter who knocks everybody out thirty seconds into the first round. But, before accepting that verdict, ask yourself what this fighter is really like.

2. **Fear of injury.** Since most fears stem from the unknown, you must find the truth about your opponent before confronting him. Watch videotapes of his previous fights to get an idea of his strengths and weaknesses. And, if possible, talk to others who have fought this same person.

3. **Fear that your conditioning is not what it should be**, and that you won't be able to perform. In order to resolve fear of conditioning and performance, you must work on it on a daily basis and maintain a disciplined effort to consistently improve your skill. Don't treat any fight lightly, and never go into a fight overconfident.

4. **Fear of how you will be viewed by your peers if you suffer a loss.** Well, just remember that you're never as bad as they say when you lose. It is easy to blow things out of proportion.

As you gain experience, the fear surrounding fighting will decrease little by little until the mystery is gone. To speed this process along, you should constantly push yourself out of your comfort zone. Try to find situations that are similar to what you will face during competition. For example, go to a rival studio or boxing gym and confront the unknown. Spar with people that you already fear, or who you perceive to be better than you.

GETTING KNOCKED OUT

Neither living, nor dead, comprehending but without comprehension, and surprisingly without pain, I heard many people: the ring announcer, the fans, my corner, all fragmented and blended into one voice. The voice that was perfectly clear, however, was the one that counted from one to ten.
~Keith Livingston

The purpose of full-contact competition kickboxing is, of course, to win. Fights can run the full length and be won by decision, but the ultimate aim is to win by knockout. When a fighter wins by knockout, he is said to have thrown a *good finisher*.

Strikes can be thought of as set-up strikes and finishing strikes. The purpose of the set-up strike is to create the opening for the finishing strike. The finishing strike won't work, however, unless it is thrown with good timing and power. If you land an uppercut to your opponent's chin, but fail to take immediate advantage of the time when your opponent's head snaps back, your are not likely to win by knockout. A good finisher lands at the precise moment when your opponent is still stunned from the blow of your previous punch.

Let's say that you throw a good finisher, and your opponent reels across the ring and collapses on the canvas. But what, exactly, is it that happens when a fighter gets knocked out?

The central nervous system consists of the brain and the spinal cord. The brain is divided into three parts: the cerebrum (your center for thinking and sensation), the cerebellum (primarily concerned with your balance), and the medulla (regulates the internal activities of your body). The spinal cord is like a cable that connects the brain to a vast network of nerves running through your body.

The brain is covered by the skull, and inside this covering the brain is also covered by layers of membranes, within which the cerebrospinal fluid bathes the central nervous system and cushions it from jarring. When you get hit in the head or on the jaw, shock waves are sent to the brain, making it bounce against the inside of the skull. The impact on the brain depends on the nature of the acceleration and the rapid turn of the head. Knockouts can also result from blows to the thorax or abdomen, stimulating the vagus nerve (either of the tenth pair of cranial nerves, arising in the medulla oblongata, and stimulating the larynx, lungs, heart, esophagus, and most of the abdominal organs). It is not uncommon to see fighters drop to the canvas when struck with a powerful hook to the abdomen.

Many activities involve cells in several areas of the brain. However, certain areas tend to be "in charge" of certain functions. The back of the brain, for example, is in charge of vision. When getting hit, depending on which part of the brain that bounces against the inside of the skull, it is possible to knock out one function only, while leaving others intact.

Knockouts can come at several levels: from getting a little dazed to total unconsciousness. A fighter who gets dazed will usually get an eight-count to recover. If he is unable to recover fully, the referee will signal an end to the fight.

Note that many of our fears of getting hurt are irrational, and the risk of serious injury or death in kickboxing is relatively low; however, the risk is there, comes with the decision of becoming a fighter, and should have been dealt with long before you face your opponent in the ring.

MENTAL TRAINING EXERCISES

Visualizing yourself in the ring is not the same as "thinking" about it. The reason imagery is so powerful is because your muscles are actually responding, even if you don't throw a full punch. You can test this by watching boxing on TV. When you get mentally involved in the fight, your body begins to respond as if you were one of the boxers. Your heart rate increases, and you tense and twitch. When watching sports, the sports fans actually live it as if they were the athletes.

Those who engage in this type of mental practice gain benefits in almost every area that the physical practice provides. Mental imagery can be extended to your senses beyond pure technique. You may feel yourself getting tired, sweaty, thirsty, and other unpleasant feelings that occur in a fight. This trains your body

and mind in advance to deal with it, so that it is a less shocking experience when it happens. Try this: Visualize your idol, the kickboxer you want to become like. How does he behave when he enters the ring? How does he take charge of the fight? What types of techniques does he throw that are effective? What about that "never say die" attitude? I used this type of imagery for a couple of my karate tests, and found that it helped my confidence tremendously. I would even visualize the muscles growing on my back and shoulders right before a sparring session. I would pretend that I were a man, and spar stronger as a result.

At one of my karate tests, one student was told he was "the most outstanding." I wanted this to be me next time. I trained with this in mind and visualized the end of the test when they would tell me that I was the most outstanding, and guess what? It happened. Prior to a kickboxing match, I really wanted to win by knockout, as I had never knocked anybody out. I kept visualizing this over and over, and guess what? You guessed right, I won by knockout in the second round. Sometimes, it is almost spooky when things happen exactly the way you visualized.

To overcome any concerns you may have about the fight, there are a number of exercises you can do to help you gain a mental edge on your opponent. Try these exercises on **BREATHING, VISUALIZATION, AND RESOLVING FEAR**:

Exercise 2

As stated earlier, learning to breathe properly is critical to the competitive fighter. Proper breathing:

1. Helps you **conserve energy** during heavy physical exertion.

2. Helps you **synchronize your strikes** for power.

Your breathing should be synchronized so that you exhale the moment your strike impacts the target. Proper breathing should also be practiced while shadow boxing. If your strikes are naturally fast, you may find it necessary to exhale at the impact of every other strike. Practice proper breathing when working on your physical conditioning exercises (jump rope, pushups, situps, frog hops, etc.).

Exercise 3

Because the mouthpiece is part of your protective gear and you have to wear it when sparring, it is a good idea to get used to it early in training. When fighting, your mouth should be closed and you should be breathing through your nose. A fighter who keeps his mouth open and takes a strike to the jaw, has much less tolerance to the blow and risks getting injured or knocked out. Some people find it difficult to breathe through their nose. Learn proper breathing by training with your mouthpiece in when running, or when working the heavy bag or focus mitts.

Exercise 4

When faced with an aggressive opponent, rely on your ability to act swiftly and spontaneously. When spontaneous action is called for, we often tighten up or freeze, inhibiting our ability to respond to the attack. By training your mind with visualization exercises, you can lessen the effect that freezing has on your performance.

To become faster, you must "think" faster. Imagine your kicks accelerating on their way to the target. Some fighters never improve on speed or power, simply because they don't train with the intent to improve; they don't allow their mind to overpower their body.

When throwing a punch or kick, imagine that your mind has moved to the part of your hand or foot that is to impact the target. "Moving" your mind in this way may help that part of your body to react faster.

Exercise 5

Word association can help you train harder when using the heavy bag or focus mitts. Try words such as explode, harder, or relax when training with equipment, and let your body follow those commands. Ideally, your mental impulses will manifest themselves in your techniques.

When training with focus mitts, you can increase the speed in your strikes by counting the strikes in your head, speeding up or slowing down your count, and making your physical body do the same.

When you feel yourself tightening up or freezing, say the word "Go!" (or some other word that you feel will help trigger a response).

Exercise 6

Most fears occur before the actual manifestation of the thing feared. Once the bell sounds for the beginning of the round, most of the energy spent on worrying about it will be converted into physical energy for fighting. However, this pre-fight fear can have a crippling effect and be difficult to deal with.

Once you analyze the fear, you may find that you are not actually as scared as you thought you were. Try rating your fear on a scale from 1-5, where 1 represents not scared at all, and 5 represents scared to death. Rating your fear helps you get a more concrete picture of it, and you will most likely find that you are not as afraid as you thought you were.

Also ask yourself, "If I were up against a fighter like myself, how scared would I be, providing that I knew little or nothing about this fighter?" In other words, rate your opponent's fear the way he ought to feel about fighting you. By doing this, you may find that your opponent has more to fear than you do.

Martina Sprague: If I were to rate my fear on a scale from 1 to 5, I would rate my first few fights as a 1 or 2. I have actually found that the less I knew about the fight or the opponent I was fighting, the less fearful I was. Later, I would rate my fear as a 3 or 4. There have been times when I have laid awake at night, three months before a fight! unable to sleep, because of negative thoughts. But I have also found that the closer I got to the fight, the less fear I would feel. I think that most fighters agree that once the first blows are exchanged, the fear is completely gone. On fight day, I usually work through every mental issue, where everything that needs to be said or done has been said or done, and my mind will be clear and ready.

Keith Livingston: If I were to rate my fear on a scale from 1 to 5, in my first few fights, I would probably rate it as a 5. Later in my career, it would be closer to a 3. And for the last few years, it would probably be a 1, because at this point I have already experienced it all and can really care less.

Exercise 7

Visualization exercises can help you feel as though you have already been through the fight before you actually get there. Before you go to sleep at night, take ten minutes and visualize yourself in the ring with your opponent. What does he look like? What is he wearing? Which corner is he in, and how large is the audience that is watching you?

Now imagine the worst possible scenario. You are fighting an opponent who has a record five times as good as yours, and most people in the audience belong to his fan club and are constantly shouting his name to cheer him on. Now experiment (in your mind) with how you can portray a confident image to the audience and your opponent.

Next, imagine yourself in total control of the fight. Your feet are light; you move fast, your strikes are lightning fast and strong, your endurance is at its peak. You can hear the crowd cheering for you. And there goes that knockout punch, which sends your opponent to the canvas . . .

WALKING THE WALK

The character of a fighter can be determined by observing his behavior after the loss of a fight. The true competitors usually have their minds set on the future, so that after a loss they immediately start training for their next fight. The true competitors also try to get a re-match with the person they lost to, so that they can win the next time.

Experiencing a loss does not necessarily mean that your opponent won. Losing may be because of something that you did wrong, and not because of something that your opponent did right. The true competitors analyze their fighting, correct what they did wrong, and take that extra step toward winning the re-match.

This section covers:

- Glove-up with Keith
- Pre-fight anxiety
- Knowledge is power
- Walking the walk

Glove Up with Keith

As a trainer setting up fights for my students, I place great emphasis on not overmatching my fighters, especially during the first few fights of their career. I always try to get an opponent who is either inferior or equal in skill to my fighter. The problem is that a lot of times the trainer part of me says, "Don't take this fight!" But the fighter part of me says, "Go for it! I really don't see that extra experience or weight difference as a problem!" The reason that I often have this conflict is because during my own kickboxing career, I would fight anybody. I didn't care if their record was a thousand and one, I would fight them!

The first time you fight is the worst. You must stay very composed at the beginning of the fight, and don't go all out right from the start. I know that's hard, but it helps you get to know your opponent, and once he lands his first strike, the mystery is gone. If you feel nervous or scared, remember that you are at this fight because you want to be there, and not because you have to. Then throw punches in bunches, keep your chin down and your guard up, and throw at least eight kicks per round. And, whatever happens, be proud of yourself when it's over.

PRE-FIGHT ANXIETY

Keith's Knockout Advice

As discussed earlier, most fighters experience pre-fight anxiety to some degree. A moderate amount of anxiety actually enhances athletic performance by increasing your alertness and raising your physical abilities to maximum performance levels. This occurs because the body releases adrenaline into the system. Too much anxiety, however, can disturb your concentration and can be detrimental to athletic performance. Anxiety can be broken down into three different levels of severity:

1. The first level is a mental reaction to stress, where uneasy thoughts about an upcoming fight can result in sleeplessness, difficulty concentrating, fear of poor performance, and expectation of failure. It is during this level that many fighters back out of their commitment to fight and find excuses not to compete.

2. The next level is a behavioral reaction to stress associated with the "fight or flight" response, where the fighter chooses to stay and fight, or to run away from the fight. This usually occurs on fight day, and in many cases right before the competition. At this point, most fighters no longer have the option of flight, and are forced by circumstance to fight. However, I have seen fighters who still experience the fight or flight syndrome when entering the ring. They immediately start looking at the canvas, and later get knocked out by a phantom punch. I believe that many fights that appear to be fixed are in fact a result of this syndrome.

3. The third and most severe level of pre-fight anxiety is a physiological reaction to stress. This involves bodily changes such as rapid heartbeat, excessive perspiration, and abnormally high tension. In some cases, the fighter becomes physically ill. Headaches and vomiting may occur, and the fighter will feel weak and fatigued.

I have seen fighters vomit prior to a fight. I have seen fighters actually disappear from the area and never return. On the other side of the spectrum are those who can care less, or at least don't show any fear. I have seen a thousand different ways that people psych themselves up: slapping their faces, screaming, ranting and raving, pounding their head on the wall and working themselves into a fury. Then there are the rituals: the guys that pray, the guys that have some kind of good luck charm, the guys that have to have the right trunks or the right mouthpiece, and the guys that have to have their hands wrapped a certain way.

All these thoughts, behaviors, and physiological changes can have a negative impact on a fighter's preparation and performance. With proper management, however, we can ally ourselves with pre-fight anxiety and gain the benefits of properly channeled adrenaline. First, you must recognize and accept what is happening to you and your body. Recognize the fact that it happens to all of us to some degree, and that it is a very normal response to a stressful situation. Most of the fears associated with pre-fight anxiety are completely without merit. Fear of failure, fear of loss of respect among family and friends, and fear of poor performance--how realistic are they? What is the worst that can happen? Are you a failure? Absolutely not! These kinds of negative thoughts only raise your anxiety level and increase the likelihood of failure.

Avoid talking to others who are negative. It's easy enough to get nervous on your own without help from others. Remember that your opponent is experiencing the same thoughts and responses that you are. Try to control your anxiety level through visualization exercises. If you feel yourself becoming uptight or overly nervous, sit back, close your eyes, take a few deep breaths, and begin to visualize your successful performance in the ring. See yourself in control and dominating your opponent from start to finish.

Finally, train and prepare properly for the contest. Through proper training, you will gain confidence in your ability and conditioning. If you are truly prepared, there is little reason to be concerned.

Martina Sprague: I once used a full wall of windows in the hallway outside of the arena to mentally pre-pare for the fight. Since it was dark outside, I could see my own reflection in the windows. I shadow boxed against my own image down the hall and back, visualizing what my opponent would see when up against me in the ring later.

KNOWLEDGE IS POWER

Keith's Corner

Besides proper training and conditioning, the next best form of preparation is knowing your opponent. By knowing as much as possible about your opponent, you can gear your training specifically toward a particular person and style. In the amateur ranks, it is often difficult to obtain this information. With a little ingenuity, however, you can find out quite a bit about your next opponent.

The process begins with your first contact with the fight promoter. Generally, you should be contacted eight to twelve weeks prior to the fight. During your conversation with the promoter, you should be asking some key questions. First, try to obtain a history on your opponent. Find out whom he has fought and, more importantly, who his most recent opponent was. Be sure to get facts and not speculation! If the promoter cannot answer these questions, ask him who can. Or have the promoter find out for you.

During your pre-fight investigation, determine your opponent's fighting style: Is he a great inside fighter, does he like to pressure, etc? And, perhaps most important, does he fight left or right-handed, and does he switch stance during the fight? It wouldn't make a lot of sense to spar right-handed fighters for eight weeks, and then arrive at the fight to find a left-handed opponent, or to have a sparring partner whose style is totally opposite of your opponent's. Remember, fighting is to a great degree subconscious. How you train is how you fight. Use the following questionnaire when initially talking with the fight promoter:

Fighter's Name: _____

Fighter's Record (try to verify through independent source):

Wins: _____ Losses: _____ Knockouts: _____
Last Fight Date: _____
Last Opponent: _____
Result: _____
Last Opponent's Phone Number:_____

Is Video Tape Available?
Yes: ____No: _____
Contact: _____
Phone:_____

Right-Handed: ____ Left-Handed: ____ Both:____

Strength: _____
Weakness: _____

Martial Arts Background And Style:
_____

The process of getting to know your opponent not only helps your fight preparation, it eliminates much of the mystery. You will be better focused, and your training will be more productive. When you have gained as much information as possible, and hopefully viewed a videotape of your opponent, you should create a *fighter profile*. The profile gives you a good overview of what type of fighter you are facing, giving you a specific method of preparation.

Once you start to physically prepare for the fight, try to find sparring partners who are similar in style to your opponent. If your opponent is left-handed, your sparring partners should also be left-handed. One of your best sources of information is the person your opponent fought last. If he won, find out how he won; if he lost, find out why he lost. Ask about specific techniques that worked or didn't work. Remember, this is just an overview for training purposes. Just because something didn't work for one fighter, it doesn't mean that it won't work for you. Concentrate mainly on style rather than on technique. For example, if your opponent appears to have the advantage on the inside, work on dominating the fight from the outside. The bottom line is, *fight your fight*.

If you study your opponent and gear your training accordingly, you should have the advantage going into the fight. Again, this may be more difficult on the amateur level, where videos are hard to come by and records are often missing or non-existent. Remember to try to verify the information through a neutral source. In many cases, the promoter may have a hidden agenda, or the fighter may even belong to the promoter. Also be aware that amateur fights are often changed at the last minute. If you have trained hard and are in great condition, however, the change should present only a minor inconvenience. This is less of a problem in the professional ranks, where a fight is generally binding through a legal contract.

Martina Sprague: I tend to disagree with the mainstream belief that you should learn as much as possible about the person you are fighting. The thing is that if you don't know anything about your opponent, you won't go into the fight with any pre-conceived ideas. And just because you have gathered all this information, it's no guarantee that your opponent will fight that way against you. If you have trained for his style only, you will have difficulty adjusting if things don't go exactly as planned. Learning about your opponent may also affect you mentally in a negative way, where you build up fears that you would otherwise not have had.

WALKING THE WALK
by Keith Livingston

There's a lot of bullshit and politics in fighting, but if you want to make it to the top, you must be prepared to put up with it. You should therefore see your amateur fights as a training period. If you're going to lose, then lose as an amateur.

I have seen the world champion get his ass kicked, and they still declared him the winner. You don't beat the world champion by decision; you win by knocking him out. If you truly want to do this, you should sit down and make a list of every fighter in your weight division. Then, work your way to the top by fighting them one at a time. You must develop a passion for fighting. When you lose, you should get a little mad and train twice as hard for your next fight. That's why so many fighters never make it to the top, because they fight only for that one fight. And if it doesn't go their way, they don't want to fight again. If you want to be a winner in this sport, you must aim for the top right from the start.

FIGHT DAY
by Keith Livingston

THE WEIGH-IN

It is Friday morning, and you have just arrived in Las Vegas with your trainer and corner men. You feel the adrenaline in your body as you enter the hotel ballroom and look at the lonely 20 by 20 foot ring amidst all the empty chairs. Tomorrow those chairs will not be empty. Tomorrow night this place will be crowded with fight fans, men and women anxiously awaiting the first knockout of the evening. As trainers and corner men are busy preparing their fighters for the bout, ring announcer and referees will mingle about with their duties, and paramedics and security guards will be on stand-by, ready to assist where needed. And yourself? Your mind will be on one thing only. You will see nothing, hear nothing, know nothing of what goes on outside of that ring. Tomorrow is fight day, and perhaps one of the biggest days in your life. Tomorrow night your mind will be on one thing only: how to outsmart your opponent and win the fight.

You look around. Already, people are furiously working to prepare the arena for the contest. In the far corner of the room, a man with a clipboard directs the workers by radio. Your trainer walks over to the man and introduces himself.

"Sir, would you know where the weigh-in is being held this morning?"

"Down the hall!" the man says flatly. "First door on your right. Ask for Dave." Without missing a beat, he goes back to coordinating the workers.

Your trainer gestures for you to follow. Before leaving, you take a last glance at the ring. "I can do it. I'll show them all!" But the butterflies have returned to your stomach, and the adrenaline is pumping high.

You follow your trainer down the hall. Your hands are cold and clammy, you feel a little queasy. You enter the weigh-in room, which is filled with fighters, trainers, and people with clipboards. You quickly size up those that appear to be fighters. Which one is Levelle "Lightning" Lewis, your opponent for tomorrow night?

A man with a clipboard walks up to you. "Hi, I'm Dave. And you are . . . ?"

"I'm Doc," says your trainer. "And this is my fighter Randy 'The Rock' Jackson. We're here for the weigh-in."

The man scribbles something on the clipboard.

"Great! Let me get Levelle and his trainer, and we'll get you guys going."

You watch with anticipation as he walks over to two men in the corner of the room. The younger of the two has a body that seems to be chiseled out of granite. As he glances your direction, it is obvious that he is Lewis. Eye contact. The pre-fight psych has begun.

Your trainer grabs you. "Come on! Let's get this over with so that we can eat."

You stare at Lewis a while longer, then step onto the scale. As you watch Dave move the little weights, you suddenly worry about the meal you had on the flight this morning. Will you make the weight limit?

"Jackson, one-hundred-seventy!" Dave announces, and you breathe a sigh of relief. You're still five pounds under the limit.

You step off and Lewis steps on. Again you watch the weights on the scale move as the arm centers itself. Part of you wishes that he is over the limit, that you will find a way out, that you can get back on that plane and leave Las Vegas.

"Lewis, one-hundred-seventy-two!" Dave announces.

Lewis steps down, walks toward you, and extends his hand. "Good luck tomorrow night!"

He gives you one of those crooked half-smiles, which you know means, "I'll whip your ass tomorrow!" You smile, too, but your glare burns holes through his body.

BREAKFAST

"Let's go eat!" says your trainer.

He takes you to the restaurant, but you can't get your mind off Levelle "Lightning" Lewis and the fight tomorrow night. "I'm too nervous to eat," you mumble, the words not hearable for anyone but yourself.

Suddenly somebody from deep within the restaurant calls your name. "Randy, Doc! Over here!" You turn and squint into the darkness. It's Ed, your cut man. "Over here, guys! I've got us a table."

Once you sit down and allow your body to relax, you realize how hungry you are. Perhaps a good meal won't be too difficult to gobble down after all. You survey the menu. The Jackpot Breakfast sounds pretty good. Eggs, toast, pancakes with plenty of syrup, sausage or bacon, and hash browns. Or how about the El-Grande Omelet?

"Give me that!" Ed rips the menu from your hands. "Not meaning any disrespect, but I took the liberty to order for all of us."

At that moment the waitress appears with bowls of oatmeal, toast, and an order of pancakes. "Can I bring you some syrup?" she asks, but Ed raises his hand.

"No syrup, thanks. This will do just fine!"

You stare at the dry pancakes.

"Look, Randy," Ed says, trying to ease your disappointment. "Look, the body is like a car, and to run efficiently it needs premium fuel. This here . . ." he points at the food in front of you, " . . . this is a high carb breakfast which will help your body run efficiently during the fight tomorrow night. Now, eat up and enjoy!"

He looks at Doc who is already diving into his El-Grande Omelet. They both chuckle as if this is some kind of conspiracy against you.

You spend the rest of the day trying not to think too much about the fight. Lunch and dinner come and go, both as tasteless as breakfast.

"How's the food?" Ed asks.

"Delicious!" you lie.

When eight o'clock approaches, Doc orders you to bed. "Got a big fight tomorrow night," he says, as if your memory is short and needs reminding. As you turn on your side and pull the covers up to your chin, he asks for the umpteenth time, "How ya feelin', Champ?"

"Great!" you say. The obligatory, "Great, ready to go!"

You close your eyes and let the fight begin to play itself out.

You awake to the smell of breakfast. Doc has ordered room service, so that you can relax and stay off your feet. You listen to music, watch TV, sleep, do everything you can to keep your mind occupied, but the day creeps by. It seems like you have just dozed off into a pleasant dream state when the phone rings. You jerk awake and sit up groggy. Doc is on the phone.

"Six o'clock? Fine! We'll be there!"

"What's up?" you ask.

"Got to be down there at six," he says. "Medical exam and a pre-fight meeting."

THE MEDICAL EXAM

You, Doc, and Ed arrive at the meeting promptly at six. The room is full of fighters, trainers, doctors, and event personnel. The whole scene is chaotic. Fighters are stretching, shadow boxing, getting their hands wrapped.

"Inexperienced amateurs!" Doc spits the words from his lips. "They'll be too tired to walk the few steps down the aisle and into the ring!" He shakes his head in disgust and points at a couple of fighters shadow boxing. "There's still two hours till show time. They should be relaxing!"

You say nothing, but secretly wish that it were time to warm up. This waiting is driving you up the walls.

"Jackson!" Your thoughts are interrupted. "Jackson, where are you?"

"Over here!" Doc replies.

An elderly man with a clipboard and a stethoscope motions for you to follow. "Take your shirt off, son! Let's check your heart and lungs."

You do as told, feeling your heart pumping harder--THUMP, THUMP! If it weren't for the commotion around you, the doctor would not need a stethoscope to hear it.

The doctor places the stethoscope against your chest. He grins and raises an eyebrow. "Nervous?"

You say nothing.

"Don't worry. Lewis' heart was also beating a little fast." Finally, the medical exam is over. "Fit as a fiddle! Good luck, son!"

Again, Doc answers before you can speak. "Thanks, but we don't believe in luck! C'mon Champ, let's find us a space!"

You find your name posted on a door marked "blue corner" and enter. The scene is the same, like a beehive: fighters warming up and stretching, trainers wrapping hands. Everybody is moving, doing something. You, Doc, and Ed make your way through the fighters and trainers and over to a table in the far corner of the room. Ed pats the table.

"Jump up here, Champ! I'll give you a massage. Will help ya relax."

You close your eyes, and again the fight begins to play in your mind. You lose all concept of time there on the table, somewhere between sleep and awake.

WARM-UP

You are awakened by a loud "thwap, thwap, thwap" and open an eye to see what is going on. The fighter next to you is kicking Thai-pads.

"Sorry to wake you, but it's getting close to fight time," he says.

You shrug. "That's okay. I wasn't really sleeping, anyway."

You spot Doc and Ed at the other end of the room, talking to a man with a clipboard. Doc glances over his shoulder and sees that you are awake. He ends the conversation and walks toward you.

"Let's get ready, Champ! Your fight has been moved up."

Doc gets some tape, gauze, and scissors from his bag and orders you to sit on a chair backwards.

"Let's get you wrapped. Rest your hands on the back of the chair and spread your fingers."

You watch as Doc wraps your right hand with precision and grace. Without a word, Ed begins tearing small strips of tape and one by one hands them to Doc, who places them between your fingers. You admire the way these two men work. The ease. Nothing is spoken, yet they understand each other perfectly.

Doc puts the finishing touches on the hand wraps. "How do they feel, Champ?"

"Great, as always!"

They do feel good, and now you really begin to feel like a fighter.

"Let's get busy," Doc says. There is enthusiasm in his voice.

Ed grabs the Thai-pads. "Kick like you mean it, Champ!"

You know from experience that a proper warm-up is essential and start kicking. "Whack!"

"Harder!"

WHAACK!

"Harder, Champ!"

WHAAACK!!

"That's it! Kick like that, and we'll be going home early!"

You feel your confidence building with each kick. **WHAAACK!!**

"That's good!" says Doc. "Now, move around!"

You begin shadow boxing. It feels good. You're in great shape! You feel unbeatable, suddenly, as you visualize Lewis in front of you.

"Jackson!" somebody calls. "You're up next. Looks like there might be a knockout. Better get ready!"

The man hands Doc the gloves. You extend your left hand, but Doc shakes his head. "C'mon Champ, you know that it is bad luck to glove the left hand first!"

You smile and extend your right hand. "Thought we didn't believe in luck!"

Doc ignores you and proceeds to glove your right hand, then your left.

"Okay kid, this is it! Tonight's your night. How do ya feel?"

"Great!"

"How do ya feel, Champ?!"

"Great! Ready to go!"

He pats you on the shoulder. "Okay, let's go do it!"

You emerge from the dressing room to a song by AC/DC called "Thunder!" and proceed to the blue corner. You barely notice the crowd of three-thousand plus. Ed jumps on to the ring apron and spreads the ropes apart for you to enter. As you climb into the ring, the music fades, and suddenly you become aware of the fight fans, thousands of faces staring at you. Suddenly it becomes real. The noise, the lights, the stained canvas.

"C'mon Randy, knock him out!" you hear from deep within the crowd.

You look across the ring at Lewis. He's got his game face on.

The ring announcer comes to the center of the ring and a microphone is lowered from the ceiling. "Good evening, ladies and gentlemen! Our next bout features two unbeaten light heavyweights. In the red corner, fighting out of Las Vegas, Nevada, with an outstanding record of fifteen wins and no losses, nine wins by knockout, ladies and gentlemen . . . Levelle 'Lightning' Lewis!"

You listen to the roar of the crowd. "His fanclub," you think. "But I'll show them tonight!"

"And his opponent . . ." the ring announcer continues, "his opponent, fighting out of the blue corner, from Los Angeles, California, with an exceptional record of eighteen wins and no defeats, ten wins by knockout. Ladies and gentlemen, please welcome Randy 'The Rock' Jackson! JACKSON!"

The referee motions you and Lewis to the center of the ring. You are standing nose-to-nose with Lewis, staring intently into his pale blue eyes. The referee is anxious to move on.

"Okay guys, I gave you your instructions in the

dressing room. Let's have a good, clean bout. Touch gloves!"

You return to your corner, and Lewis to his. You are still staring at Lewis, locking his eyes to yours.

Then the bell sounds, and the fight is on.

THE CHAMP

One minute and thirty seconds into the round, you hit Lewis with a rear cross, followed by a left hook. Lewis' knees buckle. The crowd is frantic, sensing a knockout. You barely hear Doc, "Finish him! Finish him, Champ!"

You connect with a left hook to the body. Lewis goes down, holding his right side. The referee steps in and signals you to a neutral corner. You watch as the referee begins to count, "One . . .two . . . three . . . four . . . five . . ."

At "five" Lewis stands up. You admire his courage, but sense that victory is close. The referee signals the fight to resume.

Your confidence is surging and you go after Lewis for the finish. You lead with a front kick to Lewis' mid-section. He grunts and covers up in defense of your coming barrage of punches and kicks.

Lewis is finished. You are hitting him at will now with solid lefts and rights to the body. As his guard drops for protection, you unleash a rear leg round house kick to his head, **WHAAACK!!** and for a moment time stops and you are back in the dressing room kicking the Thai-pads. The kick connects with Lewis' head, and you know that the fight is over.

You know it now . . . before he even hits the canvas . . .

QUICK REFERENCE TO CONCEPTS

DETERMINATION: When you suffer setbacks, when you're bored to death with training, when your body is screaming for you to quit, you still keep going. Determination means that you have the discipline to pursue a set training schedule that keeps you on track.

FIGHTER PROFILE: Knowledge is power. Knowing something about the person you are to fight can give you both a tactical and a mental advantage. Start to gather information about your opponent well in advance, and create a fighter profile that will help you fine tune your training program for this particular fight.

FIGHTING YOUR FIGHT: Sometimes we tend to give in to our opponent's game plan, including factors of intimidation. This places you in the inferior position from the start, making it difficult to win the fight, no matter how skilled you are. You must stick to your game plan, and not be too concerned with your opponent's attempts to control you.

GOOD FINISHER: A knockout punch is an example of a good finisher. When you throw a good finisher, you do more than just win the fight; you finish it.

TAKING THE FIGHT TO THE END: No matter how tough it gets, you don't quit. There are times when throwing in the towel is appropriate, but this is something that your corner should worry about, not you. Your mind-set should be to continue until the last bell sounds.

SECTION SEVEN
CUT KICKS, KNEES, ELBOWS, SWEEPS

BEYOND LEG KICKING
by Keith Livingston

Nobody should enter the world of kickboxing without having a healthy respect for the inherent dangers of the sport. I don't mean that you should be paranoid about getting in the ring. Rather, know the risks and train accordingly. However, some injuries border on the bizarre and are unavoidable.

I recall a fight not too long ago where the bizarre and the effective met head on. I had trained hard for this fight, especially the leg kick. Shortly after the sound of the first bell, I noticed that my opponent (we'll call him Brad) had a particularly wide stance, probably resulting from years of training in a traditional art. I decided to exploit his stance with a technique that I loved: the cut kick to the inside thigh.

Most leg kicks are thrown to the outside thigh, with the inside thigh often overlooked. I started using my lead leg like a venomous snake, biting the inside of Brad's front leg. Each time he stepped into range, I whipped my kick into his thigh. In the first round alone, I must have kicked him some thirty times.

The leg kick to the inside thigh is designed more as an irritant; much like being whipped on the ass with a wet towel. It's not likely to kill you, but it stings like hell. By the third round, it was really beginning to take a toll on Brad. He developed a slight limp and was hesitant to advance. This made him an even easier target, and I continued my assault on his injured leg. At the end of the third round when I returned to my corner, I was jolted by a sudden thud, followed by an Aw! from the crowd. I turned and saw that Brad had fallen on his way back to his corner.

As my corner fed me instructions and cooled me with water, I glanced across the ring and could see a pasty white coming over Brad's face. It was obvious that he was hurt. The bell sounded to begin the fourth round. We both stood and began our advance. Brad took a couple of steps and collapsed in front of me.

The bewildered referee began the ten count. At count six, Brad seemed to recover. He stood, and the referee wiped his gloves and signaled for us to resume.

Brad took one step toward me, and again fell face first into the canvas, bouncing as he hit. The referee stopped the match, declared me the winner, and called for medical personnel. The uninformed crowd booed their displeasure, as the medics tended to Brad and took him from the arena on a hospital gurney. Out of both concern and curiosity, I went to see him at the hospital.

I was directed to Brad's room, where I was told he was waiting to be admitted for surgery. When I entered the room, Brad was conscious, but looking concerned. He was as white as the sheets he laid upon, and there was an unbelievable amount of purple and red covering his inner thigh. I felt a certain satisfaction at the amount of damage I had inflicted. That was, until I was told of his injuries.

Apparently the repeated kicks to his inner thigh had literally crushed the femoral artery. This artery, being a major carrier of blood, was unable to complete its function of carrying blood into the lower extremities and returning the blood to the heart. However, a small amount of blood could make the journey, as long as he was lying down. This accounted for his return to consciousness while he was in a horizontal position.

I waited as the surgeons cut into Brad's thigh and used a balloon-like device to re-inflate the artery. Brad's operation went well and I've seen him compete again. Since that fight, I have thrown thousands of leg kicks, but I have yet to recreate the bizarre effects of that evening. In the fight game, the old adage "it's better to give than to receive" is a good motto to train by.

Referee questioning a fighter to determine the extent of his injuries.

CUT KICKS

Keith's Corner

Now that you have gained some ring experience, you should look at furthering your skill by learning a variety of techniques. As a purist, I seldom fight unless the rules allow for leg kicking. To me, a kickboxer without leg kicks is like a boxer without a jab. The leg kick is an integral part of the fight and highly effective for destroying your opponent's fighting spirit. If you have paid attention to the earlier sections of this book, you already know about the use and effectiveness of the cut kick (round house kick to the leg). Because a properly executed cut kick momentarily places you in an inferior position with your back turned toward your opponent, it is designed for one purpose only: **to destroy your opponent's foundation (his legs), drop him to the ground, and end the fight.** We will now look at this kick in more detail and expand on some concepts.

This section covers:

- Common errors for the cut kick
- In the gym
- Stance and power
- Body mechanics for the cut kick with a step
- Slicing your opponent's leg
- Cut kicking in close quarters (power and set-up)
- The inside thigh kick
- Stealing the moment of impact (shin blocks)
- Other defenses against the cut kick
- Summary and review

Unlike the round house kick, which is pulled back into your stance after impact, the cut kick continues (cuts) through the target, allowing you to replant your foot in the opposite stance.

COMMON ERRORS FOR THE CUT KICK

Keith's Knockout Advice

Many kickboxing matches allow the fighters to attack the legs. In many of these bouts you can kick both to the inside and outside of your opponent's thigh. A properly thrown cut kick is perhaps the most effective and vicious aspect of kickboxing but, despite its popularity, few kickboxers truly understand the nature of low kicking, and therefore fail to utilize it to its fullest. The most common errors of low kicking are:

1. Improper target
2. Improper kick
3. Improper angle

Improper target: When throwing a low kick to the outside thigh area, aim to impact the nerve cluster that is located approximately 3/4 distance vertically up from the knee (between the knee and the hip) and horizontally centered on the outside thigh. Most of us have accidentally struck this nerve cluster by bumping into furniture or being slugged on the side of the leg. A very small impact to the nerves causes a numbing sensation and a deep ache inside the thigh itself. Recall a time when this happened to you and magnify the pain ten times, and you'll have some idea as to the damage a well-placed leg kick can cause.

Studies have shown that enough impact can actually cause the other leg to react identically, causing a complete collapse of both legs. Law enforcement has used this technique to render violent offenders incapable of standing. In kickboxing, few people can go the distance with a fighter who has taken the time to learn target precision and is totally committed to the kick. In one kickboxing match, I actually finished my opponent in less than a minute with a series of well-placed leg kicks. In bouts that allow leg kicks, it is usually the better leg kicker who prevails.

Understand that you can't just kick to any target on your opponent's leg. To do actual damage, you must choose your target with care, or the kick will simply sting and be an annoyance. Practice the leg kick with a partner, taking turns impacting each other's legs lightly. Have your partner tell you when you impact the target correctly. Experimentation helps you determine whether you need to impact slightly lower or slightly higher, as well as whether you need to kick more to the front or side of your opponent's leg.

When starting out with this kick, many fighters throw it slightly high, impacting their opponent's buttocks instead of the thigh. I think this is because when we raise our knee to kick, it is automatically angled upward. It now seems natural for the kick to follow that same path. If there is some distance between yourself and your opponent, and you are impacting with your instep, the kick is more likely to land slightly high, than if you are very close and impacting with your shin. You can also impact slightly to the back of your opponent's knee joint by initiating the kick from a side angle. The back of the knee is vulnerable because of the muscles that run down the calf to the heel, and up the back of the leg to the buttocks. When kicking to the back of the knee, keep your leg slightly bent until impact, when you straighten your knee for power and target penetration.

The target for the inside thigh is often misjudged as well. There are two inside thigh targets. The first is located just above the back of the knee joint and slightly to the inside of the leg. The second target is found exactly opposite from the outside target but on the inside of the thigh. This presents an interesting problem: In order to reach the lower of these two inside thigh targets, you must allow your foot to wrap around your opponent's leg to the back of the knee. You do this by throwing the kick from a distance that is slightly closer than when kicking the higher target. In other words, you give yourself enough reach so that your foot is capable of wrapping. When kicking the higher inside thigh target, which is located about 3/4 way up your opponent's inner thigh, the kick is likely to have more of a stinging than a deep tissue effect, because the nerves on the skin on the inside thigh are very sensitive. You can test this by pinching yourself on the inside thigh, and then pinching yourself on the outside thigh. I think you will note an obvious difference. An advantage of kicking to the inside thigh, especially behind the knee joint, is that your opponent's leg is likely to be blasted sideways, making him lose balance.

Improper kick: Another problem regarding the cut kick is that we often fail to separate it from the traditional round house kick. We throw the kick, but stop the power short on impact. This often results from years of training in a traditional martial art, where the fighter gets disqualified for using too much impact in a tournament setting. A properly executed cut kick in kickboxing should be taken through the target. In other words, you should kick with total commitment and intention, as if you were concerned not only with damaging your opponent's leg, but also with using the momentum of the kick to take your opponent off balance. Because of this total commitment, the kick requires a proper set-up. It is difficult to gain momentum if you lack distance in which to initiate the kick. Many fighters tend to isolate the technique. We blast our opponent's leg and get counter-punched. A good set-up decreases your opponent's ability to counter-punch. The cut kick also requires some degree of bodily movement outside of the mechanics of the kick: either a slight step, or rotation of the hips, body, and shoulders to allow the energy of the kick to dissipate into the target.

Once you have landed the kick, your back will be turned partly toward your opponent. Providing that the kick landed on target, this should not present a problem, as your opponent will be more interested in his own well-being than in counter-striking. The problem is in knowing how to be totally committed without fear of getting countered. This is something you need to work on mentally.

When practicing the cut kick with a partner, have him hold a focus mitt at thigh height. Because of the give in his arm, you can practice commitment and total target penetration easier on a mitt than on the heavy bag. If you snap the kick from the knee, it will result in the type of round house kick used in traditional point sparring. If you focus on pivoting your hips all the way through on impact, the kick is more likely to result in a true and damaging cut kick.

Improper angle: As you start the motion of the cut kick, also start directing your hips, shoulders, and body into the kick. Generally, you should impact your opponent with your shin, which is stronger than your instep. Impacting with the shin allows you to throw the kick from a closer range where it is not detected as easily. Upon impacting your opponent's thigh, rotate your hip at a slight downward angle, as if you were going to cut through the leg and use the force of gravity to replant your foot on the floor. Pivoting your hip downward also counteracts your tendency to throw the kick slightly high to your opponent's buttocks. Improper angle happens when you throw the kick horizontally instead of at a downward angle.

Because of the position and commitment involved in throwing the cut kick, it is natural to fear getting counter-punched, which, in turn, leads to improper impact. If you pull your body away from your opponent's anticipated counter-punch or kick, you will tend to "slap" your opponent's leg with the cut kick instead of committing to it. This slap will sting, but will not destroy your opponent's foundation. Think of the cut kick as a means to get to the inside. If you kick with your shin, you are already at a closer distance than if you kick with your instep. In addition, a shin kick is not as easily telegraphed, because you don't have as much movement in the shin as in the instep. Once you have landed the kick, this closer distance makes it more difficult for your opponent to counter.

Another common error in low kicking is a lack of acceleration. Acceleration means increasing the speed of the kick through its distance to the target. The kick should move faster on impact than when you initially set it in motion. The benefit of acceleration is the primary reason for keeping your body in motion. The weight of your body should start to transfer forward into the kicking leg and help you accelerate the kick.

If you choose not to commit totally to the kick, you can throw it at a slight upward angle to the nerve cluster behind the knee instead. Impact the target with the shin. Think of it as slicing through your opponent's leg at an upward angle toward his opposite shoulder. The same kicking mechanics apply: Turn your hips and shoulders into the kick.

IN THE GYM

If I kick your legs a lot, where does your mind go? To your legs, right? The message I want to send is that every time you kick my legs, I will kick your legs harder. What separates the superior fighter from the average fighter is the ability to adapt during the fight. You have to play the thinker's game and exploit your opponent's weaknesses. If you can't find any weaknesses, you have to create them.

If I kick your legs every time you kick mine, it might be wiser for you to move in with a hand combination instead of continuing kicking my legs. Then, fire a kick once you have gotten my attention with your hands. You see, if your mind goes to your legs where the pain is, and you become obsessed with the fact that I'm kicking your legs, it will cause you to freeze and leave you open at the head. Now, once I've trained you to focus on your legs, all I have to do is fake a leg kick and then go for a knockout to your head.

STANCE AND POWER

Because kickboxing is so much about movement and kicking, you should use the cut kick to immobilize your opponent by destroying his foundation. If your opponent can't stand, he can't move. And if he can't move, he can't fight. The pain from a well-placed cut kick is likely to destroy your opponent's fighting spirit.

It is now appropriate to discuss the issue of stance. Although a few of us can switch between conventional stance and southpaw comfortably and fight well from both, most kickboxers favor one stance over the other. If you fight from a left stance, your right cut kick will be stronger than your left, because this leg is farthest from your opponent and has the most distance to travel for building power.

As mentioned earlier, the regular round house kick to your opponent's leg is usually less powerful than a cut kick, because the momentum isn't allowed to go through the target. This kick is often thrown in competition, but will not end the fight. Most fighters can go the full length even if their leg is a little bruised. However, the advantage of the regular round house kick is that you can reset into your stance quickly after landing the kick. A properly thrown cut kick, on the other hand, places you in a slightly inferior position for a moment, but has the potential to drop your opponent instantly and end the fight. Use the cut kick mainly against targets that have give, like the legs. This allows you to take your opponent's balance, and buys you time to assume a powerful stance after landing the kick. You can also throw the cut kick with full follow-through to the head with devastating results, but this requires good flexibility and speed.

In order to release your power into the target on impact, roll your hip at a diagonal angle downward. I call this the "second extension" of your leg (the first extension is the extension of the knee until the leg is straight). You can practice the second extension to both high and low targets, although low kicks are easier for the person who lacks flexibility in the hips. An additional advantage of the second extension is that you can throw your kicks to the front of your opponent's thighs effectively, which is useful when working from close quarter range, or from an angle. Extend your leg at an angle perpendicular to your opponent's thigh, with the power of the kick extending straight forward and into the target.

When throwing kicks to the front of your opponent's thighs from an angle, the kick will impact perpendicular to the thigh.

If the distance is very tight, you may need to take a step back instead of forward in order to create more distance for the kick. You do this by stepping back with your lead foot to the southpaw stance, or by taking a small adjustment step with your lead foot back into a neutral stance. The neutral stance is not as stable as the boxer's stance, and you also run the risk of exposing targets along your centerline. Still, as long as you are aware of the dangers associated with the neutral stance and make an effort to protect against strikes along your centerline, this stance is acceptable when fighting at close range, as the advantages in angle and distance usually outweigh the dangers.

BODY MECHANICS FOR THE CUT KICK WITH A STEP

When throwing the cut kick, ensure that all momentum (the full weight of your body) is going in the direction of the kick. Taking a step (or a jump-step) at a forty-five degree angle forward is appropriate. When you move your whole body in the direction of the kick, you place more weight behind the kick, and the impact has a greater effect. The kick should land at the moment your stepping foot lands, but the kick should be initiated when your stepping foot is still in the air. A common mistake is to break the kick down into two moves: stepping, followed by a slight pause, then kicking. Another common mistake when executing a jump-step is to jump upward instead of forward, directing some of the power toward the ceiling.

Step with your lead foot in the direction of line 1. This helps you close distance, allows you to impact with your shin, and increases the momentum through the use of body weight.

Throw the rear leg cut kick along line 2 to your opponent's outside thigh area. Note how the shin, rather than the instep, is used for deeper penetration. You can achieve more follow-through by rotating your supporting foot in the direction of line 3.

Because a trained opponent can easily recognize the movement of stepping and jumping, a successful cut kick requires concealment and should be blended in with the rest of your techniques. As discussed earlier, the jab is the fastest and easiest way to conceal just about any move, but other techniques also work. The important part is that you learn to use a variety of techniques, so that your opponent never really knows what to expect.

Try these exercises on **CONCEALING THE CUT KICK**:

Exercise 1

Throw multiple high and low round house kicks, impacting with your instep and stinging the target to irritate your opponent. When your opponent gets frustrated, shuffle forward and to the side with the cut kick, impacting your opponent's outside thigh area.

Exercise 2

Throw a close range hooking combination. Allow your opponent to step back, as you explode with the cut kick. Because you are moving forward while he is moving back, you have an advantage in strategy, timing, and balance.

Exercise 3

Use upper body movement, until you have bobbed and weaved to a better angle for the cut kick. Upper body movement invites your opponent to try to land a punch, and is therefore diverting his focus away from your legs.

SLICING YOUR OPPONENT'S LEG

When you are very close to your opponent and don't have enough distance to launch a fully committed kick, you can still use a variation of the cut kick using a slight upward, rather than downward, angle on impact. Think of your shin as a knife slicing diagonally up through your opponent's thigh muscle.

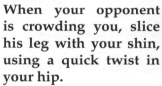

When your opponent is crowding you, slice his leg with your shin, using a quick twist in your hip.

When slicing your opponent's leg, a good rule of thumb is to use the quadriceps muscle as a guide. Most fighters have a definition of this muscle right above their knee and to the outside of their leg. For maximum effect, throw the slicing cut kick to the front of your opponent's leg where the muscle is defined, rather than to the back or side of the leg. Slicing diagonally up your opponent's leg with your shin, taking the entire quadriceps, is a devastating and quick kick that requires little movement or set-up when thrown from close range. Pivot your supporting foot enough to the outside to give your kicking foot a good angle. Your kicking foot should follow the same direction in which your supporting foot is pointed. Practice this kick when shoulder-to-shoulder with your opponent. Keep him occupied with hooks to the body, until you can blend in a slicing cut kick. Like most inside techniques, this kick works best if you are pressing forward, but you can also use it successfully when you have your back to the ropes. If you are fighting a southpaw, use your lead leg against the outside of his lead leg, with the kick concealed through the tight distance.

When fighting a southpaw, throw the cut kick to your opponent's lead leg.

Because impact is made with the shin, it is important to condition your shins properly. You do this by kicking the bottom of a heavy bag a set number of times (start with twenty on each shin), and then graduating to harder targets. Impact with the middle to lower portion of your shin, with the muscle that is slightly to the outside of the bone.

CUT KICKING IN CLOSE QUARTERS (POWER AND SET-UP)

The cut kick is usually not expected in close quarters, where most fighters rely on hooks and uppercuts. You can therefore use it to split your opponent's mind and body focus. When getting to close quarter range, first use your shoulder to bump your opponent back and create the distance you need to throw the kick effectively (about 12 inches). If you are already so close that a step is awkward, try a short jump, increasing power by rotating your body around a vertical axis. Focus your power through your opponent's thigh with full extension in your hip and leg.

To execute the jumping cut kick, initiate the jump with the non-kicking leg. For example, if you intend to throw the cut kick with your rear leg, start by raising your lead foot off the floor. As your lead foot reaches its highest point and reverses direction to replant on the floor, raise your rear foot off the floor and start the cut kicking motion. Your feet are making a scissored move, with one foot going down and the other up.

This can be likened to a tram going up a mountain. As the gondola at the top starts on its way down, the one at the bottom starts on its way up. They meet at the halfway point. This concept is important because it allows one part of your body to assist another part, with the result of less energy expenditure.

When using the *pulley-effect* (as described above) proficiently, fighting becomes economical with minimal time between strikes. When fighting is economical, it appears as though you have more speed, even though the strikes themselves aren't thrown any faster. Fighting this way also takes less effort, helping you last longer during heavy physical exertion.

Leg kicking at close quarter range is great when you are tired and need time to recover, or when your opponent has backed you up against the ropes. However, if your opponent is pushing against you, it is difficult to throw a cut kick utilizing either a step or a jump. You can now use the slicing cut kick, as discussed above. Because this kick takes very little energy to throw, you can use it to control the fight while at the same time conserving energy.

When you are backed up against the ropes, you are in a vulnerable position with limited movement and unable to use distance to your advantage. Many fighters simply cover up and hope that the attack will die out. But keep in mind that the fighter who throws the most strikes scores the most points. Action is also a great crowd pleaser. The best defense is offense, which means that in order to take the fight from your opponent, you must somehow interfere with his strikes. You do this best by counter-striking or kicking. Because your opponent's attack is likely to focus on your upper body, you can defend by covering up and using leg kicks to destroy his mind and body focus.

Most fighters don't expect to be kicked when on the inside, so you can launch the leg kick rather easily. Still, you must ensure that the kick is concealed and flows within the rhythm of your punch combination. When practicing the cut kick at close quarter range, get in the habit of concealing it within a three-punch combination. For example: **Throw a jab, a cross, a jab, and a kick** with your rear leg. Or if very close, throw three **alternating hooks, and a kick**. To speed up the kick, use the pulley-effect, and throw the kick before you have reset your body from the hook. This increases your speed by a half-beat. For example, initiate the kick as your last punch is on its way back, so that the retrieving motion of your fist pulls your kick out. This works best if you kick with the leg opposite that of your punching hand. If you threw your last punch with your left hand, kick with your right leg, and vice versa. If you practice this concept enough in training (shadow boxing and heavy bag), it will come quite naturally, and you won't need to think about it during the course of the fight.

When you have landed the cut kick, immediately follow up with additional strikes. You may also need to take additional small steps to create a better angle or position for your follow-up combination.

THE INSIDE THIGH KICK

The leg kick to the inside thigh is a valuable tool used primarily as an irritant or set-up. When thrown with intent, this kick is likely to separate your opponent's legs, destroy his balance, and open up his centerline.

Try this exercise on the **INSIDE THIGH KICK**:

Exercise 4

1. Throw a lead leg cut kick to your opponent's lead inside thigh a number of times. When it starts to bother him, he is likely to move his lead leg back or to a neutral stance. This opens up his centerline and his rear leg inside thigh area.

2. Now, fake another kick to your opponent's lead inside thigh (more about faking in Section 10), then throw a rear leg cut kick to your opponent's rear inside thigh. This is a power technique and should preferably be thrown with a step.

Because the legs are heavier than the hands, they are more difficult to set in motion, and are therefore slower than our hands. But an even more important element of the slower legs is the danger of telegraphing the kick prior to impact. However, a low kick is not quite as slow as a high kick, and not quite as likely to be telegraphed. You can reduce the time between strikes and kicks to the legs by relying on the *first touch concept*. For example, use the leg kick as a set-up for a hand technique. First throw a lead leg inside thigh kick. The moment your foot plants, follow with a rear uppercut as a finishing technique.

Set up a knockout with a lead leg cut kick to your opponent's inside thigh area. Once his focus is on the kick, shuffle forward and throw a rear uppercut to his chin.

Again, it is important to avoid breaking the technique into additional and unneeded moves. If you throw the leg kick, wait until you have planted your foot back in your fighting stance, and then move in with the uppercut, you have wasted too much time and given your opponent the opportunity to counter your move. Mechanically, it is not wrong to break the technique down into its component moves. It is only wrong because time is of the essence. A better way is to throw the inside thigh kick and, as you are in the process of replanting your foot on the floor, simultaneously shuffle forward with the uppercut. The uppercut should land on your opponent's chin the moment your lead foot lands on the floor. This concept is especially important when throwing a technique that is primarily used as a set-up. The inside thigh kick, when used as a set-up, is not likely to hurt your opponent enough to freeze him or make him unable to counter.

289

STEALING THE MOMENT OF IMPACT (SHIN BLOCKS)

Because defense goes hand in hand with offense, it is appropriate to talk about defense against the cut kick at this time. The most common defense is the shin block. Still, few kickboxers use the shin block effectively for blocking kicks to the legs. Many fighters feel they can absorb their opponent's leg kick without it slowing them down during the bout, with the pain coming after the fight when the leg begins to stiffen. This is because the fighter throwing the kick is using **improper target, improper kick, or improper angle**, as discussed at the beginning of this section. But if your opponent's kicks are lacking in power and you get in the habit of ignoring them, you may be in for a rude awakening the day you are up against a fighter who understands how to properly throw the cut kick.

Many fighters are reluctant to use the shin block, because it hurts their shins more to block than it does to actually take the kick on the thigh. The reason is that they don't understand the principle behind the *moment of impact*. This principle states that if you block your opponent's kick when it is fully extended, the impact to both you and your opponent is equal and the stronger shin will win. In order to use the shin block successfully, you must beat your opponent to the moment of impact; you must block your opponent's kick at the initiation of his kick.

It may seem as though our shins are more sensitive than our thighs, which have padding covering the bone. Still, we use our shins to block kicks to our thighs. It is interesting to note that once we get over the initial fear of impacting with our shins, we find that they are actually less sensitive to pain than the nerves in the outside thigh area. This reinforces the fact that the kick to the outside thigh is an extremely effective kickboxing weapon.

The shin block must be fast. You can build speed and explosiveness by practicing multiple shin blocks in rapid succession with a light tap of your foot on the floor between each block. Practice alternating inside and outside shin blocks, keeping your shin stiff when it meets your opponent's kick. Raise your knee high enough to form a solid defense in conjunction with your elbow. This prevents the kick from slipping through to your ribs.

Note that there is a danger in placing too much weight on your foot when planting it on the floor after blocking. Stay as light as possible when replanting your foot. If your opponent hears a loud "clomp" each time you put your foot down, he knows that all your weight is on that foot, and that he can easily sweep you to take you off balance. You will also lose mobility and be unable to follow with a second block or kick off that same leg.

You can defend the slicing leg kick (upward leg kick from close range) by pivoting your lead leg against your opponent's kick. This move is very short and quick with your foot barely off the floor. Let's look at the disadvantages of shin blocking next.

Leg kicks with the shin are difficult to detect from close range. Even if your opponent sees the kick and uses a shin block, if you are close enough, you can often redirect the kick to a higher target, and slip your shin in between his knee and elbow to the opening on his ribs.

OTHER DEFENSES AGAINST THE CUT KICK

A good reason for not using the shin block is that the block limits your mobility. When on one foot, you can't move until you have planted your other foot on the floor (concept: **COMPLETION OF MOTION**). Your foundation is also narrow, and you are in a less stable stance. Technically, when your opponent kicks and is on one leg and you raise your leg to block, your positions are equally superior with your opponent at a slight advantage, because he is the one initiating the attack with full focus on offense.

I once observed a fighter executing a cut kick, taking both his opponent's legs simultaneously. Actually, what happened was that the fighter threw a cut kick, which his opponent blocked with a shin block. The fighter immediately threw another cut kick off his other leg to his opponent's supporting leg. Because his opponent had not had time to replant his blocking foot on the floor, he lost balance and went down.

Another effective defense against the leg kick is jamming the kick simultaneous with a punch. This allows you to keep both feet on the ground, and is a way of turning defense into offense. Most fighters throw their kick slightly isolated from the combination. When your opponent initiates a committed kick and before the kick lands, step straight toward him and fire a jab to his chest (concept: **STEALING THE MOMENT OF IMPACT**). This will knock him back and off balance. You have now gained superiority and can follow with a punch or kick combination.

For jamming to work, your timing must be very good, where you initiate your attack before your opponent has extended his kick fully. When you see the first twitching in your opponent's hip, shuffle forward rapidly without worrying about blocking the kick. By moving to close range at the initiation of your opponent's kick, you will jam the power of his kick (not the kick itself). If you can land a jab while your opponent is on one leg, you may score a knockdown. Because you are starting from medium to long range and moving in, this also allows you to build momentum for power.

One may ask: Why not throw a rear cross instead of a jab? The rear cross has more power, true, but the jab is closer to your opponent and can therefore be launched faster. This goes back to the action/reaction issue, which states that it takes longer to react than it does to act. Because your opponent initiates offense with a leg kick that you react to, he has the advantage. Because the rear cross takes a bit longer to throw than the jab, your opponent is likely to land his kick before you impact with your strike. **However, it is not wrong to throw the rear cross.** The rear cross and hook are also good follow-ups when you have landed the jab.

The wallop you create when landing your strike is likely to knock your opponent down. A punch to your opponent's mid-section is just one possible technique in conjunction with jamming. When you have completed this section and learned the knee strike, you can experiment with that as well. Again, when your opponent is on one leg and off balance, the impact of any strike will have an adverse effect.

Summary and review

The cut kick to your opponent's legs is one of the most widely used techniques in kickboxing and Muay Thai. It differs from the regular round house kick by the way it cuts through the target and places you in a slightly inferior position with your back turned partially toward your opponent. However, this position is only inferior if the cut kick fails to do damage. A fully committed kick has the ability to drop your opponent instantly, and is likely to end the fight.

Cut kick practice on focus mitts

- Practice the motion of the cut kick on a focus mitt held by your partner. Do not snap the kick back after impact, but continue the motion through the target until you are in the opposite stance.

- Most cut kicks are thrown with the rear leg for power. If you start with your left foot forward, you will end up in a right stance upon completing the kick.

- When kicking the focus mitt, it is easy to take the kick through the target because your opponent's arm has give and will go with the force. When kicking your opponent's leg, kick with the same intent as you did on the focus mitt.

- Also practice the cut kick with your lead leg. This simulates a kick to your opponent's lead inside thigh area. How can you increase the power of a cut kick thrown with your lead leg? How can you use the kick to the inside thigh to take your opponent's balance?

A cut kick to the inside thigh can do significant damage, and may separate your opponent's legs and unbalance him.

Cut kicking in close quarters

- Practice backing your partner into the ropes, and intermingle cut kicks with close quarter power punching (hooks and uppercuts).

- If your opponent is good at covering his openings in close quarters, you risk tiring yourself out with punches that don't do any damage. Try to shift your opponent's focus by kicking his legs from close quarter range.

- When kicking to the legs, be careful not to lower your guard inadvertently, giving your opponent an opportunity to counter-attack.

Slicing your opponent's leg

- The slicing cut kick is thrown at an upward angle and with a quick twist of your body from very close range.

- Next time you get in a clinch, or when you're pressing your opponent back and there is little room to cut kick, slice your opponent's leg by driving your shin into his outside thigh area.

- The moment the kick starts bothering your opponent, he will step back and create distance for an upper body attack. How can you take advantage of it? How can you ensure that you stay protected against his possible counter-strikes?

Defending the cut kick

- Use the shin block to defend your opponent's cut kick. A good shin block should be thrown with intent, meeting the power of the kick through upper body movement forward.

- It is difficult to block every low kick. Sometimes, you will take one or two cut kicks before learning that your opponent is in the habit of throwing it. Once you pick up on this habit, you can look for the movement that sets it up, making the timing of your block easier.

- Good defense places you in charge. The shin block must be done with intent in order to be effective. How can you use the first touch concept to launch a follow-up after blocking your opponent's kick?

KNEES AND ELBOWS

Keith's Corner

If you have paid attention, you will remember that the elbow is one of the hardest bones in the human body and, because of its small surface area, has tremendous capability to inflict damage when used as a "striking block" against your opponent's shin or instep. The knee is similar in construction to the elbow, and is a vicious striking weapon capable of focusing a large force over a small surface area. Advanced kickboxers utilize their knees and elbows as effective and powerful weapons.

The type of competitions you choose will dictate, to some extent, the types of techniques you will use. Thai-fighters have been using elbows and knees for hundreds of years. In just the last decade, more and more kickboxing bouts in the United States have allowed the competitors to knee each other. Depending on the sanctioning body, there are some restrictions, however. In the United States, very rarely do you find competitions that allow knee strikes to the head. Generally, knees are allowed to the body only. In Europe and Asia knee strikes are more common, and in many international competitions it is legal to knee to the head. Elbow strikes are rarely used, and the tournaments that do allow them in the United States generally require the competitors to wear elbow pads.

Because of fear of the knee and elbow strike, some fighters avoid competitions that allow them. I don't recommend this. I feel that you should strive to be as well rounded as possible, so that when opportunities arise, you are trained and in position to accept fights regardless of the rules, restrictions, or sanctioning bodies. The bottom line is that to be considered a true champion, you should have the ability to compete at any level under any rules.

Because the knee is more widely used than the elbow, we will discuss it first. Although there is a variety of knee strikes, kickboxing focuses on three different types. During this phase of your training, you will study the front knee, round house knee, and side knee. These are the most common, most easy to use, and most powerful knee strikes. You will also incorporate a number of variations, including stepping, jumping, grabbing, and hands free. Some competitions allow you to grab your opponent when kneeing, while others don't, so you need to be familiar with both.

This section covers:

- Body mechanics for the front knee
- The round house knee
- Grabbing and kneeing
- Knee strikes hands free
- Multiple knee strikes
- In the gym
- The side knee
- Defending the knee strike
- Glove-up with Keith
- What's in a good knee strike?
- The knee jab
- The elbow strike
- Summary and review

BODY MECHANICS FOR THE FRONT KNEE

Body mechanics for the front knee strike are similar to the front kick, but with impact focused over the small area of the knee itself. Throw the front knee straight up along your opponent's centerline, impacting his solar plexus, ribs, or face if he is bent forward.

From a proper fighting stance, initiate the technique by thrusting your knee straight ahead, as if you were going to throw a front kick. Keep the lower portion of your leg chambered.

The momentum should force your supporting foot to pivot forty-five degrees to the outside (an alternative is to step with your supporting foot to a forty-

five degree angle to the outside).

Just prior to impact, thrust your hips forward, simultaneously inclining your upper body slightly to the rear. This gives you extension in the hips with increased target penetration.

When throwing a single knee strike, return your foot to the point of origin after impacting the target. If your intent is to throw more than one knee strike with the same leg, return the striking leg a little farther back than point of origin and immediately initiate a second strike. This greater distance gives you maximum power. If a third strike is to be thrown, its position should be identical to the second strike. Multiple knee strikes are best thrown when you grab your opponent and pull him forward and into the strike.

THE ROUND HOUSE KNEE

The round house knee strike is mechanically similar to the round house kick. Impacting with the whole thigh area allows you to take a greater target than when striking with the kneecap alone. You can therefore use the round house knee to damage your opponent's entire mid-section.

You can increase power and flexibility in the round house knee by stepping with your supporting foot (lead foot) at a forty-five degree angle forward. Simultaneously bring your rear knee forward, as though you were going to throw a rear leg round house kick, keeping the lower portion of the leg chambered. Bring your thigh across your opponent's body, impacting with the knee and thigh area. The strike should impact at the same time as your stepping foot lands. Keep your leg chambered with your toes pointed.

The round house knee strikes from the side, just like a round house kick.

Both the front knee and round house knee should be thrown with your initial step to the outside (away from your centerline). For example, when throwing the rear knee, step with your lead foot forward and to the outside of your opponent's body. This gives you a better angle for impacting the target. When throwing the lead knee, do the opposite of the above: Step with your rear foot forward and to your opponent's outside.

GRABBING AND KNEEING

You can increase the power in the knee strike by grabbing your opponent around the neck and pulling him into the strike, simultaneously thrusting your hips forward. Keep your elbows tight to your body for protection and leverage. When grabbing is permitted, landing the knee strike is much easier, but you must be cautious to avoid inadvertently exposing areas of your body or head when reaching out to grab. Conceal the knee strike with another technique. As mentioned earlier, the jab is the fastest and most versatile set-up strike:

1. First **throw the jab a couple of times** to keep your opponent occupied and gain a feel for distance.

2. On one of those jabs, **grab around your opponent's neck with your jabbing hand**, simultaneously lunging forward with the knee strike. At this time, you may reach out and grab with your other hand as well.

3. **Drive your knee into the target** at a slight upward angle. You do this by thrusting your hips forward and simultaneously pulling your opponent toward you.

Note that grabbing and kneeing could be difficult when wearing boxing gloves, because you can't interlace your fingers behind your opponent's neck. I like to cross my arms around the back of my opponent's neck rather than grabbing. This gives you a fairly strong grip for pulling, while also narrowing the space between your arms, making it more difficult for your opponent to escape the technique.

When you grab your opponent around the neck, his natural tendency is to grab back and start kneeing. Anytime you grab expect to be grabbed back. This is why the gap closure and knee strike must be dynamic. Keep your head off to one side and not on the centerline where you risk getting head butted by your opponent.

Keith's Knockout Advice

It is critical that, immediately upon grabbing, you begin to manipulate your opponent's body. Grabbing and kneeing allows you to manipulate position rather easily. Let's examine the mechanics associated with this technique. There are two types of grabs that we will use. Positions may vary.

The first grab involves interlacing your fingers behind your opponent's neck and pulling him forward and into the knee strike. You can increase power by pulling your elbows together toward your centerline, simultaneously pulling your opponent forward. This gives you leverage and narrows the gap between your arms to keep your centerline protected. Drawing your elbows together also prevents your opponent from escaping the technique by ducking and weaving to the outside.

The second type of grab involves placing both your hands on one side of your opponent's neck or shoulder and pulling him into the strike. The strike and the pulling force must be simultaneous for momentum.

Practice switching from one hand position to the other. For example, grab your opponent with both hands on the left side of his neck and throw a round house knee. Now, switch one hand to the right side of his neck and throw a front knee. Then, switch both hands

to the right side and throw a round house knee with your other leg.

Note that the round house knee is easier to throw from a tight distance than is the front knee. When grabbing and throwing the front knee, you can gain momentum by taking a step back with the leg that you are going to knee with prior to throwing the strike. This increases the distance between your hips and your opponent's body and helps you launch a powerful thrust. When your knee comes forward, simultaneously pull your opponent into the strike while raising up on the ball of your supporting foot. This gives you a diagonal upward thrust, allowing you to place the weight of your body behind the blow.

Also practice grabbing with only one hand. A one-handed grab is not as strong as a double grab, but it leaves one of your hands free for punching and blocking. You can further increase power by taking a step with your supporting foot. The step and strike should be simultaneous. Do not break the technique down into three moves by stepping, pausing, and kneeing.

The one-handed grab is not as strong, but leaves you an option to use your free hand for offense or defense.

Although the knee strike is a close range technique, you can initiate it from long range by pushing off with your rear foot and lunging toward your opponent. Regardless of whether you choose to throw a single knee or grab and throw multiple knees, the gap closure must be dynamic and done with intent.

You can also use the knee as a deterrent when your opponent is coming into close range. Your timing should be so that you catch him before he has closed distance to where he is smothering the technique. If you knee him as he is coming into close range, you will add your momentum to his, with possibly devastating effects. This technique works best with the front knee.

KNEE STRIKES HANDS FREE

You should also practice knee strikes using the hands free variation. These types of knees are a little quicker initially, and can be thrown when closing distance. Because you are not reaching out to grab your opponent, they are a little easier to conceal than the grabbing knee, and your opponent is more likely to be caught off guard and unprepared to grab you back. The drawback is that you can't pull your opponent forward and into the strike. You must therefore be dynamic and set it up with a prior technique, normally a jab. When your opponent is occupied thinking about the jab, close distance with a quick jump-step (shuffle-step with a simultaneous jump). Your knee should land on target at the same time your lead foot lands, preferably past your opponent's body, allowing you to drive your knee through the target. The knee strike should be launched at the apex (highest point) of your jump-step.

MULTIPLE KNEE STRIKES

It is difficult fighting backing up, so if you can grab your opponent and back him up as you knee, he will have difficulty countering. The more you control your opponent's body, the more difficult it is for him to maintain balance or mount any type of defense.

The fighter who can strike while moving forward usually has the advantage over the one who is moving back, because:

1. It is more **natural to move forward** than back.

2. You can **use momentum** to your advantage.

3. Moving forward is usually **seen as a strength** by the judges.

4. Backing your opponent into the ropes will **affect him mentally**.

Use the knee strike to force your opponent back. When you have thrown your first knee (with your rear leg), allow that leg to come down forward, placing you in a right fighting stance. Immediately initiate a second knee strike with your left leg, which is now in a rear position. Continue forcing your opponent back by throwing alternating rear knees, switching stance with each strike. Again, this is most practical when you have grabbed onto your opponent.

Initiate the technique by bringing your hands around your opponent's neck. Keep your elbows tight along your centerline.

Thrust your rear knee forward and pull your opponent's upper body into the strike.

After landing the knee, plant your foot forward and use your grabbing hands or forearms to return your opponent to an upright position, forcing him backward.

Repeat the sequence with your left knee, which is now your rear knee.

You can increase momentum and power by jumping as you start your rear knee forward. For best effect, impact your opponent while in the air. Again, you can use either your lead or rear knee, but the technique is more powerful if done with the rear knee. Power is also increased when grabbing and pulling simultaneous to jumping. The power of this technique comes from incorporating the entire mass of your body at impact. When replanting your foot, try to plant it in a position from where you can comfortably throw another knee strike. You can also initiate the jump knee from long range, with the jump used to launch your forward momentum.

When you pull your opponent forward, you add the momentum of his body to the momentum of your knee strike.

COMMON ERRORS WHEN JUMPING & KNEEING:

1. **Not using a proper set-up** when initiating the technique from long range, and telegraphing the technique.

2. **Not synchronizing the jump** with the kick. If you allow your foot to plant prior to impacting with the knee, the purpose of the jump is defeated.

IN THE GYM

Why is a jump knee more devastating than a regular knee strike? You get more momentum by jumping, and you also add momentums by grabbing and pulling your opponent into the strike. You can throw the jumping knee either straight or from the side like a round house knee. Impact with your thigh in addition to your knee to target your opponent's entire mid-section.

Next time you work the heavy bag, work the jumping knee strike. Either grab the bag and pull yourself forward, or knee without grabbing. Some of the kickboxing tournaments that allow knee strikes don't allow grabbing, so you need to practice both. The jumping knee strike hands free is useful when your opponent is hurt or dazed. The jumping knee, especially if thrown from long range, is now unexpected and will be a great crowd pleaser. When jumping and kneeing, impact the target when your jumping foot is at its highest point. If you wait until your foot is planted, you will lose power.

THE SIDE KNEE

The side knee is used for very tight distances, and mostly when your opponent is grabbing you. Impact your opponent's ribs, preferably the floating ribs (the lowest two pairs of ribs), which are relatively easy to break.

Use the side knee strike when your opponent grabs you and pulls you tight. Protect yourself against his knee strikes by wrapping your arms around his body and pulling him close.

The side knee is commonly thrown by bringing your knee toward your centerline, impacting with the inside of your knee and thigh. The knee should make a sweeping motion across the target. This requires some flexibility in the hips.

Start by bringing your knee forward at a forty-five degree angle toward the outside. The knee must start forward and outward to give you enough power at this range. Now bring your knee inward toward your centerline, impacting with the side of your knee against the side of your opponent's body. You can make the strike more effective by wrapping your arms around your opponent's body at the initial tie-up, and locking your hands behind his back.

Raise your opponent's arms to create openings along the sides of his body.

The side knee is also a good defensive technique against an opponent attempting to knee you. As he attacks, wrap your arms around his body and pull him tight. Then start kneeing from the side. The tight distance will hinder most of his offensive moves and create a need for him to defend himself.

DEFENDING THE KNEE STRIKE

Knowing how to throw the knee strike is not enough. In a match that allows knee striking, you must expect knees and learn to defend against them. Let's look at a variety of defenses against knee attacks:

Single hand low defense: Your opponent will often dominate with one side; for example, he will throw his right knee several times. Defend the attack by placing your hand on his hip (the hip on the same side as his kneeing leg). You have now stalled the momentum in his knee strike. Keep your other hand on the back of your opponent's neck to control him. You can also block your opponent's knee strike when he reaches out to grab and starts his knee forward. Blocking the knee will stifle his momentum. A cut kick to your opponent's supporting leg is a good follow-up, but its effectiveness depends on your timing. At this point, your opponent is likely to leave his head exposed, and an uppercut or straight strike may work well.

The single hand low defense stops your opponent's momentum.

Two hand low defense: If your opponent starts kneeing with alternating right and left knees, place both your hands on his hips or against his lower belly and start forcing him to the rear. His momentum is now halted, and he must put his foot down to brace himself. When he struggles to regain his foundation, lock both your arms around his back and pull him close. You can now continue with side knees.

Forearm blocks: As your opponent's knee thrusts upward, impact the top of his thigh with your forearm. Because the momentum of your block is meeting the momentum of his knee, the effectiveness of your defense is increased. Tuck your chin and head down and bend slightly forward at the waist. Keep your forearm horizontal, using a sawing motion into the middle of your opponent's thigh. Increase power by bending your knees slightly and lowering your weight. For best effect, block with the arm that is diagonally across your opponent's leg. If your opponent attempts to knee you with his right knee, use your right forearm to block. You can also use the double forearm block, keeping your arms parallel with your body and perpendicular to your opponent's thigh.

Use the single (left) and double (right) forearm blocks to impact the nerves in your opponent's thigh and stop the strike.

Also try blocking with your elbows. Since the elbow allows you to focus the power over a very small surface area, the damage can be devastating, with the effect of draining energy from your opponent's leg. However, you must be very precise with the block. If you miss, your opponent's knee will still impact the target.

Movement: Defend the knee and steal your opponent's balance by forcing him to move back. This is accomplished best during the initial tie-up. Lock your arms around your opponent's neck and draw both elbows toward your centerline, bringing your forearms close together and against your opponent's chest. As your opponent raises his knee, step forward and simultaneously push your forearm against his shoulder on the kneeing side. You will now force him to put his foot back down for balance. Simultaneously force him back. Follow with a series of knee strikes of your own. You can also block your opponent's knee by raising your own knee in the path of his, and block with your shin the way you would block a leg kick.

The head roll: The moment your opponent attempts to grab in preparation for a kneeing attack, instantly duck and roll (bob and weave) under either of your opponent's extended arms. Take a step back simultaneous with the roll, and mount a vicious counterattack. If using this type of defense, be careful with ducking too low. If the rules don't allow for knees to the head, and you duck into a knee strike, it will still count against you. If your opponent grabs you, try to establish the centerline with your hands between your opponent's hands. Establishing the centerline gives you the power advantage, because you have more leverage along your centerline. Once your hands are between your opponent's hands, you can also use your forearms to push his upper body back, giving you space to knee him.

The tie-up: When your opponent initiates a knee strike, immediately lock your arms around his body and pull him close. This will wear him down and eliminate his power advantage. If fighting under Western kickboxing rules, tying up may force the referee to call a break and separate the fighters. Once a lock-up occurs, you should therefore start to move your opponent to the rear immediately.

Sweep and throw: This technique requires that you lock up with your opponent. As he initiates a knee strike, tilt your body toward his supporting leg to unbalance him. Sweep his supporting leg while simultaneously pulling his upper body toward the floor (more on sweeps in the next sub-section).

Use the sweep and throw if the rules allow takedowns.

Note that rules differ between competitions. Not all fights allow knee strikes, and fights that do allow them don't always allow throws. In kickboxing matches that allow knee strikes, you are normally allowed to catch your opponent's leg when he throws a high round house kick, and to counter to his supporting leg. In these matches, sweeps are also allowed. A point is not always scored for a sweep, but the fighter who goes down must expend a considerable amount of energy getting back to his feet. Being swept is also likely to affect him mentally. Many Thai boxing matches allow elbow strikes in conjunction with knees. However, in Western style kickboxing, the elbow is normally not allowed as a striking weapon other than when used as a striking block (elbow block). Fighting by modified Thai rules is becoming more popular in the United States. You will see knee strikes and leg kicks, with elbows being more restricted. If elbow strikes are allowed, the rules usually allow for the horizontal elbow strike only, and not the downward or upward elbow. The fighters may also be required to wear elbow pads. When fighting under Muay Thai rules, clinching and throwing is allowed.

COMMON ERRORS WHEN DEFENDING THE KNEE STRIKE:

1. **Failing to time the block or defensive move to your opponent's strike.** This is perhaps especially common when using the forearm block. Because the distance between his knee and your block is so short, it is sometimes difficult to initiate your block in time to meet the strike on its way to the target.

2. **Failing to follow up after blocking.** Again, you should not be satisfied with simply knowing that you have avoided your opponent's attack. You must always stay one step ahead, so that you can take advantage of a new opening in his defense.

Glove Up with Keith

Since the knee strike is legal in some kickboxing tournaments, you should practice it meticulously. The front and round house knee are the bread and butter of knee strikes. A common way to throw these is by grabbing your opponent around the neck and pulling his upper body forward and into the knee. Most sanctioning bodies in the United States don't allow grabbing and kneeing, and the knee must be thrown with your hands kept from touching your opponent. Many fighters find it difficult to throw a powerful knee this way.

The power of the knee depends to a great extent on your angle and momentum in conjunction with synchronized body mechanics. To pull off a successful knee strike without grabbing your opponent, you must start your technique from long range and be explosive. Let's say that you are in the out-fighting zone (long range) throwing jabs to keep your opponent occupied. When you decide to move in with the knee, step up at a forty-five degree angle with your lead foot and explode forward with full intent of hurting your opponent. Whether you grab or not, there is nothing about the knee that should be pleasant. Every move should be firm and fast, so that the strike is always thrown with intent. When you land a knee, follow with a second and third knee immediately. To gain maximum power in your follow-up, you must set your foot down as far back as possible.

You can execute the knee strike with either the lead or rear leg. In general, you will get more power with your rear leg, but by the same token there is more travel distance, which could telegraph the technique and make it more difficult to land. Proficiency with both legs won't come unless you work the lead knee as well.

When closing distance, don't duck so low that you set yourself up for a knee strike to the head.

WHAT'S IN A GOOD KNEE STRIKE?

Keith's Knockout Advice

Many people think of a knee strike as simply lifting your knee and thrusting it toward the target. But there are a number of things you must do to generate maximum power. Perhaps the most difficult is getting the timing down. If the knee is thrust half-heartedly at the target, or if it is wavering on impact, the strike will lack power and you will be vulnerable to a counter-attack. The knee strike is a close range technique, but can be initiated from long range with a proper set-up. You must close distance fast and without showing your intentions. The danger lies in your opponent timing a counter-strike to your forward movement. If you close distance with a shuffle-step, you can increase the effectiveness of the knee strike by adding a jump. This is also true when grabbing and kneeing, where you can use momentum by bringing your opponent's upper body forward, simultaneously springing from the floor as you thrust your knee into the target. A powerful and sharp knee strike must land straight on impact.

Targets for the knee are the body and the legs. The head is only a target if your opponent brings his head to where his body is supposed to be; for example, when his head is low in a bob and weave.

Sometimes it is necessary to use some ingenuity and learn how to flow from one technique to the next. For example, the front knee strike and the front kick follow the same paths and differ only in distance and the striking surface of the weapon. When throwing the knee strike hands free, and your opponent steps back at the initiation of your technique, you can convert the knee strike to a longer reaching front kick simply by extending your leg. This allows you to continue on the path you have already started, and saves time by eliminating the necessity to re-chamber for another technique.

Note that the front knee has its greatest reach at mid-level. The higher you kick, the closer you must be to the target.

When throwing the front or round house knee, incline your body slightly to the rear as you thrust the knee forward. Using a thrust is more powerful than merely raising your knee to strike. It also makes it more difficult for your opponent to throw an effective counter-strike.

The knee is capable of inflicting severe damage, but the strike is often underdeveloped and failing either in set-up, distance, or timing. If you lack patience, you may throw the strike hastily, neglecting a well-calculated set-up. If you are too far from your opponent, the knee strike will be a wasted move, giving your opponent the opportunity to avoid it and counter-strike. Also beware of telegraphing the technique. When you move forward to grab your opponent's neck, he can time a counter-move to avoid getting grabbed. A better strategy is to use your jab several times first, making him respectful of the jab and unsuspecting of the grab.

A successful knee strike should be repeated, especially if you can pull your opponent forward and into the technique. Practice knee strikes on heavy bags, focus mitts, and in contact drills with a partner. The ultimate test of your abilities to use this technique comes when you get into the ring with your opponent.

THE KNEE JAB

You can also use the knee effectively as a short "jabbing" technique from a tie-up or clinch. Short, sharp movements of your knee cap into your opponent's thigh has the same effect as a cut kick, draining energy from his legs. The short jabbing knee is a technique that is often overlooked, yet it is as easy as taking a step forward. From close range, initiate a step and let your knee impact your opponent's thigh as you raise your foot off the floor. The move is very quick and almost effortless. When kneeing to the legs, impact either with the front of the knee (as in a front knee), the front and thigh (as in a round house knee), or just the side of the knee. If you initiate this technique from long range, you gain momentum by stepping to your opponent's outside with your supporting foot, just as you would when throwing the cut kick. Impact the target simultaneous to planting your stepping foot, with the step and knee synchronized for power.

While knee strikes to the mid-section can be blocked, knee strikes to the legs are more difficult to defend against. Don't neglect to take a variety of targets.

Also use the knee strike to disengage from a clinch, by thrusting your knee parallel with the floor and against your opponent's mid-section.

The short, jabbing knee is extremely painful when thrown to the nerves in your opponent's thigh.

COMMON ERRORS WHEN THROWING THE KNEE STRIKE:

1. **Failing to extend the technique.** You achieve extension by thrusting your hips forward and your upper body slightly to the rear.

2. **Using single knee strikes.** Multiple knee strikes allow you to carry your momentum forward until your opponent is cornered or goes down.

3. **Failing to manipulate your opponent's body** to achieve the best possible angle for the knee strike when grabbing and kneeing.

4. **Failing to use a proper set-up** when initiating the technique from long range. Because the knee strike is a close range technique, if you make it obvious that you are going to throw it, your opponent can counter your forward motion.

Note that you can gain more power by jumping simultaneous to kneeing, especially if you grab around your opponents neck and pull him into the technique. Pull your opponent's upper body forward and down, simultaneously elevating yourself off the ground. Another benefit to jumping is that you can initiate the technique from long range, with the jump helping you achieve a fast gap closure along with momentum. Attempt to land your knee on target prior to landing your jumping foot on the floor. If your foot plants prior to landing the kick, the main purpose of the jump is defeated. We will talk more about jumping and kicking in Section 9.

THE ELBOW STRIKE

Because more and more tournaments are beginning to allow the elbow strike (if pads are worn), it benefits the kickboxer to learn fighting according to Muay Thai rules. In tournaments that allow elbow strikes, your hooks can be substituted for elbows (and vice versa) in close quarters. The hook resembles the path of the horizontal elbow strike. You can now mix your close range fighting techniques. For example, throw a jab to set your opponent up. As you shuffle forward to close range, follow with a rear hooking elbow (instead of a rear cross or rear hook). Shift your weight to your rear foot and throw a lead uppercut. Shift your weight back to your lead foot and throw another rear elbow strike. Note that the upward elbow (which follows the path of the uppercut), the straight downward elbow, and the spinning back elbow are normally not allowed in kickboxing.

Throw the horizontal elbow to your opponent's jaw after closing distance with the jab.

The main difference between the motion of the hook and the horizontal elbow is that the hook follows a straight path through the target, while the elbow loops toward your body. You can now initiate a hook and, as the distance or target changes, change the motion of your strike and convert it to an elbow. Pivot your body as you would when throwing the hook, and snap your arm back to the guard position after impact. Also try the "two in one," where you strike with the hook first, then collapse your arm toward your body and follow with the elbow strike within the same movement.

The "two in one" allows you to throw two strikes within the motion of one: the hook (left) and the elbow (below).

The beauty of the elbow is that it has devastating power and is difficult to defend against. Impact the target with the tip of the elbow and about two inches down the forearm. Strike horizontally across your opponent's nose or jaw, or at a slight downward angle, dropping your weight simultaneously. You can also use the diagonal downward elbow to penetrate a tight guard, and the horizontal elbow to wrap around your opponent's guard and impact his jaw or temple. If you throw the elbow within another close range combination, taking a step is usually not needed. However, if your opponent backs up after being hit with one of your other strikes, you may need to step forward to close the gap. If your opponent is a master at close quarter combat, landing the elbow strike may be trickier.

If your opponent is in the habit of extending his guard slightly forward, you can wrap the horizontal elbow around his guard and impact his jaw or temple.

COMMON ERRORS WHEN THROWING THE ELBOW STRIKE:

1. Failing to judge distance correctly, or timing the strike to an inappropriate opening.

2. Not placing your body weight behind the strike.

3. Striking with the forearm instead of the elbow (the elbow is a harder weapon with more penetrating power).

4. Failing to follow up, especially if the strike has staggered your opponent.

Summary and review

The knee strike is a close range technique that follows the same motion as the front kick or round house kick. In essence, it can be said that if the range is so close that a front or round house kick are impractical, the knee strike usually works well. The knee has the capability to do great damage. The knee is small and hard, allowing you to focus a great deal of power into the strike. Targets for the knee are your opponent's body along his centerline, the ribs for the round house knee, and his head (if allowed) when pulled forward and into the strike. The nerves on your opponent's thigh are great targets for the short jabbing knee strike.

You can throw the knee both grabbing and hands free. Hands free allows you to use your hands for striking or blocking, but the knee itself may not be as powerful, because you must rely on forward momentum, rather than on pulling your opponent into the strike.

The elbow is a small, hard bone that is a devastating striking weapon. Because of the elbow's proximity to the body, it is mainly a short range technique, but can be initiated from long range with a proper set-up. Impact the target with the elbow itself and approximately two inches down the forearm.

Knee strike practice in the air

- Practice the knee strike in the air, grabbing your imaginary opponent around the neck and pulling him forward and into the strike.

- Start by throwing your rear (right) knee. Set that foot down forward and throw your left knee (which has now become your rear knee). This helps you advance while moving your opponent back.

- What can you do if your opponent is resisting when you attempt to manipulate his upper body? How can you increase the intensity of the technique? Try a jump to help launch your body momentum into the strike.

Knee strike partner practice

- Practice the knee strike on a partner, pulling him forward and into the knee. How can you manipulate his body for target accuracy? Are you more comfortable with the front knee or the round house knee? Why?

- Explore the difference between extending your hips and simply raising your knee to strike. Extending the hips when round house kneeing allows you to impact the target with your entire thigh, taking a larger target.

Quick jabbing knee strikes

- Experiment with short and quick round house knees to your opponent's outside thigh area. If your opponent clinches, is this technique still effective?

- Aside from causing pain, what are the benefits of kneeing your opponent's legs? Experiment with splitting his focus, until he leaves an opening high at the head. Can you land an elbow strike now?

The knee jab to your opponent's thigh can open up a target for the elbow strike.

- When your opponent is clinching or grabbing you in a bear hug (if fighting according to Muay Thai rules), use the side of your knee to strike the sides of his legs or the open areas at his ribs.

Setting up the knee strike from long range

- When you initiate the knee strike from long range, you must set it up with another technique. A jab usually works well.

- How can you increase the power in the knee strike when throwing it hands free from long range? Experiment with using momentum for a fast gap closure.

- Flick a quick jab toward your opponent. When he reacts, explode forward with a rear leg knee strike.

Throw the rear knee for power, unless you can get a better angle with your lead knee.

Target practice and angling off with the knee strike

- Experiment with throwing the knee strike from different angles at close range. Take a small step to the side of your opponent. What targets can you reach comfortably from here?

- When you have landed the knee strike, what follow-up strikes or kicks can you throw from your new angle?

Throw a lead knee strike to your opponent's mid-section, followed by a rear cross from a side angle.

Heavy bag work with the horizontal elbow strike

- Practice the horizontal elbow strike on the heavy bag. Make sure that power is focused into the target, and that the elbow doesn't slide against the bag.

- Try the elbow strike with a step forward to close the gap and increase momentum, or work your way to close range with jabs, hooks, and uppercuts. When you reach close range, convert the hooks to elbow strikes.

- How can you combine the left and right elbow strike into one fluid motion? When you have landed the right elbow, you gain momentum for the left elbow by pivoting your body back to the point of origin.

Shadow boxing with elbow strikes

- Shadow box, using a mix of elbows and other short range techniques. How can you flow from one to the other comfortably and with speed? In what way is the elbow similar to a hook?

- Observe yourself in a mirror and note where you leave yourself open when throwing the elbow strike. Can you tuck your chin down or turn your body to avoid exposing targets to your opponent?

Elbow strike practice on focus mitts

- Have your partner hold focus mitts while stepping forward, back, and side-to-side. Practice throwing elbow strikes while adjusting for distance and movement.

- How can you throw a powerful elbow while moving back? Experiment with using your opponent's momentum against him.

- Experiment with pivoting or stepping off the attack line to gain momentum for the elbow strike.

SWEEPS

Keith's Corner

The sweep has become an almost lost art in competition kickboxing. The opportunities to sweep are usually many, but very seldom do we see fighters take advantage of this. The benefits of sweeping extend far beyond the opportunity to get your opponent on the ground. Unlike a full takedown, the sweep is designed to briefly unbalance your opponent (concept of FREEZING), allowing you to strike when he is most vulnerable. The sweep serves as a distraction to split your opponent's mind and body focus. Because it is not possible to give full attention to more than one task at a time, a split focus creates a reaction that inhibits your opponent's ability to respond.

When separating your opponent's legs with a sweep, you will open up his centerline. On the centerline are some of the most vulnerable targets: nose, chin, chest, and solar plexus.

Some kickboxing matches allow you to sweep "boot-to-boot" only, which means that a "sweep-kick" to the calf or leg is usually not permitted. The sweep may be either inside (toward the centerline), or outside (away from the centerline). Either one will unbalance your opponent. Sweeping toward the centerline is likely to narrow your opponent's stance or take him down. If the sweep is powerful, your opponent may end up in a crossed stance, or the leg you sweep may knock his other leg off balance. Sweeping away from the centerline is likely to widen his stance, with the effect of bringing his upper body forward as he tries to regain balance. If your intent is to take your opponent down, sweep toward his centerline; if your intent is to surprise or freeze him, sweep away from his centerline. Some matches allow sweeps to the outside of your opponent's foot only.

This section covers:

- Body mechanics for the sweep
- When to execute the sweep
- In the gym
- The sweep and the hook
- Summary and review

BODY MECHANICS FOR THE SWEEP

You can sweep with either the inside or outside knife edge of your foot. To execute the sweep:

1. **Meet the knife edge of your opponent's foot with the knife edge of your foot.** It is actually better to turn your foot slightly upward, because the bottom of the foot is a little stronger than the knife edge.

2. **Pay attention to how your opponent reacts.** Does he tend to lose balance straight down or slightly sideways, and what targets are exposed?

3. **Follow up with a close range technique:** a hook, for example.

In the boot-to-boot sweep, note how the bottom of the foot of the fighter on the left is turned slightly upward.

In the inside sweep, move your leg toward the centerline of your body and impact your opponent's foot with the arch of your foot. You do this by turning the bottom of your foot upward. A common mistake when sweeping, and often a reason why the sweep seems difficult, is that we tend to make contact knife edge to knife edge. This may result in injury to your foot. It is better to use the bottom of your foot to impact the knife edge of your opponent's foot, or slightly to the back of his foot (to the Achilles tendon).When finishing the sweep, you will be in a crossed stance. If your opponent does not go down, he, too, should be in an unbalanced crossed stance. This means that, technically, your positions are equal. But because you were the one initiating the sweep, you have the advantage with your mind and body focus intact. A good follow-up from this crossed stance is a side thrust kick, because your hips are already positioned for this technique. You can also step through laterally from the crossed stance. If you used your lead foot to sweep, stepping through will place you in a good fighting stance and to the side of your opponent. If you used your rear foot to sweep, stepping through will place you in the opposite fighting stance.

The outside sweep is a little more difficult than the inside sweep, because it extends away from your centerline along which most of your power is focused.

A sweep to the inside of your opponent's leg will spread her legs with the result of her upper body coming forward.

You can increase the power of the outside sweep by combining it with the inside sweep. Try a double sweep: an inside sweep to your opponent's lead leg followed by an outside sweep with that same foot to his rear leg. Even though you are making contact boot-to-boot in the outside sweep, part of your shin will also be impacting your opponent's shin, making the outside sweep stronger. Also try planting your foot quickly between the inside and outside sweep. This isn't as fast as sweeping without planting, but allows you to use the floor to help you reverse direction (concept: FIRST TOUCH). When your opponent's legs have been separated and he is off balance, you can follow with a front kick to his mid-section or jaw, or with a round house kick to his inner thigh.

The double sweep: inside first, then outside, will quickly unbalance your opponent.

WHEN TO EXECUTE THE SWEEP

In short, sweeps have two objectives:

1. To **unbalance** your opponent
2. To **split** your opponents mind and body focus

A successful sweep depends to a great extent on timing. One of the best times to sweep is when on the inside with your opponent backed up against the ropes of the ring. A sweep, or any attack to the legs, is usually unexpected at this time and is likely to stun your opponent, momentarily freezing his offensive capabilities. A good cue to work off of is first touch. When you come to close range and make your first contact with your opponent, use this as a signal to surprise him. Sweeping is an excellent strategic move, because it destroys your opponent's balance. When he loses balance, he will have a natural tendency to lower his guard in preparation to catch himself should he go down. Knowing this in advance allows you to take the open target on his head.

Sweeping is also effective just prior to stepping back to long range. Unless you launch some sort of attack at this time, your opponent will have an opportunity to retaliate as distance is gained. When it is time to step out, first sweep, then step back until you have gained some distance, and then launch a long range attack: a side thrust kick to your opponent's head, for example. His head is likely to be slightly low, as he struggles to regain balance. Also try the sweep followed by an immediate short range attack: a series of uppercuts, for example, before stepping back to long range.

An uppercut may be effective when your opponent begins to lose balance and extends her hands to catch herself.

To make the sweep effective against a heavier adversary, sweep when your opponent has weight on the leg you intend to sweep. However, there is a fine line here. More weight does not necessarily mean an easier sweep. If your opponent has too little weight on the leg, he will retain his balance when you sweep. But if he has too much weight on the leg, his foot will not budge. The ideal time to sweep is when your opponent is beginning to place weight on that foot. If he is slightly off balance already, or is in the process of kicking, this would be a good time to sweep. Try moving in and sweeping to your opponent's supporting leg when he initiates a round house kick.

COMMON ERRORS WHEN SWEEPING:

1. **"Pushing" your foot against your opponent's foot.** An effective sweep relies on a sharp, explosive move.

2. **Poor timing**, and failing to sweep when your opponent is off balance. This is particularly important against a bigger adversary.

3. **Failing to follow up** when your opponent is off balance and is exposing targets along his centerline.

IN THE GYM

The sweep should be timed so that you sweep when your opponent is beginning to place weight on that foot. If he has no weight at all on his foot, his leg will simply swing out to the side. If he has planted his foot fully with all of his weight on it, you will have a hard time sweeping, especially if he is bigger than you. The purpose of the sweep is not necessarily to take your opponent to the ground, but to knock him off balance and place him in an inferior position.

Let's start with the lead leg sweep to your opponent's lead foot. Think of your leg as a golf club, fairly stiff and with the knee straight. Sweep all the way through. It's not enough to simply establish contact and then try to push your opponent's foot out from under him. You must use your momentum in conjunction with the moment of surprise.

Sweeping sometimes violates the principle of balance, because you end up with your feet crossed. However, if the sweep is successful, it will knock your opponent off balance, and you will have time to re-establish your stance. Most sweeps are done with your lead foot, but you can also sweep with your rear foot to your opponent's lead foot. This sweep is a little more difficult, particularly against a bigger opponent, because it moves your upper body forward of its foundation and into a crossed stance. Be careful not to telegraph it.

When sweeping with your rear foot to your opponent's rear foot, you must carry your momentum through so that, at the completion of the sweep, you are positioned behind your opponent. This forces him to readjust his position. As he turns toward you, counter with a side thrust kick.

The sweep also works great when fighting on the inside. You're in here punching to the body, concealing the fact that you're going to sweep. Now, quickly execute a rear leg sweep to your opponent's rear foot. Follow with a side thrust kick. I like to use the side thrust kick after a sweep, because when your opponent is already off balance, the kick is likely to drop him to the ground.

THE SWEEP AND THE HOOK

Sweeps and hooks go together. The sweep is essentially an in-fighting technique, as is the hook. The hook is therefore a natural follow-up off the sweep.

Try these exercises on **SWEEPS AND HOOKS**:

Exercise 1

Execute an inside sweep with your lead leg to the inside of your opponent's lead leg. This should disturb his balance. Follow with a rear hook or elbow (if allowed) to his jaw.

The hook should be synchronized with your foot movement so that, as you start to retrieve your foot back to your fighting stance (after the sweep is complete), the rear hook follows within that same movement. The hook should land on target at the same time as your lead foot plants in your fighting stance.

Exercise 2

Execute an inside sweep with your rear leg to the outside of your opponent's lead leg. Follow with a lead hook to your opponent's jaw. Again, the hook should be synchronized with your foot movement, as you bring your foot back into your fighting stance.

Exercise 3

Practice mixing your hooks and sweeps with other in-fighting techniques. For example, sweep and throw an uppercut followed by a hook, then step back and blast your opponent's thigh with a cut kick. Or bob and

Some people find the lead hook less powerful than the rear hook. As discussed earlier, you can increase power in the hook by taking a step forward at a forty-five degree angle. The step and the strike should be synchronized and happen simultaneously. When throwing your lead hook, step with your rear foot forward at a forty-five degree angle. This turns your lead hook into a rear hook and creates a powerful strike.

weave to the inside, and as you come out of the roll, throw a hook. When your opponent gets stunned from the blow, follow with a sweep to take him down.

Summary and review

A sweep is essentially a low kick to your opponent's leg. Most sweeps are done in an attempt to take your opponent down, or to distract him through an unbalancing move. Depending on what reaction you desire, you can sweep either to the inside or outside of your opponent's leg. Sweeping toward his centerline will narrow his stance and is likely to take him down. Sweeping away from his centerline will widen his stance and is likely to bring his upper body forward.

Many fighters find sweeping difficult. A successful sweep relies on timing. If your opponent has too much weight on the foot you are sweeping, he is not likely to go down. If he has too little weight on the foot you are sweeping, the sweep will have no effect. In fact, he can use the momentum you have created through the sweep to his advantage and launch a counter-attack.

Sweep practice for balance and form

- Practice the motion of the sweep in the air, keeping the sweeping foot low to the ground. This is called a "true sweep." There is also a "sweep kick," which impacts your opponent's calf rather than his foot. All matches don't permit the sweep kick.

- The true sweep is more difficult to detect, because it doesn't require that you raise your foot very far off the floor.

- Try to get a feel for balance when sweeping. Remember, you will be on one foot, so your foundation will be narrow.

- Have your partner hold a padded stick vertically straight, with one end resting on the floor. Sweep the padded stick, as if it were a leg. What is your best foot position?

- Explore how contacting with the knife edge could damage your foot, and how you can avoid this by turning the bottom of your foot at an upward angle.

Inside and outside sweep partner practice

- The inside sweep has potentially more power than the outside sweep and will feel better balanced, but both are useful and should be practiced. Get with a partner and identify the correct target for the inside and outside sweeps.

- How can you combine the inside and outside sweep without losing balance? What kinds of follow-up strikes can you use without disturbing the flow of the technique?

- The more natural a technique feels, the better it flows, and the less time it takes to execute it. Try to make the sweep explosive. Start from long range and take a quick step forward, lunging into the sweep.

Following up after the sweep

- Practice sweeping away from your partner's center-line, impacting the inside of his leg. This will widen his stance. Identify your partner's likely reaction. How can you take advantage of it?

- What kinds of follow-ups can you use if your opponent retains balance? How can you use the returning motion of your leg to position at a better angle for a follow-up technique?

- Practice sweeping toward your partner's centerline, impacting the outside of his leg. This type of sweep is easiest when done to his lead leg. Why?

- Identify your partner's likely reaction. What follow-ups can you use if he goes all the way down?

Timing the sweep

- Successful sweeps depend on good timing. Ideally, sweep when your opponent is beginning to place weight on his foot.

- Move around with your partner and watch how he is using footwork to move forward, back, and to the side. Observe how he shifts his weight from his lead foot to his rear foot depending on which direction he is moving.

- Identify the best time for initiating a sweep to his lead leg. Can you use a set-up to distract his focus away from his legs?

- It is possible to sweep from behind your opponent's foot and forward. How would you position in order to sweep this way? What is your opponent's likely reaction?

- When sweeping from behind, you can convert the low sweep to a sweep kick, targeting your opponent's calf. Try this using the bottom of your foot.

QUICK REFERENCE TO CONCEPTS

COMPLETION OF MOTION: A reason for not using the shin block as defense against the cut kick is that the block limits your mobility. When on one foot, you can't move until you have planted your other foot on the floor. Technically, when your opponent kicks and is on one leg, and you raise your leg to block, your positions are equally superior, with your opponent at a slight advantage, because he is the one initiating the attack with full focus on offense.

FIRST TOUCH CONCEPT: You can reduce the time between strikes and kicks to the legs by relying on the first touch concept. For example, use the leg kick as a set-up for a hand technique. First throw a lead leg inside thigh kick. At the moment your foot plants, follow with a rear uppercut as a finishing technique. When your opponent's legs are separated and he is off balance, you can follow with a front kick to his midsection or jaw, or with a round house kick to his inner thigh. When you come to close range and make your first contact with your opponent, use this as a signal to surprise him. Sweeping is an excellent strategic move, because it destroys your opponent's balance. When he loses balance, he will have a natural tendency to lower his guard in preparation to catch himself should he go down. Knowing this in advance allows you to take the open target on his head.

FREEZING: Unlike a full takedown, the sweep is designed to briefly unbalance your opponent, allowing you to strike when he is most vulnerable. The sweep serves as a distraction to split your opponent's mind and body focus. Because it is not possible to give full attention to more than one task at a time, a split focus creates a surprise reaction that inhibits your opponent's ability to respond.

PULLEY-EFFECT: This can be likened to a tram going up a mountain. As the gondola at the top starts on its way down, the one at the bottom starts on its way up. They meet at the halfway point. The pulley-effect is important because it allows one part of your body to assist another part, with the result of less energy expenditure. The pulley-effect makes fighting economical with minimal time between strikes. When fighting is economical, you will appear to have more speed, even though the strikes themselves aren't thrown any faster. Fighting this way also takes less effort, and you will last longer during heavy physical exertion.

STEALING THE MOMENT OF IMPACT: This principle states that if you block your opponent's kick when it is fully extended (at the moment of impact), the impact to both you and your opponent will be equal, and the stronger shin will win. In order to use the shin block successfully, you must beat your opponent to the moment of impact; you must block at the initiation of his kick.

SECTION EIGHT
UNORTHODOX TECHNIQUES

EXPECT THE UNEXPECTED
by Keith Livingston

During one phase of my career, I trained with some boxers and kickboxers in Ogden, Utah. Because I was fighting as a welterweight at the time, it wasn't uncommon to spar with lightweights and middleweights. I recall a particularly feisty lightweight, Sid Wright, who, at about 132 pounds was the smallest in our stable. However, Sid was one of the least desirable to spar with. Sid had an "in your face" type of style, and any weight difference didn't matter. Sid had only one style and one speed. He was always pressing forward, throwing punches from different angles, and seemingly without pause. My first experience with him taught me a couple of valuable lessons. First, when fighting Sid, size didn't matter. Second, expect the unexpected.

As we began our sparring session, I immediately backed up to avoid the barrage of whirlwind punches coming my way. I then found myself cornered defending the onslaught of body punches. I felt like I was doing a pretty good job blocking the body shots, but then it came: The unexpected collided with the left side of my jaw. Sid had just thrown the mother of all punches: an overhand right.

The looping strike seemed to come from nowhere. Given the distance we were fighting at, I never expected to get hit with that type of technique. As it landed, I heard a loud boom inside my head and got a sour feeling in my gut. But that wasn't the end. Sid followed with an overhand left that blasted the right side of my jaw. I am not sure if it was the punch or the sheer force that put me to one knee, but it was several minutes before I could stand.

The overhand strikes from over the top with your full body weight behind it.

I recall vividly the force with which the punch landed. Later, when I relayed my experience to Sid, he laughed. "Do you remember the wooden peg boards we played with as kids?" he asked. "You know, the ones where you practice driving the wooden peg through the hole with the wooden hammer? Well, when I was a kid, I worked on driving the peg flush with just one strike of the hammer. When throwing the overhand strike, I visualize my opponent as the wooden peg, and my strike as the hammer. I then drive my opponent through the canvas with one single blow. It works great!"

I rubbed my jaw. Of course, it worked great. He grinned, and we shook hands, and I felt richer for the experience. But, ironically, in my twenty-four years of kickboxing, I have never been hit with a true overhand strike before my experience with Sid, and I have never been hit with one since. I would like to think that is because of my defensive prowess. But in truth, I'll have to tell you I haven't seen one since. Sid was an artist.

THE OVERHAND STRIKE

Now that you have a few fights under your belt and have gained proficiency with basic striking, kicking, and defense, you can fight anywhere at any time. Understand that it is the basics that win the fight time and time again. You can even go all the way to the world championships without learning a single complex technique. Don't confuse basic with beginning. The basic techniques make up your foundation; they're your strength. We will now venture into what I call the "unorthodox." I usually refrain from using the word "advanced," as an overhand strike is not necessarily more advanced than a rear cross. Nor is a corkscrew strike more advanced than a jab, or an outside crescent kick more advanced than a round house kick. The difference is that unorthodox techniques are used more seldom than the basics, and can therefore give you a strategic advantage.

The main reason for learning unorthodox techniques is to learn about yourself and what your limitations are as a fighter. Because many of these techniques require superior balance, set-up, and speed, they will help you refine your body mechanics and gain confidence. The secondary reason is strategic, where the unorthodox often has the effect of surprising your opponent.

The overhand strike is an unorthodox technique that is relatively easy to throw, that has devastating power, and that can be launched when your opponent least expects it. A properly thrown overhand strike can level an opponent with a single blow. The combination of weight transfer and velocity makes for a lethal partnership. The punch is extremely difficult to block and equally difficult to see coming.

As we discuss various techniques, try not to get caught up in the name. Different gyms call techniques by different names. Rather than the label, look at the description. Oftentimes, the words rear cross and overhand strike are used interchangeably, but they are two distinctly different techniques.

This section covers:

- Body mechanics for the overhand strike
- Setting up the overhand strike
- Counters and follow-ups
- Defending the hook and jab with the overhand strike
- Glove-up with Keith
- Finishing with the overhand strike
- Strategy and the overhand strike
- What's in a good overhand strike?
- Summary and review

BODY MECHANICS FOR THE OVERHAND STRIKE

The overhand strike arches over the top of your opponent's guard and follows a downward trajectory. Because of the strike's curved path, it allows you to drop your weight and use gravity to your advantage.

Keith's Knockout Advice

The overhand right and left are identical, with the right thrown with your rear hand and the left thrown with your lead hand from a conventional stance. You can initiate the strike from either close range or mid-range. Let's explore the strike from close range first.

Start the punch by shifting your body weight to the right, placing approximately seventy percent of your weight on your rear foot. The movement should be subtle to avoid telegraphing your intention.

At the same time you shift right, initiate the strike by pivoting on the ball of your rear foot. Relax your shoulders, and start the punch forward and up over the top of your opponent's left hand by rolling your shoulder forward.

When your fist reaches maximum height, continue rotating your body forward and start the punch on a downward forty-five degree trajectory toward your opponent's opposite foot. Keep your free hand up as a check. The punch should strike the left side of your opponent's jaw and continue downward toward his right foot. If you immediately follow with an overhand left, the punches should create an X-pattern. Impact should come slightly past the top of the X, with full focus through the target.

In order to create the desired effect, you must develop a lot of momentum. You do this by rotating your body rapidly and dropping your weight into the strike as it begins the downward trajectory. The primary target for the overhand strike is the jaw. Unlike the hook that comes from the side, or the uppercut that comes from below, the overhand strike lands on its downward motion. It is therefore seldom expected in close quarters. You can throw the strike with either hand but, because of the power of the rear position, I prefer to throw it with the rear hand.

The overhand strike thrown from mid-range is identical with the exception of distance. Initiate the strike with a quick step forward with your lead foot. The punch and step should land approximately at the same time. As you land the punch, close the distance between your rear and lead foot. You can now throw another strike with your left hand, landing the punch at the same time as your rear foot closes distance.

SETTING UP THE OVERHAND STRIKE

The overhand strike is easily disguised, because it is often thrown after a close range attack from a low position. An effective strategy is to set up the strike with an attack to your opponent's body. First, throw a couple of vicious hooks in an attempt to make him drop his elbows for protection. When his elbows drop, even as little as an inch, his hands will drop as well, leaving an opening at the head. This is a good time to unleash the overhand strike, but your timing must be right. You can get a feel for how your opponent will react by faking a hook to the body first. For example, throw the lead hook a couple of times to make your opponent a believer and give yourself the opportunity to observe his reaction to the strike: Does he drop his hands when defending the hook?

If you determine that there is, in fact, an opening at his head, you can fake a lead hook to the mid-section by pivoting your body slightly to the left. This creates the impression that you are setting (chambering) for the hook. The moment your opponent drops his elbow to protect against the blow, you throw the overhand strike with your right hand. The set-up and strike are quickest if you throw the strike within the movement of your left pivot. This is a highly economical move, because what appears to be the "setting" for the left hook is actually the initiation of the right overhand strike.

Set up the overhand right as if you were going to throw a left hook. First throw the left hook a few times, so that your opponent associates the pivot of your body with the hook. Throw the overhand right within the movement of your left pivot.

COUNTERS AND FOLLOW-UPS

As already discussed, an important aspect of kickboxing is the counter-strike. An effective fighter does not rely only on blocking and parrying when defending, but uses his opponent's offense to create his own defense and offense. The overhand strike is a great counter-strike. Let's say that your opponent throws a jab that you parry with your lead hand. If the parry is technically correct, you should have a slight pivot in your lead foot with your heel toward your opponent. This chambers your rear hand. You can now throw the overhand right over the top of your opponent's jabbing arm and to the open target at his jaw. Remember the first touch concept? As soon as your parry connects with the inside of your opponent's jabbing arm, use this as a cue to initiate the overhand strike.

Parry your opponent's jab and use first touch to trigger the overhand strike.

Since the overhand strike is so strong, its primary purpose is to knock your opponent out. But don't assume that a knockout will occur. Since your opponent's head is likely to be in a low position after you land the strike, the uppercut is a good follow-up.

Try these exercises on the **UPPERCUT AND OVER-HAND STRIKE**:

Exercise 1

Since the overhand strike comes from over the top, it is likely to drop your opponent's head on impact. The uppercut is therefore a logical follow-up. You will now be striking your opponent from two different directions: from above with the overhand strike, and from below with the uppercut.

Initiate the technique with the overhand right. As your opponent's head drops, finish with a lead uppercut to his chin. The overhand right will chamber your body for the lead uppercut.

Exercise 2

You can also reverse the order of the overhand strike and uppercut, initiating the combination with the lead uppercut. First, throw a lead uppercut. As your opponent's head comes up, throw the overhand strike with your rear hand. Finish with a second uppercut off your lead hand. As you can see, I recommend using alternating hands for these strikes. Throwing the uppercut and the overhand strike with the same hand is not wrong, but the technique will be slightly slower, because you must re-chamber between strikes. This principle is true for all strikes.

Exercise 3

If you are very close to your opponent (shoulder-to-shoulder), you can still throw the overhand strike and be successful with it. Use your lead (left) shoulder to push your opponent back. Simultaneously step with your rear (right) foot to a forty-five degree angle forward and to the side. This creates an angle off your opponent's centerline. As you plant your foot, throw an overhand right from your now superior position to the side. You can also step forward and to the side with your left foot, and follow with an overhand left. Because your stance is perpendicular to your opponent, this actually makes the left strike a rear technique with greater power potential. Think about it!

Jab to your opponent's mid-section, and throw the overhand strike when he drops his hands to cover.

Push your opponent back with your lead shoulder, and step with your right foot in the direction of centerline B. This gives you the distance and angle you need. When your right foot plants, throw the overhand right to your opponent's jaw.

If necessary, take a short step forward with your lead foot when initiating the strike. Impact your opponent's jaw.

Exercise 4

Initiate the technique with a twisting uppercut (either hand) to your opponent's mid-section. Simultaneously step to a forty-five degree angle forward and away from your opponent's centerline, and follow with an overhand strike with your other hand.

Unlike the uppercut, you can also throw the overhand from a mid-range distance. Again, you want to get your opponent concerned with defending his mid-section, as this creates an opening at his head. You do this by throwing a number of jabs to his solar plexus. Remember, when jabbing low, you must lower your shoulders to the level of the punch to avoid exposing your head. Once you have determined your opponent's reaction, you can follow the low jab with an overhand right to his jaw.

> **By varying the "tightness" of the overhand strike (how steep or shallow you throw it), you can land it from distances ranging from a few inches to a few feet. If you initiate the strike from long range, you can also take a step forward simultaneous to striking.**

DEFENDING THE HOOK AND JAB WITH THE OVERHAND STRIKE

It is easy to get overly involved with offense and neglect defense. Even though we are aware of the importance of defense, we seldom spend the same amount of time practicing it as we do offense. This is true especially in shadow boxing and bag work. Because bags don't strike back, we don't think about how to apply defense to the routine. It is also easier to focus on offense than defense, because it seems to be the most active of the two.

When working defense in shadow boxing or on the heavy bag, you may feel as though you are not doing anything. And, yes, it is also true that in an amateur match aggressiveness scores higher, so defense often tends to come secondary. But defense does not consist solely of blocking and movement. Much of the best defense comes when applied constructively as offense. Let's look at how to use the overhand strike as a defensive move against the jab and the hook.

Even if you land a solid strike right on target, you must be ready for your opponent's counter-strike. If you have taken a few seconds to analyze your opponent's strategy, you will most likely find that there are certain counter-strikes he throws more often than others, and that he throws specific counter-strikes as defense against specific techniques. For example, you may find that every time you throw your lead leg round house kick, your opponent blocks it with an elbow block and counters with a rear cross. Since it is natural to get into a set pattern, you can anticipate which strike your opponent is most likely to throw.

Let's say that every time you throw a rear cross, your opponent slips it and moves in and counters with a lead hook. This is because he knows that whenever you throw the cross, there is an opening on the side of your head. If you have paid attention to what your opponent is doing, you can save time by calculating an appropriate defense. This is the beginning of "the chess game," which we will discuss in more detail in Section 10.

So, what is a good defense against the hook? Against a lead hook to the right side of your head, bob and weave to your right underneath the hook. This places you slightly to the side and off your opponent's attack line. Because your opponent is in an inferior position with his back turned partly toward you (since he just missed with the hook), **this is a very good opportunity for you to throw the overhand right to his jaw.**

... placing you in a superior position, from where you can easily land the overhand right. You have now turned a defensive move into an offensive move. Because you often can anticipate your opponent's counter-strike, you can pre-plan your follow-up off the bob and weave.

When weaving under your opponent's hook, if you exaggerate the move slightly so that the heel of your lead foot is turned toward your opponent, you will not only make his hook miss, you will also chamber your right hand for the overhand strike. You have now accomplished two things simultaneously: defended against the hook, and set for the counter-strike.

When your opponent counters your strike with a lead hook, bob and weave underneath the hook. As the hook misses, your opponent's back will be turned partly toward you ...

When weaving under the hook and setting for the overhand right, your weight should shift from your lead leg to your rear. As you start the overhand right toward its target, your weight should again shift to your lead leg. For maximum effect, push off with your rear foot and launch all of your body momentum into the strike. You have now used the overhand strike as defense against a hook.

Also try the overhand right as defense against a jab. When your opponent jabs, shift your weight to your rear foot. Both your feet should still be planted, but the weight distribution isn't equal anymore. When your weight shifts to your rear foot, your upper body automatically moves a few inches back. This increases the *distance of importance* between your head and your opponent's jab, but without placing you out of reach. When your upper body moves back, your opponent's jab is short of reach. In addition, the weight shift chambers your rear hand for a counter-strike. As your opponent withdraws his hand, shift your weight back to your lead foot (this closes the distance by a couple of inches) and simultaneously throw an overhand right. The overhand strike is especially effective in this scenario, because the weight shift (the forward movement of your upper body) places you at optimal distance, adding your weight and momentum to the strike.

Glove Up with Keith

Bob and weave underneath my hook. Stay low and throw the overhand right over the top of my guard. Don't loop the punch too much! Take the power of the punch straight through the target before aiming it diagonally down toward my opposite foot. Throw all of your body weight into the punch. The overhand right is a great finisher on the inside. When you hear me yell "over the top!" don't hesitate with this strike.

When you have thrown the overhand right, throw an overhand left to the right side of your opponent's jaw. Even if the first punch misses, you can still get your opponent with your follow-up. Mix your defense in with your offense, so that when you're down bobbing and weaving, you are also setting for your follow-up technique.

FINISHING WITH THE OVERHAND STRIKE

The ultimate aim of the overhand strike is to finish your opponent, to drop him to the ground and end the fight. A good time to throw a finishing technique is when your opponent is on the ropes and his mobility is limited. But if you are up against a good inside fighter, it may be difficult to find a finishing target. If your opponent is crouched forward covering his jaw and centerline well, a rear cross or uppercut may be difficult to land. You can now try the short overhand strike by keeping your elbow tight and in front of your body, and rolling the punch from your shoulder.

The strike should hit your opponent's jaw and then curve down toward his opposite foot. As his head drops from the impact of the blow, you can follow

with a lead uppercut to his jaw. If this does not finish him, it is appropriate to throw a full rear cross. Because the uppercut has a lifting effect, your opponent's head will be in the up position, increasing the distance and giving you a good target for the rear cross.

When throwing the short overhand strike, keep your elbow down until the rotation of your upper body has started. This ensures better power and protection, and also helps you direct the power of the strike into the target. Don't drop the strike until the moment of impact, when you also turn your fist into the corkscrew position (more about this in the next sub-section). Think of your hand as a drill going through the target.

Throw the short overhand strike, follow with an uppercut, and finish with a rear cross.

STRATEGY AND THE OVERHAND STRIKE

Since our hands are quicker and more coordinated than our feet, we sometimes overlook the use of our legs. Kickboxers have many strategic advantages that straight boxers lack, especially in fights that allow for leg kicks. Mixing low kicks with your hand techniques helps you split your opponent's focus. As discussed earlier, kicks to the legs can be devastating finishers. But even kicks that don't do enough damage to finish the fight can be used to strategically set up other finishing techniques.

Imagine yourself at a strategic disadvantage, backed into a corner. It is now tempting to do one of the following:

1. **Cover up** and hope that your opponent's attack will die out.

2. **Push back** against your opponent, trying to meet power with power.

If you can stay calm under pressure, you can use your disadvantaged position on the ropes to split your opponent's mind and body focus and launch a strong offensive technique, like the overhand strike. Begin by whipping round house kicks to your opponent's inside thigh area. At close range, the kicks are not likely to do much physical damage; however, the damage we're looking at is "strategic damage," where your opponent's focus goes from offense to defense (from his upper body attack on you to defending his legs). Continue attacking his inside thigh while protecting your head and upper body with your arms. When your opponent starts worrying about the assault on his leg and either steps back, looks down, or pauses, you can throw the overhand strike. Because your opponent's focus is on his lower body, the technique is unexpected, and he is likely to leave at least a bit of an opening at the head. You have now turned your inferior position on the ropes into a position of strength.

WHAT'S IN A GOOD OVERHAND STRIKE?

If you throw it mechanically correct, the overhand strike has awesome power and should be used primarily to finish your opponent. If possible, throw the strike when your opponent is dazed or off balance from a previous blow. The overhand strike has many advantages that a straight right or hook does not have. For example:

1. You can **drop your weight** with the overhand strike, using the force of gravity to your advantage.

2. Because the power is directed down, the overhand strike is a **good finishing technique** that places your opponent on the canvas quickly.

3. Because of the looping path, you can throw the overhand strike **in close quarters** easier than a straight right.

4. The overhand strike is **usually unexpected** when thrown in close quarters, where most fighters are prepared for uppercuts or hooks.

5. The overhand strike is **difficult to defend against.** Because of the curved path over the top, the strike is difficult to block or weave underneath.

How tight you throw the strike depends on your distance to the target. If you throw the strike from mid- or long range, you must throw it wider than if you are shoulder-to-shoulder with your opponent. If you are very close, you must use a tight curve over the top and angle the strike diagonally down toward your opponent's opposite foot. Balance could be an issue. If you overextend your weight and forward momentum, you can lose balance forward. The overhand strike is not an "upright" strike. In other words, you should throw it from a compact (crouched) stance.

COMMON ERRORS FOR THE OVERHAND STRIKE:

1. **Raising your body to the upright position** after throwing the strike. Aside from exposing your chin, this may also contribute to a loss of balance.

2. **Giving the strike away** when chambering for it, or failing to use a proper set-up. Avoid movement that telegraphs your intentions.

3. **Throwing the strike wide**, bringing your punching elbow to the outside of your body. Remember, a properly thrown strike is achieved by utilizing your body weight. You must therefore keep your elbow in front of your body.

4. **Looping the strike too much**. If you pull your hand in toward your body on the downward motion of the strike, the power is likely to split on impact, with some going into the target and some back toward your body. This is why we teach to aim the strike diagonally toward your opponent's opposite foot (not toward your own foot).

Keith's Corner

The overhand strike is possibly one of the most underused techniques in boxing and kickboxing. I encourage all kickboxing students to work on perfecting this highly effective technique. The strike may feel awkward at first, but I promise that with hard work the knockouts will follow. Use the overhand strike often, and you will see many opponents' looks of surprise before they hit the canvas.

Summary and review

The overhand strike is a power punch intended to level your opponent with a single blow. The strike works well from close quarter range, where most fighters are more prepared to defend against hooks or uppercuts. The fact that the strike comes from over the top makes it difficult to detect and defend against. If the first overhand strike fails to finish your opponent, you can follow with a second overhand thrown with your other hand, or with an uppercut.

Overhand strike practice on focus mitts

- Practice the overhand strike on focus mitts held by your partner. The mitts should be held face up and at a slight angle toward you.

- Although the overhand strike follows a curved path, it is important that it strikes straight on impact. In other words, don't loop the strike toward your body, and don't allow it to "brush" against the target.

- After impacting with the target, your fist should be aimed straight toward your opponent's opposite foot. If you throw the strike with your right hand, aim it at his right foot.

- Throw alternating overhand strikes on the focus mitts. When you land the overhand right, your body should be set for throwing an overhand left.

Balance analysis for the overhand strike

- Be careful not to overextend your weight when landing the strike.

- If you miss with the strike and are off balance forward, how can your opponent take advantage of you?

- Determine your balance point by dropping your weight and keeping your center of gravity above your foundation.

If you overextend your center of gravity, you will lose balance forward.

Drop your weight straight down.

Defending the hook and finishing with the overhand strike

- The overhand strike is a good finisher that can be used to defend the hook. Bob and weave under your opponent's hook and use the momentum to launch the overhand strike. If you weave to your right, you will be set for throwing an overhand right.

- When your opponent misses with the hook, his body will be in an inferior position with his back turned partly toward you. You have now established outside superiority and can throw the overhand strike without interference.

- Also use the first touch concept to launch the strike. Block your opponent's hook with an outside forearm block, using the block and first touch to trigger the overhand strike.

- Think of the overhand strike as a sledgehammer that will pound your opponent into the canvas with a single blow.

THE CORKSCREW PUNCH

Another underused and often forgotten technique is the corkscrew punch. This strike is primarily used to defeat or loosen a tight defense. Think of the corkscrew as a variation of the jab and rear cross. Traditionally, with the jab and cross, the hand is held vertical until just prior to impact, when the fist is turned horizontal. With the corkscrew punch, the fist begins in the vertical position, turns horizontal at mid-range, and continues twisting until vertically upside down on impact.

Perhaps the major difference between the jab or cross and the corkscrew, and what makes the corkscrew so versatile, is its deceptive capabilities. Unlike the jab and cross, you can throw the corkscrew effectively in close quarters, where it is often unexpected.

This section covers:

- Body mechanics for the corkscrew punch
- Why is it important to twist the hand?
- The corkscrew in close quarters
- Corkscrew exercises
- The corkscrew with the rear hand
- Summary and review

BODY MECHANICS FOR THE CORKSCREW PUNCH

Initiate the corkscrew punch by shifting your weight to the leg opposite that of the punching hand. If you throw this punch with your lead hand, shift your weight to your rear leg. Simultaneously start the rotation of your fist.

If you throw the strike in close quarters, drop your punching hand down and toward the centerline of your body. This forces your elbow to come up.

When throwing the corkscrew in close quarters, drop your hand toward your body while shifting your weight to the rear. This allows you to strike upward along your opponent's centerline.

Continue rotating your fist into the vertical upside down position. Your hand should now be twisted with your knuckles toward your centerline.

As you continue to straighten your arm, your hand will follow a twisting vertical path through your opponent's guard. If you throw the strike in close quarters, your hand will follow a twisting path of about four inches upward. Tuck your chin behind your shoulder for protection.

Impact the target with your knuckles. When throwing the strike from close range, impact the target with the bottom of your clenched fist (the side opposite the thumb).

Upon landing the strike, your hand should have made a complete 180-degree turn. If you started the punch with your fist in the vertical position with your knuckles facing away from your centerline, upon landing the blow, your fist should be in the vertical position but with your knuckles facing toward your centerline.

To further illustrate the technique, at the beginning your hand is held vertical with the thumb side up. Next, the hand turns horizontal with your thumb toward your centerline. And finally, on impact, the hand is vertical with the thumb side down. Thus, the hand has rotated a half circle by the time of impact.

Hand position when starting the corkscrew punch (left). Hand position when finishing the corkscrew punch (right).

WHY IS IT IMPORTANT TO TWIST THE HAND?

The primary purpose of the corkscrew is to penetrate a tight guard. Let's say that every time you throw the jab, your opponent parries and counters. This leads to frustration, but since the jab is such a versatile and fast punch, you are reluctant to give it up. The vertical position of the corkscrew punch allows your hand to defeat a smaller gap between your opponent's arms. First, set your opponent up by throwing a couple of traditional jabs. Allow him to block them with a tight defense. Now, throw the corkscrew jab, slipping it in between his two upheld arms.

The corkscrew can penetrate a tight guard.

Unlike a vertical jab, where there is no rotation of your fist, the additional twist of the corkscrew creates more power on impact. When throwing this strike like a jab from long range, think of it as a drill. Throw the punch straight toward the target, rotating your hand a full 180 degrees on impact. When your fist strikes your opponent's guard, it should not yet have turned a full 180 degrees. It is this final twist of your fist that allows

it to act like a drill and penetrate your opponent's guard at its weakest point: in the middle, in the space between his hands. If your opponent's guard is very tight, you can also slip the punch through on a slightly upward path.

A strategic advantage of the corkscrew punch is that you can use it to bring your opponent's arms closer to his centerline, opening the sides of his head or ribs for hooks. When your opponent notices that his guard is insufficient, he will bring his arms closer together to keep the punch from slipping through. When he tightens his guard, move in with hooks to the openings at his head or ribs. In this sense, you can use the corkscrew as a distance closer.

THE CORKSCREW IN CLOSE QUARTERS

Keith's Knockout Advice

A particularly interesting way to throw the corkscrew punch is from in-fighting range. While at close range, take a step back with your rear foot only, throw the corkscrew, and return to close range. Again, because the punch penetrates your opponent's guard rather easily, he is likely to bring his arms together. This opens the liver and spleen areas to body hooks.

As your opponent begins to defend the body with his elbows, the gap between his arms will again widen. You can now step back out with a couple of quick corkscrews, then immediately return with hooks to the body. This strategy eventually results in combinations that frustrate your opponent and present you with opportunity.

You can also throw the corkscrew from close quarters without taking a step back. The twisting motion and upward vertical path enables you to come underneath and behind your opponent's guard, rather than straight through it. The weight transfer to your rear foot at the initiation of the technique leaves you enough distance to throw the technique effectively. Remember to keep your non-working hand up as a check, and to move it slightly in front of your face.

CORKSCREW EXERCISES

As mentioned earlier, because of the jab's speed and proximity to your opponent, it is the most common and easy to use set-up technique. You can hide the corkscrew within the same movement as the jab, and can therefore use it to set your opponent up prior to closing distance.

Try these exercises on **CLOSING DISTANCE** with the corkscrew punch:

Exercise 1

Throw the jab a few times, allowing your opponent to parry. When he gets in tune with your rhythm, close distance and throw the corkscrew from close quarter range (with your fist dropping to the inside, your elbow up, and impacting with the bottom of your fist). Because your opponent is expecting a jab and is looking to parry this strike, he will leave an opening from below and along his centerline. This gives you a free path to his jaw.

Exercise 2

When you have landed the corkscrew and reset your body, you can follow with the overhand right. This is an interesting combination, because the strikes are thrown from opposite directions: the corkscrew from below and the overhand strike from above. When throwing the corkscrew, your weight will shift to your rear foot, inclining your body slightly to the rear. Initiate the overhand right simultaneous to resetting your stance forward.

Exercise 3

A common combination is the four basic strikes (two long range and two short range strikes) with alternating hands: jab, cross, hook, and uppercut. Try using four close range strikes instead: lead hook, rear uppercut, lead corkscrew, rear overhand strike. Since you can throw the corkscrew and overhand from both long and close range, this eliminates the need to close distance in the middle of the combination. The first two strikes (the hook and the uppercut) are normal close range techniques. The last two strikes (the corkscrew and the overhand) work from both close

and long range. Because your body inclines to the rear when throwing the corkscrew, your distance to your opponent increases and protects you against his retaliation.

In close quarter range, your opponent is likely to attempt to counter strike with close quarter techniques, like hooks or uppercuts. Because your body inclines to the rear when throwing the corkscrew with your lead hand in close quarters, your opponent's counter punch is less likely to land.

THE CORKSCREW WITH THE REAR HAND

Throwing the corkscrew punch with the rear hand works well from long range, where the strike follows much the same path as a rear cross. It will not have the same power as a rear cross, however. Likewise, when you throw this strike from close quarters on a vertical upward path, it will not have the same power as an uppercut. This is because, when your elbow comes up, you can't use your full body weight behind the blow.

The corkscrew with your rear hand is of somewhat limited use when thrown in close quarters. When you drop your hand and rotate your shoulder to initiate the upward path of the strike, you must also rotate your body. When throwing the strike with your rear hand, a greater rotation of your body is required than when throwing the strike with your lead hand. This is similar in concept to throwing a side thrust kick with your rear leg; it is often not done because of excessive movement. However, don't abandon the technique as long as you have a proper set-up.

At close quarter range, the corkscrew punch with the rear hand is easier to land if your stance is perpendicular to your opponent's.

COMMON ERRORS FOR THE CORKSCREW PUNCH:

1. **Failing to shift your weight** to your opposite leg for distance when throwing the strike in close quarters.

2. **Standing too upright**, or failing to tuck your chin behind your shoulder for protection as your fist drops.

3. **Throwing the strike at an inappropriate time**, or using it too often in the same fight, thus training your opponent to expect and defend against it.

Summary and review

The corkscrew punch can be used as a drill to penetrate a tight guard from long range, or as a variation to the uppercut when thrown in close quarters. The strike is easily disguised because of its unorthodox path from both long and close range. The corkscrew is not a power technique, but is used more as a set-up to bring your opponent's arms closer together, opening targets on the sides of his head and body.

Setting up the corkscrew with a jab

- Get with a partner and experiment with the jab/corkscrew combination. Take the offensive position, with your partner defending.

- Start from long range and throw the jab a few times, impacting your partner's guard. Then take a quick step forward and throw the corkscrew, drilling through your partner's guard.

- If you throw the jab too many times, your opponent will get used to it and start countering. For this combination to work, you must be determined when following with the corkscrew punch.

- The corkscrew enables you to penetrate your opponent's guard. What would be a good follow-up?

Throwing the corkscrew from close range

- Work from close range with your partner pushing against you and attempting to move you back. Experiment going with the motion of the push, taking a large step with your rear foot only, and throwing the lead corkscrew underneath your opponent's guard to his chin.

- Work on closing distance as soon as the corkscrew lands. You will now be at close range. What types of strikes can you use to finish your opponent?

When your opponent pushes against you, take a half-step to the rear with your rear foot, widening the gap between you. Throw the corkscrew to your opponent's chin.

Defending the corkscrew punch

- Take the defensive stand with your partner throwing the corkscrew from long range. Work on the first touch concept. The moment your partner throws the strike, whether it lands on or penetrates your guard, is a signal for you to counter. Your counter-strike will place you in charge of the fight.

- Avoid falling into a set pattern that your opponent can take advantage of. Be on the lookout for strikes that follow unorthodox paths, such as the corkscrew in close quarters.

UNORTHODOX KICKS

The basic techniques tend to win the fight time and time again, even on the championship level. But in order to add versatility and excitement, we will now learn some unorthodox kicks.

Every kick starts from the basic front kick position with your knee raised high. Many fighters don't think about the strategic advantages this gives you. If every kick looks the same initially, your opponent can't tell which kick is coming. Even though every kick starts from this position, the foot's path on impact differs between kicks. The round house kick, for example, impacts from the side, while the side thrust kick impacts straight like the front kick, but utilizes a different part of the foot as impact weapon. In this section, we will cover the outside crescent kick, the axe kick, the reverse round house kick, and the hook kick.

The outside crescent kick impacts the target from the side just like the round house kick, but with the outside edge of the foot and shin, rather than with the instep. The axe kick impacts the target from above, unlike any of the three basic kicks. The reverse round house kick impacts the target from the side, like the regular round house, but from the opposite direction, which makes this kick deceptive. The hook kick also impacts the target from the side, but with the heel of the foot rather than the instep.

This section covers:

- Body mechanics for the outside crescent kick
- Head vs. body
- The power of the outside crescent kick
- Exercises for the outside crescent kick
- Body mechanics for the axe kick
- What can go wrong?
- The reverse round house kick
- The hook kick
- Defending the hook kick
- Thoughts on unorthodox techniques
- Summary and review

BODY MECHANICS FOR THE OUTSIDE CRESCENT KICK

The outside crescent kick has two objectives: to hurt your opponent, and as a strategic move to take his guard down and create an opening at the head. The kick derives its name from the movement the leg makes prior to impact. A crescent is like the half circular shape of the moon just prior to or after a new moon. When initiating the crescent kick, the leg should follow this crescent shape. As discussed earlier, inside or outside is in reference to your body: inside is toward your centerline, and outside is away from your centerline. When throwing the outside crescent kick, bring your leg toward your centerline, and continue in a half-circular crescent shape up and to the outside away from your centerline. Impact the target at the apex (highest point) of the kick.

Bring your lead knee up along line 2, keeping your leg chambered until it has passed the centerline of your body. This ensures a fast and powerful kick.

Extend your leg along centerline A, but with rotation in your hips to the outside, and power focused in the direction of centerline B.

Impact the target with the outside knife edge of your foot and part of your shin.

HEAD VS. BODY

Because of the pre-conception that the outside crescent kick is designed to go through the target, many fighters feel that the kick is useless unless thrown to the head. Fighters with less flexibility are therefore not using it. But the kick can also be used strategically to the body as a distraction. For example:

1. Throw the outside crescent kick to your opponent's gloves **to momentarily freeze** her or turn her body to an inferior position.

2. Throw the outside crescent kick over the top of your opponent's guard, with **your heel landing in the crook of her arm.** Use this move to bring your opponent's guard down.

The outside crescent kick is normally thrown with your lead leg, but you can also throw it with your rear leg. The rear leg is likely to have more power, but again, it will take longer to throw, and you risk telegraphing the kick.

As with all techniques, you need to think of a proper follow-up. A follow-up punch is quicker than a kick. Why? Because the punch can be thrown simultaneous to planting your kicking foot, while a kick needs a two-count: You must plant your foot before you can throw another kick. There is an exception to this: If you throw a jump kick with your opposite leg, both your feet will be in the air at the same time, which might make the kick faster than a punch. We will discuss jump kicks in Section 9.

Throw the outside crescent kick with your lead leg to your opponent's guard. When her guard comes down, throw a rear cross in an attempt to knock her out. You will now be using opposite weapons: your left leg and your right hand. This type of technique flows naturally with no contradiction in body mechanics. If you land the kick to your opponent's body or head instead of her guard, you can try a rear cut kick to her outer thigh as a follow-up. You have now taken two targets of different height: the head and the leg.

Opposite techniques can be thought of as a tram going up a mountain. When the gondola at the top starts on its way down, the gondola at the bottom starts on its way up. They meet at the halfway mark. This is called economy of motion.

Throw the outside crescent kick to the head and follow with a rear leg cut kick.

THE POWER OF THE OUTSIDE CRESCENT KICK

You should throw the outside crescent kick with the intent of kicking through the target. Rather than initiating the move with your leg, allow your hip to lead. Because the body is so much bigger and stronger than the leg, you can attain more power by initiating the move with your body.

The power of the outside crescent kick comes mainly from three sources:

1. **Kicking through the target.** This means that, as your foot impacts the target, you should focus on continuing the motion through the target until you

have planted your foot in the opposite stance. In other words, don't stop the kick or pull it back on impact. Even if you kick to your opponent's body and are unable to go through the target, you must still kick with the intent of kicking through.

2 **Initiating the kick with a step forward.** This helps you set your hips properly for the kick and build momentum. You can step with either your lead or rear foot, but stepping with your rear foot is a little quicker and not as easily telegraphed. This may seem contradictory to what we have previously learned (step with the foot closest to the direction of travel first). However, because of the angle of your hips, a step with your lead foot requires three moves (step with your lead foot across your centerline, then step with your rear foot to adjust the distance, then throw the kick), while a step with your rear foot requires only two moves (step with your rear foot to position your hips for the kick, and throw the kick). Correct hip positioning allows your heavier body to lead.

3. **Originating the kick with your body rather than your leg.** Don't allow your leg to get ahead of your body. If you throw the kick using leg power only, you will lose much of your momentum. You will also starve the kick on impact. The leg will work on dragging the much heavier body along. This is especially true if you lack strength and flexibility in the hips.

Exercises for the outside crescent kick

In order to use the outside crescent kick proficiently, you must recognize situations from where you can comfortably throw it. The motion of the kick should not interfere with the motion of your other techniques. Because the kick requires that you turn your buttocks partly toward your opponent prior to throwing the kick (this is essentially the same move that you use when setting your hips for the side thrust kick), the kick is somewhat difficult to conceal and does not flow naturally within the movement of many other techniques.

Try these exercises on **SETTING UP AND THROWING** the outside crescent kick:

Exercise 1

Start by setting up the kick with a jab. From a distance slightly longer than normal, throw the jab as a distraction to your opponent's gloves. Simultaneously take a short step forward and to the side with your rear foot. This turns your hips partly toward your opponent. As soon as your rear foot plants, bring your lead leg up chambered and start the crescent motion toward the target. Your leg should reach full extension on impact, contacting the target with the outside knife edge of your foot and the lower part of your leg. Your knee and toes should be pointed straight toward the ceiling. If your knee points toward the target, the kick will result in a reverse round house, and not an outside crescent. Practice the set up and kick until you can achieve coordination and explosiveness. To take advantage of the set-up, avoid breaking the kick into separate moves.

Exercise 2

Take turns jabbing and throwing outside crescent kicks with your partner. Work both lead and rear legs. When you get comfortable with this combination, start throwing your jab low to the mid-section. Next, throw a three- or four-punch combination prior to throwing the kick.

Exercise 3

The set-up does not have to be a punch. Round house kicks, for example, are quite easy to throw from many different ranges and therefore have strategic value as irritants. Because the lead leg round house kick impacts from the opposite side of the lead outside crescent kick, it can be used as a set-up. First, throw the round house a few times to train your opponent to defend that side of his body. Then, throw one quick round house kick, whip your leg around (in the outside crescent motion) to the other side, and throw the outside crescent kick.

The lead leg round house and outside crescent kicks impact from opposite sides. You can therefore use the round house as a set-up for the outside crescent.

Exercise 4

When you have landed the outside crescent kick, you must also think of an immediate follow-up. If you land the kick to your opponent's head, you are likely to do more damage than if you throw the kick to the body or arms, which will serve more as an irritant. Experiment to find techniques that flow naturally within the movement of the crescent kick. If you throw the kick with your lead leg, upon planting your foot on the floor, a natural follow-up might be a rear cross or an overhand strike. You can also come back with a round house kick off that same leg, but this would take slightly longer. What other types of follow-ups can you think of? How about a knee strike?

BODY MECHANICS FOR THE AXE KICK

The purpose of the axe kick is to take your opponent's guard down and open targets on his head. It can also be used as a heel rake down the front of his face.

The axe kick is similar to the outside crescent kick in concept, but rather than bringing your leg through the target in a half-circular motion, you should bring your leg up high and drop it with your heel straight down (like an axe). Primary targets for the axe kick are the bridge of the nose and the collarbones. Secondary targets are the crook of the arm, forearms or gloves (to bring the guard down), and front of the thigh (if this is allowed). The axe kick is thrown primarily with your lead leg.

Bring your lead knee up high along line 2. The knee is pointed diagonally across your centerline and to your opponent's outside. This helps you bring your foot across and above the target. The higher you raise your knee, the easier it is to axe a high target.

Extend your leg above the target and drop your foot straight down along centerline A, impacting with

the heel. The higher the apex of the kick, the more powerful the kick will be. This is because distance allows you to build speed. You also have the aid of gravity.

Keep your leg straight on impact. Imagine a 40-pound weight tied to your heel. Don't rely on gravity alone; use the muscles in your leg to pull the kick down. Keep your body crouched to avoid contradictory moves, and drop your weight slightly with the kick.

You can throw the axe kick more effectively by taking a step. Just as with the outside crescent kick, initiate the step with your rear foot at a slight angle to the outside for fastest gap closure and set-up. This helps you raise your knee in a half circle around and above the target.

It is important to remember that your greatest reach is along the horizontal plane from your hips. Since your leg is connected to your hip, and your hip is the pivot point, if you throw the kick either high or low, you will have less reach than if you throw it directly perpendicular to your hip. Since the axe kick must be brought up high above the primary targets (bridge of nose and collarbones), your leg will have less reach than if you kick at mid-level. Don't be fooled by the distance! You may need to initiate the kick from a closer range than you expect. Experiment on a partner to find the optimal range for your legs, and train to remember this sight picture.

WHAT CAN GO WRONG?

Aside from missing with the axe kick because of incorrect distance, the kick can also get caught on your opponent's shoulder or arm. The main reason for this is because of failure to use the muscles in your leg to pull the kick through the target. When your opponent catches your kick, two dangers occur: First, you expose your supporting leg to your opponent's retaliation. Second, it is easy for your opponent to unbalance you, using your caught leg as a lever. Should you find yourself in this predicament, try the following:

1. **Bend your kicking leg at the knee and push off** against the target in an attempt to push your opponent back and unbalance him.

2. **Drop to the ground.** Don't give your opponent the opportunity to knock you down. It is better to go down freely, get it counted as a slip, and let the referee give you a chance to get back up.

3. **Move forward and grab your opponent around the neck** and press your caught foot straight down toward the ground. Because grabbing is not allowed in some kickboxing matches, this might result in a warning.

COMMON ERRORS FOR THE AXE KICK:

1. **Not bringing your leg high above the target for power**, and failing to use the muscles in your leg to bring the kick down hard on impact. Simply dropping the leg and letting gravity take over is not enough if you desire to do damage.

2. **Failing to follow up with a strike** to the created opening while your opponent is still stunned from the kick.

3. **Failing to use a proper set-up**. If your opponent sees the kick coming, he can defend it and counter with a kick to your supporting leg. Remember, the axe kick is generally thrown high, making your supporting leg an exposed target.

THE REVERSE ROUND HOUSE KICK

The reverse round house kick is used primarily as an irritant to split your opponent's focus, or to create openings for other more powerful techniques. Think of the reverse round house kick as a variation of the regular round house kick, but rather than pointing your knee to the inside, you point it to the outside away from your centerline. Because this is a contradiction in body mechanics, the reverse round house kick does not have a lot of power and should therefore be used as a "whipping kick." You can throw the kick either to the legs or body. The kick also works well when intermingled with the regular round house kick.

Note how you impact with the instep or shin, just like in the regular round house kick, but how the knee points to the outside and away from your centerline.

The beauty of the reverse round house kick is that it impacts from the opposite side of the regular round house. For example, if you are in a left fighting stance and throw a regular round house kick with your lead leg, it will impact the right side of your opponent's body. But the reverse round house thrown with your lead leg will impact the left side of your opponent's body. Because both kicks are very quick, you can reach a variety of targets in a short amount of time.

Try this exercise on the **REVERSE ROUND HOUSE KICK**:

Exercise 5

From a left fighting stance, whip a lead leg reverse round house kick to the inside thigh of your opponent's rear leg. Immediately upon landing the kick, reverse the motion and throw a regular round house kick to the inside thigh of your opponent's lead leg. You will now strike both inside thigh areas in rapid succession. If you throw the second kick with power, it will unbalance your opponent.

I recommended planting your foot briefly between kicks for power and speed.

The reverse round house kick is deceptive. When facing your opponent, you can usually tell which kick he is likely to throw just by observing the position of his feet. Because your opponent's lead foot is positioned with the toes at a forty-five degree angle toward your centerline, it is assumed that if he throws a round house kick with this leg, it will impact in the direction of his toes. This is not true with the reverse round house kick, which impacts from the opposite side.

THE HOOK KICK

The hook kick (heel kick) impacts with your heel in a hooking motion. You can throw this kick to a variety of targets including thighs, ribs, solar plexus, and head. You can also use the high hook kick to take your opponent's guard down. You do this by hooking his forearms with your heel and sweeping his hands to the side.

Start the hook kick like you would a side thrust kick, by bringing your leg up chambered and with your buttocks turned partly toward your target. But, unlike the side thrust kick, your aim should initially be slightly to the side of the target. This allows you to bring your heel in a hooking motion into the target.

A hook kick to your opponent's jaw can be devastating, with the power focused over the small area of your heel.

Initiate the hook kick by bringing your lead leg up chambered and aiming it slightly to the side of your target. Like the crescent kick, allow your hip to lead.

Extend your leg while continuing to bring it across the target in a hooking motion. Impact the target with your heel.

On impact, bend your leg at the knee to create a hooking motion, or keep your leg straight and achieve the hook by rotating your hips. There are advantages and disadvantages to both. Hooking from your knee is a little easier and faster, because of the lesser inertia of your bent leg. Hooking with the leg straight takes more energy but is also more powerful, because you are utilizing your whole body to produce the hook.

Try these exercises on the **HOOK KICK WITH FOLLOW-UPS**:

Exercise 6

Start by throwing a hook kick. Plant your foot briefly (concept: *tap and go*), and throw a side thrust kick with the same leg. What if you reversed the combination, starting with the side thrust kick and following with the hook kick? This wouldn't work as well. Since the side thrust kick is designed to move your opponent back through its linear impact, your opponent will not be in range for a follow-up hook kick. If you start with the hook kick, however, you will impact from the side, and your opponent will still be within range for the side thrust kick.

Exercise 7

When you have landed the hook kick, try following with a rear leg cut kick. Since the hook kick is thrown with the lead leg and follows a circular motion to the outside, and the cut kick is thrown with the rear leg and follows a circular motion to the inside, it creates a natural flow with no contradiction in motion. If you follow with a punch, try the overhand strike. If you throw a left hook kick, follow with a right overhand strike for flow and economy of motion. Ideally, the strike should land at the same time your kicking foot plants on the floor. If you throw the hook kick to the head, your opponent is likely to drop his head slightly low and to the side. You can now throw the overhand strike to bring your opponent down, or to knock him out.

DEFENDING THE HOOK KICK

Lastly, you must consider how to defend against the hook kick. When deciding on a defensive action, keep the following in mind:

1. The hook kick f**ollows a circular path** from the side, which enables you to step to the inside of the kick. If the kick followed a linear path, like a front kick or side thrust kick, stepping in would be riskier, as you would be walking into the kick's path of power.

2. The hook kick is normally **thrown high**. This gives you an automatic target on your opponent's supporting leg.

3. The hook kick **has a great deal of power**, because of the small and hard area of the impact weapon (the heel). It is therefore crucial to react quickly and before the kick has reached full speed.

Since the power of the hook kick is focused in your opponent's heel, a good defense is to step in and smother the kick. If you step back, you can make the kick miss but, because you also have created distance, you won't be in position to counter. If you step in, the kick will have a tendency to wrap around you instead, with the heel impacting empty space behind your body. To be successful with this defense, you must start your forward motion at the initiation of your opponent's kick. If you wait until his leg is extended, it is too late, and you will most likely take the kick. After you have smothered the kick, you must also think of an appropriate follow-up. What can you do to take advantage of your opponent? Is he in a position of weakness? Two things have happened: First, because of the hooking motion of the kick, your opponent has his back turned partly toward you. Second, he is on one leg and is therefore in a potentially unstable stance. You could move in and throw a rear cross or hook, but when your opponent is on one leg and in the process of kicking, a better way may be to attack his supporting leg. Try a rear leg cut kick to his supporting leg. The kick should be timed to your forward step, so that you smother and counter simultaneously.

Try this exercise on **DEFENDING THE HOOK KICK**:

Exercise 8

Look for the first signal that your opponent will throw the hook kick. Before he has extended his leg, move to close range to take the power out of the kick. Simultaneously cut kick the back of your opponent's supporting leg. Because your opponent's back is turned partly toward you, your kick will wrap around his leg, impacting the nerve on the outside or front of his thigh. In this sense, you can reach the same target both from the front and back.

Defend the hook kick by moving in and cut kicking your opponent's supporting leg.

You can also defend the hook kick by moving out of range so that the kick misses. However, this is not as effective, because you will lose the superior position and must again close distance before counter-striking.

THOUGHTS ON UNORTHODOX TECHNIQUES

Through comfort comes complacency. Through complacency comes death. When you think you know it all, the unexpected will reach out and grab you. Never let your guard down.

The primary reason for learning unorthodox techniques is to help you refine your balance and body mechanics, turning you into an unpredictable and strategic fighter. As time goes by, you will find that certain combinations feel more comfortable and natural than others. If you stick with these comfortable combinations only, you will become predictable. To break your habitual patterns, start by forcing yourself to practice the unorthodox in shadow boxing, then take it to the heavy bag, and finally the sparring.

As you advance as a fighter, you will learn patience. Through patience you will see more openings and opportunities. Practicing unorthodox moves will help you adapt within the fight and take openings as they occur. As mentioned in the beginning of this section, you can go all the way to the world championships without throwing one unorthodox technique. But, as they used to say in driver's ed: *Leave yourself an out.* The unorthodox can be a lifesaver.

Summary and review

The outside crescent kick strikes from the side, impacting the target with the outside of your foot and part of the shin. The primary target is the head, with the arms and legs secondary targets. Throw the outside crescent kick with full intent of going through the target. This is why it is important to allow your hip to lead.

The axe kick strikes from the top down, impacting the target with the heel of your foot. Primary targets are the bridge of the nose and collarbones, with the arms (to take a guard down) secondary targets. You can also drop the axe kick on the front of your opponent's thigh, if allowed. Both the axe kick and the outside crescent kick start with your leg brought in a half circle toward the centerline of your body. Bend your knee to facilitate speed. As you start the kick on its outward path toward the target, straighten your knee until your leg is straight on impact.

The reverse round house kick strikes from the side, but with your knee angled away from your centerline, using the instep as the impact weapon. Because of a contradiction in body mechanics, this kick is normally used more as a set-up or irritant, rather than as a power technique. Primary targets for the reverse round house kick are the mid-section and inside thigh area, with the head a secondary target.

The hook kick strikes from the side, impacting the target with the heel. The primary target is the head, with the ribs a secondary target. The hook kick is thrown with the full weight of your body behind it, and is capable of tremendous power.

Mechanics for the outside crescent kick

- Warm up for the outside crescent kick by rotating your hips and legs to the outside, alternating legs. Allow your body to lead. If the leg leads, you will exhaust the motion and starve the kick of power. Practice the kick on the heavy bag.

- The outside crescent kick should impact the target with your toes pointed toward the ceiling. Focus on kicking through the target, allowing your body to lead. Don't stop the kick on impact. You can get a more realistic sense of kicking through the target by practicing the kick on hand held focus mitts rather than the heavy bag.

- A common error is to kick upward on impact. This splits the power, with some going into the target and some toward the ceiling.

Speed and distance awareness for the outside crescent kick

- When throwing the outside crescent kick with a step to close distance, how would you step to set your hips for the kick? How can you conceal the kick within the step?

- Is it better to step with your lead or rear foot first? Why? Since the outside crescent kick is generally thrown with your lead leg, stepping with the lead foot first requires a three-count, while stepping with the rear foot first requires only a two-count and is therefore faster.

- What are the pros and cons of throwing the outside crescent kick with your lead versus rear leg?

- What types of set-ups can you use to conceal the step? In what ways do you leave yourself vulnerable?

Outside crescent kick target practice

- Practice target accuracy with the outside crescent kick on focus mitts held at different levels.

- Do you have a tendency to kick above the target? This could happen if you continue raising your leg vertically, or if you allow your leg to follow a diagonal upward path during the execution of the kick. How can you correct it?

- Practice target accuracy on a partner, using light contact. Kick his outside thigh area, body, arms, and head. How does your reach differ depending on the height of the kick? Your greatest reach is mid-level, because your leg is extended horizontally from your hip.

- After landing the outside crescent kick, what types of follow-ups can you throw? Your opponent's reaction will differ depending on which target you kick. If you kick to the head, you may need a different follow-up than if you kick to the arms to take his guard down.

Axe kick practice on focus mitts

- Practice the axe kick on a focus mitt or shield placed on the floor or on a chair, impacting with your heel.

- Work on raising your leg as high as possible prior to releasing the kick. The higher you raise your leg, the more power you can attain.

- Drop the kick straight down on the focus mitt. Rather than letting gravity do all the work, use the muscles in your leg to pull the kick down and through the target.

- Have your partner hold the focus mitt face up. Start at mid-level, bringing your leg above the mitt and dropping the kick through the mitt by pulling your leg down. Have your partner raise the mitt to head height and repeat the procedure.

- How can you increase the height of the axe kick? Try bending your supporting leg slightly. This will increase your flexibility by several inches. Can you kick above your own head level?

Distance awareness for the axe kick

- Have your partner hold a focus mitt face up at mid-level. Move side-to-side and forward and back to learn how to adjust for distance.

- Note how distance for the axe kick can be deceiving. The higher your target is above mid-level, the closer you need to be in order to land the kick.

- Throw the axe kick with a step forward to close distance. Can you throw this kick successfully with your rear leg?

- When you have landed the kick, what types of follow-ups can you use? Experiment with an axe kick followed by a strike, and an axe kick followed by a kick.

Axe kick partner practice

- Face your partner and practice throwing the axe kick over the top of his guard, dropping the kick in the crook of his arm to take his guard down.

- What is your opponent's most likely reaction? If his upper body is brought forward, which targets are exposed? Look for an opportunity to throw a follow-up strike.

- Be aware that your foot can get caught in the crook of your opponent's arm. This is one reason why it is important to use your strength to pull the kick through, rather than relying on gravity alone.

- If the axe kick gets caught on your opponent's arm, how can you save the situation? What targets are you leaving open on yourself for your opponent's retaliation?

Axe kick target practice

- Face your partner and practice target accuracy for the axe kick. Throw the kick in slow motion, impacting with your opponent's front thigh. When he is in a fighting stance with his knees bent, this target is exposed and closer than his guard, collarbone, or nose.

- If your opponent throws the axe kick often, would it benefit you to keep a higher stance with straighter legs? What are the disadvantages of keeping an upright stance to protect against the axe kick?

Reverse round house kick target practice

- Experiment with the reverse round house kick on your partner. Identify the targets for the reverse round house kick by touching each target lightly with your instep.

- If you throw the kick with your lead leg to the inside thigh area of your opponent's rear leg, you must be closer to him than if you throw the kick with your rear leg to the inside thigh area of his lead leg. Why?

- When throwing this kick to the mid-section, try impacting the floating rib, or the softer areas below the rib cage. Note that, since this is a reverse kick, you cannot increase the power by stepping laterally in the direction of the kick. A pause is required, because the same leg that is stepping will do the kicking.

- Can you throw the reverse round house kick to the head? Experiment with throwing it to your opponent's jaw from a side angle, coming underneath his guard, and impacting the opposite side of his face.

The reverse round house kick can be thrown high from a side angle to your opponent's jaw, where it is seldom expected.

Setting up the reverse round house kick

- Experiment with appropriate set-ups and follow-ups for the reverse round house kick. Try setting it up with a regular round house kick thrown with your same leg. Throw a rear round house kick to your opponent's lead outside thigh, followed by a reverse round house kick high to his jaw.

- The reverse round house kick is often used as an irritant, or to break your opponent's focus. Try to get your opponent to lower his guard by throwing multiple quick reverse round house kicks to his mid-section.

- How can you reset your stance in position to throw a finishing strike after landing the reverse round house kick? Since the kick strikes from the inside-out (away from your centerline), it is likely that your opponent's body will be blocking the path of your leg, when you try to reset your stance.

Power practice for the hook kick

- Have your partner hold focus mitts for the hook kick. Experiment with how to position in order to allow your body to lead.

- Does a step prior to throwing the kick help you position your hips for maximum power? How can you make the step and kick flow in one continuous motion?

- If the hook kick seems to lack power, experiment with bending your leg more or less on impact. What benefits and drawbacks does a straight leg give you?

- The hook kick and side thrust kick follow the same motion prior to impact. If you miss with the side thrust kick, and your opponent has stepped slightly toward your back, try converting it into a hook kick.

QUICK REFERENCE TO CONCEPTS

DISTANCE OF IMPORTANCE: You can increase the distance between your head and your opponent's jab, and still stay within reach for a follow-up strike. You do this by shifting your weight to your rear leg, without actually taking a step. Thus, the distance of importance has increased, without increasing the true distance (between your base, which determines your potential reach, and your opponent). Because your upper body has moved back, your opponent's jab will be short of reach. In addition, the weight shift will chamber your rear hand for a counter-strike.

ECONOMY OF MOTION: The most economical punching mechanics are achieved by throwing alternating strikes, using opposite sides of your body. Think of this as a tram going up a mountain. When the gondola at the top starts on its way down, the gondola at the bottom starts on its way up. They meet at the halfway mark. Thus, no time is wasted resetting your body's balance.

FIRST TOUCH: As soon as you feel your parry, block, strike, or kick connect with your opponent's parry, block, strike, or kick, use this as a cue to initiate offense. In order to take the fight from your opponent, you must constantly press him. This means staying one step ahead in speed and strategy.

TAP AND GO: Planting your foot briefly between two successive kicks thrown with the same leg allows you to bounce your foot off of the floor, increasing the speed of the second kick. The tap and go concept also gives you better balance than if you throw the second kick without first planting your foot.

SECTION NINE
SPINNING AND JUMPING

UNORTHODOX KO AT 35
by Martina Sprague

I was sitting on the bleachers feeling smug after my successful double rear cross knockout one minute and a half into the second round of a three-round amateur fight. The main event, a professional match between two skilled fighters, was about to start. The challenger in the blue corner entered first, as is the custom. He emerged from his dressing room followed by his corner team, holding his previously won belt high for all to see. He climbed into the ring and shed a full-length warm-up robe. He was wearing long traditional karate pants, displaying what looked like a less than impressive upper body.

When the reigning champion emerged from his dressing room, followed by his entourage of twenty, the cheering of the crowd was deafening. The champion stepped into the ring, slapped his face and well-cut muscular body, and continued to jump a one-legged full circle around the ring.

The referee checked the fighters' protective equipment, mainly shin guards and gloves, and called them to the center of the ring for further instructions for a clean bout. He separated the fighters and signaled for the bout to start. At the sound of the bell, the champion moved forward with an axe kick to his opponent's shoulder. The challenger retaliated with the infamous jab/rear cross combination, backing the champion into the blue corner, but failing to do damage. The fighters clinched briefly, until the referee separated them and ordered them back to the center of the ring.

The champion initiated again, this time with a quick jab. He took a step back, timed his opponent's advance, and landed a round house shin kick to the left side of the challenger's ribs. The challenger retaliated with a lead leg round house kick, which the champion countered with a rear cross/jab combination. But the challenger refused to move back, and the fighters clinched once more. The referee issued words of warning and separated the fighters to more than two arms' lengths from each other.

The round house kick thrown with the shin is a strong technique that keeps you at close range.

When the fight resumed, the champion stepped forward and laterally off the attack line with his right foot, simultaneously throwing a half-extended rear cross to measure his opponent. As his right foot landed slightly to the side of the attack line, he continued his momentum, rotating his upper body, and throwing a perfectly timed spinning back fist with his left hand, nailing his opponent with a full power shot, his arm fully extended on impact. The challenger dropped instantly to the canvas, landing on his stomach and staying there for several seconds. When he attempted to rise to all four, it was obvious that the fight was over, only 35 seconds into the first round, ended with a move that was not only unexpected, but used as a lead after the break-up from a clinch. It was probably the most impressive use I have seen of the spinning back fist, especially since it was thrown unorthodoxly from a side position, with the left hand by a right-handed fighter.

THE SPINNING BACK FIST

The first question to ask is, why would you want to spin or jump? The primary purpose is for power. A component of power comes from the ability to build momentum through distance. If you throw a straight strike: a rear cross, for example, you have a distance of approximately two to three feet in which to accelerate the strike, depending on the length of your arm (slightly longer for a straight kick). But if you can increase the distance to the target, you can achieve greater speed and more power. Because the shortest distance between two points is a straight line, you can achieve a longer distance through circular motion.

As we all know, the shortest distance between two points is a straight line. But don't let the simplicity of this thought deceive you. The circle has certain benefits in speed that a straight line can't provide.

Let's talk about jumping next. One advantage of jumping is that you can achieve greater height. But since kickboxing utilizes a lot of leg kicks, this is not really an issue. The second advantage is, just like in spinning techniques, that you can achieve greater power. You can turn your body more freely in the air than on the ground, which results in faster acceleration. Granted, spinning and jumping techniques are initially a little more time consuming than straight techniques, and are therefore a little more difficult to conceal. They also take more energy and may require you to turn your back toward your opponent. But if you can gain proficiency with these techniques, the benefits clearly outweigh the disadvantages.

Lastly, spinning and jumping teach you about your body's balance, giving you a reason to perfect your target accuracy.

This section covers:

- Body mechanics for the spinning back fist
- Landing the spinning back fist
- In the gym
- Following up off the spinning back fist
- Timing the spinning back fist off a side thrust kick
- Summary and review

BODY MECHANICS FOR THE SPINNING BACK FIST

The spinning back fist is normally a rear hand technique that gets most of its power from the rotation of your upper body. It is important not to separate the spin and the strike into two moves. In order to achieve target penetration, you must ensure that you have enough flexibility in your body and arm to spin more than 180 degrees without sliding or stepping. If you spin exactly 180 degrees, your strike will be lined up with your toe-to-heel stance, and target penetration may be difficult if your opponent is positioned slightly off center. You achieve flexibility by taking a short step with your lead foot across your centerline at the initiation of the spin. This places you in a slightly crossed stance with your lead leg to the outside of your opponent's body. Simultaneously turn your upper body in the same direction as the step, extending your arm gradually as you bring your fist around.

Targets for the spinning back fist are the side of the jaw, the temple, or the point of the chin. The spinning back fist is normally not thrown to the body.

To throw the spinning back fist, step across your centerline with your lead foot in the direction of centerline B. This gives you flexibility for spinning more than 180 degrees, allowing you to take the strike through the target.

Simultaneously rotate your head and upper body until you can see the target. A common error is to throw the strike mechanically without eye contact. The faster you can bring your head around, the faster and more accurate the strike will be.

Extend your arm fully along centerline A, impacting the target with the back of your fist. Because the fist is farther than the forearm or elbow from the axis of rotation (your body), it travels at a faster speed and can generate more power. Impacting with the elbow is not allowed in most kickboxing matches.

If your opponent is moving toward the strike (toward your left side), you can achieve flexibility without taking a step.

The spinning back fist is potentially more powerful than the rear cross or overhand strike, but you must time it to your opponent's distance and movement. Measure the distance with your jab prior to throwing the strike. Ideally, you want to impact the target with the back of your fist and with your arm fully extended. If you are too close, you risk hyper-extending the elbow by striking the air behind the target, or of fracturing your forearm, or of getting disqualified for striking with the elbow rather than the fist. If your opponent is moving toward you, your timing must be especially good in order to land the strike at its optimal range. If you are too far away, the strike will obviously not land, and your own momentum may throw you off balance.

LANDING THE SPINNING BACK FIST

Since throwing the spinning back fist requires a circular move that momentarily places you with your back toward your opponent, you must throw it at a time when your opponent least expects it. The best times to land the spinning back fist are:

1. **Off of a jab.** The primary purpose of the jab is to set up your stronger techniques. Use the jab as a distance measurer and to distract your opponent's attention away from your other techniques. Try a couple of double jabs to confuse your opponent and

get a feel for distance prior to throwing the spinning back fist.

2. **As your opponent is moving toward you.** This requires good timing, but will add his forward momentum to the momentum of your strike.

Step across your centerline and spin as your opponent is stepping toward you.

3. **When backing out from an opponent on the ropes.** This is a good time to throw the spinning back fist because, when your opponent is on the ropes, you have the superior position. However, you must still conceal the strike within a strategic move. Try backing your opponent into the ropes, and throw a series of body punches to get him to lower his guard. Step back quickly, simultaneously throwing the spinning back fist to his head.

4. **When in close, and your opponent steps back to create distance.** As he initiates his step back, step with him, moving your lead foot forward and across your centerline. This positions you for the strike. How tightly you step depends on how much distance you need to close. Simultaneously throw the spinning back fist.

5. **As a double strike from a stationary position.** When your first spinning back fist lands, reverse the direction of rotation in your upper body and throw a second spinning back fist with your other hand. Think of it as unwinding a spring. You can now nail both sides of your opponent's head with a power strike using a lot of momentum. Your second strike is actually stronger than the first, because you are in a better position for building momentum.

6. **As a follow-up off of a block.** When your opponent throws a round house kick, step in and block with the forearm that is opposite the kick. This starts the rotation in your body, building a natural flow for the spinning back fist. Because your opponent is unable to move away until the motion of his kick is complete (concept: *completion of motion*), you know that he will be there to receive the spinning back fist. It is therefore beneficial to attack when your opponent is in the process of recovering from throwing the kick.

In the gym

The spinning back fist is becoming a lost move in kickboxing. It is not seen as often as it used to, yet it is a strike that has knocked out countless fighters. The spinning back fist is easiest to land directly after a jab. Throw the jab with your lead hand and the spinning back fist with your rear hand.

You can also throw the spinning back fist in close quarters when you are shoulder-to-shoulder with your opponent. The moment your opponent steps back to create distance, you throw the spinning back fist. Distance is now optimal, and your opponent won't expect the strike in close quarters, so you can conceal it rather easily.

Another good time to throw the spinning back fist is right before a perceived clinch, when your opponent is moving toward you, but before he has actually tied you up. You will know after the first round if your opponent has a tendency to clinch. Catch him with a spinning back fist on his way in.

Be careful not to telegraph the strike. The spinning back fist is often telegraphed both physically and mentally. Physically, when you are moving your lead foot across your centerline in preparation to throw the strike. Mentally, when you are planning the strike too long in advance, rather than

just letting it go when the moment is right. When throwing unorthodox techniques, we often fidget subconsciously before throwing the strike. This will give you away.

If your opponent ducks, and you miss with the spinning back fist, a good follow-up is to reverse the direction of the spin and throw a second spinning back fist with your other hand. Because your opponent must come back up to reset his stance after ducking, your strike will land with almost certainty, as long as he doesn't shuffle back.

Throw a variation of the spinning back fist by stepping all the way around with the foot on the same side as the striking hand. Your arm and body should move together, with your rear foot in the air as you spin, and planting the moment of impact. If you started in a left stance, you will now be in a right stance. Make sure that you don't stop short on impact, but take the strike through the target.

Common errors for the spinning back fist:

1. **Not using a proper set-up,** or failing to judge distance and missing the target.

2. **Throwing the strike from too close range,** impacting with the forearm or elbow instead of the fist.

3. **Extending your arm before you can see the target,** exposing your jaw and increasing the inertia of the spin.

4. **Failing to follow up.** Because the spinning back fist is a power strike intended to finish your opponent, it is especially important to follow up right away and not give him time to recover.

FOLLOWING UP OFF THE SPINNING BACK FIST

Once you have landed the spinning back fist, you must decide on a follow-up. One of the quicker follow-ups is to reverse direction and throw a spinning back fist with your other hand. However, it is dangerous to get into a set pattern and always do the same thing. You must therefore experiment with different techniques.

Try this exercise on **FOLLOWING UP** off the spinning back fist:

Exercise 1

1. Throw the spinning back fist, then spin back into your stance, bob and weave to your left, and throw a jab and a rear cross from an angle off the attack line.

2. Throw the spinning back fist, then spin back into your stance and throw a rear leg front kick.

3. Throw the spinning back fist, then spin back into your stance and duck your opponent's counter-strike while simultaneously shuffling back. Follow with a stepping side thrust kick.

4. Throw the spinning back fist, then spin back into your stance, bob and weave to your left under your opponent's counter-strike, simultaneously shuffling left and throwing a rear round house kick to his mid-section.

TIMING THE SPINNING BACK FIST OFF A SIDE THRUST KICK

Since the spinning back fist has considerable movement, it is difficult to pull off without a proper set-up. The side thrust kick is perhaps one of the least expected set-ups, because it is designed to create distance, which places your hand techniques out of reach. The side thrust kick can therefore be used deceptively to set up the spinning back fist.

First, throw the side thrust kick. If the kick makes contact, it should knock your opponent back. If your opponent sees the kick coming, his defense will probably be to step back a few feet out of reach. This is the result you desire. As your side thrust kick misses, your opponent will have a tendency to step forward into range and try to counter with a combination. You must now wait a "two-count" to attain proper range. Throw the spinning back fist when your opponent comes forward, adding your momentum to his. The strike is likely to be unexpected.

If your opponent is back against the ropes when you throw the side thrust kick, he will be unable to move back and create distance. Upon landing the kick, side-step across your centerline (this should give you the range you need). Immediately follow with the spinning back fist.

After landing the side thrust kick on an opponent on the ropes, cross your own centerline and use the momentum to launch the spinning back fist.

Summary and review

The spinning back fist is a devastating strike that gets its power from the rotation in your upper body. When throwing this strike, keep your arm close to your body throughout the spin, and extend it fully by the moment of impact. Impact your opponent's temple, nose, or jaw with the back of your fist. The spinning back fist is seldom, if ever, thrown to the body.

Increasing the power of the spinning back fist

- The spinning back fist is capable of so much power, because it has a long distance over which to build momentum.

- If you feel that your spinning back fist is slow, what corrective action can you take? If you allow your arm to extend from your body throughout the spin, you will have difficulty accelerating the technique because of the rotational inertia. Keep your arm close to your body until it is time to land the strike.

- Try lowering your body weight slightly throughout the spin (like a descending spiral staircase). How does this allow you to maximize power and stay better protected?

Lower your weight for stability and power by bending at the knees.

- When you have landed the strike, you must reset your body's balance by "unwinding" the spin. How can you utilize that motion to throw a second spinning back fist with your other hand?

Set-up and target practice for the spinning back fist

- The spinning back fist impacts the target from the side. The primary targets for the spinning back fist are the temples and jaw.

- Make sure that you can see the target before launching the strike. Many practitioners initially throw the strike low, or miss, because they fail to look at the target. Why is the spinning back fist normally not a good body punch?

- Name two strikes and two kicks that can be used to set up the spinning back fist.

- If you were going to use a distracting kick to set up the spinning back fist, what type of kick would you throw? Why?

Heavy bag practice for the spinning back fist

- Practice the spinning back fist on the heavy bag for power. Increase the power by taking a step forward and across your centerline with your lead foot. This places your body weight behind the blow and allows you to take the strike through the target.

- You can also increase power by increasing the speed of rotation. Keep your body weight centered above your foundation to avoid the risk of getting thrown off balance.

- Practice the double spinning back fist. As soon as the first strike lands, unwind your upper body like a spring and generate momentum for a spinning back fist with your other hand. When the second strike lands, unwind your upper body to reset your stance.

Spinning back fist strategy

- Explore some of the strategic uses for the spinning back fist. How can you time the strike to your opponent's forward motion? How can you use it as a deterrent when moving from close to long range?

- If you are in a left stance, is it better to throw the strike when your opponent is moving to your left or right? Why?

Spinning back fist focus mitt practice

- Have your partner hold focus mitts. Throw the spinning back fist mixed in with the rest of your punch combinations.

- How can you make the spinning back fist flow naturally within your combination? Can you work it in with kicks comfortably?

- Experiment with timing the strike to your opponent's forward, reverse, and lateral movement. Don't throw the strike isolated. Use an appropriate set-up.

Double-end bag practice for the spinning back fist

- Practice a combination of straight strikes, followed by the spinning back fist, on the double-end bag.

- Because the bag is so responsive, it will swing toward you when striking it straight. In order to land the spinning back fist now, your timing must be very good.

- If you miss the bag, how can you use the momentum from the spin to throw another strike?

Defending the spinning back fist

- Lastly, think about how to defend the spinning back fist. Because the strike is so quick and devastating, you must react to it at the initiation of the technique.

- You can defend against the spinning back fist in two ways: You can block it, or you can avoid it. Use your peripheral vision to pick up on the movement of the strike. This is a signal for you to duck.

If you duck the spinning back fist, the momentum of the technique is likely to throw your opponent off balance.

- Ducking requires slightly better timing than blocking. Try blocking the spinning back fist with an outside forearm block.

SPINNING KICKS

Spinning kicks rely on the same principle as spinning punches: The faster you spin, the more power you generate. However, because kicking utilizes your legs, which are also your foundation, you must work a little harder to maintain balance. The most common spinning kicks are the spinning back kick and the spinning heel kick. The spinning heel kick lands from the side and is therefore similar in motion to the spinning back fist. The spinning back kick, on the other hand, lands straight, requiring two separate motions joined together for fluidity and power.

This section covers:

- Body mechanics for the spinning back kick
- The power of the spinning back kick
- In the gym
- Eight ways to set up the spinning back kick
- The spinning heel kick
- Summary and review

BODY MECHANICS FOR THE SPINNING BACK KICK

The spinning back kick uses the same rotation in your body as the spinning back fist. However, unlike the spinning back fist, which strikes from the side, the spinning back kick strikes straight from the front. In that respect, it is similar in concept to the side thrust kick. When throwing the spinning back kick, use the ball or whole bottom of your foot as a striking weapon. Power is derived both from the speed of the spin and from the big muscles in your buttocks. Targets for the spinning back kick are the solar plexus, ribs, chest, and head. Your opponent's reaction will differ depending on where you land the kick. If you kick to his solar plexus, he is likely to get the wind knocked out of him and buckle over. If you kick to his chest, he is more likely to get knocked back.

Initiate the technique with a short step with your lead foot across your centerline (same motion as for the spinning back fist). Simultaneously start the rotation in your upper body.

When you have achieved eye contact with the target, bring your rear leg up chambered and convert the circular motion of your body to linear motion with the kick extending straight through the target.

In order to build momentum for power, it is important not to separate the spin and the kick into two moves. There should be no pause between rotating your upper body and throwing the kick.

Note that because the spinning back kick is thrown with your rear leg, your lead foot becomes the pivot point in the rotating system. In order to keep your balance, upon chambering your rear leg, you must move your upper body forward until it is centered above your lead leg. This increases your reach by as much as two feet. The spinning back kick therefore has greater reach than what initially appears. If you throw it from close range, the technique may feel crammed.

THE POWER OF THE SPINNING BACK KICK

The spinning back kick is naturally powerful because of the potentially high speed in the spin, and because you are using the biggest muscle in your body (your buttocks) to throw it. This combination makes for a lethal partnership. However, the power of this kick often fails to mark an opponent for three reasons:

1. The kick **requires more movement** than a front kick or round house kick, giving your opponent time to move out of range.

2. A common tendency is to **move your upper body to the rear** (to lean away from the direction of the kick), *splitting the power* with some going forward and some backward. Leaning away from the kick also decreases your reach, giving you less penetrating force.

3. Some fighters tend to **leave the kick on the target** after impact, instead of pulling the leg back to the chambered position. This results in a push, with the kick lacking penetrating force.

Note that leaving your kick on the target is a common error with most kicks. In a full-contact art, like kickboxing, we train for maximum impact by extending the kick through the target rather than snapping it back. This eliminates the tendency to touch spar, which is common in many other martial arts. But with penetrating force comes the problem of leaving the kick in contact with the target too long, and then simply letting the foot drop to the floor. Leaving the kick on the target gives your opponent the opportunity to grab your leg. You also expose other targets unnecessarily. But the biggest drawback may be related to power. If you leave the kick on the target, the impact results in a push, and power is decreased. The faster you reverse the direction of the kick after impact, the greater your power potential. Another benefit of reversing direction, and which is especially useful with the spinning back kick, is that it counters your tendency to over-rotate on the spin. Punches are sometimes also left on the target, but it is more common with kicks. Because of the greater weight of the leg, reversing direction in a kick requires more energy.

When training for the spinning back kick, keep your body compact. As you start the rotation in your upper body, simultaneously lower your center of gravity by bending your knees. Stay low until impact is complete. If you raise your body to the upright position, you will tend to lean away from the direction of the kick, and therefore split the power. Penetrating the target when kicking a person who is heavier than you is difficult. *Staying compact* allows you to focus all your energy forward.

Staying compact is always a good idea, because you expose fewer targets to your opponent.

Don't forget to keep the kick tight throughout the spin, for the same reason that you want to keep your arm tight when throwing the spinning back fist. When you allow your leg to swing away from your body, it is difficult to accelerate the kick, and you may get thrown off balance. Work on tightening the kick by allowing your knees to brush against each other just prior to releasing the kick. This ensures that the circular motion is converted to linear, and that the kick is thrown absolutely straight. Visualize a box that is just big enough for you to fit inside. When you start to spin, your leg is not allowed to extend beyond the boundaries of the box.

IN THE GYM

Most people feel that the spinning back kick is a little more difficult to throw than the spinning back fist. This may be because a kick requires more energy and balance than a punch. A second reason is because the spinning back kick employs both circular and linear motion that must be synchronized, while the spinning back fist employs only circular motion. You can build confidence by practicing the spinning back kick on a moving target, like a heavy bag that is swinging from side to side, or on a kicking shield held by a workout partner who uses movement and angles. If you are the shield holder, do not suddenly remove the target from your partner. If he throws the kick with full power and misses, he can hyperextend his knee.

When throwing a spinning technique, we often don't see the target until right before impact. Much of your confidence comes from understanding your opponent's expected reaction. In other words, knowing where he is going to be and what he is going to do. If you throw a spinning back kick in retaliation to your opponent's round house kick, and your timing is good, you know that he will stand there on one leg for you. Also try setting the kick up with another kick to your opponent's outside thigh. First, throw the cut kick a few times. Then, fake a cut kick by raising your knee. Set your foot down across your centerline and continue the rotation into the spinning back kick.

COMMON ERRORS FOR THE SPINNING BACK KICK:

1. **Not making eye contact** with your target prior to releasing the kick. If you can't see the target, you are likely to miss.

2. **Pausing between the spin and the kick.** The purpose of the spin is to create speed for power, and any pause contradicts this. In essence, if you can't throw the kick in its entirety without pausing, the purpose of the spin is defeated, and you might as well throw a regular side thrust kick.

3. **Under- or over-rotating.** Under-rotation, or too slow rotation, is often due to lack of confidence, and allows your opponent to move out of the way. Over-rotation is often due to failing to adjust to a faster spin. If you use too much turn in the hip, you end up impacting with your toes or ball of foot rather than with your heel. Looping the kick is also a common problem, which results in the kick impacting the target from the side rather than straight.

4. **Not using an appropriate set-up**, allowing your opponent to move out of range, to jam the kick, or to take advantage of a time when your back is turned toward him. You can set up the spinning back kick with a jab, but perhaps one of the better set-ups is a fake spinning back fist. First, throw the spinning back fist a couple of times, until your opponent equates the spin in your body to the spinning back fist. When you spin, he will raise his guard to block the strike, or he will move back slightly. This opens up his mid-section and gives you distance for the kick. Now, throw the spinning back kick.

When using spinning techniques, employ a good mix, so that your opponent won't guess your next move.

EIGHT WAYS TO SET UP THE SPINNING BACK KICK

The spinning back kick is difficult to conceal because of the rotation in your upper body. It is therefore crucial that you employ some sort of set-up and don't throw the kick isolated. Still, many fighters prefer to throw it isolated, for the simple reason that the kick requires good balance and timing and is difficult to blend in with other strikes and kicks. How do you know exactly when to launch it? If you try to blend it in with punches, you will be too close, unless your opponent moves back to create distance. If you try to blend it in with kicks, you must choose kicks that allow you to flow comfortably from one kick to another, to avoid stopping your momentum. Blending the spinning back kick in with a defensive move is perhaps the trickiest part, but may be the most beneficial. You must also time the kick to your opponent's forward, back, and lateral movement. Try these set-ups for the spinning back kick:

1. **Set up the spinning back kick with a jab.** Throw the jab as an irritant and to get a feel for distance. Initiate the kick as your jabbing hand is returning to the guard position. If you pause (even briefly) between jab and kick, the purpose of the jab is defeated. The jab is a better set-up than a rear cross, because your body is already turned in the direction of the kick. If you use a rear cross to set up the kick, there will be a slight contradiction in body mechanics. Since your legs are longer than your arms, the kick is likely to feel crammed when thrown after a punch. You can work distance in two ways: Move your opponent back with the jab and, as distance is created, follow with the spinning back kick. Or position your supporting lead foot at an angle that allows you extra distance. You do this by throwing the jab first. When retrieving the jabbing hand, step across your centerline and slightly to the rear with your lead foot. Simultaneously start the rotation in your upper body. This positions you in a crossed stance for a moment, so it is especially important to eliminate any pause between jab and kick.

2. **Set up the spinning back kick with a kick.** It is important to choose kicks that don't contradict the intended motion and that allow you correct distance. Throwing the spinning back kick after an axe kick, for example, is likely to stall the kick, because

the motion of the axe kick and spinning back kick differ significantly. A lead leg round house kick may be a better set-up, because it employs a slightly circular motion and can therefore help you launch the spinning back kick easier. But the problem with the round house kick is that it strikes from the side, and often with the shin, which may position you too close for the spinning back kick. You can adjust distance with a short step across your centerline. Also try the front kick and side thrust kick as set-ups. Both these kicks are designed to move your opponent back, making the spinning back kick easier to land. Also, the side thrust kick has already turned your body and hips in the proper direction to allow a natural flow into the spinning back kick. Kicks that your opponent knows are intended to knock him back are actually really good set-up techniques. Try a front push kick. As your opponent moves back in anticipation of the kick (even if it doesn't land), distance is created, allowing you to follow with the spinning back kick.

Throw the side thrust kick. If you need additional distance, step across your centerline to shift your foundation (pivot point), and throw the spinning back kick.

When throwing the spinning back kick, your lead foot becomes your foundation and pivot point. In order to maintain balance, your upper body must move forward until it is centered above your lead foot. This increases your reach by one to two feet. So, even if your opponent is knocked back with a side thrust kick, the additional reach is still significant enough to allow the spinning back kick to land.

3. **Set up the spinning back kick with a defensive move.** This works great when your opponent is in the process of kicking. You know that his foundation is potentially unstable, because he is on one foot. Try this: When your opponent throws a round house kick to your body, block it with an inward forearm or elbow block off your opposite hand (across your centerline). As the block makes contact, initiate the spin in your upper body. Your kick should land before your opponent has retrieved his kicking foot. This move is effective, because it allows you to take advantage of your opponent's offense to throw him off balance. Furthermore, he can't move away from your kick when he is in the process of kicking.

A good follow-up off the spinning back kick is the side thrust kick. Aside from being a powerful and logical kick to throw at this time, it also keeps you from over-rotating from the spinning back kick.

4. **Set up the spinning back kick with a slip.** When your opponent throws a jab, slip (move your head) to the side and slightly to the rear to increase distance and make the jab miss. Because your opponent is thinking about the jab, and because he just missed, his mind won't be on protecting his body. Allow the slip to launch the rotation in your upper body. If you are in a left fighting stance, you must slip to your right for this to be effective, as slipping to your left would be slightly contradictory and would require a pause before throwing the kick. Throw the spinning back kick while your opponent's arm is still extended in the jab. As you get comfortable with this move, try to speed up the

rotation of the kick by throwing it within the slip itself, so that the spin starts at the initiation of your slip.

Throw the spinning back kick within the movement of a slip. Note how the fighter on the left slips to his right to avoid contradictory moves, and how he initiates the kick before his opponent has had time to retrieve his jabbing arm.

5. **Set up the spinning back kick timed to your opponent's degree of aggressiveness.** Many fighters throw the spinning back kick as their opponent moves back to create distance. But you can also throw it against an aggressive opponent who tries to crowd you. When he moves forward, a properly timed kick will add your momentum to his. Observe your opponent's movement and be aware of his likely reactions to specific strikes and kicks. Rather than standing toe-to-toe with him trying to duke it out on the inside, take a step back to create distance. Once you know that your opponent is the aggressor, you need to time your step back to the initiation of his step forward. This places you slightly ahead of your opponent (in time), and distance is created. If you throw the spinning back kick dynamically now, you should catch your opponent in the ribs, as he is moving in.

6. **Set up the spinning back kick timed to your opponent's movement.** Let's say that you throw a side thrust kick that knocks your opponent back. His natural tendency is now to come forward again. This happens because he is likely to feel flustered by the fact that you knocked him back and desires to "even the score." Because you know in advance that this is his expected reaction, you can preplan your move. There are many others instances when your opponent will be closing distance. Often, you can draw him into a kick by stepping back. If you have been fighting at striking range, and you suddenly step back and out of range, he is likely to step forward in an attempt to stay within range. Knowing this helps you launch the spinning back kick against his forward momentum. The opposite is also true. If you are fighting at close range, and you are the stronger fighter, your opponent will look for an opportunity to get outside of your striking range. The moment he gaps, follow with the spinning back kick. Again, you know in advance that he is likely to gap when you overwhelm him on the inside. You need only wait for him to initiate his move. You can even provide him with opportunities by giving him escape routes and avoid pressing him into a corner.

7. **Set up the spinning back kick timed to your opponent's attempted escape.** One of the best times to throw the spinning back kick is when your opponent is on the ropes and is trying to get away. Think like this: Which way should he move in order to walk into the kick? If you are in a left stance and your opponent moves to your left, he will walk into the kick. He will meet you halfway, allowing you to spin less than 180 degrees, making the kick more economical for you. If he moves to your right, however, you will be chasing him with the kick, so this would not be as powerful. This concept can be ap-

plied in the center of the ring as well. A fight often takes on circular movement, where one fighter tries to take up an angle to the side of his opponent. Pay attention to the direction of your opponent's movement. Whenever he moves to your left, you know that he will move into the path of power for the spinning back kick.

8. **Set up the spinning back kick with a spinning back fist.** Because the footwork in both techniques is initially identical, you can throw the spinning back fist a few times until your opponent learns to respect it and moves back when he sees it coming. This increases the range for your longer reaching legs. Now, throw the spinning back kick.

Note the similarity in stance between the spinning back fist and the spinning back kick.

THE SPINNING HEEL KICK

The spinning heel kick is similar in concept to the spinning back fist:

1. **The rotation in your body is identical.**

2. **The primary target is the head.**

3. **Both the kick and the fist strike the target from the side and at the tip of the rotating system.**

You can throw the spinning heel kick as a continuation of motion following a failed round house kick. When you miss with the round house kick, your back is turned toward your opponent. You can now throw a side thrust kick, or continue the motion into a spinning back kick or spinning heel kick with your rear leg. Because both the round house kick and the spinning heel kick strike from the side (rather than straight, like the side thrust or spinning back kick), the spinning heel kick allows you to keep your circular momentum, avoiding the need to change direction.

Because the primary target for the spinning heel kick is the jaw or temple, you must ensure that the kick has sufficient height. You can increase the height by inclining your body toward the floor. We have previously talked about crouching forward and in the direction of the kick, so inclining your body defies that principle. However, because the power of the kick is in the circular plane rather than straight, as long as you keep your body spinning, you will not sacrifice power by leaning toward the floor.

In order to achieve target penetration, you must keep the momentum (rotation) until impact is complete. Remember to *lead with the body* to avoid exhausting the power prematurely.

The spinning heel kick is a devastating technique that draws its effectiveness from the speed of the rotation and the strength of the impact weapon (the heel).

Once you have landed the kick, you must have an appropriate follow-up. A spinning heel kick that lands with accuracy can drop your opponent instantly. Still, you should be prepared to follow up. If possible, use the momentum that you have already started to launch your next technique. Throwing a strike or kick off the opposite side of your body is usually beneficial, because it allows the flow of momentum to continue. Once you plant your foot from the spinning heel kick, try a round house kick with your other leg.

If your opponent smothers the kick, try reverting to a spinning back fist. When the kick is jammed, rather than trying to continue the momentum, reverse the direction of the spin and throw a spinning back fist with your opposite hand.

Many kickboxers with a karate background are skilled at spinning and jumping, so you must also develop a strategy of defense against an opponent who favors the spinning heel kick. Because the spinning heel kick requires perfect distance to be effective, you can move back to long range and make the kick miss, but this places you out of reach to counter. I recommend moving forward to smother the kick. If your timing is good, you can move in and kick your opponent's supporting leg. You know that he will be there for you, because the spinning heel kick is always thrown high, so your opponent is unable to move until the kick is complete.

Let's look at a scenario: Your opponent throws a round house kick that you see coming from a mile away. You take a step back so that the kick misses. The kick swishes past just inches from your nose. When your opponent realizes he missed, he plants the kicking foot but continues the rotation of his body, immediately launching a spinning heel kick with his other leg. Realizing that you are up against a skilled opponent, you shuffle forward inside of his kick's path of power and kick his supporting leg. Your opponent's kick strikes the air behind you, with your guard blocking slightly above the back of his knee.

It is possible to throw continuous round house kicks and spinning heel kicks and round house kicks, using alternating legs. Start at one end of the room and throw a rear leg round house kick. As soon as your foot plants, throw a spinning heel kick with your lead leg (opposite leg). When this kicks lands, throw a round house kick with your rear leg, and so on, until you reach the other end of the room. However, throwing too many of these is counter-productive in strategy and is likely to make you dizzy.

Summary and review

The spinning back kick is, like the side thrust kick, mainly a long range weapon with the capability to do great damage, and is often used as a deterrent to keep your opponent at a distance. Impact the target with the heel or bottom of your foot. Targets are the mid-section, chest, and head. Because this technique employs a spin, it requires target accuracy. To ensure landing the kick without getting countered, the spin in your upper body must be quick and assertive. You can initiate the kick with a small step with your lead foot across your centerline. This starts the rotation in your body and assures flexibility to bring the kick through a full 180 degrees of movement. Turn your head until you have established eye-contact with your target, then bring your rear knee up in the chambered position and throw the kick straight into the target. Although the kick utilizes two moves: the spin and the extension of your leg, you should think of it as one move with no pause. A common mistake is to throw the kick wide, resulting in a looping kick impacting the side of the target instead of straight. If that is your intention, the spinning heel kick, which is designed to strike its target from the side, is a better choice.

Balance practice for the spinning back kick

- Practice the spinning back kick in the air for balance and good mechanics. If you lose balance, use a visual point of reference: a mark on the wall, for example. If you can't see the target prior to launching the kick, you are likely to miss.

- Another common cause of balance loss is failing to rotate your body around a vertical axis through your center of gravity. Leaning, or extending an arm or leg simultaneously to spinning, is likely to throw you off balance.

Concealing the spinning back kick

- Explore the difference between a wide kick (which allows your leg to strike from the side) and a tight kick (which is kept close to your axis of rotation).

- The wide kick is more likely to be telegraphed and is more difficult to accelerate because of the rotational inertia.

- Practice the tight kick by allowing your knees to rub together throughout the spin, and before you release the kick. You can achieve this by thinking of the kick as a straight back kick without the spin.

Wide kick (above), tight kick (right).

Target practice for the spinning back kick

- Place a piece of tape on the heavy bag, throw the spinning back kick, and try impacting the tape with the heel of your foot.

- How can you adjust for kicking high or low? Try manipulating the height by bending your supporting leg and crouching into the kick. Think of the spin as a downward spiral, where you lower your weight throughout the spin. This may seem contradictory if you are trying to achieve height, but it actually helps you by creating more flexibility in your supporting leg.

- How can you adjust for over- or under-spinning? Over-spinning may be a result of too much momentum, or too large a step prior to spinning. Under-spinning may be a result of too little flexibility, or of failing to bring your head around first to establish eye-contact with the target.

- Hang a tennis ball or a string from the ceiling and practice impacting it with the spinning back kick. The narrower the target, the more precise your kick must be.

- You can also practice accuracy by having your partner throw a lightweight object from across the room (a sparring glove, for example). Pay attention to your timing. Do you need to initiate the spin sooner or later in order to kick the glove? Can you speed up the spin rather than starting it sooner and achieve the same results?

- When speeding up the spin, you may have a tendency to overshoot the target before your body has adjusted and learned to release the kick sooner.

Economy of motion practice for the spinning back kick

- Practice the spinning back kick on a swinging heavy bag. Time the kick so that you strike the bag when it is coming toward you.

- When is the best time to kick: when the bag swings

left or right? Why? If you are in a left stance, the best time to kick is when the bag swings from your left and toward you, because it will be swinging into the kick's path of power. If you kick when the bag swings to your right and away from you, you will have to chase it with the kick.

- Look for your opponent's movement. It is more economical to throw the spinning back kick when your opponent moves toward your left (if you are in a left stance), because he will be moving into the kick's path of power and add his momentum to the momentum of your kick.

Setting up the spinning back kick

- Practice the side thrust kick followed by a spinning back kick on the heavy bag. The side thrust kick will set the bag swinging. Time the spinning back kick to impact when the bag is coming toward you.

- How can you make the side thrust and spinning back kick flow in one continuous motion? Is this a logical combination? Why?

- What is your opponent's likely reaction when you land the side thrust kick? If he moves back, how can you close distance for the spinning back kick without pausing or taking additional steps?

The spinning back kick at close range

- The spinning back kick is generally thrown as a long range technique. Try throwing it from close range, within an arm's length of your opponent.

- How can you increase distance without making the kick obvious? Try setting up the kick with a distraction to the head, simultaneously stepping laterally across your centerline with your lead foot. This increases the distance to your target by six to twelve inches.

- Another benefit of stepping across your centerline with your lead foot is that it sets your hips so that you are better lined up with the target, giving you more flexibility for the spin.

Set up the spinning back kick with a jab, simultaneously stepping across your centerline to gain distance.

Blocking and throwing the spinning back kick

- Have your partner throw a round house kick, which you block with an inward forearm block. As the block impacts his kick, and while your partner is still on one leg, continue the rotation of your upper body into a spinning back kick.

- Because the inward forearm block starts a rotation toward your centerline, a spinning back kick is a logical follow-up. In addition, the best time to strike or kick is when your opponent is throwing a kick and is on one leg.

Logical combinations for the spinning back kick

- Throw a round house kick with your lead leg, followed by a spinning back kick. This technique teaches you to establish a continuous flow between kicks, utilizing the momentum from the first kick to accelerate the second.

- Find kicks that flow naturally in the same direction. Since the motion of the lead round house kick is slightly circular, it helps you initiate the spin for the spinning back kick.

- If you throw a rear round house kick, you must throw the spinning back kick with your other leg in order to establish a continuous flow.

- Is the above technique logical? The round house kick strikes from the side and may not create enough distance for you to successfully land the spinning back kick. How can you fix this problem? Experiment with increasing distance by allowing your round house kick to come all the way through the target (like a cut kick), until you are in a crossed stance.

Sparring practice for the spinning back kick

- Engage in three-step sparring with your partner. Each fighter takes turns to throw a combination of three strikes or kicks, but one must be a spinning back kick.

- When is the best time to throw the spinning back kick within a combination: at the beginning, middle, or end? Why? Name a good follow-up.

- What type of technique should precede the spinning back kick? If you start the combination with the spinning back kick, how do you set it up?

Adjusting distance for the spinning back kick

- Have your partner hold a kicking shield. When he steps toward you, try to time the spinning back kick for ultimate distance and power.

- If you throw the kick too soon, your opponent will be outside of reach, and the kick will miss. If you throw it too late, he will jam the kick.

- How can you adjust if your opponent steps to the side rather than toward you? Can you still land the spinning back kick, or do you need to revert to a different kick? What other kicks lend themselves to your opponent's lateral movement?

- Have your partner move forward, back, and side-to-side without following any specific pattern. Experiment with forcing your opponent to move in a direction that lends itself to the spinning back kick. Take charge, rather than waiting for your opponent to move.

Endurance practice for the spinning back kick

- Have your partner hold a kicking shield, and set a timer for three minutes. Both the front kick, side thrust kick, and spinning back kick are designed to impact the target straight.

- Throw a side thrust kick, a spinning back kick, a front kick, and another front kick off your other leg. Replant your foot in the opposite stance and throw another spinning back kick.

- Mix the front kick, side thrust kick, and spinning back kick in any order, but try to flow smoothly from one kick to the other. Use footwork to make any necessary adjustments for distance.

- Now that you have completed these exercises on the spinning back kick, do the same exercises with the spinning heel kick. Since this kick impacts from the side with the heel of the foot, it requires slightly better distance awareness than the spinning back kick.

- If you miss with the kick, or if your opponent jams the kick, how can you salvage the situation?

JUMP KICKS

Most kickboxers stay with the three basic kicks: the front kick, the round house kick, and the side thrust kick. However, some of the fancier kicks do have application in competition kickboxing. The way a flying or jump kick looks gives your opponent a different mind-set about it. Unless you are skilled at jumping and spinning, these techniques may not land with a great deal of precision. But when you do the unorthodox, like jumping aggressively toward your opponent, your attack is likely to be feared more. This, in itself, may make your opponent tense, keeping him from defending and countering the attack effectively.

Once you get proficient at jumping and kicking, your kicks will have greater power potential than a regular kick. This is because the jump gives you additional momentum. When throwing a regular non-jump kick, you must push off against the floor with your supporting foot. Some of the power is therefore directed into the floor. When you jump, full focus is on the kicking leg. A jump kick thrown with full intent is difficult to defend against.

When you add a jump to a spinning kick, you will usually see an increase in speed, because there is less friction between your body and the air than between your foot and the floor. You can also contract your body more when airborne, which reduces the rotational inertia, making it easier to increase the rate of turn.

Before we get into the more complicated jump spinning kicks, let's look at how to execute the jump for the three basic kicks.

This section covers:

- Body mechanics for jumping
- The jump front kick
- The jump round house kick
- The jump side thrust kick
- The jump spinning back kick
- The jump spinning outside crescent kick
- Defending jump spinning kicks
- Summary and review

BODY MECHANICS FOR JUMPING

Jump kicks were originally designed for kicking men off their horses, and some martial artists can attain amazing height with these kicks. Today, when few people fight against horse back riders, you can still jump to increase the height of the kick, allowing you to reach targets on taller opponents. Most jump kicks (with the exception of the jump side thrust kick) rely on a "scissored" move. In other words, one foot comes up at a time, with the feet reversing direction at the apex of the jump:

1. Start by raising your right knee high until you are standing on one foot. Now, start to raise your left knee, simultaneously lowering your right foot toward the floor. When your left knee reaches maximum height, your right foot will plant on the floor, thus the scissored move. As you increase the speed, this can be likened to running in place with your knees high.

2. In order to execute the kick, you must now extend the kicking leg at the apex of the jump. Again, start by raising your right knee high until you are standing on one foot. **Note that your right leg is not your kicking leg. Your right leg is the leg you use to launch the kick.** Bring your left knee up, simultaneously lowering your right foot toward the floor. When your left knee reaches the apex, extend your lower leg in a front kick. As you increase the speed, this will result in a jump. Try to launch the kick slightly before your supporting foot lands. Once you have gained proficiency with this, try landing the kick when your non-kicking foot is as high as possible.

Basic mechanics for a jump front kick can be likened to running in place with your knees high.

THE JUMP FRONT KICK

The beat of the jump kick is a two-count done by alternating your feet to help launch your body into the air. The kick is therefore slightly slower from start to finish than a one-count non-jump kick. But the benefits in height and aggressiveness may outweigh the slower speed.

In order to perform the jump kick confidently, you must practice it until you have attained proper speed, balance, and agility. If you lose balance when landing from the jump, you will be in an inferior position, or you may end up on the floor.

Try these exercises on the **JUMP FRONT KICK**:

Exercise 1

Throw a stationary front kick in slow motion, keeping your supporting leg absolutely straight. Note how high your kick reaches. Now, throw another stationary front kick in slow motion, but bend your supporting leg slightly. Were you able to increase the height of the kick? In general, it can be said that a little bit of bend in your supporting leg gives you more flexibility in your kicking leg.

Exercise 2

Next, throw the jump front kick. Did the jump help you increase the height of the kick? What can you do to increase the height even more? Note that the higher you raise your knee, the higher you can kick. Start from a left fighting stance, using your right (rear) leg to launch your left front kick. Have your partner hold a focus mitt at mid-level, face down. Impact the mitt with the ball of your foot. Keep your guard up for protection. Have your partner increase the height of the focus mitt little by little until you can reach targets higher than the head.

When executing a jump kick, don't incline your upper body to the rear, as this contradicts the direction of power. Work on keeping your body compact with all motion going in the direction of the kick.

THE JUMP ROUND HOUSE KICK

The jump round house kick is similar in motion to the jump front kick. The jump is identical, but rather than extending your leg straight, you allow your hips to pivot as your jumping foot reaches the apex of the jump. Because you are relying on two different directions: upward for the jump, and sideways (perpendicular) into the target for the kick, this kick requires slightly more athletic ability than the jump front kick.

Because the jump round house kick strikes from the side, the jump must employ a combination of vertical and horizontal motion into the target, allowing you to turn your body in the air. This does not mean that the vertical jump has to be large. The jump round house kick is also effective when thrown to the legs. The jump adds height to a kick, and also easier rotation of your body, resulting in greater speed and power.

Try this exercise on the **JUMP ROUND HOUSE KICK**:

Exercise 3

Throw the kick to your opponent's outside thigh area, relying on a shallow jump with motion in both the vertical and lateral plane. Remember the stepping cut kick, where you step laterally across your opponent's centerline to gain momentum for the kick? The principle is the same, but rather than stepping, you should jump, increasing the momentum both through sideways motion and the turn of your body in the air.

THE JUMP SIDE THRUST KICK

When learning to throw the jump side thrust kick, start from medium range with a step forward rather than a jump. Think of it as a stepping side thrust kick. Then work on speeding up your gap closure by pushing off with your rear foot. Once you have learned to close the gap quickly, you can increase the distance a little at a time. Now, work on launching your body toward the target. As you increase distance even more, your step will automatically begin to turn into a jump.

Try this exercise on the **JUMP SIDE THRUST KICK**:

Exercise 4

Run toward the heavy bag from a distance of ten yards. When you get within a few feet, jump and turn your body sideways in the air. **Do not stop your forward momentum.** Simultaneously extend your lead leg in a side thrust kick toward the bag. Impact the target when your jumping foot is at the apex (highest point). The momentum you have created by running and jumping will add significant power to the kick.

If you kick with your rear leg, you must rotate your body more than if you kick with your lead leg.

The jump side thrust kick is a powerful technique that will at least knock your opponent back, if not out.

Of course, in reality you will not run from across the ring like this. When practicing the kick, the speed will help you launch your body into the air and gain height. Once your body mechanics are correct, you can shorten the distance until you can throw the jump side thrust kick using only a short shuffle-step.

The jump side thrust kick is also effective from very close range, where it is often unexpected. If you incline your body to the rear simultaneous to the jump, you will gain additional distance. The kick will not be as powerful from close range, but the strategic advantage may outweigh the benefits in power.

THE JUMP SPINNING BACK KICK

The jump spinning back kick is one of those fancy, crowd pleasers that is extremely useful when your opponent is backed up against the ropes of the ring. In general, jump spinning kicks allow you to increase the speed of the spin, and therefore the speed of the kick, due to greater ease of movement of your body through the air. The jump spinning back kick has the added advantage that it can be thrown effectively from short range.

The regular spinning back kick requires medium to long range for maximum power, but the jump spinning back kick can be thrown successfully from very close range by allowing your body to move back while airborne, thus buying distance by increasing the range to optimal for the kick. This does not mean that you should allow the impact of the kick to throw you back. For the kick to be effective, you must focus all your energy into the target. If you need to increase distance, do so simultaneously to jumping, and not at the moment of impact. If the impact throws you back, you have either failed to launch your full body momentum in the direction of the kick, or you have a fear of committing fully to the kick, and subconsciously fail to extend it.

The jump spinning back kick is seldom expected in close quarters, which gives you a strategic advantage. The faster you can bring your upper body around, the faster and more accurate the kick will be.

To throw the jump spinning back kick from close quarters:

1. **Conceal your intentions** by throwing close range techniques (hooks, uppercuts, leg kicks).

2. **Transfer your weight to your rear leg.** This creates a gap between your and your opponent's upper bodies.

3. Without pausing, **jump and spin in the air**, bringing your upper body around and landing the kick to your opponent's mid-section.

Don't loop the jump spinning back kick (like you would a spinning heel kick). Keep it tight for speed and penetration.

THE JUMP SPINNING OUTSIDE CRESCENT KICK

The jump spinning outside crescent kick is similar in principle to the jump spinning back kick (the jump is the same), but the kick strikes the target from the side rather than straight. You must therefore assure proper follow-through in the circular plane. You do this by allowing your hip to lead. If the movement originates in your leg rather than in your hip, the motion of the kick will exhaust itself before reaching the target.

Again, the kick should impact at the apex of the jump, and when your hips are aligned with your intended target. Distance is important. A spinning technique that strikes from the side has its greatest speed (linear speed) at the tip of the rotating system. If you impact with your shin, the kick may be strong, but if you impact with the side of your foot, which is farther from the axis of rotation (your hip), the kick will have a greater speed, and is therefore more likely to generate power.

The spinning outside crescent kick strikes from the side with the outside portion of your foot.

Because it is easier to turn when airborne, a jump increases the speed and power, providing that the rest of your body mechanics are correct. It is interesting to note that the kick reaches its greatest power when your leg is even (in height) with your hip. In other words, if your leg is extended diagonally upward or downward, maximum power is not possible, because the full weight of your body is not directly behind the attack line (the direction in which you throw the kick). In addition, your reach is at its maximum when your leg is extended horizontally toward the target. If your leg is diagonally low or high, you need to be closer in order to impact the target.

Strive to extend your leg when your body is at the apex of the jump. If you extend too soon (when your body is on its way up), you are likely to kick at a downward angle. If you extend too late (when your body is on its way down), you are likely to kick at an upward angle. Try to jump to where your hips are at the same height as the target you are trying to impact.

DEFENDING JUMP SPINNING KICKS

Perhaps the greatest benefit to jumping is the apparent aggressiveness of the kick. This adds a mental element to the fight game; namely the tendency for your opponent to freeze in preparation for absorbing the blow, or to flinch which may result in an incline of his upper body to the rear. Both are destructive. Freezing inhibits your opponent's ability to respond effectively, and flinching may place him in a vulnerable position in regards to balance and counter-attack. If you are on the receiving end of a jump spinning kick, being aware of these tendencies will help you counteract them. In general, it can be said that whenever your opponent throws a kick which impacts from the side (jump round house, jump spinning crescent), moving in and countering is your best strategy. Whenever he throws a kick which impacts straight (jump front kick, jump spinning back kick), it is better to move back and make the kick miss. But you must be prepared to take advantage of the element of surprise. When the kick misses, it will take your opponent a fraction of a second to regroup. Don't give him the chance! Move in and counter.

There is a third possibility: moving sideways against a linear attack. But this is more difficult and requires good timing. If you do utilize lateral movement, step forward at the same time. This places you within range to counter from an angle off your opponent's attack line. A kick to his supporting leg can be effective, but there are also a variety of strikes that you can use, including the overhand, hook, and knee strike.

Summary and review

In kickboxing, you will mostly see only the three basic kicks: the front kick, the round house kick, and the side thrust kick, with an occasional spinning back kick or spinning heel kick. Fancy jumping and flying kicks are often done for show, where the practitioner's intent is to impress the audience. Jump kicks are generally considered advanced, and can reach potentially higher targets than the regular kick. A second advantage is more power, because of easier turn of the body in the air. You should therefore practice these kicks, at least until you have determined whether they work for you. A drawback of the jump kick is that it requires greater athletic ability as well as speed to be effective.

When practicing the jump kick, attempt to impact the target at the apex (the greatest height). Keep in mind that a jump kick does not have to be thrown high to be effective. An example is the jump cut kick to your opponent's outside thigh.

INCREASING THE POWER OF THE JUMP KICK

- Jump kicks are by nature time consuming and dangerous to execute. But, providing that the jump is done correctly, it can add considerable power to the kick.

- You can increase power through a jump, because your body can turn more freely in the air.

- In general, you should launch yourself toward the target. A common mistake is to lean back when jumping, which contradicts the direction of motion and splits the power.

- Be careful not to let the non-kicking foot replant before the kicking foot makes contact, as this would split the power in two directions: into the target and into the floor. A correctly executed jump kick should impact the target at the apex.

Target practice for the jump kick

• Have a partner hold focus mitts for the jump front, round house, and side thrust kick. Practice precision kicking as your partner repositions the target from low to high. Attempt to reach greater heights by bringing your knee up high and tight to your body prior to kicking.

• Have your partner raise the mitt one inch at a time, until you have reached maximum height. At what point do you feel you must sacrifice power and flexibility for height? If you were to use this kick in a match, would you attempt it against a much taller opponent? Why, or why not?

• Work on kicking "through" the target. The kick should not stop at the moment of impact, especially when kicking a flexible target, like the head or leg. Impact slightly before your leg is fully extended, or slightly on the upward motion of the kick (for the jump front kick).

Faking and throwing the jump kick

• Another advantage of the jump kick is that it can be used as a fake for a low kick (more about fakes in Section 10).

• Jump kicks are often used to reach high targets. If your opponent thinks that you are throwing a high jump kick, he may freeze in preparation for the blow, allowing you to throw a low kick to the legs instead.

• Conceal your intentions by looking at the high target when you initiate the jump. Since a jump increases the power through easier turn of the body, it should not be used solely for the high kick.

QUICK REFERENCE TO CONCEPTS

APEX: The apex is the highest point of a jump, and the point at which you should release the kick for maximum height and power. If you release the kick prior to reaching the apex, you are cheating yourself out of motion. However, there may be an exception in the jump front kick. By releasing this kick slightly prior to reaching the apex, you can achieve more penetrating force, as long as you allow your body momentum to continue to the apex, with the kick extending through the target.

COMPLETION OF MOTION: Whenever you make a move, your body must be given the opportunity to correct itself. You can't initiate another move before the motion of your first move is complete, or you will risk losing balance. Being aware of this principle helps you take advantage of your opponent when he is the most vulnerable; for example, when he is in the process of throwing a kick.

FRICTION: This is the force that acts in the opposite direction of motion, and is created by two surfaces contacting one another. Friction on ground is greater than friction in air, so a jump kick, where no body part touches the ground, can be accelerated easier than a regular kick, providing that you have achieved proficiency with the jump.

LEADING WITH THE BODY: The body is more massive than an arm or a leg, and can therefore achieve greater power in motion, providing that it is used to accelerate the lighter arm or leg. When throwing a punch or kick, the motion should originate in the body and transfer to the arm or leg. If you start the motion in the arm or leg, you will expend more energy trying to "drag" the heavier body along. You can experience this in the spinning outside crescent kick, especially if you lack flexibility in the hips. If you allow the leg to lead, when your hip gets to its maximum range of motion, the power of the kick will die. However, if you allow your body to lead, you can maintain motion throughout the circle and impact the target with greater penetrating force.

ROTATIONAL INERTIA: Inertia is the force that resists a change in motion. In a spinning technique, where your arms or legs are extended throughout the spin, the rotational inertia resists the acceleration of the spin and therefore the power. Keep your arms and legs as close to your body's centerline and rotational axis as possible, until you must extend in order to impact the target.

SPLITTING THE POWER: Your full effort must act in the direction of motion. If you step back or allow your upper body to move to the rear simultaneous to striking, you will have a conflict with the direction of energy, and the power of the technique will split. This is commonly seen when impacting a much heavier target, or when throwing a long range technique from close range. Being aware of the effects of moving back on impact can help you counteract this tendency by training your body to stay compact and throwing all techniques with full intent.

STAYING COMPACT: Crouching, or keeping your body's mass as near its center as possible, helps you with balance, speed, and power. An upright body has a greater distribution of the mass, and therefore greater risk of losing balance when impacted by a force above or below the center of gravity. It is also difficult to accelerate a strike or kick if the arms or legs are far from the body's center of gravity, or if you rely on the strength in your arms or legs rather than on the strength in your body. Without speed and acceleration, powerful punching and kicking is difficult to achieve.

TOE-TO-HEEL LINE: This is the line that creates a slightly offset stance for stability. Your opponent's centerline is often lined up with your toe-to-heel line, which can also be thought of as the attack line, along which your power is focused. When throwing a spinning technique, keeping your feet stationary on the toe-to-heel line may limit your ability to penetrate the target. A short step with your lead foot across your centerline gives you better flexibility for a spinning technique, and should be done even at the risk of jeopardizing your stability.

Section Ten
RING GENERALSHIP

The scope on strategy
by Martina Sprague

In short, ring generalship is your ability to control the ring and the fighting environment. This involves strategy, which can be further broken down into physical strategy and mental strategy. Physical strategy involves the actual technique: how to position, when to move in and out, which specific technique to throw and when, etc. Mental strategy involves fakes and deception, and how to carry yourself to impose a threat.

Thought provoker: Because kickboxing is not organized according to a specific pattern, you must respond to the fight as it unfolds before you. You should liken the fight to a conversation and respond to "questions" as they are posed, rather than answering them before they are asked. True or false?

There are two ways to work strategy:

1. By **shaping** the situation according to a pre-determined pattern.

2. By **responding** to the situation as it unfolds before you.

Although you can never know exactly how the fight will unfold, it is not entirely true to say that kickboxing is disorganized. Most kickboxing competitions take place in a controlled environment. Already in the first round against an unknown fighter, you will start to recognize patterns, techniques, and movements that are recurrent. You can now use this bit of information as a catalyst for further strategy. Strategy consists of a combination of offense and defense. Depending on how great your chance for victory is, you may rely on one more than the other. If you have strength and endurance, you may take your opponent out with brutal offense. If your opponent is stronger, you may need to rely more on defense.

Before you get to the arena, a careful computation of your own and your opponent's tactics may be your most important life preserver. If you know whom you are fighting beforehand, make every effort to study his strengths and weaknesses, taking into account his physical strength and mental tenacity, as well as his capabilities, tactics, and weapons.

You must also develop the ability to adapt to your surroundings. Mentally, you must deal with fear, uncertainty, and exhaustion. But, as somebody once said: When a fighter thinks that he has reached the limits of what he can endure, he is really only halfway there. There is a difference between a risk and a calculated risk. When it really matters, you will often find a supply of energy that you never knew existed.

ELEMENTS OF STRATEGY

The kickboxer must have three qualities: physical strength, willpower, and strategy. Physical strength enables you to endure the rigors of the sport, and willpower helps you persevere and win against overwhelming odds. Strategy makes it easy.

Now that you have learned basic and advanced techniques and gained some proficiency in both, you may feel a need to ask, "What comes next?" Is it possible to get to the end of the journey, or is kickboxing ongoing and eternal without end? How good can a fighter get? And how do you measure how far you have come?

You must now establish a concrete goal. Many fighters equate this to winning in competition, and to eventually going for a world title. Those not interested in competing may take the alternate route of teaching. Regardless of whether you choose competition or teaching, kickboxing will now become more than a physical challenge. To further your skill, you must take the game to the next level: that of mental superiority.

As you commence your strategy training, you should focus on principles rather than techniques. Proper strategy allows you to increase the odds in your favor. As you go through the following material, bear in mind that the outcome of a fight is never certain. When you have trained to obtain maximum fitness, when you have studied your opponent's tactics, and when you finally stand face to face with your adversary . . . there, in the end, is always that bit of doubt called fate.

This section covers:

- The chess game
- Mobility
- The linear attack
- Thoughts on angles
- In the gym
- The circular attack
- Threat and response
- Strength and weakness
- The element of time
- Thoughts on speed and counter-striking
- Glove-up with Keith
- Distance
- Distance when kicking
- Timing
- Premature attacks
- Superiority
- Sizing it up
- Summary and review

THE CHESS GAME

Fighting can in many ways be likened to a game of chess. Based on an evaluation of your own and your opponent's position and strength, you must decide when to use a Pawn, a Knight, or a Bishop. Your many possible weapons and moves can be likened to the pieces on the chessboard. In fighting, as in chess, your number of effective weapons is important: how you use them, the best time to use them, and how to position to effectively reach your goal. Sometimes it is necessary to sacrifice a Pawn in order to gain a greater advantage. In fighting, as in chess, you must learn to control the chessboard. As you gain knowledge and experience, you will also gain skill in how to maneuver into a position of superiority, and how to choose the best weapons for the given situation.

It is now time to begin the chess game. Think in the following terms: **In order to end the fight quickly and in my favor, each technique must have a clear purpose. Each move should advance me a little closer toward my goal.** True, some moves may impact the target with a lesser force than what is needed to end the fight, and some moves may not impact the target at all. But there should still be purpose. For example, a fake does not physically impact the target at all, yet it has an impact on the fight as a whole. It gives you an indication of how your opponent is likely to react. A fake has purpose, and the strategic fighter notes its usefulness and employs it later in the fight. Likewise, a technique that impacts lightly but fails to knock out may still have purpose as a set-up strike for the finish that is to come.

You don't have to physically strike your opponent every time. You can also win mentally by instilling fear.

Select moves that give your opponent as many problems as possible. A move is not necessarily limited to one single technique, but can be comprised of a series of techniques: a combination, or a combination thrown simultaneous with movement forward, back, or to the side. Just like the chess master thinks a few steps ahead, so should the fighter. But, unlike chess players, fighters don't necessarily take turns to move. In fact, the strategic fighter limits his opponent's ability to execute his next move. And, unlike chess, because fighting is so dynamic, fighters don't have a lot of time to contemplate their next move.

Because no two fights are alike, fighting is initially a guessing game. Your objective in the first round is to eliminate as much as possible of the guesswork by testing your opponent to determine how he will react to specific moves. For example, you may notice that each time you step forward, he steps back and throws a jab. It is not only important to note that he places himself on the defensive by stepping back, but also that he counters with a technique that is not likely to knock you out, and that he counters with the same technique each time. You may now want to advance with a front kick. This allows you to keep your guard up in defense of your opponent's jab, and to take the open target on his ribs underneath his extended jabbing arm. In what other ways can you advance and take advantage of your opponent's retreat, without placing yourself in danger of his jab?

A successful chess player analyzes his weaknesses and determines how he can do the best with what he has. Let's say that your opponent lands his front kick time and time again. Remember, your opponent's success does not necessarily depend on what he is doing right, but may depend on what you are doing wrong. It is therefore important to understand both your weaknesses and your strengths. Your opponent's front kick may be mediocre, but is it getting in because you are exposing your centerline or telegraphing your moves?

A strength may sometimes seem like a weakness. For example, carrying your guard low may seem like a weakness. But if you carry your guard low intentionally in order to lure your opponent into throwing a strike, it is called *strategy* and is as strength.

Try this exercise on **STRATEGY**:

Exercise 1

When planning your strategy, use the analogy of the chess game. Chess masters stay several moves ahead of their opponents, they work on creating openings, and they have patience. At the beginning of the fight, size up your opponent to determine his strong and weak points, and his reactions to specific moves:

1. How experienced is he?
2. Is he aggressive or patient?
3. Does he have speed and power?
4. Which fakes does he fall for?
5. How deceptive is he?

Once you have decided what type of fighter he is, you must form a strategy to defeat him. Some fighters win based on how they affect their opponent mentally. If you hear that your opponent is twice as experienced as you, you may enter the fight with the attitude that you can't win, and may appear more timid than you are. I have witnessed this in training many times. A student may be miles ahead of his peers, but when faced with an unknown opponent, his fighting prowess, which we all envy so much, suddenly sucks. Don't let this happen to you!

Keith's Corner

In chess, the Pawn may seem like the least valuable piece. Much like the foot soldier, it is expendable. But in reality, without the Pawn little would be achieved. The Pawn plows the way for the knockout. Great chess masters use this piece to its limits. In kickboxing, the jab can be likened to the Pawn. A fighter who really knows how to use it can defeat even the most powerful adversary. But you must be crafty. It is not enough to throw the jab often, as it is easy to sacrifice power for speed. Multiple jabs may be extremely annoying to your opponent, but once the road has been paved, you must follow with a stronger force.

The lesson is that you should never throw punches just to throw punches. There is a difference between fighting and actually working on something. Economy means that there are no wasted movements: that you fight with intention and are definite in your actions.

MOBILITY

Fighting on the amateur level often boils down to basic punching and kicking, and to who can throw the most strikes. An attack that relies solely on aggressiveness may initially seem overwhelming and be difficult to defend against. Your effectiveness as a fighter is directly related to how mobile you are. Through movement comes momentum and position. Avoid countering a linear attack with a linear attack, as you will simply be trading blows with your opponent. If your opponent is very aggressive and rushes you at the beginning of the fight, all his power is focused straight ahead. Initially, you may want to cover up and wait until the attack dies down. Then take up an angle slightly away from your opponent's centerline. This limits the effectiveness of one or both of his hands, and forces him to adjust his position before firing back. By dictating the direction of the fight, you have taken the first step toward controlling the chessboard.

The positional advantage of mobility can be used to attack your opponent's weak points. When you have room to maneuver, you can employ your power more effectively and will therefore appear stronger. You can also use mobility to tire an aggressive opponent.

If you force him to chase you, or if his techniques consistently fail to land, you will tire him physically and frustrate him mentally. Your ability to use defensive movement (bobbing and weaving, slipping, ducking) helps you evade an attack and places you in a position to counter.

Try this exercise on **MOBILITY**:

Exercise 2

When up against a stronger or bigger opponent, you cannot rely on physical strength to win the fight. Mobility gives you a positional advantage that allows you to stay out of your opponent's firing range while attacking his weak points. Experiment with the following mobility concepts:

1. How to **maneuver** into a position of superiority.

2. How to **employ your power** more effectively by side-stepping or by concentrating the attack on your opponent's weak points.

3. How to use mobility **to tire** your opponent.

THE LINEAR ATTACK

Now that all your techniques are mechanically correct, your new foundation is footwork. Footwork ties directly in with mobility. The better your footwork, the more mobile you are. Superior footwork helps you land strikes effectively from a side angle. All techniques you have learned so far build upon the different concepts of footwork. Advanced footwork is especially beneficial to the fighter who lacks good upper body movement (slipping, bobbing and weaving).

When your opponent is the aggressor, try to retreat on an angle off the attack line to thwart his attack. This forces him to adjust his position, which takes both time and energy. If he doesn't, his strikes will lack accuracy and power. Likewise, when moving forward to strike, angle off slightly to thwart your opponent's counter-strike. Then, remain slightly to one side of the attack line. **Do not cross your opponent's centerline.** When your opponent attempts to reposition, you must make an adjustment as well. Generally, your adjustment should be to the outside (away from your opponent's attack line).

Shifting body weight: We have already talked about how to increase power by taking a step in the direction of the strike, or by pivoting. So, in a sense, this can be thought of as footwork. Let's take this concept a step further by using footwork to lure your opponent into throwing a strike. You can create the illusion that you have increased distance by shifting your body weight back without actually taking a step. This may lure your opponent to come forward and into your counter-strike.

The use of different angles does not mean that you must step completely off the attack line (ninety degrees). As little as a few inches to the side is often enough to thwart an attack.

Try this exercise on **SHIFTING BODY WEIGHT**:

Exercise 3

1. When your opponent throws a jab, **slip the jab by taking a half-step to the rear** with your rear foot only, leaving your lead foot planted. This moves your upper body to the rear and creates the illusion that you have moved back. Your opponent's jab will miss and tempt him to step forward with another strike.

The half-step shifts your weight to the rear and helps you avoid your opponent's strike without placing you at long range.

2. The moment your opponent steps toward you, **allow your upper body to come forward again**, but at an angle to the side of your opponent's centerline (the attack line). Your opponent's strike will pass over your shoulder, and you will be inside of his offense and at a good angle for countering.

Reset your body's balance timed to your opponent's advance, but at an angle away from his attack line.

Note that when your upper body comes forward, you can simultaneously take a short shuffle-step forward to close distance even more. Simultaneous with the step, throw your follow-up strike: an uppercut to your opponent's chin, for example. This allows you to use your body's mass to its fullest.

3. Now that you are at an angle off your opponent's attack line and to the inside of his offense, **follow with additional strikes** (hooks, for example) before he has the chance to readjust his stance.

4. When your opponent finally does adjust his stance so that he can fire back, you should also **make an adjustment to stay off the attack line.** The chess game, as it applies to footwork, has now begun. As you can see, it is extremely important to decide from the start to be the leader in this dance.

The fighter who forces his opponent to make the necessary adjustments in stance and angle has come a long way toward strategic superiority.

THOUGHTS ON ANGLES

Use angles both when retreating from an attack and for offensive superiority. In order to throw a strike from a superior position to the side, the step you use for creating the new angle must be faster than the speed of your strikes. It can therefore be said that a fighter's speed is in his footwork.

A common mistake when moving from side to side is to cross the centerline laterally, giving your opponent the opportunity to strike all your major targets. When it is necessary to cross the centerline, do so:

1. With **speed**

2. By using a **bigger step** than you normally would

3. By using a **pivot-step** rather than a straight step across the centerline

You can also step all the way back to the Safety Zone, where you and your opponent can't reach each other with any type of technique. This gives you a chance to regroup and start anew.

When you begin getting comfortable throwing strikes from different angles, transfer this knowledge to your kicks. For example: **punch-punch-punch-kick, move to a new angle, kick-punch-punch, then move, punch-punch, move out, move back in with a kick,** and so on. This helps you create the optimum angle for a powerful kick.

Also use angles when you are with your back to the ropes. When it is time to regain the center position, your footwork must be faster than your opponent's. You can increase the speed in your footwork by first establishing your opponent's cadence. You do this by taking a few steps to the side, allowing him to step with you to keep you trapped against the ropes. When he falls into your rhythm, explode with a pivot-step back to the center of the ring.

You can apply angles equally to short and long range fighting. When in close quarters, a short pivot-step with your rear foot (just enough to get off the attack line) enables you to follow with an overhand strike over the top of your opponent's guard to his jaw. When your opponent is backed up against the ropes,

keep your head off the attack line by pushing your forehead against his shoulder. From this position, you can throw strikes to the mid-section or ribs by pivoting your body only, while keeping your feet planted. Your opponent will have difficulty firing back from his inferior position on the ropes.

Side-stepping when kicking increases your power and moves you off the attack line. To facilitate speed, step with the non-kicking foot to a forty-five degree angle to your opponent's outside (away from his centerline). Synchronize the step with the kick, so that the kick lands the moment the stepping foot lands. Side-stepping works especially well with the round house kick, because your body momentum is in the direction of the kick. But angled attacks work with the front kick as well. By angling off, you will buy time, possibly eliminate your opponent's counter-strike, and set yourself up to counter from a superior position.

Try these exercises on **ANGLING OFF**:

Exercise 4

One of the first techniques you should practice when learning advanced footwork is stepping off the centerline when throwing a jab. You do this by taking a step at a forty-five degree angle forward with your lead foot. Providing that you and your opponent are fighting from left stances, this moves you toward your opponent's power side. To avoid getting struck by his rear hand, you must adjust your stance with your rear foot to a slight angle off his centerline. Your position is now superior and forces your opponent to readjust his stance. You can now fire a strong rear cross.

Throw the rear cross from a side angle off your opponent's attack line.

Exercise 5

Use the same principle when setting for a lead hook to your opponent's body. Throw the jab while stepping off the centerline to the outside. Follow with a lead hook to the back portion of your opponent's ribs. When it is time to move back out, do so with a step at an angle rather than straight back.

Throw a lead hook from a side angle off your opponent's attack line.

Exercise 6

When sparring or working focus mitts, establish the mind-set that you are in control of all movement. A common tendency, particularly when working mitts, is to let the mitt holder decide which direction to move. In other words, the mitt holder leads and you follow. He will step first and you will adjust according to his position with the mitts. The danger of training this way is that it is easily carried over into the ring. Next time you work mitts, be the one who is in control of the movement. Instead of following the mitt holder, make the mitt holder follow you.

Exercise 7

Movement in footwork should also be used to draw your opponent forward. Advance or retreat every time you jab. When retreating, your opponent will move forward to close the gap. If you step off the attack line with your lead foot now, your opponent's strike will miss, and you will be in a superior position to counter with a lead hook to his body.

IN THE GYM

Side-stepping works well both offensively and defensively. Since it is tougher to be successful when backpedaling, let's work a few exercises that will give you a strategic advantage in this area. When I throw a kick, I want you to step slightly to the side rather than straight back. If my kick is a front or side thrust kick, it will miss. If it is a round house kick, power will be stifled, even if the kick makes contact. Side-stepping keeps you within range to fire back.

Never take more than one step back in a straight line. If you mirror your opponent's step exactly, who has the advantage? Your opponent, right? This is because he is moving forward and you are moving back, and it is more difficult to fight effectively when retreating. Your opponent can also use momentum to his advantage. How do you remedy this? You take one step  *back to mirror his step forward and keep distance between you. When he starts forward again, you step back with your rear foot only, moving your upper body to the rear. When your opponent's strike misses, and he adjusts his stance and steps forward with his rear foot, you throw a punch, taking advantage of his forward momentum. In a sense, you have used your opponent's strength against him. The fact that he has momentum is what enables you to throw a powerful strike while retreating.*

THE CIRCULAR ATTACK

Most fights employ circular motion: The fighters are circling an imaginary point halfway between them. This is a natural move because, as your opponent starts to circle, you must circle with him in order to protect your back and centerline. You can think of this as dancing, with one partner leading and the other following. Except, in dancing, the person following does so willingly. In fighting, you should never follow willingly. It is amazing how easily some fighters resign to being dominated, or "led" in the ring by their opponent.

Before a fighter has gained sufficient experience (usually before he fights as a pro), he is likely to be very aggressive and constantly move forward. But this strategy only works if he has the reach and weight advantage. Circular movement allows you to move away from an aggressive opponent's power side, giving you a safer angle and distance from his longer reaching arms and legs. Remember what we have learned about keeping our opponent occupied? From your side angle, apply offense to split his mind and body focus. Because your opponent's offense is linear, it inhibits his defensive capabilities.

But your objective is not restricted to avoiding getting hit. Your objective is to play chess with your opponent, to outsmart him. If your jabs land to his gloves, they are still likely to draw enough attention to invite him to step toward you. The moment he does, halt your circular movement and unleash a powerful combination.

When your opponent picks up on your strategy, he may choose to step out of range in an attempt to lure you into closer range. The chess game is now under way. Start by taking a step toward your opponent, but only close enough to again place you at circling range. When you step forward, because of his aggressive nature, he will most likely also step forward and strike. Your timing must now be a half-beat faster than his, so that you can take the opening under his extended striking arm.

Let's sum up circular movement:

1. **Circling left and right is used against an aggressive fighter**, and enables you to move around your opponent.

2. **Use the circling move in conjunction with jabs.** When the time and angle are right, follow with a power strike.

3. **In general, circle away from your opponent's power side.** If he is in a left stance, circle to his left; if he is in a southpaw stance, circle to his right.

4. **Keep your stance when circling.** Do not expose your centerline. Squaring eliminates some of the power of your rear hand. In order to maintain your stance, your rear leg must take a slightly bigger step than your lead leg.

5. **Think of your lead foot as the pivot point**, around which the rest of your body moves. Keep your lead foot on the centerline, and your lead hand in line with your lead leg.

6. **Take many small adjustment steps**, rather than one large step with your rear foot.

Lateral movement (side-to-side) may give you an advantage over circular movement, because you eliminate the tendency to circle yourself into a trapped position. When your opponent starts to circle, practice cutting him off by stepping to the side and toward the direction he is circling.

THREAT AND RESPONSE

Fighting is by nature threatening, and the more you can make your techniques interfere with your opponent's techniques, the more threatening you will appear. At the beginning of a fight, feel your opponent out to determine his reactions to specific moves. Will your attack hurt him and force him to an inferior position? Will he respond with a strong counter-attack? The outcome of a fight is affected by your opponent's responses.

Through an understanding of which moves draw a particular response, you can create openings in your opponent's defense. For example, you may notice that every time you throw a front kick, he tenses and lowers his guard. Make a mental note of this reaction, so that later in the fight when you throw the front kick again, you know that he will lower his guard and leave an opening at the head. Tensing also implies fear, or at least respect. When your opponent is tense, he is unable to respond with a strong counter-attack.

Try these exercises on **FREEZING**:

Exercise 8

You can momentarily freeze your opponent's offensive weapons by hitting or touching that weapon. When your opponent tenses the part of his body that is struck (his hand, for example), he will momentarily be unable to use it against you. When working on this concept, start with your lead hand. Because your lead hand is closer to the target, it is usually faster than your rear hand. You can therefore use it early in the fight to determine how tense your opponent is. Start by whipping your lead hand quickly at his guard (like snatching a wet towel). Can you get him to raise or lower his hands by whipping the strike at a high or low target? Can you get him to flinch or tense? Now twitch your shoulder or hip prior to throwing a strike or kick. If your opponent tenses, he is also likely to react to a fake. You can now freeze him with a sudden, unexpected move.

Freeze your opponent's hands by whipping your jab at his guard. Throw a side thrust kick to the opening at his mid-section.

Exercise 9

Create an opening for the side thrust kick by freezing your opponent's hands. When you have touched your opponent's gloves a couple of times, make your jab "stick" to his glove, while pressing against it. His natural tendency will be to keep his hand in contact with yours and press back. You can now raise his guard just by moving your hand, and create the opening you need at the mid-section.

Note: Normally, I don't recommend keeping your hand extended. But if the move has a calculated advantage, then use it.

You must also consider how threatening your opponent is. Perhaps you can meet his threats with a strong counter-attack that will shift his mental focus? Because each situation differs, the type and number of moves you choose will vary. But if they don't hinder your opponent enough to lessen the threat, you must re-evaluate the situation. Also look at threats that have not yet been fully developed. Sometimes it is possible to see what your opponent intends to use against you later.

It is not necessarily what you are doing right that will win a fight; it can as easily be what your opponent is doing wrong. You should therefore look at it both ways: You can win by relying on your strength, but you can also win by relying on your opponent's weakness.

STRENGTH AND WEAKNESS

Every fighter has certain strengths and weaknesses. Your leg kick may be your strength, so you use it often. Your opponent's hook may be his strength, so he uses it often. Even though these techniques are not the same, the fight may become a battle of whether you can out-kick your opponent to the legs, or whether he can out-hook you to the head. If his strength is equal to your strength, and you use your strengths against each other, you will essentially be standing toe-to-toe with your opponent trading blows. In other words, not very sound strategy.

Once you learn about your opponent's strength, you have two options:

1. Work to **defeat it** (which will be difficult, since it is his strength).

2. Work to **make your strength stronger** than his strength.

The idea is to make your leg kick more destructive than his hook. No matter how much he relies on the hook, it can't out-do your leg kick. Once you start doing damage with your leg kick, your opponent's focus will begin to split, and you will take the fight from him mentally.

You can also think of the concept of strength and weakness in terms of what is worst for your opponent. If you favor a certain technique, but your opponent is proficient at defending against it, what seemed to be your strength may not be. There may be another technique that you don't think you can use proficiently, but if your opponent isn't good at defending against it, you can still use it to your advantage. Strategy is not about using your best technique; it is about using whatever technique is most difficult for your opponent to deal with at the given moment.

THE ELEMENT OF TIME

The element of time (which is not the same as timing) is important in all stages of the fight. A fight can be broken down into several "little fights," and time can be thought of as the number of moves used to win each one of these little fights. Think of time as economy of motion. If you use two moves to do something that you could have done in one move (taking an additional step before throwing a kick, for example), you waste time. When you waste time, you give your opponent additional time. Avoid prancing or telegraphing your kicks. If you have a traditional martial arts background and have fought in the point tournaments, you may have developed a habit of staying very light on your lead leg, so as to be ready to score with a lead leg kick. But, if you use this habit in kickboxing, you will lose time by telegraphing the kick, unless you do it intentionally to set your opponent up. You can also lose time by not being aggressive enough or by making needless defensive moves, as could happen if you

are timid and try to protect yourself against imaginary danger. Extra moves without purpose are also made by fighters who lack skill and simply don't know what to do. How many additional moves you make (how you utilize time) can help your opponent determine your experience level and anxiety. The same is true regarding your opponent. Because most of us fear the unknown, the more you know about your opponent, the more strategy-minded you can become. How you fight depends, to some degree, on how your opponent fights.

Moves that do not promote your power or position, or moves that do not actively interfere with your opponent's power or position, are a waste of time and give your opponent the opportunity to use his weapons more effectively. If you present your opponent with one unneeded move, his gain may be slight. But if you waste two or three moves, any worthy opponent can use the additional time to his advantage. If you come into the fight unprepared and fail to take advantage of your position, strength, and openings, you will give your opponent all the strategic advantages.

Thought provoker: Which technique takes less time:

1. A double jab followed by a lead leg front kick?
2. A jab, a rear cross, and a lead leg front kick?

Both combinations involve two strikes and a kick but, in theory, the jab/cross/lead leg front kick should be slightly faster, because the jab and the cross work off opposite hands, while two successive jabs work off the same hand, and therefore require a start/stop between strikes. However, an interesting thing occurs when adding kicks to this concept. At first, one might think that a jab followed by a lead leg front kick is slower (because they work off the same side) than a rear cross followed by a lead leg front kick, but there really is not much difference because, as you retrieve the jab, you can simultaneously extend your lead leg front kick. In fact, a jab/lead leg front kick may be slightly faster because they are closer to your opponent. There is no start/stop required, because the hand and foot are not the same body part. So, which is more beneficial? Well, it depends on the situation. Which is more powerful? In theory, a rear cross is more powerful than a jab, because it has a longer distance to travel, but again it depends on the situation. Is your opponent stationary or moving toward you? Is your speed and timing better with the jab or with the rear cross?

How far should you go defensively? It is difficult, if not impossible, to defend all targets simultaneously. You can score points by breaking your opponent's focus. Because it takes longer to react than to act, by being the one who initiates a technique, you have the added benefit of time. Giving your opponent *multiple points of pain* will inhibit his ability to fight back. One strike to one target (one point of pain) is easier to defend and counter than many strikes to multiple targets. You should therefore throw your strikes with *broken rhythm*, sometimes slowing down or pausing, and sometimes exploding with a combination. Many fighters are headhunters. By varying your targets from high to low, and from kicking to punching, you will create *sensory overload*: a state of confusion and chaos, where your opponent doesn't know what to do next.

Good defense is essential, but some moves are unnecessary and dangerous. Let's say that you are a master at upper body movement. You slip strikes with ease; your opponent seems unable to hit you. In fact, you could fight a full round without taking a single blow. (If your opponent let's you go a full round without throwing a single counter-strike with a damaging effect, he has some serious study to do on the chess game, but that's beside the point). The point is that there is a time when, no matter how good your defense, you must give your offense a chance. Fights are not won by defense alone. You must land something in order to score. As a general rule, two to three defensive moves in a row should be enough before converting to offense. Your ultimate goal is not to avoid getting hit, but to take your opponent out. This can only be accomplished with offense.

If your defense is very good, use it to trigger your offensive move. Let's talk about the *first touch concept* some more.

THOUGHTS ON SPEED AND COUNTER-STRIKING

First touch means allowing your defensive move to trigger a counter-strike. This ties directly in with speed. If you want to increase your speed, you need a catalyst, something that triggers this greater speed. The second reason to use first touch is strategic and ties directly in with timing. Let's explore first touch in conjunction with the catch.

A catch is classified as a technique that meets power with power: Your opponent's strike is stopped dead in its track. This means that his knuckles will be in the palm of your hand. While a parry relies on redirecting the strike rather than stopping it, and a block relies on a perpendicular path against the strike, the catch relies on an exact opposite path. An elbow block, for example, comes down on top of the strike or kick, and a forearm block meets the strike from the side. But, because these blocks do not meet power directly with power, they don't classify as a catch.

> Keep in mind that any block, parry, kick, replanting of the foot after kicking, or other defensive move can be worked off the first touch concept.

The catch meets power with power and stops a strike dead in its track.

So, isn't the catch contradictory to the laws of motion? Isn't it more economical to redirect the strike with a parry rather than stopping it with a catch? At this level, you must choose what is most appropriate for the situation. We are, after all, playing chess, which means that you should be as unpredictable as possible and use any means (within the rules of the game) to gain a strategic advantage. One benefit of the catch is that it stops your opponent's advance to where he can't take advantage of his momentum. An immediate follow-up is therefore not likely. When he stalls, it offsets his timing, and he must reset his body's balance before continuing. This gives you a time advantage. But your advantage in time is only as good as your ability to use it. With this in mind, we will now start working on the first touch concept for the catch to trigger your counter-strike.

The catch and counter: An effective catch stops your opponent's strike early enough to avoid the risk of it swatting your own hand into your face. Protect your centerline by bringing your hand toward it and forward at a forty-five degree angle. Keep your elbow down to ensure that the punch is caught in the palm of your hand, and does not ricochet off your hand and strike your head.

The next step is allowing the catch to trigger your counter-strike. Let's start with a lead hand catch and a rear hand counter-strike. Timing is important. If you use a two-count for the catch and counter, you take too long and are not likely to land your rear cross. Your opponent will either block your strike, or worse, launch a counter-strike to the open target created by the extension of your arm. Thus, the catch and counter should be almost simultaneous. You may need to press the attack by taking a step forward with your strike.

When you land your rear cross, it is equally important not to stop. Again, you want to take advantage of the moment your opponent is stunned from your blow. This is one reason I recommend ending a combination with a lead strike. If you throw the jab every time you have thrown a power punch, it enables you to land more strikes, because your apparent speed will increase due to the forcing of an additional strike. You will also reset your body's balance.

Next, try catching and countering with your rear hand (both moves are done with the same hand). This is a tiny bit slower than using opposite hands. Again, extend your hand slightly toward your opponent's punch and allow the force of his strike to push your hand an inch or two to the rear. This helps you re-chamber for a quick follow-up with that same hand. Again, you must keep your opponent from timing his counter-strike to the extension of your arm.

The catch and counter also works with hooks and uppercuts. When catching a hook, bring your hand across your centerline and past it toward the opposite side of your

Regardless of whether you use your lead or rear hand for catching, you must bring it forward along your centerline, catch with the palm of your hand, and rely on the first touch concept to trigger your counter-strike.

head. If your opponent throws a hook to the left side of your head, use your right hand to catch, and vice versa. Turn your body slightly to the side, which will chamber your free hand. You can now follow with a counter-hook or straight strike. Keep your free hand in the high guard position until it is ready to strike.

Catching a hook requires a larger pivot in your body and may seem awkward at first.

When catching an uppercut, drop your hand by pivoting your elbow to the outside. This momentarily leaves an opening at the side of your head. It is therefore important to bring your hand back to the high guard position as soon as you complete the catch.

Glove Up with Keith

When I first became involved in kickboxing, my coach insisted that I end all combinations with a jab. His reasoning was that by doing so, I would reset my body's balance and stance. I have since expanded on this theory. I now preach that you should always try to end your combination with a lead punch or kick. In addition to resetting your body's balance and stance, this tends to force you to throw an extra strike. All too often, we land a good rear cross or a solid rear uppercut, then stand back waiting for something to happen. If you condition yourself to ending your combinations with a lead technique, you will discover that you are usually in a much better position offensively, and as a result, defensively.

In order to make this a part of you, you must practice it in all aspects of training. Whether you are shadow boxing or working the heavy bag or the focus mitts, get in the habit of ending with a jab. Later, when you have conditioned yourself to doing that, vary your endings with different lead techniques (hook, uppercut, lead kick). When you land that big rear hand, force yourself to follow with the lead. That extra punch might just pave the way for a knockout.

DISTANCE

Remember, the fighter who controls distance controls the fight. If you can position for striking and get out of range of your opponent's retaliation, then you control the fight, regardless of how strong your opponent is. When you are too close to strike effectively, an increase in distance increases your power.

Distance is an interesting concept that is often deceiving. We normally think of distance by measuring the actual footage between ourselves and our opponent, or between our weapon and the target. Thus, distance can be decreased or increased by taking a step forward or back. But distance is also a measure of your reach. The reason this is important is because your reach is not the same all the time; your reach is not merely the length of your arm or leg. Furthermore, you can manipulate your reach without changing the actual footage to your target:

1. Increase your reach by **pivoting in the direction of the strike.** Pivoting, without pushing off or leaning toward the target, increases your reach with three to four inches. Quite significant, wouldn't you say? An additional benefit is that pivoting places the weight of your body behind the strike, and therefore increases your power.

2. Increase your reach by **bending your knees**, but without taking any steps at all. Your upper body will automatically move a few inches forward and place your shoulders closer to the target, increasing the reach of your punch significantly.

3. Increase your reach by **pushing off with your rear foot and elongating your body** toward the target. You can now use reach strategically. Circling your opponent at a distance outside of the apparent danger zone enables you to stay away from his line of attack. Yet, you can land strikes by pivoting, bending at the knees, or pushing off with your rear foot.

Try this exercise on **MANIPULATING DISTANCE**:

Exercise 10

1. Close distance by **stepping forward** with your lead foot, followed by your rear foot.

2. Close distance by **crouching**. This moves your upper body forward and increases your reach by several inches.

3. Close distance with a **shuffle-step**, pushing off with your rear foot to launch your lead foot forward, and then adjusting your stance with your rear foot.

4. Close distance with a **half-step forward with your lead foot only**, pushing off hard with your rear foot. Your stance will now be wider than normal. Once you have thrown your strike, retreat with your lead foot back to your normal stance. This allows you to land a strike and quickly get back to the Safety Zone. The disadvantage is that it doesn't allow you to land a combination easily. Stepping forward with your lead foot is only the first half of the shuffle-step. So once you land your strike, you must make a split second decision whether to step forward and follow with additional strikes, or step back to long range again. In order to throw a powerful combination, your stance can be neither too wide, nor too narrow.

5. Close distance with a **cross-over step**. This is most commonly seen with the side thrust kick. Bring your rear foot forward behind your lead foot, until your legs are crossed. I usually modify this a bit and take a half-step forward with my rear foot only, so that it is side by side with my lead foot rather than crossed behind. This eliminates the danger of losing balance from the crossed stance.

6. Close distance by **stepping with your rear foot first the way one would normally walk**. However, I usually don't recommended this, as your centerline will be vulnerable while you are in the process of stepping. This type of step would also reverse your stance from conventional to southpaw. This is not necessarily a disadvantage, but you should be aware of the consequences.

7. Close distance by **throwing a kick with your rear leg and planting the kicking foot forward** in the southpaw stance. This allows you to kick while in the process of closing distance, and therefore gives you a strategic advantage.

8. Close distance with a **switch-step, where your rear foot takes the position of your lead foot**, and vice versa, through a quick jump. You will now be in a crossed stance. What makes this technique interesting is that your upper body has not moved at all. Therefore, it appears as though the distance hasn't changed; your opponent thinks that he is still safely out of reach. But because your rear foot has taken the position of your lead foot, and because this foot is your foundation once you initiate a kick with your other leg, your upper body will automatically move forward until it is above your supporting foot, and your reach will increase by an equal distance.

The switch-step increases the reach of your kick by placing your supporting foot closer to your opponent. Because your upper body doesn't move, your opponent may not be aware of that you have reach on him.

9. When stepping back, only some of the principles apply. The **rearward shuffle** is perhaps the most common way to increase distance. I normally don't recommend the cross-over, because it doesn't serve any purpose when stepping back. Most retreats happen because your opponent moves forward. Taking a strike when you are in a crossed stance is detrimental to your balance.

10. You can also increase distance by **centering your weight above your rear foot**. This moves your upper body slightly to the rear, without moving your foundation. Use any move that places your weight above your rear foot briefly (rear slip for example) and time it to a specific strike. You are naturally vulnerable when your weight is to the rear.

DISTANCE WHEN KICKING

Your balance is your foundation. Without balance all your techniques, concepts, and strategies will fail. Balance relates directly to power, which is why it is so important to have a balanced stance before striking or kicking. But balance also directly affects your reach. If you are very close to your opponent and throw a front kick with your rear leg, you are not likely to succeed. When you raise your rear leg to kick, your upper body will automatically move a few inches forward above your supporting lead foot for balance. The kick will now be much too close. But this does not mean that you have to abandon rear front kicks at close range. By stepping with your supporting foot to the side just prior to kicking, you don't only adjust for distance, you also position off your opponent's attack line. This concept is called *positioning for kick and distance*, and has both a technical and a strategic advantage. Technical in the sense that you adjust the distance to fit the particular kick you are throwing, and strategic in the sense that you give yourself the ultimate position of power. After you land the kick, your opponent must turn toward you to again place you on the attack line.

Throwing a rear front kick from close range (left) may make the kick seem crowded. Adjust by positioning to the side and off the attack line (right).

You must also consider your opponent's movement in relation to you. There are two approaches you can take when positioning for kick and distance:

1. **Initiate** movement to a side angle.

2. **Wait** until your opponent initiates movement.

Which is better? At first, you might say that it is better to initiate movement, as this makes you the leader and places you in control of the fight. However, this also means that you are expending more energy than your opponent in an effort to move around him. If you can utilize as little movement as possible, you won't tire as quickly. But through movement comes power, so if you don't utilize movement, you are not likely to be powerful. This seems like a contradiction, but there is one factor that you should not overlook: **If your opponent moves into your kick, it has essentially the same power effect as if you move forward when throwing the kick.** As long as your timing is good, you may therefore want to allow your opponent to initiate movement.

TIMING

Timing relates directly to power and distance. If you strike an instant too late, you will jam your own strike and stifle power. If you strike an instant too soon, you will lack optimum reach and penetrating force. The same is true for defense. If you block or bob and weave an instant too late, you will absorb much of the

power of your opponent's strike. And if your counter-strike is not perfectly timed to your opponent's opening, it may ricochet off his block and lose much of the power.

Timing is the ability to take advantage of your opponent's targets, movement, or power by executing precise strikes, blocks, or movement when both your and your opponent's positions are ideal. We often don't consider that timing is also the ability to hinder your opponent's access to targets by executing precise strikes, blocks, or movement when both your and your opponent's positions are ideal.

For the purpose of kickboxing, timing is defined as **the time it takes a fighter to recognize an opening and deliver a strike before the opening disappears.** Or, if thinking defensively, to catch or intercept a strike before it reaches you, and counter to the open target on your opponent. Good timing means that you deliver the strike when it will inflict the greatest amount of damage. Timing must be precise for optimum results.

For example, an opening might exist for one or several seconds, but it is only during a precise moment that you will do the most damage.

A fighter with excellent timing delivers the strike at the precise moment his opponent is in optimum range. Many factors determine your timing, including conditioning, training regimen, and inherent ability. There is not much we can do about good genetics or inherent ability, so we should focus on conditioning and training. When a fighter begins to tire, his timing suffers. You should therefore train for muscular endurance and cardiovascular fitness, including plenty of sparring with varied opponents. This will improve your timing against different skill levels and give you the opportunity to test your timing against a variety of people: some move better than others, some have speed, and others have power. When you can hit a variety of opponents consistently, your timing is sharp.

Timing and broken rhythm: Timing is the ability to create an opening and land a strike before the opening disappears. The more you know about your opponent, the easier it is to take advantage of him. It is not possible to cover all openings at all times, and every time your opponent throws a strike or kick, he will automatically create an opening on himself, usually close to the arm or leg he extends toward you. Likewise, focusing on offense and defense simultaneously is difficult for most people, so when your opponent throws as strike, he will probably not be thinking about defending the counter right at that moment.

Timing ties in with broken rhythm. It is easy to get in tune with your own rhythm; it is more difficult to get in tune with your opponent's rhythm, at least to the point that you can exploit it. If your opponent nails you with his jab every time you get ready to advance, it gets frustrating real fast. What enables him to do this is that his timing exactly matches your rhythm, and he is waiting for you to make the first move. There are several things you can do at this point, including throwing a fake to draw his jab. But one of the more effective and simple strategies is to speed up your own strikes considerably. This will break the beat of your opponent's jab. Remember, his jab lands because he is in perfect tune with your rhythm. Your strikes don't necessarily have to be powerful, only fast. This does require that you have determination to move in, despite the risk of taking a strike in the process. You can play your timing against both your opponent's offense and defense.

Using timing to place your opponent on the canvas: Let's look at a scenario that requires you to defend against a round house kick thrown to your head. You can evade the kick, or you can block it. If you choose evasion, you can do so by stepping back or, if your timing is good, by ducking. Evasion does not only leave your hands free to pursue offense, it is also likely to leave your opponent in a vulnerable position when the momentum of his kick is allowed to continue past the target. The drawback is that you must reset your body's balance before being able to counter. Even though your hands are free, you are not likely to be within range or position to use them the moment the kick misses. Try to time a kick to your opponent's supporting leg in an attempt to place him on the canvas.

Evasion can also work against a low kick to the leg,

but is a little trickier because a low kick is usually faster and better concealed than a high kick, and therefore more difficult to pick up on in advance. If your opponent is in the habit of kicking or sweeping your lead leg, you can "give" him the leg in an attempt to draw a kick from him. It is easier to time your defense if you know in advance what is coming. When your opponent attempts to kick your lead leg, withdraw your leg so that his kick misses. The fact that you are drawing the kick from your opponent places you in charge of the fight.

When your opponent's momentum continues past the target, he will be in an inferior position with his back turned partly toward you. You can counter to his supporting leg; however, because you are also on one foot, it may be quicker to counter with a side thrust kick to his mid-section. Because of your opponent's unstable stance, such a kick is likely to knock him back or to the canvas.

Draw a leg kick from your opponent. The moment the kick misses, throw a full power side thrust kick to place him on the canvas.

You can also block your opponent's kick, or step in to jam it simultaneous to blocking. Regardless of what you do, the moment you block is the time to take advantage of your opponent's supporting leg. He will be on one foot with a narrow base, so taking his balance is easier than when he is in a solid stance.

Placing your opponent on the canvas has many benefits. When your opponent goes down, he must expend energy getting back up. Going down also affects him mentally by taking his confidence. Going down always looks bad to the crowd and judges.

The importance of speed in timing: Speed does not necessarily mean that you must be faster than your opponent. Rather, it is correct timing of speed that is important. Timing involves the ability to be precise with the speed that you do have. Whether your speed is faster or slower than your opponent's speed, it should interfere with his strikes, kicks, or movement. In other words, a slower speed will benefit you sometimes, and a faster speed at other times, and a broken or elusive speed still at other times.

You can be cursed with poor speed and still have good timing. For one thing, it is not only how fast your opponent throws his strike or kick that is important, but also how fast he withdraws his hand or foot, how well he moves, and how well he covers his openings. You can also watch and wait for your opponent to initiate a strike, and the moment he does, you parry it, let it pass over your shoulder, or simply side-step by an inch or two, placing yourself at closer range, which allows you to strike the created opening or causes your opponent to walk into your strike. Much of timing is about counter-striking, and a good way to learn this is by touching your opponent's striking weapon, using that touch as a cue to set your counter-strike in motion.

When working on speed in timing, first look to see what is happening. It is easy to fall into the trap of throwing punches just to throw punches. Once you have learned to look, tell yourself that you will not initiate a strike. Rather, when your opponent strikes, you will block, parry, redirect, make it miss, etc. and counter off that block or miss. If your opponent has superior speed, first figure out if he throws just one strike or a combination of strikes. Your opportunity to counter is in the lull between strikes or combinations. For example, if he throws a combination, you have

only to pick off his shots and counter the moment he pauses, or pick off his shots and press the attack slightly by taking small one-inch steps forward. This places you in range to counter in the middle of his combination, while he is still absorbed in offense.

Study your opponent's strengths. Nothing disturbs a fighter more than if you can mess with his superiority, because if you take this from him, he has little left to use against you.

Also consider any lapses in your opponent's mental capacity, for example, a distraction that momentarily splits his focus. My experience is that when using a mental distraction, your window of opportunity will be very small, and if you miss it, your opponent is not as likely to fall for the same trap again. In physical timing, however, you can often counter the same technique over and over, before your opponent learns to do something different.

When practicing timing, you must be prepared to move in and take advantage of your opponent's openings. To be effective with this, you must display determination and set aside any fears. I feel the underlying factor when learning timing is that it is okay to take a strike or two in training, in order to learn how to press the attack.

Keith's Knockout Advice

Every aspect of fighting has an aspect of timing. This includes blocking, movement, and footwork. Defensive timing is your ability to move or block at the precise moment, thwarting your opponent's defensive goal. Good defensive timing opens up the opportunity to turn your defensive blocks into strikes. Timing allows you to meet the strike rather than waiting for it. Good timing in your footwork allows you to be within range to strike, or out of range to be hit. As you train, fine-tune your timing in each part of your repertoire. A fighter with well-timed offense, defense, and footwork is a force to be reckoned with.

PREMATURE ATTACKS

An attack that is made without sufficient preparation is called a premature attack. Especially at the amateur ranks, fighters tend to go all out right from the start. A premature attack may be theoretically unsound, but if your opponent's defense is lacking, the attack is often successful. As a strategic fighter, I usually don't attack prematurely without a specific plan. That is not to say that I don't throw the first strike, or that I don't throw overwhelming combinations. There is a difference. The premature attacker relies on his ability to end the fight with this one explosive attack. If he doesn't, he will be physically spent within the first twenty seconds of the round.

The premature attack may be difficult to meet initially.

If your opponent engages in a *premature attack*, it is usually better to concentrate on good defense until the attack dies out. **Know that the attack will die out! Nobody can go at that pace for the whole round, and the next round, and the next . . .** Your opponent is relying on ending the fight with this one big blast; that's why it is so important that you remain calm and employ good defense, which is not as difficult as it sounds. Crouching, with weight forward, chin down, and hands high, is usually enough to protect against most blows. Furthermore, it requires very little energy. When your opponent is spent, you still have the strength to counter, and effectively so. Your positions are now unequal. In essence, through his premature attack, your opponent has turned superiority over to you. He just made a big strategic mistake!

Note that the reason premature attacks often fail against good defense is because your opponent is trying to break through without any specific plan, and with only part of his forces developed (leaving out set-up, positioning, distance, timing, and fakes). However, it is a mistake to assume that you can meet all premature attacks with good defense.

Although a premature attack may be ill prepared, the fighter who goes all out at least possesses the fighting spirit and the will to win.

Try these exercises on **PREMATURE ATTACKS**:

Exercise 11

It is important to keep your emotions in check and avoid rushing in against a strategic fighter. Practice poise by working your way in methodically. This allows you to see the full picture and not miss openings or weaknesses in your opponent's defense.

Exercise 12

Evaluate what kind of fighter you are. Are you the aggressive type who attacks without sufficient preparation, or do you have a plan? Can you keep your cool and work your way in strategically? When you get tired or hurt, do you want to quit, or does it fuel you and give you a second wind?

SUPERIORITY

Ask yourself: What is a superior fighter? Is he stronger, faster, tougher, more intelligent? Does he have better timing? If he possesses all those qualities to a greater degree than you, my advice is, don't mingle with him. But chances are that he may only be superior in one or two of those areas, and that you are superior in the others. In full-contact sparring, those fighters with superior power are usually feared the most. But superior power does not necessarily mean superiority. A weaker fighter can still win if his strategy is good, and will therefore be the superior fighter. Let's say that at the beginning of the fight, the fighters are on equal terms. If, during the course of the fight, one fighter concentrates his attack on some weak point in his opponent's position, he may succeed at reducing his opponent's strength. A fighter can also gain superiority by making smaller sacrifices for some greater advantage.

The best position is usually toward your opponent's back, as this limits the use of most of his weapons. If your opponent is in a left stance (left foot forward), try to position toward his left side to eliminate the use of his right hand. Should you move toward his right side instead, you will be moving toward his power side, and run the risk of walking into his stronger rear techniques.

In a recent sparring match, I was fighting from a left stance against an opponent who was comfortable in both left and right stances, and would switch back and forth throughout the fight. This made him very unpredictable. What bothered me the most was that he was able to land his lead hook to the side of my head time and time again. When I tried to move to a superior position toward his back, I would actually be moving into the path of his strong lead hook, thus worsening the impact of the strike. The position of superiority concept didn't work!

My opponent was skilled at both the left and right hooks. However, I noticed that regardless of which technique he used, he always used his lead hand. In other words, if he threw a left hook, he would also be in a left stance, and if he threw a right hook, he would be in a right stance. This made me realize that if I did the opposite of what I would normally do and move toward his power side rather than away from it, I could force him to switch stance whenever it suited me. If I moved toward his left, he would switch to a left stance; if I moved toward his right, he would switch to a right stance. This made fighting predictable, placing me in control of the chessboard. After deciding which stance I wanted my opponent to fight from, I could draw that stance from him by moving toward that side. In addition, I knew when he would throw the lead hook, and therefore be ready to defend against it. My strategy caused him a great deal of frustration.

Try this exercise on **SUPERIORITY**:

Exercise 13

1. You can gain superior strategy by adapting within the fight. **Work on switching from circular to linear movement within the same round.** Use circular movement when working on set-ups, and linear movement if you land a good blow and can safely come forward.

2. **Use explosive moves** when your opponent is at a distinct disadvantage. **Use short and patient moves** when working your way from the outside to the inside.

3. Sometimes you can gain superiority by sacrificing a move for some greater advantage. If you are superior at close range, you may choose to **take a strike in order to get past your opponent's long range techniques.**

SIZING IT UP

Fighting cannot be learned by rote. Don't follow rules and principles blindly, but use them as guides when selecting your moves.

When you plan your strategy, think in the following terms:

1. **What does he threaten?** Make note of your opponent's moves. Does he deliberately try to take a specific target, or does he move without purpose?

2. **What moves are available to me?** What can I do to create openings or destroy my opponent's position? Avoid wasting time and effort by throwing techniques without purpose. Focus on specific targets. Going for an open target is the first step; creating an open target is the second step. Once you learn how to create desirable targets, your opponent's movement, or the position of his guard, won't matter much.

3. **What is my opponent's best reply?** How can I counter-attack? How can I use his offense to trigger my counter-strike? (Concept: **FIRST TOUCH**)

4. **How can I intensify pressure?** How can I break through my opponent's defense while keeping my own defense intact? What are his weak points? What is the difference between a premature attack and sensory overload?

5. **How can I restrict his mobility?** Fight for room to maneuver. In what ways are angles advantageous? When should I use linear movement, and when should I use circular movement?

6. **How can I be deceptive?** Use weight shift, half-stepping, and fakes (will be discussed shortly).

7. **How can I end the fight quickly?** Never forget your final objective.

Chess masters stay several moves ahead of their opponents, they work on creating openings, and they have patience. At the beginning of a fight, size up your opponent to determine his strong and weak points, and his reactions to specific moves. Be flexible and imaginative in your fighting. Try to pick up on your opponent's set-ups, positioning, distance, timing, and fakes. After your next sparring session, ask yourself what you learned. If all you can say is that you got a couple of good shots in, and that you walked away with a bunch of bumps and bruises, you haven't really learned anything. Be ready to take advantage of your opponent's mistakes, but don't underestimate your competition.

Checkmate!

Summary and review

In kickboxing, you are your own general. Rather than knowing how to employ your people, you must know how to employ your skills. Against an average opponent, perhaps you can afford to lose some of your strength and still win, but against a skilled opponent, you must rely on strategy as well as physical skill. Techniques can be broken down into punches, kicks, and defensive blocks and moves. Strategy can be broken down into timing, footwork, movement, and mental focus.

You will face many different types of opponents during your career, and few will be exactly like you

in physical build or strategy. Studying the inherent strengths and weaknesses of each opponent can help you decide on a course of action.

Timing and counter-striking

- Much about landing a good strike or kick is about timing. The best time to strike is when your opponent is in the process of striking or kicking, as all his focus (physical and mental) is on his technique. He will also leave an opening on his body or head for your counter-strike, which saves you the step of creating the opening.

- When your opponent throws a jab or rear cross, evade it by stepping to the outside of the strike (away from his centerline). You will now be within range to counter, yet off the attack line. Counter to his ribs under his outstretched punching arm, or to his head over the top of his arm and from a side angle.

- You can also avoid a straight strike from long range by ducking or slipping. If you can counter within the same move, you will increase your chances of taking the opening. Try countering with a hook, an elbow, or a straight jab or cross to your opponent's mid-section simultaneous to your evasive move.

- You can increase power by taking a step simultaneous to countering. Because your opponent is likely to have some forward momentum, especially if he is of the aggressive type, you can add your momentum to his. Any strike to the solar plexus is likely to knock the wind out of him. If you strike higher to the chest, you are likely to knock him back.

Stepping off the attack line

- Stepping off the attack line works both against left and right punches. It is generally a little safer to step away from, rather than toward, your opponent's centerline.

- When stepping toward your opponent's centerline, and as long as you are off the attack line and throw your counter-strike while your opponent is still hung up on missing with his strike, you are still one step ahead in strategy.

- It goes without saying that you should keep your non-striking hand high in defense, and keep your chin tucked toward your chest or behind your shoulder for protection, even when you have the upper hand.

- Stepping off the attack line and throwing a strike works even if your opponent isn't throwing anything. Try it with an uppercut.

- Step to the side and throw the uppercut underneath your opponent's guard. When stepping left, throw the right uppercut, and when stepping right, throw the left uppercut.

Step to the superior position and throw an uppercut underneath your opponent's guard.

- If you have forward motion and your knees are bent, you can push off against the floor simultaneously to striking, and gain the power needed for an immediate knockout.

- Also try uppercutting to the solar plexus. Such a strike may lift your opponent off the floor and end in a knockdown.

Countering with a kick

- Time a front or side thrust kick to your opponent's jab or rear cross. Evade his strike by inclining your upper body slightly to the rear simultaneous to throwing the kick.

- Since your legs are longer than your opponent's arms, you have reach on him. Again, there will be an opening at his ribs.

- If you counter with a round house kick, you must step off the attack line first. If possible, step away from your opponent's centerline.

- Legally, you can also round house kick your opponent's legs instead of his mid-section. The same is not true for the front or side thrust kick. Since your opponent is in the middle of offense, and it's not practical to strike while on one leg, there is little risk that he will use a shin block to defend a kick to his legs.

Defending the jab with a spinning kick

- Use the spinning back kick or spinning heel kick as defense against a jab. Again, timing is important. At the initiation of your opponent's jab, start the rotation in your upper body for the spinning back kick to his mid-section.

- The spin helps you evade your opponent's jab, especially if you kick high, as this requires you to incline your upper body to the rear, increasing distance.

- If you make a wider sweeping motion of your leg, you will impact with your heel to your opponent's solar plexus, or head, if the kick is thrown high.

- The spinning heel kick may be even more effective as defense against a rear cross. Your opponent's head is exposed on the same side as his striking arm, which is also the side your kick will impact.

When your opponent throws the rear cross, start the spin for the spinning heel kick.

• If your opponent's guard is up, he will probably hold it slightly forward of his face. This will not provide adequate protection to the side of the head: your target for the spinning heel kick.

Jamming your opponent's techniques

• Use jamming as an offensive tool. The best kicks to jam are round house kicks, because they impact from the side, and you don't meet power with power.

• Jamming a kick destroys the power of the kick by eliminating full extension in the kicking leg, and places you at closer range where you can more easily follow up while your opponent is stalled from your attack.

• If your jamming technique is forceful, you will knock your opponent off balance. Even if he doesn't go all the way down, it will give you superiority of the fight.

• Try to inflict damage simultaneously to jamming; for example, drop your elbow into your opponent's shin or thigh, while using body momentum to knock him off balance.

Catching a kick

• Try catching your opponent's kick in the crook of your arm. This works best with round house kicks. The moment you catch the kick, you must follow-up. You have many opportunities, even if the rules don't allow for takedowns.

• The moment you catch the kick, attack your opponent's supporting leg. He is already concerned about his balance, so this adds to the aggravation.

• Try an upward knee strike to the back of the leg you have caught. If you catch your opponent's left leg, knee with your left leg diagonally to his leg. Make the strike quick to avoid losing your own balance.

A quick knee to the back of your opponent's caught leg is an unexpected attack that may further lift your opponent off balance.

Superiority against the aggressive opponent

• Experiment with getting the upper hand against an aggressive opponent. If he throws a barrage of blows, try to cover up and plow forward, using your momentum and weight to move him back. Keep your cool.

• When your opponent is forced to step back or gets bumped off balance, he will lose some of his aggressive edge. A well-placed strike timed to his attempt to regain balance might give you the upper hand both physically and mentally.

• If your opponent's aggressiveness doesn't accomplish the job of ending the fight, he will tire quickly. Note that when your opponent gets tired, his strikes will lose their sting and he will have a tendency to fight with his mouth open. A fighter who fails to bite down on his mouthpiece is more susceptible to a knockout.

• When your opponent is signaling to you that he is getting tired (through increased sloppiness, by leaving his mouth open, etc.), you are beginning to win the fight mentally.

Lead attack strategy

• Experiment with the benefits of using lead hand or foot attacks. The rear attack is often stronger than the lead, but the lead is quicker.

- Your lead hand or foot can keep your centerline protected, and allows you to ward off your opponent's attack and move to close range. Take advantage of first touch.

- Use a lead leg front kick to stop your opponent's kick. The moment he raises his foot off the floor, intercept it with the front kick to his shin or thigh. This will stop the kick and serve as a distraction every time he attempts to extend his leg to kick. Counter-strike the moment you have stalled your opponent's advance.

The "tip" with the ball of your foot to your opponent's shin, thigh, or hip has the effect of halting his advance.

- Quick lead kicks to the legs, body, or arms can be good strategy, even if they don't do a great deal of physical damage initially. Many successive blows to the same target will irritate and get to your opponent mentally, until he wants to protect that target.

Parrying strategy

- Attempt to establish the superior position away from your opponent's centerline. When you avoid an attack by pivoting to the outside, it places you in a superior position toward your opponent's back.

- When your opponent jabs, parry his arm behind his elbow, simultaneously stepping to the outside and throwing a rear cross.

- Parry your opponent's strike behind his elbow, stay at close range, and attack the back of his leg.

This works well against a southpaw, because you can target his lead leg without using a great deal of movement.

When fighting a southpaw, a forceful parry to her lead arm places you in the superior position for a cut kick.

FAKES AND DECEPTION

"I make the enemy see my strengths as weaknesses and my weaknesses as strengths, while I cause his strengths to become weaknesses and discover where he is not strong."
~ Ho Yen-hsi

How good a liar are you? Some people say they never lie; it is immoral. But in order to progress as a fighter, being deceptive is not only okay, it is sound strategy and, therefore, desirable. In kickboxing, it is ethical to purposely mislead your opponent for the sake of your own security.

This section covers:

- Fakes: the art of deception
- Choosing targets for the fake
- Strike and kick similarities
- Faking and the chess game
- In the gym
- Faking and the overhand strike
- To train a rat
- Summary and review

FAKES: THE ART OF DECEPTION

Faking is the art of making your opponent believe what is not there. A fake is designed to set your opponent up and create openings. Something as minor as the twitching of a leg can get your opponent to lower his guard enough to allow you to land a strike to his head. A fake can be thought of as a visual lie.

Note: Some people refer to fakes as "feints." Others say that a fake is a move intended to get your opponent to respond to a specific technique, while a feint is any subtle move intended to draw a reaction; for example, a short head movement that is not technique specific. To some people, there may be a difference between a fake and a feint, but for the purpose of this book, we will use them interchangeably.

Faking too many times in a row, without throwing an actual strike, may teach your opponent to ignore the fakes and stop reacting.

Faking without a proper follow-up is meaningless. You must also learn which fakes to use as the fight unfolds before you. All opponents are different and may not react the same to your fakes. Unless you know your opponent well, it is not possible to preplan your fakes.

There are two ways to throw your strikes:

1. **Disguise** them. Mix fakes in with the rest of your techniques, so that your opponent never knows which is a fake and which is a strike.

2. **Telegraph** them. Telegraphing is okay if you want to use the move as a set-up. Just make sure that you don't telegraph when you are not supposed to.

A fake must be convincing. If it doesn't look like a strike, your opponent will not react in the desired way. If you fake too often, your opponent will get used to the fake and stop reacting.

When you have determined your opponent's reaction to the fake, throw some actual strikes to keep him on his toes. When he becomes pre-occupied with defending against your strikes, revert back to faking in order to create the desired opening. The number of ways you can fake are many and up to your imagination. Try the following:

Faking punches: In general, faking a punch involves a short movement in your shoulder or hip. The movement is identical to throwing an actual strike, but is halted before full extension. You can fake punches by rotating your shoulder forward or by throwing a half-punch (extending the arm partially). Observe your opponent's reaction and follow with an appropriate punch or kick.

1. **Fake a jab with a half-punch** (extend your jab halfway only). Your opponent may react by moving his head slightly to the rear. When his head comes forward again, throw the jab for real. This type of fake must be done fairly quickly, so that your opponent does not have time to slip the real jab after the fake.

2. **Fake a double jab with a jab and a twitch of the same shoulder.** When your opponent reacts (by moving his hand to block, for example), follow with a lead hook.

3. **Fake a jab with a shoulder roll.** Move your lead shoulder forward in a small circle. Because your strikes originate in your body, your opponent will interpret this as a strike. Now, throw your rear cross instead.

4. **Fake both high to the head and low to the body.** Depending on your opponent's reaction, your real strike can follow either to the same target as the fake, or to a different target. In general, you should look at the target you are faking to.

Faking kicks: Faking a kick relies on a short movement in your hip, or you can raise your foot off the floor, as if you were going to throw the kick. Observe your opponent's reaction and follow with an appropriate punch or kick.

1. **Fake a round house kick by pivoting or twitching your hip.** When your opponent reacts, throw a punch instead. You can also fake the round house kick by actually throwing it a few times first to make your opponent a believer. Note his reaction each time. Does he lower his guard to block? Now fake the kick. What is your best follow up? Try raising your knee high in the round house kick motion. Now, bring your leg across your centerline and throw a spinning back kick.

2. **Fake a lead round house kick by bringing your knee up.** Then shuffle forward and throw a rear cross. The rear cross isn't the only possible follow-up. Experiment.

Fake a kick. When your opponent moves his guard, throw a rear cross to the opening.

Movement illusions: Faking also relates to your visual focus, your movement, and how you carry yourself. Can you use peripheral vision to strike a different target than what you are looking at? Can you use subtle moves and weight shifts to give your opponent a perception of movement? Can you appear timid when you are not in order to lure your opponent forward? One efficient way to fake demeanor may be to appear aggressive when you are really timid. This would also build your confidence.

Try these exercises on **MOVEMENT ILLUSIONS**:

Exercise 1

In order to strike an opening, you must first see the opening, but direct focus on the target may give away your intention. To avoid telegraphing through sight, focus directly on the target only if your purpose is to use that as a fake. Experiment with vision as a fake by looking at one target and striking to another.

Exercise 2

In general, it is easier to act (initiate a move) than to react (respond to a move). But if you know in advance which technique your opponent will throw, it will be easier to take the opening. This works especially well with the aggressive fighter. Experiment with drawing a punch through a fake. Start with a shoulder roll or a half-punch. When your opponent reacts and throws his punch, rely on the first touch concept (as discussed earlier), and time your counter-strike to the created opening.

Exercise 3

A broad shift in weight from one leg to the other creates the illusion of forward or reverse movement. Because your opponent has a tendency to mirror your moves, you can use this concept to lure him forward and into your strike, or to make him step back to create a gap.

Exercise 4

At long range, use your opponent's visual senses to lure him forward and into your strike. At short range, rely on your opponent's sense of touch. When shoulder-to-shoulder with your opponent, a weight shift to the rear will tempt him to come forward. When you feel his body press against yours, sidestep and allow his momentum to continue forward. Explode with a combination from your superior position to the side.

Exercise 5

Another fake you can try is a simple stomp with your foot, or a sudden and explosive move with your upper body. This often gives a threatening impression, making your opponent freeze.

CHOOSING TARGETS FOR THE FAKE

Many fighters are headhunters. Hunting the head is common with fakes, too. But if you always fake to the head and strike to the head, you will soon lose the element of surprise: You become predictable and your opponent stops reacting. I often see fighters fake to one area and strike to that same area. For example, you may fake a front kick to the solar plexus, and then throw the actual kick to the same target. Assuming that your opponent picks up on the fake, this will obviously not work, because the fake has trained your opponent to block this particular target. We will now look at:

1. How to successfully fake to the **same area** you intend to strike. When you fake to the same area you intend to strike, you must time the fake to your opponent's defensive move. Ask yourself how he is likely to react.

2. How to fake to a **different area** than the one you intend to strike.

Faking low, striking low: Create an opening at your opponent's ribs by raising your lead foot off the floor in the front kick motion. Your opponent drops his hand or elbow to block the kick. You wait until he retrieves his hand to the high guard position, and then throw the front kick to his ribs or gut.

Fake a front kick to the body. When your opponent raises her guard after attempting to block the fake, throw a front kick to the body.

Faking high, striking high: Fake a strike to the head and wait for your opponent to raise his guard. When the strike doesn't come, he will relax his guard again. Now, throw your strike.

Fake a strike to the head. When your opponent relaxes her guard after attempting to block the fake, throw a rear cross to the head.

A good way to create an opening at your opponent's head may be to throw the jab a couple of times and let him pick it off. Then fake the jab through a shoulder roll or half-punch, wait for your opponent to pick the strike (he will pick in the air, since no strike is actually thrown). This moves his guard away from his face for a split second. You can now throw a rear cross to the opening.

Faking low, striking high: In order to open the head, you can start by faking low to the body. Because most fighters look at the target they intend to strike, your focus must be on the target you are faking to, rather than the one you are striking. Thus, if you fake to the body but look your opponent in the eyes, the fake will probably not be realistic. When faking to the body, aim your fake low in order to draw the desired reaction. To produce a really effective fake, you must become a pretty good actor. In order to take advantage of the opening at the head, your timing between the fake and the strike must be slightly faster than if you threw the strike alone.

Fake a kick to the body. When your opponent lowers his guard, throw an overhand strike to the head.

As you can see, if you fake to an area different than the one you intend to strike, the beat between the fake and the strike must be very short. If you fake to the same area you intend to strike, the beat between the fake and the strike must be slightly longer to allow your opponent to reset his stance and create the desired opening.

Faking from different ranges: You can fake even when you are slightly out of range. This gives you an idea of how your opponent is likely to react. You will also confuse him when he never knows whether you will fake or strike. **A word of caution: Don't establish a pattern. We often fall into a set rhythm that lends predictability to our moves. Use a variety of fakes and strikes.** Staying loose in your shoulders tends to make your moves unpredictable and difficult to develop a strategy against.

The mid-range distance is the most dangerous to fight from. This is where your opponent can reach you with both short and long range techniques. Once you finish a combination, either stay on the inside, or move back to long range.

STRIKE AND KICK SIMILARITIES

Many strikes can be likened to specific kicks, and can therefore be thrown within the same movement, although not necessarily to the same target. Thus, you can fake a strike, get a reaction, and then throw a kick. For example:

1. A **jab** can be thought of as a **lead leg front kick**, because it follows the same path and is used much for the same purpose.

2. A **rear cross** can be thought of as a **rear leg front kick**.

3. A **hook** can be thought of as a **round house kick**.

Similarity between a jab and a lead leg front kick.

Similarity between a hook and a lead leg round house kick.

Try these exercises on **STRIKE AND KICK SIMILARITIES**:

Exercise 6

Throw a rear leg cut kick to your opponent's lead outside thigh. Then throw a lead leg cut kick to his lead inside thigh. When your opponent becomes a believer in the pattern of this combination, throw a hook to his ribs instead of the cut kick. Because the cut kick and the hook employ similar pivots in your body, the cut kick can be used as a fake to conceal the hook. The cut kick (or round house kick) can also be worked from close range to conceal the hook.

Note: In general, your strike must follow after you have thrown two or three kicks. If you throw the same technique too many times, your opponent will learn to defend the attack and counter.

Exercise 7

Try a couple of front kicks to your opponent's gut. When he becomes a believer in the kick, throw a jab or a rear cross to his head. Again, because of the similarity in body movement between the front kick and the jab or cross, the kick can be used as a fake.

FAKING AND THE CHESS GAME

It is through faking that the fight often develops into a chess game, particularly between experienced fighters. Let's say that every time your opponent throws a jab, you round house kick his lead leg. After a while, an inexperienced opponent would stop throwing the jab. You have now taken an important weapon from him. However, an experienced fighter who wants to play chess will now fake his jab in order to draw a leg kick from you. When you throw the kick, he will block it with an outside shin block and knock you out with a rear cross. Remember, the worst time to take a strike is when you are in the process of kicking, because your foundation is narrow.

You can take this a step further still. Let's say that you pick up on your opponent's fake jab. Rather than blocking or kicking now, fake a leg kick by twitching your hip. Your opponent will attempt to block your fake leg kick with an outside shin block. As he does so, you throw a rear cross and beat him to the punch. This time you are the one taking advantage of his narrow foundation, and so, the game goes on. As stated earlier, it is almost impossible to preplan your fakes, so you must adapt to the person you are fighting during the course of the fight.

The most difficult people to fight are those who are expecting the fake and have a counter-plan ready. There are also those who don't react to fakes at all. But most of the time, your opponent will tend to freeze momentarily when seeing the fake, especially if he has already taken a number of strikes in that round.

Whether you play on a board or in the ring, anticipating your opponent's next move is perhaps the essence of good chess.

IN THE GYM

Work on setting up your spinning back fist better. What gives you away is your foot movement. Try throwing a half-jab before throwing the spinning back fist. As with any fake, it must look realistic. When you retrieve your jab, take an adjustment step with your lead foot and throw the spinning back fist. Be careful not to jam your own strike. Your rear foot should not move. If you allow your rear foot to slide across the floor as you spin, you will decrease distance and end up striking your opponent with your elbow. Now, try a shoulder roll to fake the jab. Make sure that the movement is toward your opponent and not sideways.

Try this: Fake a front kick with your lead leg and set your foot down in position to throw a spinning back fist. This works especially well, if your opponent is in the habit of lowering his guard to block the front kick. He will now leave a perfect opening for the spinning back fist.

You can also use your feet to conceal your feet, as strange as this sounds. Because the movement of the spinning back fist and the spinning back kick are identical initially, you can fake a spinning back fist and throw a spinning back kick, and vice versa. Distance may vary, but in general, your opponent will be more concerned with your upper body movement. Thus, if you throw the spinning back fist a number of times, and then suddenly throw a spinning back kick from a slightly longer range, he is still likely to try to defend against the spinning back fist. The kick is likely to land because it utilizes a different target and strikes from the front rather than from the side.

FAKING AND THE OVERHAND STRIKE

As discussed earlier, the overhand strike is one of the more powerful techniques in your arsenal. But, unlike most other strikes, there is only one target for the overhand. You must be able to throw it at a time when your opponent is open at the jaw. You do this by using it as a counter-strike off of one of his strikes. But you may need to use a fake to create this opportunity.

Let's say that every time you throw a strike, your opponent counters to the created opening. There are a couple of ways you can keep your jaw protected and still pull off an overhand strike:

1. **Fake a punch low to the body with a shoulder roll.** As your opponent's hand drops to protect against this perceived strike, his jaw will be exposed. Now, throw the overhand strike.

   Note: One may ask why it is even necessary to throw the fake strike. Why not throw a real strike instead and get the same reaction? But if your opponent has been countering to your jaw every time you throw a strike, throwing the fake shoulder roll allows you to keep your own hands up for protection against his counter. You may also want to be out of reach of your opponent's counter-strike when faking. Then close distance with a short step simultaneous with the overhand strike.

2. **Fake a lead leg front kick by raising your foot off the floor.** As your opponent drops his guard to block, shuffle forward and throw the overhand strike. You may be able to create a better angle if you step forty-five degrees forward and to your opponent's outside, rather than straight toward him.

Fake a front kick and throw the overhand strike.

To train a rat

The art of fakes and deception is popularly referred to as *training a rat*. The idea is to train your opponent to open targets for your strikes. Once you have trained him to respond in the desired way, you build upon this and lead him farther and farther into the maze of confusion:

1. **Fake a front kick** to get your opponent to lower his guard. Now, throw a rear cross to his head.

2. Next time your opponent sees the movement of the front kick, he will not lower his guard, because he remembers being fooled and hit a moment ago. So, now you **throw the real front kick** to his gut.

3. You can either fake first and then throw the real kick, or throw the real kick first, fake the second kick to get him to drop his guard, and then throw your rear cross.

4. Now, when your opponent is expecting your rear cross, **fake a rear cross with a shoulder roll to draw a parry.** This will open the side of his head. Now, move in and throw a hook.

From now on, mix fakes in with the rest of your techniques. Instead of pausing between combinations, make the fake a part of the combination. Add fakes when shadow boxing and working the heavy bag. If you pound away at the heavy bag without any form of strategy, you may throw some very hard techniques, but you won't be training intelligently. Mitt work is great for practicing fakes. In order to absorb the impact of your strike, the mitt holder must tense and bring his hand slightly forward. When you fake, you will draw a reaction much like you would in actual fighting. The mitt holder can tell you when the fake was effective, or you may see it in the movement of his hand.

It has been said that fighting is like sex: Most of it happens between your ears. So much is mental. You must constantly try to outsmart your opponent. This is your arena. But remember that your opponent may have some brains too. If you are not careful, you may end up getting trained.

Common errors when faking:

1. Failing to make the fake look realistic. If the move is too small, your opponent may miss it and fail to react. If the fake looks too real, however, it may make contact, be defeated by a block, or trigger a counter-strike. A fake should involve just enough movement to make your opponent feel a need to defend against it.

2. Using the same fake too many times. This will train your opponent to stop reacting. However, if you take this a step further, it can be used to your advantage: When your opponent expects a fake, you throw a real strike.

3. Losing your window of opportunity by not following with a strike or kick to the created opening.

Summary and review

Faking is the art of fooling your opponent into believing in a strike that is not thrown. Fakes are used strategically to gain openings in your opponent's defense. Any twitching or sudden move usually works well, especially if done right after you have thrown a strike or kick. For example, throw a front kick, and then twitch your leg to draw a reaction. When your opponent lowers his guard, throw a strike to the opening at his head. For a fake to work, it must look convincing. If the movement is so small that it looks like a move you do regularly anyway, it will not draw the desired reaction. On the other hand, if the movement is so large that you leave an opening on yourself, a crafty opponent can take advantage of it. Fakes must also be aimed at a specific target and be thrown from a distance close enough to actually land the strike, or your opponent won't see a need to react.

Faking in shadow boxing

- Practice fakes in shadow boxing. Work on relaxing, so that the fakes come quickly and naturally.

- Avoid faking too many times in a row, as your opponent is likely to learn from this and stop reacting in the desired way.

- Practice fakes both with your hands and feet. Don't limit yourself to one or the other. Can you fake a hook through upper body movement?

Faking with broken rhythm

- Strikes thrown with broken rhythm are more likely to land. The same applies to faking. If you fall into a specific cadence, it won't take your opponent long to figure you out.

- Unless you consciously work on broken rhythm, you are likely to fall back into a specific cadence.

- Practice punches intermingled with fakes on the heavy bag. Listen to your rhythm. Make sure your fakes are logical. Are they likely to open up a target for a follow-up punch or kick?

Focus mitt practice with fakes

- In order to land a strike after a fake, you must take advantage of the opening. The strike must follow quickly.

- Have your partner hold focus mitts. Every time you strike, he must tense in order to keep the mitt from getting knocked back. If your fake looks realistic, he will tense in anticipation of the strike.

- Mix strikes and fakes, and have your partner tell you when the fake is believable (when he feels himself tense).

Partner practice with fakes

- If you know what to expect beforehand, you are more likely to land a strike. Have your partner help you determine your opponent's expected reaction to a fake.

- If you throw a punch and then twitch your shoulder, how is your opponent likely to react? If you throw a kick and then twitch your leg, how is he likely to react?

- Explore how to fake to one area and strike to the same area, or fake to one area and strike to a different area. When would you use which? Why?

MENTAL STRATEGY

There is a difference between being good and being tough. Being good means that you can throw a strike well. Being tough means that you can take a strike well. Both are important, but I tend to place slightly greater value on being tough, physically and mentally. If your mental toughness goes out the door, your physical toughness will follow, and it won't matter how good you are, because the best strike in the world can't save you.

Who is tougher: a boxer or a kickboxer? Most people would say the boxer. This is because he has trained from the beginning for both physical and mental toughness, while many kickboxers have initially trained in a traditional martial art that practiced little or no real contact. Who is tougher: a kickboxer or a Thai-boxer? Again, most people would say that the Thai-boxer is tougher. The Thai-boxer has trained under excruciating circumstances and has conditioned himself from the beginning to taking pain. The average Thai-boxer's career lasts four years. Although this book is about Western style kickboxing, we must strive to attain the same mental and physical toughness as the boxer and Thai-boxer. In the end, toughness is an individual matter. Nobody can say that just because you are a kickboxer, you are not as tough as a boxer or Thai-boxer.

You will get hit in kickboxing. Just like death, it is inevitable (but hopefully less final). Particularly in the amateur ranks, it is the number of punches you throw and how aggressive you are that win the fight. If you worry about getting hit, you will be too concerned with defense and unable to respond appropriately. Regular contact training helps your body withstand the rigors of the sport. You will get hit multiple times every time you step into the ring. You must build your ability to take your opponent's strikes and kicks to your body, arms, legs, and head. Just by the nature of the sport, with the ultimate aim of disposing of the other fighter, anybody desiring to get in the ring must possess courage. If you haven't already done so, now is the time to commit yourself to be both the best and the toughest.

It's not the fact that you will get hit that matters; it's what you do with the fact that you will get hit that matters. Does getting hit make you turn away or look for help outside of the ring? Or does getting hit fuel you to take it up a notch? Does getting hit trigger your counter-strikes? How can you use the fact that you will get hit to your advantage?

Let me tell you something about pain. As absurd as it sounds, pain is good. Use it as a learning tool. Enduring pain teaches you the extent of your limitations. Pain is a great motivator. When operating under the pressure of pain, or even imminent pain, you can't afford to take chances, your senses are heightened and you will make fewer mistakes. People who understand this actually prefer pain. Pain makes you feel alive. When you come through a difficult training exercise alive, you rise to a new level that sets you apart from the rest. I am not suggesting that you should be careless or a daredevil. There is a difference between carelessness and a calculated risk that you have come prepared to meet. When your senses are keen, when you know that pain will be present, and when you are resolute to come through it alive, nothing can stand in your way. Competing in kickboxing takes courage. Courage gives you power.

I remember a match where the audience booed a fighter for running from his opponent. The fighter's corner threw in the towel halfway through the second round. I can't imagine the embarrassment he must have felt. He hadn't even been hit once!

This section covers:

- Mental tenacity
- The truth about getting hit
- Multiple points of pain
- Shifting focus
- Mental strategy
- Evaluating the full picture
- Glove-up with Keith
- Summary and review

MENTAL TENACITY

Keith's Corner

As a child, I suffered from extreme claustrophobia. One very cold winter's day, I removed my arms from the coat sleeves, and asked my friend to zip up the front so I could hold my arms close to my body. My friend, knowing of my claustrophobia, decided it would be funny to throw me to the ground, tie my sleeves in a knot across the front of my body, and sit on me. At first, I panicked and began to plead. I could feel the life energy weakening me, and the sheer terror running to the core of my being. As silly as it sounds, I felt like I was going to die!

My supposed friend then put his hand over my mouth and pinched my nostrils shut to further the panic. At that very moment, I felt the most incredible anger, which I channeled into my life energy, creating the most powerful experience. My panic and terror suddenly stopped and became pure energy. All of my feelings now had one common goal: Defeat the threat! I exploded from the coat, throwing my friend through the air. The next moments are still somewhat hazy, but I found myself on top covering his mouth and nostrils asking, "How does it feel?" I could see the fear and terror in his eyes, which prompted me to let him up.

When I retrieved my coat, both sides were completely torn out. Since that experience, I have learned to channel this energy both in my fighting career and as a police officer. This energy that we can learn to summon at will has saved my life and brought me from the brink of a knockout to victory. The human mind is the most powerful weapon. Properly harnessed, it can take you to unimaginable heights. As a fighter, I refused to be knocked out--it wasn't an option--leading to my nickname, "The Rock." I didn't get into this sport to build somebody else's career. Now, I give you these experiences: Build your career and your life as a winner. Defeat is not an option!

THE TRUTH ABOUT GETTING HIT

Because the ultimate aim in kickboxing is to win in the ring, sparring should take up most of your time. Rather than learning a specific combination or punch technique as you would in a traditional martial art, you will learn a technique and the concepts that go along with it, and then practice it in sparring until it becomes useable in unrehearsed circumstances. Much of sparring comprises getting hit, so face it! Whether in practice or competition, you will get hit every time you enter the ring. When you get hit, how should you react? How can you turn the fight to your advantage?

Swat the strikes away as if they are nothing but flies buzzing around your nose.

First, don't show your opponent that it bothers you to get hit. When you pretend you didn't feel it, he will get frustrated and think that his blows did no damage. Of course, if your opponent is really doing damage, it may not be possible to ignore the blows. Yet, many of the reactions we generally see are unnecessary. Many new kickboxing students overreact by shaking their heads as if dazed, acknowledging a hit by touching gloves with their opponent, or saying "good strike." Pausing and acknowledging the hit is like giving your opponent the perfect opportunity to hit you again. How's my driving? Call 1-800- . . . Don't invite it! It's better to wait until after the fight to comment.

Don't contemplate a hit in the middle of a fight. Rather, put it aside and move on. Try to use your opponent's strikes to trigger your counterstrike (*first touch*, remember?) Every time your opponent lands a blow, resolve to hit him back five times.

Oftentimes, we are so concerned about getting hit that we hesitate with our offense. Unless a hesitation is a deliberate attempt to draw a reaction, it is likely to get you in trouble. When you hesitate, you are vulnerable; your opponent can and will take advantage of you. If you get hit a lot when moving in, I suggest trying to pick up the speed rather than pausing.

On the other extreme is the fighter who wants to hit his opponent so badly that he doesn't care about his own defense. Not only must there be a balance between offense and defense; you must also know when to focus more on one than the other.

If a technique works, don't give it up: When your opponent scores, it may not be because his strikes are better than yours; it may be because you have not done anything to neutralize his strikes. Let's say that every time you throw a jab, your opponent jabs you back. After a while, you will stop jabbing, because you feel exposed every time you throw. Your jab may have been a very good technique to start with, but now when you don't use it anymore, your opponent has succeeded at eliminating one of your better strikes.

Rather than stop throwing the jab, ask yourself why your opponent's jab lands every time you jab. Is it because he is faster than you? Because his reach is longer than yours? Rather than thinking about what he is doing right, think about what it is that you are not doing. Are you retrieving your hand too slowly? Are you keeping your head on the attack line?

When a technique works, your opponent will try to stop you from executing it. Your opponent's reaction may therefore be the best indicator that your technique was successful. Sometimes your opponent may try to stop you by throwing the same technique back. If it lands, you are in effect trading blows, which may deter you from throwing the technique again. Your opponent has now started to take over mentally. When a technique works, don't give it up! It is better to find a way to defend and counter. In general, it is not a good idea to mimic your opponent's moves. If you counter with the same technique he just threw, you will teach him to expect it and will, in effect, prepare his defense for him.

What to do when your opponent rushes you: If your opponent rushes you, you will have a natural tendency to move back. But, because it is more difficult to move back than forward, you can't keep distance between you for any length of time. There are two things you can do:

1. Ideally, **step to the side**. This requires good timing.

2. **Train for offense**, which allows you to hold your ground and launch an effective counter-attack that will hopefully neutralize your opponent's attack. When you hold your ground and strike back (or better, first), you establish yourself as a fighter and are likely to become an intimidation to your opponent. This gives you the psychological edge.

With one foot in the door, the rest of your body can more easily follow.

Think about this: If you can get your opponent to give just an inch (physically or mentally), he will already have started his retreat, and it is easier for you to gain another inch. Have you ever arm-wrestled? At the start, when both you and your opponent's arms are vertical, your full focus is on forcing your opponent's hand down. But if he suc-  ceeds at forcing your hand just a fraction of an inch back, it will take tremendous focus for you to make a comeback.

Multiple points of pain

It is difficult, if not impossible, to defend all targets simultaneously. You can score points by breaking your opponent's focus. Giving your opponent *multiple points of pain* inhibits his ability to fight back. One strike to one target (one point of pain) is easier to defend and counter than many strikes to multiple targets. Strikes should therefore be thrown with **broken rhythm**, where sometimes you slow down or pause, and sometimes you explode with a combination. Many fighters are headhunters, but by varying your targets from high to low, and from kicking to punching, you will create *sensory overload*: a state of confusion and chaos.

Logics: The benefit of throwing combinations is that they can be overwhelming to your opponent. Your opponent may be able to defend against one attack at a time, but not against many consecutive attacks. When your opponent concerns himself with defense, you have succeeded at inhibiting his offense. Start by throwing a simple combination of a jab, a cross, and a kick. Then add several kicks. Also try reversing the combination so that you start with a kick. Think about the logics of the techniques. This is especially important in shadow boxing and bag work, because the targets are less obvious. A kick that is designed to set your opponent back; for example, the front push kick, could not logically be followed by a jab. Also, a jab is a set-up technique and not a finishing technique. A jab should therefore precede a stronger punch or kick.

Combinations usually have a damaging effect and are great for overwhelming your opponent. But we often don't think about the secondary benefit: It allows you to flow smoothly from long range to short range, without giving away the fact that you are stepping in or out. For example, you may go from a short range hook to a long range rear cross. Normally, a hook followed by a rear cross is not a logical combination if you are stationary at close range. However, when you overwhelm your opponent with a combination, you also force him to retreat, which allows you to flow from close to long range without taking a step (your opponent steps for you). Once you have landed the rear cross, you may need to take an additional step forward, or follow with a long range kick.

The flurry: Many fighters tend to strike only when there is an opening. But there are times when it benefits you to throw a flurry of punches even when there is no opening. The effect of a flurry is usually sensory overload. First, work on blocking or parrying your opponent's strikes. Then, explode with a flurry of straight punches to his head. When his guard comes up, finish with a couple of solid hooks to the body. Another good time to use the flurry is when your opponent throws a hook that you bob and weave under. Now, follow with a series of straight punches to his head from a side angle.

Keep the following in mind:

1. **Seek out your target** from long range.
2. **Throw a strong combination** to take your opponent out.

In general, the best time to throw a combination is when your opponent is a little dazed or off balance from your previous set-up strikes. On the heavy bag, experiment with going from long to short range, and vice versa, using explosive flurries as a transition. If you pause or stutter, your opponent may take advantage of you. If your attack gets thwarted, then revert to kicking, and vice versa.

On a higher level, the flurry should be worked according to the first touch concept. You have already learned how to use a block to trigger a counter-strike. You should now use a whole technique: a series of five or six strikes to trigger your next technique. The first technique is intended to place your opponent on the defensive, to stun him, to open him up. The second technique is intended to end the fight. The second technique should be overwhelming. Step inside of the boundaries of your opponent's comfort zone. The timing between the first and second technique must be just perfect. If you wait too long, your window of opportunity will close.

SHIFTING FOCUS

Why is it so important to throw your techniques with conviction? I saw a fight tape of world champion kickboxer, Rick Roufus, when he was just nine or ten years old. At the bell, he came out of his corner, ran toward his opponent, and threw a spinning heel kick that dropped his opponent to the canvas and ended the fight. If you are point sparring, you know that most techniques don't hurt. If it wasn't for the fact that your opponent gains points for landing them, you could walk through most of what he throws, get to the inside, and start landing some power shots. But if your opponent's techniques do true damage, your focus will revert to yourself; you will be thinking more about defense than offense. Your opponent has now succeeded at placing you on the defensive. This is perhaps the easiest time to see the benefits of mental toughness. Once your opponent knows that you are hurt (because you are showing him), the fight is pretty much over. However, if you can take one more punch than your opponent can throw, if you can go one more round than he can, it won't matter how good he is; you will outlast him.

Shifting focus with kicks: Although we have talked considerably about kicking the legs, try a kick to the face to shift your opponent's focus. Kicking the face can also give you a psychological advantage.

Because our feet are meant for walking, and are therefore generally thought of as dirty, they shouldn't come anywhere near the face. A head kick is psychologically difficult to deal with, but a kick to the face is an insult!

You can also shift the focus with repeated stinging impact to your opponent's legs; for example, by whipping a round house kick to the inside thigh of your opponent's lead leg. Because this kick is thrown with your lead leg and doesn't require full follow-through, you can gain a considerable amount of speed, which makes the kick difficult to defend against. A kick doesn't have to do physical damage in order to do mental damage. Your opponent will now start worrying about his legs. He will start to favor his lead leg, and may even move it back into a neutral stance. This opens his centerline and destroys his balance.

Mental strategy

Come prepared for the worst. Never underestimate your opponent. When two fighters meet, especially if they are inexperienced, they will be anxious to get to each other right from the start. This is where you will most often find premature attacks. If your opponent attacks prematurely, keep your chin down and stay in a good balanced stance. Most importantly, keep your cool.

If your opponent has strength or weight on you and is pressing forward, you may have a hard time getting the minimum kick requirement in (if there is one). The universal round house kick is your best bet now. A short sidestep allows you to land this kick with your instep or shin from an angle, or land it with your knee, if allowed. The round house kick is great when thrown across the front of your opponent's thighs, impacting both his legs with your instep and shin.

If you are worried about the minimum kick requirement, a good rule of thumb is to finish each combination with a kick. You should now have time for about fifteen kicks in a two-minute round, plus additional time to work on your defense and movement.

Many new kickboxers are so concerned with the number of strikes they throw that they punch or kick even if they only hit their opponent's gloves or arms. As you settle into the fight, you should be concerned with choosing your targets precisely. The judges look at the number of strikes thrown to determine the aggressiveness of the fighter, but they also look at power and strategy. A strike that is powerful and hits a good target will do more damage than a hundred strikes that simply touch your opponent's gloves.

The knockdown: Another point to consider is the knockdown. Most kickboxers throw good front kicks, because it is a simple technique and usually effective at keeping an opponent at a distance. It is common to see a fighter open with the front kick: he comes out for the first round, walks toward his opponent (who is also walking forward, anxious to get going), and nails him with the front kick. I have seen fighters get knocked down five seconds into the first round, because they walked right into their opponent's front kick. I have seen one fight where both fighters were leading with the front kick and knocked each other down simultaneously! A good boxer's stance helps you absorb the impact of the front kick.

When your opponent kicks, do whatever you can to smash her foot with your elbow. If you succeed, you may end the fight just seconds into the first round.

If you do get knocked down, take the full eight-count to give yourself time to clear your head. When knocked down, we have a tendency to feel frustrated or embarrassed. What is the audience thinking?! And is your opponent getting cocky? These thoughts are dangerous because your focus will shift to yourself rather than staying on the fight. When you get back up after a knockdown, you must forget that it happened and focus on strategy. I once heard somebody say that poise is the art of raising eyebrows rather than raising the roof. Practice poise!

If your opponent gets knocked down or is dazed from a blow, take advantage of him by increasing your aggressiveness. If your first strike hits his head and you score a knockdown, you may want to hit his head again once the fight resumes. However, if your strikes have no effect because your opponent is blocking, or because he simply has a tough head, you must change your focus to another target. Then go back to hitting the head later. Don't ignore the many openings on the body and legs.

When you knock your opponent down, you will be sent to a neutral corner (a white corner). Take advantage of your opponent's eight-count and analyze the situation. Observe your opponent and the referee to determine what kind of shape your opponent is in. Is the referee reluctant to allow the fight to continue? Does your opponent look as though he has lost some confidence?

EVALUATING THE FULL PICTURE

You must now learn to outthink your opponent. If you are fighting somebody you know nothing about, try to pick up on his habits during the course of the round, and start exploiting them. Don't wait until after the fight to think through a course of action. You may not get an opportunity against this fighter again.

Most people fight better when they are absorbed in their own fight more than in their opponent's fight. True, you must look at what kind of fighter your opponent is, but without letting him lead you into his game. Don't allow him to set the pace.

You must also evaluate your own fighting habits and determine where you need improvement. I have seen fighters landing their rear cross time and time again, and the opponent losing by a lopsided decision after eating hundreds of powerful rear crosses. Why didn't the opponent do something about this fighter's rear cross? Why didn't he think of a better strategy?

Let's say that your opponent lands both his jab, rear cross, and hook. At first, you might think that you are not slipping the jab and the cross, and that you are not bobbing and weaving under the hook, so you work on upper body movement. But because the jab is a set-up for the rear cross and hook, you should not see it as an entity in itself. By keeping your opponent's jab from landing, you may well eliminate his rear cross and hook also. Without these power strikes, your opponent becomes deficient.

Fighting is a two-way street. It is not enough to look at your opponent's strategy only, nor is it enough to look at just your own strategy. By analyzing the full picture, you will discover how one strike affects another. You can now upset your opponent's entire strategy just by affecting this one strike.

Glove
Up with
Keith

What separates the superior fighter from the average fighter is the ability to adapt during the fight, the ability to think on your feet. Play the thinker's game and exploit your opponent's weaknesses. If you can't find any weaknesses, you have to create them. If your opponent kicks your legs every time you kick his, it may be wiser to move in with a hand combination first, and then fire a kick. If your mind goes to your legs where the pain is, it will cause you to freeze. Now, your opponent can fake a leg kick and then go for a knockout to the head.

Your basic strategy should be accuracy. Don't throw punches and kicks just to throw punches and kicks. Before you have had a few fights, you won't really be thinking a lot while fighting. After you get some experience, however, you will fight strategically smarter and start looking for the right time to throw that knockout punch.

Summary and review

How you approach the fight mentally may be even more important than your physical training and background. No matter how much you train or how good a shape you are in, if you lack confidence, you are not likely to win. Granted, through physical training and a lot of sparring comes confidence, but you must still prepare for those situations that require you to keep a cool head.

Evaluating the effects of getting hit

- Spar with a variety of people and evaluate how they react when taking a hit. When you hit your opponent, does it stall his attack, making him more cautious? Can you change your cadence to make him freeze and create an opening?

- Can you sense when your strikes are beginning to affect your opponent mentally? Is there a slowing in his pace? Does he try to keep his distance? Does he look away?

- If you get dazed from taking a hit, how can you regain your composure without letting your opponent know that his strike was effective?

Mental superiority practice

- Experiment with the multiple points of pain principle. Either strike different targets in rapid succession, or strike the same target multiple times.

- If your opponent is focused on attacking you with punches, how can you defend his attack and strike an open target on his legs? How does he react when you do? How many times do you need to kick his leg to stall his upper body attack?

- Listen to the rhythm of your strikes. Make an effort to explode with a flurry every twenty seconds. Note your opponent's reaction. How can you take advantage of it?

- If you really set your mind to it, is it possible to simply walk forward, forcing your opponent back by the mere threat of your advance? Oftentimes, we get stuck fighting from a particular distance. Experiment with pressing the attack.

Getting knocked down

- Next time you score a knockdown, pay attention to how your opponent reacts. Next time you slip or get knocked down, pay attention to how you react.

- Is there a sense of embarrassment for your opponent? Does he look at the floor when getting back up? Does he touch your glove to show that he is okay? Is he a bit more hesitant in his comeback?

- If you get knocked down, make an attempt to look your opponent in the eyes when getting back up. Resume the fight with speed and determination.

- If you feel that the knockdown affected you mentally, how can you ignore it until the round is over? How can you focus on what needs to be done, instead of what happened?

MORE ON COMPETITION STRATEGY

If you were to fight a clone of yourself, who do you think would win? At first, you would probably say that nobody would win, that it would be a draw, because your skills would be equally matched to your opponent's skills. But this is not true. Somebody would win because, even if you were physically identical, you wouldn't think exactly alike. All other factors being equal, the fighter who can out-think his opponent will win. This is perhaps the essence of good strategy.

This section covers:

- Study your opponent's fighting habits
- Funnel movement
- The press
- Positioning for kick and distance
- Defending your opponent's most likely technique
- Superiority against the southpaw
- Extremes and in-betweens
- Another look at targets
- Establishing your reputation
- Attributes of a winner

STUDY YOUR OPPONENT'S FIGHTING HABITS

Most fighters develop habits, or patterns, in their fighting. Once you understand your opponent's habits, you can work to exploit them. The problem is that most fighters don't take the time to learn about their opponent's habits.

Try these exercises on **FIGHTING HABITS**:

Exercise 1

Next time you watch kickboxing on TV, rather than viewing it as pure entertainment, choose one of the fighters and sit down with a pen and a piece of paper and make note of his habits. Which strikes seem to dominate? Is he the aggressive type, or does he rely more on defense? If you had to go up against this fighter next, how would you plan your strategy against him?

Exercise 2

Be aware of your own habits. Is there a particular strike, move, or combination that is working especially well for you? Have you formed any habits that are potentially dangerous? Does your opponent pick up on your habits? Is he able to exploit them? How can you turn your habits into strengths?

FUNNEL MOVEMENT

A *funnel* is considerably larger in one end than the other. Imagine placing your opponent inside a funnel, and moving him closer and closer toward the narrow end. If you are successful, you will limit his movement and cut off his escape routes. This is accomplished through superior foot positioning. When your opponent tries to move off your desired path, take a small step in the direction he is moving to force him in the opposite direction. For example, when your opponent steps to his left, position your lead foot to the outside of his lead foot, forcing him back or to his right. If he moves back, keep him moving back with a strong attack until he is on the ropes. If he steps to his right, position your lead foot to the inside of his lead foot, halting his movement and forcing him back and to his left.

In order to funnel your opponent into a corner, you must have superb control of the ring, never giving your opponent the opportunity to escape, side-step, or use your own tactics against you. Experiment with distance, footwork, determination, and staying one step ahead mentally.

Try this exercise on **FUNNEL MOVEMENT**:

Exercise 3

Strive to dominate the center of the ring. No matter how your opponent moves, his back should always be closer than your back to the ropes, so that he must make large adjustments to get around you. As you funnel your opponent into the ropes, be aware of his escape routes. Take small adjustments steps. If you can exercise control before a large adjustment is necessary, the situation will never get out of hand. How can you split your opponent's mind and body focus while giving yourself distance and angle to strike? If he attempts to escape, how can you cut him off?

THE PRESS

 **Keith's Knockout Advice** *The press* is a high pressure tactic that requires superior defensive capabilities. The primary purpose of the press is to wear your opponent down both physically and mentally. You must resolve to remain in the fighting pocket. You must move forward and apply pressure constantly. If your opponent chooses to take a stand, use your body, head, shoulders, or whatever else necessary to keep him moving back. When you press, you want to rough up your opponent and bust up his offensive weapons.

Try this exercise on **THE PRESS**:

Exercise 4

It is difficult, tiring, and aggravating to fight an opponent who constantly enters your comfort zone. Next time you spar, resolve to never take a backward step. When your opponent tries to create distance, immediately smother him while continuing with offense.

POSITIONING FOR KICK AND DISTANCE

Most fighters have few problems throwing follow-up punches (or punches in combinations). But throwing combination kicks is usually not as easy. Generally, the fighter ends with the kick, and then moves out and starts over with a new combination. But because kicks are so powerful, you can use them to stun or daze your opponent, creating an opportunity to take him out. It is therefore critical not to pause after you have landed a powerful kick.

Many kicks hurt even if your opponent's facial expressions don't tell you so. To be accurate and effective with multiple kicks, you must position for:

1. **The follow-up kick.**
2. **Distance.**

When your kick has landed and you replant the kicking foot, plant it in whatever position gives you the best distance and angle for a follow-up kick. Let's say that you throw a lead leg front kick to your opponent's gut. If your follow-up kick is going to be a rear leg round house kick to the ribs, you must plant your foot in position from where you can throw it without taking any extra steps.

Throw a left front kick. Plant your foot in position and off the angle to the left and throw a right round house kick.

A more difficult kick to position for is the side thrust kick. You can follow up easier off the side thrust kick if you plant your foot a little wide (almost in a neutral stance). You can now throw either a front kick or a round house kick with your other leg. If you pull your leg all the way back into the southpaw stance, you can follow with a side thrust kick with your other leg.

Note: When positioning for the follow-up kick, be liberal with your stance. At this level, exposing your centerline is okay as long as you are aware of the consequences. Kicking from a horse stance may conceal the kick better, because many kicks can be thrown comfortably from the horse stance.

Don't assume that your opponent will automatically be within distance for your follow-up kick. It is not enough to position for the kick; you must also position for distance. You may only have a split second to decide how to position, but with a bit of practice, your brain will begin to compute the exact distance for the kick automatically. There are also times when you will want to abandon a kick altogether, because it is simply not practical anymore.

By planting your foot in position, you will:

1. **Cut the time it takes to throw the kick combination.** The kicks will not actually be faster, but they will reach the target faster. The positioning and throwing of the kick becomes a one-step process.

2. **Smooth the transition between kicks**, especially those that require a large body movement (the side thrust kick).

3. **Smooth the transition between kick combinations and hand combinations**. Most fighters tend to throw their kicks in groups, then pause briefly, and then throw their strikes in groups. The advanced fighter knows how to transition smoothly and efficiently between kicks and punches without telegraphing his moves.

Note: When practicing advanced footwork in conjunction with kicks, it is easy to focus on the last kick only, neglecting to throw the first two or three kicks with proper spirit. But remember, unless the first kick does damage, it is useless.

Eliminating the pause between kicks does two things:

1. **Keeps your opponent from countering** or blocking the second kick.

2. **Increases your power**. The idea is to use the momentum of your first kick to launch your second kick.

Correct foot positioning enables you to conceal the kick and to throw it with power. No matter where your opponent is in the ring, or how much reach he has, once you learn to control distance, you will always be the leader.

Try these exercises on **POSITIONING FOR KICK AND DISTANCE**:

Exercise 5

Start on the heavy bag with the three basic kicks: the front kick, the round house kick, and the side thrust kick.

1. Start with the front kick and experiment with different foot positions for your follow-up kick. For example, set your foot down forward and note which follow-ups this foot position lends itself to.

2. Next, pull your foot all the way back to the opposite stance and note which kicks you can throw best from here.

3. Experiment with setting your foot down at a forty-five degree angle forward, at a reverse forty-five degree angle, and in a neutral stance, each time noting the follow-ups that best suit these foot positions.

4. Do the same exercise with the round house and side thrust kick, until you have explored all possible foot positions.

When working the heavy bag, you can also decide beforehand which kick combination to throw. If the bag swings in the wrong direction, you can clearly see that you have not positioned correctly for the follow-up. If your opponent moves after you have landed your first kick, you must make the appropriate adjustments to position for your next kick.

Exercise 6

Next, try to make one kick flow smoothly into the next. This works best with alternating kicks. For example, throw a rear leg front kick, and simultaneous to retrieving the kick, step off to your right. This widens your stance and moves your upper body off the attack line. As soon as your foot plants, follow with a lead leg round house kick. Throwing the round house kick from this angle allows you to take a bigger target: your opponent's entire mid-section, for example. After landing the lead round house kick, bring your foot back and plant it in position to follow with a side thrust kick off your rear leg. This works best if you set your lead foot down slightly to the rear for distance. There should be no pauses or extra steps between kicks.

Exercise 7

Because of the time and movement involved in throwing the side thrust kick, it is often not thrown with the rear leg. Try setting the kick up with a lead leg round house kick to your opponent's inside thigh area. When you have his attention, bring your lead leg (left leg) all the way back to a right fighting stance and throw the rear leg side thrust kick to your opponent's mid-section (your rear leg has now become your lead leg). Because you stepped back into the opposite stance with your lead foot, you have also increased distance so that you can successfully throw the side thrust kick.

Round house kick your opponent's inside thigh. Bring your foot all the way back to the southpaw stance and throw a right side thrust kick.

Exercise 8

Try a kick against an opponent who is backing up. Because he is backing up, you probably have the upper hand already, so it is crucial that you don't allow him to get away. Close distance with a rear leg side thrust kick. As your opponent steps back, raise your rear knee. When your rear leg and hips pivot through into a right fighting stance, extend your rear leg into a side thrust kick. You will gain quite a bit of reach for two reasons: First, the side thrust kick is naturally a long reaching technique. Second, because your lead leg is your foundation, your upper body must move forward above your supporting lead foot for balance. This increases your reach by a foot or two. You can test this concept by first throwing a side thrust kick with your lead leg and noting your reach. Now, from the same position, throw a side thrust kick with your rear leg and note your reach. The difference is the distance between your feet.

Exercise 9

If you are in a left fighting stance and your opponent moves toward your right, he will place himself in the line of power of your rear leg front or round house kick. If he moves toward your left, he will place himself in the line of power of your lead leg front or round house kick. Knowing this allows you to decide in advance which kick to throw. The idea is to catch your opponent while he is in the process of stepping, because it allows you to take advantage of his momentum. The side thrust and spinning back kick work best when your opponent moves toward your back. Thus, if you are in a left fighting stance, you should throw the kick when he moves toward your left. If he moves toward your right, your hips will not be lined up properly, too much movement will be required, and the kick will be uneconomical. Practice the front kick, round house kick, side thrust kick, and spinning back kick, depending on which direction your opponent moves.

Note: It is important to understand that there are times when the follow-up kick is not feasible, even though you may have taken care to position both for kick and distance. Because the human factor can never be calculated completely, there are times when your opponent does not react like you expected, and when you must abandon the kick. For example, your opponent may jam your kick and throw you off balance.

Exercise 10

Once you can transition from one kick to another, or from kicking to punching and vice versa, you may try what is called double positioning. You throw a kick, but rather than positioning for a follow-up kick, you position for a follow-up punch. Thinking of your feet as hands allows you to use either effectively. The same concept applies: Position for ultimate distance at an angle off the attack line, and eliminate any pauses between strikes and kicks.

Note: In an actual round of sparring, flowing from one technique to the next consistently is not required. There are strategic issues that need to be considered as well, some of which require pauses or successive strikes with the same hand or foot.

DEFENDING YOUR OPPONENT'S MOST LIKELY TECHNIQUE

When we discussed mental strategy, we talked about the balance between offense and defense. No fight is won by defense alone. Both offense and defense must have a clear purpose. Because only offense wins the fight, defense should be used to create offense. There are primarily three parts to good defense:

1. Cover your openings.
2. Evade or block the strike.
3. Strike when your opponent is unable to.

Covering your openings may be the most difficult of the above principles because, no matter what you do, an opening will always exist. If your opponent throws a jab that you block by moving your rear hand in front of your face, you leave an opening for a hook to the right side of your head. But if you move your hand back to the right side of your head to cover that opening, you leave an opening for a rear cross to your face instead. If you move your left hand in front of your face to cover that opening, you leave an opening for a hook to the left side of your head. And how many targets are open on your legs and body while you try to defend high? Because of the difficulty in covering all openings, you must prepare to defend against the technique that your opponent is most likely to throw. You can evade a strike by bobbing and weaving. To

decrease the risk of taking your opponent's strike, add a shallow roll (bob and weave) after each strike you throw. Rolling after every hook keeps you better protected against your opponent's expected counter-hook to your head. Be alert for counter-strikes in the slight pause between your combinations.

Be ready to strike when your opponent is unable to. A strike is usually effective when your opponent steps back after executing a close range technique because, when he steps back, he must pause briefly before reversing his momentum to strike. His move requires a two-count, while yours requires only a one-count: Step forward and strike simultaneously. If you time your strike to your opponent's initial move to the rear, you will always beat him to the punch.

SUPERIORITY AGAINST THE SOUTHPAW

A southpaw fights with his right side forward. If you fight from a conventional stance, a southpaw is like your mirror image. Many kickboxers have a traditional martial arts background and have trained with their stronger side (right side) forward, and some kickboxers are left-handed. It is therefore likely that sometime during your career you will encounter a southpaw (if you are not a southpaw yourself). Your opponent's left hand is now his power hand, and his right hand is his jab. The angle for the jab and cross will be different from what you are used to seeing. Against a conventional stance, you knew that you could move to your opponent's left to get to the superior position, but now you must move to his right. In general, to dominate the southpaw, you should keep your lead foot to the outside of your opponent's lead foot. This gives you a free shot at your opponent's lead leg, and allows you to strike and kick from an angle off the attack line. Your position is therefore great for leg kicks and sweeps.

Keep your lead foot to the outside of your opponent's lead foot when fighting the southpaw.

But fighting is seldom black and white. You must also look at the strengths of your opponent's position. Because his lead foot is to the inside of yours, he has easier access to your centerline. Use your rear hand the way you normally use your jab (to initiate the punch combination). Simultaneous to throwing the rear cross, step with your lead foot forward at a forty-five degree angle. This places your lead foot to the outside of your opponent's. The step also increases your momentum.

Initiate with a rear cross, simultaneously stepping forward. Your outside superiority allows you to throw the hook or round house kick from an angle off the attack line.

STRIKES AND TARGETS FOR FIGHTING THE SOUTHPAW

Fighting a southpaw on the inside: Fighting a southpaw on the inside may be a bit tricky as far as leg kicks go. Because your lead leg is so close to your opponent's, throwing the kick with power is difficult. This might be a good time to switch stance, so that you are also in southpaw. Keep your opponent occupied with punches to conceal the fact that you are switching stance. When the switch is complete, your lead leg has become your rear leg, you have created distance to your opponent's lead leg, and you can execute the leg kick easier.

Note: You can switch stance on the inside by taking a small step with your rear (right) foot forward first, and then step back with your left foot. If you step back with your left foot first, you will create distance between your upper body and your opponent's upper body, and may fail to conceal the switch.

Inside fighting range against the southpaw has many benefits for your hand techniques. Because your lead foot is to the outside of your opponent's lead foot, you have virtually free access to the side of his ribs with your lead hand. You also have easy access to his mid-section and chin with your rear hand. Try a lead hook simultaneous with a short step toward your opponent's back.

Fighting a southpaw at close range gives you the outside position. Hooks to the ribs and mid-section, and uppercuts can be real power shots.

Applying southpaw principles to conventional fighting: You can also apply the principle of outside superiority to a conventional opponent, even though you are both in left stances. Because your opponent is off center, he has difficulty landing his strikes. When he moves, continue keeping your lead foot to the outside of his. Be careful not to square your stance or cross your feet.

When fighting an opponent in a conventional stance, stay slightly to the outside of his lead foot (away from his centerline).

Note: One may argue that if your lead foot is to the outside of a conventional opponent, then his lead foot must also be to the outside of yours. Your positions are therefore equal. But as long as you dominate the footwork by deciding when, how, and where to move, you will dominate your opponent.

The benefits of switching stance: As you gain proficiency in the conventional stance, start to incorporate the southpaw stance. Being able to fight well from southpaw and switch from one stance to the other at any time can enhance your strategy, even if you're not a southpaw. Fighting southpaw against an opponent in a conventional stance gives you different opportunities to score with your strong hand, which has now become your lead hand. If the switch is subtle, your opponent may not even notice it, and will therefore leave many areas vulnerable.

Switching stance often enables you to find new openings. A different stance creates a slightly different angle. Switching stance is easiest on the inside where you can conceal the switch. If switching at long range, try to switch in the middle of a combination. When your opponent is focusing on defense, he is not as likely to see the switch. Some fighters don't realize that you have switched stance for some time after the fact. This allows you to land a strong left hand, without your opponent understanding why.

You can lead either with your jab or with your rear cross, depending on the angle. Try leading with a right jab while stepping forward and to your right. This positions you to throw a right hook to your opponent's ribs or head with your strong hand in the lead position. Your outside position makes your opponent feel crowded and forced toward your left into the path of your left hand, which is now your rear hand. This is the perfect opportunity to throw a double left cross.

When jabbing with your lead right hand, because you stance is mirrored to your opponent's, there may be a need to jab over the top of your opponent's lead left hand. You do this by throwing the jab slightly curved from the outside in, almost like a long hook. This enables you to go around his guard rather than above or through it. Your elbow may come up slightly prior to landing the punch, so be aware that there is an opening at your ribs.

When throwing the left cross from the southpaw stance against a conventional fighter, step forward and slightly to the right with your lead foot. This places you in the superior position to the outside of your opponent's jab and away from his power techniques.

When jabbing from the southpaw stance, throw the jab like a long hook around your opponent's guard.

Once you get used to fighting from the southpaw stance, you will find that you can build tremendous speed in your right jab. Uppercuts are also easy to throw and land from the southpaw stance, because of the proximity of your lead right side to your opponent's lead left side. Because your opponent, just like you, is likely to try to dominate the outside, he will move toward your right and into the path of power of your lead uppercut. Try a quick uppercut/hook combination with the same hand, or throw a right uppercut followed by a left rear cross, as your opponent's head snaps back.

Throw a lead uppercut followed by a left cross.

If your opponent tries to defeat your outside superiority, throw a right hook to his ribs. When he moves toward your outside, he will move into the hook's path of power. If he moves to your left instead, he will automatically position himself in the path of your left cross, which, because of the rear position, is now a power technique.

There are other reasons why a fighter would want to switch stance. For example, if your opponent cut kicks your lead leg repeatedly, you may want to switch stance to protect that leg. Some techniques, like the hook, may also be easier to land with your lead hand. Switching to southpaw may make your right hook stronger. Switching stance is useful when your opponent is pressing you. Rather than shuffling back in the same stance, switch to southpaw. This allows you to increase distance and counter-strike.

Once you become good at switching from conventional to southpaw and back, you will have a clear strategic advantage over the conventional-only fighter.

EXTREMES AND IN-BETWEENS

You will experience many different fighting styles in your career, and each one must be dealt with accordingly. Let's look at the two extremes first:

1. **Your opponent is calculating, patient, and conservative.** This usually comes from years of experience. No matter what you do, you seem unable to upset him. If his style is intentional, it will probably work to his advantage. He will look for specific opportunities, keep his cool under pressure, conserve energy, and attack ferociously when an opportunity presents itself. If it is not a result of years of training and experience, such a fighter may be of the timid type, in which case you can take advantage of him through sensory overload.

2. **Your opponent is stylish, throws overwhelming attacks, and incorporates a lot of kicks, including a variety of jumping and unorthodox kicks.** This fighter usually has a long and successful traditional karate background. Not only is he difficult to deal with because of his unpredictability, he also has the ability to get the audience on his side. His footwork may be varied, shifting from conventional to

southpaw and back. He usually strikes often and from different angles. This type of opponent must be fought with a calculating mind-set. He will take advantage of you if you let it get to you mentally.

Try this exercise on **DIFFERENT STYLES**:

Exercise 11

Most styles fall somewhere between the two extremes. Next time you watch kickboxing on TV, observe all the fighters on the card for that night and make note of the many different styles. How should each style be fought? What type of style do you have? Do you try to imitate a particular style that you admire, or have you developed your own style? If there is a fighter you admire, he can serve as a role model. Choose the parts that intrigue you about another fighter's style, and try to implement them into your own game.

There are a wide variety of in-betweens. Let's look at some of the most common:

1. **Your opponent is much taller than you.** This means that he has a significant reach advantage. Two fighters can be of roughly equal weight, with one being short and stocky, and the other tall and slender. When facing a taller opponent from long range, keep moving to avoid becoming an easy target. Quick movement in and out with attacks to your opponent's legs may prove helpful. These also help gauge distance. Try to get to the inside of your opponent's offense, with your shorter and stockier body helping you throw powerful short range strikes.

2. **Your opponent is shorter than you, or crouches to cover his openings.** I was once sparring with such a fighter. He would make himself small while advancing with tiny calculating steps. When he was within reach, he would throw an overhand or tight hook, which hurt like hell even if it landed on my arm. Don't allow this type of opponent to get to close range. Move side-to-side and kick his legs. Also try round house kicks to his head or arms to weaken them. You may be able to sneak a front kick in to his stomach or solar plexus. Be aware of elbow blocks. You may be able to use a fake to get him to lower, raise, or relax his guard.

3. **Your opponent wants to clinch.** Normally, the referee breaks you apart if the clinch lasts longer than a few seconds. But if you fight under Muay Thai rules, you are allowed to clinch and throw. Clinching can be a sign that your opponent is getting tired and is leaning on you trying to recover. It may also be because he is comfortable at close range and is trying to unbalance you, move you back, or tie up your weapons. If your opponent gets hold of your arms, use leverage to unbalance him, or to raise his arms and expose his ribs to a knee strike. The more you move, the more difficult it is for your opponent to clinch and mount an effective attack.

4. **Your opponent is quick with the jab.** You must now determine whether he uses the jab isolated in an attempt to irritate you, or if he uses it as a set-up for a stronger technique. If he uses it mainly as an irritant, you can time it through slipping or other upper body movement, or through blocking or parrying and countering. Throw your counter-strike with intent to deter your opponent from using his jab. Chances are when he takes a few brain rattling blows, he will be more cautious extending the jab.

5. **Your opponent waits for you to initiate the attack.** Or he taunts you to throw at a time when you are not ready. This kind of tactic allows your opponent to guess your approach. You must now become very active, so as not to give your opponent the opportunity to guess. Employ ferocious combinations and counter-attacks off his strikes.

6. **Your opponent is an exceptionally hard hitter.** If you know this in advance, you will probably be respectful of him from the start. Or you may get fearful as soon as the first strike lands and gives you double vision. Because of the fear factor, this type of fighter is most likely to place you on the defensive and steal your mental determination. Never become a stationary target for a hard hitter. Use kicks that have the potential to stop his advance: side thrust kick, front push kick, etc. Or, if you can increase your speed, you may have a chance to beat him to the move.

Note: When in the actual contest, it is the corner's responsibility to study your opponent's style and offer suggestions.

ANOTHER LOOK AT TARGETS

Now that you have gained an understanding of the various strikes and kicks, it may serve you well to take another good look at targets. How precise are your strikes? Do you actually aim for a specific target, or do you just hope that the strike will land in the general area of the target you are aiming for? The more precise you are with selecting your target, and the more you know about the consequences of striking a particular target, the more damaging your attack will be. Every target area has several specific targets. Even the nose has more than one specific target. Target selection also depends on how the body is angled. Thus, when striking the body, it may not always be wise to use a strike aimed for the floating rib. Is this target actually being presented, or is your opponent's elbow blocking it? The target for a kick will vary depending on the timing and circumstances. Even though the torso is a large target area, you must choose specific targets with care not only to maximize the effectiveness of your strike, but also to minimize the risk of injury to the striking weapon. Let's take another look at specific targets:

1. The **eyebrows** are easily cut and can cause bleeding, with blood getting in the eyes and clouding your opponent's vision. The lower eyelid is also prone to cuts.

2. The **bridge of the nose** extends from between the eyebrows down to the level of the eyes. Strikes that are thrown at a slight downward angle are great for impacting the bridge of the nose. These include the jab or cross, elbow strike, overhand strike, and axe kick. You can also strike the nose at an upward angle with an uppercut or knee.

3. The **philtrum** is the area directly under the nose to the upper portion of the lip. Strike the philtrum with any straight strike. Landing a blow to this area will make your opponent's eyes water.

4. The **temple** is the soft hollow area on the side of the head directly opposite the eye. Strike the temple with a hook, elbow, round house kick, hook kick, or spinning heel kick. **Caution: A good blow to the temple can cause serious injury and even death.**

5. Striking the area **above the ear** and slightly to the back of the head with a hook, elbow, or round house kick can disturb your opponent's balance or knock him out.

6. The **jaw** is a desirable target for a knockout punch. Strike the hinge of the jaw right below the ear with a hook, elbow, round house kick, hook kick, or knee strike. Striking the hinge of the jaw can also cause dislocation of the jaw.

7. Strike the **point of the chin** with a straight punch, or with an uppercut, corkscrew punch, or other strike that comes from underneath. Try the front kick and jump front knee. This could also dislocate the jaw.

8. The **collarbone** is easily broken with an axe kick. A broken collarbone will render the arm on that side useless.

9. The **solar plexus** is the soft spot where the ribs are joined at the sternum. A strike to the solar plexus can knock the wind out of your opponent. Try striking at a slight upward angle with a front kick or uppercut.

10. The **floating ribs** are the two lowest pairs of ribs and derive their name from the fact that they are attached to the backbone, but not to the sternum. They are therefore brittle and easily broken. Strike from the side and at a slight upward angle with a hooking uppercut, round house kick, front kick, or knee.

11. Strikes to the **abdomen**, including soft tissue areas on both sides of the body (liver and spleen), can cause intense pain and drop your opponent to the canvas instantly.

12. Many kickboxers don't think about targets on the arms that can have debilitating effects. A block or kick to **the wrist** can dislocate it.

13. Kick your opponent's **thighs** (front, back, and sides) with round house kicks or knees. These will drain energy from your opponent's legs and keep him from moving efficiently.

14. Kicking the **back of the knee** with a round house kick can cause a fighter's leg to collapse.

15. Strike the **shins** with elbows or shin blocks. The shins are most sensitive directly against the bone. A correctly executed shin block will not hurt your shins, only your opponent's.

16. Round house or sweep kick your opponent's **calves** to create damage or place him on the canvas.

17. Strike your opponent's **instep, ankle, and toes** with elbow blocks to make him wary of using his kicks against you.

ESTABLISHING YOUR REPUTATION

Aside from physical skill, confidence may be your most important asset, even to the point that I tend to place it ahead of physical skill. Establish your reputation early:

1. **Attack** ferociously. Attack before your opponent does. Attack with purpose.

2. **Defend** with purpose. Use defense to trigger a new attack.

3. **Don't underestimate** your opponent.

4. **Advance** quickly, **retreat** quickly.

5. **Don't show pain** or concern.

6. **Control** your temper.

7. **Listen** to your trainer.

8. **Pace** yourself; be aware of time.

9. **Be precise** with your targets.

10. **Observe** signs of weakness in your opponent.

11. Show good **sportsmanship**.

12. **Enter and exit big.** If you feel insecure, your chances of winning are minimal

ATTRIBUTES OF A WINNER

1. You must **want to win**. This may seem obvious, but many fighters can't sustain the will to win when the going gets tough.

2. You must have trained long enough to **be proficient** at the techniques you are using.

3. You must **be well-conditioned** both cardiovascularly, muscularly, and mentally. This helps you withstand whatever punishment you opponent dishes out.

4. You must **have endurance**. You must be able to go as long as is necessary. This includes the ability to know when to pace and when to explode.

5. You must **exercise mental superiority**; you must be a quick thinker and able to stay a few steps ahead of your opponent in strategy.

6. You must be able to **take the fight to the end**, to finish, no matter how tired or beat you are.

There is no easy victory. Simply hitting the heavy bag for a few months without getting actual ring experience will instill a false sense of confidence. A successful competitor must practice his fighting skills meticulously. Yes, you can attain power by kicking the bags. But toughness, stamina under pressure, and ability to think on your feet must be practiced in actual sparring.

Technique only gets you so far. When you have honed and refined your technique optimally, you must resort to your mental strength. Having gone through the battle mentally many times over will make you feel as though you have already been there. This is when your physical and mental preparation will converge . . .

. . . so that you can be that fighter with his hand raised high in victory.

QUICK REFERENCE TO CONCEPTS

ANGLING OFF: Never take more than one step back in a straight line. If you mirror your opponent's step exactly, who has the advantage? Your opponent, right? This is because he is moving forward and you are moving back, and it is more difficult to fight effectively when retreating. This also allows your opponent to use momentum to his advantage.

BROKEN RHYTHM: This involves a seemingly haphazard pattern of faster and slower rhythms, pauses, and explosions of combinations, intermingled with constant pressure to move your opponent back.

FIRST TOUCH CONCEPT: This means allowing your defensive move to trigger a counter-strike, and ties directly in with speed. If you wish to increase your speed, you need a catalyst, something that triggers this greater speed. The second reason to use first touch is strategic and ties directly in with timing. Whenever you block a strike or kick, use it as a signal to position for and throw a follow-up technique.

FREEZING: Tensing implies fear, or at least respect. When your opponent is tense, he is unable to respond with a strong counter-attack. You can freeze your opponent's offensive weapons by hitting or touching that weapon. When your opponent tenses the part of his body that is struck (his hand, for example), he will momentarily be unable to use it against you.

FUNNEL MOVEMENT: You can funnel your opponent into a corner by continually cutting off his escape routes. You do this through superior foot positioning. When your opponent steps to his left, position your lead foot to the outside of his lead foot. If he steps to his right, position your lead foot to the inside of his lead foot. This keeps him moving back in a nearly straight line.

MULTIPLE POINTS OF PAIN: One strike to one target (one point of pain) is easier to defend and counter than many strikes to multiple targets. You should therefore throw your strikes with broken rhythm, where sometimes you slow down or add a slight pause, and sometimes you explode with a combination.

POSITIONING FOR KICK AND DISTANCE: By stepping with your supporting foot to the side just prior to kicking, you will adjust for distance and position off your opponent's attack line. By planting your foot in position for a follow-up kick, you save time and can use the momentum from one kick to trigger the next.

PREMATURE ATTACK: This is an attack made without sufficient preparation. Especially at the amateur ranks, fighters tend to go all out from the start. The premature attack may be theoretically unsound, but if the opponent's defense is lacking, it is often successful. As a strategic fighter, I usually don't attack prematurely without a specific plan. That is not to say that I don't throw the first strike, or that I don't throw overwhelming combinations. There is a difference. The premature attacker relies on his ability to end the fight with this one explosive attack. If he doesn't, he will be physically spent within the first twenty seconds of the round.

SENSORY OVERLOAD: By striking and kicking with explosive combinations to as many targets as possible in the shortest amount of time, you will create sensory overload, sending your opponent into a state of confusion and chaos. Many fighters are headhunters. By varying your targets from high to low, and from kicking to punching, you become unpredictable and your opponent will not know what to do next.

STRATEGY: When planning your strategy, use the analogy of the chess game. Chess masters stay several moves ahead of their opponents, they work on creating openings, and they have patience. At the beginning of the fight, size up your opponent to determine his strong and weak points, and his reactions to specific moves

STUDY YOUR OPPONENT'S FIGHTING HABITS: You can learn much by studying patterns that seem recurrent in your opponent's fighting tactics. Train yourself to be observant of other fighters' habits by watching kickboxing matches on TV or in the gym.

THE PRESS: To press your opponent, you must resolve not to take a backward step. The press requires constant movement forward. The primary purpose of the press is to wear your opponent down physically and mentally.

TIMING: Timing is the ability to take advantage of your opponent's targets, movement, or power by executing precise strikes, blocks, or movement when both your and your opponent's positions are ideal. We often don't think about timing as the ability to hinder your opponent's access to targets by executing precise strikes, blocks, or movement when both your and your opponent's positions are ideal.

TRAIN A RAT: The art of fakes and deception is popularly referred to as training a rat. The idea is to train your opponent to open targets for your strikes. Once you have trained your opponent to respond in the desired way, you build upon this and lead him farther and farther into the maze of confusion.

WEIGHT TRANSFER: A broad shift in weight from one leg to the other will give the perception of forward or reverse movement. Because your opponent has a tendency to mirror your moves, you can use this concept to lure him forward and into your strike, or to move him back to create distance.

APPENDIX A
PHYSICAL CONDITIONING

THOUGHTS ON PHYSICAL CONDITIONING
by Keith Livingston

When asked about the most important aspect of kick-boxing, I would without hesitation say physical conditioning. I base this on my vast experience as a fighter, trainer, and spectator. Early in my career, I had a tendency to procrastinate on my training until I was notified of an upcoming event. Needless to say, my body was not physically prepared. Yet, I rationalized that my skill would see me through. I felt that I might get lucky and knock my opponent out in the early rounds. But when I took a fight on short notice, it became the eye-opener of my career. Unequivocally, I will submit to you that the most awful thing a fighter can experience is fatigue. Yes, worse than being cut or banged around for several rounds, even worse than getting knocked out.

First, you feel like you're fighting with twenty-pound ankle weights on your legs, you feel as though you are kicking in waist deep water. Your mobility is gone, and your kicks have little effect keeping your opponent at bay. Next, your lungs start to burn, and your stomach begins to tighten. Your focus is on your physical discomfort, and you lose your desire to continue. In fact, all you can think of is how much longer the round will last, and when the damn bell is going to ring. All the while, your opponent is sensing your misery, gaining confidence, and pressing the attack. Next, your shoulders begin to sag. Your guard drops, exposing you to punches and kicks that ordinarily would not find the mark. The crowd, too, senses your lack of determination and turns ugly. Boos and insults are hurled your way. You may survive the round, only to receive a tongue lashing from your corner. They try to give you water, but your labored breathing refuses the much needed liquid. Your stomach is balled up like a fist. You feel the bile building, but swallow to hold it down. Throwing up would only add to the humiliation.

You don't even hear the instructions from the corner, and you can care less about the fight plan. All you want is out of this self-imposed hell. Then the realization hits: You have only completed four rounds of a six-rounder. When the bell sounds, your primary concern is how to end the fight gracefully with your reputation still intact . . .

A fighter needs only experience this kind of fatigue once. All punching and kicking prowess is of no use if you can't muster the strength to use it. A well-conditioned fighter can compensate for a lack of skill, but a skilled fighter cannot compensate for a lack of conditioning. I have witnessed several bouts where the more skilled fighter lost because of poor conditioning. I have watched underdogs take champions the distance through conditioning. A properly conditioned fighter can give more punishment and take more punishment. Every attribute a fighter has is directly tied to conditioning. Conditioning often decides the victor. Resolve now to never take a fight without being properly conditioned.

413

STRENGTH TRAINING

In competition kickboxing, it is not your best buddy you are up against, but an opponent who wants to win as badly as you do, and who will do everything in his power to destroy your spirit. You may think it will be easy to fight for just three 2-minute rounds (for amateurs; more for professionals), but when you enter the ring for real, it is not like the sparring you do in the gym where everything and everyone is familiar. A large crowd will be watching you with a critical eye. The judges will remember best what they see last, and may judge you stricter on your performance toward the end of the last round when you are tired and hurt. In addition, you will know little or nothing about the person you are fighting. Your opponent will be a constant threat, and your head and body will take numerous blows that wear you down both physically and mentally.

In order to survive (even on the amateur level), the full-contact kickboxer must attain a high level of cardiovascular fitness, as well as a strong and supple body that can withstand the rigors of the sport. The conditioning routine may be hated, or at least disliked for the fact that it is grueling, painful, and boring. However, this portion of the training is very much necessary to prepare you for the fight.

Physical conditioning is important to help your body accomplish a variety of goals. You must develop all parts of the body to be used in the fight. Strengthening exercises train your muscles to bear heavy loads, flexibility exercises increase your muscles' ability to stretch, and aerobic exercises supply your muscles with oxygen. The exercises should be designed to give you endurance, and to strengthen your upper and lower body, as well as your abdomen and neck.

In addition to covering specific exercises to get you in shape for an upcoming fight, this section will focus on how to attain the right mind-set about physical conditioning. This involves not so much how to exercise, but rather why to exercise. We will cover both strength and cardiovascular training.

This section covers:

- Why should a kickboxer lift weights?
- Transfer of learning: the pros and cons
- Deciding on a weight training program
- Managing time
- How and what to lift
- Training with injuries
- Strengthening the upper body
- Strengthening the lower body
- Strengthening the abdomen
- Strengthening the neck
- Exercise chart
- Summing it up

WHY SHOULD A KICKBOXER LIFT WEIGHTS?

Much about training for competition involves getting in good enough shape to persevere for the duration of the fight. Because it is difficult to rise to competition level suddenly, hitting it hard for a few weeks prior to the bout while neglecting to implement a continuous training regimen is usually a bad idea. It is better to develop a program that you can stay with comfortably and look forward to for the long haul. This means that there should be a good balance. Training should not be too exhausting, yet it must be intense enough to condition your body on a continual basis. Thus, when you need to step it up for competition, the additional intensity of your workouts is not that much more than what you are already doing.

The reason you want to strength train is to develop power and endurance. Strength training also decreases the risk of injuries. The same goes for flexibility training. We often don't think about that strength and flexibility go hand in hand. Being flexible will not help you much if you lack the strength to lift your leg for a high kick.

Note that strength training is not skill specific. In other words, it will not directly improve your punching speed, timing, or strategy. But it will help you indirectly by increasing your confidence when under pressure, which, in turn, will make you a more successful competitor.

Many people equate weight lifting to bodybuilding. But weight lifting is beneficial to those who lift for no other reason than to improve physical strength. Because this book is not about weight lifting, we will approach the training slightly differently than if it were intended for bodybuilders.

As you hit the gym, remember that your main focus is on developing strength and endurance for fighting. Much of this is done through sparring and related work on heavy bag and mitts. Your weight training should be supplemental; it should not dominate your workout.

TRANSFER OF LEARNING: THE PROS AND CONS

The strength or endurance required for one activity is not necessarily the same strength or endurance required for another activity. For example, you might think that you have great endurance because you can run ten miles without breaking a sweat. Yet, when you spar, you can hardly go three rounds. Or you may go to the gym several days a week and lift weights and you have a finely toned musculature, yet, when you jab away at the heavy bag for a few rounds, you get arm weary. The strength and endurance required to kickbox is not the same strength and endurance required to lift weights or to run. Rather than spending most of your time lifting weights, you should spend the majority of your time doing exercises that directly relate to kickboxing.

Lifting weights does not necessarily make your punches stronger. However, holding weights in your hands when punching may make your punches stronger because the movement is more specific to the skill. Still, there is no proof that training with resistance will make you a better kickboxer. For example, placing weights around your ankles when practicing kicks may actually hinder your speed rather than enhancing it. The problem with using weighted objects in training is that negative transfer of learning occurs. If something is supposed to be done at a certain speed, then the movement should be practiced at that particular speed. Practicing with a weighted object at a slower speed will interfere with your timing, thus the negative transfer of learning. The required effort when using weighted objects results in a different movement than without the weights. So when you remove the weights later, you have, in effect, trained your muscles to remember a different movement.

For an exercise to carry over into a skill, the specific muscles used in the exercise and the skill must be the same, the movement must be the same, the speed must be the same, and the resistance must be the same. This is why lifting weights does not necessarily make you a better puncher. In fact, the only way you can become a better puncher is by practicing punching. However, lifting weights will increase the size of your muscles, and therefore your strength, so there is still benefit. But you should be careful not to spend too much time practicing exercises that do not directly carry over to the skill you are trying to improve. The best way to improve a skill is to practice that particular skill thousands of times, until it becomes part of your motor memory.

In general, you should train the way you intend to fight. Using heavy gloves in training and then "downsizing" to lighter gloves in the fight may not be sound, because the lighter gloves may change your timing. The feeling that you are faster after removing the weight may just be a sensory illusion.

If the above is true, then why should the kickboxer strength train? First, being strong helps you endure more; your muscles won't tire as fast. If you know which particular muscle group you are using in the skill, you should weight train to strengthen that specific muscle group. Second, a well-built body looks impressive. Being muscular or lean can be an intimidation factor to your opponent. Kickboxers fight in shorts. Male kickboxers often fight with nothing on their upper body. Female kickboxers often fight in just a sports bra on their upper body. When we see a fighter who is well defined, it also tells us something about how disciplined he is.

It is questionable how much raw power muscular strength gives you, as power is more a combination of correct body mechanics coupled with speed. But the bottom line is that strong muscles can be more powerful using less effort.

Lean and well-defined fighters take their training seriously.

DECIDING ON A WEIGHT TRAINING PROGRAM

So, if you're not lifting to be a bodybuilder, how should you tailor your conditioning program to bring maximum results? Should you lift few reps with heavy weights, or many reps with lighter weights? Does it matter whether you work upper and lower body on the same day? Does it matter in which order you do the exercises?

Personally, I prefer lifting light to moderately heavy weights that allow me to do about 12 repetitions per set. If the weights aren't heavy enough, you will probably not add any significant muscle mass. However, lighter weights tend to improve your muscular endurance, especially if you lift regularly.

One of my favorite weight lifting routines for endurance training is heavy-hands. This exercise uses light dumbbells, 3-10 pounds, for each hand. You run through a continuous series of 30-second segments for each exercise. The whole sequence takes five minutes. You are not allowed to stop and rest between segments. This gives you a really good burn and forces you to endure until the end.

Try this exercise on **HEAVY HANDS**:

Exercise 1

Each of the following exercises should be done for 30 seconds, working as fast as you can. There is no rest between sets. The exercises are designed to build your biceps, triceps, shoulders, and lats. The order in which you do the exercises is of little importance. If you are just starting out, use three-pound weights. As your strength improves, increase the weights to five pounds, and then to ten pounds.

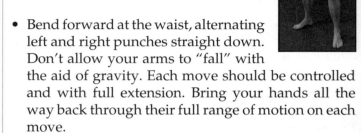

- From a neutral stance, alternate straight left and right punches. Work full extension in your arms and bring your hands all the way back to the guard position on each punch. To avoid hyper-extension or injury to the elbow, do not snap your arm. Each move should be controlled.

- Bend forward at the waist, alternating left and right punches straight down. Don't allow your arms to "fall" with the aid of gravity. Each move should be controlled and with full extension. Bring your hands all the way back through their full range of motion on each move.

- Standing upright, alternate right and left punches straight up. Control each move and avoid using gravity when lowering the weight.

- Bend forward at the waist, working flies, raising your arms as high as possible and squeezing your back muscles on each move.

- Standing upright, raise your arms alternately straight forward and up in a half circle. A slight bend in the elbow may help you avoid injury to your shoulder. Otherwise keep your arms straight for maximum rotational inertia.

- Bend forward at the waist. Start with your hands extended straight back, palms up. Bring your hands forward in a half-circle down, gradually rotating your hands until they are again palm up, extended forward. Reverse, raising your arms as high as possible to the rear.

- Standing upright, bring your arms up and back down in a jumping jack motion. Work as fast as you can without losing control of the move.

- Work triceps by bending at the waist, keeping your elbow up, and extending the lower portion of your arm to the rear. Raise as high as possible.

- Alternate left and right uppercuts/hooks, or do bicep curls. Control each move to avoid using gravity to your advantage.

• Do lateral raises with your arms extended straight to your sides. Raise your arms to shoulder height on each move. Keep your shoulders down to avoid using momentum.

Note: I have placed the exercises in an alternating upward and downward order, but any order is fine. You can also come up with your own set of exercises, or substitute those that you don't like. It is important that you work all muscle groups in the arms and shoulders, including the lats.

MANAGING TIME

Studies of people in the work place have shown that most of us only work three hours in an eight-hour day. The rest of the time is spent taking breaks and socializing, and generally being unproductive. Yet, we feel as though we are working a full day. When I go to the gym, I often see the same group of people when I come in still there when I leave. They spend hours a day at the gym, yet they don't seem to be doing much. Most of their time is spent socializing. If you can be productive in a short time, you will get a lot done and still have time left for yourself. My best workouts are 45 minutes of intense training. I don't over train. I don't burn out. I stay sharp while I'm at the gym, and I don't neglect the rest of my life.

Because weight lifting does not directly improve your kickboxing skills, your main focus should be on kickboxing. In other words, don't lift so often or so much that you sacrifice kickboxing training. A productive strength training program should include a high level of intensity. Train with the intent of tiring your muscles. If you quit the moment it begins to hurt, your time at the gym will be wasted. If you don't achieve muscular fatigue, you will not gain much strength or size. Regardless of how often you go to the gym or how much time you spend there, when there, train with intent. Because nobody can train for hours at a high intensity, the intense workout allows you to shorten the training time, lessening the risk of burnout.

When determining the effectiveness of your workouts, consider how compact they are. If you have little time to accomplish a task, you have to give an all out effort in order to get it done. Before starting a training session, know how long you are going in for. Set a timer for forty minutes, or twenty minutes even, and know that if you waste time, you will not meet your goal. By being organized and compact, you can accomplish just as much as your friends around the block, who spend hours in the gym. Make sure that you know exactly what to work on before you start your session.

Try these exercises on **MANAGING TIME**:

Exercise 2

Having a goal when you go to the gym helps you stay motivated without wasting time. Make a list of the exercises you want to work. This keeps you on track and saves time, because you won't be standing around wondering what to do next. Mark off the list as you go, noting how many reps you did and with how much weight. When you have a specific goal, training becomes meaningful, time is not wasted, and you can see your progress easier.

Exercise 3

Managing time should be part of your regular kickboxing workout as well. If you go to the gym just to beat the heavy bag for a few rounds, you won't feel nearly as productive as if you know beforehand that you are going to jump rope for three rounds as a warm-up, and then work on the spinning back kick specifically, and then finish with some good stretching. The same is true when going to class. Although your instructor is in charge of the specific exercises you do, you can still have an objective within those exercises. For example, decide to throw everything half a beat faster than your partner or opponent. Or decide to include at least one kick in every combination you throw.

Next, you must ask yourself how often you should strength train. If you exercise only once a week, your muscles won't benefit much in the long run. If you exercise every day, it will be too much, and you will fatigue the muscles and not allow them enough time to recover before your next workout.

Is it possible to reach a plateau when strength training? Sure! If you don't give your body adequate time to heal and rest between training sessions, you may actually begin to feel weaker rather than stronger.

When I go on vacation for a week and don't train at all, I allow my body to recover and get ready to train hard again. This is when I see new improvements.

If you get bored with the workouts, you probably need to vary your routine more. Keep your mind focused on the workout and not on "getting it done." If your mind is drifting, start to look for ways to bring in more variety. This can be as simple as reversing the order of the exercises.

My belief is that most of your strength training should come many weeks before the actual fight. Use the last few weeks before the fight for sparring and strategy rather than on increasing strength. Avoid putting too much weight training into your last week before a fight. You want to feel strong and ready, rather than sore and tired.

HOW AND WHAT TO LIFT

There has been much argument about whether free weights are more beneficial than machines. It is my belief that it is the intensity that determines the benefits, not free weights or machines. However, many people have a hard time getting motivated with free weights, especially if they lift alone in their home. We are well aware of the many advertisements on TV that prompt us to buy one "abdominizer" after another, but how many of these gizmos are really being used on a regular basis by the buyer? No machine will do the work for you. Your muscles don't build themselves; you have to work at it.

An increase in strength occurs when you apply a load that stimulates muscular growth. Muscular strength is also determined by inherent ability and the level of intensity in your workouts. In order to increase size and strength, the workload must be progressive. As long as the muscles are fatigued, it doesn't matter whether you use a machine or free weights.

Every exercise that can be done with barbells can also be done with dumbbells. Dumbbells have many other advantages as well. For example, they allow you to grip the weights in many different ways, so you can bring more versatility into your workout and exercise slightly different muscle groups. Gripping the weights in a different manner, or using a lighter weight on one side, may also help you while recovering from an injury. Dumbbells can add great variety to your workouts, as well as work your arms separately or with opposing movements.

You can also strength train without weights and with your partner providing resistance. Just about every exercise that can be done with weights can be done without weights with a partner. The benefit is that you can do these types of exercises anywhere. The drawback is that a partner may not provide consistent resistance throughout the exercise, or he may provide uneven resistance between the right and left sides of your body. Also, a smaller partner may not be able to give enough resistance to benefit a bigger person. A benefit for your partner is that, by providing resistance, his muscles get exercised to some extent as well. Another advantage is that the person providing resistance will feel how hard his partner works, and can encourage him. Some resistance exercises can be done by both you and your partner simultaneously. For example, grab a stick rather than your partner's arms, and sit down while your partner remains standing. Perform a pull-down against your partner's resistance; your partner, who is standing, performs an upright row. If you are both sitting, do seated rows back and forth.

Much of your ability to develop muscle size is inherited. The person who does not have favorable genetics must work harder than the person who does. So, with this in mind, if you are unable to attain the same size as your classmate, yet lift as much as him, you are actually working harder (applying yourself better) and should be commended. The person with favorable genetics doesn't have to be as disciplined in order to attain the same results.

Following a specific training program will not yield the same results for everybody. Again, it is a matter of genetics. It is therefore not necessarily wise for you to follow the same program that brought great results for the bodybuilding champion.

In general, muscles should be exercised from largest to smallest: hips and buttocks, upper legs, lower legs, upper torso, arms, abdomen, and lower back. If smaller muscles are exercised first, they will hinder the performance of the larger muscles because they will already be fatigued. For example, if you exercise the abs first, it may detract from the performance of other exercises. Exercising the lower back early may also hinder other exercises. I have often noticed that if my abs are fatigued, I don't perform as well in pushups. I therefore do pushups before I do abs. You should also strengthen the neck. Kickboxers take many blows to the head, and a strong neck decreases the risk of whiplash injuries. Strengthening the neck is often overlooked.

Many people who lift weights cheat. When I'm at the gym, I see people who use momentum on every lift. Using momentum may allow you to lift heavier weights, but it doesn't benefit you because it's not actually your muscles that do the work. It is better to decrease the weight to what you can comfortably lift. Then slow the reps to ensure that you are using your muscles rather than momentum. Be especially careful with using momentum when speeding up the reps.

Also note the benefits of muscular endurance. Strength refers to how much dead weight you can lift; endurance refers to how long you can keep going. A muscularly strong person may have less endurance than a weaker person. In a contest with very light weights (ten-pound dumbbells), where everybody does military presses for as long as they can, the muscularly strongest person will only last longest if his endurance is sufficient.

TRAINING WITH INJURIES

We all agree that injuries should be treated appropriately. But sometimes you have little nagging injuries that don't really require a physician's attention; for example, tendonitis or shoulder pain that you only feel when doing certain moves. Because of my job as a baggage handler for Delta Air Lines for eighteen years, I have mild tendonitis in my right elbow. I only feel it when I lift heavy weights in a biceps curl movement. So, when I do this exercise, I lessen the weight by a few pounds on my right arm until I don't feel any pain, or I change the angle of the movement slightly until I don't feel any pain. I still work the heavier weights with my left arm. I also have pain in my right knee when doing bicycle type moves. This is because of a martial arts injury early in my career. However, I don't feel pain when doing squats or running. So, I find an exercise that still works the legs, but doesn't aggravate the injury.

You can also train with injuries by limiting the range of motion. If you hurt only at the beginning of the move, then start with your arm or leg already slightly curled, and avoid full extension. If you have more severe injuries, like torn ligaments, you can still keep in shape with exercises that don't affect the injured area at all. I have found that it is generally better to be mobile than to sit still. Don't place stress on the injured part, and follow your doctor's advice. Don't aggravate your injuries just because you feel that you have to lift. But don't become a couch-potato either. Your injury should not be an excuse to withdraw from training completely. Working out while injured can also have a positive mental effect. I have found that I feel sicker than I am if I pamper the injury too much. When I go on with my normal life and make small adjustments wherever needed, I seem to recover faster.

Strengthening the upper body

Upper body strength, particularly in the arms and shoulders, is crucial to fighting. A regular two-minute round can have you throwing more than one-hundred punches. In addition, the offensive minded fighter usually has the upper hand over the fighter who relies mainly on defense. When you get arm weary, you are unable to keep up with the continuous and fast pace that is often necessary in order to score on a tough opponent. Try these exercises for building upper body strength:

PUSHUPS

I have found old fashion pushups to be the single most effective upper body strength and endurance building exercise. The pushup is time-economic. It can be done anywhere at any time, and allows you to lift approximately 70 percent of your body weight. Being female is no excuse for doing pushups on your knees. If you can't do even one regular pushup, start with your hands on a chair. When you can do five full pushups this way, remove the chair and do the pushups on the floor. Doing several sets of pushups throughout the day helps you get stronger fast. Work through full range of motion. Cheating by doing half pushups only hinders your goal of building strength. Don't do the pushup too fast. Faster is not better. Again, you want to avoid using momentum. If you don't already have good upper body strength, start with sets of 15, increasing, as you grow stronger, to sets of 50. Allow yourself time to recover between sets. If you have been doing cardiovascular exercises, wait until your heart rate is back to normal. Not giving yourself time to recover will hinder your ability to do the pushup.

1. Work different hand positions to condition the variety of muscles in your arms and shoulders. A wide hand position works mostly the sides of your body, while a narrow hand position works your chest and triceps.

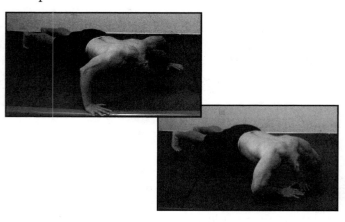

2. Try knuckle pushups to strengthen your wrists. Again, vary the width of your hands as well as the direction your hands are facing. For example, turning your hands palms forward works different muscles in your forearms and upper arms than the regular palms in pushup position.

3. When you get good at floor pushups, try them on chairs (three chairs are required for this exercise). Place your feet on one chair, and one hand on each of the other two chairs. This allows you to lower yourself below the seat of the chairs.

4. Do pushups from a handstand position with your partner holding your feet for support. This is the most difficult pushup exercise, because you are lifting one-hundred percent of your body weight. You can start this exercise with a partial incline; for example, place your hands on the floor and your feet on your partner's shoulders.

5. Work negative pushups by starting in the up position and lowering yourself through a five- or ten-count toward the floor, until you are low enough to touch your nose. Hold the down position for five seconds. The negative pushup can also be used preparatory to the regular pushup, if you are not strong enough to do the regular pushup yet.

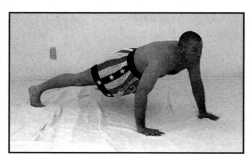

Spreading your legs, especially when working the hands narrow position, makes the pushup slightly easier and is a good way to start.

Pushups work the biceps, triceps, pectoral muscles, and lats, depending on the width between your hands. If your hands are close together, you will work more of the pectorals and triceps, and if your hands are far apart, you will work more of the lats. Pushups should be performed at a slow to medium pace with full range of motion. Tighten your abs and keep your back straight. We often mistakenly think that the faster the pushup, the better: Look at me, I can do fifty pushups in twenty seconds! But a slow pushup forces the muscles to work longer. Try it and feel the difference.

PULLUPS

Pullups require great upper body strength. Start with the assisted pullup, using either a weight machine designed for this purpose, or asking a friend to steady your body while pushing with one hand on your back. After a few weeks of practice, you should be able to perform pullups relying on your own upper body strength. Grab the pullup bar with the palms of your hands facing away from you. For a better grip, your thumb should grip the top of the bar along with your fingers. Our best gripping strength is in the pinky, ring, and middle finger, with the thumb and index finger designed more for fine motor skills, such as writing. Gripping with your thumb below the bar lessens your strength slightly.

1. Vary the width between your hands to work different muscle groups. A narrow grip works your chest muscles more, while a wide grip works your lats

(the sides of your body). Start with a set number of pullups: three sets of five, for example, increasing the sets and reps as you grow stronger.

2. To get maximum benefit from this exercise, lower yourself all the way down each time. In the beginning, you may touch the floor with your toes between each repetition, until you can do the full pullup hanging freely from the bar.

3. Pull up until your chin touches the bar. As the pullups become easier, alternate by touching the back of your neck to the bar instead of your chin.

Dips

Dips are good for building triceps strength (the back of your upper arms). The triceps are involved in the extension of the arm. Strong triceps allow you to throw more explosive punches. The triceps are often ignored in kickboxing strength training. Work a slow to medium pace, and don't cheat on the movement.

1. Place your hands behind you on the seat of a chair. Keep your arms straight (your butt should not be touching the chair). Keep your feet on the floor and your legs straight. Lower yourself toward the floor by bending your arms. Go as low as you can, then push back up until your arms are straight.

2. You can also do dips from the floor, without using any kind of equipment. Place your feet flat on the floor, keep your butt off the floor, and your hands behind you. Keep your upper body straight; do not allow your butt to sag toward the floor. Lower yourself toward the floor by bending your arms. **Do not simply drop your butt while keeping your arms straight.** You must bend your arms to get any benefit from this exercise.

3. If you are at the gym, try the dips on the triceps bars. Grab one bar with each hand and keep your arms straight. Bend your knees until your feet are off the floor and lower yourself toward the floor by bending your arms, until your lower and upper arm form a 90-degree angle. Some gyms have machines that allow you to do assisted dips with a counterweight.

Weight Training

A healthy dose of weight training will increase your upper body strength and muscular endurance. I like to use medium heavy weights that allow me to do two sets of twelve for each muscle group. I often supplement with one set of fifteen pushups between each group of exercises. When lifting weights, I focus primarily on my shoulders, upper back, and lats. I feel that the seated row is great for building a strong upper back. Also try shadow boxing with light handheld weights (5 pounds). Keep your guard high even when you begin to get arm weary. Throw all strikes with control to avoid using momentum or over-extending the elbow.

Note: There are a variety of exercises that can be done with barbells, dumbbells, or weight training machines. I have opted not to list each exercise, as there are many good reference books written specifically for weight lifting. The important part is that you use a good variety that conditions all muscles of the upper body.

Strengthening the lower body

The legs are the first to go when a fighter gets tired (some fights have a minimum kick requirement of eight kicks per round). Try these lower body exercises to develop strength in your legs for kicking:

SQUATS

Squats develop strength and endurance in the quadriceps (thighs), which are involved in lifting your leg when kicking. Strong quads allow you to throw higher and faster kicks. Work the squat with full control, lowering yourself until your thighs are parallel with the floor, until you feel a good burn.

1. Keep your back straight, feet about shoulder width and a half apart, and arms extended straight out in front of you. Start with three sets of twenty squats.

2. Come up halfway and hold for a count of five before lowering yourself back down.

3. Hold your lowest squat position for a certain length of time. Start with ten seconds, then come up halfway and hold for another ten seconds, then come back down to your lowest position and hold. As your strength builds, increase the time and number of reps.

4. Try squats while holding a light barbell: forty pounds, for example, on your shoulders.

5. Perform the squat lunge both forward and to the side. Do these with and without weights.

6. For a more challenging workout, try the jump-squat. Start with your left foot forward, your right foot back, and your hands on your hips. Lower yourself down to the low squat position. Push off until both your feet are no longer in contact with the floor. Switch the position of your feet in the air, and repeat the procedure.

TOE RAISES

Toe raises work your calf muscles and ankles. For greater effect, stand with your toes on a low object: a stairway or yellow pages phone book, for example. Your heels should not be touching.

1. Dip your heels as low as possible toward the floor without touching, and raise back up as high as possible. Start with a set of fifty and go as fast as you can. Also try this with a light barbell on your shoulders.

2. Hook one foot behind the calf of your other leg, so that one leg only supports all of your weight. Do as many one-legged toe raises as you can, as fast as you can. Switch to the other leg.

FROG HOPS

This is an excellent exercise for building strength in both the upper and lower portions of your legs. To execute the frog hop, come down in a low squat position with your hands clasped behind your head. Execute a series of jumps, springing from the balls of your feet (some people find this exercise hard on the knees. Being properly warmed up is helpful before initiating the frog hop series).

1. Frog hop in place for a set number of reps (start with twenty-five). Take a ten second break to stretch your legs. Repeat the exercise four times.

2. Get in a low squat with your left foot forward and frog hop five times. On your sixth hop, switch with your right foot forward and hop five more times. Switch back and forth in this manner for a set number of hops. You can also switch on every other hop, or on every hop.

3. Place a number of low obstacles on the floor (your boxing gloves or footpads will work well). Frog hop over these obstacles, or weave between or around them.

4. Try the frog hop in combination with the squat. Frog hop twenty-five times, then come up to a low squat position and hold for ten to twenty seconds. Repeat.

The frog hop is a low squat position with your fingers interlaced behind the back of your head. Stay low and hop like a frog. This exercise gives you a really good burn in your thighs.

BENCH RUNNING

This exercises involves stepping up and down on an obstacle (alternating feet), touching with the balls of your feet only. You do not actually place your weight on the obstacle; you just touch it with the balls of your feet. Bench running builds both your lower body strength and your cardiovascular endurance.

1. Start with a low obstacle: two yellow pages phone books, for example. Step as fast as you can for thirty seconds. Keep your hands in the high guard position. Repeat the exercise three times with a fifteen second rest between sets.

2. Increase the height of the obstacle until you are using a bench (thereof the name) or a chair. Increase the length of the rounds to one minute, then two minutes, until you can go for three 2-minute rounds with a 1-minute rest between rounds.

Bench running works both your legs and your cardiovascular endurance. Start with three one-minute rounds of stepping with a thirty-second break between rounds.

Strengthening the abdomen

A strong abdomen increases your ability to take a good blow to the mid-section. Everybody has a different potential for building strong and good looking abs, depending on genetic makeup. Rather than striving to look like others, it is better to work on making your abs look great according to your own body's balance. When you start building your abs, keep in mind that even strong abs, when relaxed, don't look overly impressive.

Building great looking abs also depends on your eating habits. I don't recommend depriving yourself of everything you enjoy. For example, protein is needed for muscle growth, but this doesn't mean that you should overload on protein and cut carbohydrates. The body is still only capable of using so much protein, and carbohydrates are your body's fuel.

There have been times when I have wanted to lose a few pounds, and have gotten on a diet low in fat and calories. But I found that the price I had to pay was feeling hungry and weak. I am a big chocolate lover, but cutting chocolate from my diet only made me feel like something was missing, and it didn't help me lose weight. When I got back on my usual daily dose of chocolate, I felt better, and did not gain any weight as a result. My recommendation is that you take other people's theories with a grain of salt.

When working the abs, focus on working the abs. I know, this sounds obvious, but I often feel that many exercises for the abs employ difficult balancing maneuvers. If you have to work too hard on keeping your balance, you can't concentrate on working the ab muscles. Make sure that you have good support when doing abdominal work. Try these abdominal exercises:

SITUPS

There are a wide variety of abdominal exercises. I am a proponent of the full situp, even though many exercise specialists recommend the crunch instead. Whichever situp exercise you choose, make sure that you use your abdominal muscles and don't cheat by using momentum. Work each rep slow and with control.

1. Lie on your back and bend your knees. Keep your feet flat on the floor. Place your hands behind your head and crunch until your shoulders are off the floor. Keep your elbows pointed to the sides. Your focus should be the ceiling (not the opposite wall). Start with a set of twenty.

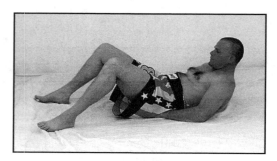

If you are just starting out, you can also do the abdominal crunch with your hands below your lower back for support.

Note: Many exercise specialists recommend against clasping your hands behind your head, as this may cause strain on your neck or lower back. You may try a variation of this exercise by crossing your arms over your chest instead. If this seems too easy, place a light weight (a ten pound sandbag, for example) on your chest underneath your crossed arms. When doing this exercise, don't come all the way up to a sitting position, but raise only your shoulders off the floor. When coming back down, don't let your shoulders touch the floor. As with all exercise routines, there is always a risk of injury. It is therefore important to use common sense and discontinue the exercise or vary your technique until you don't feel any pain.

2. Bend your knees, bring your feet off the floor, and cross them at the ankles. To get the most benefit from this type of situp, make sure that you are not rocking back and forth using momentum. Keep your lower back flat on the floor, your thighs vertical, and your shins horizontal. To help you achieve this, place your calves flat against the seat of a chair.

The double crunch, where you bring your upper and lower body together, works both your upper and lower abs simultaneously.

3. Also try situps with your legs in a variety of positions. Try extending one leg straight, resting your other foot on that leg's knee. Repeat on the other side. Also try situps with your legs off the floor, spread and extended at a forty-five degree angle upward. When you don't have the support of the floor under your feet, you are forced to work your abdominal muscles. Initially, you may want to place your hands under your lower back for support.

The weighted situp is a good way to increase difficulty without increasing time.

PELVIC THRUSTS

In general, it can be said that when the movement is in your upper body, you are working your upper abs, and when the movement is in your lower body, you are working your lower abs. The pelvic thrust is a lower ab exercise.

1. Lie on your back and grab your partner's ankles. Raise your legs to the vertical position and thrust your feet straight up toward the ceiling, until you are all the way up on your shoulders. Do this exercise with control to avoid using momentum.

2. Try the negative pelvic thrust by thrusting your feet toward the ceiling (your lower back should be off the floor), then lowering yourself slowly during a count to ten. It is important that your legs remain vertically straight for the duration of the exercise. If you allow them to tip forward over your head, or backward toward the floor, your stomach muscles will not derive the most benefit from this exercise.

3. Without a partner, place your hands on the floor or under your lower back for support and repeat the pelvic thrust exercises on your own.

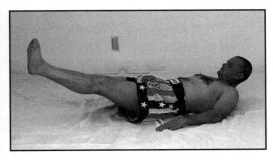

Bring your knees toward your chest and push your feet straight up toward the ceiling, until you are up on your shoulders.

LEG LIFTS

The leg lift is another lower ab exercise that requires strong abs as support for your back. Your back should be flat against the floor. You can place your hands under your lower back for support, if needed.

1. Lie on your back, extend your arms over your head, and grab the legs of a chair. Keep your legs straight and raise your feet off the floor until your legs are extended vertically. Lower your legs to six inches off the floor. Start with a set of twenty. Make sure that your lower back is pressed tightly against the floor and not arched.

2. Place your hands under your lower back for support. Raise your legs to the vertical position, then lower them back down halfway and hold for a count of five, then lower them all the way down to one inch off the floor and again hold for a count of five (keep your legs straight, and do not let your feet touch the floor). Come halfway up and hold while spreading your legs slowly. Repeat the exercise a number of times.

3. Lie on your back with your partner standing behind you. Grab his ankles, keep your legs straight and raise them to the vertical position. Have your partner push your legs back down (keep your legs straight and try not to touch your feet to the floor). Next time your legs come to the vertical position, have your partner push them back down but to the side (alternating sides). This will work your obliques (sides).

4. Raise your legs to the vertical position. Stretch your arms toward your toes, bringing your upper body off the floor. This exercise works more of your upper abs, because that's where the movement is, even though your feet are off the floor.

Note: In general, it can be said that any abdominal exercise that involves movement with your legs (leg lifts, for example) works the muscles in your lower abdomen, and any abdominal exercise that involves movement with your upper body (situps, for example) works the muscles in your upper abdomen. You should also work the sides (the obliques). You can do this by lying on your side with your knees slightly bent and your hands clasped behind your head. Now, raise your shoulders off the floor until you get a good crunch in your side. Or do V-ups from a side position, bringing your legs and shoulders off the floor simultaneously. You can also work the obliques by twisting side-to-side. Try this standing with your arms supported on a stick across your shoulders.

KNEEUPS

The kneeup is an advanced abdominal exercise that requires strong abs as support for your back. Some gyms have kneeup equipment that supports your back while you do the exercise. As you get stronger, try the free-hanging kneeup.

1. Hang from a pullup bar. Cross your ankles, round your back, and bring your knees up toward your chest.

2. As you get stronger, try this exercise with straight legs. Make sure that your back is rounded and not arched.

MEDICINE BALL

As you get stronger, you will want to add some weight or resistance to increase the difficulty of the ab exercises. The medicine ball is a good device when doing upper ab exercises, but any weight that you can hold or place on your chest will work. The medicine ball can also help you tighten your abs at the right moment in preparation for a punch. Medicine balls come at different weights ranging from 12 to 25 pounds.

1. Lie on your back and have a partner drop the medicine ball on your abdomen. Start from a distance of six inches and increase as you get stronger.

Make sure your abs are tight when absorbing the impact.

2. Stand up and have your partner throw the medicine ball against your abdomen. Let the ball hit before you catch it and throw it back to your partner.

3. You can do the same type of exercise without the medicine ball. Instead, have your partner wear boxing gloves and hit your abdomen and sides of body (lightly at first) to build up resistance to blows.

Strengthening the neck

Your neck must be strong to withstand blows to the head. If your head snaps back on impact with a punch, you risk whiplash injury. Still, my experience is that the neck is often neglected in most fighters' exercise routines. You can strengthen your neck through a variety of resistance exercises.

WITH PARTNER

Your partner can provide resistance against your head for all directions of neck strengthening exercises. The resistance should be applied smoothly and with control, and be adjusted to meet your ability to push against his hand. Avoid removing the resistance suddenly.

1. Have your partner place the palm of his hand against the side of your head and push. Keep your neck straight.

2. Have your partner repeat the same exercise against the back of your head and against your forehead. The pressure should be applied smoothly and consistently without any jerking or bouncing.

3. Place your chin in the palm of your partner's hand and press down, while he provides resistance.

WITHOUT PARTNER

Many of the neck strengthening exercises can be done alone without the help of a partner. You can also use simple homemade devices to supply the resistance.

1. Place the palm of your own hand against the sides, front, and back of your head and apply pressure.

2. Place an inner tube of a bicycle tire around the top portion of your head. Attach the other end around a steady object (the ring posts, for example), and apply pressure by walking or leaning away. Keep your neck straight for static strength building, or press in short moves forward and back against the resistance of the inner tube.

3. Also lie on your back, raising your head and pressing your chin toward your chest, then dropping your head back down. Start with a set of thirty. It doesn't sound like much but is guaranteed to give you a good burn in your neck.

EXERCISE CHART

To establish a training level for the upper body, lower body, abdomen, and neck, do as many as you can as fast as you can in one minute. Now, split that number by half. For example, if you do fifty situps in one minute, twenty-five is the number you will use during your workouts. In between each strength building exercise, do cardiovascular work for thirty seconds.

The exercises in the chart are used as examples. You may use them as is, or substitute your own exercises. The chart is provided so that you can monitor individual gains and improvements in overall fitness.

Your physical exercises should increase weekly. When planning your physical exercise schedule, you can work upper body and lower body on alternating days, or you can work them on the same day and skip a day in between. The exercises should also be done in sets. For example, you may start with three sets of 10 pushups three days a week. The second week, you may increase to three sets of 15, and so on, until you have attained a good upper and lower body physique. Work the abdomen every day.

	MON	TUE	WED	THUR	FRI	SAT	SUN	TOTAL
PUSH UPS								
PULL UPS								
DIPS								
SQUATS								
TOE RAISES								
FROG HOPS								
BENCH RUNNING								
SIT UPS								
LEG LIFTS								
NECK								

SUMMING IT UP

I have found the simplest training methods to be the best. For upper body strength, I recommend pushups, dips, and pullups. For lower body strength, I recommend running, especially on hills, and squat jumps. Running also does wonders for your heart. If I had to choose between cardiovascular strength and muscular strength, I would definitely choose the cardio. If you don't have the wind, all the muscle strength in the world won't help you. I also like endurance workouts with light dumbbells, five to ten pounds, for example, with continuous alternating punches for three minutes straight.

When supplementing your kickboxing training with weight training, remember that you are first and foremost a kickboxer. This means that the majority of your training should be in kickboxing and not in other supplementary exercises. Most of my running and weight training is 40 – 50 minutes in duration. I think that training often is more important than training long, and if you train too much with weights, you may take away valuable time that could have been spent sparring or practicing your techniques.

In a typical week, I run 10 miles (3 uphill). I also average 70 pushups a day (good full pushups, not from my knees), 20 pullups a day, and 250-300 situps of some variety a day. Today, for example, I ran three miles, did 135 pushups, 36 pullups, spent about 15 minutes on the weight machines, then went to kickboxing class in the evening where I did another 30 pushups, about 200 situps, a couple of minutes of squat jumps, and then half an hour of sparring. My total workout time today was slightly shy of two hours.

CARDIOVASCULAR TRAINING

Strength without cardiovascular fitness is meaningless. Lifting weights might give you a good muscular build, but it doesn't mean that you can last in a fight, or that you can take punches and kicks over and over and still finish. Being in good aerobic shape allows you to recover faster between rounds, and to fight harder during the round. If you are wasted aerobically, your physical strength will do you little good.

Much of a fighter's aerobic training comes from bag work and sparring. If you strength train and spar the same day, it is recommended that you do the sparring first. Because sparring is the most important component of your kickboxing training, sparring first allows you to approach it with maximum intensity. A great way to improve cardiovascular fitness for sparring is to do a lot of sparring. Spar longer rounds or more rounds with shorter rest periods in between. However, it may still benefit you to include other aerobic activity.

This section covers:

- A day in the life . . .
- Running
- Running chart
- Assessment chart
- Jumping rope
- Swimming
- Plyometrics

A DAY IN THE LIFE . . .
by Keith Livingston

The alarm is screaming for you to awake. As you bring your body into the world of the living, you feel the aches and pains from yesterday: the bruise on your shin, the pain in your jaw, and the overall stiffness in your body. You feel as though you have been sleeping on a pile of rocks all night, and for a fleeting moment you rationalize your need to stay in bed and rest. But then you think about your opponent.

"He is probably out running already!"

The thought hits you like a brick, and you hear the voice of your coach somewhere in the far reaches of your mind: Fights are won or lost in the preparation! You peel your body away from the mattress, stagger to the dresser, and don your running clothes. A faint smile creeps across your lips as you think about your drive to the mountains for this morning's scheduled altitude run. It just so happens that your route goes right past Coach's house. Coach will be sleeping, snug and warm under the covers. And it just so happens that your car horn will get stuck again . . . at the same place it always gets stuck, right outside Coach's bedroom window.

This morning's run is a three-miler at high altitude. Your next competition is in Denver (the mile-high city), and you want to prepare your lungs for the thinner air. You begin the run with some difficulty, as your body attempts to adjust to the sudden demand placed upon it. But when you have the first mile behind you, you begin to feel pretty good. Physically, your body has loosened up and adjusted, and mentally, you know that you have overcome another obstacle on the road to fight day. You finish mile three at a strong pace and are happy that you once again were able to give a hundred percent.

When you get home, you make a mental note to get your car horn fixed. It gut stuck twice this morning, ironically both times at the same place. But now it is time for breakfast. You whip up some pancakes, toast, oatmeal, and a couple of glasses of juice. Although a bowl of Lucky Charms and a cup of coffee would taste a ton better, you know it is important to fill the body's gas tank with carbohydrates (the body's fuel).

The rest of the morning and part of the afternoon are pretty ordinary as you join the human race. Finally, four o'clock rolls around and you arrive at the gym for your evening workout. As you walk through the door, you smell the sweat and listen to the thuds of leather on leather as fighters strike the bags. Then, from somewhere in the depths: C'mon, harder! What do you think this is, retirement city!?

You dress and walk into the gym. "Hi, Coach! How ya doin'?"

Coach gives you a grumpy stare. "Some asshole keeps waking me up every morning. Get ready to spar!"

You wrap your hands with precision and tape your feet, ankles, and shins. Your warm-up consists of a couple of rounds of shadow boxing and ten minutes of stretching. Coach walks toward you with a pair of 14-ounce boxing gloves and proceeds to glove your hands. As he laces and tapes your gloves, you feel his years of experience, and you feel privileged to be part of his stable. Next, he smears Vaseline on your face, pulls your head gear on, and places your mouthpiece in. He gives you a few last minute instructions.

"Get that horn fixed!" he says and winks.

For a second he seems almost affectionate.

The bell rings for round one, and Coach starts yelling again. You glance at your opponent. You are all friends at the gym . . . except during sparring.

The round begins with both you and your partner feeling each other out. Jabbing, moving. Then the distance suddenly becomes perfect and you land a big left hook to your partner's body. He counters with a hook to your head. You step back and land a rear leg front kick to his solar plexus. As you hear him gasp for air, you follow with an overhand right to his jaw, and then with another hook to his body.

"Keep those elbows in!" Coach screams to your partner, but before he finishes the sentence, you have already landed another three-punch combination.

You smell victory and remind yourself that it is just a practice fight, and that you must back off when your partner gets hurt in the gym.

You go back to the jab, as your partner tries to recover from the last barrage of punches. He is tentative now, and you know that had this been the real fight, victory would have been yours. The bell rings, and you walk over to Coach for instructions.

"Ease up a little, killer, or nobody is gonna want to spar with you!"

Your partner exits the ring and the next person enters. You can see that he is already wondering if he is up to the task.

"Work on defense this round!" Coach tells you.

Your partner, who heard Coach's instructions, is eagerly awaiting the start of round two. You work on picking his jab, slipping his right, and bobbing and weaving under his hooks. Then, suddenly, the inevitable happens and you get hit with a thundering rear cross. Instinctively, you retaliate with a vicious assault to your partner's body, then the final blow, your patented left hook to his liver. Your partner drops to the canvas, gasping for air.

"What happened to defense?" Coach asks.

"What's good defense without offense?" you retort.

"Okay, who is next?!"

You look at the row of waiting sparring partners, noticing the hesitation in their eyes. After a short debate on who's next, you finally get through with round three, four, and five. While removing your headgear and gloves, you throw advice at the others as though you have all the answers. You put in five more rounds on the heavy bag, focus mitts, air shield, and speed bag, then finish with one-hundred situps, and Coach slamming your belly with a twenty-pound medicine ball.

You say your good-byes and leave, knowing that tomorrow will be the same grind again. Back home, you eat dinner and watch some footage of your opponent for your next fight. By ten o'clock it's into bed.

"Six more weeks of this!" you groan, already fretting over tomorrow's run.

And although you are reluctant to admit it now, you know that once this fight is over, you won't regret a moment . . . You'll gladly do it all again.

RUNNING

Running helps you increase your endurance, especially leg endurance. Because the legs are usually the first to go when you get tired, running is critical to the kickboxing training process. Running also helps you build cardiovascular endurance, or wind, allowing you to carry on at a strong pace throughout the fight. Start by jogging at least three times a week for a minimum of twenty minutes to get your heart rate up. Ideally, you want to build up to where you are jogging between three and five miles. Then, rather than increasing distance, try to improve time. Vary your running routine with hills, stairs, and sprints.

The time of day you run is irrelevant. When Mike Tyson was in his prime, he used to get up and run at five o'clock in the morning, not because it made him stronger, but because it made him feel as though he had an edge; he was doing just a little more than the competition. I'm not suggesting that you get up and run in the middle of the night, but I am encouraging you to find what gives you the edge over the competition.

DISTANCE RUNNING

When running for distance, choose a running surface that is smooth but not too hard. For example, the street in your neighborhood may be too hard and cause unnecessary stress on your knees and shins, while a grassy surface may be uneven and increase the risk of injuries to your ankles. The best place to run for distance is the track at your local high school. The standard track size is one quarter of a mile. So eight laps around the track is equal to a distance of two miles.

1. Jog a set number of laps. As your endurance builds, gradually increase the number of laps, keeping the pace consistent throughout the run.

2. Jog at a set speed. As your endurance builds, gradually increase the speed, keeping the pace consistent throughout the run.

3. You should also have days that are specifically designed for muscular endurance training, where you run hills or stairs. This also keeps you from getting bored with the scenery. When not on the track, try roads with different slopes, so that sometimes you run uphill and sometimes downhill. Keep the same pace throughout the run.

4. Run on stairs, stepping on every other step on your way up, and on every step on your way down. Running downstairs causes greater stress on your joints than running upstairs. It is therefore advisable to take smaller steps when running downstairs.

5. In the winter, run on a treadmill at the gym. Try alternating the running with jumping jacks.

SPRINTING

Once you have built your endurance to where you are running between three and five miles, and you have started to decrease the time in which you do this, you should add sprints. By now you should be running four or five times a week.

Start by running at a set pace, then mix in sprints. Sprinting simulates the rhythm of the actual fight. In other words, fighting is comprised of a series of rhythms: There are times when you will be going all out, and there are times when you will be pacing. Sprinting helps you train your body to speed up and slow down, and to recover quickly when getting winded. If your opponent gets hurt or tired during the fight, you have the ability to double or triple your pace and take him out with brutal offense. If your opponent happens to recover, you can back down and begin to pace yourself, without being totally spent.

1. Sprint, then jog, then sprint, gradually increasing the sprint distance and speed.

2. Sprint a set distance, then jump over a number of small obstacles, then sprint again.

You can also do wind sprints. Mark off a yardage (a football field works well), start at zero, sprint to forty, walk back to zero, sprint to fifty, walk back to zero, and so on until you can sprint the entire field. Also, try sprinting up a steep hill a number of times and jogging back down.

Running chart

A normal training cycle runs eight weeks. When training for a three-round fight, run every other day for the first four weeks and build up to a distance of two miles. As you get closer to fight time, you will want to run almost every day. At this point, it is not necessarily the distance you run that is important. Two miles should still be sufficient. Instead, work on running faster. Shoot for a 7-8 minute mile pace. Also, work on varying your speed throughout the run, so that you sprint some and jog some. This simulates your cardiovascular performance in the fight, where you are fighting at a steady rhythm for some time, and then explode with a combination.

	MON	TUE	WED	THUR	FRI	SAT	SUN	TOTAL
TIME								
DISTANCE								
TIME								
DISTANCE								
TIME								
DISTANCE								
TIME								
DISTANCE								
TIME								
DISTANCE								
TIME								
DISTANCE								
TIME								
DISTANCE								
TIME								
DISTANCE								

ASSESSMENT CHART

Resting heart rate = total beats per minute (most accurate if taken first thing in the morning prior to any activity).

Your physical fitness is also determined by how fast your heart rate drops after strenuous exercise. A fast drop back to resting heart rate allows you to recover faster between rounds. Target heart rate is the rate you should strive for when at the peak of physical activity. Target heart rate = 220 minus your age times 0.70.

A blood pressure reading can be taken at a health facility. Many grocery stores also have blood pressure machines in their pharmacy departments.

A column has been included for the purpose of monitoring your weight for weight classification and fitness. Ideal body weight for the purpose of health is a highly controversial issue.

	WEEK 1	WEEK 2	WEEK 3	WEEK 4	WEEK 5	WEEK 6	WEEK 7	WEEK 8
RESTING HEART RATE								
DROP IN HEART RATE PER MINUTE								
BLOOD PRESSURE								
BODY WEIGHT								

JUMPING ROPE

Jumping or skipping rope develops resistance to fatigue in the legs. To jump rope, grasp the handles and position your hands about the height of your hips with your palms forward. Keep your feet together with your knees slightly bent. Stay on the balls of your feet and only jump high enough for the rope to sweep underneath your feet. There should be one jump only per sweep of the rope. Jumping rope helps you stay light on your feet and builds your endurance and cardiovascular fitness. You may notice some soreness in the arms and wrists, particularly during the early stages. Jumping rope can be done in many different fashions. To break up boredom, try the following:

ALTERNATING FEET

Jumping on one foot at a time builds your calves and ankles. You must also work to keep the rope swinging straight.

1. Jump on one foot for 20 seconds, then the other. Then alternate every other time by jumping twice on each foot.

2. Alternate by touching the floor in front of you with the ball of your foot first, then with the heel.

3. Also try alternating by kicking your heels back toward your butt, one at a time, or by bringing your knees high up (running in place).

VARYING SPEED

Keeping the same pace the whole time makes you fall into a predictable pattern, until the jump rope exercise doesn't do much to build your cardiovascular endurance. To improve, you must constantly work on it, pushing a little harder each time.

1. Jump for thirty seconds at a steady speed to warm up. Now race for five seconds, then slow down for another thirty. Repeat the procedure.

2. Try alternating feet during the thirty-second interval. When speeding up, go back to jumping on both feet simultaneously.

3. Vary the intervals. Keep the slower pace for ten seconds rather than thirty, and keep the faster pace for ten seconds rather than five.

4. As your endurance builds, race as fast as you can for one whole minute, and then keep a fairly fast and consistent pace for the next minute. Repeat the procedure.

VARYING TECHNIQUES

As your timing improves and you are able to jump continuously without stuttering, try the following jump-rope techniques:

1. Jump normally for a five-count, then bend slightly at the knees and jump for another five-count. At each five-count interval, gradually bend lower and lower at the knees until you are down in a squat position. Then gradually come back up again.

2. Try to keep the rope from touching the floor as it sweeps under your feet (but don't exaggerate your jump; jump only high enough to give the rope the clearance it needs).

3. Jump for a five-count, then cross your arms once. Jump for another five-count, then cross your legs once. Repeat the procedure.

4. Jump for a ten-count, then do a double where the rope passes twice underneath your feet. Repeat the procedure.

5. Work on lateral movement while jumping. Move left, then right while incorporating the above techniques.

Working Continuously

Have a partner or trainer set the timer without letting you know beforehand for how long you will be jumping. This helps you get used to a longer workout without anticipating the bell. The moment you look at the clock to see when the round is over, your determination will suffer.

1. Jump continuously for a set period of time. Start with five minutes, then increase to ten minutes.

2. While jumping continuously, work on different techniques, and on varying your speed.

Working Rounds

When training for a fight, you should triple (or at least double) the number of rounds. For example, if you will be fighting three two-minute rounds, then train (jump rope) for at least six rounds.

1. Set a timer for two-minute rounds, and jump for a set number of rounds.

2. Warm up during the first round by keeping a steady pace while alternating feet.

3. During subsequent rounds, vary your speed and work different techniques.

Note: I recommend using the same length rounds for training and fighting to help you develop a feel for when the round is almost over. Knowing when there are ten or twenty seconds left allows you to increase the intensity and finish big. Rather than increasing the length of the round during your workouts, decrease the rest period between rounds.

Swimming

Swimming can be excellent for building cardiovascular endurance, but you must be consistent in your training and train the way you have to perform in the actual event. If you train for competition, you must push yourself beyond your limits. An athlete who wants to compete in swimming, for example, should not swim a paced swim every day. He must push himself to

swim faster, to race. It is therefore not good enough to get in the swimming pool and go for a leisurely swim at a comfortable pace, or to simply lie there on your back and float around. For swimming to be effective (when used as a training exercise for the competitive kickboxer), it must be done with intention.

Distance Swimming

Swimming for distance increases your endurance while working all the muscles in your body. Because of the low impact, swimming is gentler on your body than running.

1. Swim a set number of laps (start with ten). As your endurance builds, gradually increase the number of laps, keeping the pace consistent throughout the swim.

2. Swim at a set speed. As your endurance builds, gradually increase the speed, keeping the pace consistent throughout the swim.

Sprinting

Just like you can sprint when running and jumping rope, you can also sprint when swimming. Sprinting simply means that you increase the speed in spurts within the swim.

1. Sprint for a set number of yards (start with one lap), gradually increasing speed and sprint distance.

2. Sprint, then swim normally, then sprint again, gradually increasing sprint distance and speed.

Varying Techniques

Varying your strokes will break up boredom and work different muscle groups.

1. Swim, using the breast stroke, for a set distance. Then switch to the side stroke or the back stroke.

2. Try using as few strokes as possible to propel you to the other end of the pool. This helps you relax while accomplishing your goal, and also teaches you economy of motion.

3. Swim under water for a set number of yards, gradu-

ally increasing the distance.

PLYOMETRICS

Plyometric exercises help you increase power by conditioning your muscles to contract more quickly and forcefully, allowing you to be more explosive in your fighting. The following plyometric exercises can be used to train your legs for endurance and explosive power:

1. Jump as high as you can, each time bringing your knees up to your chest as high and fast as possible.

2. Line up chairs side by side with about one chair-width between them. Jump over the chairs, one by one, without stopping in between.

3. Jog for ten seconds, then leap as far as you can with both legs forward, then jog again.

FLEXIBILITY

When you have achieved a proper warm-up, it is time to move on to the flexibility exercises. You should stretch both before sparring to help elongate the muscles and give you flexibility and speed, and after sparring to cool down when the muscles are already warm. Stretching also complements strength training in that strength training tends to shorten the muscle, while stretching lengthens it. The reverse is also true: Strength training complements stretching. A strong leg can throw a

higher kick than a weak but flexible leg. Some of the following flexibility exercises can be done with wrist weights or ankle weights to build strength. But remember what we talked about earlier: Strength exercises are not specific to kickboxing, so proper transfer of learning may not take place. If you use weights when kicking, you are likely to change your timing, and may not benefit in the actual fight. Experiment to find a workable medium.

Stretching should not be painful. You should feel the stretch, but any pain beyond a slight discomfort is a signal to stop. Hold each stretch for a minimum of 3-5 seconds, and ideally up to 30 seconds. Most exercise specialists recommend against bouncing in and out of stretches, as this increases the risk of tearing the muscle. My experience is that some careful "pulsing" actually helps the stretch. When you hold a stretch, you should feel the muscle relax before attempting to go farther.

This section covers:

- Why stretch?
- Upper body flexibility
- Lower body flexibility
- Stretching for warm-up
- Think on these things

WHY STRETCH?

The most common question people ask me when they find out I'm a martial artist is: Are you a black belt? Next, they ask: How high can you kick? Can you do full splits? Next, they might ask if I'm a world champion, but not until they know if I'm a black belt and if I can kick to the head.

Is it necessary to do full splits in order to be a good kickboxer? No, because many highly effective kicks are thrown low to the legs. But that is not to say that flexibility is unimportant. Flexibility does more than just allow you to kick high. Flexibility and strength go hand in hand. A strong leg is usually more flexible than a weak leg. If I asked you to extend your leg straight out in a side thrust kick and hold it there, and then, on my count, raise it five inches higher without planting your foot first, you may or may not be able to do this depending both on your strength and flexibility. If you have the flexibility but lack the strength, you will not be able to raise your leg higher. If you have the strength but lack the flexibility, you will not be able to raise it higher, either. It is interesting to note that if you build strength without working on flexibility, you will still become slightly more flexible. When working on leg strength for your kicks, do the kicks in slow motion and focus on extending and holding the kick at maximum height for a few seconds. Focus on working the muscles rather than using momentum. Flexibility also allows you greater range of motion, even for low kicks. I often see new students who are unable to extend their leg fully, no matter how low they kick. This is because they haven't done any stretching in a long time, and the tendons and muscles just don't allow full extension. Once you achieve greater range of motion, you will have a speedier kick with better follow-through, which in turn translates into more power, and you will risk fewer pulled ligaments and muscles.

Upper body flexibility

Include the following upper body stretches in your flexibility program:

NECK

1. Loosen up the neck by tilting your head side-to-side. Avoid fast or jerky moves.

2. Roll your head in a half circle from right to left and back. Note that most exercise specialists recommended against rolling your head in a full circle, or tilting your head to the rear.

SHOULDERS

1. Rotate your shoulders in a circle forward, then back.

2. Also work shoulder stretching and relaxation while shadow boxing.

ARMS

1. Swing your arms horizontally over and under in a scissor-like move.

2. Place one hand behind your neck (elbow pointed toward the ceiling), and grab your elbow with your other hand and push down. This stretches the triceps.

3. You can also stretch your arms by grabbing the ends of a towel with each hand, and working a variety of static stretches by pulling on the towel in opposite directions.

WAIST

1. Rotate your upper body in a half circle (or in a full circle all the way around).

2. Side bends help you stretch the sides of your upper body. Do not lean forward or back, but try to touch the floor directly to the side of your foot.

3. Spread your legs shoulder width and a half apart. Push your hips forward and raise your arms up and back until your body is arched backward. Next, bend forward and down, reaching between your legs as far back as you can. Hold each stretch for a few seconds and repeat.

Lower body flexibility

Include the following lower body stretches in your flexibility program:

HIPS

1. Assume a pushup position on the floor, with your legs spread about shoulder width and a half apart. Bend your arms and press your hips toward the floor. Keep your upper body from touching the floor.

2. From a standing position, step forward as far as you can with your left foot. Keep your back straight and bend your left knee until your thigh is parallel with the floor. Hold the stretch for thirty seconds. Repeat the exercise with your right foot forward.

3. Lie flat on your back. Place a towel around your left foot. Pull your foot toward you until your knee touches your chest. Extend your leg straight up while applying resistance with the towel. Repeat the exercise with your right leg.

THIGHS

1. From a standing position, lift one foot off the floor and grab your ankle. Pull your foot back with your heel toward your butt. This stretches the front of your thigh.

You can also do this stretch sitting down.

2. Also try resistance stretching with a partner. Place both your hands flat against a wall, and have your partner grab your ankle and raise your leg up and to the rear. Pull your leg down against his resistance. Don't bend your knee.

HAMSTRINGS

1. Toe touches help stretch your hamstrings. Because most people are not built completely symmetrical, a good way to do this is to cross your legs as you bend over and try to touch your toes. This allows you to stretch one leg at a time, giving each leg the most benefit of the stretch.

2. You can also do toe touches sitting down with both legs extended straight in front of you, or pull one foot back toward your butt in the hurdler's stretch.

3. Also try resistance stretching with a partner. Stand with your back against a wall and have your partner grab your leg and raise it straight up in front of you. Without bending your knee, press down with your heel against your partner's hand. Hold for a count of five, then relax and allow your partner to lift your leg a little higher.

CALVES

1. Stretch the calves from a sitting position by extending your legs straight out in front of you, curling your toes back, and raising your heels off the floor. This stretch is more effective if you grab your toes and pull the upper portion of your foot toward you.

2. You can also stretch the calves from a standing position by placing your hands flat against a wall, keeping your heels on the ground (about two feet from the wall), and leaning forward toward the wall (keep your back straight). As you become more limber, increase the distance between your feet and the wall.

GROIN

1. Sit on the floor and spread your legs. Face your partner and have him grab your wrists and pull your upper body forward, simultaneously placing his feet against the inside of your lower legs, gently pressing your legs apart.

2. You can also do the groin stretch while standing with one side against a wall. Have your partner lift your leg sideways and up. Without bending your knee, press down with the side of your foot against your partner's hand. Hold for a count of five, then relax and allow your partner to lift your leg a little higher.

3. Also try the frog stretch (some people call this butterfly stretch). Sit with your knees bent and the soles of your feet touching. Press down with your elbows against your knees, or have your partner stand behind you and gently press your knees toward the floor.

STRETCHING FOR WARM-UP

If you are serious about the sport, you must adhere to a disciplined training program. You should stretch both when warming up and when cooling down. Warming up raises the body temperature and helps muscles and ligaments to loosen and stretch for athletic activity. The warm-up should not be overdone; only enough to get the blood circulating and to get you focused on training. Jogging or jumping rope are good warm-up exercises, along with shadow boxing. I usually do controlled shadow boxing with full extension in all limbs, but without snapping the punches and kicks. I also shadow box from a partial squat position to warm up and strengthen the legs. After this, I might continue with light contact kicks on the heavy bag.

Warm-up doesn't have to last in excess of ten minutes, but can last longer. Cool-downs should be extensive enough to bring your body temperature back to normal, and should include light stretching and movement exercises.

Stretches can be either dynamic or static. An example of a dynamic stretch is controlled kicking with full extension. An example of a static stretch is partner stretching on the wall. My belief is that you can achieve results faster with dynamic stretches, especially if stretching for warm-up.

THINK ON THESE THINGS

When starting your conditioning program, don't push too hard. Your initial motivation may drive you to train harder than your body is ready for. Remember that this is a journey of many years, and that you want to present a sustained effort through all those years. Physical exhaustion may make you lose spirit. If training becomes a chore, you are not likely to prevail.

> **Quitting when you are the hungriest increases your desire to come back tomorrow.**

When resting between sets, it is a good idea to rest standing up or walking slowly back and forth, or throwing punches in the air. If you sit down, it may be difficult to get up again. Moving around also prevents stiffness and helps blood circulate.

Physical training makes the bones stronger and able to withstand the demands of the sport. It is also important to get proper rest and relaxation. Massage is great for tired muscles. Stretch frequently throughout the day. You don't have to stretch for long, just frequently and lightly to get the blood circulating and reduce stiffness. Stretch between exercises as well.

Because you will be driven to your limits in a bout, you must have the stamina to prevail. When you get tired, it is not just your physical skill that suffers; you will lose confidence as well. Regular strength training builds your stamina and confidence.

> **A well-conditioned body is a threat; it tells your opponent that you take your training seriously.**

APPENDIX B
WHAT CAN GO WRONG?

THE PROBLEM WITH THE MISSING MONEY
by Keith Livingston

To say that kickboxing is a funny business would be a gross understatement. During my twenty plus years in the game, I have seen the best of the best and certainly the worst of the worst. The one constant is that everybody is trying to turn a buck, often by exploiting the fighters.

Denver, Colorado, 1991: I had contracted seven of my fighters to compete. Add myself and two corner men, and the ten of us were on our way to Mammoth Gardens, an arena in the heart of downtown Denver. My first mistake was working with a first time promoter whom I had failed to investigate.

When we arrived, we were all weary from our long road trip into the Denver area. To top it off, the weigh-in was chaotic. It was the only weigh-in I have ever been to where they actually forgot to bring a scale! After an incredibly long wait, one of the promoter's stooges showed up with his bathroom scale. They weighed my fighters and gave us directions to what we thought would be our badly needed sleeping quarters.

We drove across town to a seedy part of Denver, and stopped in front of what only could be described as the Bates Motel right out of the movie Psycho. At first I thought I must have followed the directions wrong. That is until I noticed the weathered sign, "Carol's bed and breakfast." We grabbed our luggage and proceeded cautiously into the foyer. An elderly lady, who I assumed to be Carol, greeted us as we entered. She held her nightshirt closed with one hand as she motioned us forward with the other.

We blindly followed Carol up the old wooden staircase to our room. Yes, singular room! A twelve-by-twelve foot floor area with two beds. Two beds and ten guys . . . you do the math. We tried to adapt to the situation. Half the fighters were on the beds and the other half on the floor. My light heavyweight built himself a nest inside the closet. After a restless night, we loaded our luggage, waved to Carol, and drove straight to Holiday Inn, where I charged three-hundred dollars in rooms to my Visa card.

We spent the rest of the day sleeping and eating. When we drove to the arena, I couldn't help but wondering what would happen next. The fights went well. We won six out of seven. We then gathered the troops, found some seats, and watched the main event. All of us eagerly awaited our pay, especially me, since I was already more than three bills in the hole. The main event ended with a fifth round KO, delivered by the kid from Phoenix.

Again, we waited. Finally, the promoter emerged from the dressing room, accompanied by a single security guard. The duo walked to the ring, and as if a sign of things to come, the promoter tripped on the bottom rope as he entered. He brushed himself off, was handed a microphone, and began by clearing his throat: "Uh hum . . . ah . . . I'm afraid I have some bad news. I won't be able to pay anybody tonight." A single tear rolled down his fat little cheek. "Um . . . I'm really sorry, and goodnight."

Nobody could have predicted what happened next. As we all stood shell shocked trying to comprehend what the promoter had just announced, the biggest man I have ever seen, four-hundred pounds and nearly seven feet tall, stood up out of the front row. I could clearly see the veins protruding from his humongous neck. I later learned that he was a freestyle no-rules legend in Japan. The security guard must have sensed the danger, because in an instant he was gone. "These guys bled for you. Pay or die!" the giant yelled.

The promoter scrambled to the opposite side of the ring and started his exit. Just as he stepped through the ropes, the giant hurled a chair through the air. The chair traveled some forty feet in the air before striking the intended target squarely in the back, knocking him from the ring and flat on his face. The promoter hurried to his feet and sprinted toward the nearest exit, but the giant was amazingly quick and agile and arrived first, cutting off the escape route. His next chair toss was nearly sixty feet and missed the target by inches.

A part of me sympathized with the giant's intended prey, but not enough to get in the way. Instead, I turned to a Denver police officer that had been hired for security, and asked if he was going to intervene. His response? "Nope . . . he didn't pay us either." After a dozen more chairs, the promoter managed to beat the giant to an open window and flee into the night. I never heard from or saw him again.

Martina Sprague: One of my fights was so poorly organized that the weigh-in and physical exam were skipped entirely. I don't even think there was a physician present. Five minutes before the fight, they asked us what kind of rules we wanted to fight under. The ropes around the ring were sagging to the point that the referee had to stop the fight and allow the fighters to separate every time someone was getting close to the ropes. There was no bell signaling the start and end of the round. Instead, someone with a microphone said, "ding-ding!" at the start of the round and, "that's it, that's it!" at the end of the round. The fight took place toward the end of August, and the arena was extremely hot with no air-conditioning and hardly any air circulating, and when all was said and done, there were no trophies or belts given to the winner.

In this last section of the book, we will look at what Keith and I have learned the hard way, as well as some stories worth pondering for those of you climbing through the ranks. Enjoy!

THE FEROCIOUS FIGHTER

You have now learned countless techniques, strategies, training tips, and competition rules. If you have achieved even mediocre mastery of the information between the covers of this book, you can look forward to a successful ring career. However, no kickboxing book would be complete without mentioning Murphy's Law. Or even better: how to throw the Murphy-spell on your opponent.

Thought provoker: I don't care what anybody says, kickboxing is entertainment, and if the fighter can't put on a show for the audience, he doesn't deserve a penny of his purse! True or false?

Thought provoker: Kickboxing is for the athlete only. Kickboxing tests your physical and mental strength and makes you grow in the process. The only purpose of the audience is to heighten the pressure, forcing the fighter to find his limits. True or false?

The above statements contradict one another. Which one is correct is hard to say. If the fighter doesn't know how to market himself, or if he lacks crowd-pleasing ability, the crowd will not look forward to seeing him fight again. As a result, the promoter won't be as eager to promote the fighter, who will have a harder time getting fights. He will then earn small purses and may never get a shot at the world title. Personally, however, I care little about showing off with long introductions, fancy clothing, and fancy techniques. To me, it matters more what the audience says about my fighting skill, whether fancy or not. I would rather have all first round knockouts than ten round fights where the audience "got their money's worth." Either way, most fighters need a way to psych themselves up for the event.

This section covers:

- What's in a name?
- The entrance
- Shorts or skirts?
- Nose-to-nose
- I want it my way
- What does it hurt?
- Hanging out with the enemy
- Don't leave home without it
- In the dressing room

- It was just a joke
- The promise
- Crazy Ike
- And now, the rest of the story . . .

WHAT'S IN A NAME?
by Keith Livingston

For the past several years, I have been dealing with dragons, punishers, executioners, cobras, rattlesnakes, thunder, lightening, scorpions, destroyers, icemen, mad dogs, and firestorms. Not to mention superfeet, supermen, rocks, boom booms, bang bangs, and an occasional shark here and there. So, how is it that I'm sitting here writing to you today? Surely, I must be scarred, burned, poisoned, and maimed beyond recognition? Fortunately for me, these were mere mortal men who, like most fighters, will eventually adopt a ring name.

Some ring names are merely adopted, either because they sound good or are a copy of somebody famous who had great success with the name, others have more distinct origins. Every sport has them. In basketball you have your Mailmans, Pistols, Air Jordans, and Sir Charles. Boxing has its Golden Boys, lots of Sugars, and a few Princes. Bill "Superfoot" Wallace was called superfoot for his amazing ability to use one leg as well as most fighters use their hands. Bob "Thunder" Thurman had a lethal, thundering right hand. Jean-Yves "The Iceman" Theriault was always cool and methodical. Oftentimes, you simply get branded with a ring name. In my case, I've had two. As a welterweight, I was known as "Stinger." My corner branded me with this name, I'm told, because of a stinging left jab. As I grew in stature, and my corner team changed, I was re-branded "The Rock."

My re-naming came as a result of two consecutive fights where both opponents broke their right hands on my forehead. Somebody commented that I had a head like a rock, the name stuck, and the rest is history. I think the ring name probably serves the owner of the name more so than instilling any real fear in the opponent. However, ring names bring color and excitement to the world of sports. I hope that those of you coming through the ranks will eventually find your own name, while you continue to slay dragons, crush rocks, and laugh in the face of executioners.

THE ENTRANCE

Every fighter must make an entrance. The entrance can be powerful or spiritual, and often to the music of the fighter's choice. Either way, it must have meaning to the fighter. The idea is to get his adrenaline flowing, give him confidence, and make him anxious to get on with the fight. The cheering of the crowd, how the fighter dresses, and who enters with him all serve to heighten the thrill and bring confidence to the fighter. In professional bouts, the fighter is likely to enter with most of his entourage. In amateur bouts, he may enter with just his trainer and corner men. Usually, the trainer leads the way. The trainer climbs the stairs to the ring and spreads the ropes for the fighter to enter. The fighter might now do an introductory dance or shadow box to show his confidence to the audience. The ring announcer might also introduce the fighter at this time.

Now, some fighters make an extraordinarily long entrance, intended to irritate the opponent and break his spirit. I've seen flamboyant boxer Prince Hamed dance his way down a glittering runway for twenty minutes, while his opponent watched in dismay from the middle of the ring, getting cold while waiting for the clowning to end. Thai-boxers enter with the Wai Kruu dance to pay respect to their mentor, and to intimidate the opponent while increasing their own confidence. I observed the Wai Kruu dance at a kickboxing/Thai-boxing event in Sweden a few years ago. The fighter moved to Thai music along the inside perimeter of the ropes, stopping at every corner of the ring to perform what looked like some sort of prayer. When this part of the ceremony was over, the fighter walked to the center of the ring and performed the dance, mostly from his knees, and with different hand movements.

> **Think of the ring name as the "hood of the cobra." It is meant to instill an image that will work to the fighter's advantage and the opponent's disadvantage.**

SHORTS OR SKIRTS?

The fighter's clothing, good luck charms, hair cut, tattoos, color and design of his shorts, the writing of his name on his shirt or robe, and other frills he wears all serve to instill confidence in himself and fear in his opponent. Some fighters go to the extreme. Heavyweight world champion kickboxer, Dennis Alexio, wore a Hawaiian grass skirt instead of regulation type kickboxing shorts. He was finally forced to cut the skirt off, because his opponent couldn't see his legs, and therefore couldn't defend against his kicks.

In the amateur ranks, the fighters wear headgear that covers any fancy hair-dos, but in professional bouts, long hair must be tied back. Professional boxing seems stricter on the personal grooming rules than professional kickboxing, especially since more women have entered the sport. I have often seen women kickboxers with curls blowing every which way. This is not allowed in boxing.

NOSE-TO-NOSE

The referee calls the fighters to the center of the ring for a brief explanation of the rules, usually something like, "I gave you instructions in the dressing room. When I say break, you break. Are there any questions? Touch gloves." The fighters are standing face-to-face while the referee speaks, some literally nose-to-nose, staring each other down. Others stare at the ceiling to avoid looking their opponent in the eyes. The stare down is used either to gain a psychological edge on your opponent, or to avoid looking at him for whatever reason, and still gain a psychological edge.

It is not uncommon for fighters to get cocky once the fight is underway. The fighter may drop his guard and push his chin forward, taunting his opponent to hit him. My experience is that this most often has a negative effect, where the fighter gets struck more than he would if he protected himself properly. You will also see all kinds of dirty looks when the fighters return to their corners after a round. Sometimes a fighter hits his opponent right at the bell, or a split second after the bell. The fact that he has momentum often makes it difficult to avoid hitting after the bell, even though it is illegal. This will most certainly draw a dirty look from the opponent. The same goes for hitting low or to illegal targets. Most often this is innocent, and the referee may just give the fighter a warning. But the opponent may still give the fighter a dirty look.

I WANT IT MY WAY

Then there is the arguing with the referee when things don't go your way, which makes you or your corner team look immature. I have seen fighters take their headgear off and throw it on the canvas in the middle of a round, because they thought their opponent did something illegal he was not reprimanded for. I have seen fighters spit out their mouthpiece time and time again. Sure, the mouthpiece may be awkward and make it difficult to breathe, but it is still a requirement to keep it in. When the fighter does this repeatedly, he usually gets a warning with a threat of having a point deducted. Losing your temper hardly gives you the edge; it only makes you look ridiculous. When you are angry or upset, your emotions will rule over your reason, and you are less likely to fight strategically.

After you finish the fight, shaking your opponent's hand shows good sportsmanship. It is also a good idea to go to your opponent's corner and shake hands with his corner team. Most of the time, fighters are pretty good about doing this, but again, there are all kinds of variations. I have seen fighters win and lean over the ropes, throwing threatening remarks at the audience. Others jump up on the ropes when they are announced the winner, and some run around the ring in circles. The audience can also have a great impact on a fighter. I've had a couple of fights in my opponent's hometown, with the audience cheering for me instead of my opponent! That, of course, is a great feeling.

At a kickboxing event in Sweden (Sweden vs. Finland), they separated the Swedish spectators at one end of the ring and the Finish spectators at the other. The cheering crowd made it clear which fighter had scored on his opponent, and really heightened the intensity and thrill of the game.

WHAT DOES IT HURT?
by Keith Livingston

Most of society will have us believe that they don't believe in superstition. If you were to ask the majority of people about black cats crossing their path, walking under a ladder, or breaking a mirror, they would probably say, "I don't believe in such nonsense!" Yet, how many of us non-believers avoid walking under ladders, get a slight twinge of discomfort when a black cat crosses our path, or thinks, "Oh damn, now I've done it!" when a mirror is accidentally broken?

Sports are much the same way. Most athletes don't buy into superstition, myth, or ritual, except during the participation of their chosen sport. The most frequently heard justification is, "What can it hurt?" During my career as a fighter, I've seen every manner of bizarre behavior, superstition, and myth. Yes, I, too, have participated in what I rationally knew to be silly and childlike, but hey, what does it hurt?

My first boxing coach, Tony Bullock, was perhaps one of the most superstitious people I have ever met. Tony, a veteran of World War II, had survived the dangerous assignment of deep sea salvage diving. If not for his lucky rabbit's foot, he might not have made it home. Perhaps, in such a dangerous assignment and environment, we would all find some comfort in a lucky rabbit's foot.

During my first amateur bout, I was introduced to the strange world of pre-fight ritual and superstition. First, Tony insisted that I don his boxing shoes, assuring me that they would give me that little edge I needed to claim victory. After lacing up his 1940 throwbacks, oddly I felt less nervous. That was until the referee entered the dressing room and told us the soles were illegal in today's sport. After a heated debate, the shoes came off, much to my disappointment.

As it became my turn to glove up, I extended my left hand toward Tony, and promptly received a scolding:

"Every boxer knows that you glove the right hand first!" I extended my right hand and, tongue in cheek, retorted, "Then where's the advantage?" We began our journey to the ring, my right hand on Tony's left shoulder, head down, slow walk, everything choreographed so as to not upset the gods of boxing.

Upon entering the ring, Tony motioned me to the corner. Out of his right pocket came the lucky rabbit's foot. He rubbed the foot over my right glove, then the left, and yes, I felt less nervous. His belief seemed so deep it definitely had an effect on my psyche. After all, the rabbit's foot had gone through the war with him!

I glanced at my opponent, who was down on one knee praying to his God, and making the sign of the cross on his chest. Suddenly, a funny thought swept through my mind: "Does God take sides?" If he did, I was screwed, because God surely has more power than a rabbit's foot. I promptly went out and pounded my way to a decision. I know that it wasn't the rabbit's foot, and I believe God only helps those that help themselves. God, I'm sure, looked after both of us, but talent and training was the deciding factor . . . and yes, maybe a little luck, too . . .

Through the course of my career, I have seen fighters wrap their hands certain ways, wear a certain pair of shorts, glove their right hand first, enter the ring a given way. (In Canada, I learned that unless you enter the ring by climbing over the top rope, you are destined to lose, so for peace's sake . . .) I've seen it all: specific meals and specific ritual. In the world of sports every athlete is looking for that little edge. Be it God or a rabbit's foot, what does it hurt?

HANGING OUT WITH THE ENEMY

The fight offer had come weeks ago. I was prepared both physically and mentally . . . that was until I learned that my trainer would not be going. Could not get time off from work to take me. What to do: back out and give up months of preparation, or go alone?

It was one of those days when you don't know if you want to fight or not, so you find excuses: My opponent is fifteen pounds heavier than I. She is also four inches taller. Her kicks are better than mine. The promoter doesn't like her trainer and wants me to beat her up.

The pressure to do well was intense, and my trainer wouldn't be in my corner. I was counting hours: 72 hours from now, I'll be back home again. 48 hours from now, it will be over. 12 hours from now, I will have a win or a loss to add to my record. 6 hours from now . . .

I arrived at the weigh-in and pre-fight medical promptly at six. Blood pressure: 124 over 78. "Not bad right before a fight," the medic told me. I weighed in at 118 pounds with shoes on. My opponent weighed in at 131 pounds. "She seemed nervous," said Chad, a local who had agreed to work my corner. I was fighting from the blue corner.

I walked back out to my car and tried to nap for an hour. My opponent, who had a Tae Kwon Do background, had good legs. Think strategy. Get to the inside. Press forward. Stay away from the tip of her kicks. Get out of range by decreasing distance . . . or by using a better angle. What to do if I take a good kick to my jaw?

Darkness fell. A young man was dribbling a basketball on the parking lot, and a kid rushed by on a skateboard. I reclined the car seat and tried to rest, suddenly feeling so very alone here without my trainer. My fight was the amateur highlights. The night dragged on. I'd be lucky if I'd fought by eleven o'clock, four hours from now.

I sat up and looked at the ghost on the seat beside me. I knew this ghost. Had seen it many times, but oddly enough, today it was a black man of about 250 pounds. He looked at me with dark, glimmering eyes, shining white teeth: "Oh, baby, you've got it made!"

At eight o'clock I grabbed my gym bag from the car and walked across the lawn to the gym entrance.

When I entered the dressing room for the blue corner, I learned that my opponent had backed out of the fight. "She was pacing the hallway," they told me. "Said she had been point-sparring all day and taken a kick to the jaw. Said she wasn't feeling well . . . had female problems."

Not to worry. Chad, who was supposed to work my corner tonight, had a lady kickboxer in his stable who agreed to take a fight on short notice on the condition that we didn't use leg kicks, and that we wore sixteen ounce gloves. And there went my strategy. "And now we don't know if you want to be here in the same dressing room as your opponent," said Chad. "Oh, I don't mind," I said and dumped my gym bag on the floor. Tonight, I would hang out with the enemy.

I sat down on the floor and began wrapping my hands. My new opponent, only a few feet from me, was looking me over. I thanked her for agreeing to fight on such short notice. I wrapped my hands with care, trying to make it look professional, as if I had done it a hundred times before. I leaned against the wall, relaxed.

Chad's fighters were dominating the card, some winning and some losing, and it gave me confidence in the judges. "I hate to lose!" Chad told me. Well, who doesn't? And only minutes ago he was my friend, determined to give me full support during the fight. Now, suddenly, he was my enemy; he would work my opponent's corner instead of mine. Instead of giving me constructive advice and encouragement, he would tell my opponent how she could beat me. And, you know, it hit me that it doesn't matter whose side you're on, as long as you're on the winning side.

Twenty minutes before fight time the promoter came into the dressing room and told me that he would be in my corner himself, and that I would now be fighting out of the red corner, and to start warming up by doing some light shadow boxing. I went out in the hallway where there were one-hundred yards of windows in which I could see my mirror image. I shadow boxed the full length of the hallway. My shoulders were relaxed, my strikes snappy. My hands and feet felt light. The promoter held focus mitts that I whacked for another ten minutes. He grabbed my water bottle and towel. Chad walked past and whispered in my ear, "Don't go too hard on her!" referring to his fighter, my opponent. And just how was I supposed to obey that request right before fight time? When you fight, you fight. You go all out. There is no in-between in competition.

Up in the ring, I touched gloves with my opponent. Her forehead was glossy with sweat. Looked like she got a good warm-up. Well, maybe it would tire her early. The first round was on, and I found myself getting backed up as much as I was able to press forward. She scored on me, but her strikes lacked power and didn't hurt. I must stay calm now, must keep my mind open and clear.

In the second round, I tried moving around a bit instead of standing toe-to-toe with my opponent and trading blows. I distanced myself a few feet in hope that she would lunge forward. This was where I would throw that spinning back kick, finally, the one we had been waiting to see for three years. But she didn't step forward, and I waited, and the referee said, "Let's get it on!" I moved in at an angle and threw some round house kicks. Her legs were open for kicks, but this was not a leg kick fight, I remembered.

"You move well," they told me back in the corner. "You're using some interesting angles. In this next round, I want you to kick her in the head. All of your kicks have been to the body. Give her something to think about."

"But I lack the flexibility to kick high," I told them. In the beginning of round three, I kicked her in the head with a round house kick, anyway. Now, we were back to the inside fighting. I pressed forward, and then, WHACK! I took an uppercut to my nose. Why? Because my head was on the centerline and not off to one side. Must keep that a secret from my trainer, or he'd kill me.

"Yeah, good uppercut!" I heard from my opponent's corner. My nose turned numb and warm, and I didn't know if it was blood or snot dripping on the canvas.

It's okay, it's okay, I told myself. I'm not dazed. Not even a little. But I was afraid that the referee would stop the match or give me an eight-count. It would look bad to the judges. I kept going hard, maybe even a little harder than before. Got her backed into a corner now. She was tired. I could see it in her eyes. Her hands were down. She was mine. I threw some punches and then a side thrust kick to keep her in the corner. Then the bell sounded for the end of the fight.

The promoter jumped up in the ring and pressed a towel to my nose. I swatted his hands away. Damn it, give me a chance to catch my breath first! He unstrapped my headgear and gloves, and before I had time to collect my thoughts, I heard my name on the loud speaker, and the referee raised my hand in victory.

After thanking my opponent and her trainer, I climbed out of the ring. People in the audience were smiling at me and nodding in approval. And from somewhere in the middle, a big, black man of at least 250 pounds got out of his seat and came toward me with his hand raised for a high-five. "Best fight I've ever seen," he told me. Then Chad came toward me and hugged me and whispered in my ear, "I can't tell you how much I wish that you were my fighter!" Not bad, I thought, coming from the enemy.

I walked to the blue corner dressing room, where I had left my gym bag. As I entered, my opponent was smiling at me, telling me I was awesome. Then I noticed the towel thrown over my shoulder, more red than white from blood, my blood. "Good uppercut!" I told her, and suddenly, the enemy was not the enemy anymore.

Back at the hotel that night, I sat up startled when I realized the connection between the ghost in my car and the big, black man in the audience . . .

DON'T LEAVE HOME WITHOUT IT
by Keith Livingston

I can sit back now and laugh about all the things that have gone awry in my career, but at the time, some apparently small things caused me a great deal of stress and frustration. Once, less than an hour before fight time, when I started to dress, I realized that my most important piece of equipment was absent. I had no athletic cup! Now, that might not seem to be all that significant, but it was already approaching ten p.m., and I wasn't going to borrow one from somebody else.

While I waited impatiently in the dressing room, two of my corner men went in search of the Holy Grail. With fight time approaching quickly, my anxiety continued to mount. My trainer tried in vain to keep me focused on warming up, but my mind was fixated on one thing: my thing!

Not only was I going into battle absent my helmet, but absent two corner men. Marching toward the ring, I silently prayed that my opponent would be accurate this night and not strike below the belt. Sensing my concern, my penis hid itself the best it could. The referee brought us to the center of the ring and began the pre-fight instructions. I was happy when he admonished us to keep our blows above the belt; I just hoped my opponent hadn't missed the instructions. As we were about to touch gloves, I heard a yell from somewhere behind me: "I've got it!!!" Simultaneously, the crowd of three-thousand, the referee, my trainer, and myself turned to see Barney, my corner man, holding an athletic cup proudly over his head.

The referee looked at me with a furrowed brow, called timeout, and summoned Barney into the ring. Now, with me gloved, it was Barney's responsibility to effectively place the cup in its proper place. I was both relieved and humiliated as three-thousand pairs of eyes watched Barney reach into the front of my shorts. You could hear chuckles from the women, and a simultaneous Ooh! from the men. I knew at that point that losing wasn't an option. I was so motivated to win that I knocked my opponent out in the first round.

Another harrowing experience occurred in Las Vegas at the Union Plaza Hotel. As is my practice, my trainer is responsible for my mouthpiece. He keeps it safely tucked in his corner man's jacket. Just before I'm meeting my opponent in the center of the ring, he takes it from his pocket, gives it a good rinsing, and places it in my mouth.

It's fight time; I enter the ring, throw a few kicks to the crowd, and return to my corner for my mouthpiece. Just like clockwork, my trainer removes it from the safety of his pocket, gives it a good rinsing, and places it in my mouth. As I advance to center ring, I notice that I can't seem to get the mouthpiece to fit my teeth. By the time the opening bell sounds, I'm fighting to keep the mouthpiece in my mouth. In the first round, I lose the mouthpiece three times.

Upon returning to my corner, the referee follows and tells me, "Continue spitting out your mouthpiece, and I'm going to start taking points!" My trainer, red faced, pulls another mouthpiece from the opposite pocket and apologizes: "Whoops, I guess I gave you somebody else's mouthpiece."

Normally, that would be the end of the story, but you see, I have one particular phobia. If somebody takes a drink from my glass, I get rid of it. If somebody takes a drink from my soda can, I throw it away. I once had an awful argument with my girlfriend when I caught her using my toothbrush. She cleverly pointed out that we share germs when we kiss, so what's the difference? I astutely defended with that when we kiss I don't lick the plaque off her teeth. Anyway, that's another story, but you get my drift. I had just spent an entire round with God knows whose mouthpiece.

Upon my return to Salt Lake City, I immediately called a meeting with all the fighters and proceeded to play Cinderella, only this time it wasn't a glass slipper, but a mouthpiece. You see, I needed to know whose mouthpiece had spent the round in my mouth. One of the fighters immediately spoke up: "Oh good, you found my mouthpiece." I slowly turned to see who I had swapped spit with.

These experiences are not limited to personal equipment. I showed up in Reno once, there was no ring, and the promoter asked, "You didn't happen to bring some gloves did you?" I looked at him in utter amazement, "What good are gloves when there is no ring?" He told me they had figured that out, and pointed at four fifty-five gallon drums. Sensing my confused look, he continued, "We're going to use those as corner posts and string some ropes around them." About fifteen minutes later, we were headed home, both my trainer and I shaking our heads in disbelief.

If you're going to get into this sport, be prepared for anything. You'll meet fly-by-night promoters, equipment problems, and a myriad of things unexpected. I once got a call from a promoter who was frantic on the phone: "Keith! I know this is short notice (24 hours before the fight), but my scheduled main event is short a fighter. Can you get down to Vegas and take the fight?" Fortunately, I was in pretty good shape, and agreed.

I arrived in Vegas eight hours before fight time, and learned that I was going to fight the United States kickboxing champion. I wasn't adequately prepared to fight at that level, but hell, I'll take opportunities wherever and whenever I get them. Throughout the day, I was admittedly nervous. I knew my opponent well, he had earned the title, was always in shape, and hit like a mule.

An hour before fight time, I got to the dressing room, did some light shadow boxing, and attempted to vanquish the butterflies churning in my stomach. With about forty minutes to go, I dressed, got my hands wrapped, and seriously began to ready myself for the fight. Now, with just the fight ahead of me, game face on, and ready for battle, I waited for the gloves to arrive.

The glove runner didn't arrive, but a representative of the Nevada Athletic Commission did. "Are you Keith Livingston?" "Yes," I replied, "Is there a problem?" "Come with me." I was escorted to a side room. Once inside, I noticed several representatives from the commission, my opponent, the promoter, and another fighter.

The promoter looked up at me, "Sorry, Keith, we have a bit of a situation here. It seems I'm under a double contract on this fight." Then one of the commissioners spoke up and explained. The promoter had originally contracted with another fighter. The promoter and the fighter had an argument over the pay. The promoter then called upon me to take his spot, but now the other fighter was willing to take the fight. The commission ruled that the promoter was obligated to the first contract; therefore I would not be fighting.

There is a silver lining to this story: The commission ruled that I would be compensated at the contract amount, to include my expenses. My replacement was knocked out thirty-five seconds into the first round, and I hit the jackpot on the slot machines worth thirty-five-hundred dollars. All in all, not a bad trip!

IN THE DRESSING ROOM
by Keith Livingston

Perhaps, there is no place quite as dramatic as the dressing room with its cast of characters: from the new kid about to experience his first fight, to the aging veteran, and everyone in between. Usually, the new kid starts his warm-up far too early, and is looking to anyone for advice. I remember one guy in particular. He showed up, fresh out of the karate point circuit, looking to break into the kickboxing game.

The kid started asking me a bunch of questions. Puzzled at his line of inquiry I asked, "Where's your trainer?" "Trainer?" "Yeah, trainer, you know, the guy that works your corner, gives you advice, answers questions like the ones you're asking me." I watched as the color literally drained from the poor kid's face, "Uh . . . I don't have one." Feeling a little responsible for the kid, and pissed off at the promoter, I pulled him aside, helped him warm up, and let him borrow my corner crew. He still went out and got his ass kicked. It was about the time when he tried to execute a flying back fist point karate move that he caught a beautifully timed side kick to his rib cage. Needless to say, he was on the canvas for a while, surely realizing he had no idea what he had gotten himself into. You don't prepare for a football game by learning as much as you can about hockey!

As I'm writing this, another story comes to mind. I won't use the fighter's name, but believe me when I say that he was cockiness personified. He was a cagey old veteran who liked to intimidate people in the dressing room, especially the newbies. I liked to flip him shit right back.

One evening, he was the main event, and as was typical he had to have a grand entrance. As he was getting ready to leave the dressing room, he turned to me, "Okay, Livingston, now I'm going to show the crowd a real fighter!" I smiled, "Careful, one day your cocky attitude will crash with your karma." He put his black cape on, but before inserting his jet-black mouthpiece, he made one final remark: "Whatever!"

I went out to the arena, hoping to watch his demise, knowing, of course, that it probably wouldn't happen, as he was on top of his game and a world-class fighter. I don't recall the song, but the music began to thump, the lights went down, and the spotlights went on. The grand spectacle had begun.

As was customary with this fighter, he would enter the ring, walk straight to his opponent, get right in his face, and intimidate him with a stare. I couldn't make up this next part if I tried. After the stare down, he would go to the center of the ring and execute his trademark back flip. But this time he was a bit too close to the ropes. As he jumped over backwards, both of his feet caught the ropes and slammed his face into the canvas. You could have heard a pin drop. In an attempt to save face, he got up, brushed himself off, and executed a spinning heel kick in the air. Again his foot went over the top rope, entangling him. He fell through the ropes, over the judge's table, and to the floor. I walked over to where he lay writhing in pain: "I told you, karma!"

IT WAS JUST A JOKE
by Keith Livingston

During my years in the sport, I have witnessed and experienced every imaginable emotion. I have been front row to every imaginable behavior, from the benign to the bizarre. I have watched fighters cry, throw-up, and on one occasion sneak away just prior to the fight.

We were in Vegas. This trip I was the trainer, not the fighter. I had my best fighter and protégé, Scott Baker, with me. Scott was undefeated and on the fast track to a championship. For some odd reason, all the fighters from both corners were stabled in the same dressing room, separated by a five-foot partition.

As Scott's fight was approaching, I noticed Scott's opponent looking around the partition, overly interested in what we were doing. I started preparing Scott with a warm-up on the kicking shield. Deciding I would take advantage of our peeping tom, I told Scott to really lay his kicks into the shield. He threw the first kick, and I admonished him to kick harder. He responded by laying a beautiful round house kick into the shield. Unbeknownst to anyone, I feigned getting the air knocked out of me and dropped to the ground. As Scott came to my assistance, I peeked at Scott's opponent, whose eyes were wide open, and his jaw dropped to his knees. I chuckled inside and continued with the warm-up.

Scott entered the ring first and eagerly anticipated the fight. After several minutes of waiting, I noticed the promoter at the announcer's table. Apparently searching for the right words, but not finding them, the announcer cleared his throat: "Um . . . uh . . . Scott Baker is the winner by default, we can't find his opponent."

I guess my head game worked a little too well. I'm told the other fighter grabbed his gym bag, exited out the back door, and was last seen sprinting toward the parking lot. Scott wasn't too happy, and oh, if you're that other fighter, sorry, I was only kidding when feigning that knockdown

THE PROMISE
by Keith Livingston

I've seen special pants, magic shorts, and even a fighter who refused to wash his jock strap for fear he would wash the luck right out of it. Me? Well. . . I like to fight out of the blue corner. It seems every time I fight from the blue corner, I win! That was until I lost. It all started when I made a big stink with the promoter. It was to be one of the biggest fights of my career. I was fighting John Cronk for the I.K.A. Championship, a belt I had previously owned and desperately wanted back. It was also my last fight, my last hurrah, time to retire.

When I arrived at the arena I discovered, much to my dismay, I was slated to fight out of the red corner. This couldn't be. Not for my last fight! I quickly found the promoter and began my negotiations: "C'mon, you know I need to fight from the blue corner!" He countered: "What the hell ya talking about? What's so special 'bout the blue corner?" Not wanting to tell him about my new found superstition, I stammered, "Well . . . uh, I'm more comfortable with the fighters in the blue dressing room." After shooting me a suspicious glance he relented, "Okay, if it's that important, I'll see what I can do."

By show time, I had gotten my way, I was fighting out of the blue corner and retiring with the belt I coveted. Now, before we get into the fight, let me take a step back. Prior to leaving for Denver, I had met a new girlfriend. She knew nothing about kickboxing, other than that she was sure she didn't like it. I invited her to accompany me to Denver, and made the following statement: "You'll have a great time, I have never been hurt, I have never been knocked out, and I have never been cut. You have absolutely nothing to worry about." She reluctantly agreed, and off to Denver we went.

Fast forward to fight time: I enter the ring, and yes, from the blue corner, feeling good, feeling in shape. The opening bell sounds, and I advance landing a cracking right hand that sends Cronk into the red corner. I sense that he's slightly hurt, and ready myself to execute another. As I pivot on my rear leg, I feel a dead spot in the ring. Then there is a horrendous POP! Seconds later, I feel the most excruciating pain of my life. My ACL has torn! As the tear occurs, I buckle forward just in time to catch Cronk's shin across my forehead, cutting me above both eyes.

Hobbling across the ring trying to keep my dignity and promise to my girlfriend, all I can hear is Cronk's corner screaming, "Take out the knee!" Each time Cronk throws a leg kick, I hear the same sickening pop, feel the same excruciating pain. Now hobbling, and bleeding profusely from both eyebrows, the referee tells me he is going to stop the fight. The referee is a good friend of mine, and I ask: "Please, just let me finish the round?" He agrees, and stops the fight before the second round. I am injured, cut over both eyes, and receive a technical knockout. My girlfriend has to physically support me as I limp from the arena. Thanks a lot, blue corner!!

Did I retire? Well, we'll just have to wait and see, won't we?

CRAZY IKE
by Keith Livingston

I've had many memorable fights over the years, but perhaps the most memorable was with Ike Jenkins. Each state had selected three of its best fighters to represent their respective state in a team competition. Team Kickboxing consisted of a welterweight, a middleweight, and a light heavyweight. I was to fill the welterweight slot, "Babe" Gallegos the middleweight, and JJ Cottrell the light heavyweight. We were to meet a team from St. Louis in a nationally televised event at Caesar's Palace, Las Vegas.

We arrived in Las Vegas on Friday. The next morning, I would meet Ike for the first time. At the weigh-in, he appeared in great shape. I noticed that he had the height and reach advantage. Following the weigh-in, it became apparent that he also had a slight weight advantage. Ike walked over, introduced himself, and wished me luck. He had high cheekbones, a rugged chin, and a perfectly braided ponytail. I had heard rumors that Ike was a bit nuts, but I sensed none of that when I

shook his hand.

As it drew close to fight time, we were ushered to the dressing rooms to ready ourselves for the competition. I was up first. I began my pre-fight routine by shadow boxing. My hands had been expertly wrapped by my trainer, Ruben, who was an exceptional corner man. His simple, between rounds instruction, and his ability to stop a cut were unsurpassed.

While shadow boxing, I heard a strange thumping outside the dressing room door: thump, thump, thump. The sound grew progressively louder and more violent. A fighter nearest the door finally looked outside to investigate. There was Ike, beating his head against the wall, and slapping his gloves together. As he became aware that we were watching his antics, he stepped into the doorway. Ike was literally foaming at the mouth like a rabid dog. His eyes burned with anger and hatred. The rest of the fighters stood dumbfounded and amazed. Finally, the fighter who had opened the door slammed it shut in Ike's face. As I continued my warm-up, I could hear the muffled yelling of Ike calling me out to fight him in the hallway. When the yelling stopped, I assumed they must have led Ike to the ring, because a few minutes later I was also summoned.

During my walk to the ring, I saw Muhammad Ali and Chuck Norris sitting at ringside. The palace was filled to capacity. Upon entering the ring, I barely got my robe off when Ike rushed across the canvas and put his face in mine. We were so close, the tips of our noses were touching, and his heated breath was washing across my face. The referee summoned us to the center of the ring for the obligatory pre-fight instructions. Ike reached up, placed his gloves on my chest and shoved me backwards to a chorus of boos from the crowd. Determined not to be out-done, I returned the shove sending him reeling to the rear. The battle line had been drawn.

Ike and I met in the center of the ring, and for the next several seconds stood toe-to-toe, exchanging viciously wild hooks. I delivered the first crushing hook, sending Ike to the canvas. To my amazement, his ass barely touched down, as he popped right back up and rushed me to get back into the fight. As the round drew toward a close, we found ourselves toe-to-toe again. Just prior to the bell, I landed a beautiful spinning outside crescent kick flush on Ike's jaw. Unfortunately, he was less impressed, and the kick didn't seem to faze him. Later, during the national broadcast, the announcer stated he thought my hooks "could bend over a barrel!" Problem was, I wasn't fighting a barrel; I was fighting "Crazy" Ike Jenkins.

In round two, I stepped out of Ike's chest and threw a jump spinning back kick, which should have finished him. The kick landed square on his face, but to no avail, he continued forward. Jenkins returned the favor with a vicious uppercut to my head. The problem was he nailed the wrong head. He drove my balls into my throat! Before the round ended, I received the same uppercut at least twice more.

Ike was a great fighter, but those uppercuts turned the fight in his favor. In the third and final round, he sent me to the canvas with a perfectly delivered right cross. I, too, got back up. Toward the end of the round, he landed a series of combinations, prompting the referee to step in and stop the fight, and handing the victory to the team from St. Louis.

I tell this story for several reasons: First, expect anything in this sport. Second, never allow yourself to be psyched out by your opponent. And, finally, losing sucks! I still run into Ike from time to time, and he calls me "The Warrior." Our reunions are always pleasant. Ike is a good guy, crazy, but good.

AND NOW, THE REST OF THE STORY
by Keith Livingston

As I walked into the arena that day, I could spot almost every fighter within the crowd of five-hundred spectators. I had been there many times myself and knew well the look and attitude that fighters have just prior to the bout. In fact, I could tell the experienced ones from the first timers.

For some reason, every fighter has an inherent need to know what his opponent looks like. I guess it is supposed to take away some of the fear of the unknown, or give us a chance to size up our opponent. Although I doubt I'll change anybody's mind about this, I will say that a fighter's looks have no bearing on his performance.

I observed a few fighters scanning the crowd, trying to determine their opponent for the evening. I knew exactly how this ritual was performed. First, you look for somebody about your size and who is disinterested in whatever is occurring in the arena. He'll probably have a gym bag and may be dressed in sweats. Next to him will be an older, wiser version of himself, imparting calming advice. He may appear overly calm and relaxed. In some cases he may even be lying flat on his back with his hands interlaced across his chest. Don't be fooled. I seriously doubt he is sleeping. Inside, he is experiencing that same mild adrenaline rush as the fighter.

While making my way to the dressing room, I spotted a few of the rookies. They are the ones with their hands wrapped, warming up frantically, even though the fight will not start for another hour and a half. I wanted to tell them that the likelihood of the fight starting on time is as credible as Elvis showing up and performing a karate form tonight. However, I simply walked by, thinking that experience is the best teacher. And, on a more selfish note, I recalled that I went through it once.

Just before entering the dressing room, I spotted him, my opponent. I knew, just as he did the moment we made eye-contact, that we would meet later tonight for a showdown in the ring. Resisting the urge to voice my opinion, I couldn't help but notice his rugged, battle worn face and confident demeanor. Then it happened . . . the nod, a subtle, downward motion of his head, the kind someone you know gives you when he opts not to wave but acknowledges your presence just the same. Now I knew that he was just a bit nervous. And, tired of the pre-fight bullshit, I gave him a nod in return and entered the dressing room.

This was going to be it: my last fight. By tomorrow, I would be but a brief memory. All the people that had followed my career and showed up to cheer me on, who had won when I won and lost when I lost, would soon forget all the wars I had waged for their entertainment. Soon, they would find themselves another fighter . . . to know, to love, and most of all to live vicariously through.

THE LAST BELL

For a while
a step on your path
a star
in the corner of your eye
a glimmer
in the distant chiming
of the last bell.

The feeling that I have lost something
or won, perhaps
in the battles and hearts of those I have served.

When asking an athlete about his goals, a common answer is, "I want to be the best I can be." The problem is that, although being the best you can be may sound satisfying, it will not outdo the competition, if the competition is better than you. So, let's try again: How good do you want to be?

Being the best, and beating the competition, requires heart. Heart is the combination of courage and confidence, and is perhaps the most important aspect of kickboxing. No matter how good your physical skills, if you lack heart, you are not likely to win. Heart gives you the ability to continue against overwhelming odds, despite pain and fear. As you progress through your training program, remember that there is a difference between being good and being tough. Good means that you can throw a strike well; tough means that you can take a strike well. Both are important to success in the ring but, in my opinion, being tough is the slightly more desirable attribute. If you can't take a punch, you are not likely to win, not even against a mediocre opponent.

As stated in the beginning of this book, there are three truths about fighting and, hopefully, by now you have gained greater insight into the meaning of these truths:

1. Basic techniques are strong and practical and win the fight more often than not. Train to perfect the basics.

2. Good strategy and precision help you win over a physically stronger or more aggressive opponent. Train intellectually.

3. A tired fighter is a beaten fighter. There are no short-cuts. Don't cheat on conditioning.

I will add to this a fourth truth: There is no free lunch. If you don't put anything in, you can't expect to get anything out. You must pay your dues. Period.

So, now that you have come to the end of the book, understand that there will be many bleak moments when you will want to abandon this. It happened to me several times. Even now, today, after all these years, I still have moments when I want to throw in the towel. Quit. It happens to everybody who is aiming for the difficult. It takes courage to reach your dreams.

Tenacity is important, the will to hang on. At times you may feel as though you want to go back and change the past. But you will also learn that your experiences are yours forever, the good and the bad alike. Nobody can take from you your moments of anguish and your moments of glory, and you will have plenty of both. This world is your tormentor, but it is also your joy and what makes it possible for your heart flutter like the wings of a butterfly upon entering the ring. Accept the knowledge that, in the end, nobody can take the plunge for you.

And for how long will you keep going? For as long as is needed . . . as you always have, until the last bell signals the end of the last round.

INDEX

A

Abdominal strengthening 423-426
Acceleration 72, 92, 112, 285, 345, 360
Acceleration of kicks 112, 117, 224
Adding circular to linear 194
Adding momentums 50, 80, 98, 102, 117, 148, 156, 297, 380
Aggressiveness 240, 355, 358, 364, 368, 382
Air shield 257
Alternating hooks 65, 215
Alternating kicks 92, 97, 138
Alternating strikes 96, 315, 320
Alternating uppercuts 76-77
Angle, changing 49, 211
Angled attack 50, 61, 364
Angles 53, 181, 224, 304, 366
Angles, incorporating 178
Angling off 366-367, 411
Apex 354-357, 360
Arm trap 221-222, 225
Assessment chart 433
Attack line 80, 174, 178, 190, 205, 212, 217, 234, 305, 365, 380
Attack line, crossing 235, 239
Attitude 162, 363
Attributes of a winner 410
Awareness 214, 225
Axe kick 329-330
Axe kick target practice 335
Axe kick, targets 329

B

Bag work 253-258, 305, 342
Balance 19, 24, 57, 64, 79-80, 90, 108, 192, 220, 286, 290, 307, 310, 320, 344, 347, 351, 374
Basic movement theory 47-48, 51, 64, 80, 95, 100, 117, 149
Beat 62, 67, 77, 80, 233, 240, 355
Bench running 423
Blending 112, 192
Blending offense with defense, 231
Block, elbow 120, 156, 197
Block, forearm 124, 129, 186

Blocking, short 156
Block, lower body 131
Block, shin 131-135, 200, 204, 290
Block, shoulder 125
Block, upper body 119
Bob and weave, double 153
Bobbing and weaving 50, 77, 146, 149, 152-154, 199, 230
Body mass 57, 360, 365
Body momentum 111, 240
Body power 69
Body rotation 55, 67, 80, 217, 324
Body shots 215-217, 236
Body weight 27, 37, 45, 62, 71, 324, 365
Breathing 32-34, 46, 179, 272-273
Broken rhythm 37-38, 46, 53, 63-64, 80, 142, 150, 162, 166, 171, 235, 371, 376, 391, 394, 411

C

Cadence 63, 80
Canceling momentums 50, 80
Cardiovascular training 429
Catch 145, 184-185, 209, 371-372
Catch, downward, 146, 230
Catching a kick 382
Catch, straight 146
Centerline 21, 25-26, 42, 69-70, 80, 108, 129, 140, 151, 201, 306, 364
Centerline, protecting 212, 295
Chambering 89, 94, 100, 108, 114, 125, 153, 211, 231, 237
Changing the angle 49, 211
Chess game 317, 362-363, 368, 388, 411
Chipping ice 222
Choosing a gym 245
Choosing a heavy bag 253
Choosing your targets 171, 205, 216, 283, 386-387, 396
Circling 26, 38-40
Circling strategy 52, 228
Circular attack 368
Circular motion 194-195, 368
Circular to linear 194, 205, 344-345,
Close range 71, 91, 97, 132, 138
Closing distance 38, 51, 66, 78, 108, 155-156, 165, 202, 208, 214, 240, 324, 403
Combination kicking 114, 213, 401-404
Combination, logical 79, 114, 160-161, 163, 315, 352-353, 395

<u>NOTES</u>

NOTES

<u>NOTES</u>

NOTES

<u>NOTES</u>

NOTES

NOTES

<u>NOTES</u>

<u>NOTES</u>

NOTES

<u>NOTES</u>

NOTES

ABOUT THE AUTHORS

Martina Sprague began her martial arts training in 1987. She is an athlete and analytical writer with black belts in kickboxing, modern freestyle, and Kenpo karate. She is the author of the best selling title *Fighting Science*.

In addition to her martial arts training and writing, Martina is a scholar of history, leadership, and the tactics and philosophies of modern warfare. You can reach Martina via her website www.modernfighter.com.

Keith Livingston is a 20 year veteran of law enforcement and the master instructor for the S. Salt Lake Police Department defensive tactics training, including force on force, close quarter combat, pepper spray and taser instruction. he has been involved in the martial arts for 28 years and holds black belts in Tae-Kwon-Do and kickboxing, with advanced training in Kenpo karate, boxing, Aikido, and Ju-Jitsu. He is the former Utah State kickboxing champion and former I.K.A. light heavyweight Rocky Mountain champion. He retired from competition kickboxing in 1999.

Also Available from Turtle Press:

Ultimate Flexibility
Boxing: A 12 Week Course
The Fighter's Body: An Owner's Manual
The Science of Takedowns, Throws and Grappling for Self-defense
Fighting Science
Martial Arts Instructor's Desk Reference
Guide to Martial Arts Injury Care and Prevention
Solo Training
Fighter's Fact Book
Conceptual Self-defense
Martial Arts After 40
Warrior Speed
The Martial Arts Training Diary
The Martial Arts Training Diary for Kids
TeachingMartial Arts
Combat Strategy
The Art of Harmony
Total MindBody Training
1,001 Ways to Motivate Yourself and Others
Ultimate Fitness through Martial Arts
A Part of the Ribbon: A Time Travel Adventure
Herding the Ox
Neng Da: Super Punches
Taekwondo Kyorugi: Olympic Style Sparring
Martial Arts for Women
Parents' Guide to Martial Arts
Strike Like Lightning: Meditations on Nature
Everyday Warriors

For more information:
Turtle Press
PO Box 290206
Wethersfield CT 06129-206
1-800-77-TURTL
e-mail: sales@turtlepress.com

http://www.turtlepress.com